AI-Powered Search

AI-Powered Search

TREY GRAINGER
DOUG TURNBULL
MAX IRWIN
FOREWORD BY GRANT INGERSOLL

MANNING
SHELTER ISLAND

For online information and ordering of this and other Manning books, please visit
www.manning.com. The publisher offers discounts on this book when ordered in quantity.
For more information, please contact

    Special Sales Department
    Manning Publications Co.
    20 Baldwin Road
    PO Box 761
    Shelter Island, NY 11964
    Email: orders@manning.com

Manning Publications Co.
20 Baldwin Road
PO Box 761
Shelter Island, NY 11964

Development editor:	Marina Michaels
Technical development editor:	John Guthrie
Review editors:	Adriana Sabo and Dunja Nikitović
Production editor:	Keri Hales
Copy editor:	Andy Carroll
Proofreader:	Mike Beady
Technical proofreaders:	Alex Ott, Daniel Crouch
Typesetter and cover designer:	Marija Tudor

ISBN 9781617296970
Printed in the United States of America

brief contents

v

contents

foreword

For the past two decades, search has been at the heart of nearly every aspect of our technical existence as humans. Need to find a fact? Do a search. Want to try a new restaurant? Do a search. Need directions to that trailhead in the mountains for your weekend hike? Do a search. Yet, for many engineers, the underpinnings of how search works or goes beyond simple keyword matching to truly unlock what users need out of an information system is a mystery, left untaught in almost all computer science courses and bootcamps. Given this relative lack of instruction and the new golden age of AI, there is no better time for *AI-Powered Search* to make its mark on the world by teaching all of the core principles required for readers to unlock AI in any application.

At the heart of all search systems is the goal of doing just that: unlocking information to help users make better decisions that help them understand and navigate their world. This unlocking primarily takes place in four ways:

1 Combing through data, finding relevant pieces of information, and ranking and returning the most important bits for the user to synthesize
2 Summarizing data into smaller, more digestible forms for sharing and collaboration via visualizations and other abstractions
3 Relating data to other, ideally familiar, pieces of information and concepts
4 Feeding any of these three, along with other context from the user, into a large language model (LLM) for further synthesis, summarization, and insights, all while interacting and updating based on user feedback

In these same two decades that search has become ubiquitous in our lives at the consumer level, the engines powering this world, like Google, Elasticsearch, Apache Solr, and others, have evolved to tackle not only the retrieval and ranking part above, but also the other three challenges, and not just on text data, but on all forms of data.

Search engines have leaped forward to tackle these problems by deeply incorporating statistical analysis, machine learning, large language models, and natural language processing; in other words, integrating artificial intelligence techniques into every aspect of their core. And yet, despite their depth and breadth of capabilities, they are all too often overlooked as that thing that does "keyword search."

In *AI-Powered Search*, Trey, Doug, and Max have crafted a rich and thorough guide designed to take engineers through all aspects of building intelligent information systems using all means available: LLMs, domain-specific knowledge, knowledge bases and graphs, and finally, user- and crowdsourced signals. Examples in the book highlight key concepts in accessible, easy-to-understand ways.

As someone who has spent the better part of their career building, teaching, and promoting search as a means to help solve some of the most important challenges of our time, I've witnessed firsthand the *A-ha!* moments that launch engineers (after they push through the fuzziness inherent in dealing with messy, multimodal data) into life-long careers working on one of the hardest and most interesting problems of our time. My hope in your reading this book is that you too will find endless fascination in the world of search.

Happy searching!

—GRANT INGERSOLL, CEO & FOUNDER OF DEVELOMENTOR LLC, OPENSEARCH LEADERSHIP COMMITTEE

preface

Thanks for purchasing *AI-Powered Search*! This book will teach you the knowledge and skills you need to deliver highly intelligent search applications that can automatically learn from every content update and user interaction, delivering continuously more relevant search results.

There is no better time than now to learn how to implement AI-powered search. With the rise of generative AI, techniques like retrieval augmented generation (RAG) have arisen as the de facto way to ground AI systems with up-to-date and reliable data from which to drive responses. Yet the "R" in RAG is often the least-well-understood aspect of building such systems. This book provides a deep dive into how to do AI-powered information *retrieval* well, whether you're using it to power an AI system, building a traditional search application, or creating a novel new application requiring intelligent ranking and matching.

Over my career, I've had the opportunity to dive deep into search relevance, semantic search, personalized search and recommendations, behavioral signals processing, semantic knowledge graphs, learning to rank, LLMs and other foundation models, dense vector search, and many other AI-powered search capabilities, publishing research in top journals and conferences and, more importantly, delivering working software at massive scale. As founder of Searchkernel and as Lucidworks' former chief algorithms officer and SVP of engineering, I've also helped deliver many of these capabilities to hundreds of the most innovative companies in the world to help them power search experiences you probably use every single day.

I'm thrilled to also have Doug Turnbull (Reddit, previously Shopify) and Max Irwin (Max.io, previously OpenSource Connections) as contributing authors on this book, pulling from their many years of hands-on experience helping companies and clients with search and relevance engineering.

In this book, we distill our many decades of combined experience into a practical guide to help you take your search applications to the next level. You'll discover how to enable your applications to continually learn to better understand your content, users, and domain in order to deliver optimally relevant experiences with each and every user interaction.

Best wishes as you begin putting AI-powered search into practice!

—TREY GRAINGER

acknowledgments

First and foremost, I want to thank my wife, Lindsay, and my children Melodie, Tallie, and Olivia. You've supported me through all the long nights and weekends I've spent writing this book, and I couldn't have done it without you. I love you all!

Next, I'd like to thank Doug Turnbull and Max Irwin for their contributions to this book, and to the field of AI-powered search (and to Information Retrieval in general). Doug contributed most of chapters 10–12, and Max contributed most of chapters 13–14 and some of 15. I've learned a lot from both of you and your careers, and I'm grateful for the opportunity to work with you on this book.

Next, I'd like to acknowledge my development editor at Manning, Marina Michaels. Thank you for your encouragement and patience, especially as the timelines stretched on this massive undertaking due to me working at multiple startups during the course of this project. The quality of the book is in large part attributable to your experience and guidance.

Thanks as well to all the other folks at Manning who worked with me on development and promotion: John Guthrie on technical development, Ivan Martinović on early-access releases, Michael Stephens on overall vision and direction, and the entire Manning marketing team. I also thank the Manning production team for all their hard work in the formatting and typesetting of this book.

Special thanks to Grant Ingersoll for writing the foreword. I've learned a tremendous amount from you over the years, and I'm very grateful for your support.

I'd next like to thank the additional technical contributors to the book:

- Daniel Crouch, for his thorough review of the book's manuscript, his extensive refactoring of the book's codebase, and his work to make the book mostly search-engine agnostic by integrating plug-and-play support for multiple popular search engines and vector databases

- Alex Ott, for his many technical reviews of the book and for his many rounds of contributions to improve the book's codebase
- Mohammed Korayem, PhD, for his collaboration and implementation of the algorithms for knowledge graph learning from user signals (chapter 6) and personalized search techniques leveraging embeddings (chapter 9)
- Chao Han, PhD, for her collaboration on the design of the signals-based algorithms for domain-specific phrase detection and spelling correction

I'd also like the thank the many readers who provided feedback on the early-access versions of this book while it was in development. Your feedback made a significant impact on the quality of the book.

Finally, I'd also like to thank the reviewers who took their valuable time to read the manuscript at various stages during its development and who provided invaluable feedback: Abdul-Basit Hafeez, Adam Dudczak, Al Krinker, Alain Couniot, Alfonso Jesus Flores Alvarado, Austin Story, Bhagvan Kommadi, David Meza, Davide Cadamuro, Davide Fiorentino, Derek Hampton, Gaurav Mohan Tuli, George Seif, Håvard Wall, Ian Pointer, Ishan Khurana, John Kasiewicz, Keith Kim, Kim Falk Jorgensen, Maria Ana, Mark James Miller, Martin Beer, Matt Welke, Maxim Volgin, Milorad Imbra, Nick Rakochy, Pierluigi Riti, Richard Vaughan, Satej Kumar Sahu, Sen Xu, Sriram Macharla, Steve Rogers, Sumit Pal, Thomas Hauck, Tiklu Ganguly, Tony Holdroyd, Venkata Marrapu, Vidhya Vinay, Yudhiesh Ravindranath, and Zorodzayi Mukuya. Your suggestions helped make this a better book.

—TREY GRAINGER

about this book

AI-Powered Search shows you how to build cutting-edge search engines that continuously learn from both your users and your content to drive more domain-aware and intelligent search. You'll learn modern, data-science-driven search techniques, such as

- Semantic search using dense vector embeddings from foundation models
- Retrieval augmented generation (RAG)
- Question answering and summarization combining search and large language models (LLMs)
- Fine-tuning Transformer-based LLMs
- Personalized search based on user signals and vector embeddings
- Collecting user behavioral signals and building signals-boosting models
- Semantic knowledge graphs for domain-specific learning
- Multimodal search (hybrid queries on text, image, and other types)
- Implementing generalizable machine-learned ranking models (learning to rank)
- Building click models to automate machine-learned ranking
- Vector search optimization techniques like ANN search, quantization, representation learning, and bi-encoders versus cross-encoders
- Generative search, hybrid search, and the search frontier

Today's search engines are expected to be smart, understanding the nuances of natural language queries as well as each user's preferences and context. This book empowers you to build search engines that take advantage of user interactions and the hidden semantic relationships in your content to automatically deliver better, more relevant search experiences. You'll even learn how to integrate LLMs and multimodal foundation models to massively accelerate the capabilities of your search technology.

Who should read this book

This book is for search engineers, software engineers, and data scientists who want to learn how to build cutting-edge search engines integrating the latest machine learning techniques to drive more domain-aware and intelligent search. The book also provides a thorough overview of AI-powered search for product managers and business leaders who may not be able to implement the techniques themselves, but who want to understand the possibilities and limitations of AI-powered search.

Technical readers who want to get the most out of this book can follow along with the Python code examples. Familiarity with SQL (Structured Query Language) syntax is assumed, as we've chosen to implement many of the data aggregations in this standardized representation when possible. A basic understanding of how search engines (such as Elasticsearch, Apache Solr, or OpenSearch) or vector databases work is also helpful, but not required.

How this book is organized: A road map

The book has 4 sections that include 15 chapters. Part 1 introduces AI-powered search and modern search relevance:

- Chapter 1 provides an overview of AI-powered search, including the core concepts and techniques that underpin the rest of the book.
- Chapter 2 covers working with natural language, providing a foundational background on the structure of language and how it enables intelligence to be learned from data.
- Chapter 3 covers the basics of search relevance, explaining matching and ranking techniques leveraging vector embeddings and keyword matching.
- Chapter 4 introduces crowdsourced relevance, covering how to collect and process user interaction signals and providing a survey of reflected intelligence approaches that will be utilized in later chapters to automatically optimize search relevance algorithms.

Part 2 covers domain-specific intent, focusing on leveraging content and user interactions to optimize query understanding:

- Chapter 5 introduces knowledge graph learning, focusing both on extracting explicit knowledge graphs and implicit semantic knowledge graphs for nuanced query understanding and expansion.
- Chapter 6 teaches query intent classification, disambiguation of different meanings of words and phrases, and how to leverage both content and user behavioral

signals to learn domain-specific terminology, related terms, misspellings, and alternate forms of terms.

- Chapter 7 ties everything you've learned together as you build a query pipeline to parse domain-specific intent from your users' queries to perform semantic search.

Part 3 covers reflected intelligence, the process of automatically optimizing search relevance algorithms based on ongoing user interactions:

- Chapter 8 covers signals boosting models, popularized relevance models that automatically optimize ranking for your most important queries.
- Chapter 9 covers personalized search, leveraging collaborative filtering and dense vector embeddings to deliver personalized relevance models for each user.
- Chapter 10 introduces machine-learned ranking (also known as learning to rank), the process of training a ranking classifier, based on user relevance judgments, to act as a generalized relevance model.
- Chapter 11 extends learning to rank by training click models on incoming user behavioral signals to generate implicit user relevance judgments to continuously retrain the ranking model.
- Chapter 12 introduces active learning and A/B testing to overcome inherent bias in machine-learned ranking models.

Part 4 covers the search frontier, exploring the latest techniques and emerging paradigms in AI-powered search:

- Chapter 13 covers how Transformers and LLMs work and how dense vector search and approximate nearest neighbor (ANN) search on embeddings can be used and optimized to deliver efficient semantic search leveraging bi-encoders and cross-encoders.
- Chapter 14 demonstrates fine-tuning an LLM for question answering and demonstrates how to implement a system for answering questions that extracts answers directly from search results.
- Chapter 15 wraps up our journey by exploring the latest techniques and emerging paradigms in AI-powered search, including generative search, retrieval augmented generation (RAG), multimodal search leveraging foundation models, synthetic data generation, and results summarization.

Appendix A covers running the code examples, and appendix B covers supported search engines and vector databases, in case you want to swap in your preferred technology choice.

In general, readers should read all of part 1 (especially chapters 1–3) to ensure the foundational concepts are well understood before moving on to other parts of the book. If you want to jump around after that, keep in mind the following dependencies between chapters:

- Chapter 1: no dependencies
- Chapter 2: no dependencies
- Chapter 3: builds on chapter 2
- Chapter 4: builds on chapters 1, 2, 3
- Chapter 5: builds on chapters 1, 2, 3
- Chapter 6: builds on chapters 1, 2, 3, 4, 5
- Chapter 7: builds on chapters 1, 2, 3, 4, 5, 6
- Chapter 8: builds on chapters 1, 2, 3, 4
- Chapter 9: builds on chapters 1, 2, 3, 4, 8
- Chapter 10: builds on chapters 1, 2, 3
- Chapter 11: builds on chapters 1, 2, 3, 4, 10
- Chapter 12: builds on chapters 1, 2, 3, 4, 10, 11
- Chapter 13: builds on chapters 1, 2, 3
- Chapter 14: builds on chapters 1, 2, 3, 13
- Chapter 15: builds on chapters 1, 2, 3, 4, 13, 14

We also highly recommend loading the Jupyter notebooks and following along so that you can get hands-on experience with the data and code examples in the book.

About the code

While the techniques in this book are broadly applicable for use in most search engines and vector databases, we have chosen to standardize on the following key technologies for the code examples:

- *Programming language*—Python
- *Data processing framework*—Spark (PySpark)
- *Delivery mechanism*—Docker containers
- *Code setup and walk-throughs*—Jupyter notebooks
- *Search engine/vector database*—Apache Solr (with plug-and-play support for using many other popular search engines and vector databases)

RUNNING THE CODE EXAMPLES

All of the book's code is written in Python and shipped in Jupyter notebooks running in Docker containers. This enables readers to run the code examples from the book locally in a web browser with no additional configuration required. The notebooks are all designed so you can run them as many times as you like and get the same results, enabling you to focus on reading and understanding each chapter while following along by executing the corresponding code in a fully preconfigured environment.

See appendix A for instructions on how to run the Docker containers. The source code is all open sourced under the Apache 2.0 license and is available at https://github.com/treygrainger/ai-powered-search.

CODING CONVENTIONS

Coding convention-wise, we have chosen to omit most boilerplate code from the book, since all the code is easily accessible for reference in the Jupyter notebooks. Python imports, for example, are usually omitted from code listings for brevity unless they add significant context to the code example, such as avoiding potential confusion between namespaces.

Likewise, you will find that very long code listings or outputs may be abbreviated with an ellipsis (...) and that some helper functions may have their code omitted to save space when the excluded sections are not important for understanding the point of the code example.

In some cases, the original source code has been reformatted; we've added line breaks and reworked indentation to two spaces (versus the Python standard of four spaces) to accommodate the available page space in the book. In rare cases, even this was not enough, and listings include line-continuation markers (➥). When possible, however, we have used Python line continuations (\) instead to keep the codebase and book listings consistent.

Code annotations accompany many of the listings, highlighting important concepts. Additionally, comments in the source code have usually been removed from the listings when the code is described in the text or accompanying code annotations.

The complete code for the examples in the book is available for download from the Manning website at https://www.manning.com/books/ai-powered-search. The most current and up-to-date code repository is hosted on Github and is still being actively improved. Readers can always download a zip file of the latest code at this URL: https://github.com/treygrainger/ai-powered-search/archive/refs/heads/main.zip.

SUPPORT FOR OTHER SEARCH ENGINES AND VECTOR DATABASES

The book also includes plug-and-play support for many popular search engines and vector databases, enabling you to run the code examples in the book against your engine of choice. Most of the book uses a generic engine and collection abstraction to ensure the code and concepts are as broadly applicable as possible to the wide variety of matching and ranking technologies available today. Unfortunately, it isn't practical to include duplicate code examples in the book targeting every available search engine technology, so in the few cases where search-engine-specific syntax is required in examples, we chose to standardize on the open source Apache Solr search engine.

We use Solr's JSON query syntax for all query examples, making them highly readable and reasonably easy to conceptually map to other engines. If you would like to use a different search engine, see appendix B for instructions on how to toggle between different engines or implement your own.

SYSTEM REQUIREMENTS FOR RUNNING CODE EXAMPLES

To comfortably run the examples in the book, you will need a Mac, Linux, or Windows computer, and we recommend a minimum of 8 GB of RAM to be able to run through some of the more heavy-duty Spark jobs. The only dependency you will need to install is Docker, after which you can pull or build the Docker containers for the book. The Docker containers and datasets are quite large, so we recommend a minimum of 25 GB of available disk space to pull and process all examples in the book. You may need to modify your system settings for Docker to ensure you have these minimum memory and storage amounts allocated.

liveBook discussion forum

Purchase of *AI-Powered Search* includes free access to liveBook, Manning's online reading platform. Using liveBook's exclusive discussion features, you can attach comments to the book globally or to specific sections or paragraphs. It's a snap to make notes for yourself, ask and answer technical questions, and receive help from the authors and other users. To access the forum, go to https://livebook.manning.com/book/ai -powered-search/discussion. You can also learn more about Manning's forums and the rules of conduct at https://livebook.manning.com/discussion.

Manning's commitment to our readers is to provide a venue where a meaningful dialogue between individual readers and between readers and the authors can take place. It is not a commitment to any specific amount of participation on the part of the authors, whose contribution to the forum remains voluntary (and unpaid). We suggest you try asking the authors some challenging questions lest their interest stray! The forum and the archives of previous discussions will be accessible from the publisher's website as long as the book is in print.

Other online resources

Join our growing community! While this book serves as a timely and comprehensive guide to building AI-powered search, the world of AI-powered search continues to grow and evolve quickly. In order to stay up to date with the latest and greatest new AI-powered search techniques and technologies for years to come, we invite you to join our *AI-Powered Search Community*.

aipoweredsearch.com/community

When you join the AI-Powered Search Community, you'll be able to interact with thousands of Search and AI practitioners, including many of the top experts (who have already joined) from the fields of AI and Information Retrieval. You can join for free at https://aipowered search.com/community.

The AI-Powered Search website (https://aipoweredsearch.com) is centered around three key pillars:

- Providing the ultimate *Guide* to building AI-powered search (this book and follow-on updates)

- Being the ultimate *Hub* for AI-powered search content (ongoing posts and content updates from across the industry)
- Building the ultimate *Community* for AI-powered search

With the purchase of this book, you now have the *Guide*. The AI-Powered Search website serves as the *Hub* and as a continually updating appendix for this book, adding in new and emerging techniques that you'll be ready for after reading this book. Our invitation is now for you to *join the Community*, where you can both share what you're working on and interact with other readers, this book's authors, and the world's other leading AI-powered search experts.

about the authors

TREY GRAINGER is the founder of Searchkernel, a software company and consultancy building the next generation of AI-powered search. He is also an advisor to several startups and an adjunct professor of computer science at Furman University. He previously served as CTO of Presearch, a decentralized web search engine, and as chief algorithms officer and SVP of engineering at Lucidworks, an AI-powered search company whose search technology powers hundreds of the world's leading organizations. He is also the co-author of *Solr in Action* (Manning, 2014), the leading book on Apache Solr. Trey has over 17 years of experience in search and data science, including significant work developing semantic search, personalization, and recommendation systems, and building self-learning search platforms leveraging content and behavior-based reflected intelligence. This work resulted in the publication of dozens of research papers, journal articles, conference presentations, and books at the cutting edge of intelligent search systems.

Doug Turnbull is principal engineer at Reddit, former staff relevance engineer at Spotify, and former chief technical officer at OpenSource Connections. He is the co-author of the book *Relevant Search* (Manning, 2016), and he contributed most of chapters 10–12 of this book.

Max Irwin is the founder of Max.io, focused on scaling production AI models, and former managing consultant at OpenSource Connections, a leading search relevance consultancy. Max contributed most of chapters 13–14 and part of chapter 15 of this book.

about the cover illustration

The figure on the cover of *AI-Powered Search* is "Homme des Environ's de Rome," or "Man from the Vicinity of Rome," taken from a collection by Jacques Grasset de Saint-Sauveur, published in 1788. Each illustration is finely drawn and colored by hand.

In those days, it was easy to identify where people lived and what their trade or station in life was just by their dress. Manning celebrates the inventiveness and initiative of the computer business with book covers based on the rich diversity of regional culture centuries ago, brought back to life by pictures from collections such as this one.

Part 1

Modern search relevance

Search engines serve as the gateway to accessing most of human knowledge. Web search engines offer a queryable cache of the internet, allowing you to instantly find information on any topic across billions of websites. Generative AI (artificial intelligence) relies heavily on search engines to perform retrieval augmented generation (RAG), which is the process of using search to find relevant context to provide to AI models so that they generate accurate responses for incoming prompts.

Search algorithms also power matching and ranking in most data-driven applications: from e-commerce, to email, to social media, to company intranets and private filesystems. Performing search well requires optimizing search relevance—the ability to find and rank the most relevant results for a given query.

In this first part of the book, we will explore modern search relevance. Chapter 1 provides an introduction to AI-powered search, highlighting the major topics you'll learn throughout the book. Chapter 2 is about working with natural language, providing background into key natural language processing (NLP) concepts needed to implement AI-powered search. Chapter 3 then dives into relevance ranking, covering the mechanics of how search engines and vector databases find and rank the best results for a given query. Finally, chapter 4 covers crowdsourced relevance, the process of using ongoing user interactions with your search results to learn models that improve relevance ranking.

Introducing
AI-powered search

This chapter covers

- What is AI-powered search?
- Understanding user intent
- How AI-powered search works
- Content and behavioral intelligence
- Architecting an AI-powered search engine

The search box has become the default user interface for interacting with data in most modern applications. If you think of every major app or website you use daily, one of the first things you likely do on each visit is enter a query to find the content or actions most relevant to you.

When you're not explicitly searching, you may instead be consuming streams of content customized to your tastes and interests. Whether these be video recommendations, items for purchase, prioritized emails, news articles, or other content, you're likely still looking at filtered or ranked results and given the option to either page through or explicitly filter the content with your own query.

For most people, the phrase "search engine" brings up thoughts of a website like Google, Bing, or Baidu that enables queries based on a crawl of the entire public internet. However, the reality is that search is now available in nearly all our digital interactions every day across the numerous websites and applications we use.

These search engines are far from static. We're seeing commercial technologies like OpenAI's ChatGPT, Anthropic's Claude, and Google's Gemini, as well as hundreds of other more open large language models (LLMs), like Meta's Llama and Mistral's Mixtral, with source code and model weights published for public use. These all serve as models of the world's information that can generate interpretations and responses to arbitrary queries. These models are being actively integrated into major search engines and will continue to heavily influence the evolution of AI-powered search.

While the expected response from a search box may have historically been to return "ten blue links"—a list of ranked documents for a user to investigate further to find information in response to their query—expectations for the intelligence level of search technologies have skyrocketed in recent years.

Users today expect search technology to be

- *Domain-aware*—Search technology should understand the entities, terminology, categories, and attributes of each specific use case and corpus of documents, not just use generic statistics on strings of text.
- *Contextual and personalized*—It should be able to take into account user context (location, last search, profile, previous interactions, user recommendations, and user classification), query context (other keywords, similar searches), and domain context (inventory, business rules, domain-specific terminology) to better interpret user intent.
- *Conversational*—It should be able to interact in natural language and guide users through a multi-step discovery process while learning and remembering relevant new information along the way.
- *Multi-modal*—It should be able to resolve queries issued by text, voice, images, video, or other content types, and to use those queries to also search across the other content types.
- *Intelligent*—It should be able to deliver predictive type-ahead and to understand what users mean (spelling correction, phrase and attribute detection, intent classification, conceptual searching) to deliver the right answers at the right time and to constantly get smarter.
- *Assistive*—It should move beyond delivering just links to delivering answers, summaries, explanations, and available actions.

Many of these capabilities are enabled by LLMs, while others are driven by analyzing user behavior and building domain-specific personalization profiles, knowledge graphs, and ranking models.

Search interfaces are also evolving to include more chatbot and conversational information discovery sessions as LLMs become more ubiquitous, but even today's best models struggle with hallucinating (making up bad answers) and going off the rails unless tethered to an actual information source, such as a search engine index, to reliably find and return information from trusted sources. *Retrieval augmented generation*

(RAG), the technique of using a search engine or vector database as a knowledge source to provide LLMs accurate and up-to-date information as context, is one of the most reliable techniques for improving the accuracy of generative AI models today.

The goal of AI-powered search is to use automated machine learning techniques to deliver on all these desired capabilities. While many organizations start with basic text search and spend many years trying to manually optimize synonym lists, business rules, ontologies, field weights, and countless other aspects of their search configuration, some are beginning to realize that most of this process can be automated.

Throughout the book, you'll learn to implement many key AI-powered search techniques, such as

- Using LLMs for query interpretation, embeddings, question answering, and results summarization
- Fine-tuning LLMs for search and question answering
- Collecting and using user signals for crowdsourced relevance
- Signals-boosting models
- Knowledge graph learning from both signals and content
- Semantic knowledge graphs
- Query intent classification and query-sense disambiguation
- Personalized search and recommendations
- Machine-learned ranking (learning to rank)
- Click models for implicit relevance feedback
- Avoiding bias in ranking models through active learning
- Hybrid search and multimodal search across text, images, and mixed content types
- Semantic search using both knowledge graphs and LLMs

This book is an example-driven guide through the most applicable machine learning algorithms and techniques commonly used to build intelligent search systems. We'll not only walk through key concepts but will also provide reusable code examples to cover data collection and processing techniques, as well as the self-learning query interpretation and relevance strategies employed to deliver AI-powered search capabilities across today's leading organizations—hopefully soon to include your own!

1.1 What is AI-powered search?

Prior to November 2022, when OpenAI released ChatGPT to the world as a generalizable algorithm that non-technical users could talk with to solve many problems, the definition of "artificial intelligence" was a bit nebulous to the general public. It was understood to include things like self-driving cars, autonomous robots, and other futuristic technologies that made computers appear to be intelligent, but AI appeared to many to be more of a marketing buzzword than a well-defined term. A more concrete definition has existed in the software industry for years, however.

In the context of software development, the term *artificial intelligence* generally describes any computer program that can perform a task that previously required human intelligence. That program often includes machine learning techniques, allowing it to learn from data and improve its performance over time. That said, even rules-based systems that do not involve machine learning techniques but generate human-like feedback have also traditionally been considered "AI" systems. We'll adopt this more general definition of AI in this book, though we'll be primarily discussing the machine-learning aspects of AI.

The term *search* (or *search engine*) is likewise considered by the general public to refer to web search engines like Google or Bing. In software development, the term is also used to describe any technology that enables users to query for and find information. Search typically involves at least two critical steps—finding documents that match a query (*matching*) and then ordering those documents by relevance to the query (*ranking*). Search can also include many preprocessing steps to better understand the query, and postprocessing steps to extract answers or summarize results from the matched documents. Search is often the primary way users find information, whether conducting general web search, product search, enterprise search, video/image search, or any of hundreds of other common use cases for finding and ranking information. It is also the primary way generative AI systems quickly find updated factual content to use as context for their prompts.

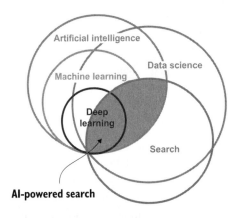

Figure 1.1   AI-powered search includes all the technologies and techniques at the intersection of the fields of search and AI. These overlap heavily with and use the fields of data science, machine learning, and deep learning.

But what is AI-powered search, and how does it differ from traditional "search"? Many buzzwords such as "AI", "machine learning", "data science", and "deep learning" are often thrown around interchangeably, and it's important to understand the distinctions and how they overlap with AI-powered search. Figure 1.1 demonstrates the important relationships between these related areas.

Machine learning is a subset of AI that focuses on using data to train models to perform tasks based on insights learned from the training data. Deep learning is a further subset of machine learning that focuses on training artificial neural networks—algorithms that partially mimic the structure of the human brain—to learn to solve complex problems. In figure 1.1, notice that deep learning is a fully contained subset of machine learning, which is then a fully contained subset of artificial intelligence. Data science is a discipline that overlaps heavily with AI and search, but it also contains other distinct focus areas, so it is not completely a superset or subset of either.

Our focus in this book is specifically on the intersection of search (also known as *information retrieval*) and AI, and in particular on the application of machine learning

and deep learning techniques to improve the relevance of search results and to automate the process of tuning search relevance. Building AI-powered search involves many
well-known machine learning techniques, but also many that are specific to information retrieval and the search domain. Figure 1.2 provides a categorized list of some key
AI-powered search techniques we'll cover in this book, broken down by whether they
are deep learning techniques, other machine learning techniques not requiring deep
learning, or other artificial intelligence techniques not requiring machine learning.

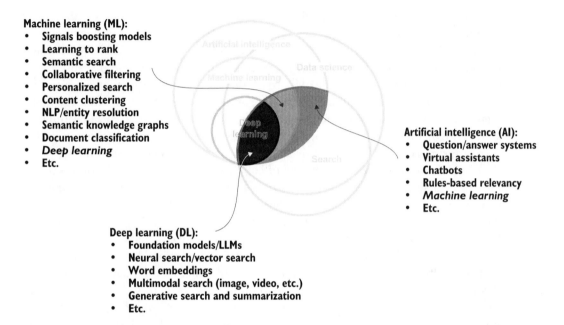

Machine learning (ML):
- **Signals boosting models**
- **Learning to rank**
- **Semantic search**
- **Collaborative filtering**
- **Personalized search**
- **Content clustering**
- **NLP/entity resolution**
- **Semantic knowledge graphs**
- **Document classification**
- *Deep learning*
- **Etc.**

Artificial intelligence (AI):
- **Question/answer systems**
- **Virtual assistants**
- **Chatbots**
- **Rules-based relevancy**
- *Machine learning*
- **Etc.**

Deep learning (DL):
- **Foundation models/LLMs**
- **Neural search/vector search**
- **Word embeddings**
- **Multimodal search (image, video, etc.)**
- **Generative search and summarization**
- **Etc.**

Figure 1.2   Specific AI-powered search techniques, broken down by whether they are deep learning techniques, other machine learning techniques not requiring deep learning, or other artificial intelligence techniques not requiring machine learning

In the AI-only category, question-answering systems, virtual assistants, chatbots, and
rules-based relevancy are all examples of AI techniques that are often built using
machine learning, but which do not *require* machine learning. Many have built chatbots based entirely on rules to understand different user utterances and intents, and
likewise question-answering systems can be built solely on rules and ontologies. That
said, machine learning is often used to learn these kinds of rules and ontologies, so
the lines between these categories are often blurred.

When algorithms begin to use data to train models, we enter into the machine
learning subcategory of AI-powered search. We use behavioral signals from search
engine users (clicks, likes, add-to-carts, purchases, etc.) to build models that can learn
to better rank documents. This can include signals-boosting models (top documents

per query or category), collaborative filtering models that generate recommendations or personalize search results, and ranking classifiers (learning to rank) that learn from content and behavioral signals to better rank results. Machine learning is also used to learn knowledge graphs, which are graphs of entities, concepts, and their relationships that can be used to better understand the domain and to better interpret user queries. Semantic search (search on meaning, not just keywords) can be enabled by such knowledge graphs, along with traditional natural language processing approaches, query intent classification, document clustering, and other techniques driven by user queries, documents, and user behavioral signals.

Finally, in the deep learning subcategory of AI-powered search, we see the use of neural networks to build models that can understand user queries and documents, as well as rank and summarize search results. Here, text is used to train LLMs to understand the meaning of words and phrases, to generate answers to questions, and to generate summaries of documents. LLMs are a type of *foundation model* that can interpret text content and are often trained on massive amounts of text from the internet. Foundation models can also be trained on other types of content beyond just text (images, audio, video) to enable multimodal search across those content types: text-to-image search, text-to-audio, image-to-video, and so on. LLMs are also used to generate *embeddings*, which are vector representations of content that represent the content's meaning. Since a search engine's primary job is to find and rank content similar to an incoming query, these embeddings enable a sophisticated ability to search on a query's meaning and significantly improve query understanding and ranking. Further fine-tuning of foundation models on specific goals or domain-specific datasets will also make them significantly better at understanding the nuances of those domains or use cases.

Foundation models compress a large amount of human knowledge (often much of the internet), providing them with a broad understanding across most domains. This compression of knowledge, however, is a lossy compression—the original data is not stored, and specific facts and concepts can be easily confused. Foundation models are well known to hallucinate answers to questions, making them generally unreliable for answering factual questions. As a result, in addition to search engines using foundation models to improve query understanding and ranking, we're also seeing them used heavily for RAG—where search serves as a knowledge source that foundation models can rely on for accurate and up-to-date information as context for generative AI tasks.

We'll cover each of these AI-powered search techniques in detail throughout this book. But first, let's discuss the goals of AI-powered search and how it differs from traditional search.

1.2 *Understanding user intent*

To deliver AI-powered search, we'll need a cohesive understanding of the dimensions involved in interpreting user intent and returning content matching that intent. Within the field of information retrieval, search engines and recommendation engines are the two most popular technologies employed to deliver the relevant content required to satisfy users' information need. Many organizations think of search engines and recommendation engines as separate technologies solving different use cases. Commonly, different teams within the same organization—often with different skill sets—work independently on separate search engines and recommendation engines. In this section, we'll discuss why separating search and recommendations into independent functions and teams can often lead to less-than-ideal outcomes.

1.2.1 What is a search engine?

A search engine is typically thought of as a technology for explicitly entering queries and receiving a response (figure 1.3). It is usually exposed to end users through a text box into which a user can enter keywords or questions. The results are often returned in a list, alongside additional filtering options that enable further refinement of the initial query. Using this mechanism, search is used as a tool for direct discovery of relevant content. When a user is finished with their search session, they can usually issue a new query and start with a blank slate, ignoring the context of previous searches.

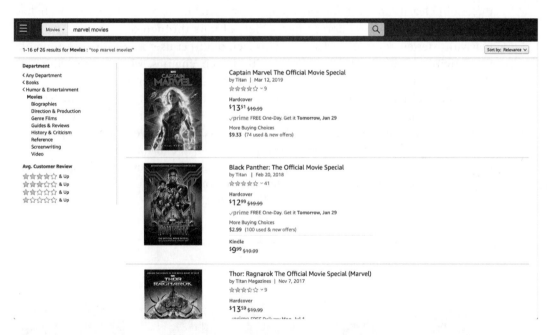

Figure 1.3   A typical search experience, with a user entering a query and seeing search results with filtering options to support further refinement of the search results

A search engine is one of the most cross-functional kinds of systems within the software engineering world. Most underlying search engine technology is designed to operate in a massively scalable way, serving large volumes of queries against millions, billions, or even trillions of documents, and delivering results in hundreds of milliseconds or less. In many cases, real-time processing and near-real-time searching on newly ingested data is required, and all of this must be parallelizable across numerous servers to scale out and meet such high-performance requirements.

Implementing search engines also requires substantial work building search-specific data structures like an inverted index or ANN-based vector store, an understanding of linear algebra and vector similarity scoring, experience with text analysis and natural language processing, and knowledge of numerous search-specific types of data models and capabilities (spell checking, autosuggest, faceting, text highlighting, embeddings, and so on).

For a search engine to fully interpret user intent, it's critical that you combine a thorough understanding of your content, your users, and your domain. We'll revisit why this is important after briefly discussing the related topic of recommendation engines.

1.2.2   *What do recommendation engines offer?*

Most people think of recommendation engines (or "recommendation systems") as systems that don't accept direct user input and instead deliver content based upon what the engine learns about them, calculating best matches for their interests and behaviors. These interests are inferred in a variety of ways through user preferences, user behavior, viewed content, and so on. This lack of direct user input for recommendation engines stands in direct contrast with search engines, which are traditionally thought of as technology that requires explicit user-driven queries.

If you routinely visit Amazon.com or any other major e-commerce website, you are no doubt familiar with recommendation engine sections stating that "based on your interest in this item, you may also like . . ." or otherwise just recommending a list of items based upon your collective browsing and purchase history, like the example in figure 1.4. These recommendations often drive significant revenue for companies, and they help customers discover relevant, personalized, and related content that often complements what they are searching for explicitly.

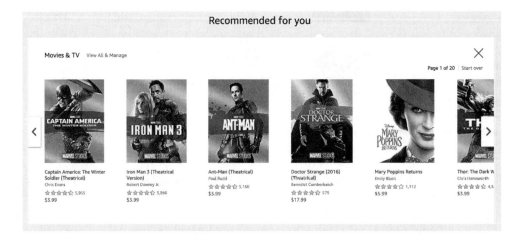

Figure 1.4   Recommendations based upon users expressing interest in similar items

Recommendation algorithms can roughly be divided into three categories:

- *Content-based recommenders*—These match based on attributes of items or users
- *Behavior-based recommenders*—These match based upon the overlap of interactions from similar users with similar items
- *Multimodal recommenders*—These perform hybrid matching based on both similar content-based attributes and overlapping behavior-based interactions.

1.2.3   *The personalization spectrum between search and recommendations*

The key difference between search engines and recommendation engines is that search engines are typically guided by users and match the users' explicitly entered queries, whereas recommendation engines typically accept no direct user input and instead recommend—based upon already-known or inferred knowledge—what a user may want to see next.

But these two systems are really two sides of the same coin, and treating them as separate systems creates a false dichotomy. The goal, in both cases, is to understand what a user is looking for and to deliver relevant results to meet that user's information need. A broad range of personalization capabilities lies within the spectrum between search and recommendation systems.

Assuming you have both explicit queries and a user-specific personalization profile available when trying to find content for your end users, you can do any of the following:

- *Traditional keyword search*—Ignore the profile and only use explicit inputs.
- *Personalized search*—Use the profile implicitly along with other explicit user input.
- *User-guided recommendations*—Use the profile explicitly and provide the user with the ability to adjust it.
- *Traditional recommendations*—Use the profile explicitly with no ability for a user to adjust it.

Figure 1.5 shows this personalization spectrum.

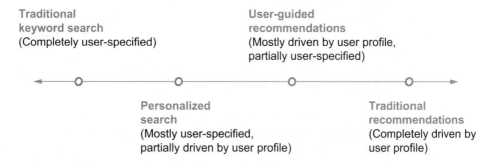

Figure 1.5   The personalization spectrum, showing traditional keyword search and traditional recommendations as two ends of a larger continuum

While the two ends of this personalization spectrum represent the extremes, they are also the two most common approaches. Unfortunately, one of the biggest mistakes we see in many organizations is teams built around the belief that search and recommendations are separate problems. This often leads to data science teams building complicated personalization and segmentation models only capable of recommendations and not search, and engineering teams building large-scale keyword matching engines that can't easily take advantage of the robust models built by the recommendations teams.

More often than not, the recommendation teams are staffed by data scientists with minimal information retrieval background, and the search teams are often staffed by engineers with minimal data science background. Due to Conway's law ("organizations which design systems ... are constrained to produce designs which are copies of the communication structures of these organizations"), this ultimately results in challenges solving problems along the personalization spectrum (particularly in the middle) that need the best from both teams. In this book, we focus on the shared techniques that make it possible for search to become smarter and for recommendations to become more flexible through a unified approach. AI-powered search platforms need to be able to continuously learn from both your users and your content and then enable your users to guide the results so they continue to improve.

1.2.4   *Semantic search and knowledge graphs*

We presented search and recommendations as a personalization spectrum in figure 1.5, with personalized search and user-guided recommendations in between, but there's one more dimension that is critical for building a good AI-powered search system—a deep understanding of the given domain. It's not enough to match on keywords and to recommend content based upon how users collectively interact with documents. The engine must also learn as much as it can about the domain. This includes

- Learning all the important domain-specific phrases, synonyms, and related terms
- Identifying entities in documents and queries
- Generating a knowledge graph that relates those entities
- Disambiguating the many nuanced meanings represented by domain-specific terminology
- Being able to effectively parse, interpret, and conceptually match the nuanced intent of users within your domain.

Figure 1.6 shows an example of semantic parsing of a query, with the goal being to search for "things" (known entities) instead of "strings" (just text matching).

To make their searches smarter, many companies spend considerable money employing large teams to manually create dictionaries and knowledge graphs to identify the relationships between entities in their users' queries. This book focuses on a

Goal: search on "things", not "strings"...

Figure 1.6 Semantic parsing of a query, demonstrating an understanding of the entities ("things") represented by query terms

more scalable approach: building an AI-powered search engine that can automatically learn these relationships continuously. We also dive into additional techniques for semantic search, including dense vector search on embeddings and generative search using LLMs.

1.2.5 Understanding the dimensions of user intent

We've discussed the important roles of traditional keyword search, recommendations, and the personalization spectrum in between. We also discussed the need for semantic search to provide domain-specific understanding of your content and your users' queries. All of these are key pillars of a singular, larger goal: fully understanding user intent. Figure 1.7 demonstrates the interplay between each of these key pillars of user intent.

The top-left circle in figure 1.7 represents *content understanding*—the ability to find the right content based on keywords, language patterns, and known attribute matching. The top-right circle represents *user understanding*—the ability to understand each user's specific preferences and use those to return more personalized results. Finally, the lower circle represents *domain understanding*—the ability to interpret words, phrases, concepts, entities, and nuanced interpretations and relationships between each of these within your own domain-specific context.

A query only in the content understanding circle represents traditional *keyword search*, enabling matching on keywords but without using any domain or user-specific context. A query only in the user understanding circle would be recommendations from collaborative filtering, with no ability for the user to override the inputs and no understanding of the domain or content of the underlying documents. A query only in the domain understanding circle might be a structured query on known tags, catego-

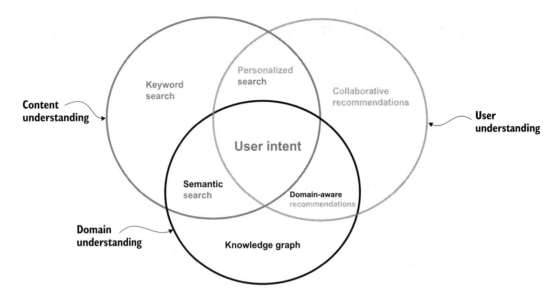

Figure 1.7   The dimensions of user intent: a combination of content understanding, user understanding, and domain understanding

ries, or entities, or even a browse-like interface that allowed for exploration of a *knowl-edge graph* of these domain-specific entities and their relationships, but without any user-specific personalization or ability to find arbitrary terms, phrases, and content.

When traditional keyword search and recommendations overlap, we get *personalized search* or guided recommendations. When traditional keyword search and knowledge graphs overlap, we get *semantic search*: a smart, domain-specific search experience. Finally, when recommendations and knowledge graphs overlap, we get smarter *domain-aware recommendations* that match on crowdsourced user interactions across similar documents and also on a domain-specific understanding of the important attributes of those documents.

The holy grail for AI-powered search is to harness the intersection of all three categories: semantic search, personalized search, and domain-aware recommendations. That is to say, to truly understand user intent, we need all of the following:

- An expert understanding of the domain the user is searching
- An expert understanding of the user and their preferences
- An expert ability to match and rank arbitrary queries against any content

AI-powered search starts with the three pillars of user intent (content, domain, and user), and then employs intelligent algorithms to constantly learn and improve in each of these areas. This learning includes techniques like automatically learning ranking criteria, automatically learning user preferences, and automatically learning knowledge graphs and language models of the represented domain. At the end of the day, a balanced combination of these three approaches provides the key to optimal understanding of users and their query intent, which is the end goal of our AI-powered search system.

1.3 How does AI-powered search work?

We laid out our end goal of matching user intent through content understanding, user understanding, and domain understanding. With that background established, let's wrap up this chapter with an overview of the actual components needed to deliver an AI-powered search platform. Search intelligence typically matures along a predictable progression iteratively over time, as shown in figure 1.8. Basic keyword search is a typical starting point for organizations. Once in production, they realize their search relevancy needs to be improved, and they start manually tuning field weights, boosts, text and language analysis, and introducing additional features and functions.

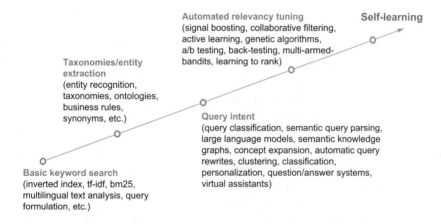

Figure 1.8 The typical search intelligence progression, from basic keyword search to a full self-learning search platform

Eventually, they realize they need to inject domain understanding into their search capabilities, at which point organizations begin to invest in synonym lists, taxonomies, lists of known entities, and domain-specific business rules. While these all help, organizations eventually also discover that relevant search is very much dependent upon successfully interpreting user queries and understanding user intent, so they begin investing in techniques for query classification, semantic query parsing, knowledge graphs, personalization, and other attempts to correctly interpret user queries.

Because these tasks yield improvements, this success often results in the creation of large teams investing significant time manually tuning lists and parameters, and eventually organizations may realize that it is possible (and more expedient) to automate as much of that process as possible through learning from user signals, user testing

(A/B testing, offline relevancy simulations, and active learning), and building of machine-learned relevancy models. The end goal is to completely automate each of these steps along the search intelligence progression and enable the engine to be self-learning.

1.3.1 The core search foundation

The first step in building a search platform is almost always to get traditional keyword search working (the "content understanding" part in figure 1.7). Teams often spend years tuning and improving this step, and a whole discipline called *relevance engineering* has arisen that has historically focused significant effort into understanding content; improving content for search; adjusting boosts, query parameters, and query functions; and otherwise trying to maximize the relevance of the traditional search experience. For a deep dive into this world of relevance engineering and tuning traditional keyword search relevance, we recommend the book *Relevant Search* by Doug Turnbull and John Berryman (Manning, 2016).

As relevance engineers become more sophisticated, their work often moves into the realms of user understanding and recommendations, as well as into domain-understanding and semantic search. The rise of large language models has made it easy in recent years to implement out-of-the-box semantic search, but getting to the next level in optimizing the relevance and matching requires much more sophisticated approaches, as you'll learn throughout this book. Our focus in *AI-Powered Search* will be on automating the process of learning and optimizing search relevance so it operates as a continuous feedback loop. We essentially want to automate much of the relevance engineer's job, relying on algorithms, where possible, to continually learn optimal matching and ranking strategies.

So, what characteristics differentiate a well-tuned search engine from an AI-powered search engine? A well-tuned search engine is the foundation upon which AI-powered search is built, but AI-powered search goes far beyond that, continuously learning and improving through reflected intelligence. *Reflected intelligence* is the idea of using continual feedback loops of user input, content updates, and user interactions with content to continually learn and improve the quality of your search application.

1.3.2 Reflected intelligence through feedback loops

Feedback loops are critical to building an AI-powered search solution. Imagine if your entire education (elementary school through to your highest degree) had consisted of nothing more than you reading textbooks: no teachers to ask questions, no exams to test your knowledge and provide feedback, and no classmates or others with which to interact, study, or collaborate. You would have probably hit endless walls where you were unable to fully grasp certain concepts or even understand what you were reading, and you would have understood many ideas incorrectly and never had the opportunity to realize this or to adjust your assumptions.

Search engines often operate this same way. Smart engineers push data to the search engine and tune certain features and feature weights, but the engine just reads those configurations and acts upon them the same way every time for repeated user queries. Search engines are the perfect kind of system for interactive learning, however, when we introduce feedback loops.

Figure 1.9 shows the typical flow of information through a search feedback loop. First, a user issues a query. This query executes a search, which returns results, such as a specific answer, a list of answers, or a list of links to pages, to an end user. Once presented with the list, the user then takes one or more actions. These actions usually start with clicks on documents, but those clicks can ultimately lead to adding an item to a shopping cart and purchasing it (e-commerce), giving the item a thumbs up or thumbs down (media consumption website), liking or commenting on the result (social media website), or any number of other context-specific actions.

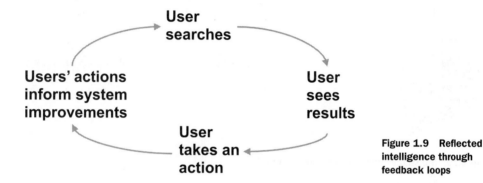

Figure 1.9   Reflected intelligence through feedback loops

These actions can then be used to generate an improved relevance ranking model for future searches. Your search application can automatically adjust the ranking of future search results, delivering an improved search experience for the next user's search.

1.3.3   Signals boosting, collaborative filtering, and learning to rank

The searches, clicks, likes, add to carts, purchases, comments, and other interactions with your search application are critical data that you need to capture. We collectively refer to these data points as *signals*. Signals provide a constant stream of feedback to your search application, recording every meaningful interaction with your end users. These digital moments can then be used by machine learning algorithms to generate models to power user understanding, content understanding, and domain understanding.

Figure 1.10 shows the data flow for the collection and processing of signals in a typical AI-powered search application. You can see signals being collected for each search, as well as resulting clicks and purchases. Unique signals can also be recorded for any other kind of user interaction (add-to-cart, facet click, bookmark, hover, or even page dwell time).

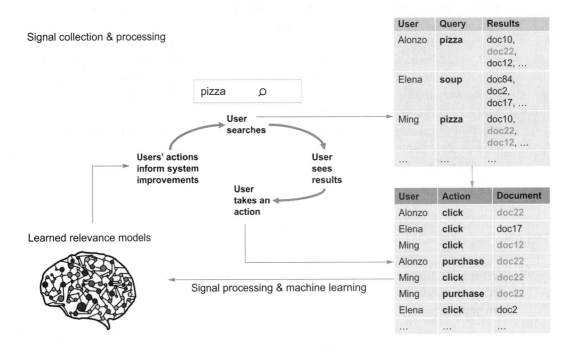

Figure 1.10   **Signal collection and processing data flow**

Signals are one of the two sources of data that power the intelligence engine of an AI-powered search application, with the other being content. Many AI-powered search algorithms incorporate signals feedback loops to build reflected intelligence models. Some of these key types of reflected intelligence algorithms include

- Popularized relevance—*Signals-boosting* algorithms create models that use aggregated signals to boost the rankings of the most important documents for your most popular queries.
- Personalized relevance—*Collaborative filtering* algorithms create models using matrix factorization or similar techniques that use signals to generate recommendations and user profiles to personalize search results for each user.
- Generalized relevance—*Learning to rank* algorithms train *ranking classifiers* to perform machine-learned ranking based on relevance judgments generated from user-signals-based click models. This process learns a set of features and ranking weights that can be applied generally to all queries—even ones that have not been previously seen.

These algorithms enable your search application to learn from user interactions and to automatically adjust rankings for future search results, delivering an improved search experience for the next users' searches.

1.3.4   *Content and domain intelligence*

While signals provide a constant stream of usage and feedback data to your search application, your content is also a rich source of information that can be incorporated in your feedback loops. For example, if someone searches for a particular keyword, the other keywords and top categories in the documents returned serve as valuable data points. Those data points can be used to tag or categorize the query and can be shown to other end users (as facets, for example), leading to further interactions that generate signals from which the engine can learn.

The content of your documents forms a representative textual model of your domain. Entities, domain-specific terminology, and the sentences contained within your documents serve as a rich, semantic graph. That graph can be utilized to drive powerful conceptual and semantic search that better understands your domain. We'll dive more deeply into understanding your content in chapter 2, and into semantic search capabilities using this rich semantic knowledge graph (SKG) in chapter 5.

In recent years, LLMs have revolutionized how search engines can interpret queries and responses. LLMs are deep neural networks trained on massive amounts of text data. They can recognize, translate, summarize, predict, and generate new data based on incoming prompts and any additional context provided. Often, LLMs are trained on text, receive a prompt as text, and return a response as text, though similar multimodal models can also be trained on images, audio, other data, or all the above. LLMs often contain billions of parameters within the neural network, and this number is likely to continue to grow in the future so long as model performance continues to improve with more parameters.

Today's most successful LLMs are based on the Transformer architecture, introduced by Google researchers in 2017, which applies the concept of "attention" to language learning ("Attention is All You Need", Ashish Vaswani et al.). Massive amounts of textual data are fed into a neural network, and a representation of the words and their relationships within each context are modeled using unsupervised learning. Once the model is built, it's able to interpret an incoming string of text, a *prompt*, as a context and to encode the context into embeddings, which are numerical vector representations of the meaning of the prompt. In addition to being able to encode prompts into embeddings, Transformers also contain a decoder layer, which can convert embeddings back into text. Transformers can be used to solve many kinds of problems, from similarity search on embeddings (text search, image search, etc.), to question answering, to classification, to summarization of content, and even to generation of new content (writing, code, poems, images, etc.).

Transformers are context-sensitive. An LLM tuned for question answering might respond to the prompt "What is the difference between a capital and capitol?" with the answer "A capital is a city or town that serves as the seat of government for a state or country. A capitol is a building in which a state legislature meets." However, the same LLM may respond to the question "What is the difference between a capital and lowercase word?" with the following context-based answer: "The difference between a capital and lowercase word is that a capital letter is used at the beginning of a sentence or proper nouns, while a lowercase letter is used for all other letters in a word."

Many LLMs are open sourced, but for optimal output quality, LLMs benefit from being fine-tuned for the task at hand with domain-specific content and prompts. Fine-tuning is the act of taking a pretrained model, which already has a strong general understanding of language and general concepts, and "teaching" it about new content and tasks. The original pretrained models are often referred to as *foundation models*, as they form the foundation upon which the domain-specific fine-tuning will be applied. The process of fine-tuning usually takes a small fraction of the time necessary to train the original LLM. Some LLMs have been trained on so much data and such a wide variety of data (such as a comprehensive web crawl of the internet) that they can perform quite well without retraining, but retraining for the task at hand almost always improves performance.

1.3.5 *Generative AI and retrieval augmented generation*

Generative AI is accelerating at a rapid pace, and search engines both benefit from it and serve as a key component of generative AI systems. LLMs (and other foundation models) serve as reasoning engines, having enough knowledge of the world to interpret language and generally reason about most concepts, but without the ability to reliably recall factual information without the risk of hallucinating (making up false information).

As a result, search engines are used in retrieval augmented generation (RAG) pipelines as a knowledge source for LLMs, allowing relevant context to be retrieved and passed to the LLM to ensure it has up-to-date and accurate data from which to answer. This entire book is effectively about using AI to optimize the "retrieval" part of RAG, and we'll cover the "generative" part in chapter 15.

While RAG makes search engines a critical component of generative AI systems, LLMs also serve as critical components of search engines. LLMs can be used to interpret queries, generate embeddings for vector search, generate summaries of search results, and even generate answers to questions directly from search results.

The transition from traditional information retrieval to these new *generative search* capabilities is shown in figure 1.11. For decades, traditional search has returned a list of search results ("ten blue links"), showing the top-ranked documents most relevant for a query. For queries on entities and well-known topics, search engines often show precalculated info boxes with summary information or show predetermined answers to known questions. Search engines often also extract words, sentences, or paragraph snippets out of search results to answer questions instead of forcing users to open and read the search results to find the answer. This process is known as *extractive question answering*, and it is a more targeted form of search, since it additionally searches and ranks answers found within documents.

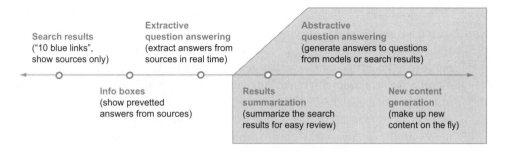

Figure 1.11   The transition from traditional information retrieval to generative search

However, there's a fine line between extracting answers from search results and synthesizing new content to return in the results, and this is where we transition into the realm of generative search. *Results summarization* is the process of rewriting search results into a more concise and readable format, often combining information from multiple sources and even providing citations for the sources within the summarized response. *Abstractive question answering* is the process of generating answers to questions by synthesizing information from one or more ranked search results into an answer to a user's question. The difference between extractive question answering and abstractive question answering is that extractive question answering finds relevant content within documents to return as answers ("extracting it"), whereas abstractive question answering writes a synthesized response by interpreting results and generating an answer that may look different than what's written in any of the documents. *New content generation* is also possible within a generative search experience, such as responding to queries with creative new prose, code, poems, images, or other content, based on the keywords or prompts being submitted by users.

In summary, generative AI and AI-powered search are tightly intertwined. Generative AI is a critical component of "AI-powered search" (powering answer generation and results summarization), and AI-powered search is a critical component of "search-powered AI" (RAG). Both heavily utilize LLMs and other foundation models, and both are critical components of intelligent and accurate AI systems.

1.3.6   *Curated vs. black-box AI*

Like LLMs, many modern AI techniques rely heavily on deep learning based on artificial neural networks. Unfortunately, it is often challenging for a human to understand the specific factors that go into any particular prediction or output from a deep learning model due to the internal complexity of the learned model.

This sometimes results in a "black-box AI" system, where the results may be correct or impressive, but they are not easy to debug or correct when the model makes an incorrect judgment. An entire field of *explainable AI* (sometimes called *interpretable AI* or *transparent AI*) has arisen out of a need to be able to understand, curate, and trust these models.

In this book, we'll cover deep learning approaches to search, such as dense vector search on embeddings, question answering, synthetic training data generation, and results summarization using LLMs. We'll mostly focus our efforts, however, on creating intelligence that can be expressed in human terms and then corrected and augmented by human intelligence. You can think of this as "AI-assisted human curation", or as "human-assisted AI", but either way, the overriding philosophy of this book is to use AI to automate the process of search intelligence while keeping the human in the loop with the ability to take control and augment or override the system.

As a learning exercise, this approach also leads to a deeper, intuitive understanding of how search ranking and relevance work, and how you can integrate many different AI-driven approaches without forfeiting control of the system.

1.3.7 *Architecture for an AI-powered search engine*

The architecture for an AI-powered search engine often requires numerous building blocks to be assembled to form a smart end-to-end system. You start with a core search engine like Apache Solr, OpenSearch, or one of the other search engines or vector databases identified in appendix B. You then feed your searchable content into the engine, running various transformations to make it more useful. These index-time transformations might include changes like these:

- Interpreting the meaning of your documents into embeddings using LLMs
- Classifying the document, adding the classification as a field
- Normalizing field values
- Extracting entities from text, adding entities in separate fields
- Clustering content, adding clusters as a field
- Detecting and annotating phrases
- Pulling in additional data from a knowledge graph, external API, or other data source
- Performing part of speech (POS) detection and other natural language processing steps
- Extracting facts (such as RDF triples)
- Applying other machine learning models or ETL rules to enrich the document

Once the data is in the engine, your goal is to make it available for searching. This requires query pipelines, which can interpret incoming queries; identify concepts, phrases, and entities; correct misspellings; expand the query to include related terms, synonyms, concepts, or embedding representations; and then rewrite the query so your core engine can find the most relevant results. Individual search documents may then be returned to the end user, summaries of results may be generated from language models, or answers may be explicitly extracted from the results.

Much of this query intelligence requires a robust understanding of your domain, however. This requires running batch jobs on your content and user signals to learn patterns and derive domain-specific intelligence. What are the most common misspellings from your users, and what do they choose as the correct spelling among multiple candidates? When a user searches for specific queries, which documents should be boosted as the most popular? For unknown queries, what is the ideal ranking among all the attributes or features available for matching?

We need access to most of these answers at query time (either precomputed or quickly computable) because we expect queries to return within milliseconds to seconds. This requires a job processing framework (we use Apache Spark in this book) and a workflow scheduling mechanism to keep the jobs running in sequence.

You'll also need a mechanism for collecting the constant stream of incoming user signals (capturing them on the frontend application and then storing them in your search engine or other backend datastore).

The signals will then be used to generate all kinds of models—from signals boosting models that boost the most popular items for top queries, to learning to rank models that apply a generalizable ranking function to all queries, to personalization models that output user-specific recommendations and personalization preferences for each user or segment of users.

AI-powered search is way more than just using the latest LLM to interpret queries. It's about engineering an end-to-end system for continuous learning. Ultimately, you'll end up with a system that receives constant streams of document changes and user signals, continually processes those streams to improve models, and then constantly adjusts future search results and measures the effect of changes in order to deliver more intelligent results. That is the key behind AI-powered search: implementing a process of continual learning and improvement based upon real user interactions, updating content patterns, and evolving models to optimally understand current user intent and to deliver an ever-improving search experience.

Summary

- Expectations for search sophistication are evolving with the rise of LLMs, with end users expecting search to now be domain-aware, contextual and personalized, conversational, multimodal, intelligent, and assistive.
- Search and recommendations are the two extreme ends of a continuous personalization spectrum within information retrieval, and it's important to consider the opportunities in between to optimize relevance.
- Correctly interpreting user intent requires simultaneous understanding of your content, your user and their preferences, and the knowledge domain in which your platform operates.
- Optimal search relevance lies at the intersection of personalized search (traditional keyword search plus collaborative recommendations), semantic search (traditional keyword search plus knowledge graphs), and domain-aware recommendations (collaborative recommendations plus knowledge graphs).

- AI-powered search operates on and learns from two key types of data: content and user signals.
- Search and generative AI go hand in hand. Generative search capabilities, such as RAG, are a critical component of modern generative AI systems (to prevent hallucinations); and generative AI capabilities, such as results summarization, are critical components of modern search engines (to return better answers).
- Reflected intelligence—the use of feedback loops to continually collect signals, tune results, and measure improvements—is the engine that enables AI-powered search to learn and constantly improve.

Working with natural language

This chapter covers

- The hidden structures in unstructured data
- A search-centric philosophy of language
- Exploring distributional semantics and vector-based embeddings
- Modeling domain-specific knowledge
- Challenges with natural language and querys
- Applying natural language understanding techniques to both content and signals

In the first chapter, we provided a high-level overview of what it means to build an AI-powered search system. Throughout the rest of the book, we'll explore and demonstrate the numerous ways your search application can continuously learn from your content and your users' behavioral signals to better understand your content, your users, and your domain, and to ultimately deliver users the answers they need. We will get much more hands-on in chapter 3, firing up a search server of your choice and a data processing layer (Apache Spark) and starting with the first of our Jupyter notebooks, which we'll use throughout the book to walk through many step-by-step examples.

Before we dive into those hands-on examples and specific implementations, however, it is important in this chapter that we first establish a shared mental model for the higher-level problems we're trying to solve. Specifically, when it comes to intelligent search, we have to deal with many complexities and nuances in natural language—both in the content we're searching and in our users' search queries. We have to deal with keywords, entities, concepts, misspellings, synonyms, acronyms, initialisms, ambiguous terms, explicit and implied relationships between concepts, hierarchical relationships usually found in taxonomies, higher-level relationships usually found in ontologies, and specific instances of entity relationships usually found in comprehensive knowledge graphs.

While it might be tempting to dive immediately into some specific problems, like how to automatically learn misspellings from content or how to discover synonyms from mining user search sessions, it will be more prudent to first establish a conceptual foundation that explains what *kinds* of problems we have to deal with in search and natural language understanding (NLU). Establishing that philosophical foundation will enable us to build better end-to-end solutions in our AI-powered search system, where all the parts work together in a cohesive and integrated way. This chapter will thus provide the philosophical underpinnings for how we tackle the problems of natural language understanding throughout this book and how we apply those solutions to make our search applications more intelligent.

We'll begin by discussing some common misconceptions about the nature of free text and other unstructured data sources.

2.1 *The myth of unstructured data*

The term "unstructured data" has been used for years to describe textual data, because it does not appear to be formatted in a way that can be readily interpreted and queried. The widely held idea that text, or any other data that doesn't fit a pre-defined schema ("structure"), is actually "unstructured", however, is a myth that we'll spend time reconsidering throughout this section.

If you look up *unstructured data* in Wikipedia, it is defined as "information that either does not have a pre-defined data model or is not organized in a pre-defined manner". The entry goes on to say that "unstructured information is typically text-heavy, but may contain data such as dates, numbers, and facts as well".

The phrase "unstructured data" is a poor term to describe textual content, however. In reality, the terms and phrases present in text encode an enormous amount of meaning, and the linguistic rules applied to the text to give it meaning serve as their own structure. Calling text unstructured is a bit like calling a song playing on the radio "arbitrary audio waves". Even though every song has unique characteristics, most exhibit common attributes (tempo, melodies, harmonies, lyrics, and so on). Though these attributes may differ or be absent from song to song, they nevertheless fit common expectations that enable meaning to be conveyed by and extracted from each song. Textual information typically follows similar rules—sentence structure, grammar, punctuation, interaction between parts of speech, and so on. Figure 2.1 shows an example of text we'll explore a bit more in the upcoming sections as we investigate this structure.

Trey Grainger works at Searchkernel.
He spoke at the Haystack 2023 conference.
#haystackconf (Haystack) was held in
Charlottesville, VA April 25–26, 2023. Trey got
his masters degree from Georgia Tech.

Figure 2.1   Unstructured data. This text represents typical unstructured data you may find in a search engine.

While text is the most commonly recognized type of unstructured data, there are several other kinds of unstructured data with similar characteristics, as we'll see in the next section.

2.1.1   *Types of unstructured data*

Free text content is considered the primary type of unstructured data, but search engines also commonly index many other kinds of data that similarly don't fit neatly into a structured database. Common examples include images, audio, video, and event logs. Figure 2.2 expands on our text example from figure 2.1 and includes several other types of unstructured data, such as audio, images, and video.

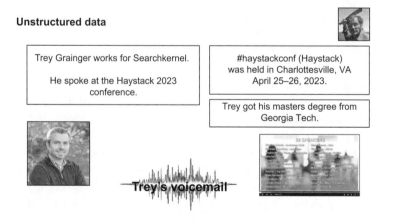

Figure 2.2   Multiple types of unstructured data. In addition to the text from the last figure, we now see images, audio, and video, which are other forms of unstructured data.

Audio is the most similar to text content, since it is often just another way to encode words and sentences. Of course, audio can include much more than just spoken words—it can include music and non-language sounds, and it can more effectively encode nuances such as emotion, tone of voice, and simultaneously overlapping communication.

Images are another kind of unstructured data. Just as words form sentences and paragraphs to express ideas, images form grids of colors that, taken together, form pictures.

Video, then, serves as yet another kind of unstructured data, as it is a combination of multiple images over time, as well as optional audio that coincides with the progression of images.

When unstructured data is found mixed with structured data, we typically refer to this as *semi-structured* data. Log data is a great example of such semi-structured data. Often, log messages contain a structured event date, structured event types (such as warning versus error or search versus click), and then some kind of unstructured message or description in free text.

Technically speaking, virtually any kind of file could be considered unstructured data, but we'll primarily deal with the aforementioned types. Search engines are often tasked with handling each of these kinds of unstructured data, so we'll discuss strategies for handling them throughout the book.

2.1.2 *Data types in traditional structured databases*

To better deal with our unstructured data, it may be useful to first contrast it with structured data in a SQL database. This will allow us to later draw parallels between how we can query unstructured data representations versus structured ones.

A record (row) in a SQL database is segmented into columns, which can each be of a particular data type. Some of these data types represent discrete values—values that come from an enumerated list, such as IDs, names, or textual attributes. Other columns may hold continuous values, such as date/time ranges, numbers, and other column types that represent ranges without a finite number of possible values.

Generally speaking, when one wants to relate different rows together or to relate them to rows in other database tables, "joins" will be performed on the discrete values. *Joins* use a shared value (often an ID field) to link two or more records together to form a composite record.

For example, if someone had two tables of data, one representing employees and another representing companies, then there would likely be an `id` column on the `companies` table, and a corresponding `company_id` column on the `employees` table. The `company_id` field on the employees table is known as a *foreign key*, which is a value in one table that refers to an entity in another table, linking the records together based upon a shared identifier. Figure 2.3 demonstrates this, showing examples of discrete values, continuous values, and a join across tables using a foreign key.

This notion of joining different records together based upon known relationships (keys and foreign keys) is a powerful way to work with relational data across explicitly

Structured data

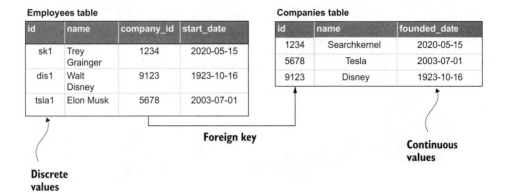

Figure 2.3   **Structured data in a typical database. Discrete values represent identifiers and enumerated values, continuous values represent data that falls within ranges, and foreign keys exist when the same value exists across two tables and can thus be used as a shared attribute that creates a relationship between corresponding rows from each table.**

modeled tables, but as we'll see in the next section, very similar techniques can also be applied to free-form unstructured data.

2.1.3   Joins, fuzzy joins, and entity resolution in unstructured data

Whereas structured data in a database is already in an easily queryable form, the reality is that unstructured data suffers less from a lack of structure, and more from having a large amount of information packed into a very flexible structure. In this section, we'll walk through a concrete example that uncovers this hidden structure in unstructured data and demonstrates the ways it can similarly be used to find and join relationships between documents.

FOREIGN KEYS IN UNSTRUCTURED DATA

We've discussed how foreign keys can be used to join two rows together in a database, based on a shared identifier between the two records. In this section, we'll show how the same objective can be achieved with text data.

For example, we can easily map the idea of foreign keys used in a SQL table to the unstructured information we explored in figure 2.2. Notice in figure 2.4 that two different sections of text both contain the word "Haystack", which refers to a technology conference focused on search relevance.

The first instance indicates a conference being spoken at, while the second block of text contains general information about the event. For the purposes of our example, let's assume that every piece of information (block of text, image, video, and audio clip) is represented as a separate document in our search engine. There is functionally very little difference between having two rows in a database table that each contain a column with the value "Haystack", and having separate documents in our

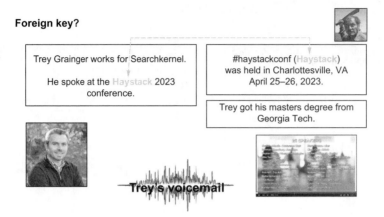

Figure 2.4
**Foreign keys in unstructured data.
In this example, the same term is being used to join across two related text documents.**

search engine that each contain the value "Haystack". In both cases, we can think of these documents as related by a foreign key.

FUZZY FOREIGN KEYS IN UNSTRUCTURED DATA

With unstructured data, however, we have much more power than with traditional structured data modeling. In figure 2.5, for example, notice that now two documents are linked and that they both refer to the lead author of this book—one using my full name of "Trey Grainger", and one simply using my first name of "Trey".

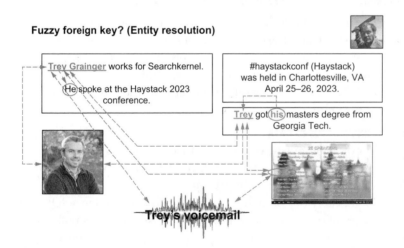

Figure 2.5   **Fuzzy foreign keys. In this example, the same entity is being referenced using different terms, and a join is occurring based upon multiple phrases resolving to the same entity.**

This is an example of *entity resolution*, where there are two different representations of the entity, but they can still be resolved to the same meaning, and therefore can still be used to join information between two documents. You can think of this as a "fuzzy foreign key", since it's still a foreign key, but not in a strict token-matching sense, as it requires additional natural language processing and entity resolution techniques to resolve.

Once we've opened this door to advanced text processing for entity resolution, we can learn even more from our unstructured information. For example, not only do the names "Trey" and "Trey Grainger" in these documents refer to the same entity, but so do the words "he" and "his".

You'll also notice that both an image of me (in the bottom-left corner, in case you have no idea what I look like) and a video containing a reference to my name are identified as related and joined back to the textual references. We're relying on the hidden structure present in all of this unstructured data to understand the meaning, relate the documents together, and learn even more about each of the referenced entities in those documents.

DEALING WITH AMBIGUOUS TERMS

So far, so good, but in real-world content it's not always appropriate to assume that the same term in multiple places carries the same meaning, or even that our entity resolution always resolves entities correctly. This problem of the same spelling of words and phrases having multiple potential meanings is called *polysemy*, and dealing with these ambiguous terms can be a huge problem in search applications.

You may have noticed an odd image in the upper-right corner of the previous figures that seemed a bit out of place. This image is of a fairly terrifying man holding a machete. Apparently, if you go to Google and search for `Trey Grainger`, this image comes back. If you dig in further, you'll see in figure 2.6 that there's an x.com (formerly Twitter) user also named "Trey Grainger", and this image is his profile picture.

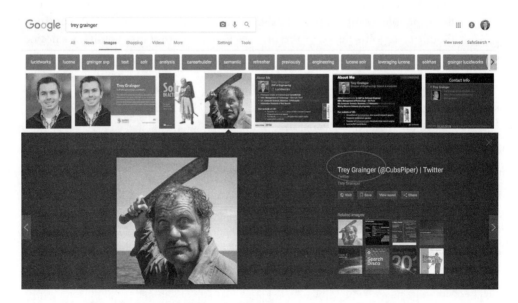

Figure 2.6   Polysemy. This image shows a Google search for `Trey Grainger`. Pictures of multiple different people are returned because those people's names share the same spelling, making the phrase "Trey Grainger" ambiguous.

The picture is apparently of Robert Shaw (who plays Quint in the 1975 movie *Jaws*), but it's definitely not the kind of thing you want people to first come across when they search for you online!

There are two key lessons to take away here. First, perhaps never Google yourself (you might be terrified at what you find!). Second, and on a more serious note, polysemy is a major problem in search and natural language understanding. It's not safe to assume a term has a single meaning or even a consistent meaning across different contexts, so our AI-powered search engine needs to use context to differentiate these various meanings.

UNSTRUCTURED DATA AS A GIANT GRAPH OF RELATIONSHIPS

In the previous sections, we saw that unstructured data not only contains rich information (entities and their relationships) but also that it's possible to relate different documents by joining them on shared entities, similar to how foreign keys work in traditional databases. Typical unstructured data contains so many of these relationships, however, that instead of thinking in terms of rows and columns, it may be more useful to think of the collection of data as a giant graph of relationships, as we'll explore in this section.

At this point, it should be clear that there is much more structure hidden in unstructured data than most people appreciate. Unstructured information is really more like "hyper-structured" information—it is a graph that contains much more structure than typical "structured data".

Figure 2.7 demonstrates this giant graph of relationships that is present in even the small handful of documents in our example. You can see names, dates, events, locations, people, companies, and other entities, and you can infer relationships between them, using joins between the entities across documents. You'll also notice that the

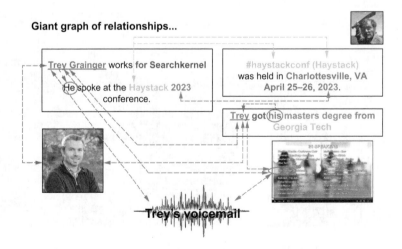

Figure 2.7 Giant graph of relationships. A rich graph of relationships emerges from even a small collection of related documents.

images have been correctly disambiguated so that the machete guy is now discon-nected from the graph. If all of this can be learned from just a few documents, imag-ine what can be learned from the thousands, millions, or billions of documents you have within your search engine.

Part of the value of an AI-powered search platform is being able to learn insights like this from your data. The question is, how do you use this enormous graph of semantic knowledge to drive this intelligence?

One of the most powerful ways to use a graph from text data is through a large lan-guage model (LLM), such as a Transformer model, which was introduced in section 1.3.4. These models use deep learning to learn billions of parameters across massive datasets, such as crawls of most of the internet, to build a detailed understanding of language. This understanding includes both the meanings of words in different con-texts and the linguistic and conceptual connections between words. These models internally represent the giant graph of relationships found in all the data they are trained on, which is usually more general than your dataset, so the models must be fine-tuned to learn any domain-specific relationships from your data. This need for fine-tuning can create some challenges due to LLMs being somewhat of a black box, as they otherwise don't optimally represent your dataset, and the information they return could be erroneous.

Fortunately, the inherent structure of the inverted index in your search engine makes it very easy to traverse the large graph of relationships in your data without any additional explicit data modeling required. An *inverted index* is the primary data struc-ture used for lexical search, mapping each keyword or term in the fields of your docu-ments to lists (called *postings lists*) of all the documents containing those keywords. The inverted index enables very fast lookups of the set of documents containing any given term (or term sequences, when considering positional matching and Boolean logic implemented through set operations). With those lookups, it is possible to tra-verse between different term sequences using their shared documents to calculate a weighted edge in a graph. We will dive deep into how to harness this semantic knowl-edge graph hidden in your data in chapter 5.

2.2 The structure of natural language

In the last section, we discussed how text and unstructured data typically contain a giant graph of relationships, which can be derived by looking at shared terms between different records. If you've been building search engines for a while, you're used to thinking about content in terms of "documents", "fields", and "terms" within those fields. When interpreting the semantic meaning of your content, however, there are a few more levels to consider.

Figure 2.8 walks through these additional levels of semantic meaning. At the most basic level, you have *characters*, which are single letters, numbers, or symbols, such as the letter "e" in the figure. One or more characters are then combined to form *character sequences* such as "e", "en", "eng", ... "engineer", and "engineers". Some character sequences form terms, which are completed words or tokens that carry an identifiable meaning, such as "engineer", "engineers", "engineering", or "software". One or more terms can then be combined into *term sequences*—usually called *phrases* when the terms are all sequential. These include things like "software engineer", "software engineers", and "senior software engineer". For simplicity in this book, we also consider single terms to be "term sequences", so any time we refer to "phrases", this includes single terms.

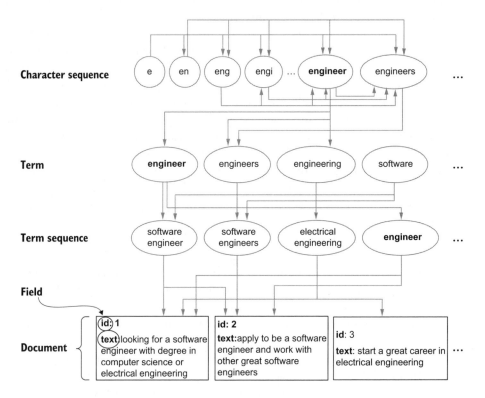

Figure 2.8   Semantic data encoded into free text content. Characters form character sequences, which form terms, which form term sequences, which form fields, which form documents, which form a corpus.

Term sequences vs. phrases

You may be wondering what the difference is between a "term sequence" and a "phrase". Quite simply, a phrase is a term sequence where all of the terms appear sequentially. For example, `"chief executive officer"` is both a phrase and a term sequence, whereas `"chief officer"~2` (meaning "officer" within two positions, or edit distances, of "chief") is only a term sequence, since it specifies a sequence of terms that is not necessarily sequential. In the vast majority of cases, you will only be dealing with sequential term sequences, so we'll mostly use the word "phrase" for simplicity throughout the book when referring inclusively to both single terms and multi-term sequential sequences. To avoid confusion, note that the word "term" is

> separately used to refer to "a unique value in a field in the search engine". As such, we will sometimes also refer to unsplit strings with multiple words in them in the search engine as "terms", even though linguistically they are considered "phrases" or "term sequences".

Of course, we know that a number of term sequences together can form sentences, multiple sentences can form paragraphs, and paragraphs can then be rolled up into even larger groups of text. For a search engine, though, the next higher-level level of grouping we'll typically focus on after term sequences is a field. A *field* in a search engine is a partitioned and labeled section of a document, usually for purposes of searching on or returning as an independent portion of the document. Fields containing text can be analyzed in any number of ways using a text analyzer, which typically includes techniques like splitting on white space and punctuation, lowercasing all terms so they are case-insensitive, stripping out noise (stop words and certain characters), stemming or lemmatization to reduce terms to a base form, and removing accents. If the text analysis process is unfamiliar to you, or you would like a refresher, we recommend checking out chapter 6 of *Solr in Action* by Trey Grainger and Timothy Potter (Manning, 2014).

One or more fields are then composed together into a *document*, and multiple documents form a *corpus* or collection of data. Whenever a query is executed against the search index, it filters the corpus into a *document set*, which is a subset of the corpus that specifically relates to the query in question.

Each of these linguistic levels—character sequences, terms, term sequences, fields, documents, document sets, and the corpus—provides unique insights into understanding your content and its unique meaning within your specific domain.

2.3   *Distributional semantics and embeddings*

Distributional semantics is a research area within the field of natural language processing that focuses on the semantic relationships between terms and phrases based on the distributional hypothesis. The distributional hypothesis is that words that occur in similar contexts tend to share similar meanings. It is summarized well by the popular quote, "You shall know a word by the company it keeps."[1]

When applying machine learning approaches to your text, these distributional semantics become increasingly important, and the search engine makes it incredibly easy to derive the context for most linguistic representations present in your corpus. For example, if someone wants to find all documents about C-level executives, they could issue a query like this:

```
c?o
```

---

[1] John Rupert Firth, "A synopsis of linguistic theory, 1930–1955," in J.R. Firth et al., *Studies in Linguistic Analysis*, Special Volume of the Philological Society (Oxford University Press, 1957).

This query would match "CEO", "CMO", "CFO", or any other CXO-style title, as it is asking for any character sequence starting with "c" and ending with "o" with a single character in between.

The same kind of freedom exists to query for arbitrarily complex term sequences:

```
"VP Engineering"~2
```

This query would match "VP Engineering", "VP of Engineering", "Engineering VP", or even "VP of Software Engineering", as it is asking to find "VP" and "Engineering" within two positions (edit distances) of each other.

Of course, the nature of a search engine's inverted index also makes it trivial to support arbitrary Boolean queries. For example, if someone searches for the term "Word", but we want to ensure any matched documents also contain either the term "Microsoft" or "MS" somewhere in the document, we could issue the following query:

```
(Microsoft OR MS) AND Word
```

Search engines support arbitrarily complex combinations of queries for character sequences, terms, and term sequences throughout your corpus, returning document sets that serve as a unique context of content matching that query. For example, if you run a query for pizza, the documents returned are more likely going to be restaurants than car rental companies, and if you run a query for machine learning, you're more likely to see jobs for data scientists or software engineers than for accountants, food service workers, or pharmacists. This means that you can infer a strong relationship between "machine learning" and "software engineering", and a weak relationship between "machine learning" and "food service worker". If you dig deeper, you'll also be able to see what other terms and phrases most commonly co-occur within the machine learning document set relative to the rest of your corpus, and thereby better understand the meaning and usage of the phrase "machine learning". We'll dive into hands-on examples of using these relationships in chapter 5.

Introducing vectors

A basic understanding of vector operations will be important as you progress through this book. A *vector* is a list of values describing some attributes of an item. For example, if your items are houses, you may have a list of attributes like price, size, and number of bedrooms. If you have a home costing $100,000 with 1,000 square feet and 2 bedrooms, this could be represented as the vector [100000, 1000, 2].

These attributes (price, size, and number of bedrooms in this example) are called *dimensions* or *features*, and a specific collection of dimensions is called a *vector space*. You can represent any other items (like other homes, apartments, or dwellings) within the same vector space if you can assign them values within the dimensions of the vector space.

If we consider other vectors within the same vector space (such as a house [1000000, 9850, 12] and another house [120000, 1400, 3]), we can perform mathematical operations on the vectors to learn trends and compare vectors. For example, you may intuitively look at these three example vectors and determine that "home prices tend to increase as the number of rooms increases" or that "the number of rooms tends to increase as home size increases". We can also perform similarity calculations on vectors to determine that the $120,000 home with 1,400 square feet and 3 bedrooms is more similar to the $100,000 home with 1,000 square feet and 2 bedrooms than to the $1,000,000 home with 9,850 square feet and 12 bedrooms.

In recent years, the distributional hypothesis has been applied to create semantic understandings of terms and term sequences through what are known as embeddings. An *embedding* is a set of coordinates in a vector space into which we map (or "embed") a concept. More concretely, that set of coordinates is a numerical vector (a list of numbers) that is intended to represent the semantic meaning of your data (text, image, audio, behavior, or other data modalities). Text-based embeddings can represent term sequences of any length, but when representing individual words or phrases, we call those embeddings *word embeddings*.

The term sequence is often encoded into a reduced-dimension embedding that can be compared with the vectors for all of the other embeddings within the corpus to find the most semantically related documents.

To understand this process, it may be useful to think of how a search engine works out of the box. Let's imagine a vector exists for each term that contains a value (dimension) for every word in your corpus. It might look something like figure 2.9.

Query	apple	caffeine	cheese	coffee	drink	donut	food	juice	pizza	tea	water
latte	0	0	0	0	0	0	0	0	0	0	0
cappuccino	0	0	0	0	0	0	0	0	0	0	0
apple juice	1	0	0	0	0	0	0	1	0	0	0
cheese pizza	0	0	1	0	0	0	0	0	1	0	0
donut	0	0	0	0	0	1	0	0	0	0	0
soda	0	0	0	0	0	0	0	0	0	0	0
green tea	0	0	0	0	0	0	0	0	0	1	0
water	0	0	0	0	0	0	0	0	0	0	1
cheese bread sticks	0	0	1	0	0	0	0	0	0	0	0
cinnamon sticks	0	0	0	0	0	0	0	0	0	0	0

Figure 2.9 Vectors with one dimension per term from the inverted index. Every query on the left maps to a vector on the right, with a value of 1 for any term from the index that is also in the query, and a 0 for any term from the index that is not in the query.

Figure 2.9 demonstrates conceptually how document matching works in lexical search engines by default. A *lexical search* is a search where documents are matched and ranked based on the degree to which they contain the actual keywords or other attributes specified in the query. For every keyword query, a vector exists that contains a dimension for every term in the inverted index. If that term exists in the query, the value in the vector is 1 for that dimension, and if that value does not exist in the query, then the value is 0 for that dimension. A similar vector exists for every document in the inverted index, with a 1 value for any term from the index that appears in the document, and a 0 for all other terms.

When a query is executed, a lookup occurs in the index for any matched terms, and then a similarity score is calculated based on a comparison of the vector for the query and the vector for the document that is being scored relative to the query. We'll walk through the specific scoring calculation in chapter 3, but this high-level understanding is sufficient for now.

There are obvious downsides to this approach. While it's great for finding documents with exact keyword matches, what happens when you want to find "related" things instead? For example, you'll notice that the term "soda" appears in a query, but never in the index. Even though there are other kinds of drinks ("apple juice", "water", "cappuccino", and "latte"), the search engine will always return zero results because it doesn't understand that the user is searching for a drink. Similarly, you'll notice that even though the term "caffeine" exists in the index, queries for latte, cappuccino, and green tea will never match the term "caffeine", even though they are related.

For these reasons, it is now common practice to use reduced-dimension dense embeddings to model a semantic meaning for term sequences in your index and queries. A *dense embedding* (also known as a *dense vector embedding*) is a vector of more abstract features that encodes an input's conceptual meaning in a semantic space. Figure 2.10 demonstrates the terms now mapped to a dimensionally reduced vector that can serve as a dense embedding.

	food	drink	dairy	bread	caffeine	sweet	calories	healthy
apple juice	0	5	0	0	0	4	4	3
cappuccino	0	5	3	0	4	1	2	3
cheese bread sticks	5	0	4	5	0	1	4	2
cheese pizza	5	0	4	4	0	1	5	2
cinnamon bread sticks	5	0	1	5	0	3	4	2
donut	5	0	1	5	0	4	5	1
green tea	0	5	0	0	2	1	1	5
latte	0	5	4	0	4	1	3	3
soda	0	5	0	0	3	5	5	0
water	0	5	0	0	0	0	0	5

Figure 2.10 **Dense embeddings with reduced dimensions. In this case, instead of one dimension per term (exists or missing), now higher-level dimensions exist that score shared attributes across items such as "healthy", contains "caffeine" or "bread" or "dairy", or whether the item is "food" or a "drink".**

With a new embedding vector now available for each term sequence in the leftmost column of figure 2.10, we can now score the relationship between each pair of term sequences, using the similarity between their vectors. In linear algebra, we use a cosine similarity function (or another similarity measure) to score the relationship between two vectors. Cosine similarity is computed by performing a dot product between the two vectors and scaling it by the magnitudes (lengths) of each of the vectors. We'll visit the math in more detail in the next chapter, but for now, figure 2.11 shows the results of scoring the similarity between several of these vectors.

Term Sequence:	Vector:
apple juice:	[1, 5, 0, 0, 0, 4, 4, 3]
cappuccino:	[0, 5, 3, 0, 4, 1, 2, 3]
cheese bread sticks:	[5, 0, 4, 5, 0, 1, 4, 2]
cheese pizza:	[5, 0, 4, 4, 0, 1, 5, 2]
cinnamon bread sticks:	[5, 0, 4, 5, 0, 1, 4, 2]
donut:	[5, 0, 1, 5, 0, 4, 5, 1]
green tea:	[0, 5, 0, 0, 2, 1, 1, 5]
latte:	[0, 5, 4, 0, 4, 1, 3, 3]
soda:	[0, 5, 0, 0, 3, 5, 5, 0]
water:	[0, 5, 0, 0, 0, 0, 0, 5]

Vector Similarity (*a, b*):

$$\cos(\theta) = \frac{a \cdot b}{|a| \times |b|}$$

Vector Similarity Scores:

Green Tea	
0.94	water
0.85	cappuccino
0.80	latte
0.78	apple juice
0.60	soda
...	...
0.19	donut

Vector Similarity Scores:

Cheese Pizza	
0.99	cheese bread sticks
0.91	cinnamon bread sticks
0.89	donut
0.47	latte
0.46	apple juice
...	...
0.19	water

Vector Similarity Scores:

Donut	
0.99	cinnamon bread sticks
0.89	cheese bread sticks
0.89	cheese pizza
0.57	apple juice
0.51	soda
...	...
0.07	water

Figure 2.11 Similarity between embeddings. The cosine between vectors shows the items list sorted by similarity with "green tea", with "cheese pizza", and with "donut".

As you can see in figure 2.11, since each term sequence is encoded into a vector that represents its meaning in terms of higher-level features, this embedding can now be used to score the similarity of that term sequence with any other similar vector. You'll see three vector similarity lists at the bottom of the figure: one for "green tea", one for "cheese pizza", and one for "donut".

By comparing the vector similarity of "green tea" with all the other term sequences, we find that the top related items are "water", "cappuccino", "latte", "apple juice", and "soda", with the least related being "donut". This makes intuitive sense, as "green tea" shares more attributes with the items higher in the list. For the "cheese pizza" vector, we see that the most similar other embeddings are for "cheese bread sticks", "cinnamon bread sticks", and "donut", with "water" being at the bottom of the list. Finally, for the term "donut", we find the top items to be "cinnamon bread sticks", "cheese bread sticks", and "cheese pizza", with "water" once again being at the bottom of the list. These results do a great job of finding the most similar items to our original query.

It's worth noting that this vector scoring is only used in the calculation of similarity between items. In your search engine, there's usually a two-phase process whereby you first filter to a set of documents (the *matching* phase) and then score those resulting documents (the *ranking* phase). Unless you're going to skip the first step and score all of your documents relative to your query vectors (which can be time- and processing-intensive), you'll still need some form of initial matching prior to the ranking phase to filter the query to a reasonable number of documents to score. We'll dive more into the mechanics for successfully implementing embeddings and vector search in chapters 3, 9, 13, 14, and 15.

Embeddings might represent queries, portions of documents, or even entire documents. It is commonplace to encode terms and term sequences into word embeddings, but *sentence embeddings* (encoding a vector with the meaning of a sentence), *paragraph embeddings* (encoding a vector with the meaning of a paragraph), and *document embeddings* (encoding a vector with the meaning of an entire document) are also common techniques.

It's also very common for dimensions to be more abstract than our examples here. For example, deep learning models like LLMs may detect seemingly unintelligible features from character sequences and the way that documents cluster together within the corpus. We wouldn't be able to easily apply a human-readable label to these dimensions in the embedding vector, but as long as it improves the predictive power of the model and increases relevance, this is usually not a concern for most search teams. In fact, since vectors encode "meaning" through different abstract numeric features, it's also possible to create and search on vectors representing different types (or *modalities*) of data, such as images, audio, video, or even signals and activity patterns. We'll cover *multimodal search* (searches on different data modalities) in section 15.3.

Ultimately, combining multiple models for harnessing the power of distributional semantics and embeddings tends to create the best outcomes, and we'll dive further into numerous graph and vector-based approaches to using these techniques throughout the rest of this book.

2.4   *Modeling domain-specific knowledge*

In chapter 1, we discussed the search intelligence progression (refer to figure 1.8), whereby organizations start with basic keyword search and progress through several additional stages of improvement before they ultimately achieve a full self-learning system. The second stage in that search intelligence progression was building taxonomies and ontologies, and the third stage ("query intent") included the building and use of knowledge graphs. Unfortunately, there can sometimes be significant confusion among practitioners in the industry on proper definitions and key terminology, like "ontology", "taxonomy", "synonym lists", "knowledge graphs", "alternative labels", and so on. It will benefit us to provide some definitions for use in this book to prevent any ambiguity. Specifically, we'll lay out definitions for the key terms of "knowledge graph", "ontology", "taxonomy", "synonyms", and "alternative labels". Figure 2.12 shows a high-level diagram of how they relate.

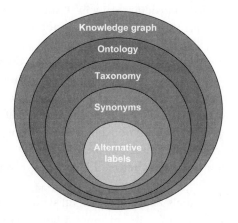

Figure 2.12 Levels of domain-specific knowledge modeling. Knowledge graphs extend ontologies, which extend taxonomies. Synonyms extend alternative labels and map to entries in taxonomies.

We define each of these knowledge modeling techniques as follows:

- *Alternative labels (or alt. labels)*—Replacement term sequences with identical meanings.

  ```
  Examples:
      CTO => Chief Technology Officer
      specialise => specialize
  ```

- *Synonyms*—Replacement term sequences that can be used to represent the same or very similar things.

  ```
  Examples:
      human => homo sapiens, mankind
      food => sustenance, meal
  ```

- *Taxonomy*—A classification of things into categories.

  ```
  Examples:
      human is mammal
      mammal is animal
  ```

- *Ontology*—A mapping of relationships between types of things.

  ```
  Examples:
      animal eats food
      food contains ingredients
  ```

- *Knowledge graph*—An instantiation of an ontology that also contains the things that are related.

  ```
  Examples:
      John is human
      John eats food
  ```

Creating alternative labels is the most straightforward of these techniques to under-stand. Initialisms (such as "RN" => "Registered Nurse") and acronyms virtually always serve as alternative labels, as do misspellings and alternative spellings. Sometimes it is useful to store these mappings in separate lists, particularly if you're using algorithms to determine them and you expect to allow for human modification of them or if you plan to rerun the algorithms later.

Synonyms are the next most common of the techniques, as virtually every search engine will have some implementation of a synonym list. Alternative labels are a sub-set of a synonym list and are the most obvious kind of synonym. Most people consider "highly related" term sequences to be synonyms, as well. For example, "software engi-neer" and "software developer" are often considered synonyms since they are usually used interchangeably, even though there are some nuances in meaning between the two. Sometimes, you'll even see translations of words between languages showing up in synonyms for bilingual search use cases.

One key difference between alternative labels and more general synonyms is that alternative labels can be seen as *replacement terms* for the original, whereas synonyms are more often used as *expansion terms* to add alongside the original. Implementations can vary widely, but this ultimately boils down to whether you are confident that two term sequences carry exactly the same meaning (and you want to normalize them), or whether you're just trying to include additional related term sequences so you don't miss other relevant results.

Taxonomies are the next step up from synonyms. Taxonomies focus less on substi-tute or expansion words and instead focus on categorizing your content into a hierar-chy. Taxonomical information will often be used to drive website navigation, to change behavior for a subset of search results (for example, to show different faceting or filtering options based upon a parent product category), or to apply dynamic filter-ing based upon a category to which a query maps. For example, if someone searches for range on a home improvement website, the site might automatically filter down to "appliances" to remove the noise of other products that contain phrases like "fall within the range" in their product description. Synonyms then map into a taxonomy, pointing to particular items within the taxonomy.

Whereas taxonomies tend to specify parent-child relationships between categories and then map things into those categories, ontologies provide the ability to define much richer relationships between things (term sequences, entities) within a domain. Ontologies typically define more abstract relationships, attempting to model the rela-tionships between kinds of things in a domain, such as "employee reports to boss," "CMO's boss is CEO," "CMO is employee". This makes ontologies really useful for deriving new information from known facts by mapping the facts into the ontology and then drawing logical conclusions based on relationships in the ontology that can be applied to those facts.

Knowledge graphs are the relative newcomer to the knowledge management space. Whereas ontologies define high-level relationships that apply to types of things, knowledge graphs tend to be full instantiations of ontologies that also include each of the specific entities that fall within those types. Using our previous ontology example, a knowledge graph would additionally have "Michael is CMO," "Michael reports to Marcia," and "Marcia is CEO" as relationships in the graph. Before knowledge graphs came to the forefront, it was common for these more detailed relationships to be modeled into ontologies, and many people still do this today. As a result, you'll often see the terms "knowledge graph" and "ontology" used interchangeably, though this is becoming less common over time.

Throughout this book, we will mostly focus our discussions on alternative labels, synonyms, and knowledge graphs, since taxonomies and ontologies are mostly subsumed into knowledge graphs. We'll explore knowledge graphs more thoroughly in chapter 5.

2.5 Challenges in natural language understanding for search

In the last few sections, we've discussed the rich graph of meaning embedded within unstructured data, like text, as well as how distributional semantics and embeddings can be used to derive and score semantic relationships between term sequences in queries and documents. We also introduced key techniques for knowledge modeling and defined related terminology we'll use throughout this book. In this section, we'll discuss a few key challenges associated with natural language understanding that we'll seek to overcome in the coming chapters.

2.5.1 The challenge of ambiguity (polysemy)

In section 2.1.3, we introduced the idea of polysemy, or ambiguous terms. In that section, we were dealing with an image tagged with the name "Trey Grainger" but that referred to a different person than the author of this book. In textual data, however, we have the same problem, and it can get very messy.

Consider a word like "driver". It can refer broadly to a "vehicle driver", a kind of golf club for hitting the ball off a tee, software that enables a hardware device to work, a kind of tool (screwdriver), or the impetus for pushing something forward ("a key driver of success"). There are many potential meanings for this word, and you could explore even more granular meanings. For example, within the "vehicle driver" category, it could mean a taxi driver, Uber driver, Lyft driver, professional trucker like a CDL driver (someone with a commercial drivers license), or even a bus driver. Within the subset of bus drivers, it could mean a school bus driver, a driver of a public city bus, a driver of a tour bus, and so on. We could continue breaking down this list into dozens of additional categories at a minimum.

When building search applications, engineers will often naively create static synonym lists and assume terms have a singular meaning that can be applied universally. The reality, however, is that every term (word or phrase) takes on a unique meaning that is based on the specific context in which it is being used.

TIP   Every term takes on a unique meaning that is based on the specific context in which it is being used.

It's not often practical to support an infinite number of potential meanings, though we discuss techniques to approximate this with a semantic knowledge graph in chapter 5. Nevertheless, whether you support many meanings per phrase or just a few, it's important to recognize the clear need to be able to generate an accurate (and often nuanced) interpretation for any given phrase your users may encounter.

2.5.2   *The challenge of understanding context*

I like to say that every term (word or phrase) you ever encounter is a "context-dependent cluster of meaning with an ambiguous label". That is to say, there is a label (the textual representation of the term) that is being applied to some concept (a cluster of meaning) that is dependent upon the context in which it is found. By this definition, it's impossible to ever precisely interpret a term without understanding its context. As a result, creating fixed synonym lists that aren't able to take context into account is likely to create suboptimal search experiences for your users.

Transformer models largely operate on this premise by using input prompts as the context in which to interpret each word part (or token) in the prompt. Attention is paid to every token, based on the surrounding tokens and how they relate to the learned representation in the model, which is also contextual. We'll dive into the nuances of how Transformers work in chapter 13, and we'll fine-tune a Transformer for a question-answering task in chapter 14.

Just because context is important doesn't mean it's always easy to apply correctly. It's often necessary to perform basic keyword search as a fallback when your search engine doesn't understand a query, and it's almost always useful to have prebuilt domain understanding that can similarly be relied upon to help interpret queries. This prebuilt domain understanding then ends up overriding some of the default keyword-based matching behavior (such as joining individual keywords into phrases, injecting synonyms, and correcting misspellings).

As we discussed in chapter 1, the context for a query includes more than just the search keywords and the content within your documents. It also includes an understanding of your domain, as well as an understanding of your user. Queries can take on entirely different meanings based on what you know about your user and any domain-specific understanding you may have. This context is necessary both to detect and resolve the kinds of ambiguity we discussed in the last section, as well as to ensure your users are receiving the most intelligent search experience possible. Throughout this book, our focus will be on techniques to automatically learn contextual interpretations of each query, based on the unique context in which it's being used.

2.5.3   *The challenge of personalization*

When considering user-specific context as a tool for enhancing query understanding, it's not always obvious how to apply user-specific personalization on top of the preexisting content and domain-specific scoring. For example, say you learn that a particular user really likes Apple as a brand because they keep searching for iPhones. Does this mean that Apple should also be boosted when they are searching for watches, computers, keyboards, headphones, and music players? It could be that the user only likes Apple-branded phones and that by boosting the brand in other categories you may frustrate the user. For example, even if the user did search for an iPhone previously, how do you know they weren't just trying to compare the iPhone with other phones they were considering?

Out of all of the dimensions of user intent (figure 1.5), personalization is the easiest one to trip up on, and, as a result, it is the one that is least commonly seen in modern AI-powered search applications (outside of recommendation engines, of course). We'll work through these problems in detail in chapter 9 to highlight how we can strike the right balance when rolling out a personalized search experience.

2.5.4   Challenges interpreting queries vs. documents

One common problem we see when engineers and data scientists first get started with search is a propensity to apply standard natural language processing techniques, like language detection, part-of-speech detection, phrase detection, and sentiment analysis to queries. Usually, those techniques were trained to operate on longer blocks of text—often at the document, paragraph, or at least sentence level.

Documents tend to be longer and to supply significantly more context to the surrounding text, whereas queries tend to be short (a few keywords only) in most use cases. Even when they are longer, queries tend to combine multiple ideas as opposed to supplying more linguistic context. As a result, when trying to interpret queries, you need to use external context as much as possible.

Instead of using a natural language processing library that relies on sentence structure to interpret the query, for example, you can try looking up the phrases from your query in your corpus of documents to find their most common domain-specific interpretations. Likewise, you can use the co-occurrence of terms within your query across previous user search sessions by mining user behavioral signals. This enables you to learn real intent from similar users, which would be very challenging to reliably derive from a standard natural language processing library.

In short, queries need special handling and interpretation due to their tendency to be short and to often imply more than they state explicitly, so fully using search-centric data science approaches to queries is going to generate much better results than traditional natural language processing approaches.

2.5.5   Challenges interpreting query intent

While the process of parsing a query to understand the terms and phrases it contains is important, there is often a higher-level intent behind the query—a query intent, if you will. For example, let's consider the inherent differences between the following queries:

```
who is the CEO?
support
iphone screen blacked out
iphone
```

```
verizon silver iphone 8 plus 64GB
sale
refrigerators
pay my bill
```

The intent of the first query for who is the CEO? is clearly to find a factual answer and not a list of documents. The second query for support is trying to navigate to the support section of a website, or to otherwise contact the support team. The third query for iphone screen blacked out is also looking for support, but it is for a specific problem, and the person likely wants to find troubleshooting pages that may help with that specific problem before reaching out to the actual support team.

The next two queries for iphone and for verizon silver iphone 8 plus 64GB are quite interesting. While they are both for iPhones, the first search is a general search, likely indicating a browsing or product research intent, whereas the second query is a much more specific variant of the first search, indicating the user knows exactly what they are looking for and may be closer to making a purchasing decision. The general query for iphone may be better to return a landing page providing an overview of iphones and the available options, whereas the more specific query may be better for going straight to a product page with a purchase button. As a general rule of thumb, the more general a query, the more likely the user is just browsing. More specific queries—especially when they refer to specific items by name—often indicate a purchase intent or desire to find a particular known item.

The query for sale indicates that the user is looking for items that are available for purchase at a discounted rate, which will invoke some specially implemented filter or redirect to a particular landing page for an ongoing sale event. The query for refrigerators indicates that the user wants to browse a particular category of product documents. Finally, the query for pay my bill indicates that the user wants to take an action—the best response to this query isn't a set of search results or even an answer, but instead a redirect to a bill review and payment section of the application.

Each of these queries contains an intent beyond just a set of keywords to be matched. Whether the intent is to redirect to a particular page, apply particular filters, browse or purchase items, or even take domain-specific actions, the point is that there is domain-specific nuance to how users may express their goals to your search engine. Oftentimes, it can be difficult to derive these domain-specific user intents automatically. It is fairly common for businesses to implement specific business rules to handle these as one-off requests. Query intent classifiers can certainly be built to handle subsets of this problem, but successfully interpreting every possible query intent still remains challenging when building out natural language query interpretation capabilities.

2.6   *Content + signals: The fuel powering AI-powered search*

In the first chapter, we introduced the idea of reflected intelligence—using feedback loops to continually learn from both content and user interactions. This chapter has focused entirely on understanding the meaning and intelligence embedded within your content, but it's important to recognize that many of the techniques we'll apply to the "unstructured data" in your documents can also be just as readily applied to your user behavioral signals. For example, we discussed in section 2.3 how the meanings of phrases can be derived from finding the other phrases they most commonly appear with across your corpus. We noted that "machine learning" appears more commonly with "data scientist" and "software engineer" than it does with "accountants," "food service workers," or "pharmacists".

If you abstract the distributional hypothesis beyond documents and also apply it to user behavior, you might expect that similar users querying your search engine are likely to exhibit similar query behavior. Specifically, people who are data scientists or who are searching for data scientists are far more likely to also search for or interact with documents about machine learning, and the likelihood of a food service worker or accountant searching for machine learning content is much lower than the likelihood of a software engineer doing so. We can thus apply these same techniques to learn related terms and term sequences from query logs, where instead of thinking of terms and term sequences mapping to fields in documents, we think of terms in queries and clicks on search results mapping to user sessions, which then map to users. We'll follow this approach in chapter 6 to learn related terms, synonyms, and misspellings from user query logs.

Some search applications are content-rich but have very few user signals. Other search applications have an enormous number of signals but either very little content or content that poses challenges from an automated learning perspective. In an ideal scenario, you'll have great content and an enormous quantity of user signals to learn from, which allows you to combine the best of both worlds into an even smarter AI-powered search application. Regardless of which scenario you're in, keep in mind that your content and your user signals can both serve as fuel to power learning algorithms, and you should do your best to maximize the collection and quality of each.

As a final note on natural language understanding: with the rise of LLMs, which are deep neural networks trained on a large percentage of human knowledge (much of the internet, plus selected sources), we now have the ability to interpret the meaning and intent of general-knowledge questions at an unprecedented level of quality. LLMs do not handle domain-specific understanding very well out of the box, at least for information that is not part of their training sets, but with the ability to fine-tune LLMs on domain-specific data, these models can often be quickly adapted to more closed-domain data. LLMs represent a large leap forward in our ability to learn the nuances of natural language, interpret arbitrary documents and queries based on those nuances, and drive more relevant search.

LLMs, while generally the most impressive technique for wide-scale natural language understanding, are far from the only powerful tools in our AI-powered search toolbox. We'll dive into using LLMs for search in chapters 9, 13, 14, and 15. In the meantime, we have many other critical algorithms and techniques to explore for natural language and domain understanding, interpreting user behavior, and learning optimal relevance ranking models.

Now that we've covered all the background needed to begin extracting meaning from your natural language content, it's time to roll up our sleeves and get hands-on. In the next chapter, we'll dive into lots of examples as we begin to explore content-based relevance in an AI-powered search application.

Summary

- Unstructured data is a misnomer—it is really more like hyper-structured data, as it represents a giant graph of domain-specific knowledge.
- Search engines can use distributional semantics—interpreting the semantic relationships between terms and phrases based upon the distributional hypothesis—to harness rich semantic meaning at the level of character sequences, terms, term sequences (typically phrases), fields, documents, document sets, and an entire corpus.
- Distributional semantics approaches enable us to learn the nuanced meaning of our queries and content from their larger surrounding context.
- Embeddings are a powerful technique for search results ranking based on the semantic meaning of text (and other data modalities) instead of just the existence and occurrence counts of specific keywords.
- Domain-specific knowledge is commonly modeled through a combination of alternative labels, synonym lists, taxonomies, ontologies, and knowledge graphs. Knowledge graphs typically model the output from each of the other approaches into a unified knowledge representation of a particular domain.
- Polysemy (ambiguous terms), context, personalization, and query-specific natural language processing approaches represent some of the more interesting challenges in natural language search.
- Content and user signals are both important fuel for our AI-powered search applications to use when solving natural language challenges.

Ranking and content-based relevance

This chapter covers

- Executing queries and returning search results
- Ranking search results based on how relevant they are to an incoming query
- Keyword match and filtering versus vector-based ranking
- Controlling and specifying custom ranking functions with function queries
- Catering ranking functions to a specific domain

Search engines fundamentally do three things: ingest content (*indexing*), return content matching incoming queries (*matching*), and sort the returned content based on some measure of how well it matches the query (*ranking*). Additional layers can be added, allowing users to provide better queries (autosuggest, chatbot dialogs, etc.) and to extract better answers from the results or summarize the results by using large language models (see chapters 14–15), but the core functions of the search engine are matching and ranking on indexed data.

Relevance is the notion of how well the returned content matches the query. Normally, the content being matched is documents, and the returned and ranked content is the matched documents along with corresponding metadata. In most search engines, the default relevance sorting is based upon a score indicating how well each keyword in a query matches the same keyword in each matched document. Alternatively, queries can be mapped into numerical vector representations, with the score then representing how similar the query vector is to each matched document. The best matches yield the highest relevance score, and they are returned at the top of the search results. The relevance calculation is highly configurable and can be adjusted on a per-query basis, allowing sophisticated ranking behavior.

In this chapter, we'll provide an overview of how relevance is calculated, how the relevance function can be easily controlled and adjusted through function queries, and how we can implement popular domain-specific and user-specific relevance ranking features.

3.1 Scoring query and document vectors with cosine similarity

In section 2.3, we demonstrated the idea of measuring the similarity of two vectors by calculating the cosine between them. We created vectors (lists of numbers, where each number represents the strength of some feature) that represented different food items, and we then calculated the cosine (the size of the angle between the vectors) to determine their similarity. We'll expand upon that technique in this section, discussing how text queries and documents can map into vectors for ranking purposes. We'll then explore some popular text-based feature-weighting techniques and how they can be integrated to create an improved relevance-ranking formula.

> **Running the code examples**
>
> All the code listings in the book are available in Jupyter notebooks running in preconfigured Docker containers. This enables you to run interactive versions of the code with a single command (`docker compose up`) without needing to spend time on complicated system configuration and dependency management. The code examples can also run with multiple search engines and vector databases. See appendix A for instructions on how to configure and launch the Jupyter notebooks and follow along in your web browser.
>
> For brevity, the listings in this book may leave out certain lines of code, such as imports or ancillary code, but the notebooks contain all implementation details.

In this section, we'll dive into our first code listings for the book. It will be helpful to start up the Docker containers needed to run the accompanying Jupyter notebooks so you can follow along with the interactive code examples. Instructions for doing this are provided in appendix A.

3.1.1   Mapping text to vectors

In a typical search application, we start with a collection of documents, and we then try to rank documents based on how well they match some user's query. In this section, we'll walk through the process of mapping the text of queries and documents into vectors.

In the last chapter, we used the example of a search for food and beverage items, like `apple juice`, so let's reuse that example here. Let's assume we have two different documents we would like to sort based on how well they match this query.

Query: `apple juice`

```
Document 1:
  Lynn: ham and cheese sandwich, chocolate cookie, ice water
  Brian: turkey avocado sandwich, plain potato chips, apple juice
  Mohammed: grilled chicken salad, fruit cup, lemonade
Document 2:
  Orchard Farms apple juice is premium, organic apple juice made from the
  freshest apples, never from concentrate. Its juice has received the
  regional award for best apple juice three years in a row.
```

If we mapped both documents (containing a combined 48 words) to vectors, they would map to a 48-word vector space with the following dimensions:

```
[a, and, apple, apples, avocado, award, best, brian, cheese, chicken, chips,
 chocolate, concentrate, cookie, cup, farms, for, freshest, from, fruit,
 grilled, ham, has, ice, in, is, its, juice, lemonade, lynn, made,
 mohammed, never, orchard, organic, plain, potato, premium, received,
 regional, row, salad, sandwich, the, three, turkey, water, years]
```

If you recall in section 2.3, we proposed thinking of a query for the phrase "apple juice" as a vector containing a feature for every word in any of our documents, with a value of 1 for the terms "apple" and "juice", and a value of 0 for all other terms.

Since the term "apple" is in the 3rd position, and "juice" is in the 28th position of our 48-word vector space, a query vector for the phrase "apple juice" would look as shown in figure 3.1.

Query: [0 0 1 0 0 0 0 0 0 0 0 0 0 0 0 0 0 0 0 0 0 0 0 0 0 0 0 1 0 0 0 0 0 0 0 0 0 0 0 0 0 0 0 0 0 0 0 0]

     apple   **juice**

Figure 3.1   Query vector. The query for `apple juice` is mapped to a vector containing one dimension for every known term, with a value of 1 for the terms "apple" and "juice" and a value of 0 for all other terms.

Even though the query vector only contains a nonzero value for two dimensions (representing the positions of "apple" and "juice"), it still contains values of 0 for all other possible dimensions. Representing a vector like this, including every possible value, is known as a *dense vector representation*.

Each of the documents also maps to the same vector space based upon each of the terms it contains:

```
Document 1:
[0 1 1 0 1 0 0 1 1 1 1 1 0 1 1 0 0 0 0 1 1 1 0 1
 0 0 0 1 1 1 0 1 0 0 1 1 1 0 0 0 0 1 1 0 0 1 1 0]

Document 2:
[1 0 1 1 0 1 1 0 0 0 0 0 1 0 0 1 1 1 1 0 0 0 1 0
 1 1 1 1 0 0 1 0 1 1 0 0 0 1 1 1 1 0 0 1 1 0 0 1]
```

With these dense vector representations of our query and documents, we can now use linear algebra to measure the similarity between our query vector and each of the document vectors.

3.1.2 *Calculating similarity between dense vector representations*

To rank our documents, we just need to follow the same process we used in chapter 2 to calculate the cosine between each document and the query. This cosine value will then become the relevance score by which we'll be able to sort each document.

The following listing shows how we would represent the query and document vectors in code, and how we would calculate the cosine similarity between the query and each document.

Listing 3.1 Calculating cosine similarity between vectors

```
query_vector = numpy.array(
    [0, 0, 1, 0, 0, 0, 0, 0, 0, 0, 0, 0, 0, 0, 0, 0, 0, 0, 0, 0, 0, 0, 0,
     0, 0, 0, 1, 0, 0, 0, 0, 0, 0, 0, 0, 0, 0, 0, 0, 0, 0, 0, 0, 0, 0, 0])

doc1_vector = numpy.array(
    [0, 1, 1, 0, 1, 0, 0, 1, 1, 1, 1, 1, 0, 1, 1, 0, 0, 0, 0, 1, 1, 1, 0, 1,
     0, 0, 0, 1, 1, 1, 0, 1, 0, 0, 1, 1, 1, 0, 0, 0, 0, 1, 1, 0, 0, 1, 1, 0])

doc2_vector = numpy.array(
    [1, 0, 1, 1, 0, 1, 1, 0, 0, 0, 0, 0, 1, 0, 0, 1, 1, 1, 1, 0, 0, 0, 1, 0,
     1, 1, 1, 1, 0, 0, 1, 0, 1, 1, 0, 0, 0, 1, 1, 1, 1, 0, 0, 1, 1, 0, 0, 1])

def cosine_similarity(vector1, vector2):
    return dot(vector1, vector2) / (norm(vector1) * norm(vector2))

doc1_score = cosine_similarity(query_vector, doc1_vector)
doc2_score = cosine_similarity(query_vector, doc2_vector)

print_scores([doc1_score, doc2_score])
```

Output:

```
Relevance Scores:
  doc1: 0.2828
  doc2: 0.2828
```

Interesting . . . both documents received the same relevance score, even though the documents contain lengthy vectors with very different content. It might not be immediately obvious what's going on, so let's simplify the calculation by focusing only on the features that matter.

3.1.3   Calculating similarity between sparse vector representations

The key to understanding the calculation in the last section is realizing that the only relevant features are the ones shared between the query and the document. All other features (words appearing in documents that don't match the query) have zero effect on whether one document is ranked higher than another. As a result, we can remove all the other insignificant terms from our vector to simplify the example, converting from a dense vector representation to what is known as a *sparse vector representation,* as shown in figure 3.2.

Sparse vector
representation: [1 1]

apple   juice

Figure 3.2   Sparse vector representations only contain the "present" features, unlike dense vector representations, which also contain the 0-valued entries for every feature.

In most search engine scoring operations, we tend to deal with sparse vector representations because they are more efficient to work with when scoring based on the small number of features.

In addition, we can further simplify our calculations by creating vectors that only include "meaningful entries"—the terms that are present in the query—as shown in the following listing.

Listing 3.2   Cosine similarity of sparse vector representations

```
query_vector = [1, 1] #[apple, juice]
doc1_vector  = [1, 1]
doc2_vector  = [1, 1]

doc1_score = cosine_similarity(query_vector, doc1_vector)
doc2_score = cosine_similarity(query_vector, doc2_vector)

print_scores([doc1_score, doc2_score])
```

Output:

```
Relevance Scores:
  doc1: 1.0
  doc2: 1.0
```

Notice that doc1 and doc2 still yield equal relevance scores, but now the score for each is 1.0. If you remember, a 1.0 score from a cosine calculation means the vectors are perfect matches, which is sensible considering that both vectors are identical ([1, 1]).

In fact, you'll notice several very interesting things:

- This simplified sparse vector representation calculation still shows both doc1 and doc2 returning equivalent relevance scores, since they both match all the words in the query.
- Even though the absolute score between the dense vector representation similarity (0.2828) and the sparse vector representation similarity (1.0) are different, the scores are still the same relative to each other within each vector type.
- The feature weights for the two query terms ("apple", "juice") are the same between the query and each of the documents, resulting in a cosine score of 1.0.

Vectors vs. vector representations

We've been careful to refer to "dense vector representations" and "sparse vector representations" instead of "dense vectors" and "sparse vectors". This is because there is a conceptual distinction between the idea of a vector and its representation, and this distinction often causes confusion.

The sparsity of a *vector* refers to the proportion of the vector's features that have meaningful values. Specifically, a dense vector is any vector whose features have mostly nonzero values, whereas a sparse vector is any vector whose features have mostly zeros, regardless of how they are stored or represented. Vector *representations*, on the other hand, deal with the data structures used to work with the vectors. For sparse vectors, it can be wasteful to allocate memory and storage space for all the zeros, so we will often use a sparse data structure (such as an inverted index) to only store the nonzero values. Here is an example:

dense vector:
feature_1: 1.1, feature_2: 2.3, feature_3: 7.1, feature_4: 5.2, feature_5: 8.1
dense vector representation: [1.1, 2.3, 7.1, 5.2, 8.1]
sparse vector representation: N/A (the vector is not sparse, so it can't be represented sparsely)

sparse vector: feature_1: 1.1, feature_2: 0, feature_3: 0, feature_4: 5.2, feature_5: 0
dense vector representation: [1.1, 0.0, 0.0, 5.2, 0.0]
sparse vector representation: { 1: 1.1, 4: 5.2 }, or just [1.1, 5.2] if feature positions aren't needed

Because a sparse vector contains predominantly zeros, and its corresponding sparse vector representation contains nearly the opposite (only the nonzero values), it is unfortunately common for people to confuse these concepts and incorrectly refer to dense vector representations (of sparse vectors) as "dense vectors", or even refer to any vector with many dimensions as a "dense vector" and with few dimensions as a "sparse vector". You may find this confusion in other literature, so it's important to be aware of the distinction.

Since our query and document vectors are all sparse vectors (most values are zero, since the number of features is the number of keywords in the search index), it makes sense to use a sparse vector representation when doing keyword search.

Search engines adjust for these problems by not just considering each feature in the vector as a `1` (exists) or a `0` (does not exist), but instead by providing a score for each feature based upon how *well* the feature matches.

3.1.4 Term frequency: Measuring how well documents match a term

The problem we encountered in the last section is that the features in our term vectors only signify *if* the word "apple" or "juice" exists in a document, not how well each document represents either of the terms. A side effect of representing each term from the query with a value of `1` if it exists is that both doc1 and doc2 will always have the same cosine similarity score for the query, even though, qualitatively, doc2 is a much better match, since it talks about apple juice much more.

Instead of using a value of `1` for each existing term, we can emulate "how well" a document matches by using the *term frequency* (TF), which is a measure of the number of times a term occurs within each document. The idea here is that the more frequently a term occurs within a specific document, the greater the likelihood that the document is more related to the query.

The following listing shows vectors with a count of the number of times each term occurs within the document or query as the feature weights.

Listing 3.3 Cosine similarity of raw TF vectors

```
query_vector    = [1, 1] #[apple:1, juice:1]
doc1_tf_vector = [1, 1] #[apple:1, juice:1]
doc2_tf_vector = [3, 4] #[apple:3, juice:4]

doc1_score = cosine_similarity(query_vector, doc1_tf_vector)
doc2_score = cosine_similarity(query_vector, doc2_tf_vector)

print_scores([doc1_score, doc2_score])
```

Output:

```
Relevance Scores:
  doc1: 1.0
  doc2: 0.9899
```

Contrary to what you might expect, doc1 is considered a better cosine similarity match than doc2. This is because the terms "apple" and "juice" both occur "the same proportion of times" (one occurrence of each term for every occurrence of the other term) in both the query and in doc1, making them the most textually similar. In other words, even though doc2 is intuitively more about the query, since it contains the terms in the query significantly more, cosine similarity returns doc1, since it's an exact match for the query, unlike doc2.

Since our goal is for documents like doc2 with higher TF to score higher, we can accomplish this by switching from cosine similarity to another scoring function, such as *dot product* or *Euclidean distance*, that increases as feature weights continue to increase. Let's use the dot product $(a \cdot b)$, which is equal to the cosine similarity multiplied by the length of the query vector times the length of the document vector: $a \cdot b = |a| \times |b| \times \cos(\theta)$. The dot product will result in documents that contain more matching terms scoring higher, as opposed to cosine similarity, which scores documents higher when they contain a more similar proportion of matching terms between the query and documents.

Phrase matching and other relevance tricks

By now, you may be wondering why we keep treating "apple" and "juice" as independent terms and why we don't just treat "apple juice" as a phrase to boost documents higher that match the exact phrase. Phrase matching is one of many easy relevance-tuning tricks we'll discuss later in the chapter. For now, we'll keep our query-processing simple and just deal with individual keywords to stay focused on our main goal—explaining vector-based relevance scoring and text-based keyword-scoring features.

In the next listing, we replace cosine similarity with a dot product calculation to consider the magnitude of the document vectors (which increases with more matches for each query term) in the relevance calculation.

Listing 3.4   Dot product of TF vectors

```
query_vector    = [1, 1] #[apple:1, juice:1]
doc1_tf_vector = [1, 1] #[apple:1, juice:1]
doc2_tf_vector = [3, 4] #[apple:3, juice:4]

doc1_score = dot(query_vector, doc1_tf_vector)
doc2_score = dot(query_vector, doc2_tf_vector)

print_scores([doc1_score, doc2_score])
```

Output:

```
Relevance Scores:
  doc1: 2
  doc2: 7
```

As you can see, doc2 now yields a higher relevance score for the query than doc1, an improvement that aligns better with our intuition. Note that the relevance scores are no longer bounded between 0 and 1, as they were with cosine similarity. This is because the dot product considers the magnitude of the document vectors, which can increase unbounded with additional matching keyword occurrences.

While using the TF as the feature weight in our vectors certainly helps, textual queries exhibit additional challenges that need to be considered. Thus far, our documents have all contained every term from our queries, which does not match with most real-world scenarios. The following example will better demonstrate some of the limitations still present when using only term-frequency-based weighting for our text-based sparse vector similarity scoring. Let's start with the following three text documents:

Document 1:
> In light of the big reveal in her interview, the interesting
> thing is that the person in the wrong probably made a good
> decision in the end.

Document 2:
> My favorite book is the cat in the hat, which is about a crazy
> cat in a hat who breaks into a house and creates the craziest
> afternoon for two kids.

Document 3:
> My careless neighbors apparently let a stray cat stay in their
> garage unsupervised which resulted in my favorite hat that I
> let them borrow being ruined.

Let's now map these documents into their corresponding (sparse) vector representations and calculate a similarity score. The following listing ranks text similarity based on raw TFs (term counts).

Listing 3.5   Ranking text similarity based on term counts

```
def term_count(content, term):
  tokenized_content = tokenize(content)
  term_count = tokenized_content.count(term.lower())
  return float(round(term_count, 4))

query = "the cat in the hat"
terms = tokenize(query)

query_vector = list(numpy.repeat(1, len(terms)))
doc_vectors = [[term_count(doc, term) for term in terms] for doc in docs]
doc_scores = [dot(v, query_vector) for v in doc_vectors]

print_term_count_scores(terms, doc_vectors, doc_scores)
```

Output:

```
labels:  ['the', 'cat', 'in', 'the', 'hat']

query vector: [1, 1, 1, 1, 1]

Document Vectors:
  doc1: [5.0, 0.0, 4.0, 5.0, 0.0]
  doc2: [3.0, 2.0, 2.0, 3.0, 2.0]
  doc3: [0.0, 1.0, 2.0, 0.0, 1.0]

Relevance Scores:
  doc1: 14.0
  doc2: 12.0
  doc3: 4.0
```

While we receive different relevance scores now for each document, based on the number of times each term matches, the ordering of the results doesn't necessarily match our expectations about which documents are the best matches. Intuitively, we would instead expect the following ordering:

1 *doc2:* because it is about the book *The Cat in the Hat*
2 *doc3:* because it matches all the words "the", "cat", "in", and "hat"
3 *doc1:* because it only matches the words "the" and "in", even though it contains them many times

The problem here is that since a term is considered just as important every time it appears, the relevance score is indiscriminately increasing with every additional occurrence of that term. In this case, doc1 is getting the highest score, because it contains 14 total term matches (the first "the" five times, "in" four times, and the second "the" five times), yielding more total term matches than any other document.

It doesn't really make sense that a document containing these words 14 times should be considered 14 times as relevant as a document with a single match, though. Instead, a document should be considered more relevant if it matches many different terms from a query versus the same terms over and over. Often, real-world TF calculations dampen the effect of each additional occurrence of a word by calculating TF as a log or square root of the number of occurrences of each term (as we do in figure 3.3). Additionally, TF is often also normalized relative to document length by dividing the TF by the total number of terms in each document. Since longer documents are naturally more likely to contain any given term more often, this helps normalize the score to account for those document length variabilities (per the denominator for figure 3.3). Our final, normalized TF calculation can be seen in figure 3.3.

$$TF(t, d) = \sqrt{\frac{f_{t,d}}{\sum_{t' \in d} f_{t',d}}}$$

Figure 3.3 Normalized TF calculation. *t* represents a term and d represents a document. *TF* equals the square root of the number of times the term appears in the current document ($f_{t,d}$) divided by the number of terms in the document ($\sum_{t' \in d} f_{t',d}$). The square root dampens the additional relevance contribution of each additional occurrence of a term, while the denominator normalizes that dampened frequency to the document length so that longer documents with more terms are comparable to shorter documents with fewer terms.

Many variations of the TF calculation exist, only some of which perform document-length normalization (the denominator) or dampen the effect of additional term occurrences (the square root here, or sometimes using a logarithm). Apache Lucene (the search library powering Solr, OpenSearch, and Elasticsearch), for instance, calculates TF as only the square root of the numerator, but then multiplies it by a separate document-length norm (equivalent to the square root of the denominator in our equation) when performing certain ranking calculations.

Going forward, we'll use this normalized TF calculation to ensure additional occurrences of the same term continue to improve relevance, but at a diminishing rate. The following listing shows the new TF function in effect.

Listing 3.6   Ranking text similarity based on TF

```
def tf(term, doc):
  tokenized_doc = tokenize(doc)
  term_count = tokenized_doc.count(term.lower())
  doc_length = len(tokenized_doc)
  return numpy.sqrt(term_count / doc_length)

query = "the cat in the hat"
terms = tokenize(query)

query_vector = list(numpy.repeat(1, len(terms)))
doc_vectors = [[tf(term, doc) for term in terms] for doc in docs]
doc_scores = [dot(dv, query_vector) for dv in doc_vectors]

print_term_frequency_scores(terms, doc_vectors, doc_scores)
```

Output:

```
Document TF Vector Calculations:
    doc1: [tf(doc1, "the"), tf(doc1, "cat"), tf(doc1, "in"),
          tf(doc1, "the"), tf(doc1, "hat")]
    doc2: [tf(doc2, "the"), tf(doc2, "cat"), tf(doc2, "in"),
          tf(doc2, "the"), tf(doc2, "hat")]
    doc3: [tf(doc3, "the"), tf(doc3, "cat"), tf(doc3, "in"),
          tf(doc3, "the"), tf(doc3, "hat")]

Document TF Vector Values:
Labels: ['the', 'cat', 'in', 'the', 'hat']
    doc1: [0.4303, 0.0, 0.3849, 0.4303, 0.0]
    doc2: [0.3111, 0.254, 0.254, 0.3111, 0.254]
    doc3: [0.0, 0.1961, 0.2774, 0.0, 0.1961]

Relevance Scores:
    doc1: 1.2456
    doc2: 1.3842
    doc3: 0.6696
```

The normalized `tf` function shows an improvement, as doc2 is now ranked the highest, as expected. This is mostly because of the dampening effect on the number of term occurrences in doc1 (which matched "the" and "in" so many times), such that each additional occurrence contributes less to the feature weight than prior occurrences. Unfortunately, doc1 is still ranked second-highest, so even the improved TF calculation wasn't enough to get the better matching doc3 higher.

The next step for improvement will be to factor in the relative importance of terms, as "cat" and "hat" are intuitively more important than common words like "the" and "in". Let's modify our scoring calculation to fix this oversight by introducing a new variable that incorporates the importance of each term.

3.1.5 *Inverse document frequency: Measuring the importance of a term in the query*

While TF has proven useful at measuring how well a document matches each term in a query, it does little to differentiate between the importance of the terms in the query. In this section, we'll introduce a technique using the significance of specific keywords based on their frequency of occurrence across documents.

The *document frequency* (DF) for a term is defined as the total number of documents in the search engine that contain the term, and it serves as a good measure of a term's importance. The idea here is that more specific or rare words (like "cat" and "hat") tend to be more important than common words (like "the" and "in"). The function used to calculate document frequency is shown in figure 3.4.

$$DF(t) = \sum_{i=1}^{|D|} \quad \text{if} \quad t \in D_i : 1; \quad \text{if} \quad t \notin D_i : 0$$

Figure 3.4 Document frequency calculation. D is the set of all documents, t is the input term, and D_i is the *i*th document in D. The lower the document frequency for a term (DF(t)), the more specific and important the term is when seen in queries.

Since we would like more important words to score higher, we take the *inverse document frequency* (IDF), as defined in figure 3.5.

$$IDF(t) = 1 + \log\left(\frac{|D| + 1}{DF(t) + 1}\right)$$

Figure 3.5 Inverse document frequency. |D| is the total count of all documents, t is the term, and DF(t) is the document frequency. The lower the IDF(t), the more insignificant the term, and the higher, the more the term in a query should count toward the relevance score.

Carrying forward our the cat in the hat query example from the last section, a vector of IDFs would thus look like the following listing.

Listing 3.7 Calculating inverse document frequency

```
def idf(term):
    df_map = {"the": 9500, "cat": 100,          Mocked document counts simulating
             "in": 9000, "hat": 50}             realistic statistics from an inverted index
    total_docs = 10000
    return 1 + numpy.log((total_docs+1) / (df_map[term] + 1))      The IDF function, which
                                                                   dictates the importance
terms = ["the", "cat", "in", "the", "hat"]                        of a term in the query
idf_vector = [idf(term) for term in terms]
                                                                   IDF is term-dependent,
print_inverse_document_frequency_scores(terms, idf_vector)         not document-dependent,
                                                                   so it is the same for both
                                                                   queries and documents.
```

Output:

```
IDF Vector Values:
  [idf("the"), idf("cat"), idf("in"), idf("the"), idf("hat")]

IDF Vector:
  [1.0513, 5.5953, 1.1053, 1.0513, 6.2786]
```

These results look encouraging. The terms can now be weighted based on their relative descriptiveness or significance to the query:

1 "hat": `6.2786`
2 "cat": `5.5953`
3 "in": `1.1053`
4 "the": `1.0513`

We'll next combine the TF and IDF ranking techniques you've learned thus far into a balanced relevance ranking function.

3.1.6 *TF-IDF: A balanced weighting metric for text-based relevance*

We now have the two principal components of text-based relevance ranking:

- TF measures how well a term describes a document.
- IDF measures how important each term is.

Most search engines, and many other data science applications, use a combination of these factors as the basis for textual similarity scoring, using a variation of the function in figure 3.6.

$$\text{TF-IDF} = TF \cdot IDF^2$$

Figure 3.6   TF-IDF score. Combines both the TF and IDF calculations into a balanced text-ranking similarity score.

With this improved feature-weighting function in place, we can finally calculate a balanced relevance score as follows.

Listing 3.8   Calculating TF-IDF for the query `the cat in the hat`

```
def tf_idf(term, doc):
    return TF(term, doc) * IDF(term)**2

query = "the cat in the hat"
terms = tokenize(query)

query_vector = list(numpy.repeat(1, len(terms)))
doc_vectors = [[tf_idf(doc, term) for term in terms] for doc in docs]
doc_scores = [[dot(query_vector, dv)] for dv in doc_vectors]

print_tf_idf_scores(terms, doc_vectors, doc_scores)
```

Output:

```
Document TF-IDF Vector Calculations
  doc1: [tf_idf(doc1, "the"), tf_idf(doc1, "cat"), tf_idf(doc1, "in"),
         tf_idf(doc1, "the"), tf_idf(doc1, "hat")]
  doc2: [tf_idf(doc2, "the"), tf_idf(doc2, "cat"), tf_idf(doc2, "in"),
         tf_idf(doc2, "the"), tf_idf(doc2, "hat")]
  doc3: [tf_idf(doc3, "the"), tf_idf(doc3, "cat"), tf_idf(doc3, "in"),
         tf_idf(doc3, "the"), tf_idf(doc3, "hat")]

Document TF-IDF Vector Scores
Labels: ['the', 'cat', 'in', 'the', 'hat']
  doc1: [0.4756, 0.0, 0.4703, 0.4755, 0.0]
  doc2: [0.3438, 7.9521, 0.3103, 0.3438, 10.0129]
  doc3: [0.0, 6.1399, 0.3389, 0.0, 7.7311]

Relevance Scores:
  doc1: 1.4215
  doc2: 18.9633
  doc3: 14.2099
```

Finally, our search results make sense! doc2 gets the highest score, since it matches the most important words the most, followed by doc3, which contains all the words, but not as many times, followed by doc1, which only contains an abundance of insignificant words.

This TF-IDF calculation is at the heart of many search engine relevance algorithms, including the default similarity algorithm, known as BM25, which is currently used for keyword-based ranking in most search engines. We'll introduce BM25 in the next section.

3.2 Controlling the relevance calculation

In the last section, we showed how queries and documents can be represented as vectors and how cosine similarity, or other similarity measurements like the dot product, can be used as a relevance function to compare queries and documents. We introduced TF-IDF ranking, which can be used to create a feature weight that balances both the strength of occurrence (TF) and significance of a term (IDF) for each term in a term-based vector.

In this section, we'll show how a full relevance function can be specified and controlled in a search engine, including common query capabilities, modeling queries as functions, ranking versus filtering, and applying different kinds of boosting techniques.

3.2.1 BM25: The industry standard default text-similarity algorithm

BM25 is the name of the default similarity algorithm in Apache Lucene, Apache Solr, Elasticsearch, OpenSearch, and many other search engines. BM25 (short for Okapi "Best Matching" version 25) was first published in 1994, and it demonstrates improvements over standard TF-IDF cosine similarity ranking in many real-world, text-based ranking evaluations. For now, it still beats ranking models using embeddings from most non-fine-tuned LLMs, so it serves as a good baseline for keyword-based ranking.

BM25 still uses TF-IDF at its core, but it also includes several other parameters, giving more control over factors like TF saturation point and document length normalization. It also sums the weights for each matched keyword instead of calculating a cosine.

The full BM25 calculation is shown in figure 3.7. The variables are defined as follows:

- t = term; d = document; q = query.
- $freq(t, d)$ is a simple TF, $\sum_{t \in d} 1$ showing the number of times term t occurs in document d.
- $IDF(t) = \log\left(\dfrac{N - N(t) + 0.5}{N(t) + 0.5} + 1\right)$

  is a variation of IDF used in BM25, where N is the total number of documents and $N(t)$ is the number of documents containing term t.
- $|d|$ is the number of terms in document d.
- $avgdl$ is the average number of terms per document in the index.
- k is a free parameter that usually ranges from 1.2 to 2.0 and increases the TF saturation point.
- b is a free parameter usually set to around 0.75. It increases the effect of document normalization.

$$BM25(q,d) = \sum_{t \in q} IDF(t) \cdot \frac{freq(t,d)}{freq(t,d) + k \cdot (1 - b + b \cdot |d| / avgdl))}$$

Figure 3.7   BM25 scoring function. It still predominantly uses a simplified *TF* and a variation of *IDF*, but it provides more control over how much each additional occurrence of a term contributes to the score (the k parameter) and how much scores are normalized based on document length (the b parameter).

You can see that the numerator contains *freq* (simplified TF) and *IDF* parameters, while the denominator adds the new normalization parameters k and b. The TF saturation point is controlled by k, making additional matches on the same term count less as k is increased, and by b, which controls the level of document length normalization more as it increases. The *TF* for each term is calculated as $freq(t, d) / (freq(t, d) + k \cdot (1 - b + b \cdot |d| / avgdl))$, which is a more complex calculation than the one we used in figure 3.3.

Conceptually, BM25 just provides a heuristically determined better way to normalize the TF than traditional TF-IDF. It's also worth noting that several variations of the BM25 algorithm exist (BM25F, BM25+), and, depending on the search engine you use, you might see some slight alterations and optimizations.

Instead of reimplementing all this math in Python as we test out BM25, let's now switch over to using our search engine and see how it performs the calculation. Let's start by creating a collection in the search engine (listing 3.9). A collection contains a specific schema and configuration, and it is the unit upon which we will index documents, search, rank, and retrieve search results. Then we'll index some documents (using our previous the cat in the hat example), as shown in listing 3.10.

Listing 3.9   Creating the `cat_in_the_hat` collection

```
engine = get_engine()
collection = engine.create_collection("cat_in_the_hat")
```

> The engine is set to Apache Solr by default. See appendix B to use other supported search engines and vector databases.

Output:

```
Wiping "cat_in_the_hat" collection
Creating "cat_in_the_hat" collection
Status: Success
```

Listing 3.10   Adding documents to a collection

```
docs = [{"id": "doc1",
        "title": "Worst",
        "description": """The interesting thing is that the person in the
                          wrong made the right decision in the end."""},
       {"id": "doc2",
        "title": "Best",
        "description": """My favorite book is the cat in the hat, which is
                          about a crazy cat who breaks into a house and
                          creates a crazy afternoon for two kids."""},
       {"id": "doc3",
        "title": "Okay",
        "description": """My neighbors let the stray cat stay in their
                          garage, which resulted in my favorite hat that
                          I let them borrow being ruined."""}]
collection.add_documents(docs)
```

Output:

```
Adding Documents to 'cat_in_the_hat' collection
Status: Success
```

With our documents added to the search engine, we can now issue our query and see the full BM25 scores. The following listing searches with the query the cat in the hat and requests the relevance calculation explanation for each document.

Listing 3.11   Ranking by and inspecting the BM25 similarity score

```
query = "the cat in the hat"
request = {"query": query,
          "query_fields": ["description"],
          "return_fields": ["id", "title", "description", "score"],
          "explain": True}
```

```
response = collection.search(**request)
display_search(query, response["docs"])
```

Output:

Query: the cat in the hat
Ranked Docs:
```
[{'id': 'doc2',
'title': ['Best'],
'description': ['My favorite book is the cat in the hat, which is about a
➡crazy cat who breaks into a house and creates a crazy afternoon for
➡two kids.'],
'score': 0.68231964, '[explain]': '
  0.68231964  = sum of:
    0.15655403 = weight(description:the in 1) [SchemaSimilarity], result of:
      0.15655403 = score(freq=2.0), product of:
        2.0 = boost
        0.13353139 = idf, computed as log(1 + (N - n + 0.5) / (
          n + 0.5)) from:
          3 = n, number of documents containing term
          3 = N, total number of documents with field
        0.58620685 = tf, computed as freq / (freq + k1 * (
          1 - b + b * dl / avgdl)) from:
          2.0 = freq, occurrences of term within document
          1.2 = k1, term saturation parameter
          0.75 = b, length normalization parameter
          28.0 = dl, length of field
          22.666666 = avgdl, average length of field
    0.19487953 = weight(description:hat in 1) ...
    0.27551934 = weight(description:cat in 1) ...
    0.05536667 = weight(description:in in 1) ...
'}, {'id': 'doc3',
'title': ['Okay'],
'description': ['My neighbors let the stray cat stay in their garage, which
➡resulted in my favorite hat that I let them borrow being ruined.'],
'score': 0.62850046, '[explain]': '
  0.62850046 = sum of:
    0.21236044  = weight(description:the in 2) ...
    0.08311336 = weight(description:hat in 2) ...
    0.21236044 = weight(description:cat in 2) ...
    0.120666236 = weight(description:in in 2) ...
'}, {'id': 'doc1',
'title': ['Worst'],
'description': ['The interesting thing is that the person in the wrong made
➡the right decision in the end.'],
'score': 0.3132525,
'[explain]': '
  0.3132525 = sum of:
    0.089769006 = weight(description:the in 0) ...
    0.2234835 = weight(description:in in 0) ...
'}]
```

For the top-ranked document, doc2, you can see a portion of the score calculation using the `tf` and `idf` components, and you can see the high-level scores for each matched term in the query for the other two documents. If you would like to dig deeper into the math, you can examine the full calculations in the Jupyter notebook.

While the BM25 calculation is more complex than the TF-IDF feature weight calculations, it still uses TF-IDF as a core part of its calculation. As a result, the BM25 ranking is in the same relative order as our TF-IDF calculations from listing 3.8:

```
Ranked Results (Listing 3.8: TF-IDF Cosine Similarity):
  doc2: 0.998
  doc3: 0.9907
  doc1: 0.0809

Ranked Results (Listing 3.9: BM25 Similarity):
  doc2: 0.6878265
  doc3: 0.62850046
  doc1: 0.3132525
```

Our query for `the cat in the hat` can still very much be thought of as a vector of the BM25 scores for each of the terms: `["the", "cat", "in", "the", "hat"]`.

What may not be obvious is that the feature weights for each of these terms are actually overridable functions. Instead of thinking of our query as a bunch of keywords, we can think of our query as a mathematical function composed of other functions, where some of those functions take keywords as inputs and return numerical values (scores) to be used in the relevance calculation. For example, our query could alternatively be expressed as this vector:

```
[ query("the"), query("cat"), query("in"), query("the"), query("hat") ]
```

The `query` function here simply calculates the BM25 of the term passed in, relative to all the documents scored. So the BM25 of the entire query is the sum of the TF-IDFs of each term. In Solr query syntax, this would be

```
{!func}query("the") {!func}query("cat") {!func}query("in")
{!func}query("the") {!func}query("hat")
```

If we execute this "functionized" version of the query, we get the exact same relevance score as if we had executed the query directly. The following listing shows the code that performs this version of the query.

> **Listing 3.12   Text similarity using the `query` function**

```
query = '{!func}query("the") {!func}query("cat") {!func}query("in")
    ➥{!func}query("the") {!func}query("hat")'
request = {"query": query,
           "query_fields": "description",
           "return_fields": ["id", "title", "score"]}
```

```
response = collection.search(**request)
display_search(query, response["docs"])
```

Output:

```
Query:
 {!func}query("the") {!func}query("cat") {!func}query("in")
  {!func}query("the") {!func}query("hat")
Results:
 [{'id': 'doc2', 'title': ['Best'], 'score': 0.6823196},
   {'id': 'doc3', 'title': ['Okay'], 'score': 0.62850046},
   {'id': 'doc1', 'title': ['Worst'], 'score': 0.3132525}]
```

As expected, the scores are the same as before—we've simply substituted explicit functions where implicit functions were previously.

3.2.2 *Functions, functions, everywhere!*

We just encountered the query function (at the end of the previous section), which performs the default (BM25) similarity calculation on keywords. Understanding that every part of the query is actually a configurable scoring function opens tremendous possibilities for manipulating the relevance algorithm. What *other* kinds of functions can be used in queries? Can we use other features in our scoring calculation—perhaps some that are not text-based?

Here is a partial list of functions and scoring techniques commonly applied to influence relevance scores:

- *Geospatial boosting*—Documents near the user running the query should rank higher.
- *Date boosting*—Newer documents should get a higher relevance boost.
- *Popularity boosting*—More popular documents should get a higher relevance boost.
- *Field boosting*—Terms matching in certain fields should get a higher weight than in other fields.
- *Category boosting*—Documents in categories related to query terms should get a higher relevance boost.
- *Phrase boosting*—Documents matching multi-term phrases in the query should rank higher than those only matching the words separately.
- *Semantic expansion*—Documents containing other words or concepts that are highly related to the query keywords and context should be boosted.

> **Using the book's search-engine-agnostic search API**
>
> Throughout the book and codebase, we've implemented a set of Python libraries providing a generic API for indexing documents (collection.add_documents(documents) or collection.write(dataframe)), querying documents (collection.search(**query_parameters)), and performing other search engine

(continued)

operations. This allows you to execute the same code in the book and corresponding notebooks regardless of which supported search engine or vector database you have selected, delegating the creation of engine-specific syntax to the client library. See appendix B for details about how to switch seamlessly between engines.

While these generic methods for invoking AI-powered search against your favorite engine are powerful, it's also helpful in some cases to see the details of the underlying implementation within the search engine, and for more complicated examples it can even be difficult to express the full power of what's going on using the higher-level engine-agnostic API. For this reason, we will occasionally also include the raw search engine syntax for our default search engine (Apache Solr) in the book. If you're unfamiliar with Apache Solr and its syntax, please don't get too bogged down in the details. The important thing is to understand the concepts well-enough that you can apply them to your search engine of choice.

These techniques (and many more) are supported by most major search engines. For example, field boosting can be accomplished in our search client by appending a `^BOOST_AMOUNT` after any of the fields specified in `query_fields` for a query:

```
Generic search request syntax:
 {"query": "the cat in the hat",
  "query_fields": ["title^10", "description^2.5"]}
```

This query request provides a 10X relevancy boost for matches in the `title` field and a 2.5X relevancy boost for matches in the `description` field. When mapped into Solr syntax, it looks like this:

```
Solr request syntax:
 {"query": "the cat in the hat",
  "params": {"defType": "edismax",
             "qf": "title^10 description^2.5"}}
```

Every search engine is different, but many of these techniques are built into specific query parsers in Solr, either through query syntax or through query parser options, as with the `edismax` query parser just shown.

Boosting on full phrase matching, on two-word phrases, and on three-word phrases is also a native feature of Solr's `edismax` query parser:

- Boost docs containing the exact phrase `"the cat in the hat"` in the `title` field:

  ```
  Solr request syntax:
   {"query": "the cat in the hat",
    "params": {"defType": "edismax",
               "qf": "title description",
               "pf": "title"}}
  ```

- Boost docs containing the two-word phrases `"the cat"`, `"cat in"`, `"in the"`, or `"the hat"` in the `title` or `description` field:

```
Solr request syntax:
 {"query": "the cat in the hat",
  "params": {"defType": "edismax",
             "qf": "title description",
             "pf2": "title description"}}
```

- Boost docs containing the three-word phrases `"the cat in"` or `"in the hat"` in the `description` field:

```
Solr request syntax:
 {"query": "the cat in the hat",
  "params": {"defType": "edismax",
             "qf": "title description",
             "pf3": "description"}}
```

Many of the other relevance-boosting techniques require constructing custom features using function queries. For example, if we want to create a query that only boosts the relevance ranking of documents geographically closest to the user running the search, we can issue the following Solr query:

```
Solr request syntax:
 {"query": "*",
  "sort": "geodist(location, $user_latitude, $user_longitude) asc",
  "params": {"user_latitude": 33.748,
             "user_longitude": -84.39}}
```

That last query uses the `sort` parameter to strictly order documents by the `geodist` function, which takes the document's location field name along with the user's latitude and longitude as parameters. This works great when considering a single feature, but what if we want to construct a more complex sort based on many features? To accomplish this, we can update our query to apply several functions when calculating the relevance score, and then sort by the relevance score:

```
Solr request syntax:
 {"query": "{!func}scale(query($keywords),0,25)
            {!func}recip(geodist($lat_long_field,$user_latitude,
            $user_longitude),1,25,1)
            {!func}recip(ms(NOW/HOUR,modify_date),3.16e-11,25,1)
            {!func}scale(popularity,0,25)",
  "params": {"keywords": "basketball",
             "lat_long_field": "location",
             "user_latitude": 33.748,
             "user_longitude" -84.391}}
```

That query has a few interesting characteristics:

- It constructs a query vector containing four features: BM25 relevance score for the keywords (higher is better), geographical distance (lower is better), publication date (newer is better), and popularity (higher is better).
- Each of the feature values is scaled between 0 and 25 so they are all comparable, with the best score for each feature being 25, and the worst score near 0.

- Thus, a "perfect score" will add up to 100 (all 4 features scoring 25), and the worst score will be approximately 0.
- Since the relative contribution of 25 is specified as part of the query for each function, we can easily adjust the weights for any features on the fly to influence the final relevance calculation.

With the last query, we have fully taken the relevance calculation into our own hands by modeling the relevance features and giving them weights. While this is very powerful, it still requires significant manual effort to determine which features matter most for a given domain and to tune their weights. In chapter 10, we'll walk through building machine-learned ranking models to automatically make those decisions for us (a process known as *learning to rank*). For now, our goal is just to understand the mechanics of modeling features in query vectors and how to programmatically control their weights.

> ### Deeper dives on function queries
> If you'd like to learn more about how to utilize Solr's function queries, we recommend reading chapter 7 of *Solr in Action*, one of our previous books, by Trey Grainger and Timothy Potter (Manning, 2014; https://mng.bz/n0Y5). For a full list of available function queries in Solr, you can also check out the documentation in the function query section of the Solr Reference Guide (https://mng.bz/vJop). If you're using a different search engine, check out their documentation for similar guidance.

We've seen the power of utilizing functions as features in our queries, but so far our examples have all been what are called "additive" boosts, where the sum of the values of each function calculation comprises the final relevance score. It is also frequently useful to combine functions in a fuzzier, more flexible way through "multiplicative" boosts, which we'll cover in the next section.

3.2.3 *Choosing multiplicative vs. additive boosting for relevance functions*

One last topic to address, concerning how we control our relevance functions, is multiplicative versus additive boosting of relevance features.

In all our examples to this point, we have added multiple features into our query vector to contribute to the score. For example, the following Solr queries will all yield equivalent relevance calculations, assuming they are filtered down to the same result set (i.e., filters=["the cat in the hat"]):

```
Text query (score + filter):
 {"query": "the cat in the hat"}

Function Query (score only, no filter):
 {"query": '{!func}query("the cat in the hat")'}

Multiple Function Queries (score only, no filter):
 {"query": '{!func}query("the")
        ➥{!func}query("cat")
```

```
⇒{!func}query("in")
⇒{!func}query("the")
⇒{!func}query("hat")'}
```

```
Boost Query (score only, no filter):
 {"query": "*",
  "params": {"bq": "the cat in the hat"}}
```

The kind of relevance boosting in each of these examples is known as *additive boosting*, and it maps well to our concept of a query as nothing more than a vector of features that needs to have its similarity compared across documents. In additive boosting, the relative contribution of each feature decreases as more features are added, since the total score is just the sum of all the features' scores.

Multiplicative boosting, in contrast, allows a document's entire calculated relevance score to be scaled (multiplied) by one or more functions. Multiplicative boosting enables boosts to "pile up" on each other, preventing the need for individually constraining the weights of different sections of the query, as we did in section 3.2.2. There, we had to ensure that the keyword scores, geographical distance, age, and popularity of documents were each scaled to 25% of the relevance score so that they would add up to a maximum score of 100%.

To supply a multiplicative boost in Apache Solr, you can either use the boost query parser (syntax: {!boost …}) in your query vector or, if you are using the edismax query parser, the simplified boost query param. The following two queries will multiply a document's relevance score by ten times the value in the popularity field:

```
{"query": "the cat in the hat",
 "params": {"defType": "edismax",
            "boost": "mul(popularity,10)"}}
```

```
{"query": "{!boost b=mul(popularity,10)} the cat in the hat"}
```

In this example, the query for the cat in the hat still uses additive boosting (the BM25 value of each keyword is added together), but the final score is multiplied by 10 times the value in the popularity field. This multiplicative boosting allows the popularity to scale the relevance score independently of any other features.

In general, multiplicative boosts offer you greater flexibility to combine different relevance features without having to explicitly predefine a relevance formula accounting for every potential contributing factor. On the other hand, this flexibility can lead to unexpected consequences if the multiplicative boost values for particular features get too high and overshadow other features. In contrast, additive boosts can be a pain to manage, because you need to explicitly scale them so that they can be combined while still maintaining a predictable contribution to the overall score. However, with this explicit scaling, you maintain tight control over the relevance scoring calculation and range of scores. Both additive and multiplicative boosts can be useful, so it's best to consider the problem at hand and experiment with what gets you the best results.

We've now covered the major ways of controlling relevance ranking in the search engine, but the matching and filtering of documents can often be just as important, so we'll cover them in the next section.

3.2.4 *Differentiating matching (filtering) vs. ranking (scoring) of documents*

We've spoken of queries and documents as feature vectors, but we've mainly discussed search thus far as a process of either calculating a vector similarity (such as cosine or dot product) or adding up document scores for each feature (keyword or function) in the query.

Once documents are indexed, there are two primary steps involved in executing a query:

- *Matching*—Filtering results to a known set of possible answers
- *Ranking*—Ordering all the possible answers by relevance

We can often completely skip the first step (matching) and still see the exact same results on page one (and for many pages), since the most relevant results should generally rank the highest and thus show up first. If you think back to chapter 2, we even saw some vector scoring calculations (comparing feature vectors for food items—i.e., "apple juice" versus "donut") where we would have been unable to filter results at all. We instead had to first score every document to determine which ones to return based upon relevance alone. In this scenario (using dense vector embeddings), we didn't even have keywords or other attributes that could be used as a filter.

So, if the initial matching phase is effectively optional, why do it at all? One obvious answer is that it provides a significant performance optimization. Instead of iterating through every single document and calculating a relevance score, we can greatly speed up both our relevance calculations and the overall response time of our search engine by first filtering the initial results to a smaller set of documents that are logical matches.

There are additional benefits to being able to filter result sets, in that we can provide analytics, such as the number of matching documents or counts of specific values found in documents (known as *facets* or *aggregations*). Returning facets and similar aggregated metadata from the search results helps the user subsequently filter down by specific values to further explore and refine their result set. Finally, there are plenty of scenarios where "having logical matches" should be considered among the most important features in the ranking function, so simply filtering on logical matches upfront can greatly simplify the relevance calculation. We'll discuss these trade-offs in the next section.

3.2.5 *Logical matching: Weighting the relationships between terms in a query*

We just mentioned that filtering results before scoring them is primarily a performance optimization and that the first few pages of search results would likely look the same regardless of whether you filter the results or just do relevance ranking.

This only holds true, however, if your relevance function successfully contains features that already appropriately boost better logical matches. For example, consider the difference between expectations for the following queries:

1 `"statue of liberty"`
2 `statue AND of AND liberty`
3 `statue OR of OR liberty`
4 `statue of liberty`

From a logical matching standpoint, the first query will be very precise, only matching documents containing the *exact* phrase "statue of liberty". The second query will only match documents containing all the terms "statue", "of", and "liberty", but not necessarily as a phrase. The third query will match any document containing any of the three terms, which means documents *only* containing "of" will match, but documents containing "statue" and "liberty" should rank much higher due to the BM25 scoring calculation.

In theory, if phrase boosting is turned on as a feature, documents containing the full phrase will likely rank highest, followed by documents containing all terms, followed by documents containing any of the words. Assuming that happens, you should see a similar ordering of results regardless of whether you filter them to logical Boolean matches or whether you only sort based on a relevance function.

In practice, though, users often consider the logical structure of their queries to be highly relevant to the documents they expect to see, so respecting this logical structure and filtering *before* ranking allows you to remove results that users' queries indicate are safe to remove.

Sometimes the logical structure of user queries is ambiguous, however, such as with our fourth example: the query `statue of liberty`. Does this logically mean `statue AND of AND liberty`, `statue OR of OR liberty`, or something more nuanced like `(statue AND of) OR (statue AND liberty) OR (of AND liberty)`, which essentially means "match at least two of three terms". Using the "minimum match" (`min_match`) parameter in our search API enables you to control these kinds of matching thresholds easily, even on a per-query basis:

- 100% of query terms must match (equivalent to `statue AND of AND liberty`):

  ```
  Generic search request syntax:
   {"query": "statue of liberty",
    "min_match": "100%"}
  ```

  ```
  Solr request syntax:
   {"query": "statue of liberty",
     "params": {"defType": "edismax",
                "mm": "100%"}}
  ```

- At least one query term must match (equivalent to `statue OR of OR liberty`):

  ```
  Generic search request syntax:
   {"query": "statue of liberty",
    "min_match": "1"}
  ```

```
Solr request syntax:
 {"query": "statue of liberty",
  "params": {"defType": "edismax",
             "mm": "1"}}
```

- At least two query terms must match (equivalent to (statue AND of) OR (statue AND liberty) OR (of AND liberty)):

```
Generic search request syntax:
 {"query": "statue of liberty",
  "query_parser": "edismax",
  "min_match": "2"}
```

```
Solr request syntax:
 {"query": "statue of liberty",
  "params": {"defType": "edismax",
             "mm": "2"}}
```

The min_match param in our Python API supports specifying either a minimum percentage (0% to 100%) of terms or a number of terms (1 to *N* terms) that must match. This parameter corresponds with Solr's mm parameter and OpenSearch's and Elasticsearch's minimum_should_match parameter. In addition to accepting a percentage or number of terms to match, those engines also support a step function like mm=2<-30% 5<3. This example step function means "all terms are required if there are less than 2 terms, up to 30% of terms can be missing if there are less than 5 terms, and at least 3 terms must exist if there are 5 or more terms". When using Solr, the mm parameter works with the edismax query parser, which is the primary query parser we will use for text-matching queries in this book if Solr is configured as your engine (per appendix B). You can consult the "Extended DisMax Parameters" section of the Solr Reference Guide for more details on how to fine-tune your logical matching rules with these minimum match capabilities (https://mng.bz/mRo8).

When thinking about constructing relevance functions, the ideas of filtering and scoring can often get mixed up, particularly since most search engines perform both for their main query parameter. We'll attempt to separate these concerns in the next section.

3.2.6   *Separating concerns: Filtering vs. scoring*

In section 3.2.4, we differentiated between the ideas of matching and ranking. Matching of results is logical and is implemented by filtering search results down to a subset of documents, whereas ranking of results is qualitative and is implemented by scoring all documents relative to the query and then sorting them by that calculated score. In this section, we'll cover some techniques to provide maximum flexibility in controlling matching and ranking by cleanly separating out the concerns of filtering and scoring.

Our search API has two primary ways to control filtering and scoring: the query and filters parameters. Consider the following request:

```
Generic search request syntax:
 {"query": "the cat in the hat",
  "query_fields": ["description"],
  "filters": [("category", "books"), ("audience", "kid")],
  "min_match": "100%"}
```

```
Solr request syntax:
 {"query": "the cat in the hat",
  "filters": ["category:books", "audience:kid"],
  "params": {"qf": ["description"],
             "mm": "100%",
             "defType": "edismax"}}
```

In this query, the search engine is being instructed to filter the possible result set down to only documents with both a value of "books" in the `category` field and a value of "kid" in the `audience` field. In addition to those filters, however, the query also acts as a filter, so the result set gets further filtered down to only documents containing (100%) of the values "the", "cat", "in", and "hat" in the `description` field.

The logical difference between the `query` and `filters` parameters is that `filters` only acts as a filter, whereas `query` acts as *both* a filter and a feature vector for relevance ranking. This dual use of the `query` parameter is helpful default behavior for queries, but mixing the concerns of filtering and scoring in the same parameter can be suboptimal for more advanced queries, especially if we're simply trying to manipulate the relevance calculation and not arbitrarily removing results from our document set.

There are a few ways to address this:

- Model the `query` parameter as a function (functions only count toward relevance and do not filter):

```
Solr request syntax:
 {"query": '{!func}query("{!edismax qf=description mm=100%
   ➥v=$user_query}")',
  "filters": "{!cache=false v=$user_query}",
  "params": {"user_query": "the cat in the hat"}}
```

- Make your query match all documents (no filtering or scoring) and apply a boost query (`bq`) parameter to influence relevance without scoring:

```
Solr request syntax:
 {"query": "*",
  "filters": "{!cache=false v=$user_query}",
  "params": {"bq": "{!edismax qf=description mm=100% v=$user_quer}",
             "user_query": "the cat in the hat"}}
```

The `query` parameter both filters and then boosts based upon relevance, `filters` only filters, and `bq` only boosts. The two preceding approaches are logically equivalent, but we recommend the second option, since it's a bit cleaner to use the dedicated `bq` parameter, which was designed to contribute toward the relevance calculation without filtering.

You may have noticed that both versions of the query also contain a filter query `{!cache=false v=$user_query}` that filters on the `user_query`. Since the `query` parameter intentionally no longer filters our search results, this `filters` parameter is now required if we still want to filter to the user-entered query. The special `cache=false` parameter is used to turn off caching of the filter. Caching of filters is turned on by default in Solr, since filters tend to be reused often across requests. Since the `user_query` parameter is user-entered and is wildly variable in this case (not frequently reused across requests), it doesn't make sense to pollute the search engine's caches with these values. If you try to filter on user-entered queries without turning the cache off, it will waste system resources and likely slow down your search engine.

The overarching theme here is that it's possible to cleanly separate logical filtering from ranking features to maintain full control and flexibility over your search results. While going through this effort may be overkill for simple text-based ranking, separating these concerns becomes critical when attempting to build out more sophisticated ranking functions.

Now that you understand the mechanics of how to construct these kinds of purpose-built ranking functions, let's wrap up this chapter with a brief discussion of how to apply these techniques to implement user- and domain-specific relevance ranking.

3.3   *Implementing user and domain-specific relevance ranking*

In section 3.2, we walked through how to modify the parameters of our query-to-document similarity algorithm dynamically. That included passing in our own functions as features that contribute to the score, in addition to text-based relevance ranking.

While text-based relevance ranking using BM25, TF-IDF, vector cosine similarity, or some other kind of statistics-based approach on word occurrences can provide decent generic search relevance out of the box, it can't hold its own against good domain-specific relevance factors. Here are some domain-specific factors that often matter the most within various domains:

- *Restaurant search*—Geographical proximity, user-specific dietary restrictions, user-specific taste preferences, price range
- *News search*—Freshness (date), popularity, geographical area
- *E-commerce*—Likelihood of conversion (click-through, add-to-cart, and/or purchase)
- *Movie search*—Name match (title, actor, etc.), popularity of movie, release date, critic review score
- *Job search*—Job title, job level, compensation range, geographical proximity, job industry
- *Web search*—Keyword match on page, popularity of page, popularity of website, location of match on page (in title, header, body, etc.), quality of page (duplicate content, spammy content, etc.), topic match between page and query

These are just examples, but most search engines and domains have unique features that need to be considered to deliver an optimal search experience. This chapter has barely scratched the surface of the countless ways you can control the matching and ranking functions to return the best content. An entire profession exists—called *relevance engineering*—that is dedicated in many organizations to tuning search relevance. If you'd like to dive deeper, we highly recommend one of our prior books, *Relevant Search* by Doug Turnbull and John Berryman (Manning, 2016), which is a guide to this kind of relevance engineering.

Every search engine and domain have unique features that need to be considered to deliver an optimal search experience. Instead of having to manually model these relevance features, an AI-powered search engine can utilize machine learning to automatically generate and weight such features.

The goal of this chapter was to give you the knowledge and tools you'll need in the coming chapters to affect relevance ranking as we begin integrating more automated machine learning techniques. We'll begin applying this in our next chapter on crowdsourced relevance.

Summary

- We can represent queries and documents as dense or sparse numerical vectors and assign documents a relevance rank based on a vector similarity calculation (such as cosine similarity).
- Using TF-IDF or the BM25 similarity calculations (also based upon TF-IDF) for our text similarity scores provides a more meaningful measure of feature (keyword) importance in our queries and documents, enabling improved text ranking over just looking at term matches alone.
- Text similarity scoring is one of many kinds of functions we can invoke as a feature within our queries for relevance ranking. We can inject functions within our queries, along with keyword matching and scoring, as each keyword phrase is effectively just a ranking function.
- Treating "filtering" and "scoring" as separate concerns provides better control when specifying our own ranking functions.
- To optimize relevance, we need to both create domain-specific relevance functions and use user-specific features instead of relying just on keyword matching and ranking.

Crowdsourced relevance

This chapter covers

- Harnessing your users' collective insights to improve the relevance of your search platform
- Collecting and working with user behavioral signals
- Using reflected intelligence to create self-tuning models
- Building an end-to-end signals boosting model

In chapter 1, we introduced the dimensions of user intent as content understanding, user understanding, and domain understanding. To create an optimal AI-powered search platform, we need to be able to combine each of these contexts to understand our users' query intent. The question, though, is how do we derive these understandings?

We can learn from many sources of information: documents, databases, internal knowledge graphs, user behavior, domain experts, and so on. Some organizations have teams that manually tag documents with topics or categories, and some even outsource these tasks using tools like Amazon Mechanical Turk, which allows them to crowdsource answers from people all around the world. For identifying malicious behavior or errors on websites, companies often allow their users to report problems and even suggest corrections. All of these are examples of crowdsourcing—relying upon input from many people to learn new information.

When it comes to search relevance, crowdsourcing can play a vital role, though it is usually important not to annoy your valued customers by constantly asking them for help. Fortunately, it is often possible to learn implicitly from your users, based on their behaviors. For example, to discover the most relevant documents for a query, we can examine logs to determine the documents most clicked on by other users when running that same search. Those clicks provide signals of which results are the most relevant for the query.

In this chapter, we'll explore how we can collect, analyze, and generate insights from these signals to crowdsource relevance. We'll also cover the reflected intelligence process, introducing three key types of models for popularized relevance (signals boosting), for personalized relevance (collaborative filtering), and for generalized relevance (learning to rank). You'll also index an e-commerce dataset and build your very first reflected intelligence model.

4.1 Working with user signals

Every time a customer takes an action—such as issuing a query or purchasing a product—this provides a signal of that user's intent. We can log and process these signals to learn insights about each user, different groups of users, or our entire user base.

This section introduces the power of using user signals with a sample e-commerce dataset we'll use throughout the book, and it walks you through the mechanics of collecting, storing, and processing these signals.

4.1.1 Content vs. signals vs. models

When building search engines, two high-level sources of data affect search relevance: content and signals. Most content is in the form of documents, which can represent web pages, product listings, computer files, images, videos, facts, or any other type of searchable information. Content documents usually contain text or embedding fields that are used to search, along with other fields representing attributes related to the content (author, size, color, dates, and so on). The defining characteristic of the content documents is that they contain information users search on and ideally the answers to their queries.

When a user sees content in response to a query, they may click on a result, add it to their shopping cart, or take some other actions. These actions are signals, and they're key to providing insights into how users engage with the content. These signals can later be aggregated and used to build models to improve the relevance of your matching and ranking algorithms. The defining characteristic of signals is that they are user-supplied insights for demonstrating how users want to interact with content.

Sometimes it can also be useful to rely on external data sources—or *models*—as part of the search experience. This can include querying a knowledge graph, referencing a list of entities, or invoking a large language model (LLM) or other foundation model that has been trained on external data sources. These external models can be used to better interpret user queries, reason about and understand the content, or even summarize or generate new content to return. While we can consider models as a third source of data for our search engine, they are trained on content and/or signals and thus serve as a derivative and refined representation of those two original data sources.

In summary, we use three main sources of information to improve search: the attributes of the items (content), the observed user interactions with content (signals), and external models (which are derived from content and/or signals).

For many tasks we undertake when building AI-powered search, we can derive similar outcomes using either content or signals, but they give us two different perspectives of relevance. In ideal cases, we can apply both perspectives to build an even smarter system, but it is useful to understand their strengths and weaknesses to best employ them.

For example, when trying to find a synonym for the word "driver", we can look through the text content for words that commonly appear in the same documents. We may, in this case, find words (in priority order by the percentage of documents they appear within) like "taxi" (40%), "car" (35%), "golf" (15%), "club" (12%), "printer" (3%), "linux" (3%), and "windows" (1%). Similarly, we can look at the signals from users who searched for "driver" and aggregate common keywords from their other searches in priority order like "screwdriver" (50%), "printer" (30%), "windows" (25%), "mac" (15%), "golf" (2%), and "club" (2%). The lists derived from signals versus content might be similar, or they could look very different. The content-based approach tells us the most-represented meanings within our documents, whereas the signals-based approach tells us the most-represented meanings being looked for by our users.

Since our end goal is to present users with what they are looking for, it's often more effective to rely on the signals-derived meanings than the content-derived meanings. But what if we don't have good content that maps to the signals-derived meaning? Do we use the content-derived meaning, or do we try to suggest other related searches based on the signals data? What if we don't have enough signals or if the signals data is not very clean? Can we somehow clean up the signals-derived data using the content-derived data?

We run into similar issues with recommendations. Content-based recommendations use attributes in documents but don't understand users, whereas signals-based recommendations don't understand content attributes and won't work without sufficient interactions. Content-based recommendations may be based on features that are unimportant to users, whereas signals-based recommendations can create self-reinforcing loops where users only interact with items they are recommended, but those items are only recommended because users are interacting with them.

Ideally, we want to create a balanced system that can use the best of both content-derived and signals-derived intelligence. While this chapter focuses primarily on signals-derived, crowdsourced intelligence, a major goal of this book is to show you how to balance and combine both approaches to yield a more optimal AI-powered search experience.

4.1.2 Setting up our product and signals datasets (RetroTech)

We'll use various datasets throughout this book as we explore different use cases, but it is also valuable to have a consistent example that we can build on as we progress. We'll benefit by having a robust search use case with lots of data and user interactions, and we'll set that up in the section.

It's worth noting that most techniques in this book apply across almost all search cases. The deciding factor for when to use a particular technique typically depends more on the volume and variety of content and signals than on the specific use case.

E-commerce search provides one of the most concrete use cases for the value of AI-powered search techniques, and it is also one of the most well-understood problems among likely readers, so we've created an e-commerce dataset to help us explore this domain: the RetroTech dataset.

THE RETROTECH USE CASE

With aggressive competition among retailers selling cutting-edge electronics, multimedia, and tech products, it is hard for a small online business to compete. However, a niche but emerging segment of the population chooses to avoid the latest and greatest products and instead falls back to the familiar technology of decades past. The RetroTech company was launched to meet the needs of this unique group of consumers, offering vintage hardware, software, and multimedia products that may be hard to find on today's shelves.

Let's load the dataset for the RetroTech company so we can get started learning about the relationships between documents and user signals, and about how crowdsourced intelligence can improve our search relevance.

LOADING THE PRODUCT CATALOG

The RetroTech website has around 50,000 products available for sale, which we need to load into our search engine. If you built the AI-Powered Search codebase to run the chapter 3 examples, then your search engine is already up and running. Otherwise, the instructions for building and running all the book's examples can be found in appendix A.

With your search engine up, the next thing you need to do is download the RetroTech dataset that accompanies this book. The dataset includes two CSV files, one containing all of RetroTech's products, and another containing one year of signals data from RetroTech's users. The following listing shows a few rows of the product catalog dataset to get you familiar with the format.

> Listing 4.1   Exploring the RetroTech product catalog

```
"upc","name","manufacturer","short_description","long_description"
"096009010836","Fists of Bruce Lee - Dolby - DVD", , ,
"043396061965","The Professional - Widescreen Uncut - DVD", , ,
"085391862024","Pokemon the Movie: 2000 - DVD", , ,
"067003016025","Summerbreeze - CD","Nettwerk", ,
```

```
"731454813822","Back for the First Time [PA] - CD","Def Jam South", ,
"024543008200","Big Momma's House - Widescreen - DVD", , ,
"031398751823","Kids - DVD", , ,
"037628413929","20 Grandes Exitos - CD","Sony Discos Inc.", ,
"060768972223","Power Of Trinity (Box) - CD","Sanctuary Records", ,
```

You can see that the products are identified by a UPC (Universal Product Code) and also have a name, a manufacturer, and both a short description (used as a teaser in search results) and a long description (the full description used on the product details pages).

Since we're trying to search for products, our next step is to send them to the search engine to be indexed. To enable search on our RetroTech product catalog, let's run the document indexing code in the following listing to send the product documents to the search engine.

Listing 4.2 Send product documents to the search engine

```
products_collection = engine.create_collection("products")
products_dataframe = load_dataframe("data/retrotech/products.csv")
products_collection.write(products_dataframe)
```

Output:

```
Wiping "products" collection
Creating "products" collection
Status: Success
Loading Products
Schema:
root
 |-- upc: long (nullable = true)
 |-- name: string (nullable = true)
 |-- manufacturer: string (nullable = true)
 |-- short_description: string (nullable = true)
 |-- long_description: string (nullable = true)

Successfully written 48194 documents
```

Finally, to verify that the documents are now indexed and searchable, let's run an example keyword search. The following listing shows an example search for ipod, a true classic device!

Listing 4.3 Running a search on the product catalog

```
def product_search_request(query, param_overrides={}):
  request = {"query": query,
             "query_fields": ["name", "manufacturer", "long_description"],
             "return_fields": ["upc", "name", "manufacturer",
                               "short_description", "score"],
             "limit": 5,
             "order_by": [("score", "desc"), ("upc", "asc")]}
  return request | param_overrides
```

```
query = "ipod"
request = product_search_request(query)
response = products_collection.search(**request)
display_product_search(query, response["docs"])
```

The results of the preceding `ipod` search are shown in figure 4.1, demonstrating that our products are now indexed and searchable. Unfortunately, the relevance of the results is quite poor.

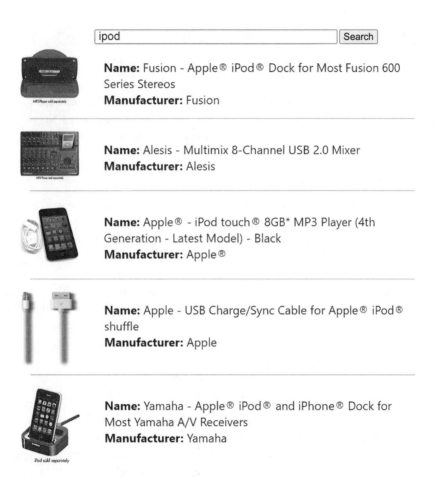

Figure 4.1 Product search results. We can see that the product catalog has been indexed and a query for `ipod` now returns search results.

While the quality of the search results ranking is not yet very good, we have an out-of-the-box "keyword matching" search engine that we can begin improving. We'll use this as our base and start introducing more intelligent AI-powered search features throughout the rest of the book. Our next step is to introduce our signals data.

Because RetroTech is running on your computer, no live users are searching, clicking, or otherwise generating signals. Instead, we've generated a dataset that approximates the kind of signal activity you'd expect in similar real-world datasets.

For simplicity, we'll store our signals in the search engine so they can be accessed both in real-time search scenarios and for external processing. Running the following listing will simulate and index some sample signals that we can use throughout the rest of the chapter.

Listing 4.4 Indexing the user signals dataset

```
signals_collection = engine.create_collection("signals")
signals_collection.write(from_csv("data/retrotech/signals.csv"))
```

With our RetroTech product and signals data all loaded, we'll soon begin exploring ways we can use the signals data to enhance search relevance. Let's first familiarize ourselves with the signals data so we can understand how signals are structured, used, and collected in real-world systems.

4.1.3 *Exploring the signals data*

Different types of signals have different attributes that need to be recorded. For a "query" signal, we want to record the user's keywords. For a "click" signal, we want to record which document was clicked upon, as well as which query resulted in the click. For later analysis, we'd also want to record which documents were returned to and possibly viewed by a user after a query.

To make the examples more extensible and avoid custom code for every new signal type, we've adopted a generic format for representing signals in this book. This format may differ from how you currently log signals, but as long as you can ultimately map your signals into this format, all the code in this book should work without requiring use-case-specific modifications.

The signals format we use in this book is as follows:

- query_id—A unique ID for the query signal that originated this signal
- user—An identifier representing a specific user of the search engine
- type—What kind of signal ("query", "click", "purchase", and so on)
- target—The content to which the signal at this signal_time applies
- signal_time—The date and time the signal occurred

As an example, assume a user performed the following sequence of actions:

1 Issued a query for ipad and had three documents (doc1, doc2, and doc3) returned.
2 Clicked on doc1.
3 Went back and clicked on doc3.
4 Added doc3 to the shopping cart.

5 Went back and searched for `ipad cover` and had two documents returned (doc4 and doc5).

6 Clicked on doc4.

7 Added doc4 to the shopping cart.

8 Purchased the items in the shopping cart (doc3 and doc4).

These interactions would result in the signals shown in Table 4.1.

Table 4.1   Example signals format

query_id	user	type	target	signal_time
1	u123	query	ipad	2024-05-01-09:00:00
1	u123	results	doc1,doc2,doc3	2024-05-01-09:00:00
1	u123	click	doc1	2024-05-01-09:00:10
1	u123	click	doc3	2024-05-01-09:00:29
1	u123	add-to-cart	doc3	2024-05-01-09:03:40
2	u123	query	ipad cover	2024-05-01-09:04:00
2	u123	results	doc4,doc5	2024-05-01-09:04:00
2	u123	click	doc4	2024-05-01-09:04:40
2	u123	add-to-cart	doc4	2024-05-01-09:05:50
1	u123	purchase	doc3	2024-05-01-09:07:15
2	u123	purchase	doc4	2024-05-01-09:07:15

There are a few things to note about the format of the signals:

- *The "query" type and the "results" type are broken into separate signals.* This isn't necessary, as they occur at the same time, but this allows us to keep the table structure consistent and not have to add an extra results column that would only apply to the query signal. Also, if the user clicks the Next Page link or scrolls down the page and sees additional results, this structure allows us to create a new signal without having to go back and modify the original signal.

- *Every signal ties back to the* `query_id` *of the original "query" signal that started the series of content interactions.* The `query_id` is not merely a reference to the keywords entered by the user but is instead a reference to the specific "query" signal identifying a time-stamped instance of the user's query keywords. Because results for the same query keywords can change over time, this enables us to do more sophisticated processing of how users reacted to the specific set of results they were shown for a query.

- *Most signal types contain one item in the* `target`, *but the "results" signal type contains an ordered list of documents.* The order of results will matter for some algorithms we introduce later in the book, to measure relevance. It's thus important to preserve the exact ordering of the search results. The `target` is an ordered list of documents in this case, instead of a single document.

- *The checkout resulted in a separate "purchase" signal for each item instead of just one "checkout" signal.* This is done so we can track whether each purchase originated from separate queries. A "checkout" signal type could additionally be added to track the transaction, and possibly could list the two purchases as the `target`, but this is superfluous for our needs in this book.

With these raw signals available as our building blocks, we can now start thinking about how we could link the signals together to begin learning about our users and their interests. In the next section, we'll discuss ways to model users, sessions, and requests within our search platform.

4.1.4   *Modeling users, sessions, and requests*

In the last section, we looked at the structure of user signals as a list of independent interactions tied back to an original query. We assumed that a "user" was present with a unique ID, but how does one identify and track a unique user? Furthermore, once you have identified how to track unique users, what is the best way to break their interactions up into sessions to understand when their context may have changed?

The concept of a user in web search can be quite fluid. If your search engine has authenticated (logged-in) users, then you already have an internal user ID to track them. If your search engine supports unauthenticated access or is publicly available, however, you'll have many users running searches with no formal user ID. That doesn't mean you can't track them, however; it just requires a more fluid interpretation of what a "user" means. A unified tracking identifier allows us to relate multiple signals from the same user to learn their interaction patterns.

If we think of the trackable information as a hierarchy from the most durable representation of a user to the least, it will look something like this:

- *User ID*—A unique user ID that persists across devices (authenticated)
- *Device ID*—A unique ID that persists across sessions on the same device (such as a device ID or an IP address plus a device fingerprint)
- *Browser ID*—A unique ID that persists across sessions in the same application or browser only (a persistent cookie ID)
- *Session ID*—A unique ID that persists across a single session (such as a cookie in a browser's incognito mode)
- *Request ID*—A unique ID that only persists for a single request (a browser with cookies turned off)

In most modern search applications, and certainly in most e-commerce applications, we typically need to deal with all of these. As a rule of thumb, you want to tie a user to the most durable identifier—the one as high up the list as possible. Both the links between request IDs and session IDs, as well as the links between session IDs and browser IDs, are through the user's cookie, so ultimately the browser ID (persistent unique ID stored in the cookie) is the common denominator for each of these.

Specifically,

- If a user has persistent cookies enabled, one browser ID can have many session IDs, which can have many request IDs.
- If a user clears cookies after each session (such as by using incognito mode), each browser ID has only one session ID, which can have many request IDs.
- If a user turns off cookies, then each request ID has a new session ID and a new browser ID.

When building search platforms, most organizations do not properly plan for and design their signals-tracking mechanisms. If they're not able to correlate visitors' queries with subsequent actions, it becomes difficult to maximize the capabilities of their AI-powered search platform. In some cases, it's possible to derive missing signals-tracking information after the fact (such as by modeling signals into likely sessions using timestamps), but it's usually best to design the system upfront to better handle user tracking to prevent potential information loss. In the next section, we'll discuss how these rich signals can be used to improve relevance through a process known as "reflected intelligence".

4.2   Introducing reflected intelligence

In the last section, we covered how to capture signals from users as they interact with our search engine. While the signals themselves are useful to help us understand how our search engine is being used, they also serve as the primary inputs for building models that can continually learn from user interactions and enable our search engine to self-tune its relevance model. In this section, we'll introduce how these self-tuning models work through the concept of reflected intelligence.

4.2.1   What is reflected intelligence?

Imagine you are an employee at a hardware store. Someone asks you where they can find a hammer, and you tell them "aisle two". A few minutes later you see the same person walk from aisle two to aisle five without a hammer, and then they walk out of aisle five holding a hammer. The next day someone else asks for a hammer, you again tell them "aisle two", and you observe a nearly identical pattern of behavior. You would be a lousy employee if you didn't spot this pattern and adjust your advice going forward to provide a better experience for your customers.

Unfortunately, most search engines function in this manner by default—they have a largely static set of documents that are returned for each query, regardless of who each user is or how prior users have reacted to the list of documents shown. By applying machine learning to the collected signals, however, we can learn about users' intent and reflect that knowledge to improve future search results. This process is called *reflected intelligence.*

Reflected intelligence is all about creating feedback loops that constantly learn and improve based on evolving user interactions. Figure 4.2 demonstrates a high-level overview of a reflected intelligence process.

Reflected intelligence process

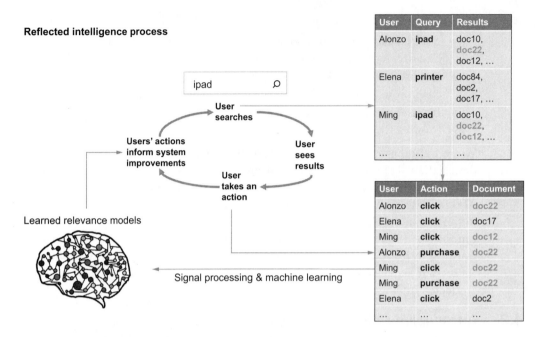

User	Query	Results
Alonzo	**ipad**	doc10, doc22, doc12, ...
Elena	**printer**	doc84, doc2, doc17, ...
Ming	**ipad**	doc10, doc22, doc12, ...
...	...	...

User	Action	Document
Alonzo	**click**	doc22
Elena	**click**	doc17
Ming	**click**	doc12
Alonzo	**purchase**	doc22
Ming	**click**	doc22
Ming	**purchase**	doc22
Elena	**click**	doc2
...	...	...

Figure 4.2   The reflected intelligence process. A user issues a query, sees results, and takes a set of actions. Those actions (signals) are then processed to create learned relevance models that improve future searches.

In figure 4.2., a user (Alonzo) runs a search, entering the query `ipad` in the search box. A query signal is logged, containing the list of all search results displayed to Alonzo. Alonzo then sees the list of search results and takes two actions: clicking on a document (doc22) and then purchasing the product that document represents. Those two additional actions are logged as additional signals. All Alonzo's signals, along with the signals from every other user, can then be aggregated and processed by various machine learning algorithms to create learned relevance models.

These learned relevance models may boost the most popular results for specific queries, personalize results for each user, or even learn which document attributes are generally most important across all users. The models could also learn how to better interpret user queries, such as identifying common misspellings, phrases, synonyms, or other linguistic patterns and domain-specific terminology.

Once these learned relevance models are generated, they can then be deployed back into the production search engine and immediately applied to enhance the outcomes of future queries. The process then begins again, with the next user running a search, seeing (now hopefully improved) search results, and interacting with those results. This process creates a self-learning system that improves with every additional user interaction, getting continually smarter and more relevant over time and automatically adjusting as user interests and content evolve.

In the following sections, we'll explore a few categories of reflected intelligence models, including signals boosting (popularized relevance), collaborative filtering (personalized relevance), and learning to rank (generalized relevance). We'll start with one of the simplest and most effective: signals-boosting models.

4.2.2   *Popularized relevance through signals boosting*

The most popular queries sent to your search engine tend to also be the most important ones to optimize from a relevance standpoint. Thankfully, since more popular queries generate more signals, we can often aggregate and boost the relevance of documents with the highest number of signals for each query. This kind of *popularized relevance* is known as *signals boosting*. It is one of the simplest forms of reflected intelligence and also one of the most effective for improving the relevance of your most popular, highest-volume queries. The following listing demonstrates an out-of-the-box search with the query `ipad` in our RetroTech search engine, prior to any signals boosting being applied.

> **Listing 4.5   Executing a keyword search for products matching `ipad`**

```
query = "ipad"
request = product_search_request(query)
response = products_collection.search(**request)
display_product_search(query, response["docs"])
```

As expected, this query returns many documents containing the keyword `ipad`, with the documents containing `ipad` typically ranking highest. Figure 4.3 shows the results for this query.

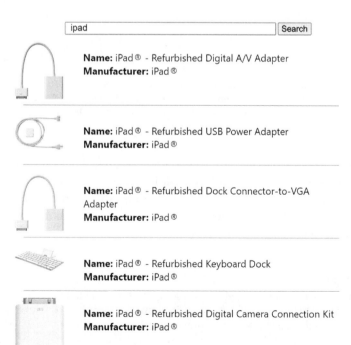

Figure 4.3   Results of a keyword search for the query `ipad`. Results are returned primarily based on the number of occurrences of the keyword, so accessories mentioning the keyword multiple times rank higher than the actual product the user intended to see.

While these results all contain the word "ipad" in their content multiple times, most users would be disappointed with these results, since they are secondary accessories as opposed to the main product type that was the focus of the search. This is a significant limitation when ranking just by document text. For very popular queries, however, it's likely that many customers will run the same queries repeatedly and fight through the frustrating search results to find the actual products they are seeking. We can tie these repeated searches into a feedback loop that continuously updates a signals-boosting model based on new signals, as shown in figure 4.4.

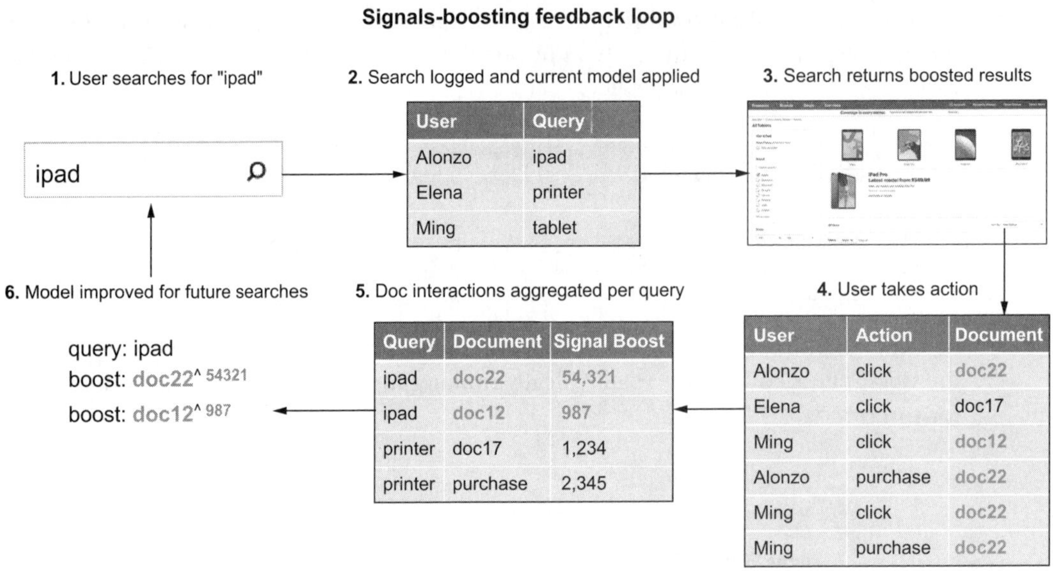

Signals-boosting feedback loop

1. User searches for "ipad"

2. Search logged and current model applied

User	Query
Alonzo	ipad
Elena	printer
Ming	tablet

3. Search returns boosted results

6. Model improved for future searches

query: ipad
boost: doc22^ 54321
boost: doc12^ 987

5. Doc interactions aggregated per query

Query	Document	Signal Boost
ipad	doc22	54,321
ipad	doc12	987
printer	doc17	1,234
printer	purchase	2,345

4. User takes action

User	Action	Document
Alonzo	click	doc22
Elena	click	doc17
Ming	click	doc12
Alonzo	purchase	doc22
Ming	click	doc22
Ming	purchase	doc22

Figure 4.4 **Signals-boosting feedback loop. A user's search is logged, and the current signals-boosting model is applied to return the boosted results. After users take action on those results, all user interaction signals with documents are aggregated by the originating query to generate an updated model to further improve future searches.**

Once your products are indexed and you've started collecting signals for your users' queries and document interactions, the only additional steps necessary for implementing signals boosting are to aggregate your signals and then add your aggregated signals as boosts to either your queries or your documents. Listing 4.6 demonstrates a simple model for aggregating signals into a sidecar collection.

Sidecar collections

Sidecar collections are additional collections that sit in your search engine alongside a primary collection and that contain other useful data to improve your search application. In our e-commerce example, our primary collection is `products`. Our `signals` collection, which has already been added, can be considered a sidecar collection. We'll add another sidecar collection, `signals_boosting`, which we'll use at query time to enhance our queries. Throughout the book, we'll introduce many other sidecar collections to store the inputs for and outputs of our generated models.

Listing 4.6 Creating a signals-boosting model by aggregating signals

```
signals_collection = engine.get_collection("signals")
create_view_from_collection(signals_collection, "signals")

signals_aggregation_query = """
SELECT q.target AS query, c.target AS doc,
COUNT(c.target) AS boost
FROM signals c LEFT JOIN signals q ON c.query_id = q.query_id
WHERE c.type = 'click' AND q.type = 'query'
GROUP BY q.target, doc
ORDER BY boost DESC"""

dataframe = spark.sql(signals_aggregation_query)
signals_boosting_collection = \
  engine.create_collection("signals_boosting")
signals_boosting_collection.write(dataframe)
```

Creates a view to make the signals collection queryable with SQL

Counts total clicks for each document for each keyword

Executes the signals aggregation SQL query

Writes the results to a new signals_boosting collection

The most important part of listing 4.6 is the `signals_aggregation_query`, defined as a SQL query for readability. For every query, we will get the list of documents that users have clicked on in the search results for that query, along with a count of how many times the document has been clicked on. By ordering the documents by the click count for each query, we get an ordered list of the documents ranked by popularity.

The idea here is that users tend to choose the products they believe are the most relevant, so if we were to boost these documents, we would expect our top search results to become more relevant. We'll test this theory in the next listing by using these aggregated counts as signals boosts. Let's revisit our previous query for `ipad`.

Listing 4.7 Searching with signals boosting to improve relevance

```
def search_for_boosts(query, collection, query_field="query"):
  boosts_request = {"query": query,
                    "query_fields": [query_field],
                    "return_fields": ["query", "doc", "boost"],
                    "limit": 10,
                    "order_by": [("boost", "desc")]}
  response = collection.search(**boosts_request)
  return response["docs"]

def create_boosts_query(boost_documents):
  print(f"Boost Documents: \n{boost_documents}")
  boosts = " ".join([f'"{b["doc"]}"^{b["boost"]}'
                     for b in boost_documents])
```

```
    print(f"\nBoost Query: \n{boosts}\n")
    return boosts

query = "ipad"
boost_docs = search_for_boosts(query, signals_boosting_collection)
boosts_query = create_boosts_query(boost_docs)
request = product_search_request(query)
request["query_boosts"] = boosts_query

response = products_collection.search(**request)
display_product_search(query, response["docs"])
```

Boost documents:

```
[{"query": "ipad", "doc": "885909457588", "boost": 966},
 {"query": "ipad", "doc": "885909457595", "boost": 205},
 {"query": "ipad", "doc": "885909471812", "boost": 202},
 {"query": "ipad", "doc": "886111287055", "boost": 109},
 {"query": "ipad", "doc": "843404073153", "boost": 73},
 {"query": "ipad", "doc": "635753493559", "boost": 62},
 {"query": "ipad", "doc": "885909457601", "boost": 62},
 {"query": "ipad", "doc": "885909472376", "boost": 61},
 {"query": "ipad", "doc": "610839379408", "boost": 29},
 {"query": "ipad", "doc": "884962753071", "boost": 28}]
```

Boost query:

```
"885909457588"^966 "885909457595"^205 "885909471812"^202 "886111287055"^109
"843404073153"^73 "635753493559"^62 "885909457601"^62 "885909472376"^61
"610839379408"^29 "884962753071"^28
```

The query in listing 4.7 does two noteworthy things:

- It queries the `signals_boosting` sidecar collection for ranked documents by boost and transforms those signals boosts into another query.
- It then passes that boosting query to the search engine as a query-time boost in the `query_boosts` parameter. In the case of Solr (our default search engine), this translates internally to a `boost` parameter of `sum(1,query($boost_query))` being added to the search request to multiply the relevance score by `1` (so it always increases) plus the calculated relevance score of the `boost_query`. (See section 3.2 if you want a refresher on influencing ranking like this through functions and multiplicative boosts.)

If you remember from figure 4.3, our original keyword search for `ipad` returned mostly iPad accessories, as opposed to actual iPad devices. Figure 4.5 demonstrates the improved results after signals boosting is applied to that original query.

The new results are significantly better than the keyword-only results. We now see products that the user was more likely looking for—iPads! You can expect to see similar improvements for most other popular queries in your search engine. Of course, as we move further down the list of popular products, the relevance improvements from

| ipad | Search |

Name: Apple® - iPad® 2 with Wi-Fi - 16GB - Black
Manufacturer: Apple®

Name: Apple® - iPad® 2 with Wi-Fi - 32GB - Black
Manufacturer: Apple®

Name: Apple® - iPad® 2 with Wi-Fi - 16GB - White
Manufacturer: Apple®

Name: ZAGG - InvisibleSHIELD for Apple® iPad® 2 - Clear
Manufacturer: ZAGG

device sold separately

Name: Apple® - iPad® 2 with Wi-Fi - 64GB - Black
Manufacturer: Apple®

Figure 4.5 Search results with signals boosting enabled. Instead of iPad accessories showing up as before, we now see actual iPads, because we have crowdsourced the answers based on the documents that users choose to interact with.

signals boosting will start to decline, and with insufficient signals we may even reduce relevance. Thankfully, we'll introduce many other techniques to improve relevance for queries with inadequate signals volume.

The goal of this section was to walk you through an initial, concrete example of implementing an end-to-end reflected intelligence model. The signals aggregation used in this implementation was very simple, though the results speak for themselves. There are many considerations and nuances to consider when implementing a signals-boosting model—whether to boost at query time or index time, how to increase the weight of newer signals versus older signals, how to avoid malicious users trying to boost particular products in the search results by generating bogus signals, how to introduce and blend signals from different sources, and so on. We'll cover each of these topics in detail in chapter 8.

Let's move on from popularized relevance and signals boosting for now and discuss a few other types of reflected intelligence models.

4.2.3   *Personalized relevance through collaborative filtering*

Let's now look at a reflected intelligence approach called collaborative filtering, which we'll categorize as *personalized relevance*. Whereas popularized relevance determines which results are usually the most popular across many users, personalized relevance focuses on determining which items are most likely to be relevant for a specific user.

Collaborative filtering is the process of using observations about the preferences of some users to predict the preferences of other users. It is the most popular type of algorithm used by recommendation engines, and it is the source of the common "users who liked this item also liked these items" recommendation lists that appear on many websites. Figure 4.6 demonstrates how collaborative filtering follows this same reflected intelligence feedback loop that we saw for signals-boosting models.

Collaborative filtering (recommendations)

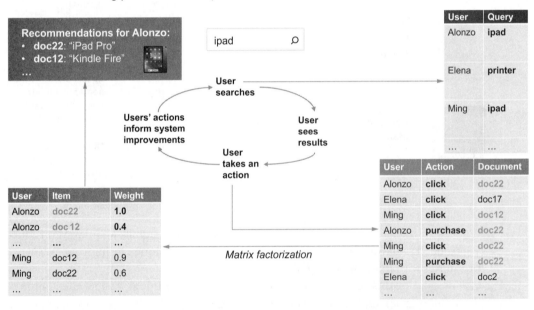

Figure 4.6   Collaborative filtering for user-to-item recommendations. Based upon his past behavior, our user (Alonzo) receives recommendations based on items other users liked, where those users also interacted with some of the same items as Alonzo.

Like signals boosting, collaborative filtering involves a continuous feedback loop. Signals are collected, models are built by those signals, recommendations are generated by those models, and interactions against those recommendations are then logged again as additional signals. Collaborative filtering approaches typically generate a user-item interaction matrix, mapping each user to each item (document), with the relationship strength between each user and item being based on the strength of the positive interactions (clicks, purchases, ratings, and so on).

If the interaction matrix is sufficiently populated, it's possible to infer recommendations from it for any user or item with interaction data. This is done by directly looking up the other users who interacted with the same item and then boosting other items (similar to signals boosting) that those users also interacted with. If the user-item interaction matrix is too sparse, however, a matrix factorization approach will typically need to be applied.

Matrix factorization is the process of breaking the user-item interaction matrix into two matrices: one mapping users to latent features (or *factors*), and another mapping those latent factors to items. This is similar to the dimensionality reduction approach we described in chapter 3, where we switched from representing food items with many exact keywords (a vector including a feature for every word in the inverted index) to using a much smaller number of meaningful dimensions (a vector with eight features describing the food items) that we compressed the data into. This matrix factorization makes it possible to derive user preferences for items, as well as the similarity between items, by distilling limited signals data into a smaller number of more meaningful dimensions that better generalize the similarity between items.

In the context of matrix factorization for collaborative filtering, the latent factors represent attributes of our documents that are learned to be important indicators of shared interests across users. By matching other documents based on these factors, we are using crowdsourcing to find other similar documents matching the same shared interests.

As powerful as collaborative filtering can be for learning user interests and tastes based entirely on crowdsourced relevance, it suffers from a major flaw known as the *cold start problem*. This is a scenario where the returning of results is dependent upon the existence of signals, but where new documents that have never generated signals will not be returned. This creates a catch-22 situation where new content is unlikely to be shown to users (a prerequisite for generating signals) because it has not yet generated any signals (which are required for the content to be shown). To some degree, signals-boosting models demonstrate a similar problem, where documents that are already popular tend to receive a higher boost, resulting in them getting even more signals, while unseen documents continue to not receive signals boosting. This process creates a self-reinforcing cycle that can lead to a lack of diversity in search results. This problem is called *presentation bias*, and we'll show how to overcome it in chapter 12.

You can also generate recommendations in other ways, such as through content-based recommendations, which we'll explore in the next chapter (section 5.4.6). Collaborative filtering is unique, however, in that it can learn the preferences and tastes of users for other documents without having to know anything about the content of the documents. This is because all decisions are made entirely by observing the interactions of users with content and determining the strength of the similarity based on those observations. We'll take a deeper dive into collaborative filtering when implementing personalized search in chapter 9.

Instead of only utilizing popularized and personalized relevance models (which function best when documents already have signals), a search engine can also benefit from a more generalized relevance model that can apply to all searches and documents. This goes a long way toward solving the cold-start problem. We'll next explore how crowdsourced relevance can be generalized through a technique called "learning to rank".

4.2.4 Generalized relevance through learning to rank

Because signals boosting (popularized relevance, section 4.2.2) and collaborative filtering (personalized relevance, section 4.2.3) only work on documents that already have signals, a substantial proportion of queries won't benefit until documents receive traffic. This is where learning to rank proves valuable as a form of generalized relevance.

Learning to rank (LTR), also known as *machine-learned ranking*, is the process of building and using a ranking classifier that can score how well any document matches any arbitrary query. You can think of the ranking classifier as a trained relevance model. Instead of manually tuning search boosts and other parameters, the LTR process trains a machine learning model that can understand the important features of your documents and then score search results appropriately. Figure 4.7 shows the general flow for rolling out LTR.

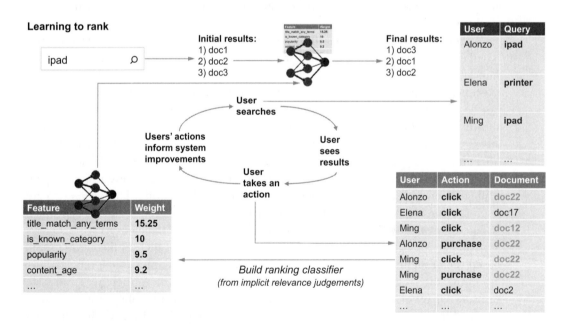

Figure 4.7 Learning to rank (generalized relevance). A ranking classifier is built from user judgments about the known relevance of documents for each query (training set). That ranking classifier model is then used to rerank search results so that the top-ranked documents are more relevant.

In an LTR system, the same high-level reflected intelligence process applies as in signals boosting and collaborative filtering (refer to figure 4.2). The difference is that LTR can use relevance judgment lists (maps of queries to their ideal ranked set of documents) to automatically train a relevance model that can then be applied generally to all queries. You'll see that the output of the "Build ranking classifier" step in figure 4.7 is a model of relevance features (`title_match_any_terms`, `is_known_category`, `popularity`, and `content_age`), and that model is deployed into the production search engine periodically to enhance search results ranking. The features in a very simple machine-learned ranking model might be readable like this, but there is no requirement that a ranking classifier be interpretable or explainable, and many advanced, deep-learning-based ranking classifiers are not.

In figure 4.7, notice that the live user flow starts with a query for `ipad`. The initial search results are then run through the deployed learning-to-rank classifier, which returns the final reranked set of search results. Since the ranking classifier is typically much more intelligent and uses more complicated ranking parameters than a traditional keyword-ranking relevance model, it is usually way too slow to use the ranking classifier to score all the matching documents in the search engine. Instead, LTR will often use an initial, faster ranking function (such as BM25) to find the top-N documents (usually hundreds or thousands of documents) and then only run that subset of documents through the ranking classifier. It is possible to use the ranking classifier as the main relevance function instead of applying this reranking technique, but it's more common to see a reranking approach, as it's typically much faster while still yielding approximately the same results.

LTR can use either explicit relevance judgments (created manually by experts) or implicit judgments (derived from user signals), or some combination of the two. We'll cover examples of implementing LTR from both explicit and implicit judgment lists in chapters 10–12.

4.2.5 *Other reflected intelligence models*

In addition to diving deeper into signals boosting (chapter 8), collaborative filtering (chapter 9), and learning to rank (chapter 10), we'll explore many other kinds of reflected intelligence throughout this book. In chapter 6, we'll explore mining user queries to automatically learn domain-specific phrases, common misspellings, synonyms, and related terms, and in chapters 11–12 we'll explore automated ways of learning relevance judgments from users' interactions so we can automatically generate training data for interesting machine learning approaches.

In general, every interaction between a user and content creates a connection—an edge in a graph—that we can use to understand emerging relationships and derive deeper insights. Figure 4.8 demonstrates some of the various relationships we can learn by exploring this interaction graph. The same incoming signals data can be processed differently, through various signals aggregation and machine learning approaches, to learn

- The similarity between users and items (user-item recommendations)
- The similarity between items and other items (item-item recommendations)
- Specific attribute-based preferences that can generate a profile of a user's interests
- The similarity between queries and items

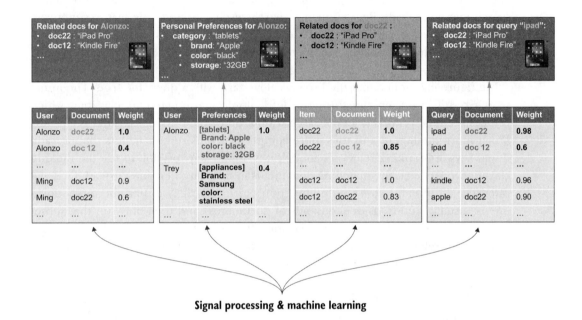

Signal processing & machine learning

Figure 4.8   Many reflected intelligence models. The leftmost box represents user-to-item similarity for recommendations, the next shows learning specific attribute-based preferences for a user's profile, the third shows learning item-to-item–based similarity for recommendations, and the rightmost shows learning query-to-item recommendations.

We'll continue to explore these techniques in the chapters to come, but it's good to keep in mind that signals data contains a treasure trove of potential insights and often provides just as much benefit as the content of the documents receiving the user interactions. Reflected intelligence and crowdsourcing are not limited to only the signals boosting, collaborative filtering, and learning-to-rank techniques we've described. They can also be derived from content instead of signals, as we'll discuss in the next section.

4.2.6   *Crowdsourcing from content*

While we typically think of crowdsourcing as asking users to provide input, we've seen in this chapter that implicit feedback can often provide as much or even more value in aggregate across many user signals. While this chapter has been entirely focused on using user signals to do this crowdsourcing, it's also important to point out that content itself can be used as crowdsourced intelligence for your AI-powered search platform.

For example, if you're trying to figure out the general quality of your documents, you may be able to look at customer reviews to generate a product rating or to see if the product has been reported as abusive or spam. If the customer has left comments, you may be able to run a *sentiment analysis* algorithm on the text, denoting if the comments are positive, neutral, or negative. Based on the detected sentiment, you can boost or penalize the source documents accordingly. This process is essentially deriving signals from user-submitted content, so it's still a form of crowdsourcing, albeit from other content provided by the users.

We mentioned that in chapter 6 we'll walk through how we can mine user signals to automatically learn domain-specific terminology (phrases, misspellings, synonyms, and so on). Just as you can take user queries and interactions to learn this terminology, you should also realize that documents are typically written by people and that very similar kinds of relationships between terminology are therefore reflected in the written content. We'll explore these content-based relationships further in the next chapter.

One of the best-known search algorithms in existence is the *Page Rank* algorithm—the breakthrough algorithm that initially enabled Google to rise to prominence as the most relevant web search engine. Page Rank goes beyond the text of any given web page and looks at the implied behavior of all other web page creators to see how they have linked to other web pages. By measuring the incoming and outgoing links, it's possible to measure a web page's "quality" on the assumption that websites are more likely to link to higher-quality, more authoritative sources and that those higher-quality sources are less likely to link to lower-quality sources. This idea of going beyond the content within a single document and relating it to other documents—whether by direct links between them, user comments or feedback, any other user interactions, or even just the use of terminology in different, nuanced ways across documents—is incredibly powerful. The art and science of using all the available information about your content and from your users is key to building a highly relevant AI-powered search engine. In chapter 5, we'll look into the concept of knowledge graphs and how we can use some of the relationships embedded within the implied links between documents to automatically further domain understanding.

Summary

- Content, signals, and models (which are derived from content and signals) are the three main sources of "fuel" to power an AI-powered search engine, with signals being the primary source for crowdsourced relevance.
- Reflected intelligence is the process of creating learning feedback loops that improve from each user interaction and reflect that learned intelligence back, to continuously increase the relevance of future results.

- Signals boosting is a form of "popularized relevance", which usually has the biggest effect on your highest-volume, most popular queries.
- Collaborative filtering is a form of "personalized relevance", which can use patterns of user interaction with items to learn user preferences or the strength of relationships between items and to then recommend similar items based upon those learned relationships.
- Learning to rank (LTR) is a form of "generalized relevance" and is the process of training a ranking classifier based on relevance judgment lists (queries mapping to correctly ranked documents). LTR can be applied to rank all documents and avoid the cold-start problem.
- Other kinds of reflected intelligence exist, including techniques for using content (instead of just signals) for crowdsourced relevance.

Part 2

Learning domain-specific intent

In part 1, you learned the mechanics of matching and ranking on keywords (using TF-IDF and BM25) and numerical vectors (using cosine and dot product). You were also introduced to an overview of crowdsourced relevance ranking. Before performing these ranking techniques, however, it's important to be able to correctly interpret a user's query and run an appropriate search that understands the user's intent. If an incorrect query is run and the wrong documents are matched, no amount of ranking logic on those bad results is going to overcome a misinterpreted query.

Properly interpreting the user's query is the focus of part 2. This step is often overlooked because it is very domain-specific, but it's crucial for meeting a user's information need. In chapter 5, you'll learn to traverse semantic knowledge graphs, the giant graphs of hyperstructured data inside your search engine that were introduced in chapter 2. These graphs underpin search engines and enable inference of the nuanced meaning of domain-specific terms within your data. In chapter 6, you'll learn to perform query intent classification, using these graphs to disambiguate different meanings of words and phrases, and how to leverage both your content and user behavioral signals to learn domain-specific terminology, related terms, misspellings, and alternate forms of terms. In chapter 7, we'll tie everything you've learned together and build a query pipeline to perform semantic search. This pipeline will parse the domain-specific intent of your users' queries and rewrite them to represent a more accurate semantic interpretation of the user's intent to the search engine, resulting in far more relevant search results.

Knowledge graph learning

In the last chapter, we primarily focused on learning the similarity between queries and documents based on users' behavioral signals. In chapter 2, we also discussed how textual document content, instead of being "unstructured data", is more like a giant graph of hyper-structured data containing a rich graph of semantic relationships connecting the many character sequences, terms, and phrases that exist across our collections of documents.

In this chapter, we'll demonstrate how to use this giant graph of semantic relationships within our content to better interpret domain-specific terminology. We'll accomplish this by using both traditional knowledge graphs, which enable explicit modeling of relationships within a domain, and semantic knowledge graphs, which enable real-time inference of nuanced semantic relationships within a domain.

A semantic knowledge graph is a simple kind of *language model* (a language model represents a probability distribution over sequences of words). We'll use a semantic knowledge graph as a stepping stone to understanding large language models (LLMs) in later chapters. LLMs are deep neural networks typically trained on billions of parameters and massive amounts of data (often much of the known internet) to model a general representation of human knowledge. Semantic knowledge graphs, however, are queryable language models representing only the relationships that are actually within your search index. While semantic knowledge graphs don't contain the ability to reason in general about language, they can be very powerful for domain-specific contextual inference, as we'll see.

We'll also play with several fun datasets in this chapter, to show some variety in how knowledge graphs can be built and applied to improve query understanding across different domains.

5.1   Working with knowledge graphs

In section 2.4, we introduced the idea of *knowledge graphs* and discussed how they relate to other types of knowledge models, such as ontologies, taxonomies, synonyms, and alternative labels. Knowledge graphs, if you recall, integrate each of those other types of knowledge models, so we'll be referring to them all collectively as "knowledge graphs" as we build throughout this chapter.

A knowledge graph (or any graph, for that matter) is represented through the concept of nodes (also known as *vertices*) and edges. A *node* is an entity represented in the knowledge graph (such as a term, person, place, thing, or concept), whereas an *edge* represents a relationship between two nodes. Figure 5.1 shows an example of a graph displaying nodes and edges.

In this figure, you can see four nodes representing authors, one node representing a research paper they wrote together, one node representing the academic conference at which the paper was presented and published, and then nodes representing the city, province, country, and dates during which the conference was held. By traversing (or "following") the independent edges between nodes, you might infer that one of the authors was in Montreal, Canada in October 2016. While any structure with nodes and edges like this is considered a graph, this particular graph represents factual knowledge and is therefore also considered a knowledge graph.

There are numerous ways to build and represent knowledge graphs, both through explicitly modeling data as nodes and edges and through dynamically materializing (discovering) nodes and edges from your data in real time. The latter is what's known as a *semantic knowledge graph*. In this chapter, we'll walk through various examples

A graph

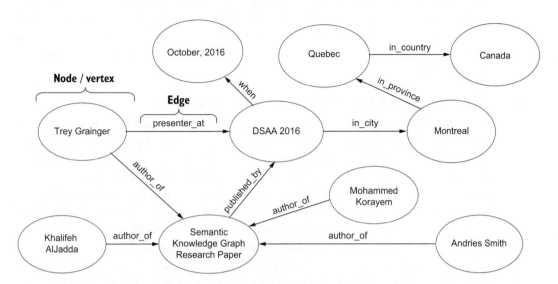

Figure 5.1 A graph structure. Graphs are composed of nodes (also known as "vertices") that represent entities and of edges that represent a node's relationship with another node. Graphs provide a way to model knowledge and infer new insights by traversing (or "following") the edges between nodes.

including building an explicit knowledge graph by hand, autogenerating an explicit knowledge graph, and using a semantic knowledge graph that is already present within your search index.

To get started with knowledge graphs, you have essentially three options:

- Build a knowledge graph from scratch using a graph database (Neo4j, Apache TinkerPop, ArangoDB, etc.)
- Plug in a preexisting knowledge graph (ConceptNet, DBpedia, a large language model, etc.)
- Autogenerate a knowledge graph from your data, using your content directly to extract knowledge

Each approach has its strengths and weaknesses, though the approaches are not necessarily mutually exclusive. If you are building a general-knowledge search engine (such as a web search engine), utilizing a preexisting knowledge graph or large language model is a great place to start. If your search engine is more domain-specific, however, your domain-specific entities and terminology may not be present in a preexisting graph, requiring you to create a custom knowledge graph.

In this chapter, we will focus primarily on the third option: autogenerating a knowledge graph from your content. The other two techniques are already covered well in external materials, using technologies like SPARQL, RDF Triples, and Apache

Jena or preexisting knowledge graphs like DBpedia and Yago. You will still need to be able to override your knowledge graph and add custom content, so we will include examples of how you can integrate both explicitly defined knowledge graphs (built with a specific list of predefined relationships) and implicitly defined knowledge graphs (autogenerated relationships discovered dynamically from the data) into your search platform.

5.2   *Using our search engine as a knowledge graph*

Many organizations spend considerable resources building out knowledge graphs for their organizations but have trouble integrating them within their search engines. We have fortunately chosen a default search engine implementation (Apache Solr) for our examples that has explicit graph traversal capabilities built in, so there is no need to pull in a new, external system to implement or traverse our knowledge graphs.

While there may be some advantages to using an external graph database, such as Neo4J or ArangoDB, that supports more sophisticated graph traversal semantics, using an external system like this makes coordinating requests, keeping data in sync, and infrastructure management more complex. Additionally, because some kinds of graph operations can only be done effectively in the search engine (like the semantic knowledge graph traversals using an inverted index, which we'll encounter shortly), using the search engine as a unified platform for both search and knowledge graph capabilities reduces the number of systems we'll need to manage.

We will focus extensively on implementing a semantic search system in chapter 7, including semantic query parsing, phrase extraction, misspelling detection, synonym expansion, and query rewriting, all of which will be modeled into an explicitly built knowledge graph. Since the purpose of the current chapter is to focus on knowledge graph *learning*, we'll save most of the discussion of query-time integration pattens until chapter 7 when we can tie everything from this chapter and chapter 6 together into the appropriate knowledge graph structure.

5.3   *Automatically extracting knowledge graphs from content*

While you'll need to be able to modify nodes and edges in your knowledge graphs, manually maintaining a large-scale knowledge graph is very challenging. Manually maintained knowledge graphs require substantial subject matter expertise, must be actively kept up to date with changing information, and are subject to the biases and errors of those maintaining them.

Open information extraction is an evolving area of natural language processing (NLP) research. Open information extraction aims to extract facts directly from your text content. This is often done using NLP libraries and language models to parse sentences and assess the dependency graph between them. A *dependency graph* is a breakdown of the parts of speech for each word and phrase in a sentence, along with an indication of which words refer to which other words.

More recent approaches to knowledge graph extraction tend to use LLMs specifically trained for entity extraction, such as UniRel (unified representation and interaction for joint relational triple extraction) and REBEL (relation extraction by end-to-end language generation). LLM-based approaches are likely to become the standard for knowledge graph extraction over time due to their ability to represent and extract more nuanced relationships between entities than traditional dependency graph–based approaches. For the sake of learning in this chapter, however, we'll focus on the dependency graph–based approach, as it will provide a better foundation for understanding the mechanics of knowledge graph extraction from text and the ability to craft custom relationship extraction patterns. You can always switch to a more advanced LLM-driven approach later if it better suits your needs.

In this section, we'll use a language model and dependency graphs to extract two different types of relationships: arbitrary relationships and hyponym relationships.

5.3.1 *Extracting arbitrary relationships from text*

Given the hyper-structured nature of text and the rich relationships expressed within typical sentences and paragraphs, it stands to reason that we should be able to identify the subjects and objects of sentences and how they are related. In this section, we'll focus on extracting arbitrary relationships between the entities described within the sentences of our text content.

By analyzing the nouns and verbs within a sentence, it is often possible to infer a fact that is present in the sentence and map that fact into an RDF triple (also known as a semantic triple). The Resource Description Framework (RDF) is a data model used to represent graphs and relationships. An *RDF triple* is a three-part data structure representing a subject (starting node), relationship (edge), and object (ending node). For example, in the sentence "Colin attends Riverside High School", the verb "attends" can be extracted as a relationship type connecting the subject ("Colin") with the object ("Riverside High School"). The RDF triple is therefore (`"Colin"`, `"attends"`, `"Riverside High School"`).

Listing 5.1 walks through an example of using the Python-based spaCy library to extract facts from text content. SpaCy is a popular natural language processing library that ships with state-of-the-art statistical neural network models for part-of-speech tagging, dependency parsing, text categorization, and named-entity recognition.

Listing 5.1 Extracting relationships and resolving co-references

```
def extract_relationships(text, lang_model, coref_model):
    resolved_text = resolve_coreferences(text, coref_model)
    sentences = get_sentences(resolved_text, lang_model)
    return resolve_facts(sentences, lang_model)

text = """
Data Scientists build machine learning models. They also write code.
Companies employ Data Scientists.
```

Resolves entities, such as replacing pronouns with nouns

Classifies parts of speech for the text

Generates RDF triples

```
Software Engineers also write code. Companies employ Software Engineers.
"""
lang_model = spacy.load("en_core_web_sm")
coref_model = spacy.load("en_coreference_web_trf")    ◁─┐
graph = extract_relationships(text, lang_model, coref_model)
print(graph)
```
The spaCy-experimental model used for co-reference resolution

Output:

```
sentence: Data Scientists build machine learning models.
dependence_parse: ['nsubj', 'ROOT', 'dobj', 'punct']
--------------------
sentence: Data Scientists also write code.
dependence_parse: ['nsubj', 'advmod', 'ROOT', 'dobj', 'punct']
--------------------
sentence: Companies employ Data Scientists.
dependence_parse: ['nsubj', 'ROOT', 'dobj', 'punct']
--------------------
sentence: Software Engineers also write code.
dependence_parse: ['nsubj', 'advmod', 'ROOT', 'dobj', 'punct']
--------------------
sentence: Companies employ Software Engineers.
dependence_parse: ['nsubj', 'ROOT', 'dobj', 'punct']
--------------------
[['Data Scientists', 'build', 'machine learning models'],
 ['Data Scientists', 'write', 'code'],
 ['Companies', 'employ', 'Data Scientists'],
 ['Software Engineers', 'write', 'code'],
 ['Companies', 'employ', 'Software Engineers']]
```

As you can see, the example code has taken the text content, parsed it into sentences, and then determined the subjects, relationships, and objects within those sentences. Those RDF triples can then be saved into an explicitly built knowledge graph and traversed.

Figure 5.2 provides a visualization of this extracted graph. Though this example is basic, advanced algorithms can extract facts from more sophisticated linguistic patterns. We are using the spaCy library in the code example, which uses a deep-learning-based neural language model to detect parts of speech, phrases, dependencies, and co-references within the input text. The mechanism we then employ to parse those linguistic outputs into RDF triples is more rules-based, following known semantic patterns within the English language.

Unfortunately, when parsing arbitrary verbs into relationships this way, the extracted relationships can become quite noisy. Since verbs conjugate differently, have synonyms, and have overlapping meanings, it is often necessary to prune, merge, and otherwise clean up any list of arbitrary extracted relationships.

In contrast, some relationship types are much simpler, such as statistical relationships ("is related to") and hyponyms ("is a"). We'll spend the rest of the chapter focusing primarily on using these two special types, starting with hyponyms.

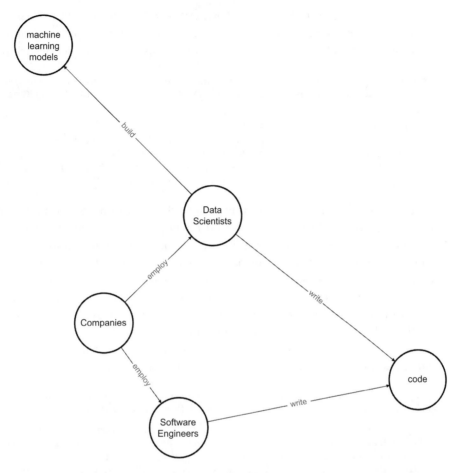

Figure 5.2   Extracted knowledge graph. The nodes and edges in this graph were automatically extracted from textual content based upon part-of-speech patterns.

5.3.2   *Extracting hyponyms and hypernyms from text*

While it can be challenging mapping arbitrary verbs to clean lists of relationships within a knowledge graph, extracting hyponyms and hypernyms can be much easier. *Hyponyms* are entities that maintain an "is a" or "is instance of" relationship with a more general form of the entities, with the more general form being called a *hypernym*. For example, for the relationships between the terms "phillips head", "screwdriver", and "tool", we would say that "phillips head" is a hyponym of "screwdriver", that "tool" is a hypernym of "screwdriver", and that "screwdriver" is both a hypernym of "phillips head" and a hyponym of "tool".

One common and fairly accurate way to extract hyponym/hypernym relationships from text is through the use of Hearst patterns, described by Marti Hearst in "Automatic Acquisition of Hyponyms from Large Text Corpora" (in *COLING 1992 Volume 2:*

The 14th International Conference on Computational Linguistics, 1992). These patterns describe common linguistic templates that reliably indicate the presence of hyponyms within sentences. The following listing demonstrates a few examples of such patterns.

Listing 5.2   Hearst patterns that identify semantic relationships

```
simple_hearst_patterns = [
    ("(NP_\\w+ (, )?such as (NP_\\w+ ?(, )?(and |or )?)+)", "first"),
    ("(such NP_\\w+ (, )?as (NP_\\w+ ?(, )?(and |or )?)+)", "first"),
    ("((NP_\\w+ ?(, )?)+(and |or )?other NP_\\w+)", "last"),
    ("(NP_\\w+ (, )?include (NP_\\w+ ?(, )?(and |or )?)+)", "first"),
    ("(NP_\\w+ (, )?especially (NP_\\w+ ?(, )?(and |or )?)+)", "first")]
```

Each of these five simple patterns is represented as a Python tuple, with the first entry being a *regular expression* and the second being a position within the pattern match (i.e., `first` or `last`). If you are unfamiliar with regular expressions, they provide a common and powerful syntax for pattern matching within strings. Anywhere you see the *NP* characters, this stands for the existence of a *noun phrase* within a sentence. The position specified in the second element of the tuple (`first` or `last`) indicates which noun phrase in the sentence represents the hypernym, with all other noun phrases matching the pattern considered the hyponyms.

In the following listing, we run through almost 50 of these Hearst patterns to match many combinations of "is a" relationships within our content.

Listing 5.3   Extracting hyponym relationships using Hearst patterns

```
text_content = """Many data scientists have skills such as machine learning,
python, deep learning, apache spark, among others. Job candidates most
prefer job benefits such as commute time, company culture, and salary.
Google, Apple, or other tech companies might sponsor the conference.
Big cities such as San Francisco, Miami, and New York often appeal to
new graduates. Job roles such as Software Engineer, Registered Nurse,
and DevOps Engineer are in high demand. There are job benefits including
health insurance and pto."""

extracted_relationships = HearstPatterns().find_hyponyms(text_content)
facts = [[pair[0], "is_a", pair[1]] for pair in extracted_relationships]
print(*facts, sep="\n")
```

Output:

```
['machine learning', 'is_a', 'skill']
['python', 'is_a', 'skill']
['deep learning', 'is_a', 'skill']
['apache spark', 'is_a', 'skill']
['commute time', 'is_a', 'job benefit']
['company culture', 'is_a', 'job benefit']
['salary', 'is_a', 'job benefit']
['Google', 'is_a', 'tech company']
['Apple', 'is_a', 'tech company']
['San Francisco', 'is_a', 'big city']
```

```
['Miami', 'is_a', 'big city']
['New York', 'is_a', 'big city']
['Software Engineer', 'is_a', 'Job role']
['Registered Nurse', 'is_a', 'Job role']
['DevOps Engineer', 'is_a', 'Job role']
['health insurance', 'is_a', 'job benefit']
['pto', 'is_a', 'job benefit']
```

As you can see from this listing, by focusing on extracting a fixed type of relationship (and the most prevalent one—the "is a" relationship), we can generate a nice, clean list of taxonomical facts with the more specific term (the hyponym) pointing to the more general term (the hypernym) with an is_a edge. Figure 5.3 demonstrates this generated graph visually.

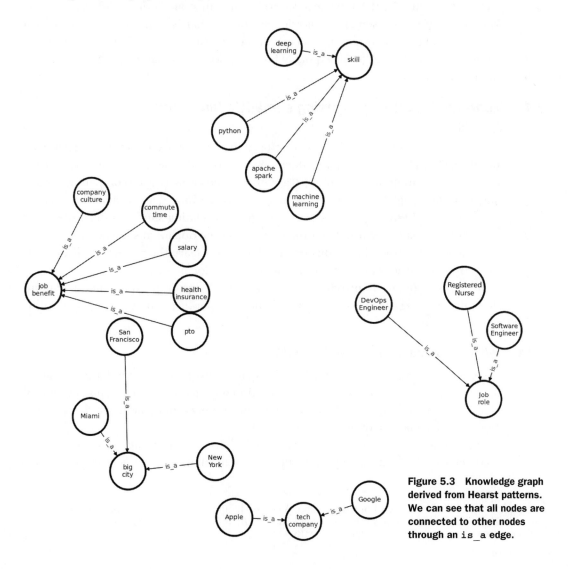

Figure 5.3 Knowledge graph derived from Hearst patterns. We can see that all nodes are connected to other nodes through an is_a edge.

The inconsistency and noise that exists with arbitrary relationship extraction is significantly reduced by utilizing Hearst patterns. We could still have ambiguity about the relationship between similar terms (for example, misspellings, alternative spellings, known phrases, or synonyms), but those are much easier to resolve. In fact, we'll spend the entire next chapter discussing how to learn this kind of domain-specific language from your signals and content to use it when interpreting incoming user queries.

Although it can be useful to extract information from our text into an explicit knowledge graph for later traversal, the reality is that this kind of extraction is a lossy process, as the representation of the items gets disconnected from the originating context of those items within our content (the surrounding text and documents containing the text). In the next section, we'll introduce an entirely different kind of knowledge graph—a semantic knowledge graph—that is optimized to enable real-time traversal and ranking of the relationships between terms and phrases within our content without having to be explicitly built and without separating terms from their original textual context.

5.4   *Learning intent by traversing semantic knowledge graphs*

In chapter 2, sections 2.1 and 2.2, we discussed the myth of text content being "unstructured data" and how, in reality, text documents represent hyper-structured data. We discussed the distributional hypothesis ("a word shall be known by the company it keeps") and walked through how character sequences, terms, phrases, and other arbitrary term sequences can be thought of as fuzzy foreign keys relating similar concepts between documents. We also discussed how these links between documents can be thought of as edges in a giant graph of relationships, enabling us to learn the contextual meaning of the terms and entities present within our corpus of documents.

In this section, we'll introduce a semantic knowledge graph, a tool and technique that will enable us to traverse that giant graph of semantic relationships present within our documents.

5.4.1   *What is a semantic knowledge graph?*

A *semantic knowledge graph* (SKG) is a "compact, auto-generated model for real-time traversal and ranking of any relationship within a domain".[1] We can think of an SKG as a search engine that, instead of matching and ranking documents, finds and ranks *terms* that best match a query.

For example, if we indexed a collection of documents about health topics and searched for `advil`, instead of returning documents that contain the term for the pain

---

[1] Grainger, et al., "The Semantic Knowledge Graph: A compact, auto-generated model for real-time traversal and ranking of any relationship within a domain." In *2016 IEEE International Conference on Data Science and Advanced Analytics (DSAA)*, pp. 420–429. IEEE, 2016.

reliever "advil", an SKG would automatically (with no manual list creation or data modeling required) return values like these:

```
advil   0.71
motrin  0.60
aleve   0.47
ibuprofen  0.38
alleve  0.37
```

Such results can be thought of as "dynamic synonyms", but instead of the terms having the same meaning, they are more like conceptually related terms. You could expand a lexical search engine query for `advil` to include these other terms to improve the recall of your search results or to boost documents that conceptually match the meaning of "advil", instead of just the string containing the five characters `a, d, v, i, l`.

In addition to finding related terms, an SKG can traverse between fields in your inverted index ("find the most-related skills to this job title"), traverse multiple levels deep ("find the most-related job titles to this query and then find the most-related skills for this query and each of those job titles"), and use any arbitrary query you can send to the search engine as a node in the graph traversal to find semantically related terms in any field.

The use cases for SKGs are diverse. They can be used for query expansion, generating content-based recommendations, query classification, query disambiguation, anomaly detection, data cleansing, and predictive analytics. We'll explore several of these in the remainder of this chapter, but let's first set up some datasets for testing our SKG.

5.4.2 Indexing the datasets

An SKG works best on datasets where there is more overlap of terms being used together across documents. The more often two words tend to appear within documents, the better we can determine whether those terms appear statistically more often than we would expect.

Although Wikipedia is often a good starting dataset for many use cases, it usually has a single page about a major topic that is supposed to be authoritative, so there isn't significant overlap across most documents, making Wikipedia a poor dataset for this use case. In contrast, most other websites where users submit the content (questions, forum posts, job postings, social media posts, reviews) tend to have excellent datasets for an SKG use case.

For this chapter, we have selected two primary datasets: a jobs dataset (job board postings) and a series of Stack Exchange data dumps including posts from the following forums:

- health
- scifi
- devops
- travel
- cooking

5.4.3   Structure of an SKG

To best utilize an SKG, it is useful to understand how the graph works based on its underlying structure.

Unlike a traditional knowledge graph, which must be explicitly modeled into nodes and edges, an SKG is *materialized* from the underlying inverted index of your search engine. This means that all you need to do to produce an SKG is to index documents into a search engine. No extra data modeling is required.

The inverted index and a corresponding forward index then serve as the underlying data structure that enables real-time traversal and ranking of any arbitrary semantic relationships present within your collection of documents.

Figure 5.4 demonstrates how documents get added into both the forward index and the inverted index. On the left of the figure, you can see three documents, each of which has a `job_title` field, a `desc` field, and a `skills` field. The right side of the figure

Documents

id: 1
job_title: Software Engineer
desc: software engineer at a great company
skills: .Net, C#, java

id: 2
job_title: Registered Nurse
desc: a registered nurse at hospital doing hard work
skills: oncology,phlebotemy

id: 3
job_title: Java Developer
desc: a software engineer or a java engineer doing work
skills: java,scala, hibernate

Docs-terms forward index

field	doc	term
	1	a
		at
		company
		engineer
		great
		software
	2	a
		at
		doing
		hard
desc		hospital
		nurse
		registered
		work
	3	a
		doing
		engineer
		java
		or
		software
		work
job_title	1	Software Engineer
...	...	...

Terms-docs inverted index

field	term	postings list	
		doc	pos
	a	1	4
		2	1
		3	1, 5
	at	1	3
		2	4
	company	1	6
	doing	2	6
		3	8
	engineer	1	2
		3	3, 7
desc	great	1	5
	hard	2	7
	hospital	2	5
	java	3	6
	nurse	2	3
	or	3	4
	registered	2	2
	software	1	1
		3	2
	work	2	10
		3	9
job_title	java developer	3	1
...	...	...	...

Figure 5.4 Inverted index and forward index. Documents get added to an inverted index, which maps documents to lists of terms, and to a forward index, which maps terms back to lists of documents. Having the ability to map both directions will prove important for graph traversal and relationship discovery.

shows how these documents are mapped into your search engine. We see that the inverted index maps each field to a list of terms, and then maps each term to a postings list containing a list of documents (along with positions in the documents, as well as some other data not included in the figure). This makes it quick and efficient to look up any term in any field and find the set of all documents containing that term.

In addition to the well-known inverted index, you can also see the less-well-known *forward index* in the center of figure 5.4. A forward index can be thought of as an *uninverted index*: for each field, it maps each document to a list of terms contained within that document. A forward index is what search engines use to generate *facets* (also called *aggregations*) on search results, which show the top values per field from a set of documents. In Lucene-based search engines like Solr, OpenSearch, and Elasticsearch, a forward index is usually generated at index time for a field by enabling a feature called *doc values* on the field. Alternatively, Apache Solr also allows you to generate the same forward index by "uninverting" the inverted index in memory at query time, enabling faceting even on fields for which doc values weren't added to the index.

If you have the ability to search for arbitrary queries and find sets of documents through an inverted index (traversing from terms to documents), and you also have the ability to take arbitrary sets of documents and look up terms in those documents (traversing from documents to terms), this means that by doing two traversals (terms to documents to terms) you can find all of the related terms that appear across any documents matching the query. Figure 5.5 demonstrates how such a traversal can occur, including a data structure view, a set-theory view, and a graph view.

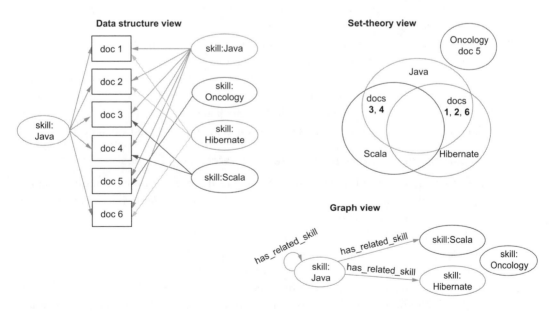

Figure 5.5 Three representations of an SKG. The data structure view shows terms mapped to sets of documents, the set-theory view shows how the intersection of sets of documents forms the relationship between them, and the graph view shows the nodes and edges.

In the data structure view, which represents our inverted and forward indices, we see how terms are related to documents based on whether they appear within them. Those relationship links are only present if there is an intersection between the docs that any two nodes (terms, in this case) appear within in the set-theory view. The graph view, finally, demonstrates a third view into the same underlying data structures, but in this case we see nodes (instead of document sets) and edges (instead of intersecting document sets). Essentially, the SKG exists as an abstraction on top of the inverted index that is already built and updated anytime the search engine indexes content.

We typically consider the primary function of search engines to be accepting a query, finding matching documents, and returning those documents in a relevance-ranked order. We devoted all of chapter 3 to discussing this process, walking through matching (sections 3.2.4–3.2.6), TF-IDF ranking (section 3.1), and the commonly used BM25 ranking function (section 3.2.1). However, with an SKG, we focus on matching and ranking related *terms*, as opposed to related documents.

Any arbitrary query (anything you can resolve to a document set) can be a node in your graph, and you can traverse from that node to any other term (or arbitrary query) in any document field. Additionally, since each traversal of an edge between two nodes uses both an inverted index (terms to docs) and a forward index (docs to terms), it is trivial to chain these traversals together into a multilevel graph traversal, as shown in figure 5.6.

In the figure, the data structure view shows a traversal from a skill node (Java) to a layer of other skills nodes (Java, Oncology, Hibernate, and Scala), to a layer of job title nodes (Software Engineer, Data Scientist, and Java Developer). You can see that not all nodes are connected—the node for Oncology, for example, does not appear in the graph view because none of the original nodes can connect to it through any edges—there are no overlapping documents.

Given that not all possible nodes are going to be relevant for any given traversal, it is also important that SKGs be able to score and assign a weight to the relationships between nodes so that those edges can be prioritized during any graph traversal. We will cover the scoring and assignment of weights to edges in the next section.

5.4.4 *Calculating edge weights to measure the relatedness of nodes*

Given that the primary function of an SKG is to discover relevant semantic relationships between nodes, the ability to calculate *semantic similarity* is critical. But what exactly is semantic similarity?

If you recall, the distributional hypothesis, introduced in section 2.3, says that words appearing together in the same contexts and with similar distributions tend to share similar meanings. Intuitively, this makes sense—the terms "pain" or "swelling" will be more likely to occur in documents that also mention "advil", "ibuprofen", or "ice pack" than in some random documents. Interestingly, though, "ice pack" may also occur in documents containing terms like "cooler", "road trip", or "cold", whereas "advil" and "ibuprofen" likely would not.

Data structure view

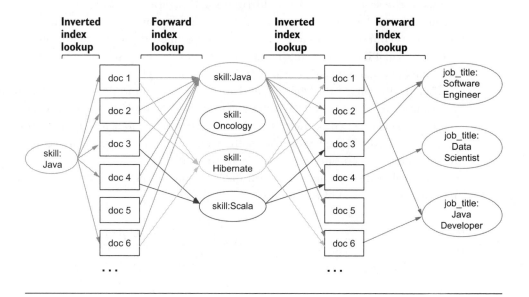

Graph view

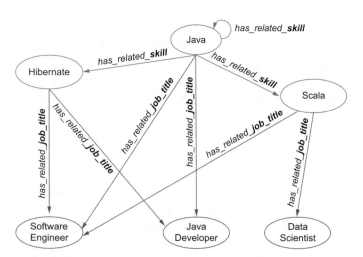

Figure 5.6 Multilevel graph traversal. In the data structure view, we see two traversals: through the inverted index and then the forward index each time. In the graph structure view, we see the corresponding two-level traversal: from skills to skills to job titles.

These examples show words (and their contexts) with similar meanings, but let's also consider words like "a", "the", "of", "and", "if", "they", and countless other very common stop words. These words will also appear heavily within the same contexts of "pain", "swelling", "advil", "ibuprofen", or any of the other words we examined. This points to the second part of the distributional hypothesis—that the words must also occur with similar distributions. In essence, this means that given some number of documents containing a first term, any second term tends to be semantically similar to the first term if it co-occurs in the same documents as the first term more often than it co-occurs in documents with other random terms.

Practically, since "the" or "a" tend to co-occur commonly with almost all other terms, they are not considered semantically similar to those terms even though their level of co-occurrence is high. Terms like "pain" and "ibuprofen", however, occur together statistically way more often than either term appears with random other terms, so they are considered semantically similar.

The following equation demonstrates one way to calculate the semantic relatedness of a term to a set of documents:

$$\text{relatedness}(x, fg, bg) = \frac{|D_x \cap D_{fg}| - |D_{fg}| \cdot P_x}{\sqrt{|D_{fg}| \cdot P_x \cdot (1 - P_x)}}$$

where

- x is a query (usually a term or term sequence) for which the relatedness is calculated relative to another query, the foreground query fg. D_x is the set of documents matching the query x.
- D_{fg} is the set of documents matching the foreground query fg. The relatedness of x is calculated relative to this foreground set.
- D_{bg} is the set of documents matching the background query bg. This bg query should be uncorrelated with x and fg and is usually set to match the entire collection of documents D or a random sample from D.
- P_x is the probability of finding x in a random document in the background set, calculated as $(D_{bg} \cap D_x) / |D_{bg}|$

This relatedness calculation (conceptually similar to a z-score in a normal distribution) relies on the concept of a "foreground" set of documents and a "background" set of documents and enables the distribution of the term x to be statistically compared between the two sets. For example, if the foreground set was all documents matching the query pain, and the background set was all documents, then the relatedness of the term "advil" would be a measure of how much more often "advil" occurs in documents also containing the word "pain" (foreground set) versus in any random document (background set). It's most common to normalize the relatedness score using a sigmoid function to map values between –1.0 and 1.0, with 0.0 indicating no relationship between the terms. For simplicity, we'll rely on this normalized range of values in the code and all subsequent examples.

If two terms are highly related, their relatedness will be a positive number approaching 1.0. If the terms are highly unrelated (meaning they tend to occur in divergent domains only), the score would be closer to –1.0. Finally, terms that aren't semantically related at all—like stop words—will tend to have a relatedness score close to zero.

Apache Solr has SKG capabilities built directly into its faceting API. Faceting provides the ability to traverse from terms to sets of documents to terms, and a relatedness aggregation function (RelatednessAgg) implements the semantic similarity calculation we just described. The following listing demonstrates searching for semantically related terms to "advil" within the Stack Exchange health dataset.

Listing 5.4 Discovering semantically related terms to advil

```
health_skg = get_skg(engine.get_collection("health"))

nodes_to_traverse = [{"field": "body",
                      "values": ["advil"]},
                     {"field": "body",
                      "min_occurrences": 2,
                      "limit": 8}]

traversal = health_skg.traverse(*nodes_to_traverse)
print_graph(traversal, "advil")
```

The field in which to find values for the starting node

Our starting node is the query "advil".

Reduces noise by excluding terms not found at least this many times

How many nodes (terms) will be returned

Performs the graph traversal

Prints the results of the SKG traversal

Output:

```
advil   0.70986
motrin  0.59897
aleve   0.4662
ibuprofen  0.38264
alleve  0.36649
tylenol 0.33048
naproxen 0.31226
acetaminophen 0.17706
```

As you can see, of all the terms within the forum posts in the Stack Exchange health dataset, the ranked order of the most semantically related terms to advil was a list of similar painkillers. This is the magic of using the distributional hypothesis to discover and rank terms by semantic similarity—it provides us with the ability to automatically discover relationships in real time that can be used to further improve our understanding of incoming queries.

The following is a Solr SKG request, which uses Solr's JSON faceting API and ability to sort on a function—the relatedness calculation we just discussed.

```
{
  "limit": 0,
  "params": {
    "q": "*",
    "fore": "{!${defType} v=$q}",
    "back": "*",
    "defType": "edismax",
```

```
    "f0_0_query": "advil"
  },
  "facet": {
    "f0_0": {
      "type": "query",
      "query": "{!edismax qf=body v=$f0_0_query}",
      "field": "body",
      "sort": {"relatedness": "desc"},
      "facet": {"relatedness": {"type": "func",
                                "func": "relatedness($fore,$back)"},
        "f1_0": {
          "type": "terms",
          "mincount": 2,
          "limit": 8,
          "sort": {"relatedness": "desc"},
          "facet": {"relatedness": {"type": "func",
                                    "func": "relatedness($fore,$back)"}
}}}}}}
```

The `skg.traverse(*nodes_to_traverse)` function in listing 5.4 abstracts away this engine-specific syntax, but if you're trying to understand the nuances of how your specific search engine or vector database internally handles these kinds of knowledge graph traversals, you can inspect the function in the notebooks. We'll mostly show the `skg.traverse` abstraction going forward, but you can always call the `skg.transform_request(*nodes_to_traverse)` function directly to see and debug the internal, engine-specific request.

In the next section, we'll discuss how we can apply the related terms returned from this SKG traversal to improve query relevance.

5.4.5   *Using SKGs for query expansion*

Matching and ranking solely on the keywords entered during a search doesn't always provide sufficient context to find and rank the best results. In these cases, you can significantly improve the quality of search results by dynamically expanding or otherwise augmenting queries to include conceptually related terms. In this section, we'll walk through how you can generate these related terms, and we'll demonstrate several strategies for applying the terms to enhance the quality of your search results.

Given its ability to start with any keyword or query and to find other highly related terms in any field, one obvious use case for an SKG is to dynamically expand queries to include related terms. This kind of expansion is sometimes referred to as *sparse lexical expansion,* as it operates on sparse vectors of query tokens made of term-based (lexical) features. One well-known technique for implementing this kind of query expansion is SPLADE (the Sparse Lexical and Expansion model), which we'll cover in section 7.4.3. Semantic knowledge graphs also provide a great way to generate contextual, sparse lexical expansions and have the benefit that they require no additional fine-tuning to your dataset. This enables documents to match even if they don't necessarily contain the exact keywords entered by the user, but they do contain other terms that carry a very similar meaning. For example, instead of a user's query for `advil`, an expanded query with boosted terms generated by the SKG might look something like `advil OR motrin^0.59897 OR aleve^0.4662 OR ibuprofen^0.3824 OR . . ..`

Let's walk through the steps for implementing this kind of query expansion, using a dataset from a different domain this time (the Stack Exchange scifi dataset). The following listing shows the first step in this process: searching for an obscure term (as a node in the SKG) and finding related other terms (as related nodes in the SKG). In this case, we'll use the query for `vibranium` as our starting node.

Listing 5.5   Discovering context for the unknown term "vibranium"

```
stackexchange_skg = get_skg(engine.get_collection("stackexchange"))

query = "vibranium"
nodes_to_traverse = [{"field": "body", "values": [query]},
                     {"field": "body", "min_occurrences": 2, "limit": 8}]

traversal = stackexchange_skg.traverse(*nodes_to_traverse)

print_graph(traversal, query)
```

Response:

```
vibranium  0.94237
wakandan  0.8197
adamantium  0.80724
wakanda  0.79122
alloy  0.75724
maclain  0.75623
klaw  0.75222
america's  0.74002
```

For anyone unfamiliar with the term "vibranium", it is a strong, fictional metal that exists in Marvel comic books and movies (best popularized through the 2018 Hollywood hit *Black Panther*). The most related terms that came back were related to "Wakandan" and "Wakanda", the fictional culture and country from which vibranium originates, "adamantium", another strong (fictional) metal from Marvel comics, and the names "Maclain" and "Klaw", characters in the Marvel comic books that are heavily associated with the metal vibranium. Maclain created the vibranium "alloy" used to make Captain "America's" shield, hence the relatedness of those words.

An autogenerated knowledge graph is very effective at identifying related pieces of information. By using an SKG and expanding your query to include additional related context, you can drastically improve the recall of your search requests. By boosting results that best match your query conceptually (as opposed to just the text), you may also be able to improve the precision of your top-ranked search results.

The following listing demonstrates an example of translating this original query, along with the SKG output, into an expanded query.

Listing 5.6   Expanding a query with nodes in an SKG

```
expansion = ""
for term, stats in traversal["graph"][0]["values"][query] \
                   ["traversals"][0]["values"].items():
  expansion += f'{term}^{stats["relatedness"]} '
expanded_query = f"{query}^5 " + expansion

print(f"Expanded Query:\n{expanded_query}")
```

Expanded query:

```
vibranium^5 vibranium^0.94237 wakandan^0.8197 adamantium^0.80724
wakanda^0.79122 alloy^0.75724 maclain^0.75623 klaw^0.75222 america's^0.74002
```

In this case, we are doing a simple Boolean OR search for any of the keywords related to the original query `vibranium`, boosting the original query term's weight by a factor of 5x and weighting each subsequent term's effect on the relevance score based upon its semantic similarity score. The choice to boost the original term by 5x is arbitrary—you can choose any value here to assign a relative relevance boost compared to the other (expanded) terms.

You might also notice that the term "vibranium" appears twice—first as the original term, and then again as an expanded term (since the term is *also* the most semantically similar to itself). This will almost always be the case if you are searching for individual keywords, but since your query might have phrases or other constructs that make the original query different from the returned terms (if any), it is usually a good idea to include the original query as part of the expanded (rewritten) query, so the user's actual query is always represented in the results.

Although the prior expanded query should rank the results reasonably well (prioritizing documents matching multiple related terms), it is also heavily focused on *recall* (expanding to include anything relevant) as opposed to *precision* (ensuring everything included is relevant). An augmented query can be constructed in many ways, depending on your primary goals.

Rewritten queries can perform a simple expansion, require a minimum percentage or number of terms to match, require specific terms like the original query to match, or even just change the ranking of the same initial results set. The following listing demonstrates several examples, using minimum match thresholds and percentages, which can tilt the scale between precision and recall as needed.

Listing 5.7   Different query augmentation strategies

```
def generate_request(query, min_match=None, boost=None):
  request = {"query": query,
             "query_fields": ["title", "body"]}
  if min_match:
```

```
    request["min_match"] = min_match
  if boost:
    request["query_boosts"] = boost
  return request

simple_expansion = generate_request(f"{query} {expansion}", "1")
increased_conceptual_precision = \
  generate_request(f"{query} {expansion}", "30%")
increased_precision_same_recall = \
  generate_request(f"{query} AND ({expansion})", "2")
slightly_increased_recall = generate_request(f"{query} {expansion}", "2")
same_results_better_ranking = generate_request(query, "2", expansion)
```

Let's look at the final search queries for each of the preceding query expansion techniques.

Simple query expansion: `simple_expansion`

```
{"query": "vibranium vibranium^0.94237 wakandan^0.8197 adamantium^0.80724
        ➥wakanda^0.79122 alloy^0.75724 maclain^0.75623 klaw^0.75222
        ➥america's^0.74002 ",
 "query_fields": ["title", "body"],
 "min_match": "0%"}
```

This simple query expansion is the same as previously described, matching any documents containing either the original query or any of the semantically related terms.

Increased-precision, reduced-recall query: `increased_conceptual_precision`

```
{"query": "vibranium AND (vibranium^0.94237 wakandan^0.8197
        ➥adamantium^0.80724 wakanda^0.79122 alloy^0.75724
        ➥maclain^0.75623 klaw^0.75222 america's^0.74002)",
 "query_fields": ["title", "body"],
 "min_match": "30%"}
```

This increased-precision, reduced-recall example specifies a "minimum match" threshold of 30%, meaning that for a document to match, it must contain at least 30% (rounded down) of the terms in the query.

Increased precision of top results, no reduction in recall: `increased_precision_same_recall`

```
{"query": "vibranium AND (vibranium^0.94237 wakandan^0.8197
        ➥adamantium^0.80724 wakanda^0.79122 alloy^0.75724
        ➥maclain^0.75623 klaw^0.75222 america's^0.74002)",
 "query_fields": ["title", "body"],
 "min_match": "2"}
```

This increased-precision, same-recall query requires the term "vibranium" to match, and it will rank documents higher when other expansion terms match, leading to an increase in precision for the top results.

Slightly increased-recall query: `slightly_increased_recall`

```
{"query": "vibranium vibranium^0.94237 wakandan^0.8197
        ➥adamantium^0.80724 wakanda^0.79122 alloy^0.75724
        ➥maclain^0.75623 klaw^0.75222 america's^0.74002",
```

```
"query_fields": ["title", "body"],
"min_match": "2"}
```

This slightly increased recall query requires two terms to match, but it does not explicitly require the original query, so it can expand to other documents that are conceptually similar but don't necessarily contain the original query term. Since the term "vibranium" is repeated twice, any documents containing just "vibranium" will also match.

Same results, better conceptual ranking: `same_results_better_ranking`

```
{"query": "vibranium",
 "query_fields": ["title", "body"],
 "min_match": "2",
 "query_boosts": "vibranium^0.94237 wakandan^0.8197 adamantium^0.80724
                ➥wakanda^0.79122 alloy^0.75724 maclain^0.75623
                ➥klaw^0.75222 america's^0.74002 "}
```

This final query returns the same documents as the original query for `vibranium`, but it ranks them differently according to how well they match the semantically similar terms from the knowledge graph. This ensures the keyword exists in all matched documents and that all documents containing the user's query are returned, while also greatly improving ranking by boosting more contextually relevant documents.

Of course, there are an unlimited number of possible query permutations you can explore when rewriting your query to include enhanced semantic context, but the preceding examples should provide a good sense of the kinds of options available and the tradeoffs you'll want to consider.

5.4.6   *Using SKGs for content-based recommendations*

In the last section, we explored how we could augment queries by discovering and using related nodes from the SKG, including multiple ways of structuring rewritten queries to optimize for precision, recall, or even improved conceptual ranking over the same results. In addition to expanding queries with semantically related terms, it's also possible to use the SKG to generate content-based recommendations by translating documents into queries based on the semantic similarity of the terms within the documents.

Since nodes in the SKG can represent any arbitrary query, we can take terms from documents and model them as arbitrary nodes to be scored relative to some known context about the document. This means we can take dozens or hundreds of terms from a document, score them all relative to the topic of the document, and then use the most semantically similar terms to generate a query best representing the nuanced, contextual meaning of the document.

The following listing walks through an example of translating a document classified as "star wars" and ranking all the terms in the document relative to that topic.

Listing 5.8 Calculating how related document terms are to "star wars"

```
from aips import extract_phrases

stackexchange_skg = get_skg(engine.get_collection("stackexchange"))

classification = "star wars"
document = """this doc contains the words luke, magneto, cyclops,
              darth vader, princess leia, wolverine, apple, banana,
              galaxy, force, blaster, and chloe."""
parsed_document = extract_phrases(document)
nodes_to_traverse = [{"field": "body", "values": [classification]},
                     {"field": "body", "values": parsed_document}]

traversal = stackexchange_skg.traverse(*nodes_to_traverse)

print_graph(traversal, classification)
```

Scored nodes:

```
luke   0.75212
force   0.73248
darth vader   0.69378
galaxy   0.58693
princess leia   0.50491
blaster   0.47143
this   0.19193
the   0.17519
words   0.10144
and   0.09709
contains   0.03434
doc   0.00885
chloe   0.0
cyclops   -0.01825
magneto   -0.02175
banana   -0.0319
wolverine   -0.03362
apple   -0.03894
```

In these results, you can see a list of terms from the document that is nicely ordered based upon semantic similarity to the topic of "star wars". Terms with lower scores will have no relatedness or negative relatedness with the specified topic. The following listing filters terms with at least a relatedness above 0.25 to get a very clean list of relevant terms from the document.

Listing 5.9 Generating a recommendation query from scored phrases

```
def get_scored_terms(traversal):
  return {term: data["relatedness"]
          for term, data in traversal["graph"][0]["values"]["star wars"] \
                            ["traversals"][0]["values"].items()}
```

```
rec_query = " ".join(f'"{term}"^{score}'
                     for term, score in get_scored_terms(traversal).items()
                     if score > 0.25)

print(f"Expanded Query:\n{rec_query}")
```

Expanded query:

```
"luke"^0.75212 "force"^0.73248 "darth vader"^0.69378 "galaxy"^0.58693
"princess leia"^0.50491 "blaster"^0.47143
```

The next listing demonstrates the last step in this process—running the search to return the top documents most semantically similar to the original document.

Listing 5.10   Running the content-based recommendations query

```
stackexchange_collection = engine.get_collection("stackexchange")

request = {"query": rec_query,
           "query_fields": ["title", "body"],
           "return_fields": ["title"],
           "limit": 5,
           "filters": [("title", "*")]}

response = stackexchange_collection.search(**request)

print(json.dumps(response["docs"], indent=2))
```

Output:

```
[{"title": "At the end of Return of the Jedi, did Darth Vader learn
        that Princess Leia was his daughter?"},
 {"title": "Did Luke know the &quot;Chosen One&quot; prophecy?"},
 {"title": "Was Darth Vader at his strongest during Episode III?"},
 {"title": "Why couldn't Snoke or Kylo Ren trace Luke using the Force?"},
 {"title": "Does Kylo Ren know that Darth Vader reconciled with Luke?"}]
```

What we have just created is a content-based recommendations algorithm. When there's an insufficient amount of user behavioral signals for signal-based recommendations like collaborative filtering (see section 4.2.3), a content-based approach can generate recommendations that are still context- and domain-aware.

The example in this section generated a content-based recommendations query based on terms found in the starting document, but it is worth keeping in mind that the SKG is not restricted to using the terms passed in. You could add an extra level to the traversal to find additional terms that are semantically related to the terms in the original document, but not actually contained within it. This can be particularly useful for niche topics where not enough documents match the recommendations query—traversing further will open new possibilities for exploration.

In the next section, we'll take a quick step beyond the "is related to" graph relationships and see if we can use the SKG to also generate and traverse some more interesting edges.

5.4.7 *Using SKGs to model arbitrary relationships*

Thus far, all our SKG traversals have used an "is related to" relationship. That is to say, we've been finding the strength of the semantic relationship between two words or phrases using the `relatedness` function, but we have only measured that the nodes are "related", not *how* they are related. What if we could find other kinds of edges between nodes instead of just "is related to" type edges?

If you recall, the nodes in an SKG are materialized on the fly by executing a query that matches a set of documents. If the node you start with is `engineer`, that node is internally represented as the set of all documents containing the word "engineer". If the node is labeled as `software engineer`, that node is internally represented as the set of all documents containing the term "software" intersected with all documents containing the term "engineer". If the search is for `"software engineer" OR java` then it is internally represented as the union of the set of all documents containing the term "software" one position before the term "engineer" (a phrase) with the set of all documents containing the term "java". All queries, regardless of their complexity, are internally represented as a set of documents.

You may also recall that an edge is formed by finding the set of documents containing both nodes. This means that *both* nodes and edges are internally represented using the same mechanism—a set of documents. Practically speaking, this means that if we can construct a node using a query that approximates an interesting relationship (as opposed to an entity), we can relate two nodes together through the "relationship node" in a similar way to how an edge would be used to relate the nodes together in a traditional graph structure.

Let's work through an example. Revisiting our scifi dataset, let's say we wanted to ask a question about Jean Grey, one of the popular characters from Marvel Comics' X-Men franchise. Specifically, let's say that we wanted to figure out who was in love with Jean Grey.

We can accomplish this by using a starting node of `jean grey`, traversing to the node `in love with`, and then requesting the top related terms associated with `in love with` within the context of `jean grey`. Listing 5.11 demonstrates this query. By traversing through a node designed to capture an explicit linguistic relationship (`in love with`, in this case), we can use the intermediate node to model an edge between the starting and terminating nodes.

> **Listing 5.11 Materializing an edge through a "relationship node"**

```
scifi_skg = get_skg(engine.get_collection("scifi"))

starting_node = "jean grey"
relationship = "in love with"
nodes_to_traverse = [{"field": "body", "values": [starting_node]},
                     {"field": "body", "values": [relationship],
                      "default_operator": "OR"},
                     {"field": "body",
                      "min_occurrences": 25, "limit": 10}]
```

```
traversal = scifi_skg.traverse(*nodes_to_traverse)

print_graph(traversal, starting_node, relationship)
```

Output:

```
jean  0.84915
grey  0.74742
summers  0.61021
cyclops  0.60693
xavier  0.53004
wolverine  0.48053
mutant  0.46532
x  0.45028
mutants  0.42568
magneto  0.42197
```

In case you're unfamiliar with these characters, here's the relevant background on Jean Grey: she has recurring relationships with two mutants, one named Cyclops (real name: Scott Summers) and one named Wolverine. Additionally, and unknown to most fans, two of Jean Grey's mentors, Professor Charles Xavier and Magneto, were known to have a love interest in Jean Grey at points throughout the comic books.

If we examine the results from listing 5.11, we'll see all of these expected names listed. The first two terms, "jean" and "grey", are the most related, since we are searching for in love with relative to jean grey. Her name is going to be highly semantically related to itself. The next two terms, "summers" and "cyclops", both refer to the same person, Jean's most prominent love interest. Then we see "xavier" and "wolverine", and the last result in the list is "magneto". Figure 5.7 illustrates some of the underlying graph relationships for this traversal.

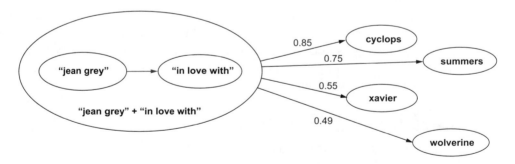

Figure 5.7 Traversing arbitrarily defined edge types. By materializing a new node with the combined context of both the originating node ("jean grey") and a new node ("in love with"), we can traverse from that combined node ("jean grey" + "in love with") to other nodes. This is equivalent to saying we are traversing from "jean grey" through an edge of "in love with" to the other nodes.

By using an intermediate node (i.e., `in love with`) to model a relationship between other nodes, we can form any arbitrarily typed edge between nodes, as long as we can express that edge as a search query.

While the results of our graph traversal in listing 5.11 were pretty good, we do see the terms "x" (presumably from "x-men") and "mutant" also showing up. Jean Grey and all the other listed people are mutants in the X-Men comics, which is why these terms are so semantically related. However, these terms are not great answers to the question "Who is in love with Jean Grey?"

This brings up an important point: the SKG is a statistical knowledge graph. The existence of the `in love with` relationship is purely based upon statistical correlations of terms within our collection, so just as with any ontology learning approach, there is going to be noise. That said, for an autogenerated graph with no explicit modeling of entities, these results are quite good.

If we wanted to improve the quality of these results, one of the easiest things to do would be to run preprocessing on the content to identify entities (people, places, and things) and index those instead of just single-term keywords. This would cause actual people's names (e.g., "Scott Summers", "Charles Xavier", "Jean Grey") to be returned instead of just individual keywords ("summers", "xavier", "jean", "grey").

It is also worth pointing out that the traversal of relationships depends entirely on whether those relationships were discussed in the underlying corpus of documents. In this case, plenty of forum posts discuss each of these peoples' relationships with Jean Grey. Had insufficient documents existed, the results returned may have been poor or nonexistent. To avoid noise in our results, we set a `min_occurrences` threshold of 25, indicating that at least 25 documents must exist discussing `jean grey`, `in love with`, and the other nodes found and scored. We recommend setting a `min_occurrences` to some number greater than 1 to avoid false positives.

While traversing arbitrary linguistic relationships like "in love with" can be useful from an exploratory standpoint, it is usually sufficient from a query understanding standpoint to stick with the default "is related to" relationship and use the relatedness scores between terms for most semantic search use cases. It can still be useful to traverse through multiple levels of relationships to generate better context, however. Specifically, it can be useful to traverse from a term to a classification field to provide some additional context, and then to related meanings of the term within that category. We'll cover this strategy in more detail in chapter 6, where we'll focus on disambiguating terms with multiple meanings.

5.5 Using knowledge graphs for semantic search

By providing the ability to accept arbitrary queries and dynamically discover related terms in a context-sensitive way, SKGs become a key tool for query interpretation and relevance ranking. We've seen that not only can SKGs help interpret and expand queries, they can also provide the abilities to classify queries and keywords in real time and to disambiguate multiple meanings of the terms in each query.

Early in the chapter, we also explored how to build explicit knowledge graphs through open information extraction techniques. What may not be obvious yet is how to parse arbitrary incoming queries and look up the appropriate context and entities in the knowledge graph. We'll spend the majority of chapter 7 covering how to build an end-to-end semantic search system that can parse queries and integrate these knowledge graph capabilities.

There are still some critical kinds of relationships we need to add to our knowledge graph that are important for search engines, such as misspellings, synonyms, and domain-specific phrases. We'll cover how to automatically learn each of these sources of domain-specific terminology from user signals or content in the next chapter, which focuses on learning domain-specific language.

Summary

- Knowledge graphs model the relationships between entities within your domain and can be built explicitly with known relationships or can be extracted dynamically from your content.
- Open information extraction, the process of extracting facts from your content (subject, relationship, object triples) can be used to learn arbitrary relationships (which typically results in noisy data) or to extract hyponym and hypernym relationships (less noisy) from text into an explicit knowledge graph.
- Semantic knowledge graphs (SKGs) enable the traversal and ranking of arbitrary semantic relationships between any content within your search index. This allows you to use your indexed content directly as a knowledge graph and language model without any additional data modeling required.
- Content-based recommendations that don't rely on user signals can be generated by ranking the most semantically interesting terms and phrases from documents and using them as a query to find and rank other related documents.
- SKGs enable a better understanding of user intent by powering domain-sensitive and context-sensitive relationship discovery and query expansion.

Using context to learn
domain-specific language

In chapter 5, we demonstrated both how to generate and use a semantic knowledge graph (SKG) and how to extract entities, facts, and relationships explicitly into a knowledge graph. Both techniques rely on navigating either the linguistic connections between terms in a single document or the statistical co-occurrences of terms across multiple documents and contexts. You learned to use knowledge graphs to find related terms, and how those related terms can integrate into various query-rewriting strategies to increase recall or precision.

In this chapter, we'll dive deeper into understanding query intent and the nuances of using different contexts to interpret domain-specific terminology in queries. We'll start by exploring query classification and then show how those classifications can be used to disambiguate queries with multiple potential meanings. Both approaches will extend our use of SKGs from the last chapter.

While those SKG-based approaches are more effective at contextualizing and interpreting queries, they continue to rely on having high-quality documents that accurately represent your domain. As a result, their efficacy for interpreting user queries depends on how well the queries overlap with the content being searched.

For example, if 75% of your users are searching for clothing, but most of your inventory is films and digital media, then when they search for the query shorts and all the results are videos with short run times (known as "digital shorts"), most of your users will be confused by the results. Given the data in your query logs, it would be better if "shorts" could map to other related terms more commonly found in your query signals, like "pants", "clothing", and "shirts".

It can be very beneficial to not only rely on the content of your documents to learn relationships between terms and phrases, but to also use your user-generated signals. In this chapter, we'll demonstrate techniques to extract key phrases, learn related phrases, and identify common misspellings or alternative spellings based on user signals. By using both content-based context and behavioral context from real user interactions, your search engine will better understand domain-specific terminology and actual user intent.

6.1 *Classifying query intent*

The goal or intent of a query usually matters more than the keywords. A search for driver crashed can mean two *very* different things in the context of news or travel content versus a computer technology context. Similarly, someone searching in e-commerce for a specific product name or product ID is probably searching for a very specific item with a high likelihood of wanting to purchase it. A general search like kitchen appliances could indicate the user just intends to browse available products to see what's available.

In both contexts, a query classifier can be effective at determining the general kind of query being issued. Depending on the domain, a query's context could be automatically applied (e.g., filtering the category of documents), used to modify the relevance algorithm (automatically boosting specific products), or even used to drive a different user experience (skipping the results page and going directly to a specific product's page). In this section, we'll show how to use the SKG from chapter 5 as a classifier for incoming queries to build a query classifier.

An SKG traversal does a *k*-nearest neighbor search at each level of the graph traversal. *K*-nearest neighbor is a type of classification that takes a data point (such as a query or term) and tries to find the top *k* most similar other data points in a vector space. If we have a field like category or classification on our documents, we can ask the SKG to "find the category with the highest relatedness to my starting node". Since the starting node is typically a user's query, an SKG can classify that query.

We'll continue to use the indexed Stack Exchange datasets as an SKG to be extended for query classification (in this section) and query-sense disambiguation (in section 6.2).

Listing 6.1 shows a function that takes a user query and traverses the SKG to find semantically related categories to classify the query. Since we've indexed multiple different Stack Exchange categories (scifi, health, cooking, devops, etc.), we'll use those categories as our classifications.

Listing 6.1   Query classification using the SKG

The initial node of the graph based on a query matching against a field

The field from which we'll find related classifications. In this case, we traverse to the category field.

```
def print_query_classification(query, classification_field="category",
        classification_limit=5, keywords_field="body", min_occurrences=5):

    nodes_to_traverse = [{"field": keywords_field,
                          "values": [query]},
                         {"field": classification_field,
                          "min_occurrences": min_occurrences,
                          "limit": classification_limit}]

    traversal = skg.traverse(*nodes_to_traverse)
    print_classifications(query, traversal)

skg = get_skg(get_engine().get_collection("stackexchange"))

print_query_classification("docker", classification_limit=3)
print_query_classification("airplane", classification_limit=1)
print_query_classification("airplane AND crash", classification_limit=2)
print_query_classification("vitamins", classification_limit=2)
print_query_classification("alien", classification_limit=1)
print_query_classification("passport", classification_limit=1)
print_query_classification("driver", classification_limit=2)
print_query_classification("driver AND taxi", classification_limit=2)
print_query_classification("driver AND install", classification_limit=2)
```

Sets the number of classifications to return

Only classifications occurring in at least this number of documents will be returned.

Traverses the SKG to classify the query

Prints a query and its classifications

Example query classifications:

```
Query: docker
  Classifications:
    devops  0.87978

Query: airplane
  Classifications:
    travel  0.33334

Query: airplane AND crash
  Classifications:
    scifi  0.02149
    travel  0.00475
```

```
Query: vitamins
  Classifications:
    health  0.48681
    cooking  0.09441

Query: alien
  Classifications:
    scifi  0.62541

Query: passport
  Classifications:
    travel  0.82883

Query: driver
  Classifications:
    travel  0.38996
    devops  0.08917

Query: driver AND taxi
  Classifications:
    travel  0.24184
    scifi  -0.13757

Query: driver AND install
  Classifications:
    devops  0.22277
    travel  -0.00675
```

This request uses the SKG to find the top *k* nearest neighbors based on a comparison of the semantic similarity between the query and each available classification (within the `category` field).

We see classification scores for each potential category for each query, with `airplane` and `passport` classified to "travel", `vitamins` classified to "health" and "cooking", and `alien` classified to "scifi". When we refine the `airplane` query to a more specific query like `airplane AND crash`, however, we see that the classification changes from "travel" to "scifi", because documents about airplane crashes are more likely to occur within "scifi" documents than "travel" documents.

As another example, `driver` could have multiple meanings. It returns two potential classifications ("travel" or "devops"), with the "travel" category being the clear choice when no other context is provided. When additional context *is* provided, however, we can see that the query `driver AND taxi` gets appropriately classified to the "travel" category, while `driver AND install` gets appropriately classified to the "devops" category.

This ability for the SKG to find semantic relationships between arbitrary combinations of terms makes it useful for on-the-fly classification of incoming queries. You can auto-apply the classifications as query filters or boosts, route queries to a context-specific algorithm or landing page, or automatically disambiguate query terms. We'll explore using a two-level graph traversal in the next section to implement query-sense disambiguation.

6.2   Query-sense disambiguation

When interpreting users' intent from their queries, understanding exactly what they meant by each word is challenging. The problem of polysemy, or ambiguous terms, can significantly affect your search results.

If someone searches for `server`, this could refer to someone who takes orders and waits on tables at a restaurant, or it could mean a computer that runs software on a network. Ideally, we want our search engine to be able to disambiguate each of these word senses and generate a unique list of related terms within each disambiguated context. Figure 6.1 demonstrates these two potential contexts for the word "server" and the kinds of related terms one might find within each context.

Server

Devops	**Travel**
server: servers, docker, code, configuration, deploy, nginx, jenkins, git, ssh	**server**: tipping, tip, servers, vpn, tips, restaurant, bill, wage, restaurants

Figure 6.1   Differentiating multiple senses of the ambiguous term "server"

In section 6.1, we demonstrated how to use an SKG to automatically classify queries into a set of known categories. Given that we already know how to classify our queries, adding a second-level traversal can provide a contextualized list of related terms for each query classification.

In other words, by traversing from query to classification and then to terms, we can generate a list of terms that describe a contextualized interpretation of the original query within each of the top classifications. The following listing shows a function that disambiguates a query this way utilizing an SKG.

Listing 6.2   Disambiguating query intent across different contexts

```
def print_query_disambigutaion(query,
    context_field="category", context_limit=5,
    keywords_field="body", keywords_limit=10, min_occurrences=5):

    nodes_to_traverse = [{"field": keywords_field,
                          "values": [query]},
                         {"field": context_field,
                          "min_occurrences": min_occurrences,
                          "limit": context_limit},
```

The starting node of the graph traversal (the user's query)

The first traversal returns the contexts for disambiguating the query.

```
                        {"field": keywords_field,
                         "min_occurrences": min_occurrences,
                         "limit": keywords_limit}]

         traversal = skg.traverse(*nodes_to_traverse)
         print_disambigutaions(query, traversal)
```

> **The second traversal is from keywords related to both the query AND each related context.**

You can see from this listing that a context field (the `category` field by default) and a keywords field (the `body` field by default) are used as part of a two-level traversal. For any query that is passed in, we first find the most semantically related category and then the terms most semantically related to the original query within that category.

The following listing demonstrates how to call this function, passing in three different queries containing ambiguous terms for which we want to find differentiated meanings.

Listing 6.3   Running query-sense disambiguation for several queries

```
print_query_disambigutaion("server")
print_query_disambigutaion("driver", context_limit=2)
print_query_disambigutaion("chef", context_limit=2)
```

The results of the queries in listing 6.3 can be found in tables 6.1–6.3, followed by the search-engine-specific SKG request used to disambiguate `chef` in listing 6.4. Each disambiguation context (`category` field) is scored relative to the query, and each discovered keyword (`body` field) is scored relative to both the query and the disambiguation context.

Table 6.1   Related terms lists contextualized by category for the query `server`

Query: server	

Context: devops 0.83796
  Keywords:
    server 0.93698
    servers 0.76818
    docker 0.75955
    code 0.72832
    configuration 0.70686
    deploy 0.70634
    nginx 0.70366
    jenkins 0.69934
    git 0.68932
    ssh 0.6836
	Context: cooking -0.1574
	  Keywords:
	    server 0.66363
	    restaurant 0.16482
	    pie 0.12882
	    served 0.12098
	    restaurants 0.11679
	    knife 0.10788
	    pieces 0.10135
	    serve 0.08934
	    staff 0.0886
	    dish 0.08553

Context: travel -0.15959
  Keywords:
    server 0.81226
    tipping 0.54391
    vpn 0.45352
    tip 0.41117
	Context: scifi -0.28208
	  Keywords:
	    server 0.78173
	    flynn's 0.53341
	    computer 0.28075
	    computers 0.2593

Table 6.1 Related terms lists contextualized by category for the query `server` *(continued)*

Query: server	
servers 0.39053	flynn 0.24963
firewall 0.33092	servers 0.24778
restaurant 0.21698	grid 0.23889
tips 0.19524	networking 0.2178
bill 0.18951	shutdown 0.21121
cash 0.18485	hacker 0.19444

Table 6.1 shows the top most semantically related categories for the query `server`, followed by the most semantically related keywords from the `body` field within each of those category contexts. Based on the data, we see that the category of "devops" is the most semantically related (positive score of `0.83796`), whereas the next three categories all contain negative scores (`-0.1574` for "cooking", `-0.15959` for "travel", and `-0.28208` for "scifi"). For the query `server`, the "devops" category is thus overwhelmingly the most likely category to be relevant.

If we look at the different term lists that come back for each of the categories, we also see several distinct meanings arise. In the "devops" category, the meaning of the term "server" is focused on tools related to managing, building, and deploying code to a computer server. In the "scifi" category, the meaning revolves around computer grids being hacked and having their networks shut down. In the "travel" category, on the other hand, the overwhelming sense of the word "server" is related to someone working in a restaurant, with terms like "tipping", "restaurant", and "bill" showing up.

When implementing an intelligent search application using this data, if you know the user's context is related to travel, it makes sense to use the specific meaning within the "travel" category. If the context is unknown, the best choice is usually either the most semantically related category or the most popular category among your users.

Table 6.2 Contextualized related terms lists by category for the query `driver`

Query: driver	
Context: travel 0.38996	Context: devops 0.08917
Keywords:	Keywords:
driver 0.93417	ipam 0.78219
drivers 0.76932	driver 0.77583
taxi 0.71977	aufs 0.73758
car 0.65572	overlayfs 0.73758
license 0.61319	container_name 0.73483
driving 0.60849	overlay2 0.69079
taxis 0.57708	cgroup 0.68438
traffic 0.52823	docker 0.67529
bus 0.52306	compose.yml 0.65012
driver's 0.51043	compose 0.55631

Table 6.2 demonstrates a query-sense disambiguation for the query `driver`. In this case, there are two related categories, with "travel" being the most semantically related (`0.38996`) versus "devops" (`0.08917`). We can see two very distinct meanings of "driver" appear within each of these contexts, with "driver" in the "travel" category being related to "taxi", "car", "license", "driving", and "bus", whereas within the "devops" category "driver" is related to "ipam", "aufs", and "overlayfs", which are all different kinds of computer-related drivers.

If someone searches for `driver`, they usually do not intend to find documents about both meanings of the word in the search results. There are several ways to deal with multiple potential meanings for queried keywords, such as grouping results by meaning to highlight the differences, choosing only the most likely meaning, carefully interspersing different meanings within the search results to provide diversity, or providing alternative query suggestions for different contexts. An intentional choice here is usually much better than lazily lumping multiple different meanings together.

Table 6.3 Contextualized related terms lists by category for the query `chef`

Query: chef	

Context: cooking 0.37731
    Keywords:
        chef 0.93239
        chefs 0.5151
        www.pamperedchef.com 0.41292
        kitchen 0.39127
        restaurant 0.38975
        cooking 0.38332
        chef's 0.37392
        professional 0.36688
        nakiri 0.36599
        pampered 0.34736
	Context: devops 0.34959
	    Keywords:
	        chef 0.87653
	        puppet 0.79142
	        docs.chef.io 0.7865
	        ansible 0.73888
	        www.chef.io 0.72073
	        learn.chef.io 0.71902
	        default.rb 0.70194
	        configuration 0.68296
	        inspec 0.65237
	        cookbooks 0.61503

As a final example, table 6.3 demonstrates the query disambiguation for the query `chef`. The top two contexts both show reasonably positive relatedness scores, indicating that both meanings are likely interpretations. While the "cooking" context has a slightly higher score (`0.37731`) than the "devops" context (`0.34959`), it would still be important to consider the user's context as far as possible when choosing between these two meanings. The meaning of `chef` within the "devops" context is related to the Chef configuration management software used to build and deploy servers (related terms include "puppet" and "ansible"), whereas within the "cooking" context it refers to a person who prepares food ("cooking", "taste", "restaurant", "ingredients"). The Chef software borrows inspiration from the cooking domain as a metaphor for how to prepare and serve software, so it's not surprising to see a term like "cookbooks" appear in the "devops" category.

The search-engine-specific SKG request used to disambiguate a query can be seen by invoking the `print_disambigutaion_request` function. This can be useful for understanding and running the internal SKG request directly against your configured search engine or vector database. The Solr-specific SKG request syntax printed for this `chef` query-sense disambiguation function call is shown in the following listing.

Listing 6.4 Solr SKG disambiguation request for the query `chef`

```
print_disambigutaion_request("chef", context_limit=2)
```

Result:

```
{"limit": 0,
 "params": {"q": "*",
            "fore": "{!${defType} v=$q}",
            "back": "*",
            "defType": "edismax",
            "f0_0_query": "chef"},
 "facet": {
   "f0_0": {
     "type": "query",
     "query": "{!edismax qf=body v=$f0_0_query}",
     "field": "body",
     "sort": {"relatedness": "desc"},
     "facet": {"relatedness": {"type": "func",
                               "func": "relatedness($fore,$back)"},
       "f1_0": {
         "type": "terms",
         "field": "category",
         "mincount": 5, "limit": 2,
         "sort": {"relatedness": "desc"},
         "facet": {"relatedness": {"type": "func",
                                   "func": "relatedness($fore,$back)"},
           "f2_0": {
             "type": "terms",
             "field": "body",
             "mincount": 5, "limit": 10,
             "sort": {"relatedness": "desc"},
             "facet": {"relatedness":{"type": "func",
                                      "func": "relatedness($fore,$back)"}}
}}}}}}
```

The starting node is a query for chef.

The first SKG traversal finds terms from the category field most related to the starting node. These categories are the disambiguation contexts.

The final SKG traversal finds the terms from the body field related to the disambiguation context.

This is the internal Solr SKG request used for disambiguating the query `chef` with a `context_limit` of 2. The request will be specific to whichever search engine or vector database is configured, or it will fall back on Solr if the engine does not have SKG capabilities. See appendix B for instructions on changing your configured search engine.

By combining query classification, term disambiguation, and query expansion, an SKG can power enhanced domain-specific and highly contextualized semantic search capabilities within your AI-powered search engine. We'll dive into using these techniques further in chapter 7 when we apply them in a live semantic search application.

6.3   *Learning related phrases from query signals*

Thus far, you've seen how to use your content as a knowledge graph to discover related terms, classify queries, and disambiguate terms. While these techniques are powerful, they are also entirely dependent upon the quality of your documents. Throughout the rest of this chapter, we'll explore the other major source of knowledge about your domain—user signals (queries, clicks, and subsequent actions). Often, user signals can lead to similar, if not even more useful, insights than document content for interpreting queries.

As a starting point for learning domain-specific terminology from real user behavior, let's consider what your query logs represent. For every query to your search engine, a query log contains an identifier for the person running the search, the query that was run, and the timestamp of the query. This means that if a single user searches for multiple terms, you can group those searches together and also know in which order the terms were entered.

While it's not always true, one reasonable assumption is that if someone enters two different queries within a very short timespan, the second query is likely to be either a refinement of the first query or about a related topic. Figure 6.2 demonstrates a realistic sequence of searches you might find for a single user in your query logs.

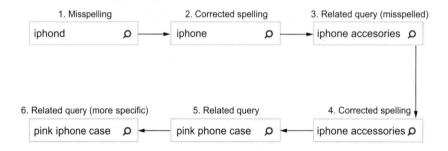

Figure 6.2   A typical sequence of searches from query logs for a particular user

When looking at these queries, we intuitively understand that `iphond` is a misspelling of `iphone`, that `iphone accesories` is a misspelling of `iphone accessories`, and that `iphone`, `pink phone case`, and `pink iphone case` are all related queries. We'll deal with the misspellings in a later section, but we can consider those to also be related terms for now.

While it's not wise to depend on a single user's signals to deduce that two queries are related, similar query patterns across many users indicate likely relationships. As we demonstrated in section 5.4.5, queries can be expanded to include related terms to improve recall. In this section, we'll explore techniques for learning related queries, first through mining query logs and then through cross-referencing product interaction logs.

6.3.1   *Mining query logs for related queries*

Before we start mining user signals for related queries, let's first convert our signals into a simpler format for processing. The following listing provides a transformation from our generic signal structure to a simple structure that maps each occurrence of a query term to the user who searched for that term.

> **Listing 6.5   Mapping signals into keyword, user pairs**

```
signals_collection = engine.get_collection("signals")
create_view_from_collection(signals_collection, "signals")
query = """SELECT LOWER(searches.target) AS keyword, searches.user
        FROM signals AS searches
        WHERE searches.type='query'"""
spark.sql(query).createOrReplaceTempView("user_searches")
print_keyword_user_pairs()
```

Loads all documents from the signals corpus into a Spark view

Selects keyword and user data from query signals

Output:

```
Number of keyword user pairs: 725459

Keyword user pairs derived from signals:
User "u10" searched for "joy stick"
User "u10" searched for "xbox"
User "u10" searched for "xbox360"
```

You can see from this listing that over 725,000 queries are represented. Our goal is to find pairs of related queries based on how many users entered both queries. The more frequently two queries co-occur across different users' query logs, the more related those queries are presumed to be.

The next listing shows each query pair where both queries were searched by the same user, along with the number of users that searched for both queries (users_cooc).

> **Listing 6.6   Total occurrences and co-occurrences of queries**

```
query = """SELECT k1.keyword AS keyword1, k2.keyword AS keyword2,
        COUNT(DISTINCT k1.user) users_cooc
        FROM user_searches k1
        JOIN user_searches k2 ON k1.user = k2.user
        WHERE k1.keyword > k2.keyword
        GROUP BY k1.keyword, k2.keyword"""
spark.sql(query).createOrReplaceTempView("keywords_users_cooc")
```

Limits keyword pairs to only one permutation to avoid duplicate pairs

Counts the number of users that searched for both k1 and k2

Joins the user_searches view with itself on the user field to find all keyword pairs searched by the same user

```
query = """SELECT keyword, COUNT(DISTINCT user) users_occ FROM
            user_searches GROUP BY keyword"""
spark.sql(query).createOrReplaceTempView("keywords_users_oc")
print_keyword_cooccurrences()
```

Output:

```
+-----------+---------+
|    keyword|users_occ|
+-----------+---------+
|     lcd tv|     8449|
|       ipad|     7749|
| hp touchpad|    7144|
|   iphone 4s|    4642|
|   touchpad|     4019|
|     laptop|     3625|
|    laptops|     3435|
|      beats|     3282|
|       ipod|     3164|
|  ipod touch|    2992|
+-----------+---------+
```

Number of co-occurring keyword searches: 244876

```
+-------------+---------------+----------+
|     keyword1|       keyword2|users_cooc|
+-------------+---------------+----------+
|green lantern|captain america|        23|
|    iphone 4s|         iphone|        21|
|       laptop|      hp laptop|        20|
|         thor|captain america|        18|
|         bose|          beats|        17|
|    iphone 4s|       iphone 4|        17|
|    skullcandy|         beats|        17|
|      laptops|         laptop|        16|
|      macbook|            mac|        16|
|         thor|  green lantern|        16|
+-------------+---------------+----------+
```

In listing 6.6, the first query produces the most searched-for keywords, as seen in the results. While these may be the most popular queries, they aren't necessarily the queries that co-occur the most often with other queries. The second query produces the total number of query pairs (244,876) where both queries were searched by the same user at least once. The final query ranks these query pairs by popularity. These top query pairs are highly related.

Notice, however, that the top result only has 23 co-occurring users, which means the number of data points is sparse and will likely include more noise further down the list. In the next section, we'll explore a technique to combine signals along a different axis (product interactions), which can help with this sparsity problem.

While directly aggregating the number of searches into co-occurrences by users helps find the most popular query pairs, the popularity of searches isn't the only metric useful for finding relatedness. The keywords "and" and "of" are highly co-occurring, as are "phones", "movies", "computers", and "electronics", because they are all general words that many people search. To additionally focus on the strength of the relationship between terms independent of their individual popularity, we can use a technique called *pointwise mutual information.*

Pointwise mutual information (PMI) is a measure of association between any two events. In the context of natural language processing, PMI predicts the likelihood of two words occurring together because they are related versus the likelihood of them occurring together by chance. Many formulas can be used to calculate and normalize PMI, but we'll use a variation called PMI^k, where k = 2, which does a better job than PMI at keeping scores consistent regardless of word frequencies.

The formula for calculating PMI^2 is shown in figure 6.3.

$$PMI^2(k1, k2) = \log \frac{P(k1, k2)^2}{P(k1) \cdot P(k2)}$$

Figure 6.3 PMI² score

In our implementation, k1 and k2 represent two different keywords that we want to compare. P(k1,k2) represents how often the same user searches for both keywords, whereas P(k1) and P(k2) represent how often a user only searches for the first keyword or second keyword, respectively. Intuitively, if the keywords appear together more often than they would be expected to, based on their likelihood of randomly appearing together, then they will have a higher PMI^2 score. The higher the score, the more likely the terms are to be semantically related.

The following listing demonstrates the PMI^2 calculation on our co-occurring query pairs dataset.

Listing 6.7 PMI² calculation on user searches

```
query = """
SELECT k1.keyword AS k1, k2.keyword AS k2, k1_k2.users_cooc,
k1.users_occ AS n_users1, k2.users_occ AS n_users2,
LOG(POW(k1_k2.users_cooc, 2) /                     The PMI calculation
    (k1.users_occ * k2.users_occ)) AS pmi2
FROM keywords_users_cooc AS k1_k2
JOIN keywords_users_oc AS k1 ON k1_k2.keyword1 = k1.keyword
JOIN keywords_users_oc AS k2 ON k1_k2.keyword2 = k2.keyword"""
spark.sql(query).createOrReplaceTempView("user_related_keywords_pmi")

spark.sql("""SELECT k1, k2, users_cooc, n_users1,
                n_users2, ROUND(pmi2, 3) AS pmi2
         FROM user_related_keywords_pmi
         WHERE users_cooc > 5 ORDER BY pmi2 DESC, k1 ASC""").show(10)
```

Output:

```
+-----------------+---------------------+----------+--------+--------+------+
|              k1|                   k2|users_cooc|n_users1|n_users2|  pmi2|
+-----------------+---------------------+----------+--------+--------+------+
|  iphone 4s cases|       iphone 4 cases|        10|     158|     740|-7.064|
|     sony laptops|           hp laptops|         8|     209|     432|-7.252|
|otterbox iphone 4|             otterbox|         7|     122|     787| -7.58|
|    green lantern|      captain america|        23|     963|    1091|-7.594|
|          kenwood|               alpine|        13|     584|     717|-7.815|
|      sony laptop|          dell laptop|        10|     620|     451|-7.936|
|    wireless mouse|            godfather|         6|     407|     248|-7.939|
|        hp laptops|          dell laptops|         6|     432|     269| -8.08|
|       mp3 players|          dvd recorder|         6|     334|     365|-8.128|
|          quicken|  portable dvd players|         6|     281|     434|-8.128|
+-----------------+---------------------+----------+--------+--------+------+
```

The results from listing 6.7 are sorted by PMI^2 score, and we set a minimum occurrences threshold at >5 to help remove noise. "hp laptops", "dell laptops", and "sony laptops" show up as related, as well as brands like "kenwood" and "alpine". Notably, there is also noise in the pairs, like "wireless mouse" with "godfather" and "quicken" with "portable dvd players". One caveat of using PMI is that a small number of occurrences together across a few users can lead to noise more easily than when using co-occurrence, which is based upon the assumption of terms commonly co-occurring.

One way to blend the benefits of both the co-occurrence model and the PMI^2 models is to create a composite score. This will provide a blend of popularity and likelihood of occurrence, which should move query pairs that match on both scores to the top of the list. Listing 6.8 demonstrates one way to blend these two measures together. Specifically, we take a ranked list of all co-occurrence scores (r1) along with a ranked list of all PMI^2 scores (r2) and blend them together to generate a composite ranking score as shown in figure 6.4.

$$\text{comp\_score}(q1, q2) = \frac{\left(\frac{r1(q1, q2) + r2(q1, q2)}{r1(q1, q2) \cdot r2(q1, q2)}\right)}{2}$$

Figure 6.4   Composite ranking score combining co-occurrence and PMI^2 ranking

The comp_score, or composite rank score, shown in figure 6.4 assigns a high score to query pairs (query q1 and query q2) where their rank in the co-occurrence list (r1) and their rank in the PMI^2 list (r2) is high, and it assigns a lower rank as the terms move further down in the rank lists. The result is a blended ranking that considers both the popularity (co-occurrence) and the likelihood of the relatedness of queries regardless of their popularity (PMI^2). The following listing shows how to calculate the comp_score based on the already-calculated co-occurrence and PMI^2 scores.

> ## Listing 6.8 Calculating a composite score from co-occurrence and PMI

```
query = """
SELECT *, (r1 + r2 / (r1 * r2)) / 2 AS comp_score
FROM (
  SELECT *,
  RANK() OVER (PARTITION BY 1
          ORDER BY users_cooc DESC) r1,
  RANK() OVER (PARTITION BY 1
          ORDER BY pmi2 DESC) r2
  FROM user_related_keywords_pmi)"""
spark.sql(query).createOrReplaceTempView("users_related_keywords_comp_score")

spark.sql("""SELECT k1, k2, users_cooc, ROUND(pmi2, 3) as pmi2,
          r1, r2, ROUND(comp_score, 3) as comp_score
          FROM users_related_keywords_comp_score
          ORDER BY comp_score ASC, pmi2 ASC""").show(20)
```

The composite score calculation combines the sorted ranks of the PMI2 score and the co-occurrences.

Ranks the co-occurrence scores from best (highest co-occurrence) to worst (lowest co-occurrence)

Ranks the PMI2 scores from best (highest PMI2) to worst (lowest PMI2 score)

Output:

k1	k2	users_cooc	pmi2	r1	r2	comp_score
green lantern	captain america	23	-7.594	1	8626	1.0
iphone 4s	iphone	21	-10.217	2	56156	1.25
laptop	hp laptop	20	-9.133	3	20383	1.667
thor	captain america	18	-8.483	4	13190	2.125
iphone 4s	iphone 4	17	-10.076	5	51964	2.6
bose	beats	17	-10.074	5	51916	2.6
skullcandy	beats	17	-9.001	5	18792	2.6
laptops	laptop	16	-10.792	8	80240	4.063
macbook	mac	16	-9.891	8	45464	4.063
thor	green lantern	16	-8.594	8	14074	4.063
headphones	beats by dre	15	-9.989	11	49046	5.545
macbook pro	macbook	15	-9.737	11	39448	5.545
macbook air	macbook	15	-9.443	11	26943	5.545
ipod touch	ipad	13	-11.829	14	200871	7.036
ipad 2	ipad	13	-11.765	14	196829	7.036
nook	kindle	13	-9.662	14	36232	7.036
macbook pro	macbook air	13	-9.207	14	21301	7.036
kenwood	alpine	13	-7.815	14	9502	7.036
beats by dre	beats	12	-10.814	19	82811	9.526
macbook	apple	12	-10.466	19	62087	9.526

Overall, the composite rank score does a reasonable job of blending our co-occurrence and PMI^2 metrics to overcome the limitations of each. The top results shown in listing 6.8 all look reasonable. One problem we already noted in this section, however, is that the co-occurrence numbers are very sparse. Specifically, the highest co-occurrence of any query pairs, out of over 700,000 query signals, was 23 overlapping users for "green lantern" and "captain america", as shown in listing 6.6.

In the next section, we'll show a way we can overcome this sparse data problem, where there is a lack of overlap between users for specific query pairs. We'll accomplish this by aggregating many users together into a larger group with similar behaviors. Specifically, we'll switch our focus to the products where user queries overlap, as opposed to focusing on the individual users issuing the overlapping queries.

6.3.2   *Finding related queries through product interactions*

The technique used to find related terms in section 6.3.1 depends on many users searching for overlapping queries. As we saw, with over 700,000 query signals, the highest overlap of any query pair was 23 users. Because the data can be so sparse, it can often make sense to aggregate on something other than users.

In this section, we'll demonstrate how we can use the same technique (using co-occurrence and PMI[2]) but rolling up based on product click signals instead of users. Since you'll hopefully have many more users than products, and since particular products are likely to be clicked in response to similar keywords, this technique helps overcome the data sparsity problem and generates higher overlaps between queries.

The transformation in listing 6.9 combines separate query and click signals into single rows with three key columns: keyword, user, and product.

Listing 6.9   Mapping raw signals into keyword, user, product groupings

```
query = """SELECT LOWER(searches.target) AS keyword, searches.user AS user,
        clicks.target AS product FROM signals AS searches
        RIGHT JOIN signals AS clicks
        ON searches.query_id = clicks.query_id
        WHERE searches.type = 'query'
        AND clicks.type = 'click'"""
spark.sql(query).createOrReplaceTempView("keyword_click_product")
print_signals_format()
```

> Utilizes click signals to produce keyword, user, and product groupings

Output:

```
Original signals format:
+------------------+-----------+----------------+-----------+-----+-------+
|                id|   query_id|     signal_time|     target| type|   user|
+------------------+-----------+----------------+-----------+-----+-------+
|000001e9-2e5a-4a...|u112607_0_1|2020-04-18 16:33|        amp|query|u112607|
|00001666-1748-47...|u396779_0_1|2019-10-16 10:22|Audio stand|query|u396779|
|000029d2-197d-4a...|u466396_0_1|2020-05-07 11:39|alarm clock|query|u466396|
+------------------+-----------+----------------+-----------+-----+-------+


Simplified signals format:
+-------------+----+------------+
|      keyword|user|     product|
+-------------+----+------------+
|   joy stick| u10|097855018120|
|        xbox| u10|885370235876|
|virgin mobile|u100|799366521679|
+-------------+----+------------+
```

Using this data, we'll now be able to determine the strength of the relationship between any two keywords based on their use across independent users searching for the same products. Listing 6.10 generates pairs of keywords to determine their potential relationship for all keyword pairs where both keywords were used in a query for the same document. The idea behind looking for overlapping queries for each user in section 6.3.1 was that each user is likely to search for related items. Each product is also likely to be searched for by related queries, though, so we can shift our mental model from "find how many users searched for both queries" to "find how many documents were found by both queries across all users".

The result of this transformation in listing 6.10 now includes the following columns:

- `k1`, `k2`—The two keywords that are potentially related because they both resulted in a click on the same product.
- `n_users1`—The number of users who searched for `k1` that clicked on a product that was also clicked on after a search by some user for `k2`.
- `n_users2`—The number of users who searched for `k2` that clicked on a product that was also clicked on after a search by some user for `k1`.
- `users_cooc`—Represents the total number of users who searched for either `k1` or `k2` and visited a product visited by other searchers for `k1` or `k2`. Calculated as `n_users1 + n_users2`.
- `n_products`—The number of products that were clicked on by searchers for both `k1` and `k2`.

> **Listing 6.10 Keyword pairs leading to the same product being clicked**

```
query = """
SELECT k1.keyword AS k1, k2.keyword AS k2, SUM(p1) n_users1, sum(p2) n_users2,
SUM(p1 + p2) AS users_cooc, COUNT(1) n_products FROM (
   SELECT keyword, product, COUNT(1) AS p1 FROM keyword_click_product
   GROUP BY keyword, product) AS k1 JOIN (
   SELECT keyword, product, COUNT(1) AS p2 FROM keyword_click_product
   GROUP BY keyword, product) AS k2 ON k1.product = k2.product
WHERE k1.keyword > k2.keyword GROUP BY k1.keyword, k2.keyword"""
spark.sql(query).createOrReplaceTempView("keyword_click_product_cooc")
print_keyword_pair_data()
```

Output:

```
Number of co-occurring queries: 1579710
```

k1	k2	n_users1	n_users2	users_cooc	n_products
laptops	laptop	3251	3345	6596	187
tablets	tablet	1510	1629	3139	155
tablet	ipad	1468	7067	8535	146
tablets	ipad	1359	7048	8407	132

```
|          cameras|       camera|    637|    688|   1325|    116|
|             ipad|        apple|   6706|   1129|   7835|    111|
|         iphone 4|       iphone|   1313|   1754|   3067|    108|
|       headphones|  head phones|   1829|    492|   2321|    106|
|           ipad 2|         ipad|   2736|   6738|   9474|     98|
|        computers|     computer|    536|    392|    928|     98|
|   iphone 4 cases|iphone 4 case|    648|    810|   1458|     95|
|          netbook|       laptop|   1017|   2887|   3904|     94|
|           laptop|    computers|   2794|    349|   3143|     94|
|          netbook|      laptops|   1018|   2781|   3799|     91|
|       headphones|    headphone|   1617|    367|   1984|     90|
|           laptop|           hp|   2078|    749|   2827|     89|
|           tablet|    computers|   1124|    449|   1573|     89|
|          laptops|    computers|   2734|    331|   3065|     88|
|              mac|        apple|   1668|   1218|   2886|     88|
|        tablet pc|       tablet|    296|   1408|   1704|     87|
+--------------+-------------+--------+--------+----------+----------+
```

The `users_cooc` and `n_products` calculations are two different ways to look at overall signal quality for how confident we are that any two terms `k1` and `k2` are related. The results are currently sorted by `n_products`, and you can see that the top of the list of relationships is quite clean. These keyword pairs represent multiple kinds of meaningful semantic relationships, including the following:

- *Spelling variations*—"laptops" ⇒ "laptop" ; "headphones" ⇒ "head phones" ; etc.
- *Brand associations*—"tablet" ⇒ "ipad" ; "laptop" ⇒ "hp" ; "mac" ⇒ "apple" ; etc.
- *Synonyms/alternate names*—"netbook" ⇒ "laptop" ; "tablet pc" ⇒ "tablet"
- *Category expansion*—"ipad" ⇒ "tablet" ; "iphone 4" ⇒ "iphone" ; "tablet" ⇒ "computers" ; "laptops" ⇒ "computers"

You can write custom, domain-specific algorithms to identify some of these specific types of relationships, as we'll do for spelling variations in section 6.5.

It's also possible to use `n_users1` and `n_users2` to identify which of the two queries is more popular. In the case of spelling variations, we see that `headphones` is used more commonly than `head phones` (1,829 versus 492 users) and is also more common than `headphone` (1,617 versus 367 users). Likewise, we see that `tablet` is much more common in usage than `tablet pc` (1,408 versus 296 users).

While our current list of keyword pairs looks clean, it only represents the keyword pairs that both occurred together in searches that led to the same products. Determining the popularity of each keyword overall will provide a better sense of which specific keywords are the most important for our knowledge graph. The following listing calculates the most popular keywords from our query signals that resulted in at least one product click.

Listing 6.11   Computing keyword searches that resulted in clicks

```
query = """SELECT keyword, COUNT(1) AS n_users FROM keyword_click_product
    GROUP BY keyword"""
```

```
spark.sql(query).createOrReplaceTempView("keyword_click_product_oc")
print_keyword_popularity()
```

Output:

```
Keyword searches that resulted in clicks: 13744

+------------+-------+
|     keyword|n_users|
+------------+-------+
|        ipad|   7554|
| hp touchpad|   4829|
|      lcd tv|   4606|
|    iphone 4s|  4585|
|      laptop|   3554|
|       beats|   3498|
|     laptops|   3369|
|        ipod|   2949|
|  ipod touch|   2931|
|      ipad 2|   2842|
|      kindle|   2833|
|    touchpad|   2785|
|   star wars|   2564|
|      iphone|   2430|
|beats by dre|   2328|
|     macbook|   2313|
|  headphones|   2270|
|        bose|   2071|
|         ps3|   2041|
|         mac|   1851|
+------------+-------+
```

This list is identical to the list from listing 6.6, but instead of showing the number of users who searched for a keyword, this list shows the number of users who searched for a keyword and also clicked on a product. We'll use this as our master list of queries for the PMI^2 calculation.

With our query pairs and query popularity now based on queries and product interactions, the rest of our calculations (PMI^2 and composite score) are the same as in section 6.3.1, so we'll omit them here (they are included in the notebooks for you to run). After calculating the PMI^2 and composite scores, the following listing shows the final results of our product-interaction-based related terms calculations.

Listing 6.12 Related terms scoring based on product interactions

```
query = """SELECT k1, k2, n_users1, n_users2, ROUND(pmi2, 3) AS pmi2,
        ROUND(comp_score, 3) AS comp_score
        FROM product_related_keywords_comp_score
        ORDER BY comp_score ASC"""
dataframe = spark.sql(query)
print("Number of co-occurring queries:", dataframe.count(), "\n")
dataframe.show(20)
```

Output:

```
Number of co-occurring queries: 1579710

+----------+-----------+--------+--------+-----+----------+
|       k1|         k2|n_users1|n_users2| pmi2|comp_score|
+----------+-----------+--------+--------+-----+----------+
|      ipad|hp touchpad|    7554|    4829|1.232|       1.0|
|    ipad 2|       ipad|    2842|    7554|1.431|      1.25|
|    tablet|       ipad|    1818|    7554|1.669|     1.667|
|  touchpad|       ipad|    2785|    7554|1.223|     2.125|
|   tablets|       ipad|    1627|    7554|1.749|       2.6|
|     ipad2|       ipad|    1254|    7554|1.903|     3.083|
|      ipad|      apple|    7554|    1814|  1.5|     3.571|
|  touchpad|hp touchpad|    2785|    4829|1.394|     4.063|
|      ipad|  hp tablet|    7554|    1421|1.594|     4.556|
|ipod touch|       ipad|    2931|    7554|0.863|      5.05|
|      ipad|      i pad|    7554|     612|2.415|     5.545|
|    kindle|       ipad|    2833|    7554|0.828|     6.042|
|    laptop|       ipad|    3554|    7554|0.593|     6.538|
|      ipad| apple ipad|    7554|     326|2.916|     7.036|
|    ipad 2|hp touchpad|    2842|    4829|1.181|     7.533|
|   laptops|     laptop|    3369|    3554| 1.29|     8.031|
|      ipad|         hp|    7554|    1125|1.534|     8.529|
|     ipads|       ipad|     254|    7554|3.015|     9.028|
|      ipad|  htc flyer|    7554|    1834|1.016|     9.526|
|      ipad|    i pad 2|    7554|     204| 3.18|    10.025|
+----------+-----------+--------+--------+-----+----------+
```

The results of listings 6.11 and 6.12 show the benefit of aggregating at a less granular level. By looking at all queries that led to a particular product being clicked on, the list of query pairs is now much larger than in section 6.3.1, where query pairs were aggregated by individual users. You can see that there are now 1,579,710 query pairs under consideration versus 244,876 (per listing 6.6) when aggregating by user.

Further, you can see that the related queries include more fine-grained variations for top queries (ipad, ipad 2, ipad2, i pad, ipads, i pad 2). Having more granular variations like this will come in handy if you are combining this related term discovery with other algorithms, like misspelling detection, which we'll cover in section 6.5.

Between the SKG approach in the last chapter and query log mining in this chapter, you've now seen multiple techniques for discovering related phrases. Before we can apply the related phrases, however, we first need to be able to identify such known phrases in incoming queries. In the next section, we'll cover how we can generate a list of known phrases from our query signals.

6.4   *Phrase detection from user signals*

In section 5.3, we discussed several techniques for extracting arbitrary phrases and relationships from documents. While this can go a long way toward discovering all the relevant domain-specific phrases within your content, this approach suffers from two different problems:

- *It generates a lot of noise*—Not every noun phrase across your potentially massive set of documents is important, and the odds of identifying incorrect phrases (false positives) increase as your number of documents increases.
- *It ignores what your users care about*—The real measure of user interest is communicated by what they search for. They may only be interested in a subset of your content or may be looking for things that aren't even represented well within your content.

In this section, we'll focus on how to identify important domain-specific phrases from your user signals.

6.4.1 Treating queries as entities

The easiest way to extract entities from query logs is to treat the entire query as one entity. In use cases like our RetroTech e-commerce site, this works very well, as many of the queries are product names, categories, brand names, company names, or people's names (actors, musicians, etc.). Given that context, most of the high-popularity queries end up being entities that can be used directly as phrases without needing any special parsing.

Looking back at the output of listing 6.11, you'll find the following most popular queries:

```
+------------+-------+
|     keyword|n_users|
+------------+-------+
|        ipad|   7554|
| hp touchpad|   4829|
|      lcd tv|   4606|
|   iphone 4s|   4585|
|      laptop|   3554|
|         ... |   ... |
+------------+-------+
```

These are entities that belong in a known-entities list, with many of them being multi-word phrases. In this case, the simplest method for extracting entities is also the most powerful—just use the queries as your entities list. The higher the frequency of each query across users, the more confident you can be about adding it to your entities list.

One way to reduce potential false positives from noisy queries is to find phrases that overlap in both your documents and queries. Additionally, if you have different fields in your documents, like a product name or company, you can cross-reference your queries with those fields to assign a type to the entities found within your queries.

Depending on the complexity of your queries, using the most common searches as your key entities may be the most straightforward way to achieve a high-quality entities list.

6.4.2   *Extracting entities from more complex queries*

In some use cases, the queries may contain more noise (Boolean structure, advanced query operators, etc.) and therefore may not be directly usable as entities. In those cases, the best approach to extracting entities may be to reapply the entity extraction strategies from chapter 5, but on your query signals.

Out of the box, a lexical search engine parses queries as individual keywords and looks them up in the inverted index. For example, a query for `new york city` will be automatically interpreted as the Boolean query `new AND york AND city` (or if you set the default operator to `OR`, then `new OR york OR city`). The relevance ranking algorithms will then score each keyword individually instead of understanding that certain words combine to make phrases that then take on a different meaning.

Being able to identify and extract domain-specific phrases from queries can enable more accurate query interpretation and relevance. We already demonstrated one way to extract domain-specific phrases from documents in section 5.3, using the spaCy NLP library to do a dependency parse and extract out noun phrases. While queries are often too short to perform a true dependency parse, it's still possible to apply some part of speech filtering on any discovered phrases in queries to omit non-noun phrases. If you need to split sections of queries apart, you can also tokenize the queries and remove query syntax (`AND`, `OR`, etc.) before looking for phrases to extract. Handling the specific query patterns for your application may require some domain-specific query parsing logic, but if your queries are largely single phrases or easily tokenizable into multiple phrases, your queries likely represent the best source of domain-specific phrases to extract and add to your knowledge graph. We'll walk through code examples of phrase identification when parsing queries in section 7.4.

6.5   *Misspellings and alternative representations*

We've covered detecting domain-specific phrases and finding related phrases, but there are two very important subcategories of related phrases that typically require special handling: misspellings and alternative spellings (also known as *alternative labels*). When entering queries, users will commonly misspell their keywords, and the general expectation is that an AI-powered search system will be able to understand and properly handle those misspellings.

While general related phrases for "laptop" might be "computer", "netbook", or "tablet", misspellings would look more like "latop", "laptok", or "lapptop". *Alternative labels* are functionally no different than misspellings but occur when multiple valid variations for a phrase exist (such as "specialized" versus "specialised" or "cybersecurity" versus "cyber security"). In the case of both misspellings and alternative labels, the end goal is usually to normalize the less common variant into the more common, canonical form and then search for the canonical version.

Spell-checking can be implemented in multiple ways. In this section, we'll cover the out-of-the-box document-based spell-checking that is found in most search engines, and we'll also show how user signals can be mined to fine-tune spelling corrections based upon real user interactions with your search engine.

6.5.1 Learning spelling corrections from documents

Most search engines contain some spell-checking capabilities out of the box, based on the terms found within a collection's documents. Apache Solr, for example, provides file-based, dictionary-based, and index-based spell-checking components. The file-based spell-checker requires assembling a list of terms that can be spell-corrected. The dictionary-based spell-checker can build a list of terms to be spell-corrected from fields in an index. The index-based spell-checker can use a field on the main index to spell-check directly without having to build a separate spell-checking index. Additionally, if someone has built a list of spelling corrections offline, you can use a synonym list to directly replace or expand any misspellings to their canonical form.

Elasticsearch and OpenSearch have similar spellchecking capabilities, even allowing specific contexts to refine the scope of the spelling suggestions to a particular category or geographical location.

While we encourage you to test out these out-of-the-box spell-checking algorithms, they all unfortunately suffer from a major problem: lack of user context. Specifically, anytime a keyword is searched that doesn't appear a minimum number of times in the index, the spell-checking component begins looking at all terms in the index that are *off by the minimum number of characters*, and they then return the most prevalent keywords in the index that match the criteria. The following listing shows an example of where out-of-the-box index-based spell-checking configuration falls short.

> **Listing 6.13 Using out-of-the-box spelling corrections on documents**

```
products_collection = engine.get_collection("products")
query = "moden"
results = engine.spell_check(products_collection, query)
print(results)
```

Output:

```
{'modes': 421, 'model': 159, 'modern': 139, 'modem': 56, 'mode6': 9}
```

In listing 6.13, you can see a user query for moden. The spell-checker returns the suggested spelling corrections of "modes", "model", "modern", and "modem", plus one suggestion that only appears in a few documents, which we'll ignore. Since our collection is tech products, it may be obvious which of these is likely the best spelling correction: it's "modem". In fact, it is unlikely that a user would intentionally search for "modes" or "model" as standalone queries, as those are both generic terms that would usually only make sense within a context containing other words.

The content-based index has no way to distinguish easily that end users would be unlikely to search for "modern" or "model". Thus, while content-based spell-checkers can work well in many cases, it is often more accurate to learn spelling corrections from users' query behavior.

6.5.2   *Learning spelling corrections from user signals*

Returning to our core thesis from section 6.3 that users tend to search for related queries until they find the expected results, it follows that a user who misspelled a particular query and received bad results would then try to correct their query.

We already know how to find related phrases (discussed in section 6.3), but in this section we'll cover how to specifically distinguish a misspelling based on user signals. This task largely comes down to two goals:

1 Find terms with similar spellings.

2 Figure out which term is the correct spelling versus the misspelled variant.

For this task, we'll rely solely on query signals. We'll perform some up-front normalization to make the query analysis case-insensitive and filter duplicate queries to avoid signal spam. (We'll discuss signal normalization in sections 8.2–8.3.) The following listing shows a query that grabs our normalized query signals.

Listing 6.14   Getting all queries searched by users

```
def get_search_queries():
    query = """SELECT searches.user AS user,
            LOWER(TRIM(searches.target)) As query
            FROM signals AS searches WHERE searches.type = 'query'
            GROUP BY searches.target, user"""
    return spark.sql(query).collect()
```

> **Lowercasing the queries makes the query analysis ignore uppercase vs. lowercased variants.**

> **Grouping by user prevents spam from a single user entering the same query many times.**

For the purposes of this section, we're going to assume that the queries can contain multiple different keywords and that we want to treat each of these keywords as a potential spelling variant. This will allow individual terms to be found and substituted within a future query, as opposed to treating the entire query as a single phrase. It will also allow us to throw out certain terms that are likely to be noise, such as stop words or standalone numbers.

The following listing demonstrates the process of tokenizing each query to generate a word list upon which we can do further analysis.

Listing 6.15   Finding words by tokenizing and filtering query terms

```
from nltk import tokenize, corpus, download
download('stopwords')
stop_words = set(
  corpus.stopwords.words("english"))

def is_term_valid(term, minimum_length=4):
    return (term not in stop_words and
            len(term) >= minimum_length and
            not term.isdigit())
```

> **Defines stop words that shouldn't be considered as misspellings or corrections utilizing the Natural Language Toolkit (nltk)**

> **Removes noisy terms including stop words, very short terms, and numbers**

```
def tokenize_query(query):
    return tokenize.RegexpTokenizer(r'\w+').tokenize(query)

def valid_keyword_occurrences(searches, tokenize=True):
    word_list = defaultdict(int)
    for search in searches:
        query = search["query"]
        terms = tokenize_query(query) if tokenize else [query]
        for term in terms:
            if is_term_valid(term):
                word_list[term] += 1
    return word_list
```

Splits the query on whitespace into individual terms if tokenizing

Aggregates the occurrences of valid keywords

Once the list of tokens has been cleaned up, the next step is to distinguish high-occurrence tokens from infrequently occurring tokens. Since misspellings will occur relatively infrequently and correct spellings will occur more frequently, we will use the relative number of occurrences to determine which version is most likely the canonical spelling and which variations are the misspellings.

To ensure our spell correction list is as clean as possible, we'll set some thresholds for popular terms and some for low-occurrence terms that are more likely misspellings. Because some collections may contain hundreds of documents and other collections could contain millions, we can't just look at an absolute number for these thresholds, so we'll use quantiles instead. The following listing shows the calculations for each of the quantiles between `0.1` and `0.9`.

Listing 6.16 Calculating quantiles to identify spelling candidates

```
def calculate_quantiles(word_list):
    quantiles_to_check = [0.1, 0.2, 0.3, 0.4, 0.5, 0.6, 0.7, 0.8, 0.9]
    quantile_values = numpy.quantile(numpy.array(list(word_list.values())),
                                     quantiles_to_check)
    return dict(zip(quantiles_to_check, quantile_values))

query_signals = get_search_queries()
word_list = valid_keyword_occurrences(query_signals, tokenize=True)
quantiles = calculate_quantiles(word_list)
display(quantiles)
```

Output:

```
{0.1: 5.0,
 0.2: 6.0,
 0.3: 8.0,
 0.4: 12.0,
 0.5: 16.0,
 0.6: 25.0,
 0.7: 47.0,
 0.8: 142.20000000000027,
 0.9: 333.2000000000007}
```

Here we see that 80% of the terms are searched for `142.2` times or less. Likewise, only 20% of terms are searched for `6.0` times or less. Using the Pareto principle, let's assume that most of our misspellings fall within the bottom-searched 20% of our terms and that the majority of our most important terms fall within the top 20% of queries searched. If you want higher precision (only generate spelling corrections for high-value terms and only if there's a low probability of false positives), you can push these to the `0.1` quantile for misspellings and the `0.9` quantile for correctly spelled terms. You can also go the other direction to attempt to generate a larger misspelling list with a higher chance of false positives.

In Listing 6.17, we'll divide the terms into buckets, assigning low-frequency terms to the `misspellings` bucket and high-frequency terms to the `corrections` bucket. These buckets will be a starting point for finding high-quality spelling corrections when enough users search for both the misspelling candidate and the correction candidate.

Listing 6.17 Identifying spelling correction candidates

```
def create_spelling_candidates(word_list):
  quantiles = calculate_quantiles(word_list)
  misspellings = {"misspelling": [],
                  "misspell_counts": [],
                  "misspell_length": [],
                  "initial": []}
  corrections = {"correction": [],
                 "correction_counts": [],
                 "correction_length": [],
                 "initial": []}
  for key, value in word_list.items():
    if value <= quantiles[0.2]:
      misspellings["misspelling"].append(key)
      misspellings["misspell_counts"].append(value)
      misspellings["misspell_length"].append(len(key))
      misspellings["initial"].append(key[0])
    if value >= quantiles[0.8]:
      corrections["correction"].append(key)
      corrections["correction_counts"].append(value)
      corrections["correction_length"].append(len(key))
      corrections["initial"].append(key[0])
  return (pandas.DataFrame(misspellings), pandas.DataFrame(corrections))
```

> **Terms at or below the 0.2 quantile are added to the misspellings list.**

> **The number of searches is retained to keep track of popularity.**

> **The length of the term will be used later to set thresholds for edit distance calculations.**

> **The first letter of the term is stored to limit the scope of the misspellings checked.**

> **The top 20% of terms have the same data stored but in the corrections list.**

To efficiently compare all of the `misspellings` and the `corrections` values, we first load them into dataframes in listing 6.17. You can imagine that `corrections` is a pristine list of the most popular searched terms, while the `misspellings` list should provide a good candidate list for less commonly searched terms that are more likely to be misspellings.

When we compare misspelled candidates with correctly spelled candidates and decide how many character differences (or *edit distances*) are allowed, we need to consider the term length. The following listing shows a simple `good_match` function, which defines a general heuristic for how many edit distances a term match can be off by while still considering the misspelling a likely permutation of the correction candidate.

Listing 6.18 Finding proper spellings by lengths and edit distance

```
def good_match(word_length_1, word_length_2, edit_dist):
  min_length = min(word_length_1, word_length_2)
  return ((min_length < 8 and edit_dist == 1) or
          (min_length >= 8 and min_length < 11 and edit_dist <= 2) or
          (min_length >= 11 and edit_dist == 3))
```

With our `misspellings` and `corrections` candidates loaded into dataframes and the `good_match` function defined, it's time to generate our spelling correction list. Just like in section 6.5.1, where spelling corrections were generated from edit distances and counts of term occurrences within our collection of documents, listing 6.19 generates spelling corrections based on edit distances and term occurrences within our query logs.

Listing 6.19 Mapping misspellings to their correct spellings

```
from nltk import edit_distance

def calculate_spelling_corrections(word_list):
  (misspellings, corrections) = create_spelling_candidates(word_list)
  matches_candidates = pandas.merge(misspellings,
                  corrections, on="initial")
  matches_candidates["edit_dist"] = matches_candidates.apply(
     lambda row: edit_distance(row.misspelling,
                 row.correction), axis=1)
  matches_candidates["good_match"] = matches_candidates.apply(
     lambda row: good_match(row.misspell_length,
                 row.correction_length,
                 row.edit_dist),axis=1)
  cols = ["misspelling", "correction", "misspell_counts",
          "correction_counts", "edit_dist"]
  matches = matches_candidates[matches_candidates["good_match"]] \
    .drop(["initial", "good_match"],axis=1) \
    .groupby("misspelling").first().reset_index() \
    .sort_values(by=["correction_counts", "misspelling",
                "misspell_counts"],
              ascending=[False, True, False])[cols]
  return matches

query_signals = get_search_queries()
word_list = valid_keyword_occurrences(query_signals, tokenize=True)
corrections = calculate_spelling_corrections(word_list)
display(corrections.head(20))
```

Groups the misspelling and correction candidates on the first letter of the word

Calculates the edit distance between each misspelling and correction candidate

Applies the good_match function using the lengths of the terms and the edit distance

Aggregates all the misspellings by name

Gets the 20 most misspelled words

Output:

```
misspelling   correction  misspell_counts correction_counts edit_dist
50   iphone3     iphone      6               16854             1
61   laptopa     laptop      6               14119             1
62   latop       laptop      5               14119             1
...
76   moden       modem       5               3590              1
77   modum       modem       6               3590              1
135  tosheba     toshiba     6               3432              1
34   gates       games       6               3239              1
84   phono       phone       5               3065              1
```

As you can see, we now have a relatively clean list of spelling corrections based on user signals. Our query of `moden` maps correctly to "modem", as opposed to unlikely search terms like "model" and "modern", which we saw in the document-based spelling correction in listing 6.13.

There are numerous other ways that you could go about creating a spelling correction model. If you wanted to generate multiterm spelling corrections from documents, you could generate bigrams and trigrams to perform chained Bayesian analysis on probabilities of consecutive terms occurring. Likewise, to generate multiterm spelling corrections from query signals, you could remove the tokenization of queries by setting `tokenize` to `False` when calling `valid_keyword_occurrences`.

Listing 6.20   Finding multiterm spell corrections from full queries

```
query_signals = get_search_queries()
word_list = valid_keyword_occurrences(query_signals, tokenize=False)
corrections = calculate_spelling_corrections(word_list)
display(corrections.head(20))
```

Output:

```
misspelling       correction     misspell_counts  correction_counts edit_dist
181 ipad.         ipad           6                7749              1
154 hp touchpad 32 hp touchpad   5                7144              3
155 hp toucpad   hp touchpad     6                7144              1
153 hp tochpad   hp touchpad     6                7144              1
190 iphone s4    iphone 4s       5                4642              2
193 iphone4 s    iphone 4s       5                4642              2
194 iphones 4s   iphone 4s       5                4642              1
412 touchpaf     touchpad        5                4019              1
406 tochpad      touchpad        6                4019              1
407 toichpad     touchpad        6                4019              1
229 latop        laptop          5                3625              1
228 laptopa      laptops         6                3435              1
237 loptops      laptops         5                3435              1
205 ipods touch  ipod touch      6                2992              1
204 ipod tuch    ipod touch      6                2992              1
165 i pod tuch   ipod touch      5                2992              2
173 ipad 2       ipad 2          6                2807              1
215 kimdle       kindle          5                2716              1
```

```
206 ipone        iphone      6              2599          1
192 iphone3      iphone      6              2599          1
```

You can see some of the common multiword misspellings and their corrections in list-ing 6.20, now that the queries are no longer being tokenized. Note that the single-term words are largely the same, but multiword queries have also been spell-checked. This is a great way to normalize product names, so that "iphone4 s", "iphones 4s", and "iphone s4" are all correctly mapped to the canonical "iphone 4s". Note that in some cases this can be a lossy process, as "hp touchpad 32" maps to "hp touchpad", and "iphone3" maps to "iphone". Depending on your use case, you may find it beneficial to only spell-correct individual terms, or to include special handling in your good_match function for brand variations to ensure the spell-check code doesn't mis-takenly delete relevant query context.

6.6 *Pulling it all together*

In this chapter, we dove deeper into understanding the context and meaning of domain-specific language. We showed how to use SKGs to classify queries and disam-biguate terms that have different or nuanced meanings based on their context. We also explored how to mine relationships from user signals, which usually provides a better context for understanding your users than looking at your documents alone. We also showed how to extract phrases, misspellings, and alternative labels from query signals, enabling domain-specific terminology to be learned directly from users as opposed to only from documents.

At this point, you should feel confident about learning domain-specific phrases and related phrases from documents or user signals, classifying queries to your avail-able content, and disambiguating the meaning of terminology based on the query classification. These techniques are critical tools in your toolbox for interpreting query intent.

Our goal isn't just to assemble a large toolbox, though. Our goal is to use each of these tools where appropriate to build an end-to-end semantic search layer. This means we need to model known phrases into our knowledge graph, extract those phrases from incoming queries, handle misspellings, classify queries, disambiguate incoming terms, and ultimately generate a rewritten query for the search engine that uses each of our AI-powered search techniques. In the next chapter, we'll show you how to assemble each of these techniques into a working semantic search system designed to best interpret and model query intent.

Summary

- Classifying queries using a semantic knowledge graph (SKG) can help interpret query intent and improve query routing and filtering.
- Query-sense disambiguation can deliver a more contextual understanding of a user's query, particularly for terms with significantly divergent meanings across different contexts.

- In addition to learning from documents, domain-specific phrases and related phrases can also be learned from user signals.
- Misspellings and spelling variations can be learned from both documents and user signals, with document-based approaches being more robust and user-signal-based approaches better representing user intent.

Interpreting query intent through semantic search

In chapters 5 and 6, we used content and signals to interpret the domain-specific meaning of incoming user queries. We discussed phrase identification, misspelling detection, synonym discovery, query intent classification, related-terms expansion, and even query-sense disambiguation. We mostly discussed these techniques in isolation to demonstrate how they each work independently.

In this chapter, we'll put all those techniques into practice, integrating them into a unified query interpretation framework. We'll show an example search interface that accepts real queries, interprets them, rewrites them to better express the end user's intent, and then returns ranked results.

We should note that multiple paradigms have evolved for implementing semantic search, including embedding-based query interpretation and question answering (returning extracted or generated answers instead of documents) using large language models (LLMs) and pretrained Transformers. These typically involve encoding queries into vectors, searching for an approximate nearest neighborhood of vectors, and then performing a vector similarity calculation to rank documents. The ranked documents are often then analyzed to summarize, extract, or generate answers. We'll cover these LLM-based approaches for semantic search and question answering in chapters 13–15.

We'll focus in this chapter on the mechanics of integrating each of the AI-powered search strategies you've already learned to deliver an end-to-end semantic query pipeline. We'll implement the pipeline in four phases:

- *Parsing* the user's query
- *Enriching* the parsed query with improved context
- *Transforming* the query to optimize for relevance in our target search engine
- *Searching* using the optimized query

These steps don't have to be implemented linearly (sometimes they repeat, and sometimes steps can be skipped), and they can also be broken down further (for example, searching could be broken down into matching, ranking, and reranking). Having this consistent framework through which we can integrate any combination of AI-powered search techniques will nevertheless be invaluable as you mix and match approaches in your own search applications.

7.1   *The mechanics of query interpretation*

There is no one "right way" to build a query interpretation framework. Every organization building an intelligent search platform is likely to build something a bit different, depending on their business needs and the expertise of their search team. There are, however, some consistent themes across implementations worth exploring:

- *Pipelines*—Both when indexing documents and processing queries, it's useful to model all of the necessary parsing, interpretation, and ranking logic as modular stages in a workflow. This allows for easy experimentation by swapping out, rearranging, or adding processing stages within the pipeline at any time.
- *Models*—Whether you are fine-tuning a complex deep-learning-based LLM (chapters 13–14), a learning-to-rank model (chapters 10–12), a signals-boosting or personalization model (chapters 8–9), or a knowledge graph containing synonyms, misspellings, and related terms (chapters 5–6), proper query interpretation requires plugging in the right models in the right order within the indexing and query pipelines.
- *Conditional fallbacks*—You'll never be able to interpret every query perfectly. You could have many models helping interpret one query, while having no clue

what another query means. It's usually best to start with a base or "fallback" model (usually keyword-based) that can handle any query imperfectly, and to layer in more sophisticated models on top, to enhance precision of interpretation. Additionally, if no results are found, it might be useful to return recommendations to ensure the searcher sees *something* that might be useful, even if it is not exactly what they were seeking.

Figure 7.1 shows an example query pipeline demonstrating each of these themes of combining pipeline stages, models, and conditional fallbacks.

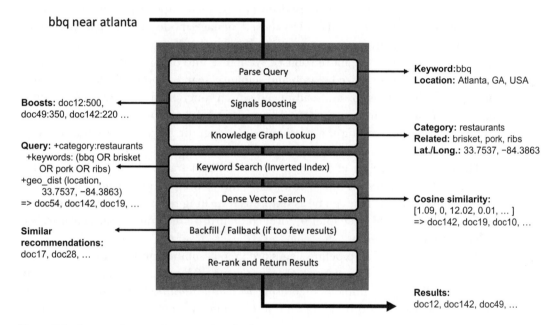

Figure 7.1 An example query interpretation pipeline

Figure 7.1 takes in the query bbq near atlanta and begins with a parse-query stage that performs entity extraction on known keywords, locations, or other known terms from the query. It then hits a signals-boosting stage, which checks with a signals-boosting model (which was introduced in chapter 4 and will be covered in much greater detail in chapter 8) to boost the most popular documents for the given query.

Three different, but complementary, approaches are commonly used to interpret individual keywords and relate them to each other, all of which are included in the example pipeline:

- *Lexical search,* such as BM25 ranking on Boolean query matches in an inverted index

- *Knowledge graph search,* such as ranking the entities found within a query and their relationships with the most similar entities in your index using a semantic knowledge graph (SKG) or explicitly built knowledge graph
- *Dense vector search,* such as cosine similarity of vectors found with an approximate nearest neighborhood of embeddings

Of the three, the most common "default" matching layer tends to be lexical search on an inverted index, as this approach allows matching on *any* term that exists in the corpus of documents, whether that term is understood or not. The knowledge graph and dense vector approaches both rely on being able to relate the terms in each query to concepts or entities, and this simply can't be done in all cases.

In fact, BM25 ranking often outperforms dense vector approaches on embeddings even from state-of-the-art LLMs unless those language models are initially trained or fine-tuned on domain-specific content (this may change over time, as pretrained LLMs continue to become more robust). We'll dive into using LLMs starting in chapters 9 and 13 for personalized search and semantic search, and we'll spend time fine-tuning and using LLMs for more advanced search functionality like question answering and generative search in chapters 14 and 15. We'll keep our focus in this chapter primarily on demonstrating the mechanics of integrating lexical search and knowledge graphs.

The figure 7.1 pipeline ends with a backfill/fallback stage, which can be useful for inserting additional results in the case that none of the previous stages were able to return a full result set. This can be as simple as returning recommendations instead of search results (covered in chapter 9), or it could involve returning a partially matched query with lower precision.

The final results of all pipeline stages are then combined and reranked as needed to yield a final set of relevance-ranked search results. The reranking stage can be simple, but it will often be implemented using *machine-learned ranking* through a ranking classifier. We'll dive into building and automating the training of learning to rank models in chapters 10–12.

While the example pipeline in this section may provide good results in many cases, the specific logic of a pipeline should always depend on the needs of your application. In the next section, we'll set up an application to search local business reviews, and then we'll implement a unified pipeline capable of semantic search over this domain.

7.2   Indexing and searching on a local reviews dataset

We're going to create a search engine that aggregates product and business reviews from across the web. If a business has a physical location (restaurant, store, etc.), we want to find all of the reviews associated with the business and make them available for searching.

The following listing shows the ingestion of our crawled local reviews data into the search engine.

Listing 7.1 Loading and indexing the reviews dataset

```
reviews_collection = engine.create_collection("reviews")
reviews_data = reviews.load_dataframe("data/reviews/reviews.csv")
reviews_collection.write(reviews_data)
```

Output:

```
Wiping "reviews" collection
Creating "reviews" collection
Status: Success

Loading Reviews...
root
 |-- id: string (nullable = true)
 |-- business_name: string (nullable = true)
 |-- city: string (nullable = true)
 |-- state: string (nullable = true)
 |-- content: string (nullable = true)
 |-- categories: string (nullable = true)
 |-- stars_rating: integer (nullable = true)
 |-- location_coordinates: string (nullable = true)

Successfully written 192138 documents
```

The data model for a review can be seen in the listing's output. Each review has the business name, location information, review content, review rating (number of stars from 1 to 5), and categories of the type of entity being reviewed.

Once the data has been ingested, we can run a search. In this chapter, we provide a more interactive application than in prior chapters, launching a web server to power a dynamic search interface. Running listing 7.2 will launch the web server.

Listing 7.2 Launching the web server and loading the search page

```
start_reviews_search_webserver()

%%html
<iframe src="http://localhost:2345/search" width=100% height="800"/>
```

Figure 7.2 shows the loaded search interface from listing 7.2. You can run the embedded search page from the Jupyter notebook, but if you're running on your local computer on port 2345, you can also just navigate to http://localhost:2345/search in your web browser to get a better experience.

Figure 7.2   Visiting the review search page from a local web browser

Let's first try a simple query for `bbq near charlotte`. For now, let's pretend you haven't gone through the knowledge graph learning process (chapter 6) and don't yet know how to apply an SKG (chapter 5) to your query interpretation. In this case, we're just doing out-of-the-box lexical keyword matching. Figure 7.3 shows the top lexical search result for the query `bbq near charlotte`.

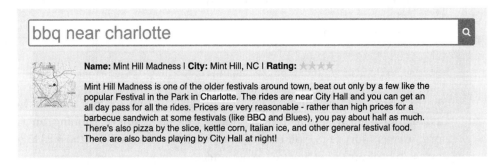

Figure 7.3   Basic lexical keyword search for `bbq near charlotte`, only matching keywords

In our reviews dataset, this is the only review that matches our query, even though multiple BBQ (also known as barbecue) restaurants exist in or near the city of Charlotte, NC, USA. The reason only this result is returned is that it's the only document containing all three terms (bbq, near, and charlotte). If you look at the review, it is not even for a restaurant that serves barbecue—it's actually for a festival whose review just happens to reference another festival with "BBQ" in the name!

The main problem here is that most relevant restaurants do not contain the word near. Figure 7.4 shows that more results do exist if we take out the word near and search instead for bbq charlotte.

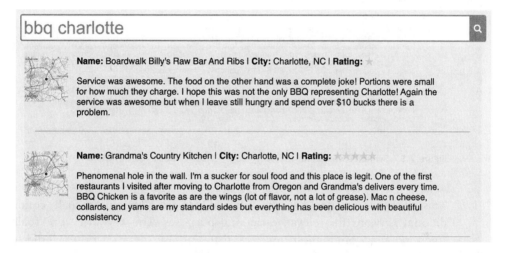

Figure 7.4   Basic lexical keyword search for bbq charlotte. **More results matching with the word "near" removed.**

Both of the top results contain the term "bbq", but the first one has a low (1-star) rating, and the second one mentions "bbq chicken" (chicken with barbecue sauce on it) but not "bbq" (barbecue), which would typically refer more to smoked meat like pulled pork, pulled chicken, rib, or brisket. Additionally, while the results are all in the city Charlotte, NC, this is only because they match the keyword charlotte in the review text, which means many good results are missing that didn't reference the city by name in the review. It is clear from the results that the search engine hasn't properly interpreted the user's query intent.

We can do so much better than this! You've already learned how to extract domain-specific knowledge and how to classify queries (for example, bbq implies a restaurant), so we just need to integrate these techniques and learned models end-to-end.

7.3   An end-to-end semantic search example

The last section showed the shortcomings of relying on pure keyword search. How might we improve upon the search engine's ability to interpret queries? Figure 7.5 demonstrates the results of a reasonably specific query that traditional keyword search would struggle to correctly interpret: `top kimchi near charlotte`.

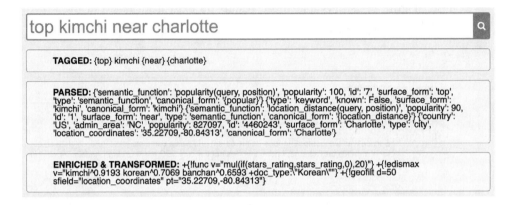

Figure 7.5   Semantic search for the query `top kimchi near charlotte`

This query is interesting, because only one keyword ("kimchi") actually contains a traditional keyword for relevance ranking purposes. The keyword "top" really means "most popular" or "highest rated", and the phrase "near charlotte" indicates a geographical filter to apply to search results. You can see in the figure that the original query is parsed as `{top} kimchi {near} {charlotte}`. We're using this curly-brace syntax to indicate that the terms "top", "near", and "charlotte" were all identified from our knowledge graph, whereas "kimchi" was not tagged and is, therefore, an unknown.

After these keywords and phrases are parsed, you can see that they are enriched and transformed into the following search-engine-specific syntax (Solr):

- *top*: `+{!func v="mul(if(stars_rating,stars_rating,0),20)"}`. This syntax will boost all documents based on their reviews (1 to 5 stars), multiplying by 20 to generate a score between 0 and 100.

- *kimchi*: `+{!edismax v="kimchi^0.9193 korean^0.7069 banchan^0.6593 +doc_type:\"Korean\""}`. This is an expansion of the unknown term "kimchi" using the SKG expansion approach from chapter 5. The SKG, in this case, identifies "Korean" as the category in which to filter results, and the top related terms to "kimchi" are "korean" and "banchan".

- *near charlotte*: `+{!geofilt d=50 sfield="location_coordinates" pt="35.22709,-80.84313"}`. This geographical filter limits results to documents only within a 50 km radius of the latitude/longitude of Charlotte, NC, USA.

Had the original query been executed as a traditional lexical search *without* the query interpretation layer, no results would have matched, as shown in figure 7.6.

Figure 7.6   Traditional lexical search returns no results due to no documents containing all keywords

However, figure 7.7 demonstrates the results after executing the semantically parsed and enriched version.

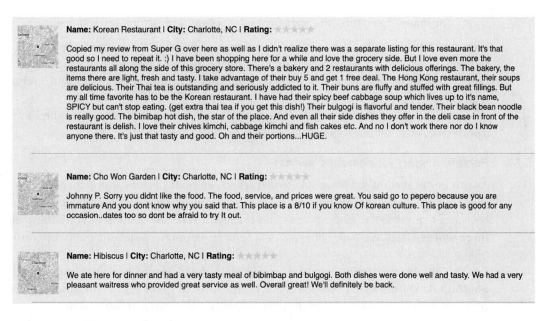

Figure 7.7   Semantic search example returns relevant results by better interpreting and executing the query

The results look quite good! You'll notice that

- There are many results (instead of zero).
- All results have *top* ratings (5 stars).

- All results are in *Charlotte.*
- Some results match even without having the main keyword ("kimchi"), and they are clearly for Korean restaurants that would serve kimchi because similar terms were used in the review.

We'll spend the remainder of the chapter walking through how we can implement this level of semantic query interpretation, starting with a high-level query interpretation pipeline.

7.4   *Query interpretation pipelines*

While we often need to integrate multiple models and diverse query-understanding approaches in a query pipeline, most query pipelines share a similar set of high-level phases:

1 *Parsing*—Extracting key entities and their logical relationships from the query
2 *Enriching*—Generating an understanding of the query context, queried entities, and their semantic relationships
3 *Transforming*—Rewriting the user's query for the search engine to optimize recall and ranking
4 *Searching*—Executing the transformed query and returning ranked results

You can think of each phase as a different type of pipeline stage. As in the example pipeline in section 7.1, some pipelines may invoke multiple stages to parse or enrich a query, and some pipelines may even run multiple conditional searches and merge results.

In the coming subsections, we'll implement each phase to demonstrate the inner workings of our end-to-end semantic search example from section 7.3.

7.4.1   *Parsing a query for semantic search*

As you saw in section 3.2.5, most keyword search engines perform some form of Boolean parsing on incoming queries by default. The query statue of liberty thus becomes a query for statue AND of AND liberty, where any document containing all three words ("statue", "of", "liberty") will match, assuming a default query operator of AND.

This Boolean matching alone does not yield great results, but when paired with BM25 ranking (discussed in section 3.2.1), it can yield great results for a naive algorithm that doesn't have any true understanding of the terms within the domain.

In contrast to this Boolean parsing, it's also possible to convert an entire query into a numerical vector embedding, as discussed in section 3.1.1. We'll cover dense vector search using LLMs and embeddings later in chapters 13–14. One benefit of using LLMs and embedding-based query interpretation is that these techniques provide a better representation of the query as one unit of meaning. The logical structure of the query can sometimes be lost using this approach, though, so it may not work well for scenarios where your Boolean logic must be preserved or you must ensure certain keywords appear in the search results.

A final way to parse a query is by extracting the known terms and phrases from a knowledge graph. We took this approach in our end-to-end example in section 7.3. One benefit of this approach is that, in addition to offering fine-grained control over known vocabulary, it also allows for the interpretation of specific phrases and trigger words (top, in, near) to be modeled explicitly, to reflect their functional meaning instead of just keyword matching. The downside of this approach is that any terms or phrases *not* existing in the knowledge graph can't be as easily extracted and interpreted.

Since we'll dive into LLMs in later chapters, we'll focus in this chapter on explicit query parsing using a knowledge graph, as explicit parsing enables significant customization for a domain, it's cheap to implement, and it enables us to incorporate all the other AI techniques we've already learned.

IMPLEMENTING A SEMANTIC QUERY PARSER

The first step when semantically interpreting a query is identifying the terms and phrases in the query (the *parsing* phase). In chapter 6, we walked through how to identify important domain-specific terms and phrases from our content and user behavioral signals. These can be used as the known entities list for powering entity extraction on incoming queries.

Because there can be potentially millions of entities in the known phrases list, an efficient structure such as a *finite state transducer* (FST) makes it possible to perform entity extraction at this scale in just milliseconds. We won't get into the nuances of how FSTs work here, but they enable very compact compression of many term sequences and very quick lookups on those term sequences, enabling lightning-fast entity extraction.

Our example search engine, Apache Solr, implements a *text tagger* request handler, which is purpose-built for fast entity extraction. It enables you to index any number of terms into a lookup index, so you can build that index into an FST and extract terms from that index on any incoming stream of text.

In chapter 6, we generated lists of domain-specific phrases, which also included alternative spellings. We can map all these terms into a specially configured entities collection, along with any spelling variations, to enable seamless entity extraction from incoming queries. The following listing explores several types of entity data within our entities collection.

Listing 7.3   Entity data used for tagging and extraction

```
entities_dataframe = from_csv("data/reviews/entities.csv", log=False)
display_entities(entities_dataframe, limit=20)
```

Output:

```
Entities
+---+-------------------+--------------------+-----------------+----------+
| id|       surface_form|      canonical_form|             type|popularity|
+---+-------------------+--------------------+-----------------+----------+
|  1|               near| {location_distance}|semantic_function|        90|
|  2|                 in| {location_distance}|semantic_function|       100|
|  3|                 by| {location_distance}|semantic_function|        90|
|  4|                 by|{text_within_one_...|semantic_function|        10|
|  5|               near|     {text_distance}|semantic_function|        10|
|  6|            popular|           {popular}|semantic_function|       100|
|  7|                top|           {popular}|semantic_function|       100|
|  8|               best|           {popular}|semantic_function|       100|
|  9|               good|           {popular}|semantic_function|       100|
| 10|             violet|              violet|            color|       100|
| 11|       violet crowne|       violet crowne|            brand|       100|
| 12|violet crowne cha...|violet crowne cha...|    movie_theater|       100|
| 13|       violet crown|       violet crowne|            brand|       100|
| 14|violet crown char...|violet crowne cha...|    movie_theater|       100|
| 15|           haystack| haystack conference|            event|       100|
| 16|      haystack conf| haystack conference|            event|       100|
| 17| haystack conference| haystack conference|            event|       100|
| 18|           heystack| haystack conference|            event|       100|
| 19|      heystack conf| haystack conference|            event|       100|
| 20| heystack conference| haystack conference|            event|       100|
+---+-------------------+--------------------+-----------------+----------+
only showing top 20 rows

... Entities continued
+---+----------------------------------------------+
|id |semantic_function                             |
+---+----------------------------------------------+
|1  |location_distance(query, position)            |
|2  |location_distance(query, position)            |
|3  |location_distance(query, position)            |
|4  |text_within_one_edit_distance(query, position)|
|5  |text_distance(query, position)                |
|6  |popularity(query, position)                   |
|7  |popularity(query, position)                   |
|8  |popularity(query, position)                   |
|9  |popularity(query, position)                   |
+---+----------------------------------------------+
```

The fields represented within the table for entities in listing 7.3 include

- surface_form—The specific text of any spelling variation we want to match on future queries.
- canonical_form—The "official" version of any term that may have potentially multiple surface forms.
- type—A classification (category) for the term within our domain.
- popularity—Used to prioritize different meanings of the same surface form.
- semantic_function—Only present for entities of type "semantic_function". This is used to inject programmatic handling of special combinations of keywords.

In most cases, the `surface_form` and `canonical_form` will be the same, but our entity extractor will always match on a `surface_form` and map it to a `canonical_form`, so this mechanism is used to map multiple variations of an entity's spelling to one official or "canonical" version. This can be used to handle misspellings ("amin" ⇒ "admin"), acronyms and initialisms ("cto" ⇒ "chief technology officer"), ambiguous terms ("cto" ⇒ "chief technology officer" versus "cto" ⇒ "cancelled-to-order"), or even mapping terms to specific interpretation logic (semantic functions) like "near" ⇒ {location_distance}.

The "semantic_function" type is a special type that we'll explore in section 7.4.2; it enables nonlinear, conditional query parsing rules. For example, "if the word *near* is followed by an entity that has a *geographical location*, interpret that section of the query as a geography filter".

In the event of an ambiguous term, multiple entries will exist containing the same surface form mapped to different canonical forms. In this case, the `popularity` field will specify a relative value indicating which meaning is more common (the higher, the more popular).

This format is also extensible—you can add a `vector` field representing the semantic meaning of a canonical form, or a `related_terms` field that contains other terms with similar meanings. This would enable caching a static representation of the meaning of the `canonical_form`, which can be much more efficient at query time than referencing external models or knowledge graphs for known terms on every request.

INVOKING THE ENTITY EXTRACTOR

In addition to the `reviews` collection created in listing 7.1, we also need to create an `entities` collection containing the known entities to be extracted. This collection will serve as an explicit knowledge graph containing all of the entities from listing 7.3, as well as a list of all major cities in the world. The next listing configures and populates the `entities` collection.

Listing 7.4 Creating the `entities` collection

```
entities_collection = engine.create_collection("entities")
entities_dataframe = from_csv("data/reviews/entities.csv")
cities_dataframe = cities.load_dataframe("data/reviews/cities.csv")
entities_collection.write(entities_dataframe)
entities_collection.write(cities_dataframe)
```

Explicit entities and city entities are indexed to the entities collection to be used for entity extraction.

Output:

```
Wiping "entities" collection
Creating "entities" collection
Status: Success
Loading data/reviews/entities.csv
Schema:
root
 |-- id: integer (nullable = true)
 |-- surface_form: string (nullable = true)
 |-- canonical_form: string (nullable = true)
```

Creates the entities collection and configures it to hold our explicit knowledge graph of entities to extract from queries

```
|-- type: string (nullable = true)
|-- popularity: integer (nullable = true)
|-- semantic_function: string (nullable = true)

Loading Geonames...
Successfully written 21 documents
Successfully written 137581 documents
```

One configuration point we should highlight is the setting up of entity extraction, which occurs within `engine.create_collection("entities")`. In the default case where Solr is being used to serve the explicit knowledge graph for entity extraction from queries, Solr's text tagger functionality is enabled by internally making the following configuration changes:

- Adding an `/entities/tag` endpoint using the `TaggerRequestHandler` in Solr. We can pass queries to this endpoint to perform entity extraction of any entities found in the `entities` collection.
- Adding a `tags` field type in the schema that is configured to use an in-memory FST, enabling compact and fast tagging from a collection of potentially millions of entities in milliseconds.
- Adding a `name_tag` field that the `surface_form` field is copied into. The `name_tag` field is a `tags` field type and is used by the `/entities/tag` endpoint to match entities from the query.

If your search engine has native text tagging capabilities, the configuration will differ, but the following listing shows the code corresponding to these changes for the default implementation of the text tagger using Apache Solr.

Listing 7.5   Configuring the Solr text tagger for entity extraction

```
add_tag_type_commands = [{
  "add-field-type": {
    "name": "tag",
    "class": "solr.TextField",                       The tag field type is configured using
    "postingsFormat": "FST50",                       the Lucene FST50 index format,
                                                     enabling fast in-memory matching
    "omitNorms": "true",
    "omitTermFreqAndPositions": "true",
    "indexAnalyzer": {
      "tokenizer": {"class": "solr.StandardTokenizerFactory"},
      "filters": [
        {"class": "solr.EnglishPossessiveFilterFactory"},
        {"class": "solr.ASCIIFoldingFilterFactory"},     The ConcatenateGraphFilter
        {"class": "solr.LowerCaseFilterFactory"},        is a special filter used by
        {"class": "solr.ConcatenateGraphFilterFactory",  the text tagger to facilitate
        "preservePositionIncrements": "false"}]},        entity extraction.
    "queryAnalyzer": {
      "tokenizer": {"class": "solr.StandardTokenizerFactory"},
      "filters": [{"class": "solr.EnglishPossessiveFilterFactory"},
                  {"class": "solr.ASCIIFoldingFilterFactory"},
                  {"class": "solr.LowerCaseFilterFactory"}]}}
  },
```

```
    {"add-field": {"name": "name_tag", "type": "tag",
                   "stored": "false"}},
    {"add-copy-field": {"source": "surface_form",
                        "dest": ["name_tag"]}}]
add_tag_request_handler_config = {
  "add-requesthandler": {
    "name": "/tag",
    "class": "solr.TaggerRequestHandler",
    "defaults": {
      "field": "name_tag",
      "json.nl": "map",
      "sort": "popularity desc",
      "matchText": "true",
      "fl": "id,surface_form,canonical_form,type,semantic_function,
      popularity,country,admin_area,*_p"
}}}
```

> **We add the name_tag field, which we'll use to tag queries against the index.**

> **The name_tag field is populated using the surface_form value.**

> **A /tag request handler is configured to use values indexed in the name_tag field as entities to extract from incoming queries.**

> **If multiple entities match (polysemy), return the most popular one by default.**

With the `entities` collection created, the text tagger configured, and the entities all indexed, we're now ready to perform entity extraction on a query. In the following listing, we run a query for `top kimchi near charlotte`.

Listing 7.6 Extracting entities for a given query

```
query = "top kimchi near charlotte"
entities_collection = engine.get_collection("entities")
extractor = get_entity_extractor(entities_collection)
query_entities = extractor.extract_entities(query)
print(query_entities)
```

Output:

```
{"query": "top kimchi near charlotte",
 "tags": [
  {"startOffset": 0, "endOffset": 3, "matchText": "top", "ids": ["7"]},
  {"startOffset": 11, "endOffset":15, "matchText":"near", "ids":["1","5"]},
  {"startOffset": 16, "endOffset": 25, "matchText": "charlotte",
   "ids": ["4460243", "4612828", "4680560", "4988584", "5234793"]}],
 "entities": [
  {"id":"1", "surface_form":"near", "canonical_form":"{location_distance}",
   "type": "semantic_function", "popularity": 90,
   "semantic_function": "location_distance(query, position)"},
  {"id": "5", "surface_form": "near", "canonical_form": "{text_distance}",
   "type": "semantic_function", "popularity": 10,
   "semantic_function": "text_distance(query, position)"},
  {"id": "7", "surface_form": "top", "canonical_form": "{popular}",
   "type": "semantic_function", "popularity": 100,
   "semantic_function": "popularity(query, position)"},
  {"id":"4460243", "canonical_form":"Charlotte", "surface_form":"Charlotte",
   "admin_area": "NC", "popularity": 827097, "type": "city",
   "location_coordinates": "35.22709,-80.84313"},
  {"id":"4612828", "canonical_form":"Charlotte", "surface_form":"Charlotte",
```

```
        "admin_area": "TN", "popularity": 1506, "type": "city",
        "location_coordinates": "36.17728,-87.33973"},
     {"id":"4680560", "canonical_form":"Charlotte", "surface_form":"Charlotte",
        "admin_area": "TX", "popularity": 1815, "type": "city",
        "location_coordinates": "28.86192,-98.70641"},
     {"id":"4988584", "canonical_form":"Charlotte", "surface_form":"Charlotte",
        "admin_area": "MI", "popularity": 9054, "type": "city",
        "location_coordinates": "42.56365,-84.83582"},
     {"id":"5234793", "canonical_form":"Charlotte", "surface_form":"Charlotte",
        "admin_area": "VT", "popularity": 3861, "type": "city",
        "location_coordinates": "44.30977,-73.26096"}]}
```

The response includes three key sections:

- query—The query that has been tagged
- tags—A list of text phrases found within the incoming query, along with the character offsets within the text (start and end positions) and a list of all possible entity matches (canonical forms) for each tag (surface form)
- entities—The list of doc IDs for matching entities that may correspond with one of the matched tags

We've previously described ambiguous terms, where one surface form can map to multiple canonical forms. In our example, the first tag is {'startOffset': 0, 'endOffset': 3, 'matchText': 'top', 'ids': ['7']}. This states that the text "top" was matched starting at position 0 and ending at position 3 in the input top kimchi near charlotte. It also lists only one entry in the ids, meaning that there is only one possible meaning (canonical representation). For the other two tags, however, multiple ids are listed, making them ambiguous tags:

- {"startOffset": 11, "endOffset": 15, "matchText": "near",
  "ids": ["1", "5"]}
- {"startOffset": 16, "endOffset": 25, "matchText": "charlotte",
  "ids": ["4460243", "4612828", "4680560", "4988584", "5234793"]}

This means that there were two canonical forms (two ids listed) for the surface form "near" and five canonical forms for the surface form "charlotte". In the entities section, we can also see all of the different entity records associated with the lists of ids in the tags.

In this chapter, we'll keep things simple by always using the canonical form with the highest popularity. For cities, we supplied the city's population in the popularity field, which means that the "charlotte" selected is Charlotte, NC, USA (the most populated Charlotte in the world). For our other entities, the popularity was specified manually in entities.csv from listing 7.3. You can alternatively specify the popularity using the signals-boosting value (if you derived your entities from signals, which will be covered in detail in chapter 8) or using the count of documents containing the entity in your index as a proxy for popularity.

You may also find it beneficial to use user-specific context or query-specific context to choose the most appropriate entity. For example, if you are disambiguating locations, you could boost the popularity with a geographical distance calculation so locations closer to the user receive a higher weight. If the entity is a keyword phrase, you can alternatively use an SKG to classify the query or load a term vector and boost the canonical form that is a better conceptual match for the overall query.

With our `query_entities` available from the knowledge graph, we can now generate a user-friendly version of the original query with the tagged entities identified. The following listing implements this `generate_tagged_query` function.

Listing 7.7   Generating a tagged query

```
def generate_tagged_query(extracted_entities):          ◁──┐  Reconstructs the query
  query = extracted_entities["query"]                        with tagged entities
  last_end = 0
  tagged_query = ""
  for tag in extracted_entities["tags"]:
    next_text = query[last_end:tag["startOffset"]].strip()
    if len(next_text) > 0:
      tagged_query += " " + next_text
    tagged_query += " {" + tag["matchText"] + "}"        ◁──┐  Wraps known entities
    last_end = tag["endOffset"]                               in braces to offset them
  if last_end < len(query):                                   from regular keywords
    final_text = query[last_end:len(query)].strip()
    if len(final_text):
      tagged_query += " " + final_text
  return tagged_query

tagged_query = generate_tagged_query(query_entities)
print(tagged_query)
```

Output:

```
{top} kimchi {near} {charlotte}
```

From this tagged query, we can now see that the keywords "top", "near", and "charlotte" map to known entities, while "kimchi" is an unknown keyword. This format is a useful user-friendly representation of the query, but it is too simple to represent the metadata associated with each entity. Because we need to process the entities and their semantic interactions programmatically to enrich the query, we will also implement a more structured representation of the semantically parsed query, which we'll call a `query_tree`.

Instead of a pure text query, this `query_tree` is a structure of strongly typed nodes within the query represented as JSON objects. Listing 7.8 demonstrates the `generate_query_tree` function, which returns a query tree from the incoming entity extraction data (`query_entities`).

Listing 7.8   Generating a typed query tree from a user query

```
def generate_query_tree(extracted_entities):
  query = extracted_entities["query"]
  entities = {entity["id"]: entity for entity            │  Creates a mapping of
             in extracted_entities["entities"]}           │  entity IDs to entities
```

```
query_tree = []
last_end = 0

for tag in extracted_entities["tags"]:
    best_entity = entities[tag["ids"][0]]
    for entity_id in tag["ids"]:                        Chooses the most popular
        if (entities[entity_id]["popularity"] >         canonical form for the
            best_entity["popularity"]):                 entity by default
            best_entity = entities[entity_id]

    next_text = query[last_end:tag["startOffset"]].strip()
    if next_text:
        query_tree.append({"type": "keyword",           Assigns a keyword type to any
                           "surface_form": next_text,    untagged text as a fallback
                           "canonical_form": next_text})
    query_tree.append(best_entity)          ◁          Adds the entity object to the query tree in
    last_end = tag["endOffset"]                        the appropriate position in the query

if last_end < len(query):
    final_text = query[last_end:len(query)].strip()
    if final_text:                                      Any text after the last
        query_tree.append({"type": "keyword",           tagged entity will also be
                           "surface_form": final_text,  considered a keyword.
                           "canonical_form": final_text})
return query_tree

parsed_query = generate_query_tree(query_entities)
display(parsed_query)
```

Output:

```
[{"semantic_function": "popularity(query, position)", "popularity": 100,
  "id": "7", "surface_form": "top", "type": "semantic_function",
  "canonical_form": "{popular}"},
 {"type": "keyword", "surface_form": "kimchi", "canonical_form": "kimchi"},
 {"semantic_function":"location_distance(query, position)", "popularity":90,
  "id": "1", "surface_form": "near", "type": "semantic_function",
  "canonical_form": "{location_distance}"},
 {"country": "US", "admin_area": "NC", "popularity": 827097,
  "id": "4460243", "surface_form": "Charlotte", "type": "city",
  "location_coordinates": "35.22709,-80.84313",
  "canonical_form": "Charlotte"}]
```

We now have multiple representations of the query and tagged entities:

- `tagger_data`—Output of listing 7.6
- `tagged_query`—Output of listing 7.7
- `parsed_query`—Output of listing 7.8

The `parsed_query` output is a serialization of the underlying `query_tree` object, fully representing all keywords and entities along with their associated metadata. At this point, the initial *parsing* phase that maps the query into typed entities is complete, and we can begin to use the relationships between the entities to better enrich the query.

7.4.2   *Enriching a query for semantic search*

The *enriching* phase of our query interpretation pipeline focuses on understanding the relationships between entities in a query and how to best interpret and represent them for optimal search results relevance.

Much of this book has already been, and will continue to be, focused on the enriching phase. Chapter 4 introduced crowdsourced relevance, which is a way to enrich specific keyword phrases with information about which documents are the most relevant, based on prior user interactions. Chapter 5 focused on knowledge graphs, which provide a way to enrich specific keyword phrases with topic classifications and to find other terms that are highly related. In chapter 6, we implemented algorithms to find synonyms, misspellings, and related terms that can be used to enrich queries by augmenting or replacing parsed terms with better, learned versions. Upcoming chapters on signals boosting, personalization, and dense vector search on embeddings will likewise introduce new ways to interpret parsed entities and enrich queries to optimize relevance.

These techniques are all tools in your toolbox, but the best way to combine them for any specific implementation will be domain-specific, so we'll avoid overly generalizing in our examples. Instead, we'll focus on a simple end-to-end implementation to tie things together in a way that other models can be easily plugged into. Our simple implementation will consist of two components:

- A *semantic function* implementation that enables dynamic and nonlinear semantic rules to be injected for each domain
- An SKG to find related terms for unknown keywords and query classifications

You already have the tools you need to extend the query-parsing framework to handle other enrichment types from previous chapters. For example, you can use the mappings from surface form to canonical form to handle all alternate representations learned in chapter 6. Likewise, by adding additional fields to each entity in the `entities` collection, you can inject signals boosts, related terms, query classifications, or vectors, making them available for use as soon as queries are parsed.

Let's kick off our enrichment implementation with a discussion of semantic functions.

IMPLEMENTING SEMANTIC FUNCTIONS

A *semantic function* is a nonlinear function that can be applied during query parsing and enrichment to better interpret the meaning of the surrounding terms. Our previous example of `top kimchi near charlotte` contains two terms that map to semantic functions: "top" and "near". The term "top" has a very domain-specific meaning: prioritize documents with the highest rating (number of stars on the review). Likewise, the term "near" isn't a keyword that should be matched; instead, it modifies the meaning of the succeeding terms to attempt to marshal them into a geographic location. From listing 7.3, you will see the following entities referencing semantic functions:

```
Semantic Function Entities
+-------+------------------+----------+---------------------------------+
|surface|canonical_form    |popularity|semantic_function                |
+-------+------------------+----------+---------------------------------+
|near   |{location_distance}|90        |location_distance(query, position)|
|in     |{location_distance}|100       |location_distance(query, position)|
|by     |{location_distance}|90        |location_distance(query, position)|
|by     |{text_within_on...}|10        |text_within_one_edit_distance(...)|
|near   |{text_distance}   |10        |text_distance(query, position)   |
|popular|{popular}         |100       |popularity(query, position)      |
|top    |{popular}         |100       |popularity(query, position)      |
|best   |{popular}         |100       |popularity(query, position)      |
|good   |{popular}         |100       |popularity(query, position)      |
+-------+------------------+----------+---------------------------------+
```

You'll note that the surface forms "top", "popular", "good", and "best" all map to the {popularity} canonical form, which is represented by the popularity(query, position) semantic function in the following listing.

Listing 7.9   A semantic function that accounts for popularity

Another query tree node must follow the popularity node ("top mountain" and not "mountain top").

Replace the {popularity} node in the query tree with a new node that represents a relevance boost for popularity.

```
def popularity(query, position):
  if len(query["query_tree"]) -1 > position:
    query["query_tree"][position] = {
      "type": "transformed",
      "syntax": "solr",
      "query": '+{!func v="mul(if(stars_rating,stars_rating,0),20)"}'}
    return True
  return False
```

Returns whether the semantic function was triggered. If False, then another overlapping function with lower precedence could be attempted.

This popularity function allows us to apply semantic interpretation logic to manipulate the query tree. Had the query tree ended with the keyword "top", the function would have returned False and no adjustments would have been made. Likewise, if another function had been assigned higher precedence (as specified in the entities collection), it might have removed the {popularity} entity before its function was even executed.

The location_distance function is a bit more involved, as shown in the next listing.

Listing 7.10   A semantic function that accounts for location

```
def location_distance(query, position):
  if len(query["query_tree"]) -1 > position:
    next_entity = query["query_tree"][position + 1]
    if next_entity["type"] == "city":
```

The function must modify the next entity to succeed.

The next entity must be of a location type (city).

```
            query["query_tree"].pop(position + 1)
            query["query_tree"][position] = {
Add in the          "type": "transformed",
replacement         "syntax": "solr",
entity with the     "query": create_geo_filter(
radius filter.         next_entity['location_coordinates'],
                      "location_coordinates", 50)}
            return True
        return False

def create_geo_filter(coordinates, field, distance_KM):
    return f'+{!geofilt d={distance_KM} sfield="{field}" pt="{coordinates}"}'
```

Remove the next entity, since it is a location that will now be replaced by a radius-based filter.

If the next entity was not a city, then don't apply the function.

As you can see, our implementation of semantic functions allows for any arbitrary logic to be conditionally applied when interpreting queries. If you want, you can even call external knowledge graphs or other data sources to pull in additional information to better interpret the query.

You may have noticed that the surface forms "near", "in", and "by" all map to the {location_distance} canonical form, which is represented by the location_distance(query, position) function. This function works well if one of those terms is followed by a location, but what if someone searches for chief near officer? In this context, the end user may have meant "find the term *chief* close to the term *officer* within a document"—essentially an edit distance search. Note that there is also an entity mapping "near" ⇒ {text_distance} that can be invoked conditionally for this fallback use case if the {location_distance} entity's semantic function returns False.

Semantic functions can be implemented in many different ways, but our example implementation provides a highly configurable way to code dynamic semantic patterns into your query interpretation pipeline to best tie into the many different AI-powered search approaches available to your search application. We show this implementation in the process_semantic_functions function in the following listing, which loops through the query tree to invoke all matched semantic functions.

Listing 7.11 Processing all semantic functions within the query tree

```
def process_semantic_functions(query_tree):
    position = 0
    while position < len(query_tree):
        node = query_tree[position]
        if node["type"] == "semantic_function":
            query = {"query_tree": query_tree}
            command_successful = eval(node["semantic_function"])
            if not command_successful:
                node["type"] = "invalid_semantic_function"
        position += 1
    return query_tree
```

Iterates through all items in the query tree, searching for semantic functions to execute

The query and position variables are passed to the semantic function on eval.

Dynamically evaluates semantic functions, which augment the query tree

Updates the type of any unsuccessful semantic functions

Since the semantic functions are stored as part of their entity from the `entities` collection, we perform late binding on these functions (using Python's `eval` function). This allows you to plug new semantic functions into the `entities` collection at any time without needing to modify the application code.

Because semantic functions may or may not succeed depending on the surrounding context nodes, each semantic function must return `True` or `False` to allow the processing logic to determine how to proceed with the rest of the query tree.

INTEGRATING AN SKG

In this section, we'll integrate an SKG (discussed in chapter 5) into our query enrichment process.

Your `entities` collection is likely to contain many learned entities using the techniques from chapter 6. You may also use an SKG or other approach to classify known entities or to generate lists of related terms. If you do, we recommend adding the classifications and related terms as additional fields in the `entities` collection to cache the responses for quicker lookup at query time.

For our implementation, we'll invoke an SKG in real time to enrich *unknown* terms. This approach injects related keywords for all unknown keyword phrases in a query, which can generate a lot of false positives. You'll likely want to be more conservative in any production implementation, but implementing this is useful for learning and experimentation purposes. The following listing demonstrates how to look up keyword phrases and traverse our reviews collection as an SKG.

Listing 7.12   Getting related terms and categories from the SKG

```
def get_enrichments(collection, keyword, limit=4):
  enrichments = {}
  nodes_to_traverse = [{"field": "content",
                        "values": [keyword],
                        "default_operator": "OR"},
                       [{"name": "related_terms",
                         "field": "content",
                         "limit": limit},
                        {"name": "doc_type",
                         "field": "doc_type",
                         "limit": 1}]]
  skg = get_semantic_knowledge_graph(collection)
  traversals = skg.traverse(*nodes_to_traverse)
  if "traversals" not in traversals["graph"][0]["values"][keyword]:
    return enrichments

  nested_traversals = traversals["graph"][0]["values"] \
                                 [keyword]["traversals"]

  doc_types = list(filter(lambda t: t["name"] == "doc_type",
                    nested_traversals))
  if doc_types:
    enrichments["category"] = next(iter(doc_types[0]["values"]))
```

The starting node for the SKG traversal is a query for the passed-in keyword in the content field.

Returns the top 4 related terms for the keyword

Returns the top 1 doc_type (category) for the keyword

Returns empty when no enrichments are found

Returns discovered categories from the traversal

```
related_terms = list(filter(lambda t: t["name"] == "related_terms",
                            nested_traversals))
if related_terms:
  term_vector = ""
  for term, data in related_terms[0]["values"].items():
    term_vector += f'{term}^{round(data["relatedness"], 4)} '
  enrichments["term_vector"] = term_vector.strip()

return enrichments
```

> **Constructs a boosted query from discovered related terms boosted by their relatedness**

```
query = "kimchi"
get_enrichments(reviews_collection, query)
```

> **Gets enrichments for the keyword "kimchi"**

The output of listing 7.12 for the keyword "kimchi" is as follows:

```
{"category": "Korean",
 "term_vector": "kimchi^0.9193 korean^0.7069 banchan^0.6593 bulgogi^0.5497"}
```

Here are some sample SKG outputs for other potential keywords:

- *bbq*:

  ```
  {"category": "Barbeque",
   "term_vector": "bbq^0.9191 ribs^0.6187 pork^0.5992 brisket^0.5691"}
  ```

- *korean bbq*:

  ```
  {"category": "Korean",
   "term_vector": "korean^0.7754 bbq^0.6716 banchan^0.5534 sariwon^0.5211"}
  ```

- *lasagna*:

  ```
  {"category": "Italian",
   "term_vector": "lasagna^0.9193 alfredo^0.3992 pasta^0.3909
                  italian^0.3742"}
  ```

- *karaoke*:

  ```
  {"category": "Karaoke",
   "term_vector": "karaoke^0.9193 sing^0.6423 songs^0.5256 song^0.4118"}
  ```

- *drive through*:

  ```
  {"category": "Fast Food",
   "term_vector": "drive^0.7428 through^0.6331 mcdonald's^0.2873
                  window^0.2643"}
  ```

To complete our *enriching* phase, we need to apply the `get_enrichments` function and the previously discussed `process_semantic_functions` function to our query tree.

Listing 7.13 Enriching the query tree nodes

```
def enrich(collection, query_tree):
  query_tree = process_semantic_functions(query_tree)
  for item in query_tree:
```

> **Loops through the query tree and processes all semantic functions**

```
if item["type"] == "keyword":
   enrichments = get_enrichments(collection, item["surface_form"])
   if enrichments:
      item["type"] = "skg_enriched"
      item["enrichments"] = enrichments
return query_tree
```

If enrichments
are found,
apply them to
the node.

Takes all unknown
keyword phrases,
and looks them
up in the SKG

This `enrich` function encompasses the entire enrichment phase, processing all semantic functions and then enriching all the remaining unknown keywords using the SKG. Before we move on to the transformation phase, however, let's quickly look at an alternative approach to the SKG-based keyword expansion we've implemented.

7.4.3   *Sparse lexical and expansion models*

We've covered two main approaches to search so far in this book: *lexical search*—matching and ranking based on specific terms or attributes in a query—and *semantic search*—matching and ranking based on the meaning of the query. You've also been introduced to two main approaches for representing queries: as sparse vectors (vectors with very few nonzero values) and dense vectors (vectors with mostly nonzero values). Lexical keyword search is usually implemented using an inverted index, which holds a sparse vector representation of every document with a dimension for every term in the index. Semantic search is likewise usually implemented using a dense vector representation searching on embeddings.

> **Sparse vector vs. dense vector vs. lexical search vs. semantic search**
>
> Due to computational cost, dense vector representations usually have a limited number of dimensions (hundreds to thousands) that densely compress a semantic representation of the data, whereas sparse vector representations can easily have hundreds of thousands to tens of millions of dimensions that represent more identifiable terms or attributes. Lexical keyword search is usually implemented using an inverted index, which holds a sparse vector representation of every document with a dimension for every term in the index. Semantic search is likewise usually implemented using a dense vector representation searching on embeddings. Due to these trends, many people mistakenly treat the term "semantic search" as synonymous with dense vector search on embeddings, but this throws away the rich history of much more explainable and flexible sparse-vector and graph-based semantic search approaches. This chapter highlights some of those approaches, with chapters 13–15 covering the dense vector search techniques in more depth.

As you've seen already in this chapter, however, semantic search can also be implemented using sparse vectors, and within the context of typical lexical queries. While we've implemented semantic query parsing that operates directly on user queries, we've also generated query expansions using an SKG to generate sparse vectors of terms and weights to power semantic search.

Other techniques exist for this kind of query expansion, such as SPLADE (Sparse Lexical and Expansion). Instead of using an inverted index as its language model, the SPLADE approach (https://arxiv.org/pdf/2107.05720) uses a prebuilt language model to generate contextualized tokens. We won't use SPLADE (or SPLADE V2 or subsequent versions) because it wasn't released under a license enabling commercial use, but listing 7.14 demonstrates sample output from an alternative open source implementation (SPLADE++) for the same example queries we just tested with the SKG approach in section 7.4.2.

Listing 7.14 Expanding queries with SPLADE++

```
from spladerunner import Expander
expander = Expander('Splade_PP_en_v1', 128)      ◁──┐  Specifies the SPLADE++
queries = ["kimchi", "bbq", "korean bbq",              model name and maximum
          "lasagna", "karaoke", "drive through"]        sequence length

for query in queries:                            │  Generates the
  sparse_vec = expander.expand(query,            ◁──┘  sparse lexical vector
                  outformat="lucene")[0]         ◁──┐  Returns token labels (strings)
  print(sparse_vec)                                 │  instead of token IDs (integers)
```

Here are the outputs from the SPLADE++ expansion:

- *kimchi*:

  ```
  {"kim": 3.11, "##chi": 3.04, "ki": 1.52, ",": 0.92, "who": 0.72,
   "brand": 0.56, "genre": 0.46, "chi": 0.45, "##chy": 0.45,
   "company": 0.41,  "only": 0.39, "take": 0.31, "club": 0.25,
   "species": 0.22, "color": 0.16, "type": 0.15, "but": 0.13,
   "dish": 0.12, "hotel": 0.11, "music": 0.09, "style": 0.08,
   "name": 0.06, "religion": 0.01}
  ```

- *bbq*:

  ```
  {"bb": 2.78, "grill": 1.85, "barbecue": 1.36, "dinner": 0.91,
   "##q": 0.78, "dish": 0.77, "restaurant": 0.65, "sport": 0.46,
   "food": 0.34, "style": 0.34, "eat": 0.24, "a": 0.23, "genre": 0.12,
   "definition": 0.09}
  ```

- *korean bbq*:

  ```
  {"korean": 2.84, "korea": 2.56, "bb": 2.23, "grill": 1.58, "dish": 1.21,
   "restaurant": 1.18, "barbecue": 0.79, "kim": 0.67, "food": 0.64,
   "dinner": 0.39, "restaurants": 0.32, "japanese": 0.31, "eat": 0.27,
   "hotel": 0.16, "famous": 0.11, "brand": 0.11, "##q": 0.06, "diner": 0.02}
  ```

- *lasagna*:

  ```
  {"las": 2.87, "##ag": 2.85, "##na": 2.39, ",": 0.84, "she": 0.5,
   "species": 0.34, "hotel": 0.33, "club": 0.31, "location": 0.3,
   "festival": 0.29, "company": 0.27, "her": 0.2, "city": 0.12,
   "genre": 0.05}
  ```

- *karaoke*:

```
{"kara": 3.04, "##oke": 2.87, "music": 1.31, "lara": 1.07,
 "song": 1.03, "dance": 0.97, "style": 0.94, "sara": 0.81,
 "genre": 0.75, "dress": 0.48, "dish": 0.44, "singer": 0.37,
 "hannah": 0.36, "brand": 0.31, "who": 0.29, "culture": 0.21,
 "she": 0.17, "mix": 0.17, "popular": 0.12, "girl": 0.12,
 "kelly": 0.08, "wedding": 0.0}
```

- *drive through*:

```
{"through": 2.94, "drive": 2.87, "driving": 2.34, "past": 1.75,
 "drives": 1.65, "thru": 1.44, "driven": 1.22, "enter": 0.81,
 "drove": 0.81, "pierce": 0.75, "in": 0.72, "by": 0.71, "into": 0.64,
 "travel": 0.59, "mark": 0.51, ";": 0.44, "clear": 0.41,
 "transport": 0.41, "route": 0.39, "within": 0.36, "vehicle": 0.3,
 "via": 0.15}
```

Note that the `outputformat=lucene` parameter results in the tokens (keywords or partial keywords) being returned instead of the integer IDs of the tokens, because seeing the tokens helps us better interpret the results.

When comparing this output with the previously shown SKG output for the same queries, you may notice the following differences:

- The SKG output returns actual terms in the index, whereas the SPLADE-style output returns tokens from the LLM. This means that you can use the SKG output ("lasagna", "alfredo", "pasta") directly to search on the fields on your documents, whereas the SPLADE tokens (`las`, `##ag`, `na##`) will need to be generated from SPLADE for all documents and indexed in order for a SPLADE-style query to match on the right tokens at query time.

- The SKG sparse vectors tend to look cleaner and more relevant to the dataset (restaurant reviews) for in-domain terms. For example, for the query `bbq`, the SKG returns {`"bbq"`: 0.9191, `"ribs"`:0.6186, `"pork"`:0.5991, `"brisket"`:0.569}, whereas SPLADE returns {`'bb'`: 2.78, `'grill'`: 1.85, `'barbecue'`: 1.36, `'dinner'`: 0.91, `'##q'`: 0.78, `'dish'`: 0.77, `'restaurant'`: 0.65, `'sport'`: 0.46, `'food'`: 0.34, …}. This underperformance of the SPLADE model relative to the SKG model is mostly due to SPLADE not being trained on the data in the search index, whereas the SKG uses the data in the search index directly as its language model. Fine-tuning the SPLADE-based model would help to close this gap.

- The SKG model is more flexible, as it can return relationships across multiple dimensions. Notice in the last section that we not only returned the sparse vector of related terms, but also a classification of the query.

- Both the SPLADE and SKG models are context-aware. SPLADE natively weights each token based on the entire context of the query (or document) being encoded, and the SKG request can likewise (optionally) use any passed-in context for the query or document to contextualize the weights of its tokens. SPLADE-based models tend to shine more with longer well-known contexts (like general documents), whereas the SKG model is more optimized for shorter, domain-specific contexts (like in-domain queries), but they both work and represent novel techniques for sparse-vector-based or lexically oriented semantic search.

We've chosen to use an SKG-based approach instead of SPLADE in this chapter due to its ability to also classify queries and further contextualize queries for query sense disambiguation, but similar concepts apply for implementing sparse-vector-based semantic search regardless of which model you choose, so it's good to be familiar with multiple techniques.

In the next section, we'll walk through the transformation of the enriched query tree into a search-engine-specific query syntax for sending to the search engine.

7.4.4 *Transforming a query for semantic search*

With the user's query now parsed and enriched, it's time to transform the query tree into an appropriate search-engine-specific syntax.

During this *transforming* phase, we invoke an adapter to convert the query tree to the most useful engine-specific representation of the query—Solr in our default implementation. In the case of our semantic functions (the `popularity` and `location_distance` functions), we already injected this engine-specific syntax (`{"type":"transformed"`, `"syntax":"solr"}`) directly into the enriched nodes in the query tree. We could have alternatively abstracted this a bit by creating a generic intermediate representation of each semantic function's output and then waiting until the transforming phase to convert to engine-specific syntax (Solr, OpenSearch, etc.), but we chose to avoid the intermediate representations to keep the examples simpler. If you run the code using a different engine (as explained in appendix B), you'll see the syntax for that engine in the transformed nodes instead.

The following listing shows a `transform_query` function that takes an enriched query tree and transforms each of its nodes into search-engine-specific nodes.

> **Listing 7.15 Transforming a query tree into engine-specific syntax**

```
def transform_query(query_tree):
  for i, item in enumerate(query_tree):
    match item["type"]:
      case "transformed":
        continue
      case "skg_enriched":
        enrichments = item["enrichments"]
        if "term_vector" in enrichments:
          query_string = enrichments["term_vector"]
          if "category" in enrichments:
            query_string += f' +doc_type:"{enrichments["category"]}"'
          transformed_query =
        ➥'+{!edismax v="' + escape_quotes(query_string) + '"}'
        else:
          continue
```

If a query tree element has already been transformed to search-engine-specific syntax, there is no need to process it further.

Generates an enriched query for enriched nodes

For all other types without custom transformation logic, just search on their surface form.

```
        case "color":
            transformed_query = f'+colors:"{item["canonical_form"]}"'
        case "known_item" | "event":
            transformed_query = f'+name:"{item["canonical_form"]}"'
        case "city":
            transformed_query = f'+city:"{str(item["canonical_form"])}"'
        case "brand":
            transformed_query = f'+brand:"{item["canonical_form"]}"'
        case _:
            transformed_query = "+{!edismax v=\"" +
            ➥escape_quotes(item["surface_form"]) + "\"}"
    query_tree[i] = {"type": "transformed",
                     "syntax": "solr",
                     "query": transformed_query}
    return query_tree

enriched_query_tree = enrich(reviews_collection, query_tree)
processed_query_tree = transform_query(enriched_query_tree)
display(processed_query_tree)
```

Denotes each transformed query tree node with the engine-specific syntax and query

Handles the transformation of other potential query-tree elements with custom type-handling logic

Output:

```
[{"type": "transformed",
  "syntax": "solr",
  "query": "+{!func v=\"mul(if(stars_rating,stars_rating,0),20)\"}"},
 {"type": "transformed",
  "syntax": "solr",
  "query": "{!edismax v=\"kimchi^0.9193 korean^0.7069 banchan^0.6593
  ➥+doc_type:\\\"Korean\\\"\"}"},
 {"type": "transformed",
  "syntax": "solr",
  "query": "+{!geofilt d=50 sfield=\"location_coordinates\"
  ➥pt=\"35.22709,-80.84313\"}"}]
```

At this point, all nodes in the query tree have been transformed into {'type': 'transformed', 'syntax': engine} nodes, which means they internally contain the search-engine-specific syntax needed to generate a final query to the configured engine. We're now ready to convert the query tree into a string and send the request to the search engine.

7.4.5 Searching with a semantically enhanced query

The final step of our semantic search process is the *searching* phase. We convert the fully transformed query_tree to a query, run the query against the search engine, and return the results to the end user.

Listing 7.16 Running the query

```
def to_query(query_tree):
    return [[node["query"] for node in query_tree]
```

```
transformed_query = to_query(query_tree)
reviews_collection = engine.get_collection("reviews")
reviews_collection.search(query=transformed_query)
```

The search results for our query `top kimchi near charlotte` will return exactly what was shown in our end-to-end example in section 7.3. Since we know we can now handle variations of semantic functions ("in" versus "near" for locations, "good" versus "popular" versus "top" for popularity), we'll show the output for a slightly modified query: `good kimchi in charlotte`. If you contrast the output for this variant, shown in figure 7.8, with the output for the original query of `top kimchi near charlotte`, you'll see that they yield the exact same transformed query and final set of search results as figures 7.5 and 7.7 earlier in the chapter.

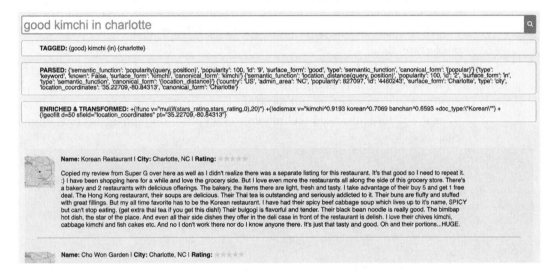

Figure 7.8 **Search results for** `good kimchi in charlotte`, **interpreted as semantically identical to the results for the** `top kimchi near charlotte` **end-to-end example**

Congratulations, you've now implemented an end-to-end semantic search pipeline that can semantically parse, enrich, transform, and run searches. This chapter didn't introduce any fancy new machine-learning algorithms but instead provided a concrete implementation of how the many models, algorithms, and other techniques you've learned throughout the book can be integrated into an end-to-end system.

Throughout the remainder of the book, we'll continue to explore more advanced approaches that can plug into this framework to enhance relevance ranking and improve query intent understanding.

Summary

- Query interpretation requires appropriately mixing query pipelines with learned models while ensuring an adequate fallback model for matching unknown keywords.
- Matching only on keywords can sometimes work, but it results in poor matches when the intent expressed by connecting words isn't understood (top, near, etc.). One way to solve this is by implementing domain-specific semantic functions to overcome those limitations.
- A semantic query parser, which is aware of known terms and phrases learned within your domain, allows you to move from a keyword-based search to a semantic search on entities and their relationships.
- Extracting known entities enables the seamless integration of models into your query interpretation pipeline, using mappings between surface forms of keywords to canonical representations of entities generated from your learned models (signals boosts, alternative spellings, related terms, and other knowledge graph data).
- Semantic search involves *parsing* known entities, *enriching* with learned models, *transforming* the query to optimize matching and relevance for the target search engine, and then *searching* and returning results to the end user. We'll continue to explore more advanced techniques to plug into these phases in the coming chapters.

Part 3

Reflected intelligence

Search ranking shouldn't be a static function. Every query and user interaction with search results is a signal that can be used to improve the relevance of future results. In the last part, we learned domain-specific knowledge from content and signals, and we used that knowledge to interpret query intent.

In this part, we'll take a deeper dive into the topic of reflected intelligence, the process of learning from user interactions with search results to improve relevance ranking models. We'll extend our coverage of crowdsourced relevance algorithms from chapter 4, with chapters dedicated to three key types of reflected intelligence: popularized relevance (signals boosting), personalized relevance (collaborative filtering), and generalized relevance (learning to rank).

Chapter 8 covers various approaches to signals boosting to better rank your most popular queries. Chapter 9 then leverages signals to build more personalized relevance ranking, catering to your users' specific interests based on their behavior. Chapter 10 begins a three-chapter journey into the world of machine-learned ranking, also known as "learning to rank". In chapter 10, you'll learn how to build a ranking classifier model from relevance judgments and how to deploy that model as a generalized relevance ranking algorithm. Chapter 11 introduces click models—leveraging user search and click signals to learn implicit relevance judgments—and it uses them to automate the process of learning to rank. Finally, chapter 12 introduces active learning and A/B testing approaches to overcome biases in those implicitly trained models by intelligently exploring previously unseen results and gathering live user feedback.

Signals-boosting models

In chapter 4, we covered three different categories of reflected intelligence: signals boosting (popularized relevance), collaborative filtering (personalized relevance), and learning to rank (generalized relevance). In this chapter, we'll dive deeper into the first of these, implementing signals boosting to enhance the relevance ranking of your most popular queries and documents.

In most search engines, a relatively small number of queries tend to make up a large portion of the total query volume. These popular queries, called *head queries*, also tend to lead to more signals (such as clicks and purchases in an e-commerce use case), which enable stronger inferences about the popularity of top search results.

Signals-boosting models directly harness these stronger inferences and are the key to ensuring your most important and highest-visibility queries are best tuned to return the most relevant documents.

8.1 Basic signals boosting

In section 4.2.2, we built our first signals-boosting model on the RetroTech dataset, enabling a significant boost in relevance for the most frequently searched and clicked search results. In this section, we'll quickly recap the process of creating a simple signals-boosting model, which we'll build upon in the upcoming sections to tackle some more advanced needs.

You'll recall from section 4.2.2 that signals-boosting models aggregate useful user behavioral signals on documents (such as click signals) that occur as the result of a specific query. We used a search for `ipad` and boosted each document based on how many times it was previously clicked in the results for that search. Figure 8.1 demonstrates the before (no signals boosting) and after (signals boosting on) search results for the query `ipad`.

Figure 8.1   Before and after applying a signals-boosting model. Signals boosting improves relevance by pushing the most popular items to the top of the search results.

The signals-boosting model that led to the improved relevance in figure 8.1 is a basic signals-boosting model. It looks at each document ever clicked for a given query and applies a boost equal to the total number of past clicks on that document for that query.

While this basic signals-boosting model covered in section 4.2.2 provides greatly improved relevance, it is unfortunately susceptible to some data biases and even manipulation. In section 8.2, we'll discuss some techniques for removing noise in the signals to maximize the quality of your signals-boosting models and reduce the likelihood of undesirable biases.

8.2 Normalizing signals

It is important to normalize incoming user queries prior to aggregation so that variations are treated as the same query. Given that end users can enter any arbitrary text as a query, the aggregated signals are inherently noisy. The basic signals-boosting model from chapter 4 (and recapped in section 8.1) does no normalization. It generates aggregated boosts for each query and document pair, but since incoming queries haven't been normalized into a common form, variations of a query will be treated as entirely separate queries. The following listing produces a list of top queries that boost the most popular iPad model in their search results.

Listing 8.1 Aggregating signals and retrieving relevant queries

```
def create_boosting_collection(collection_name):
  basic_signals_aggregation_query = """
  SELECT q.target AS query, c.target AS doc,
  COUNT(c.target) AS boost
  FROM signals c LEFT JOIN signals q
  ON c.query_id = q.query_id
  WHERE c.type = 'click' AND q.type = 'query'
  GROUP BY q.target, doc
  ORDER BY boost DESC
  """
  collection = engine.get_collection(collection_name)
  return aggregate_signals(collection, "basic_signals_boosts",
                    basic_signals_aggregation_query)


def search_for_boosts(query, collection, query_field="query"):
  boosts_request = {"query": query,
                    "query_fields": [query_field],
                    "return_fields": ["query", "doc", "boost"],
                    "limit": 20, 3((CO1-16))
                    "order_by": [("boost", "desc")]}
  response = collection.search(**boosts_request)
  return response["docs"]

signals_boosting_collection = create_boosting_collection("signals")
query = "885909457588"
signals_docs = search_for_boosts(query, signals_boosting_collection, "doc")
show_raw_boosted_queries(signals_docs)
```

Defines the signals aggregation query

Runs the aggregation from the signals collection to the basic_signals_boosts collection

Loads signals boosts for the specified query and collection

The most popular iPad model

Returns the list of top signals boosts for the specified document

Output:

```
Raw Boosted Queries
"iPad" : 1050
"ipad" : 966
"Ipad" : 829
```

```
"iPad 2" : 509
"ipad 2" : 347
"Ipad2" : 261
"ipad2" : 238
"Ipad 2" : 213
"I pad" : 203
"i pad" : 133
"IPad" : 77
"Apple" : 76
"I pad 2" : 60
"apple ipad" : 55
"Apple iPad" : 53
"ipads" : 43
"tablets" : 42
"apple" : 41
"iPads" : 38
"i pad 2" : 38
```

This listing aggregates all signals by their queries and stores each query along with the number of occurrences into a new collection. You can see from the output that many variations of the same queries exist in the basic signals-boosting model. The biggest culprit of the variations seems to be case-sensitivity, as we see iPad, ipad, Ipad, and IPad as common variants. Spacing appears to be another problem, with ipad 2 versus i pad 2 versus ipad2. We even see singular versus plural representations in ipad versus ipads.

Keyword search fields usually normalize queries to be case-insensitive, use stemming to ignore plural versions of terms, and split on case changes and letter-to-number transitions between words. It is likewise useful to normalize signals, as keeping separate query terms and boosts for variations that are non-distinguishable by the search engine can be counterproductive. Failing to normalize terms diffuses the value of your signals, since the signals are divided across variations of the same keywords with lower boosts, as opposed to being coalesced into more meaningful queries with stronger boosts.

It is up to you to figure out how sophisticated your query normalization should be prior to signals aggregation, but even just lowercasing incoming queries to make the signals aggregation case-insensitive can go a long way. The following listing demonstrates the same basic signals aggregation as before, but this time with the queries lowercased first.

Listing 8.2   Case-insensitive signals aggregation

```
normalized_signals_aggregation_query = """        Normalizing case by
SELECT LOWER(q.target) AS query,                   lowercasing each query
c.target AS doc, COUNT(c.target) AS boost
FROM signals c LEFT JOIN signals q ON c.query_id = q.query_id
WHERE c.type = 'click' AND q.type = 'query'
GROUP BY LOWER(q.target), doc
ORDER BY boost DESC
"""
```

Grouping by normalized query increases the count of signals for those queries, increasing the signals boost

```
normalized_collection = \
  aggregate_signals(signals_collection, "normalized_signals_boosts",
                    normalized_signals_aggregation_query)

query = "885909457588"        ⟵──────────────
signals_documents = search_for_boosts(query, normalized_collection, "doc")
show_raw_boosted_queries(signals_documents)
```

**The most popular
iPad model**

Output:

```
Raw Boosted Queries
"ipad" : 2939
"ipad 2" : 1104
"ipad2" : 540
"i pad" : 341
"apple ipad" : 152
"ipads" : 123
"apple" : 118
"i pad 2" : 99
"tablets" : 67
"tablet" : 61
"ipad 1" : 52
"apple ipad 2" : 27
"hp touchpad" : 26
"ipaq" : 20
"i pad2" : 19
"wi" : 19
"apple computers" : 18
"apple i pad" : 15
"ipad 2 16gb" : 15
"samsung galaxy" : 14
```

The list of raw boosted queries is already looking much cleaner! Not only is there less redundancy, but notice that the strength of the signals boosts has increased, because more signals are being attributed to a canonical form of the query (the lowercased version).

Lowercasing the queries and maybe removing whitespace or extraneous characters is often sufficient normalization for queries prior to aggregating signals. The important takeaway from this section, though, is that the signals-boosting model becomes stronger the more you can ensure that identical queries are treated as the same when aggregated.

Variations in queries aren't the only kind of noise we need to worry about in our data. In the next section, we'll talk about how we can overcome significant potential problems caused by spam in our user-generated click signals.

8.3   *Fighting signal spam*

Anytime we use crowdsourced data, such as click signals, to influence the behavior of the search engine, we need to ask ourselves "How might the data inputs be manipulated to create an undesirable result?" In this section, we'll demonstrate how the search engine can be spammed with click signals to manipulate search results, and how you can stop it.

8.3.1   *Using signal spam to manipulate search results*

Let's imagine we have a user who, for whatever reason, really hates *Star Wars* and thinks that the most recent movies are complete garbage. They feel so strongly, in fact, that they want to ensure any searches for star wars return a physical trash can for purchase as the top search result. This user knows a thing or two about search engines and has noticed that your killer relevance algorithms seem to be using user signals and signals boosting. Figure 8.2 shows the default response for the query star wars, with signals boosting bringing the most popular products to the top of the search results.

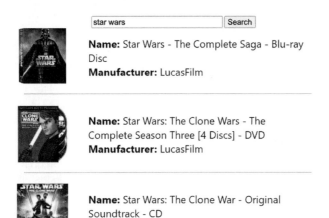

| star wars | Search |

Name: Star Wars - The Complete Saga - Blu-ray Disc
Manufacturer: LucasFilm

Name: Star Wars: The Clone Wars - The Complete Season Three [4 Discs] - DVD
Manufacturer: LucasFilm

Name: Star Wars: The Clone War - Original Soundtrack - CD
Manufacturer: Sony Classics

Figure 8.2   The most popular search results for the query star wars, with signals boosting turned on. These are the expected results when there is no malicious signal spam.

The user decides that since your search engine ranking is based upon popular items, they will spam the search engine with a bunch of searches for star wars. They will follow up each search with fake clicks on the Star Wars–themed trash can they found, attempting to make the trash can show up at the top of the search results.

In order to simulate this scenario, we'll run a simple script in the following listing to generate 5,000 queries for star wars and 5,000 corresponding clicks on the trash can after running that query.

Listing 8.3   Generating spam query and click signals

```
signals_collection = engine.get_collection("signals")
spam_user = "u8675309"
spam_query = "star wars"
spam_signal_boost_doc_upc = "45626176"    ◁─┐

signal_docs = []
for num in range(5000):
    query_id = f"u8675309_0_{num}"
    query_signal = {
```

Document for the trash can the spammer wants to move to the top of the search results

Generates and sends 5,000 query and click signals to the search engine

```
    "query_id": query_id,
    "user": spam_user,
    "type": "query",
    "target": spam_query,
    "signal_time": datetime.now().strftime("%Y-%m-%dT%H:%M:%SZ"),
    "id": f"spam_signal_query_{num}"}
  click_signal = {                                    Generates and sends 5,000
    "query_id": query_id,                              query and click signals to
    "user": spam_user,                                   the search engine
    "type": "click",
    "target": spam_signal_boost_doc_upc,
    "signal_time": datetime.now().strftime("%Y-%m-%dT%H:%M:%SZ"),
    "id": f"spam_signal_click_{num}"}
  signal_docs.extend([click_signal, query_signal])

signals_collection.add_documents(signal_docs)

spam_signals_collection = \
  aggregate_signals(signals_collection, "signals_boosts_with_spam",
    normalized_signals_aggregation_query)
                                               Runs the signals aggregation to
                                             generate the signals-boosting model
                                                 including the spammy signals
```

Listing 8.3 sends thousands of spammy query and click signals to our search engine, modeling the same outcome we would see if a user searched and clicked on a particular search result thousands of times. The listing then reruns the basic signals aggregation.

To see the effect of the malicious user's spammy click behavior on our search results, the following listing runs a search for the query star wars, now incorporating the manipulated signals-boosting model.

Listing 8.4 Search results affected by spam user signals

```
                                         Loads signals boosts from the signals-boosting
                                            model that included the spammy signals

def boosted_product_search_request(query, collection, boost_field=None):
  signals_documents = search_for_boosts(query, collection)
  signals_boosts = create_boosts_query(signals_documents)
  boosted_request = product_search_request(query)
  if boost_field:                                    Boosts the star wars
    signals_boosts = (boost_field, signals_boosts)    query using the
  boosted_request["query_boosts"] = signals_boosts    signals-boosting model
  return boosted_request

query = '"star wars"'
boosted_request = boosted_product_search_request(query,
                  spam_signals_collection, "upc")
response = products_collection.search(**boosted_request)
display_product_search(query, response["docs"])
```

Figure 8.3 shows the new manipulated search results generated from listing 8.4, with the Star Wars trash can in the top spot.

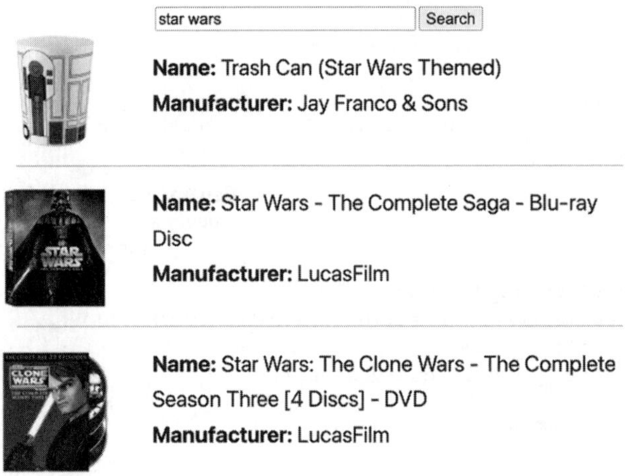

star wars   [Search]

Name: Trash Can (Star Wars Themed)
Manufacturer: Jay Franco & Sons

Name: Star Wars - The Complete Saga - Blu-ray
Disc
Manufacturer: LucasFilm

Figure 8.3   Search results manipulated by a user spamming the search engine with fake signals to affect the top result. The user was able to modify the top result just by clicking on it many times.

Name: Star Wars: The Clone Wars - The Complete
Season Three [4 Discs] - DVD
Manufacturer: LucasFilm

The spammer was successful, and these manipulated search results will now be seen by every subsequent visitor who searches for star wars on the RetroTech website! Looks like we're going to need to make our signals-boosting model more robust to combat this kind of signal spam.

8.3.2 *Combating signal spam through user-based filtering*

If you are going to use crowdsourced data like user signals to influence the search engine ranking, it's important to take steps to minimize users' ability to manipulate your signals-based ranking algorithm.

To combat the Star Wars trash can problem we just demonstrated, the simplest technique is to ensure that duplicate clicks by the same user only get one "vote" in the signals-boosting aggregation. That way, whether a malicious user clicks one time or a million times, their clicks only count as one signal and therefore have no material effect on the signals-boosting model. The following listing reworks the signals aggregation query to only count unique click signals from each user.

Listing 8.5   Deduplicating noisy user signals

```
anti_spam_aggregation_query = """
SELECT query, doc, COUNT(doc) AS boost FROM (
  SELECT c.user unique_user, LOWER(q.target) AS query, c.target AS doc,
  MAX(c.signal_time) AS boost                          ◁──────────────
  FROM signals c LEFT JOIN signals q ON c.query_id = q.query_id
  WHERE c.type = 'click' AND q.type = 'query'                    Signal date is the
  GROUP BY unique_user, LOWER(q.target), doc)   ◁─────            most recent
GROUP BY query, doc                                                signal from the
ORDER BY boost DESC"""      Group by user to limit each user      user if there
                           to one "vote" per query/doc pair      are duplicates.
anti_spam_collection = \     in the signals-boosting model.
  aggregate_signals(signals_collection, "signals_boosts_anti_spam",
                    anti_spam_aggregation_query)
```

If we rerun the `star wars` query from listing 8.3 with this new `signals_boosts_anti_spam` model, we'll see that our normal search results have returned and look the same as in figure 8.2. This is because the extra, spammy signals from our malicious user have all been reduced to a single bad signal, as shown in table 8.1.

Table 8.1   The 5,000 spammy signals have been deduplicated to 1 signal in the antispam signals-boosting model.

model	query	doc	boost
Before spam signals (`normalized_signals_boosts`)	star wars	400032015667	0 (no signals yet)
After spam signals (`normalized_signals_boosts`)	star wars	400032015667	5000
After spam signals cleanup (`signals_boosts_anti_spam`)	star wars	400032015667	1

You can see that the aggregated signals count in the `signals_boosts_anti_spam` model has a total much closer to the `normalized_signals_boosts` model that we built before the spam signals were generated. Since each user is limited to one signal per query/document pair in the `signals_boosts_anti_spam` model, the ability for users to manipulate the signals-boosting model is now substantially reduced.

You could, of course, identify any user accounts that appear to be spamming your search engine and remove their signals entirely from your signals-boosting aggregation, but reducing the reach of the signals through deduplication is simpler and often accomplishes the same end goal of restoring a good, crowdsourced relevance ranking.

In listing 8.5, we used user IDs as the key identifier to deduplicate spammy signals, but any identifier will work here: user ID, session ID, browser ID, IP address, or even some kind of browser fingerprint. As long as you find some value to uniquely identify users or to otherwise identify low-quality traffic (like bots and web scrapers), you can use that information to deduplicate signals. If none of those techniques work, and you have too much noise in your click signals, you can also choose to only look at click signals from known (authenticated) users who you can presumably be much more confident are legitimate traffic.

One final way to mitigate signal spam is to find a way to separate the important signal types from the noisy ones that can be easily manipulated. For example, generating signals from running queries and clicking on search results is easy. Signals from purchasing a product are much harder to manipulate, as they require users to log in or enter payment information before a purchase will be recorded. The odds of someone maliciously purchasing 5,000 Star Wars trash cans are quite low, because there are multiple financial and logistical barriers to doing this.

Not only is it valuable to weight purchases as stronger signals than clicks from the standpoint of fighting spam, it is also valuable from a relevance standpoint, because purchases are more clear indicators of intent. In the next section, we'll walk through how we can combine different signal types into a signals-boosting model that considers the relative importance of each different signal type.

8.4   *Combining multiple signal types*

Thus far we've only worked with two signal types—queries and clicks. For some search engines (such as web search engines), click signals may be the only good source of crowdsourced data available to build a signals-boosting model. Many different signal types exist, however, which can provide additional and often much better inputs for building a signals-boosting model.

In our RetroTech dataset, we have several kinds of signals that are common to e-commerce use cases:

- query
- click
- add-to-cart
- purchase

While clicks in response to queries are helpful, they don't necessarily imply a strong interest in the product, as someone could just be browsing to see what's available. If someone adds a product to their shopping cart, this typically represents a much stronger signal of interest than a click. A purchase is an even stronger signal that a user is interested in a product, as the user is willing to pay money to receive the item for which they searched.

While some e-commerce websites may receive enough traffic to ignore click signals entirely and only focus on add-to-cart and purchase signals, it is often more useful to include all signal types when calculating signals boosts. Thankfully, combining multiple signal types is as simple as assigning relative weights as multipliers to each signal type when performing the signals aggregation:

```
signals_boost = (1 * sum(click_signals)) +
                (10 * sum(add_to_cart_signals)) +
                (25 * sum(purchase_signals))
```

By counting each click as 1 signal, each add-to-cart as 10 signals, and each purchase as 25 signals, a purchase carries 25 times as much weight and an add-to-cart carries 10 times as much weight as a click in the signals-boosting model. This helps reduce noise from less reliable signals and boosts more reliable signals while still making use of the large volume of less reliable signals in cases where better signals are less prevalent (like new or obscure items).

The following listing demonstrates a signals aggregation designed to combine different signal types with different weights.

Listing 8.6   Combining multiple signal types with different weights

```
mixed_signal_types_aggregation_query = """
SELECT query, doc, ((1 * click_boost)
        + (10 * add_to_cart_boost) +
        (25 * purchase_boost)) AS boost FROM (
   SELECT query, doc,
     SUM(click) AS click_boost,
     SUM(add_to_cart) AS add_to_cart_boost,
     SUM(purchase_boost) AS purchase_boost FROM (
       SELECT lower(q.target) AS query, cap.target AS doc,
         IF(cap.type = 'click', 1, 0) AS click,
         IF(cap.type = 'add-to-cart', 1, 0) AS  add_to_cart,
         IF(cap.type = 'purchase', 1, 0) AS purchase
       FROM signals cap LEFT JOIN signals q on cap.query_id = q.query_id
       WHERE (cap.type != 'query' AND q.type = 'query')
     ) raw_signals
   GROUP BY query, doc) AS per_type_boosts"""

type_weighted_collection = \
   aggregate_signals(signals_collection, "signals_boosts_weighted_types",
                     mixed_signal_types_aggregation_query)
```

> **Multiple signals are combined with different relative weights to calculate a total boost value.**

> **Each signal type is summed independently before being combined.**

You can see from the SQL query that the overall boost for each query/document pair is calculated by counting all clicks with a weight of 1, counting all add-to-cart signals and multiplying them by a weight of 10, and counting all purchase signals and multiplying them by a weight of 25.

These suggested weights of 10x for add-to-cart signals and 25x for purchase signals should work well in many e-commerce scenarios, but these relative weights are also fully configurable for each domain. Your website may be set up such that almost everyone who adds a product to their cart purchases the product (for example, a grocery store delivery app, where the only purpose of using the website is to fill a shopping cart and purchase). In these cases, you could find that adding an item to a shopping cart adds no additional value, but that *removing* an item from a shopping cart should potentially carry a penalty, indicating that the product is a bad match for the query.

In this case, you may want to introduce the idea of *negative signals boosts*. Just as we've discussed clicks, add-to-carts, and purchases as signals of user intent, your user experience may also have numerous ways to measure user dissatisfaction with your search results. For example, you might have a thumbs-down button or a remove-from-cart button, or you may be able to track product returns after a purchase. You may even want to count documents in the search results that were skipped over and record a "skip" signal for those documents to indicate that the user saw them but didn't show interest. We'll cover the topic of managing clicked versus skipped documents in chapter 11 when we discuss click modeling.

Thankfully, handling negative feedback is just as easy as handling positive signals: instead of just assigning increasingly positive weights to signals, you can also assign increasingly negative weights to negative signals. Here's an example:

```
positive_signals = (1 * sum(click_signals)) +
                   (25 * (purchase_signals)) +
                   (10 * sum(add_to_cart_signals)) +
                   (0.025 * sum(seen_doc_signals))

negative_signals = (-0.025 * sum(skipped_doc_signals)) +
                   (-20 * sum(remove_from_cart_signals)) +
                   (-100 * sum(returned_item_signals)) +
                   (-50 * sum(negative_post_about_item_in_review_signals))

type_based_signal_weight = positive_signals + negative_signals
```

This simple, linear function provides a highly configurable signals-based ranking model, taking in multiple input parameters and returning a ranking score based on the relative weights of those parameters. You can combine as many useful signals as you want into this weighted signals aggregation to improve the robustness of the model. Of course, tuning the weights of each of the signal types to achieve an optimal balance may take some effort. You can do this manually, or you can use a machine learning technique called learning to rank to do this. We'll explore learning to rank in chapters 10 and 11.

Not only is it important to weight different kinds of signals relative to each other, but it can also sometimes be necessary to weight the *same* kind of signals differently against each other. In the next section, we'll discuss one key example of doing this: assigning higher value to more recent interactions.

8.5   *Time decays and short-lived signals*

Signals don't always maintain their usefulness indefinitely. In the last section, we showed how signals-boosting models can be adjusted to weight different kinds of signals as more important than others. In this section, we'll address a different challenge—factoring in the "temporal value" of signals as they age and become less useful.

Imagine three different search engine use cases:

- An e-commerce search engine with stable products
- A job search engine
- A news website

For an e-commerce search engine, like RetroTech, the documents (products) often stay around for years, and the best products are often those that have a long track record of interest.

In a job search engine, the documents (jobs) may only stick around for a few weeks or months until the job is filled, and then they disappear forever. While the documents are present, however, newer clicks or job applications aren't necessarily any more important as signals than older interactions.

In a news search engine, while the news articles stick around forever, newer articles are generally much more important than older articles, and newer signals are also more important than older signals, as people's interests change on a daily, if not hourly, basis.

Let's dive into these use cases and demonstrate how to best handle the time-sensitivity of signals when performing signals boosting.

8.5.1　*Handling time-insensitive signals*

In our RetroTech use case, our documents are intentionally old, having been around for a decade or more, and interest in them likely only increases as the products become older and more "retro". As a result, we don't often have massive spikes in popularity for items, and newer signals don't necessarily carry significantly more importance than older signals. This type of use case is a bit atypical, but plenty of search use cases do deal with "static" document sets like this. The best solution in this case is the strategy we've already taken in this chapter: process all signals within a reasonable period of months or years and give them equal weight. When all time periods carry the same weight, the signals-boosting model likely doesn't need to be rebuilt very often, since the model changes slowly over time. The frequent processing of signals is unnecessary computational overhead.

In a job search use case, however, the scenario is very different. For the sake of argument, let's say that on average it takes 30 days to fill a job opening. This means the document representing that job will only be present in the search engine for 30 days, and any signals collected for that document are only useful for signals boosting during that 30-day window. When a job is posted, it will typically be very popular for the first few days, since it is new and is likely to attract many existing job seekers, but all interactions with that job at any point during the 30 days are just as useful. In this case, all click signals should get equal weight, and all job application signals should likewise receive an equal weight (at a weight higher than the click signals). Given the very short lifetime of the documents, however, it is important that all signals be processed as quickly as possible to make the best use of their value.

Use cases with short-lived documents, like in the job search use case, aren't usually the best candidates for signals boosting, as the documents may be deleted by the time the signals-boosting model becomes any good. As a result, it can often make more sense to look at personalized models (like collaborative filtering, covered in chapter 9) and generalizable relevance models (like learning to rank, covered in chapters 10 and 11) for these use cases.

In both the RetroTech and the job search use cases, the signals were just as useful for the entire duration of the document's existence. In the news search use case, which we'll look at next, the value of the signals declines over time.

8.5.2　*Handling time-sensitive signals*

In a news search engine use case, the most recently published news usually gets the most interaction, so more recent signals are considerably more valuable than older signals. Some news items may be very popular and relevant for days or longer, but generally the signals from the last ten minutes are more valuable than the signals from the last hour, which are more valuable than the signals from the last day, and so on. News search is an extreme use case where signals both need to be processed quickly and where more recent signals need to be weighted as substantially more important than older signals.

One easy way to model this is by using a decay function, such as a half-life function, which cuts the weight assigned to a signal by half (50%) over equally spaced time spans. For example, a decay function with a half-life of 30 days would assign 100% weight to a signal that happens "now", 75% weight to a signal from 15 days ago, 50% weight to a signal from 30 days ago, 25% weight to a signal from 60 days ago, 12.5% weight to a signal from 90 days ago, and so on. The math for calculating a signal's time-based weight using a decay function is

```
starting_weight × 0.5 (signal_age / half_life)
```

When applying this calculation, the `starting_weight` will usually be the relative weight of a signal based upon its type, such as a weight of `1` for clicks, `10` for add-to-cart signals, and `25` for purchase signals. If you are not combining multiple signal types, then the `starting_weight` will just be `1`.

The `signal_age` is how old the signal is, and the `half_life` is how long it takes for the signal to lose half of its value. Figure 8.4 demonstrates how this decay function affects signal weights over time for different half-life values.

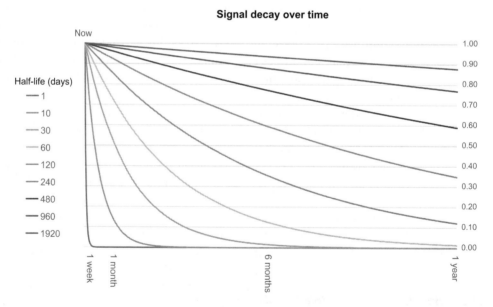

Figure 8.4 Signal decay over time based upon various half-life values. As the half-life increases, individual signals maintain their boosting power for longer.

The 1-day half-life is very aggressive and is impractical in most use cases, as it is unlikely you would be able to collect enough signals in a day to power meaningful signals boosting, and the likelihood of your signals becoming irrelevant that quickly is low.

The 30-day, 60-day, and 120-day half-lives are effective at aggressively discounting older signals while still keeping residual value from the discounted signals over a six to twelve month period. If you have very long-lived documents, you could push out even longer, making use of signals over the course of many years. The following listing demonstrates an updated signal aggregation query that implements a half-life of 30 days for each signal.

Listing 8.7 Applying time decay to the signals-boosting model

```
half_life_days = 30
target_date = '2024-06-01'      The latest possible signal date. This should be
signal_weight = 1                now() in a live system, but it can be set to a
                                 fixed date for a frozen dataset like RetroTech.

                                 A function could be added here to differentiate
                                 weights for different signal types.
time_decay_aggregation = f"""
SELECT query, doc, sum(time_weighted_boost) AS boost FROM (
  SELECT user, query, doc, {signal_weight} *
  POW(0.5, (DATEDIFF('{target_date}', signal_time) /      The half-life
                {half_life_days}))                        calculation
  AS time_weighted_boost FROM (
    SELECT c.user AS user, lower(q.target) AS query, c.target AS doc,
    MAX(c.signal_time) as signal_time
    FROM signals c LEFT JOIN signals q ON c.query_id = q.query_id
    WHERE c.type = 'click' AND q.type = 'query'
        AND c.signal_time <= '{target_date}'
    GROUP BY c.user, q.target, c.target
  ) AS raw_signals
) AS time_weighted_signals
GROUP BY query, doc
ORDER BY boost DESC"""

time_weighted_collection = \
    aggregate_signals(signals_collection, "signals_boosts_time_weighted",
                        time_decay_aggregation)
```

Only includes signals up to the target date

Gets the most recent unique signal per user, query, and product combination

This decay function has a few unique configurable parameters:

- It contains a `half_life_days` parameter, which calculates a weighted average using a configurable half-life, which we've set as 30 days to start.
- It contains a `signal_weight` parameter, which can be replaced with a function returning a weight by signal type, as shown in the last section ("click" = 1, "add-to-cart" = 10, "purchase" = 25, etc.).
- It contains a `target_date` parameter, which is the date at which a signal gets the full value of 1. Any signals before this date will be decayed based on the half-life, and any signals after this date will be ignored (filtered out).

Your `target_date` will usually be the current date, so that you are making use of your most up-to-date signals and assigning them the highest weight. However, you could also apply it to past periods if your documents have seasonal patterns that repeat monthly or yearly.

While our product documents don't change very often, and the most recent signals aren't necessarily any more valuable than older signals, there are potentially annual patterns we could find in a normal e-commerce dataset. For example, certain types of products may be more popular around major holidays like Mother's Day, Father's Day, and Black Friday. Likewise, searches for something like a "shovel" may take on a different meaning in the summer (shovel for digging dirt) versus the winter (shovel for removing snow from the sidewalk). If you explore your signals, any number of trends may emerge for which time sensitivity should affect how your signals are weighted.

Ultimately, signals are a lagging indicator. They reflect what your users just did, but they are only useful as predictions of future behavior if the patterns learned are likely to repeat themselves.

Having now explored techniques for improving our signals models through query normalization, mitigating spam and relevance manipulation, combining multiple signal types with different relative weights, and applying time decays to signals, you should be able to flexibly implement the signals-boosting models most appropriate for your use case. When rolling out signals boosting at scale, however, there are two different approaches you can take to optimize for flexibility versus performance, which we'll cover in the next section.

8.6   Index-time vs. query-time boosting: Balancing scale vs. flexibility

All the signals-boosting models in the chapter have been demonstrated using *query-time boosting*, which loads signals boosts for each query from a separate sidecar collection at query time and modifies the query to add the boosts before sending it to the search engine. It's also possible to implement signals-boosting models using *index-time boosting*, where boosts are added directly to documents for the queries to which those boosts apply. In this section, we'll show you how to implement index-time boosting and discuss the benefits and tradeoffs of query-time boosting versus index-time boosting.

8.6.1   Tradeoffs when using query-time boosting

Query-time boosting, as we've seen, turns each query into a two-step process. Each incoming user query is looked up in a signals-boosting collection, and any boosted documents found are used to modify the user's query. Query-time boosting is the most common way to implement signals boosting, but it comes with benefits and drawbacks.

BENEFITS OF QUERY-TIME BOOSTING

Query-time boosting's primary architectural characteristic is that it keeps the main search collection (`products`) and the signals-boosting collection (`*_signals_boosts`) separate. This separation provides several benefits:

- It allows the signals for each query to be updated incrementally by only modifying the one document representing that query.

- It allows boosting to be turned on or off easily by just not doing a lookup or modifying the user's query.
- It allows different signals-boosting algorithms to be swapped in at any time.

Ultimately, the flexibility to change signals boosts at any point in time based on the current context is the major advantage of query-time signals boosting. This enables easier incorporation of real-time signals and easier experimentation with different ranking functions.

DRAWBACKS OF QUERY-TIME BOOSTING

Although it's flexible, query-time boosting also introduces some significant downsides affecting query performance, scale, and relevance, which may make it inappropriate for certain use cases:

- It requires an extra search to look up boosts before the boosted search is executed, adding more processing (executing two searches) and latency (the final query must wait on the results of the signals lookup query before being processed).
- It leads to unfortunate tradeoffs between relevance (boosting all relevant documents) and scalability (limiting the number of boosted documents to keep query times and query throughput reasonable).
- It makes pagination inefficient and potentially inaccurate, as increasing the number of boosts to account for the increasing document offset while paging through results will slow the query down and possibly result in documents being pushed to earlier pages (missed by the user) or later pages (seen as duplicates by the user).

The first downside is straightforward, as each query essentially becomes two queries executed back-to-back, increasing the total search time. The second downside may not be as obvious. In query-time boosting, we look up a specific number of documents to boost higher in the search results for a query. In our `ipad` search example from figure 8.1 (see listing 4.7 for the code), the boost for the query ultimately becomes

```
"885909457588"^966 "885909457595"^205 "885909471812"^202 "886111287055"^109
"843404073153"^73 "885909457601"^62 "635753493559"^62 "885909472376"^61
"610839379408"^29 "884962753071"^28
```

This boost contains 10 documents, but only because that is the number of boosts we requested. Assuming we only showed ten documents on the first page, the whole first page will look good, but what if the user navigates to page 2? In this case, no boosted documents will be shown, because only the first 10 documents with signals for the query were boosted!

To boost documents for the second page, we would need to ensure we have at least enough document boosts to cover the full first two pages, which means increasing from 10 boosts to 20 boosts (modifying the `limit` parameter to 20 on the boost lookup query):

```
"885909457588"^966 "885909457595"^205 "885909471812"^202 "886111287055"^109
"843404073153"^73 "635753493559"^62 "885909457601"^62 "885909472376"^61
"610839379408"^29 "884962753071"^28 "635753490879"^27 "885909457632"^26
"885909393404"^26 "716829772249"^23 "821793013776"^21 "027242798236"^15
"600603132827"^14 "886111271283"^14 "722868830062"^13 "092636260712"^13
```

You can mostly solve this problem by increasing the number of boosts looked up every time someone navigates to the "next" page, but this will aggressively slow down subsequent queries, as page 3 will require looking up and applying 30 boosts, page 10 will require 100 boosts, and so on. For a use case where only a small number of boosted documents exist for each query, this is not a big problem, but for many use cases, there may be hundreds or thousands of documents that would benefit from being boosted. In our query for `ipad`, there are more than 200 documents that contain aggregated signals, so most of those documents will never be boosted unless someone pages very deep into the search results. At that point, the queries are likely to be slow and could even time out.

Only including a subset of the boosts presents another problem: search results aren't always strictly ordered by the boost value! We've assumed that requesting the top 10 boosts will be enough for the first page of 10 results, but the boost is only one of the factors that affects relevance. It could be that documents further down in the boost list have a higher base relevance score and that if their boosts were also loaded, they would jump up to the first page of search results.

As a result, when a user navigates from page 1 to 2 and the number of boosts loaded increases, unwanted reranking may occur, where results might jump up to page 1 and never be seen or jump down to page 2 and be seen again as duplicates.

Even if these results are much more relevant than search results without signals boosting applied, it doesn't make for an optimal user experience. Index-time signals boosting can help overcome these drawbacks, as we'll show in the next section.

8.6.2   Implementing index-time signals boosting

Index-time signals boosting turns the signals-boosting problem on its head—instead of boosting popular documents for queries at query time, we boost popular queries for documents at indexing time. This is accomplished by adding popular queries to a field in each document, along with their boost value. Then, at query time, we simply search on the new field, and if the field contains the term from our query, it gets automatically boosted based on the boost value indexed for the term.

When implementing index-time boosting, we use the exact same signals aggregations to generate pairs of documents and boost weights for each query. Once those signals boosts have been generated, we just have to add one additional step to our workflow: updating the products collection to add a field to each document containing each term for which the document should be boosted, along with that term's associated signals boost. The following listing demonstrates this additional step.

Listing 8.8 Indexing boosts into the main product collection

```
from aips.data_loaders import index_time_boosts

boosts_collection = engine.get_collection("normalized_signals_boosts")
create_view_from_collection(boosts_collection,
                            boosts_collection.name)

boosted_products_collection = \
  engine.get_collection("products_with_signals_boosts")
create_view_from_collection(boosted_products_collection,
                            boosted_products_collection.name)

boosted_products = index_time_boosts.load_dataframe(
    boosted_products_collection,
    boosts_collection)

boosted_products_collection.write(boosted_products)
```

Loads a previously generated signals-boosting model

Registers the product table so we can load from it and save back to it with boosts added

Inserts all keywords with signals boosts for each document into a new signals_boosts field on the document

Saves the products back to the boosted products collection, with the updated signals_boosts added

The code reads all previously generated signals boosts for each product document and then maps the queries and boosts into a new signals_boosts field on that document. The signals_boosts field has a comma-separated list of terms (user queries) with a corresponding weight for each term.

When using Solr as your search engine (the default), this signals_boosts field is a specialized field containing a DelimitedPayloadBoostFilter filter, which allows for terms (queries) to be indexed with associated boosts that can be used to influence query-time scoring. For example, for the most popular iPad, the product document will now be modified to look as follows:

```
{...
  "id": "885909457588",
  "name": "Apple® - iPad® 2 with Wi-Fi - 16GB - Black"
  "signals_boosts": "ipad|2939,ipad 2|1104,ipad2|540,i pad|341,apple ipad|
    152,ipads|123,apple|118,i pad 2|99,tablets|67,..."
  ...
  }
```

This format for specifying index-time term boosts will vary from search engine to search engine. At query time, this signals_boosts field will be searched upon, and if the query is present in the field, the relevance score for that document will be boosted by the indexed payload for the matched query. The following listing demonstrates how to perform a query utilizing index-time signals boosts.

Listing 8.9 Ranking search results with index-time boosts

```
def get_boosted_search_request(query, boost_field):
  request = product_search_request(query)
  request["index_time_boost"] = (boost_field, query)
  return request
```

Boosting the relevance score based upon the indexed signals boosts for the query

```
query = "ipad"
boosted_query = get_boosted_search_request(query, "signals_boosts")
response = boosted_products_collection.search(**boosted_query)
display_product_search(query, response["docs"])
```

While support for querying on index-time boosted terms is handled differently by various search engines, in the case of Solr (our default search engine), this translates internally into a `boost` parameter value of `payload("signals_boosts", "ipad", 1, "first")` being added to the search request to boost documents by the payload attached to the *first* match of the query `ipad` in the `signals_boosts` field (or 1 if no payload was indexed). See section 3.2 if you want a refresher on influencing ranking like this through functions and multiplicative boosts.

Figure 8.5 shows the results of this index-time signals boosting. As you can see, the results now look similar to the query-time signals-boosting output shown previously in figure 8.1.

Figure 8.5   Index-time signals boosting, demonstrating similar results as query-time index boosting

The relevance scores will likely not be identical when performing index-time boosting versus query-time boosting, as the math is different when scoring an indexed payload versus a boosted query term. The relative ordering of results should be very similar, though. The index-time signals boosting will also apply to all documents with a matching signals-boost payload, whereas query-time signals boosting only applies to the top-*N* documents that are explicitly boosted in the query.

8.6.3   *Tradeoffs when implementing index-time boosting*

Index-time boosting, as we've seen, moves most of the work of performing signals boosting from the query execution phase to the indexing phase of your searches. This solves some of the problems inherent in query-time boosting, but it also introduces some new challenges, which we'll discuss in this section.

BENEFITS OF INDEX-TIME BOOSTING

Index-time boosting solves most of the drawbacks of query-time boosting:

- The query workflow is simpler and faster because it doesn't require doing two queries—one to look up the signals boosts and another to run a boosted query using those signals boosts.
- Each query is more efficient and faster as the number of boosted documents increases, because the query is a single keyword search against the `signals_boosts` field as opposed to a longer query containing the increasing list of boosted documents.
- Results paging is no longer a problem, because *all* documents matching the query are boosted, not just the top-N that can be efficiently loaded and added to the query.

Given these characteristics, index-time boosting can substantially improve the relevance and consistency of results ordering by ensuring all queries receive consistent and complete boosting of all their matching documents. It can also substantially improve query speed by removing query terms (the doc boosts) and eliminating extra lookups prior to execution of the main query.

DRAWBACKS OF INDEX-TIME BOOSTING

If index-time boosting solves all the problems of query-time boosting, why wouldn't we always use index-time signals boosting?

The main drawback of index-time boosting is that since the boost values for a query are indexed onto each document (each document contains the terms for which that document should be boosted), adding or removing a keyword from the signals-boosting model requires reindexing all documents associated with that keyword. If signals-boosting aggregations are updated incrementally (on a per-keyword basis), this means potentially reindexing all the documents within your search engine on a continuous basis. If your signals-boosting model is updated in batch for your entire index, this means potentially reindexing all your documents every time your signals-boosting model is regenerated.

This kind of indexing pressure adds operational complexity to your search engine. To keep query performance fast and consistent, given this indexing pressure, you may want to separate the indexing of documents onto separate servers from where the search indexes are hosted for serving queries.

Separation of concerns: Indexing vs. querying

When performing high-volume indexing, it may be architecturally best to isolate your indexing servers from your querying servers if possible. Otherwise, memory or CPU pressure from busy indexing operations can affect query latency and throughput. Not

(continued)

all search engines support this separation of concerns between indexing and query servers, but many do.

Elasticsearch and OpenSearch, for instance, support this separation of concerns using the concept of *follower indexes*, while Solr does it through supporting different *replica types*. All three of these engines have the concepts of *shards*, which are partitions containing a subset of the documents in a collection, and *replicas*, which are exact copies of all the data belonging to their shard. Each shard has a leader that is responsible for receiving updates and forwarding them to all replicas.

By default, leaders send all document updates to every replica of a shard, and each replica then (redundantly) indexes the document so that it is available immediately to be searched on that replica. Unfortunately, the tradeoff for immediate availability is that high-volume indexing will consume resources on every replica, which can slow down query performance across the entire search engine.

By changing the replica type in Solr for replicas on query servers from NRT (near-real-time) to either TLOG (transaction log) or PULL, you'll instruct replicas to pull prebuilt index files from the shard's leader (which is already indexing documents) instead of performing duplicate indexing. Similarly in Elasticsearch and OpenSearch, if you configure a follower index, the servers hosting the follower index will replicate prebuilt index files from the leader index instead of redundantly indexing the document. Some other search engines and vector databases have similar abilities to segregate indexing operations and query operations across servers that you can explore.

If you plan to do index-time signals boosting and expect to be constantly reindexing signals at high volumes, you should strongly consider isolating index and query-time operations. This ensures your query performance isn't negatively affected by the significant additional indexing overhead from ongoing signals-boosting aggregations.

The other drawback of index-time boosting is that making changes to your signals-boosting function can require more planning. For example, if you want to change your weight for click versus purchase signals from 1:25 to 1:20, you'll need to create a `signals_boosts_2` field with the new weights, reindex all your documents adding the new boosts, and then flip over your query to use the new field instead of the original `signals_boosts` field. Otherwise, your boost values and ranking scores will fluctuate inconsistently until all your documents' scores have been updated.

If those drawbacks can be worked around, however, implementing index-time signals boosting can solve all the drawbacks of query-time signals boosting, leading to better query performance, full support for results paging, and the use of all signals from all documents as opposed to just a sampling from the most popular documents.

As we've seen in this chapter, signals boosting allows for popularized relevance—boosting the most important items for specific queries. In the next chapter, we'll implement personalized relevance—adjusting ranking on a per-user basis, using each user's signals (relative to other users) to learn their specific interests.

Summary

- Signals boosting is a type of ranking algorithm that aggregates user signal counts per query and uses those counts as relevance boosts for that query in the future. This ensures the most popular items for each query are pushed to the top of the search results.

- Normalizing queries by treating different variations (case, spelling, etc.) as the same query helps clean up noise in user signals and builds a more robust signals-boosting model.

- Crowdsourced data is subject to manipulation, so it is important to explicitly prevent spam and malicious signals from affecting the quality of your relevance models.

- You can combine different signal types into a single signals-boosting model by assigning relative weights to each type and doing a weighted sum of values across signal types. This enables you to give more relevance to stronger signals (positive or negative) and reduce noise from weaker signals.

- Introducing a time-decay function enables recent signals to carry more weight than older signals, allowing older signals to phase out over time.

- Signals-boosting models can be productionized using query-time signals boosting (more flexible) or index-time signals boosting (more scalable and more consistent relevance ranking).

Personalized search

9

This chapter covers

- The personalization spectrum between search and recommendations
- Implementing collaborative filtering and personalization using latent features from users' signals
- Using embeddings to create personalization profiles
- Multimodal personalization from content and behavior
- Applying clustering-based personalization guardrails
- Avoiding the pitfalls of personalized search

The better your search engine understands your users, the more likely it will be able to successfully interpret their queries. In chapter 1, we introduced the three key contexts needed to properly interpret query intent: content understanding, domain understanding, and user understanding. In this chapter, we'll dive into the user understanding context.

We've already focused on learning domain-specific context from documents (chapter 5) and on the most popular results according to many different users (chapter 8), but it's not always reasonable to assume that the "best" result is agreed upon across all users. Whereas signals-boosting models find the most *popular* answers across all users, personalized search instead attempts to learn about each *specific* user's interests and to return search results catering to those interests.

For example, when searching for restaurants, a user's location clearly matters. When searching for a job, each user's employment history (previous job titles, experience level, salary range) and location may matter. When searching for products, particular brand affinities, colors of appliances, complementary items purchased, and similar personal tastes may matter.

In this chapter, we'll use user signals to learn latent features describing users' interests. *Latent features* are features hidden within data, but which can be inferred about users or items by modeling the data. These latent features will be used to generate product recommendations and boosts to personalized search results. We'll also use content-based embeddings to relate products and we'll use embeddings of the products each user interacts with to generate vector-based personalization profiles to personalize search results.

Finally, we'll cluster products by their embeddings to generate personalization guardrails to ensure that users don't see personalized search results based on products from unrelated categories.

Personalization should be applied to search results very carefully. It's easy to frustrate users by overriding their explicit intent (usually specified as search keywords) with assumptions based on their previous search activity. We'll dive into the nuances of balancing the benefits of better-personalized search against potential user frustration caused by an engine trying too hard to read their minds. Not all searches should be personalized, but when it's done well, you'll see how it can greatly improve the search experience.

9.1 Personalized search vs. recommendations

Search engines and recommendation engines represent two ends of a personalization spectrum, which we introduced in chapter 1 (see figure 1.5). We also discussed the dimensions of user intent in chapter 1 (see figure 1.7), noting that fully understanding user intent requires content understanding, user understanding, and domain understanding. Figure 9.1 resurfaces these two mental models.

While keyword search represents only content understanding, and collaborative recommendations represent only user understanding, they both can and should be combined when possible. *Personalized search* lies at the intersection between keyword search and collaborative recommendations.

Personalization spectrum

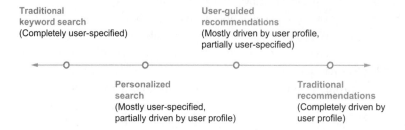

Dimensions of user intent

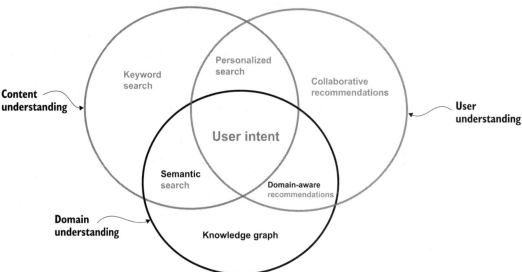

Figure 9.1   The personalization spectrum and the dimensions of user intent

Figure 9.2 superimposes the personalization spectrum on top of the diagram of the dimensions of user intent to paint a more nuanced picture of how personalized search fits along the personalization spectrum.

The key differentiating factor between search engines and recommendation engines is that search engines are typically guided by users and match their explicitly entered queries, whereas recommendation engines typically accept no direct user input and instead recommend content based on already known or inferred knowledge. The reality, however, is that these two kinds of systems form two sides of the same coin. The goal in both cases is to understand what a user is looking for and deliver relevant results to meet that user's information need. In this section, we'll

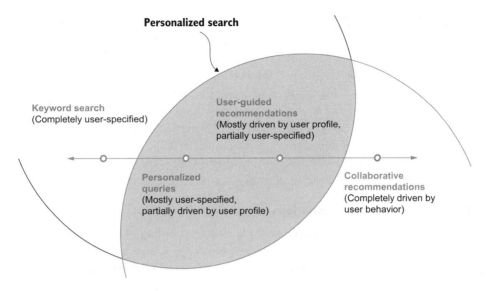

Figure 9.2   Personalized search lies at the intersection between keyword search and collaborative recommendations

discuss the broad spectrum of capabilities that lie within the personalization spectrum between search and recommendation systems.

9.1.1   Personalized queries

Let's imagine we're running a restaurant search engine. Our user, Michelle, is on her phone in New York at lunchtime, and she types in a keyword search for steamed bagels. She sees top-rated steamed bagel shops in Greenville, South Carolina (USA); Columbus, Ohio (USA); and London (UK).

What's wrong with these search results? Well, in this case, the answer is clear—Michelle is looking for lunch in New York, but the search engine is showing her results hundreds to thousands of kilometers away. But Michelle never *told* the search engine she only wanted to see results in New York, nor did she tell the search engine that she was looking for a lunch place close by because she wants to eat now. Nevertheless, the search engine should be able to infer this information and personalize the search results accordingly.

Consider another scenario—Michelle is at the airport after a long flight, and she searches on her phone for driver. The top results that come back are for a golf club for hitting the ball off a tee, followed by a link to printer drivers, followed by a screwdriver. If the search engine knows Michelle's location, shouldn't it be able to infer her intended meaning—that she is searching for a ride?

Using our job search example from earlier, let's assume Michelle goes to her favorite job search engine and types in nursing jobs. Like our restaurant example earlier, wouldn't it be ideal if nursing jobs in New York showed up at the top of the list? What if she later types `jobs in Seattle`? Wouldn't it be ideal if—instead of seeing random jobs in Seattle (doctor, engineer, chef, etc.)—nursing jobs now showed up at the top of the list, since the engine previously learned that she is a nurse?

Each of these is an example of a personalized query: the combining of both an explicit user query *and* an implicit understanding of the user's intent and preferences into a search that serves results specifically catering to that user. Doing this kind of personalized search well is tricky, as you must carefully balance your understanding of the user without overriding anything they explicitly want to query. When it's done well, though, personalized queries can significantly improve search relevance.

9.1.2   *User-guided recommendations*

Just as it's possible to sprinkle an implicit understanding of user-specific attributes into an explicit keyword search to generate personalized search results, it's also possible to enable user-guided recommendations by allowing user-overrides of the inputs into automatically generated recommendations.

It is becoming increasingly common for recommendation engines to allow users to see and edit their recommendation preferences. These preferences usually include a list of items the user interacted with before by viewing, clicking, or purchasing them. Across a wide array of use cases, these preferences could include both specific item preferences, like favorite movies, restaurants, or places, as well as aggregated or inferred preferences, like clothing sizes, brand affinities, favorite colors, preferred local stores, desired job titles and skills, preferred salary ranges, and so on. These preferences make up a user profile: they define what is known about a customer, and the more control you can give a user to see, adjust, and improve this profile, the better you'll be able to understand your users and the happier they'll likely be with the results.

9.2   *Recommendation algorithm approaches*

In this section, we'll discuss the different types of recommendation algorithms. Recommendation engine implementations come in different flavors depending on what data is available to drive their recommendations. Some systems only have user behavioral signals and very little content or information about the items being recommended, whereas other systems have rich content about items, but very few user interactions with the items. We'll cover content-based, behavior-based, and multi-modal recommenders.

9.2.1   *Content-based recommenders*

Content-based recommendation algorithms recommend new content based on attributes shared between different entities (often between users and items, between items and items, or between users and users). For example, imagine a job search website. Jobs may have properties on them like "job title", "industry", "salary range", "years of experience", and "skills". Users will have similar attributes on their profile or resume/

CV. Based upon these properties, a content-based recommendation algorithm can figure out which of these features are most important and can then rank the best matching jobs for any given user based on the user's desired attributes. This is what's known as a user-item (or user-to-item) recommender.

Similarly, if a user likes a particular job, it is possible to use this same process to recommend similar jobs based on how well those jobs match the attributes of the first job. This type of recommendation is popular on product details pages, where a user is already looking at an item and it may be desirable to help them explore related items. This kind of recommendation algorithm is known as an item-item (or item-to-item) recommender.

Figure 9.3 demonstrates how a content-based recommender might use attributes about items with which a user has previously interacted to match similar items for that user. In this case, our user viewed the "detergent" product and was then recommended "fabric softener" and "dryer sheets" based upon these items matching within the same category field (the "laundry" category) and containing similar text to the "detergent" product within their product descriptions.

We demonstrated this kind of related attribute and category matching in chapter 5 when covering knowledge graph learning and in chapter 6 when covering query expansion using knowledge graphs. In those cases, we were mostly expanding the keyword query to include additional related terms, but you could match items based on any other attributes, like brand, color, or size.

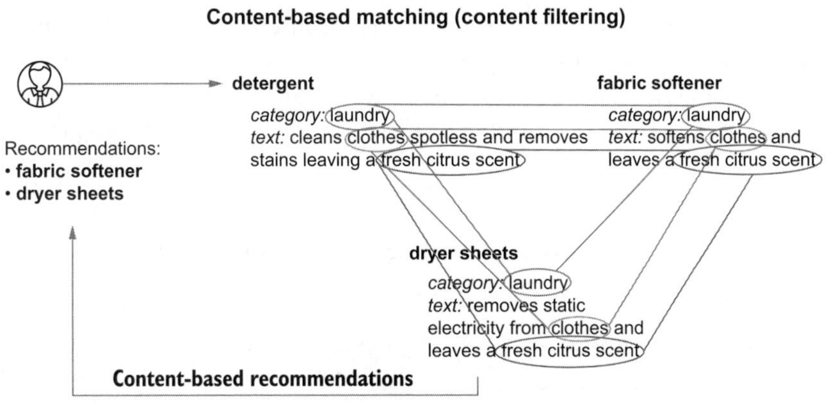

Figure 9.3 Content-based recommendations based upon matching attributes of an item of interest to a user, such as categories and text keywords

It's also possible to match users to other users, or any entity to any other entity. In the context of content-based recommenders, all recommendations can be seen as item-item recommendations, where each item is an arbitrary entity that shares attributes with the other entities being recommended.

9.2.2   *Behavior-based recommenders*

Behavior-based recommenders use user interactions with items (documents) to discover similar patterns of interest among groups of items. This process is called *collaborative filtering*, referring to the use of a multiple-person (collaborative) voting process to filter matches to those demonstrating the highest similarity, as measured by how many overlapping users interacted with the same items. The idea here is that similar users (i.e., those with similar preferences) tend to interact with the same items, and when users interact with multiple items, they are more likely to be interacting with similar items as opposed to unrelated items.

One amazing characteristic of collaborative filtering algorithms is that they fully crowdsource the relevance scoring process from your end users. In fact, features of the items themselves (name, brand, color, text, and so on) are not needed—all that is required is a unique ID for each item and knowledge of which users interacted with which items. Further, the more user-interaction signals you have, the smarter these algorithms tend to get, because more people are continually voting and informing your ranking algorithm. This often leads to collaborative filtering algorithms significantly outperforming content-based algorithms.

Figure 9.4 demonstrates how overlapping behavioral signals from multiple users can be used to drive collaborative recommendations. In this figure, a new user is expressing interest in fertilizer, and because other users who have previously expressed interest in fertilizer tended to also click on, add-to-cart, or purchase soil and mulch, then soil or mulch will be returned as recommendations. Another behavior-based cluster of items including a screwdriver, hammer, and nails is also depicted, but they don't sufficiently overlap with the user's current interest (fertilizer), so they are not returned as recommendations.

We'll implement an end-to-end collaborative filtering example in section 9.3, covering the process of discovering latent user and item features from user behavioral

Behavior-based matching (collaborative filtering)

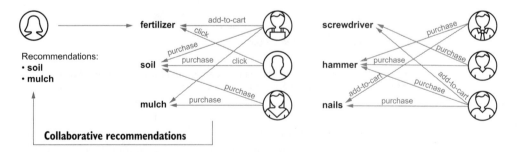

Figure 9.4   Recommendations based on collaborative filtering, a technique using the overlap between behavioral signals across multiple users

signals and using those to generate item recommendations for users. Because collaborative filtering is completely crowdsourced, it is immune to data quality problems with your documents or associated content attributes that may be missing or incorrect.

Unfortunately, the same dependence upon user behavioral signals that makes collaborative filtering so powerful also turns out to be its weakness. What happens when there are only a few interactions with a particular item—or possibly none at all? The answer is that the item either never gets recommended (when there are no signals), or it will be likely to generate poor recommendations or show up as a bad match for other items (when there are few signals). This situation is known as the *cold-start problem,* and it's a major challenge for behavior-based recommenders. To solve this problem, you typically need to combine behavior-based recommenders with content-based recommenders, as we'll discuss next.

9.2.3   *Multimodal recommenders*

Multimodal recommenders (also sometimes called *hybrid recommenders*) combine both content-based and behavior-based recommender approaches. Since collaborative filtering tends to work best for items with many signals, but works poorly when few or no signals are present, it is often most effective to use content-based features as a baseline and then layer a collaborative filtering model on top. This way, if few signals are present, the content-based matcher will still return results, whereas if there are many signals, the collaborative filtering algorithm will take greater prominence when ranking results. Incorporating both approaches can give you the best of both worlds: high-quality crowdsourced matching, while avoiding the cold-start problem for newer and less-well-discovered content. Figure 9.5 demonstrates how this can work in practice.

Content-based matching (content filtering) + behavior-based matching (collaborative filtering)

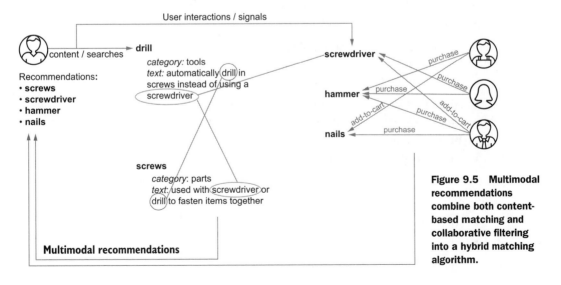

Figure 9.5   Multimodal recommendations combine both content-based matching and collaborative filtering into a hybrid matching algorithm.

You can see in figure 9.5 that the user could interact with either the drill (which has no signals) or the screwdriver (which has previous signals from other users, as well as content), and the user would receive recommendations in both cases. This provides the benefit that signals-based collaborative filtering can be used, while also enabling content-based matching for items with insufficient signals.

We'll implement a collaborative filtering model in the next section, followed by a hybrid personalized search system in section 9.4.

9.3   *Implementing collaborative filtering*

In this section, we'll implement a collaborative filtering algorithm. We'll use user-item interaction signals and demonstrate how to learn latent (hidden) features from those signals that represent users' preferences. We'll then use those learned preferences to generate recommendations.

Pure collaborative filtering, as in figure 9.2, allows us to learn the similarity between items based entirely on user-interaction patterns with those items. This is a powerful concept, as it allows learning about items without any knowledge of the items themselves (such as titles, text, or other attributes).

9.3.1   *Learning latent user and item features through matrix factorization*

Collaborative filtering often uses a technique called *matrix factorization* to learn latent features about items based on user interactions. Latent features are features that are not directly observed but are inferred from other observed features. For example, assume you have four users with the following movie purchase history:

- User 1—*Avengers: Endgame, Black Panther*, and *Black Widow*
- User 2—*Black Widow, Captain Marvel*, and *Black Panther*
- User 3—*Black Widow, The Dark Knight*, and *The Batman*
- User 4—*The Little Mermaid, The Lion King*, and *Toy Story*
- User 5—*Frozen, Toy Story*, and *The Lion King*

Are there patterns to these purchases? If you know the titles or descriptions, you could infer the following:

Users 1–3:

- All of these are movies about superheroes.
- Most of them were made by Marvel Studios, though some were made by Warner Brothers (DC Comics).
- They are all action movies.
- They are not suitable for small children due to violence and/or language.

Users 4–5:

- All of them are animated movies.
- All of them are suitable for small children.
- All of them are made by Disney/Pixar.

Imagine you don't have access to anything other than the product IDs, though. By using matrix factorization, it is possible to observe how users interact with items and to infer latent features about those items. If the features listed in the previous bullet points are the most predictive of the purchasing behavior of similar users, they are likely to be represented in the latent features learned by matrix factorization. Matrix factorization is also likely to discover other features that are not as obvious.

As a different example, in the RetroTech dataset, user signals may show one group of users purchasing stainless-steel microwaves, stainless-steel refrigerators, and stainless-steel dishwashers. Another group of users may be purchasing black microwaves, black refrigerators, and black dishwashers. By clustering the user-item interactions together, it's possible to statistically determine a latent feature that separates these items by color. Additionally, one group may be purchasing televisions, PlayStations, and DVD players, and another group may be purchasing iPhones, phone cases, and screen protectors. By clustering these behaviors together, we can differentiate these product categories (home theaters versus mobile phones) into one or more latent features.

Figure 9.6 demonstrates an example user-item interaction matrix for a few products and users. The numbers are ratings representing how strongly a user (y-axis) is interested in an item (x-axis), with a purchase being weighted higher than an add-to-cart action, and an add-to-cart signal being weighted higher than a click. The empty cells represent no interaction between the user and the item.

Items

	Avengers: Endgame (Movie)	Black Panther (Movie)	Notting Hill (Movie)	The Notebook (Movie)	Minecraft (Game)	The Bachelor (TV Show)
	9	7		1	7	
	2		9	10		10
Users	9	6	3	4	8	1
	10	7	6	8	1	9
	1	3	9		1	7

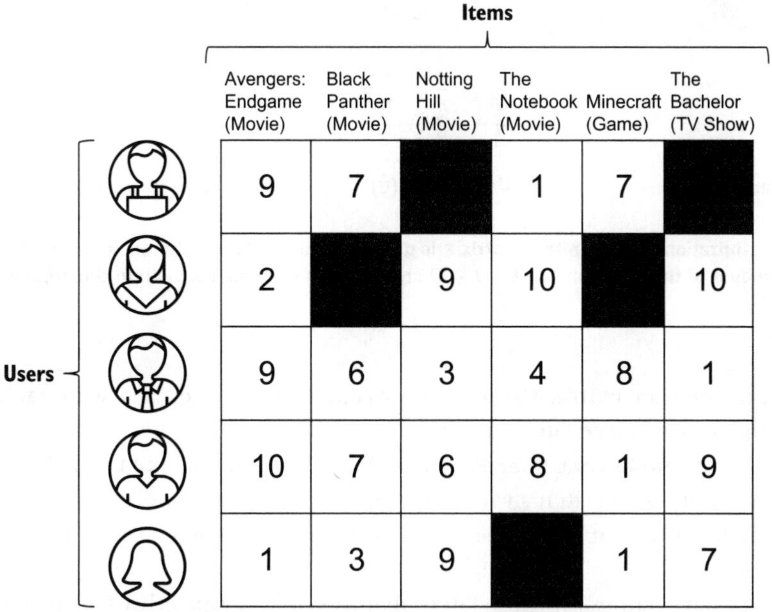

Figure 9.6 A user-item interaction matrix. Numbers represent a user's preference for an item on a scale of 1 (very unfavorable) to 10 (very favorable). Empty cells represent no interaction between the user and the item.

Given the user-item interaction matrix, our goal is to figure out *why* particular items are preferred by each user. We assume that some combination of user interests and item similarities explain these preferences. Matrix factorization, therefore, takes the user-item ratings matrix and breaks it into two separate matrices—one mapping each user to a set of features, and one mapping each item to a set of features.

Figure 9.7 demonstrates the matrix factorization process, resulting in the conversion of the user-item rankings matrix R into a corresponding user feature matrix U and item feature matrix I.

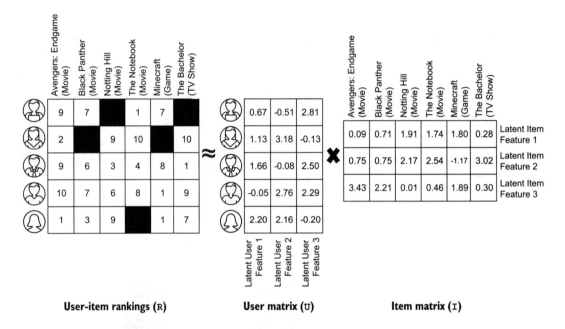

Figure 9.7   Matrix factorization. The user-item matrix R is decomposed into two matrices, a user matrix U and an item matrix I. The product of these two matrices (U · I) should be as close as possible to the original user-item matrix R.

Each row in the user matrix (U) is a vector representing one user, with each column representing one of three latent user features (labeled Latent User Feature 1, Latent User Feature 2, and Latent User Feature 3). In the item matrix (I), each column is a vector representing one item, with each row representing one of three latent item features (labeled Latent Item Feature 1, Latent Item Feature 2, and Latent Item Feature 3).

We don't have names for these latent features or know exactly what they represent, but they are discovered mathematically and are predictive of actual user-item interests. The number of latent features is a hyperparameter that can be tuned, but it is set to 3 in this example. This means that each user is represented by a vector with three dimensions (latent features), and each item is also represented by a vector with three dimensions (latent features).

Once matrices U and I are learned, they can thereafter be used independently to predict the similarity between any user and item (by comparing users in U with items in I), between any two users (by comparing a user in U with another user in U), or between any two items (by comparing an item in I with another item in I). We will focus only on the user-item similarity as a means of personalizing recommendations for each user. Figure 9.8 demonstrates how to generate an item rating prediction for any user.

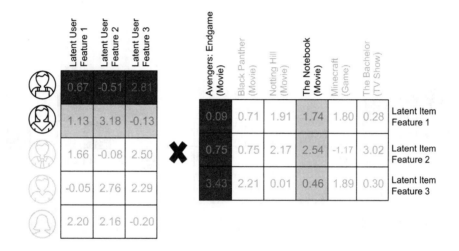

Calculating preferences from latent factors:

Figure 9.8 Calculating a user-item preference from the factorized matrices. Multiply each latent user feature value (first, second, and third values in the row for the user) by the corresponding latent item feature value (first, second, and third values in the column for the item), and then sum the results. This is the predicted user-item preference for the chosen user and item.

For the first user (first row in U), we can generate a predicted rating for the movie *Avengers: Endgame* (first column in I) by performing a dot product between the first row of the user matrix U (0.67, -0.51, 2.81) and the first column of the item matrix I (0.09, 0.75, 3.43), which results in a predicted rating of (0.67 * 0.09) + (-0.51 * 0.75) + (2.81 * 3.43) = 9.32. Likewise, for the second user (second row in U), we can generate a predicted rating for the movie *The Notebook* (fourth column in I) by performing a dot product between the second row of the user matrix U (1.13, 3.18, -0.13) and the fourth column of the item matrix I (1.74, 2.54, 0.46), which results in a predicted rating of 9.98.

While performing individual predictions between a single user and item may be helpful in some cases, such as for generating real-time recommendations immediately after an incremental user interaction, it is often more useful to generate a full user-item matrix R' of predicted ratings for all users and items. Figure 9.9 demonstrates a final user-item matrix R' generated (on the far-right) by performing a dot product of the user matrix U with the item matrix I.

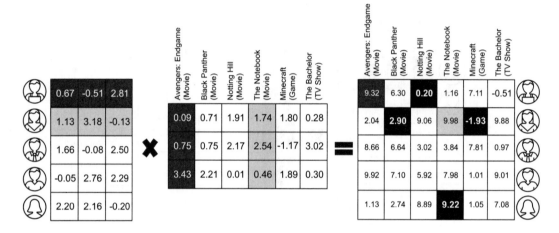

Figure 9.9   Reconstituted user-item matrix R', with previous calculations from figure 9.8 highlighted. Note that the empty values from the original user-item matrix R are now filled in with predicted values (highlighted in black).

When taking the dot product of the user matrix and the item matrix (U · I), the resulting user-item matrix R' should be as close as possible to the original user-item matrix R. Minimizing the difference between the original matrix R and predicted matrix R' is the training optimization goal of matrix factorization. The closer the two matrices are, the better the model's ability to predict similar personalized recommendations in the future.

In practice, the latent features don't perfectly represent all the potentially relevant features. By training with a loss function that reduces the difference between the original R and predicted R', however, the model will maximize the chances of representing R and thus be able to best predict future recommendations based upon past user-item interactions.

9.3.2   *Implementing collaborative filtering with Alternating Least Squares*

One popular algorithm for pure collaborative filtering (based only on user interaction with items) is *Alternating Least Squares* (ALS). ALS is an iterative algorithm that performs matrix factorization by alternating between learning the latent features of items and the latent features of users.

The logic behind ALS is that latent features in a user-item ratings matrix are a combination of the user's latent features and the items' latent features. While the relative weights between users and items for each latent feature are not known upfront, it is possible to begin learning user feature weights by initially using random item weights and freezing them (keeping them constant). As the user feature weights begin to coalesce, they can be frozen and used as inputs when learning the item feature weights. ALS then continues to alternate between further training the user features matrix (with the latest item feature weights frozen) and the item features matrix (with the latest user feature weights frozen). This process is repeated for a configurable number of iterations until the weights of both matrices are well-balanced and optimized. By alternating between learning the latent features of items and users, ALS can iteratively learn the best combined weights of both matrices to improve the predictive power of the model.

The number of latent features learned using matrix factorization is a hyperparameter, called the *rank*. The higher the rank, the more granular the features you can learn, but you also tend to need more data points to reliably learn more granular features. While you won't be able to apply a label to each latent feature (features are just represented as numbers), it's still possible to discover meaningful categories in the data that best predict similar items. ALS is a popular algorithm for collaborative filtering because it is relatively easy to implement and can scale to large datasets.

In this section, we'll discuss how to implement ALS using Spark to generate a recommendations model based on user-item interactions. We'll use the RetroTech dataset, since it contains user-item interactions for a set of products. We'll use user-item interactions to learn latent features about both users and items, and then we'll use those latent features to generate future recommendations.

We'll start by generating a list of implicit preferences for each user-item pair using Spark's built-in ALS implementation. Listing 9.1 generates a `user_product_implicit_preferences` collection, assigning a rating based on the strength of the user interaction.

Listing 9.1 Generating implicit user-item ratings from user signals

```
click_weight = 1
add_to_cart_weight = 0          Only click signals are currently weighted,
purchase_weight = 0             but weights can be set per signal type.

signals_collection = engine.get_collection("signals")

mixed_signal_types_aggregation = f"""
SELECT user, product,
  (click_boost + add_to_cart_boost + purchase_boost) AS rating
FROM (
  SELECT user, product,
    SUM(click) AS click_boost,
    SUM(add_to_cart) AS add_to_cart_boost,
    SUM(purchase) AS purchase_boost
```

```
      FROM (
        SELECT s.user, s.target AS product,
          IF(s.type = 'click', {click_weight}, 0) AS click,
          IF(s.type = 'add-to-cart', {add_to_cart_weight}, 0) AS add_to_cart,
          IF(s.type = 'purchase', {purchase_weight}, 0) AS purchase
        FROM signals s
        WHERE (s.type != 'query')) AS raw_signals
      GROUP BY user, product) AS per_type_boosts"""
```

> Aggregates all signals to generate a single rating per user-item pair

```
signals_agg_collection = \
  aggregate_signals(signals_collection, "user_product_implicit_preferences",
                    mixed_signal_types_aggregation)
```

We modeled support for clicks, add-to-cart, and purchase signals, though we only assigned a weight of 1 to clicks and 0 to both add-to-cart and purchase signals. We did this to keep the math more straightforward for the ALS algorithm, but you can experiment with turning on add-to-cart or purchase signals by increasing their weights to a positive number. These weights are somewhat arbitrary, but the idea is to differentiate the strength of the user's product interest based on their level of interaction. You could also simplify by just assigning a rating of 1 for each user-item pair if you don't have confidence that more interactions by a user necessarily indicates a stronger rating or that the weights you've chosen are meaningful.

With our user-item ratings prepared, we'll generate a dataframe from the prepared collection to train and test the model. Our dataset contains less than 50,000 products, and we'll be using all of them in listing 9.2; however, you may want to modify the `top_product_count_for_recs` to a substantially lower number if you want to run through it quickly. Depending on your hardware and Docker resource configuration, it could take anywhere from several minutes to several days to run. For a quick (but low-quality) run, consider testing with 1,000 products initially (`top_product_count_for_recs=1000`) and then scaling up as you feel comfortable.

Listing 9.2 Preparing the user-product-ratings data for training

```
create_view_from_collection(signals_agg_collection,
                            "user_product_implicit_preferences")

top_product_count_for_recs = 50000
user_preference_query = f"""
SELECT user, product, rating
FROM user_product_implicit_preferences
WHERE product IN (
  SELECT product FROM (
    SELECT product, COUNT(user) user_count
    FROM user_product_implicit_preferences
    GROUP BY product
    ORDER BY user_count DESC
    LIMIT {top_product_count_for_recs}
  ) AS top_products)
ORDER BY rating DESC"""

user_prefs = spark.sql(user_preference_query)
```

> Decreasing the number of products can speed up training, but with reduced accuracy.

> Returns the user, product, and rating

> Limits the number recommendations to the most popular products

Our dataframe contains three columns: `user`, `product`, and `rating`. For performance reasons, many machine learning algorithms (including Spark's ALS implementation, which we will be using) prefer to deal with numeric IDs instead of strings. Spark contains a `StringIndexer` helper object that can be used to convert string IDs to numeric IDs, and a corresponding `IndexToString` object that can be used to convert the numeric IDs back to string IDs. Listing 9.3 integrates this ID conversion into our dataframe.

> **Listing 9.3 Converting IDs to integers for Spark's ALS algorithm**

```
def order_preferences(prefs):
  return prefs.orderBy(col("userIndex").asc(),
                       col("rating").desc(),
                       col("product").asc())

def strings_to_indexes(ratings, user_indexer,
                       product_indexer):
  transformed = product_indexer.transform(
    user_indexer.transform(ratings))
  return order_preferences(transformed)

def indexes_to_strings(ratings, user_indexer,
                       product_indexer):
  user_converter = IndexToString(inputCol="userIndex",
                                 outputCol="user",
                   labels=user_indexer.labels)
  product_converter = IndexToString(inputCol="productIndex",
                                    outputCol="product",
                      labels=product_indexer.labels)
  converted = user_converter.transform(
    product_converter.transform(ratings))
  return order_preferences(converted)

user_indexer = StringIndexer(inputCol="user",
      outputCol="userIndex").fit(user_prefs)
product_indexer = StringIndexer(inputCol="product",
         outputCol="productIndex").fit(user_prefs)

indexed_prefs = strings_to_indexes(user_prefs, user_indexer, product_indexer)
indexed_prefs.show(10)
```

- **Transforms user and product columns into index columns for the dataframe** — `strings_to_indexes`
- **The numeric index-to-string mappings for product and user**
- **Performs the index-to-string transformation for the user identifier**
- **Maps the string user field to an integer index named userIndex**
- **Maps the string product field to an integer index named productIndex**

Output:

```
+-------+------------+------+---------+------------+
|  user |    product |rating|userIndex|productIndex|
+-------+------------+------+---------+------------+
|u159789|008888345435|    1|      0.0|      5073.0|
|u159789|014633196870|    1|      0.0|      4525.0|
|u159789|018713571687|    1|      0.0|     10355.0|
|u159789|024543718710|    1|      0.0|       263.0|
|u159789|025192979620|    1|      0.0|     12289.0|
|u159789|025193102324|    1|      0.0|      9650.0|
|u159789|085391163121|    1|      0.0|      9196.0|
|u159789|720616236029|    1|      0.0|      2781.0|
|u159789|801213001996|    1|      0.0|     28736.0|
|u159789|813985010007|    1|      0.0|      5819.0|
+-------+------------+------+---------+------------+
only showing top 10 rows
```

As you can see from listing 9.3, our dataframe now contains two additional columns: userIndex and productIndex. We'll use these numeric IDs going forward in the ALS implementation code, before we call the indexes_to_strings function at the very end to convert back to our original string IDs.

Now that our user-item preferences dataframe is prepared, it's time to invoke the ALS algorithm. ALS requires three parameters: userCol, itemCol, and ratingCol, which correspond to the userIndex, productIndex, and rating columns in our dataframe. We'll also set a few other parameters, including the following:

- maxIter=3 (the maximum number of iterations to run)
- rank=10 (the number of latent features to learn)
- regParam=0.15 (the regularization parameter)
- implicitPrefs=True (whether to treat the ratings as implicit or explicit)
- coldStartStrategy=drop (how to handle new users or items that were not present in the training data)

Listing 9.4 demonstrates how to invoke ALS with these parameters.

Listing 9.4 Training an ALS model using Spark

```
from pyspark.ml.evaluation import RegressionEvaluator
from pyspark.ml.recommendation import ALS                    Trains the ALS model
from pyspark.sql import Row                                   with the user preferences
                                                             in the training set
als = ALS(maxIter=3, rank=10, regParam=0.15, implicitPrefs=True,
          userCol="userIndex", itemCol="productIndex", ratingCol="rating",
          coldStartStrategy="drop", seed=0)

(training_data, test_data) = \              Splits the preferences, 95% as
  user_prefs.randomSplit([0.95, 0.05], 0)   training data and 5% as test data

training_data = strings_to_indexes(training_data, user_indexer, product_indexer)
test_data = strings_to_indexes(test_data, user_indexer, product_indexer)

model = als.fit(training_data)
predictions = model.transform(test_data)
evaluator = RegressionEvaluator(metricName="rmse",
                                labelCol="rating",          Measures the trained
                     predictionCol="prediction")            model against the user
rmse = evaluator.evaluate(predictions)                      preferences in the test set
print(f"Root-mean-square error = {rmse}")
```

Output:

```
Root-mean-square error = 1.0007877733299877
```

You have now trained a recommendation model! We split the data into a training set (95%) and a test set (5%), built the ALS model, and then ran an evaluator to calculate a root mean square error (RMSE) loss function to measure the quality of the model. The RMSE is a measure of how far off the predicted ratings are from the actual ratings, so the lower the RMSE, the better the model. The absolute value of the RMSE is less important than the relative value across different model training passes, as the calculation depends on the scale used in the underlying data. If you increase the maxIter, find an optimal rank, and increase the top_product_count_for_recs when preparing the user-product-ratings data, you'll likely see the RMSE decrease a bit due to improvement in the model.

Now that the model is trained, we can use it to generate recommendations. Listing 9.5 demonstrates how to generate item recommendations for all users. We'll generate 10 recommendations for each user and display the top 5 users' recommendations.

Listing 9.5   Generating user-item recommendations from the ALS model

```
indexed_user_recs = model.recommendForAllUsers(10) \
                        .orderBy(col("userIndex").asc())
indexed_user_recs.show(5, truncate=64)
```

Output:

```
+----------+----------------------------------------------------------------+
|userIndex|                                                  recommendations|
+----------+----------------------------------------------------------------+
|        0|[{6, 0.022541389}, {13, 0.015104328}, {36, 0.010634022}, {20,...|
|        1|[{13, 0.009001873}, {3, 0.007981183}, {23, 0.0050935573}, {31...|
|        2|[{9, 0.06319133}, {17, 0.04681776}, {3, 0.041046627}, {14, 0....|
|        3|[{17, 0.0145240165}, {14, 0.01413305}, {12, 0.012459144}, {39...|
|        4|[{14, 0.006752351}, {4, 0.004651022}, {10, 0.004487163}, {17,...|
+----------+----------------------------------------------------------------+
only showing top 5 rows
```

Note that the format of the recommendations is a bit awkward. We're stuck with the userIndex instead of our original user, and the recommendations column is an array of structs, with each struct containing a productIndex and a rating. Let's clean this up by converting each user-item recommendation into a row and replacing the userIndex and productIndex values with our original user and product IDs. Listing 9.6 demonstrates how to do this.

Listing 9.6   Converting recommendations into a final, cleaned-up format

```
column_exploder = explode("recommendations").alias("productIndex_rating")
user_item_recs = indexed_user_recs.select("userIndex", column_exploder) \
                    .select("userIndex", col("productIndex_rating.*"))
user_item_recs = indexes_to_strings(user_item_recs, user_indexer,
                                    product_indexer)
user_item_recs = user_item_recs.select("user", "product",
                                    col("rating").alias("boost"))
```

In this listing, we first explode the recommendations into separate rows for each recommendation with rec.productIndex and rec.rating columns. After selecting userIndex onto each row, we select rec.productIndex as productIndex and rec

.rating as rating. Finally, we convert back to user and product from userIndex and productIndex, and we return user, product, and boost.

Let's save our recommendations to a collection for future use. This will enable us to serve the recommendations instantly from the search engine or to use them as boosts to personalize search results. Listing 9.7 writes our user-item recommendations dataframe to a user_item_recommendations collection in the search engine, following a data format similar to the one we used in chapter 8 to represent signal boosts.

Listing 9.7   Indexing the recommendations into the search engine

```
recs_collection = engine.create_collection("user_item_recommendations")
recs_collection.write(user_item_recs)
```

You have now generated item recommendations for users based on their interactions with items, and you've saved them for future use in the user_item_recommendations collection in the search engine. Next, we'll demonstrate how we can serve these recommendations and use them to personalize search results.

9.3.3   *Personalizing search results with recommendation boosting*

With user-item recommendations generated, we can now personalize search results. The only difference between our collection schema for the signals_boosts collection in chapter 8 and the user_item_recommendations collection here is the replacement of the query column with a user column. In other words, whereas signals boosting is based on matching a particular keyword query and applying associated item relevance boosts, personalization is based on matching a particular user and applying associated item relevance boosts.

With our recommendations collection now populated from listing 9.7, we can either serve the recommendations directly (no keyword query) or use the recommendations to personalize search results by boosting them based on the user's recommendations.

PURE COLLABORATIVE RECOMMENDATIONS

Serving recommendations directly is straightforward, so we'll start there. Listing 9.8 shows recent signals for one of our users, for whom we'll demonstrate these personalization techniques.

Listing 9.8   Interaction history for our target user

```
def signals_request(user_id):
  return {"query": "*",
          "return_fields": ["signal_time", "type", "target"],
          "order_by": [("signal_time", "asc")],
          "filters": [("user", user_id)]}

user_id = "u478462"                                          ◁── User for whom we'll be
signals_collection = engine.get_collection("signals")            personalizing results

request = signals_request(user_id)
```

```
previous_signals = signals_collection.search(**request)["docs"]
print_interaction_history(user_id, previous_signals)
```

```
Previous Product Interactions for User: u478462
+-----------+-----------+-----------+-----------------------------------+
|signal_time|       type|     target|                                 name|
+-----------+-----------+-----------+-----------------------------------+
|05/20 06:05|      query|      apple|                                apple|
|05/20 07:05|      click|885909457588|Apple® - iPad® 2 with Wi-Fi - 16GB...|
|05/20 07:05|add-to-cart|885909457588|Apple® - iPad® 2 with Wi-Fi - 16GB...|
|05/20 07:05|   purchase|885909457588|Apple® - iPad® 2 with Wi-Fi - 16GB...|
|05/25 06:05|      query|    macbook|                              macbook|
|05/25 07:05|      click|885909464043|Apple® - MacBook® Air - Intel® Cor...|
+-----------+-----------+-----------+-----------------------------------+
```

Based on the user's history, it's clear that they are interested in Apple products, tablets, and computers. The following listing demonstrates how to serve up recommendations for this user from our `user_item_recommendations` collection.

Listing 9.9 Serving recommendations using a signals boosting query

```
def get_query_time_boosts(user, boosts_collection):
  request = {"query": "*",
             "return_fields": ["product", "boost"],
             "filters": [("user", user)] if user else [],
             "limit": 10,
             "order_by": [("boost", "desc")]}

  response = boosts_collection.search(**request)
  signals_boosts = response["docs"]
  return " ".join(f'"{b["product"]}"^{b["boost"] * 100}'
                  for b in signals_boosts)

def search_for_products(query, signals_boosts):
  request = product_search_request(query if query else "*")     ◁─┐ Function omitted
  if signals_boosts:                                               │ for brevity; it can be
    request["query_boosts"] = ("upc", signals_boosts)             │ seen in listing 4.3.
  return products_collection.search(**request)

user = "u478462"
boosts = get_query_time_boosts(user, recs_collection)
response = search_for_products("", boosts)     ◁─┐ Queries the recommendation
                                                 │ collection for indexed
print(f"Boost Query:\n{boosts}")                 │ product boosts
display_product_search("", response["docs"])
```

Figure 9.10 shows the output from listing 9.9. At the top, you'll notice a "Boost Query" listed, showing the top-recommended products for the user, along with their relative boost for the user (which was calculated as `rating * 100`). Under that boost query, you'll see the boosted search results for this blank keyword search, which are the raw recommendations for the user.

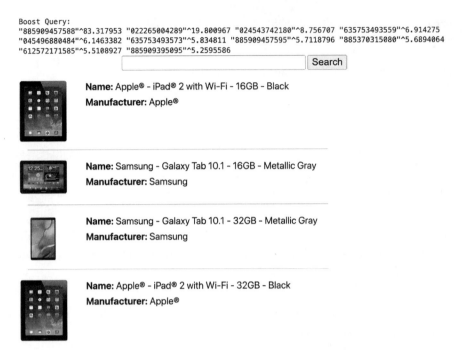

```
Boost Query:
"885909457588"^83.317953 "022265004289"^19.800967 "024543742180"^8.756707 "635753493559"^6.914275
"045496880484"^6.1463382 "635753493573"^5.834811 "885909457595"^5.7118796 "885370315080"^5.6894064
"612572171585"^5.5108927 "885909395095"^5.2595586
```

Figure 9.10   Recommendations for a user based only on collaborative filtering

The recommendations boost a 16 GB iPad to the top, which makes sense given that the user previously searched for and clicked on the 16 GB iPad, with another Apple iPad (a 32 GB model) ranked fourth. You also see other tablets made by competing manufacturers with similar configurations within the top recommendations. This is a good example of how collaborative filtering can help surface items that might not directly match the user's previous interactions (with only an Apple laptop and iPads), but which may still be relevant to the user's interests (similar tablets to iPads).

Recommendations like these can be useful to integrate alongside traditional search results, or possibly to even insert into a set of search results. But it's also possible to use them as boosts to your keyword ranking algorithm to personalize search results, which we'll explore next.

PURE KEYWORD SEARCH VS. PERSONALIZED SEARCH

Instead of serving recommendations independently of keyword search, it can also be useful to blend them in as additional signals in your search ranking algorithm to personalize the results. Going back to our last example, imagine that our user who is interested in iPads and MacBooks from Apple performs a keyword search for `tablet`. How would this look different than if the tablet recommendations were used to personalize the search results? Listing 9.10 runs the query before and after applying signals boosts based on the user's personalized recommendations.

Listing 9.10 Non-personalized vs. personalized search results

```
query = "tablet"
response = search_for_products(query, None)        ◁─── Non-personalized search
print(f"Non-personalized Query")                         results (keyword search only)
display_product_search(query, response["docs"])

response = search_for_products(query, boosts)      ◁─── Personalized search results
print(f"Personalized Query")                             (keyword + user-item
display_product_search(query, response["docs"])          recommendations boosting)
```

Figure 9.11 shows the output of the non-personalized query for `tablet`, whereas figure 9.12 shows the output once the recommendation boosts have been applied to personalize the search results.

The personalized search results are likely much more relevant for this user than the non-personalized results. It's worth noting that in our implementation, the personalization is *only* applied as a relevance boost. This means products that don't match the user's explicit query will not be returned, and all items that do match the query will still be returned; the only difference is the ordering of the products, as items personalized to the user should now show up on the first page.

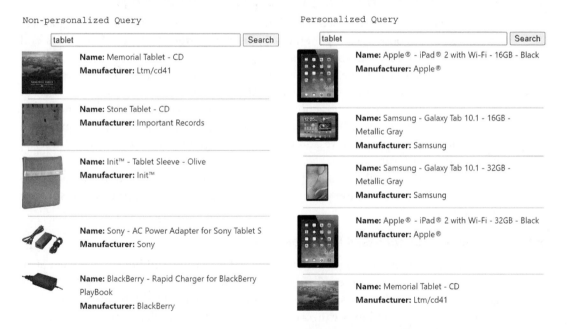

Figure 9.11 Traditional keyword search for `tablet` with no personalization applied

Figure 9.12 Personalized search for `tablet`, where the user has shown an interest in the Apple brand

Also note that after the boosted recommendations (tablets from the recommendation example) the fifth search result is an item from the non-personalized search results, the "Memorial Tablet" titled CD.

This implies two things:

- If you are personalizing search results and not just serving pure recommendations, you'll likely want to generate more than 10 recommendations per user, particularly since recommendations only show up if they also match a user's explicit query.
- The non-personalized relevance algorithm is still critical. If signals boosting based on the query (per chapter 8) was applied in addition to recommendations boosting (based on the user), you would see popular tablets at the top (and not the tablet sleeve and CD), with the personalized tablets then moving up higher among the popular results because of the personalization.

We've now learned how collaborative filtering works through matrix factorization, we've implemented recommendations based on a collaborative filtering algorithm (ALS), and we've demonstrated how to use those recommendations to personalize search results. In the next section, we'll explore another technique for personalization based on document embeddings.

9.4 *Personalizing search using content-based embeddings*

In the previous section, we used user signals to learn personalized boosts for particular items. These boosts were generated by learning latent features about users and items using matrix factorization on user-item interaction patterns.

You could also use these latent factors directly to cluster users or items together. Unfortunately, there isn't a great way to reliably map queries into particular clusters of items based only on user-interaction signals without having already seen the corresponding queries before (the cold-start problem, again). Thankfully, it is quite rare for a search engine to *not* have additional knowledge of items such as titles, descriptions, and other attributes.

In this section, we'll look at a hybrid approach using both content-based understanding and user-interaction patterns to build an evolving user profile to personalize search results.

9.4.1 *Generating content-based latent features*

We've covered many techniques for utilizing fields to filter and boost on explicit attributes in documents. Chapters 5–7, in particular, focused on generating knowledge graphs and parsing domain-specific entities to help with context-dependent relevance.

While those techniques can certainly be useful for implementing personalized search (and we encourage you to experiment with them), we're going to explore a different approach in this section. Instead of using explicit attributes, we're going to use latent features learned from the content of documents to generate personalized search results. We'll use a large language model (LLM) to generate embeddings for each document, and then we'll use those embeddings along with user interactions with documents to build an evolving user profile. Finally, we'll use that user profile to personalize search results.

Figure 9.13 demonstrates conceptually how using an LLM to generate embeddings for documents works. Similar to how we used matrix factorization in section 9.3.1 to create a matrix that mapped each item to its list of latent features, we'll use an LLM to generate a vector of latent features for each document. We'll extract these latent features based on the text of the document mapped into a vector space that has already been learned by the LLM. Don't worry for now about the mechanics of *how* the LLM is trained—we will cover that in depth in chapters 14 and 15. Just know that it is trained on a large corpus of text, and it learns how to map words and phrases into a vector space using some number of latent features that represent the meaning of the text. Each of the dimensions in the vector space represents a latent feature, and the value of each dimension represents how strongly that latent feature is represented in the text.

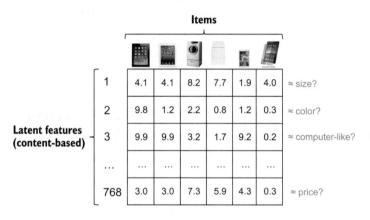

Figure 9.13 Item embeddings from an LLM. Each dimension in the vector space represents a latent feature, and the value of each dimension represents how strongly that latent feature is represented in the text for that item.

The values in figure 9.13 are for illustration purposes and are not the actual values that would be generated by our LLM. We have assigned simplified labels to the features to describe what they seem to represent ("size", "color", "computer-like", and "cost"), but in a real-world scenario, these features would be unlabeled and would represent more complex latent features combining many different aspects learned by the LLM's deep neural network during its training process.

For our examples, we'll be using the `all-mpnet-base-v2` LLM, a publicly available model (https://huggingface.co/sentence-transformers/all-mpnet-base-v2) that serves as a good general-purpose LLM for semantic search and clustering over sentences and short paragraphs, like those in our RetroTech dataset. It is a lightweight model (only 768 dimensions) that was trained on over 1.17 billion sentence pairs from across the web, providing a good general-knowledge base.

The following listing retrieves the fields we need to pass to the LLM.

Listing 9.11   Retrieving product data to generate embeddings

```
query = "SELECT DISTINCT name, string(upc), short_description FROM products"
spark.sql(query).createOrReplaceTempView("products_samples")
product_names = dataframe.select("name").rdd.flatMap(lambda x: x).collect()
product_ids = dataframe.select("upc").rdd.flatMap(lambda x: x).collect()
```

To generate embeddings, we first use Spark to create a new `products_samples` table containing a subset of fields useful for generating embeddings and identifying the associated products. Listing 9.12 demonstrates how we can generate embeddings for each product using the `all-mpnet-base-v2` LLM and the `Sentence_Transformers` library. We'll generate a `product_embeddings` object containing a 768-dimension vector for each product, along with a `product_names` object containing the name of each product and a `product_ids` object containing the ID of each product.

Listing 9.12   Generating product embeddings

```
from sentence_transformers import SentenceTransformer          Loads the all-mpnet-base-v2 LLM
transformer = SentenceTransformer("all-mpnet-base-v2")
...                                                             Optimization
                                                               code to cache
                                                               generated
def get_embeddings(texts, model, cache_name, ignore_cache=False):  embeddings is
    ...                                                            omitted for
        embeddings = model.encode(texts)                           brevity.
    ...
    return embeddings                                    Generates the 768-dimension
product_embeddings = get_embeddings(product_names,       vector embedding for all products
 transformer, cache_name="all_product_embeddings")
```

Because we're using the out-of-the-box `all-mpnet-base-v2` model, loading and generating embeddings for all our products is as simple as the code in listing 9.12. Because the process of generating embeddings for all products can take a while, the notebooks additionally contain some omitted code optimizations to cache and reuse embeddings to save extra processing time.

If we want to compare the similarity of two products, we can directly compare their vectors using dot product or cosine similarity calculations. The 768 features in the vector are pretrained latent features of each document, similar to the latent features represented in the item feature matrix in figure 9.7. This means that we can now

- Generate embeddings for any item or query to get a vector representation of that item or query.
- Perform semantic search starting with any query embedding and find the closest (cosine or dot product) other embeddings.
- Use an item's embedding to generate recommendations for other items by finding the ones with the most similar (cosine or dot product) embeddings.

But what about generating user-based recommendations or personalized search results? In figure 9.7, we not only factored out latent item features, but we also factored out latent user features. The whole idea behind collaborative filtering in section

9.2 is that similar users interact with similar items precisely *because* the items share features that overlap with those users' interest. In other words, a vector representing a user's interests should be similar to the vectors representing the items for which the user has expressed interest.

To personalize search results based on embedding vectors, we thus need to generate a vector representing the user's interests. One way to do this is by taking the average of the vectors representing the items with which the user has interacted. This is a simple way to generate a vector representing *all* the user's past interests, and it works surprisingly well in practice. Unfortunately, personalizing *every* future search based on every past search can be a bit too aggressive, as users often perform unrelated searches for different types of items at different times. To avoid unhelpful over-personalization in these cases, it can be useful to first apply some guardrails across different item categories, which we'll cover next.

9.4.2 *Implementing categorical guardrails for personalization*

The fact that someone searches for an item doesn't always mean they want to see similar items. But if they do want personalization, it is usually a very bad idea to apply personalization across conceptual or categorical boundaries. For example, if someone watches the movie *The Terminator*, which contains violent time-traveling robots, it doesn't mean they want to purchase a robot vacuum cleaner or a gun. As a concrete example from our dataset, imagine that someone previously expressed interest in a "Hello Kitty Water Bottle", a "GE Electric Razor (Black)", a "GE Bright White Light Bulbs", and a "Samsung Stainless-steel Refrigerator". If they subsequently perform a search for `microwave`, which of the items from figure 9.14 would be most appropriate to recommend?

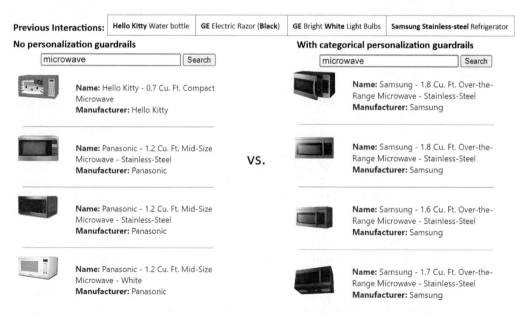

Figure 9.14 Personalization guardrails can help prevent unrelated past interests from unexpectedly influencing future searches

While the user previously looked at "white" lights and a "black" electric shaver, there is no good reason to apply those color preferences to the unrelated category of "kitchen appliances". Additionally, it is questionable whether the interest in a "Hello Kitty Water Bottle" would transfer over to an interest in a "Hello Kitty microwave", or whether looking at "light bulbs" and an "electric shaver" made by the company "GE" would in any way translate into a user having a brand affinity for "GE" when looking at "kitchen appliances". Given that this particular user has already shown an interest in another appliance (a refrigerator that is "stainless-steel") made by the company "Samsung", however, it is very reasonable to assume they would be more interested in other "stainless-steel" appliances made by "Samsung" (or at least by other companies beyond "GE"), such as the microwave for which they are now searching.

Personalization should be applied with a light touch. It is easy to make mistakes and to apply personalization in ways that are not helpful to the user (or are even frustrating and counterproductive), so it's usually better to err on the side of caution and ensure that personalization is only applied when it is likely to be helpful. One simple way to do this is to only apply personalization within similar categories as the query. This is one way of applying *guardrails* to personalization, and it is a very effective way to avoid applying personalization in ways that are likely to be unhelpful to the user.

While your data may or may not have an explicit category field to filter on, it's also possible to dynamically generate categories by clustering items together based on their similarity. This can be done by taking the embeddings for all items and clustering them to dynamically create a data-driven set of categories. The following listing demonstrates a simple method for generating clusters of items from their embeddings.

Listing 9.13   Generating dynamic categories from clustered products

```
def get_clusters(data, algorithm, args):
  return algorithm(**args).fit(data)

def assign_clusters(labels, product_names):
  clusters = defaultdict(lambda:[], {})
  for i in range(len(labels)):
    clusters[labels[i]].append(product_names[i])
  return clusters

args = {"n_clusters": 100, "n_init": 10, "random_state": 0}
algo = get_clusters(product_embeddings, cluster.KMeans, args)
labels = algo.predict(product_embeddings)
clusters = assign_clusters(labels, product_names)
```

Generates 100 clusters using a KMeans clustering algorithm

Assigns each product name to its corresponding cluster label

To ensure that our clustering worked well, we can inspect the top words in each cluster to ensure they are related and form a coherent category. Listing 9.14 demonstrates code to identify the top words in each cluster and to generate a 2D visualization of the clusters using principal component analysis (PCA) to map the 768-dimension embeddings down to two dimensions for visualization purposes.

Listing 9.14 Inspecting popular terms from each product cluster

```
import collections, numpy as np, matplotlib.pyplot as plt
from adjustText import adjust_text
from sklearn.decomposition import PCA

plt.figure(figsize=(15, 15))
pca = PCA(100, svd_solver="full")
centers = algo.cluster_centers_
plot_data = pca.fit_transform(centers)

points = []
for i, cluster_name in enumerate(plot_data):
    plt.scatter(plot_data[i,0], plot_data[i, 1],
                s=30, color="k")
    label = f"{i}_{"_".join(top_words(clusters[i], 2))}"
    points.append(plt.text(plot_data[i, 0],
                           plot_data[i, 1],
                           label, size=12))
adjust_text(points, arrowprops=dict(arrowstyle="-",
                     color="gray", alpha=0.3))
plt.show()
```

- Performs PCA to reduce embeddings down to two dimensions for visualization
- The top words function gets the most common words from a cluster.
- Loops through each cluster and plots it on the graph
- Adds a text label for each cluster with the cluster ID and top-N words in each cluster
- Display improvement: adjusts the text labels to minimize overlap

Figure 9.15 shows the output of listing 9.14. Each dot represents a cluster, with the text label for each cluster including the cluster ID and the top words in that cluster.

While figure 9.15 may appear chaotic, representing all 100 clusters into which our nearly 50,000 products are categorized, you can see clear patterns in the semantic space. The top left of the graph contains kitchen appliances, and music tends to be at the top right of the remaining populated area of the graph (CDs in the top right, musical instruments and speakers in the top middle), and items related to video and data storage tend to be at the bottom of the graph (DVDs and Blu-ray at the bottom right, home theaters and cameras in the bottom middle, computer memory cards and storage in the bottom left along with other computer peripherals). Feel free to inspect the various categories and relationships between the clusters, but realize that they have been mapped down from 768 dimensions into 2 dimensions, so much of the richness represented by the KMeans clustering algorithm will be lost in the visualization.

Now that we have clusters available to categorize products (and signals corresponding to interacted-with products), we need to ensure that we can map queries into the correct clusters. There are multiple ways to do this:

- *Model-driven*—Just pass the query through the LLM, and use the resulting embedding vector to find the closest categories.
- *Behavior-driven*—Use query signals and corresponding interaction signals (such as clicks) to determine the most likely categories for popular queries.
- *Content-driven*—Run a keyword or semantic search, and find the top categories in the results.
- *Hybrid*—Use any combination of these approaches.

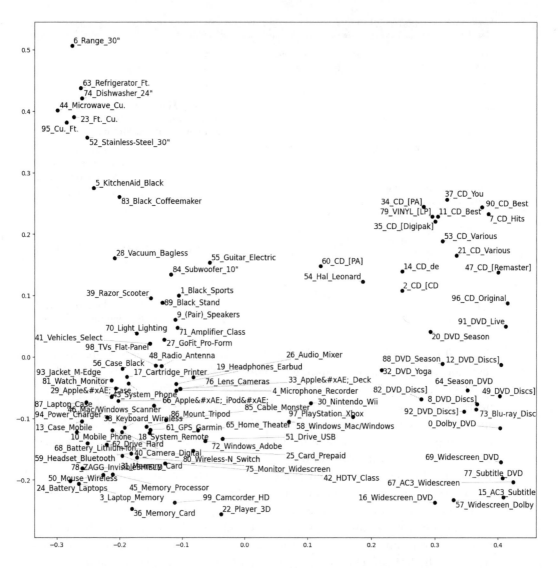

Figure 9.15   Clusters generated by KMeans clustering of all product embeddings, to be used for categorizing all queries and products

The behavior-driven approach follows the signals-boosting methodology from chapter 8, but it aggregates by the categories associated with the top boosted documents instead of by queries. The content-driven approach enables you to use the other semantic search techniques explored in chapters 5–7. For simplicity, we'll use the model-driven approach here and give deference to the LLM to determine the meaning of the query. The following listing demonstrates three different approaches for deriving the top categories for a query based on the embedding vectors.

Listing 9.15 Comparing techniques for mapping queries to clusters

```
import sentence_transformers, heapq                    Gets the top N clusters
                                                       based on cosine similarity
def get_top_labels_centers(query, centers, n=2):  ⟵┘  with the cluster centroids
  query_embedding = transformer.encode([query], convert_to_tensor=False)
  similarities = sentence_transformers.util.cos_sim(
                            query_embedding, centers)
  sim = similarities.tolist()[0]
  return [sim.index(i) for i in heapq.nlargest(n, sim)]
                                                     Gets the cluster based on the
def get_query_cluster(query):                    ⟵   KMeans model's prediction
  query_embedding = transformer.encode([query], convert_to_tensor=False)
  return algo.predict(query_embedding)
                                                       Option 2: Finds the
def get_cluster_description(cluser_num):               most-similar cluster
  return "_".join(top_words(clusters[cluser_num], 5))  (cosine similarity)

                                               Option 1: Predicts the
query = "microwave"                            nearest cluster (KMeans)
kmeans_predict = get_query_cluster(query)[0]  ⟵┘
print("K-means Predicted Cluster:")
print(f"    {kmeans_predict} ({get_cluster_description(kmeans_predict)})")

closest_sim = get_top_labels_centers(query, centers, 1)[0]        ⟵
print(f"\nCosine Predicted Cluster:")
print(f"    {closest_sim} ({get_cluster_description(closest_sim)})")

knn_cosine_similarity = get_top_labels_centers(query, centers, 5)   ⟵┐
print(f"\nKNN Cosine Predicted Clusters: {knn_cosine_similarity}")
for n in knn_cosine_similarity:
  print(f"    {n} ({get_cluster_description(n)})")    Option 3 (recommended):
                                                      Finds N-most-similar clusters
                                                      (cosine similarity)
```

Output:

```
K-means Predicted Cluster:
   44 (Microwave_Cu._Ft._Stainless-Steel_Oven)

Cosine Predicted Cluster:
   44 (Microwave_Cu._Ft._Stainless-Steel_Oven)

KNN Cosine Predicted Clusters: [44, 52, 5, 83, 6]
   44 (Microwave_Cu._Ft._Stainless-Steel_Oven)
   52 (Stainless-Steel_30"_Black_Range_Cooktop)
   5 (KitchenAid_Black_White_Stand_Mixer)
   83 (Black_Coffeemaker_Maker_Coffee_Stainless-Steel)
   6 (Range_30"_Self-Cleaning_Freestanding_Stainless-Steel)
```

In listing 9.15, we see three predictions being calculated: nearest cluster (K-means), most-similar cluster (cosine similarity), and the *N*-most-similar clusters (cosine similarity). The `get_top_labels_centers` function calculates the top *N* clusters based on the cosine similarity with the cluster centroids. The clustering function `get_query_cluster` calculates a cluster based on a K-means prediction.

The output from these three approaches demonstrates an important point. While the query is for `microwave`, we know that the categories were generated dynamically and may have overlap between products. The K-means model and cosine similarity approaches both choose category 44 (`Microwave_Cu._Ft._Stainless-Steel_Oven`) in this example. While you're likely to find better results by relying on the cosine similarity to measure semantic similarity versus the K-means prediction, the categories returned from each are likely to be closely related. Thus, any personalization would benefit by being applied *across* each of the relevant categories instead of only one. Products can be split across multiple, related categories, and meaningful categories can be arbitrarily split based upon the number of items and nuances of the item descriptions.

To overcome the overlaps between similar categories, we recommend using the top-N cosine predicted clusters (Knn, option 3) instead of filtering to a single cluster. In the results from listing 9.15, this miscellaneous approach returns five related categories: 44 ("microwaves"), 52 ("stoves"), 5 ("miscellaneous appliances"), 83 ("counter appliances"), and 33 ("ovens").

We'll next use these predicted categories, along with the embeddings from a user's previous interactions, to personalize search results.

9.4.3   *Integrating embedding-based personalization into search results*

The final step in our personalization journey is to execute the personalized search. We could accomplish this in many different ways:

- Perform a weighted average between the query vector (embedding for `microwave`) and the vectors for the user's previous interactions within the predicted clusters. This would generate a single vector representing a personalized version of the user's query, so all results would be personalized.
- Perform a standard search, but then boost the results based on the average of the embeddings from a user's previous interactions within the predicted clusters. This would be a hybrid keyword- and vector-based ranking function, where the keyword search would be the primary driver of the results, but the user's previous interactions would be used to boost related results higher.
- Do one of the above, but then only personalize a few items in the search results instead of all the results. This follows a light-touch mentality so as not to disturb all of the user's search results, while still injecting novelty to enable the user to discover personalized items they may not have otherwise found.
- Perform a standard search (keyword or vector), but then rerank the results based on the weighted average between the query vector and the vectors for the user's previous interactions within the predicted clusters. This uses the original search to find the candidate results using the default relevance algorithm, but those results are reranked to boost personalized preferences higher.

We'll demonstrate the last technique, as it is easy to replicate across any search engine, since the personalization/reranking pass can be done as a final step after the original search. This technique will thus work well with both traditional search engines and vector databases.

Listing 9.16 demonstrates the two key functions we'll use to generate our personalization vector: a `get_user_embeddings` function that looks up the embeddings for a list of products and also returns the cluster associated with each product, and a `get_personalization_vector` function that can combine embeddings between a query and all relevant user-item interaction vectors.

Listing 9.16   Functions for generating personalization vectors

```
def top_clusters_for_embedding(embedding, n=2):
  similarities = sentence_transformers.util.cos_sim(embedding, centers)
  sim = similarities.tolist()[0]
  return [sim.index(i) for i in heapq.nlargest(n, sim)]

def get_user_embeddings(products=[]):
  values = []
  embeddings = get_indexed_product_embeddings()
  for p in products:
    values.append([embeddings[p],
                top_clusters_for_embedding(embeddings[p], 1)[0]])
  return pandas.DataFrame(data=numpy.array(values), index=products,
                  columns=["embedding", "cluster"])

def get_personalization_vector(query=None,
                    user_items=[],
                    query_weight=1,
                  user_items_weights=[]):
  query_embedding = transformer.encode(query) if query else None

  if len(user_items) > 0 and len(user_items_weights) == 0:
    user_items_weights = numpy.full(shape=len(user_items),
                    fill_value=1 / len(user_items))

  embeddings = []
  embedding_weights = []
  for weight in user_items_weights:
    embedding_weights.append(weight)
  for embedding in user_items:
    embeddings.append(embedding)
  if query_embedding.any():
    embedding_weights.append(query_weight)
    embeddings.append(query_embedding)

  return numpy.average(embeddings, weights=numpy.array(embedding_weights),
                axis=0).astype("double") if len(embeddings) else None
```

Annotations:
- **Returns a dataframe with the embedding and guardrail cluster for each product** ← (points to `return [sim.index...]`)
- **Returns a vector that combines (weighted average) an embedding for the query with the embeddings for the passed-in user_items** ← (points to `def get_personalization_vector`)
- **You can optionally specify a query_weight and user_item_weights to influence how much each embedding influences the personalization vector.**
- **By default, the weight is split 1:1 (50% each) between the query embedding and the user_items_weight.** ← (points to `if len(user_items)...`)

With the ability to combine embeddings and to look up the guardrail cluster for any product, it's time to generate a personalization vector for a user based on their incoming query and past product interactions. We'll generate a personalization vector with guardrails as well as one without guardrails to compare the results side by side.

Listing 9.17 demonstrates how to generate personalization vectors. In this case, the user has previously interacted with two products: a Hello Kitty water bottle and a stainless-steel electric range. They are now running a new query for the keyword `microwave`.

Listing 9.17 Generating personalization vectors from user queries

```
product_interests = ["7610465823828", #hello kitty water bottle
                     "36725569478"]   #stainless steel electric range

user_embeddings = get_user_embeddings(product_interests)
query = "microwave"

unfiltered_personalization_vector =
  get_personalization_vector(query=query,
  user_items=user_embeddings['embedding'].to_numpy())
print("\nPersonalization Vector (No Cluster Guardrails):")
print(format_vector(unfiltered_personalization_vector))
```
> **Personalization vector with no guardrails (uses query and all past item interactions)**

```
query_clusters = get_top_labels_centers(query,
                         centers, n=5)
print("\nQuery Clusters ('microwave'):\n" + str(query_clusters))
```
> **Gets the top 5 clusters for the query to use as guardrails**

```
clustered = user_embeddings.cluster.isin(query_clusters)
products_in_cluster = user_embeddings[clustered]
print("\nProducts Filtered to Query Clusters:\n" + str(products_in_cluster))
```
> **Filters down to only items in the guardrail query clusters**

```
filtered_personalization_vector = get_personalization_vector(query=query,
  user_items=filtered['embedding'].to_numpy())
print("\nFiltered Personalization Vector (With Cluster Guardrails):")
print(format_vector(filtered_personalization_vector))
```
> **Generates a personalization vector with guardrails (uses query and only items related to the query)**

Output:

```
Products Interactions for Personalization:
product       embedding                                        cluster
7610465823828 [0.06417941, 0.04178553, -0.0017139615, -0.020...  1
36725569478   [0.0055417763, -0.024302201, -0.024139373, -0.... 6

Personalization Vector (No Cluster Guardrails):
[0.016, -0.006, -0.02, -0.032, -0.016, 0.008, -0.0, 0.017, 0.011, 0.007 ...]

Query Clusters ('microwave'):
[44, 52, 5, 83, 6]

Products Filtered to Query Clusters:
product       embedding                                        cluster
36725569478   [0.0055417763, -0.024302201, -0.024139373, -0.... 6

Filtered Personalization Vector (With Cluster Guardrails):
[0.002, -0.023, -0.026, -0.037, -0.025, 0.002, -0.009, 0.007, 0.033, -0 ...]
```

Listing 9.17 performs a four-step process for generating a personalization vector for a user's query:

1 Get the list of product interactions, along with the associated product embeddings and clusters.
2 Find the N (5 in this case) most similar clusters for the query.
3 Filter the list of user interactions down to only items in the query clusters.
4 Generate the personalization vector (`filtered_personalization_vector`) by combining the query and filtered user-item interaction vectors. (Note: we also generated an `unfiltered_personalization_vector` that does not apply categorical guardrails, for later side-by-side comparison.)

The final `filtered_personalization_vector` could be used directly for a vector search across embeddings, as it represents an embedding for the query that has been pulled toward the user's interests in the 768-dimension embedding vector space. In our case, we are going to run an independent search for the query instead, and then use the `filtered_personalization_vector` to rerank the top results. The following listing demonstrates this search and reranking process.

Listing 9.18 Using the personalization vector to rerank results

```
def rerank_with_personalization(docs,
               personalization_vector):
  embeddings = get_indexed_product_embeddings()
  result_embeddings = numpy.array(
    [embeddings[docs[x]["upc"]]
    for x in range(len(docs))]).astype(float)
    similarities = sentence_transformers.util.cos_sim(
            personalization_vector, result_embeddings).tolist()[0]
  reranked = [similarities.index(i)
            for i in heapq.nlargest(len(similarities), similarities)]
  reranked, _ = zip(*sorted(enumerate(similarities),
                        key=itemgetter(1), reverse=True))
  return [docs[i] for i in reranked]

query = "microwave"
request = product_search_request(query, {"limit": 100})

response = products_collection.search(**request)
docs = response["docs"]
print("No Personalization:")
display_product_search(query, docs[0:4])

print("Global Personalization (No Category Guardrails):")
reranked_seach_results_no_guardrails = \
  rerank_with_personalization(docs,
    unfiltered_personalization_vector)
display_product_search(query, reranked_seach_results_no_guardrails[0:4])

print("Contextual Personalization (with Category Guardrails):")
```

> **Reranks all search results based upon cosine similarity to the personalized query vector**

> **Displays the original search results (no personalization)**

> **Personalized search with no guardrails (uses unfiltered_personalization_vector)**

```
reranked_seach_results_with_guardrails = \
    rerank_with_personalization(docs,
        filtered_personalization_vector)
display_product_search(query, reranked_seach_results_with_guardrails[0:4])
```

**Personalized search with guardrails
(uses filtered_personalization_vector)**

Listing 9.18 walks through the entire process of applying personalization vectors to rerank the search results. The `rerank_with_personalization` function takes the original search results and a personalization vector and then reranks the search results based on the cosine similarity between the personalization vector and the embedding vectors for each search result. We invoke reranking twice for comparison purposes: once with and once without guardrails applied to the personalization vector. The final sets of ranked results are each passed to the `display_product_search` function to render the three result sets compared in figure 9.16: the non-personalized search results, personalized search results with no guardrails, and personalized search results with guardrails.

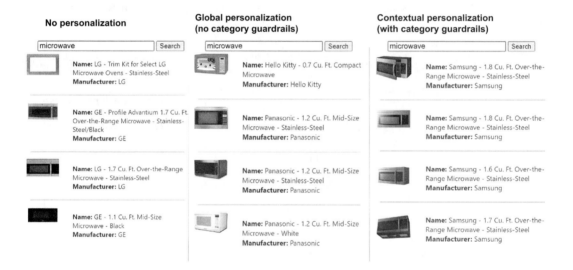

Figure 9.16   Comparing non-personalized, always personalized (no guardrails), and contextually personalized (with guardrails) search results

On the left, we see the original search results for `microwave`, including a microwave cover, some stainless-steel microwaves, and a basic microwave. In the middle, we see personalized search results with no categorical guardrails. The user's personalization vector includes embeddings for a stainless-steel microwave, as well as a Hello Kitty water bottle. As you can see, the Hello Kitty microwave jumped straight to the top of the results, even though the user has previously looked at a stainless-steel refrigerator, and their interest in a water bottle is unlikely to translate into an interest in a Hello Kitty microwave. On the right, we see personalization with guardrails applied. We see that all of these results are now for stainless-steel microwaves, reflecting the user's previous interest in a stainless-steel refrigerator, which was automatically identified as a similar category.

You have now implemented an end-to-end personalized search algorithm. Personalized search can significantly improve relevance when implemented carefully and with a light touch, but it is important to not frustrate your users by over-personalizing. In the next section, we'll review some of the pitfalls and challenges with personalization that you'll need to keep in mind to avoid potential user frustration.

9.5 Challenges with personalizing search results

Throughout this chapter, we've highlighted many of the challenges with personalizing search results. While personalization can be a powerful tool for driving more relevant search results, it is important to be aware of the potential pitfalls and to ensure that personalization is only applied when it is likely to be helpful to the user. We touched on the following key challenges in this chapter:

- *The cold-start problem*—When using collaborative filtering, users who have interacted with no items lack any information on which to base personalization. For such users, it's important to fall back to non-personalized search results. Combining a content-based filtering approach (search or attribute-based matching) with collaborative filtering can help overcome the cold-start problem.

- *Guardrails are important*—Applying personalization across categorical boundaries is generally a bad idea. Otherwise, as a user switches context to look at unrelated items, search results are going to look strange and be counterproductive. Looking at "white paper" or "white light bulbs" doesn't mean a user wants to later see "white" refrigerators when searching for appliances. Similarly, liking the movie *The Terminator* doesn't mean someone wants to purchase a gun or a robot vacuum. When personalizing search results, it is important to understand the relevant scope in which learned user preferences should be applied. Modeling related categories for items and queries and restricting personalization to only using items related to the query is a good way to avoid these problems.

- *Over-personalization is frustrating*—When someone types in a search query, they expect the search engine to return the most relevant results for their specific query. While applying personalization can be very helpful in certain use cases (e.g., location personalization in a restaurant), it can also be very frustrating if the amount of personalization interferes with the user's control over the search experience. As an extreme case, imagine if every query were boosted by features from every previous query or item interaction; the search experience would quickly degrade into an unusable mess that would prevent the user from finding what they're looking for. Consider only personalizing a few of the top results instead of the entire set of search results so that if the personalization is ever wrong, the non-personalized results are still available. Also, consider providing a way for users to turn off personalization if they find it frustrating.

- *Feedback loops are critical*—User interests change over time. Whether you're showing recommendations or building personalization profiles for search, users need to be able to provide feedback to the system to help it learn and adapt to their changing interests. This can be done by allowing users to provide explicit feedback (e.g., thumbs up or thumbs down) on recommendations, or by just continuing to collect implicit feedback from behavioral signals (clicks, purchases, and so on) and using newer interactions to update the personalization profile. In either case, it is important to provide a way for users to provide feedback to the system so that it can learn and adapt to their changing interests over time.

- *Privacy can be a concern*—Because personalization is based on previous user-interaction patterns, showing personalized recommendations and search results means collecting and exposing a user's past behavior. Imagine a movie-streaming service suggesting violent or adult-themed movies, a bookstore suggesting romance novels or self-improvement titles, or a grocery store boosting junk food and alcohol. This could both be embarrassing and demoralizing for the user, eroding both trust and confidence in the service. It is important to be transparent about what signals are being collected and how they are being used. It is also important to provide a way for users to opt out of personalization if they are concerned about their privacy.

- *Apply personalization with a light touch*—Most search engines do not personalize search results, leaving the user in full control of expressing their interests through their current query. Deviating from this paradigm can be beneficial in many cases, but it is important to ensure that personalization is only applied when it is likely to be helpful to the user. One strategy for ensuring a light touch is to apply personalization only to the top few results. It is usually better to err on the side of caution with personalization and apply it very conservatively. Most users will be less frustrated by a lack of personalization than by a search engine that tries too hard to read their minds and gets it wrong.

Out of all the techniques in AI-powered search, personalization is both one of the most underutilized ways to better understand user intent and one of the most challenging. While recommendation engines are prevalent, the personalization spectrum between search and recommendations is more nuanced and less explored. So long as personalized search is implemented with care, it can be a powerful tool to drive more relevant search results and save the user time discovering the items that best meet their particular interests.

Summary

- Personalized search sits in the middle of the personalization spectrum between keyword search (driven by explicit user input) and collaborative recommendations (driven by implicit input derived from user behavior).
- Collaborative recommendations can be learned entirely from user-interaction patterns across documents, but they suffer from the cold-start problem.

Combining collaborative filtering with content-based attributes can overcome the cold-start problem and drive more flexible personalized search experiences.

- Representing documents and users as embedding vectors enables building dynamic personalization profiles that can be used to drive better-personalized search results.

- Clustering products by their embedding vectors can be used to generate dynamic categories to serve as guardrails for personalized search, ensuring that users are not shown results that are personalized too far outside of their interests.

- Incorporating feedback loops to learn from user interactions is important, as long as user privacy is preserved and it is applied with a light touch to avoid over-personalizing.

- Personalized search can drive more relevant search results, but it's important to balance the benefits of personalization with the potential for user frustration if the personalization is too aggressive. Striking the right balance can drive significant improvements to your search engine's understanding of user intent.

Learning to rank
for generalizable
search relevance

10

This chapter covers

- An introduction to machine-learned ranking, also known as learning to rank (LTR)
- How LTR differs from other machine learning methods
- Training and deploying a ranking classifier
- Feature engineering, judgment lists, and integrating machine-learned ranking models into a search engine
- Validating an LTR model using a train/test split
- Performance tradeoffs for LTR-based ranking models

It's a random Tuesday. You review your search logs, and the searches range from the frustrated runner's `polar m430 running watch charger` query to the worried hypochondriac's `weird bump on nose - cancer?` to the curious cinephile's `william shatner first film`. Even though these may be one-off queries, you know each user expects nothing less than amazing search results.

You feel hopeless. You know many query strings, by themselves, are distressingly rare. You have very little click data to know what's relevant for these searches. Every day gets more challenging: trends, use cases, products, user interfaces, and even user terminology evolve. How can anyone hope to build search that amazes when users seem to constantly surprise us with new ways of searching?

Despair not, there is hope! In this chapter, we'll introduce generalizable relevance models. These models learn the underlying patterns that drive relevance ranking. Instead of memorizing that the article entitled "Zits: bumps on nose" is the answer for the query `weird bump on nose - cancer?` we observe the underlying pattern—that a strong title match corresponds to high probability of relevance. If we can learn these patterns and encode them into a model, we can give relevant results *even for search queries we've never seen.*

This chapter explores *learning to rank* (LTR): a technique that uses machine learning to create generalizable relevance ranking models. We'll prepare, train, and search with LTR models using the search engine.

10.1 What is LTR?

Let's explore what LTR does. We'll see how LTR creates generalizable ranking models by finding patterns that predict relevance. We'll then explore more of the nuts and bolts of building a model.

10.1.1 Moving beyond manual relevance tuning

Recall manual relevance tuning from chapter 3. We observe factors that correspond with relevant results, and we combine those factors mathematically into a *ranking function.* The ranking function returns a relevance score that orders results as closely as possible to our ideal ranking.

For example, consider a movie search engine with documents like those in the following listing. This document comes from TheMovieDB (tmdb) corpus (http://themoviedb.org), which we'll use in this chapter. If you wish to follow along with the code for this chapter, use this chapter's first notebook to index the tmdb dataset.

> **Listing 10.1 A document for the movie *The Social Network***

```
{"title": ["The Social Network"],
 "overview": ["On a fall night in 2003, Harvard undergrad and computer
    programming genius Mark Zuckerberg sits down at his computer and
    heatedly begins working on a new idea. In a fury of blogging and
    programming, what begins in his dorm room as a small site among
    friends soon becomes a global social network and a revolution in
    communication. A mere six years and 500 million friends later,
    Mark Zuckerberg is the youngest billionaire in history... but for
    this entrepreneur, success leads to both personal and legal
    complications."],
 "tagline": ["You don't get to 500 million friends without making a few
    enemies."],
 "release_year": 2010}
```

Through endless iterations and tweaks, we might arrive at a generalizable movie ranking function that looks something like the next listing.

> **Listing 10.2   A generalizable ranking function using manual boosts**

```
keywords = "some example keywords"
{"query": f"title:({keywords})^10 overview:({keywords})^20
➥{!func}release_year^0.01"}
```

Manually optimizing the feature weights of general ranking functions like this to work over many queries can take significant effort, but such optimizations are perfect for machine learning.

This is where LTR comes in—it takes our proposed relevance factors and learns an optimal ranking function. LTR takes several forms, from a simple set of linear weights (like the boosts here) to a complex deep learning model.

To learn the ropes, we'll build a simple LTR model in this chapter. We'll find the optimal weights for `title`, `overview`, and `release_year` in a scoring function like the one in listing 10.2. With this relatively simple task, we'll see the full lifecycle of developing an LTR solution.

10.1.2 *Implementing LTR in the real world*

As we continue to define LTR at a high level, let's quickly clarify where LTR fits into the overall picture of a search system. Then we can look at the kinds of data we'll need to build an LTR model.

We'll focus on building LTR for production search systems, which can be quite different from a research context. We not only need relevant results, but results returned suitably quickly, with mainstream, well-understood search techniques.

Conceptually, invoking LTR usually involves three high-level steps:

1. Training an LTR model
2. Deploying the model to production
3. Using the model to rank (or rerank) search results

Most modern search engines support deploying ranking models directly into the search engine, allowing the LTR model to be invoked efficiently "where the data lives". Usually, LTR models are significantly slower at ranking than basic keyword-based ranking functions like BM25, so LTR models are often only invoked for subsequent-pass ranking (or reranking) on a subset of the top search results ranked by an initial, faster ranking function. Pushing the LTR model into the engine (if supported) prevents the need to return hundreds or thousands of documents and their metadata from the search engine to an external model service for reranking, which can be slow and inefficient compared to doing the work in-engine and at scale.

For this reason, our `ltr` library in this chapter implements pluggable support for deploying and invoking each supported search engine or vector database's native LTR model integration capabilities when available. The code in each listing will work with any supported engine (see appendix B to change it), but the listing output you'll see in this chapter will reflect Solr's LTR implementation, since Solr is configured by default. If you change the engine, you'll see the output from your chosen engine when you run the Jupyter notebooks.

Solr was one of the first major open source search engines to natively support LTR model serving, with the capabilities later being ported to a community-developed Elasticsearch LTR plugin (https://github.com/o19s/elasticsearch-learning-to-rank) and then forked to the OpenSearch LTR plugin (https://github.com/opensearch -project/opensearch-learning-to-rank-base). As such, the Elasticsearch and Open-Search LTR plugins implement nearly identical concepts as those in Solr. Vespa implements phased ranking (reranking) and the ability to invoke models during each phase, and Weaviate also implements various reranking capabilities. Other engines that support native LTR will follow similar patterns.

Figure 10.1 outlines the workflow for developing a practical LTR solution.

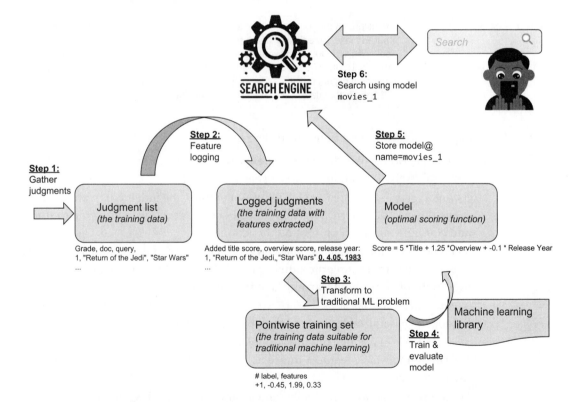

Figure 10.1 LTR systems transform our training data (judgment lists) into models that generalize relevance ranking. This type of system lets us find the underlying patterns in our training data.

You may notice similarities between LTR and traditional machine learning–based classification or regression system workflows. But the exceptions are what make it interesting. Table 10.1 maps definitions between traditional machine learning objectives and LTR.

Table 10.1   Traditional machine learning vs. LTR

Concept	Traditional machine learning	LTR
Training data	Set of historical or "true" examples the model should try to predict, e.g., stock prices on past days, like "Apple" was $125 on June 6th, 2021.	A *judgment list*: A *judgment* simply labels a document as relevant or irrelevant for a query. In figure 10.2, *Return of the Jedi* is labeled relevant (grade of 1), for the query star wars.
Feature	The data we can use to predict the training data, e.g., Apple had 147,000 employees and revenue of $90 billion.	Data used so that relevant results rank higher than irrelevant ones and, ideally, values the search engine can compute quickly. Our features are search queries like title: ({keywords}) from listing 10.2.
Model	The algorithm that takes features as input to make a prediction. Given that Apple has 157,000 employees on July 6th, 2021, with $95 billion in revenue, the model might predict a stock price of $135 for that date.	Combines the ranking features (search queries) together to assign a relevance *score* to each potential search result. Results are sorted by score descending, hopefully placing more relevant results first.

This chapter follows the steps in figure 10.1 to train an LTR model:

1 *Gather judgments*—We derive judgments from clicks or other sources. We'll cover this step in depth in chapter 11.

2 *Feature logging*—To train a model, we must combine the judgments with features to see the overall pattern. This step requires us to ask the search engine to store and compute queries representing the features.

3 *Transform to a traditional machine learning problem*—You'll see that most LTR really is about translating the ranking task into something that looks more like the "traditional machine learning" column in table 10.1.

4 *Train and evaluate the model*—Here we construct our model and confirm that it is, indeed, generalizable, and thus will perform well for queries it hasn't seen.

5 *Store the model*—We upload the model to our search infrastructure, tell the search engine which features to use as input, and enable it for users to use in their searches.

6 *Search using the model*—We finally can execute searches using the model!

The rest of the chapter will walk through each of these steps in detail to build our first LTR implementation. Let's get cracking!

10.2   Step 1: A judgment list, starting with the training data

You already saw what LTR is at a high level, so let's get into the nitty-gritty. Before implementing LTR, we must first learn about the data used to train an LTR model: the judgment list.

A *judgment list* is a list of relevance labels or *grades*, each indicating the relevance of a document to a query. Grades can come in a variety of forms. For now, we'll stick to simple *binary judgments*—a 0 indicates an irrelevant document and a 1 indicates a relevant one.

Using the Judgment class provided with this book's code, we'll label *The Social Network* as relevant for the query social network by creating a Judgment:

```
from ltr.judgments import Judgment
Judgment(grade=1, keywords="social network", doc_id=37799)
```

It's more interesting to look over multiple queries. In listing 10.3, we have social network and star wars as two different queries, with movies graded as relevant or irrelevant.

Listing 10.3   Labeling movie judgments as relevant or irrelevant

```
sample_judgments = [
  # for 'social network' query
  Judgment(1, "social network", 37799),  # The Social Network
  Judgment(0, "social network", 267752), # #chicagoGirl
  Judgment(0, "social network", 38408),  # Life As We Know It
  Judgment(0, "social network", 28303),  # The Cheyenne Social Club

  # for 'star wars' query
  Judgment(1, "star wars", 11),      # Star Wars
  Judgment(1, "star wars", 1892),    # Return of the Jedi
  Judgment(0, "star wars", 54138),   # Star Trek Into Darkness
  Judgment(0, "star wars", 85783),   # The Star
  Judgment(0, "star wars", 325553)   # Battlestar Galactica
]
```

You can see that we labeled *Star Trek into Darkness* and *Battlestar Galactica* as irrelevant for the query star wars, but *Return of the Jedi* as relevant.

You're hopefully asking yourself "where did these grades come from?" Hand labeled by movie experts? Based on user clicks? Good questions! Creating a good training set, based on user interactions with search results, is crucial for getting LTR to work well. To get training data in bulk, we usually derive these labels from click traffic using a type of algorithm known as a *click model*. As this step is so foundational, we'll dedicate all of chapter 11 to diving deeper into the topic. In this chapter, however, we'll start with manually labeled judgments so we can initially focus on the mechanics of LTR.

Each judgment also has a features vector, which can be used to train a model. The first feature in the features vector could be made to correspond to the title BM25 score, the second to the overview BM25 score, and so on. We haven't populated the `features` vectors yet, so if you inspect `sample_judgments[0].features`, it's currently empty (`[]`).

Let's use the search engine to gather some features.

10.3   *Step 2: Feature logging and engineering*

Feature engineering requires identifying patterns between document attributes and relevance. For example, we might hypothesize that "relevant results in our judgments correspond to strong title matches". In this case, "title match" would be a feature we'd need to define. In this section, you'll see what features (like "title match") are and how to use a modern search engine to engineer and extract these features from a corpus.

For the purposes of LTR, a *feature* is some numerical attribute of the document, the query, or the query-document relationship. Features are the mathematical building blocks we use to build a ranking function. You've already seen a manual ranking function with features in listing 10.2: the keyword score in the `title` field is one such feature, as are the `release_year` and `overview` keyword scores:

```
{"query": f"title:({keywords})^10 overview:({keywords})^20
⮕ {!func}release_year^0.01"}
```

Of course, the features you end up using could be more complex or domain-specific, such as the commute distance in a job search, or some knowledge graph relationship between query and document. Anything you can compute relatively quickly when a user searches might be a reasonable feature.

Feature logging takes a judgment list and computes features for each labeled query-document pair. If we computed the values of each component of listing 10.2 for the query `social network`, we would arrive at something like table 10.2.

Table 10.2   Features logged for the keywords `social network` for relevant (`grade=1`) and irrelevant (`grade=0`) documents

Grade	Movie	`title:({keywords})`	`overview:({keywords})`	`{!func}release_year`
1	Social Network	8.243603	3.8143613	2010.0
0	#chicagoGirl	0.0	6.0172443	2013.0
0	Life As We Know It	0.0	4.353118	2010.0
0	The Cheyenne Social Club	3.4286604	3.1086721	1970.0

A machine learning algorithm might examine the feature values from table 10.2 and converge on a good ranking function. From just the data in table 10.2, it seems such an algorithm might produce a ranking function with a higher weight for the `title` feature and lower weights for the other features.

Before we get to the algorithms, however, we need to examine the feature logging workflow in a production search system.

10.3.1 Storing features in a modern search engine

Modern search engines that support LTR help us store, manage, and extract features. Engines like Solr, Elasticsearch, and OpenSearch track features in a *feature store*—a list of named features. It's crucial that we log features for training in a manner consistent with how the search engine will execute the model.

As shown in listing 10.4, we generate and upload features to the search engine. We use a generic feature store abstraction in the book's codebase, allowing us to generate various search-based features and upload them as a *feature set* to the feature store of a supported search engine. Here we create three features: a title field relevance score `title_bm25`, an overview field relevance score `overview_bm25`, and the value of the `release_year` field. BM25 here corresponds to the BM25-based scoring defined in chapter 3, which will be our default method for scoring term matches in text fields.

Listing 10.4   Creating three features for LTR

```
feature_set = [
  ltr.generate_query_feature(feature_name="title_bm25",
                             field_name="title"),
  ltr.generate_query_feature(feature_name="overview_bm25",
                             field_name="overview"),
  ltr.generate_field_value_feature(feature_name="release_year",
                                    field_name="release_year")]

ltr.upload_features(features=feature_set, model_name="movie_model")
display(feature_set)
```

Engine-specific feature set definition (for `engine=solr`):

```
[{"name": "title_bm25",                          ◁── The name of
  "store": "movies",                                  the feature
  "class": "org.apache.solr.ltr.feature.SolrFeature",   ◁── The feature store where
  "params": {"q": "title:(${keywords})"}},                    the feature will be saved
 {"name": "overview_bm25",                       ◁──
  "store": "movies",                                  A parametrized feature taking
  "class": "org.apache.solr.ltr.feature.SolrFeature",   the keywords (e.g., star wars)
  "params": {"q": "overview:(${keywords})"}},         and searching the title field
 {"name": "release_year",                        ◁──
  "store": "movies",                                  Another feature that searches
  "class": "org.apache.solr.ltr.feature.SolrFeature",   against the overview field
  "params": {"q": "{!func}release_year"}}]      ◁──
                                                      A document-only feature, the
                                                      release_year of the movie

                                                      params are the same params for a Solr
                                                      query, allowing you to use the full power of
                                                      Solr's extensive Query DSL to craft features.
```

The output of listing 10.4 shows the feature set that's uploaded to the search engine—in this case, a Solr feature set. This output will obviously look different based on which search engine implementation you configure (as discussed in appendix B). The first two features are parameterized: they each take the search keywords (`social network`, `star wars`) and execute a search on the corresponding field. The final one is a field value feature utilizing the release year of a movie, which will boost more recent movies higher.

10.3.2 Logging features from our search engine corpus

With features loaded into the search engine, our next focus will be to log features for every row in our judgment list. After we get this last bit of plumbing out of the way, we will then train a model that can observe relationships between each relevant and irrelevant document for each query.

For each unique query in our judgment list, we need to extract the features for the query's graded documents. For the query `social network` in the sample judgment list from listing 10.3, we have one relevant document (37799) and three irrelevant documents (267752, 38408, and 28303).

The following listing shows an example of feature logging for the query `social network`.

Listing 10.5   Logging feature values for `social network` results

```
ids = ["37799", "267752", "38408", "28303"]          ⟵— Relevant and irrelevant documents
options = {"keywords": "social network"}                  for the "social network" query
ltr.get_logged_features("movie_model", ids,
                        options=options, )           Queries the search engine for
                        fields=["id", "title"])      feature values contained in
display(response)                                     the movies feature store
```

Engine-specific search request (for `engine=solr`):

```
                                                     Example Solr query syntax to
                                                     retrieve feature values from
                                                     each returned document
{"query": "{!terms f=id}37799,267752,38408,28303",
 "fields": ["id", "title",
   '[features store=movies efi.keywords="social network"]']}    ⟵—
```

Documents with logged features:

```
[{"id": "37799",
  "title": "The Social Network",
  "[features]": {"title_bm25": 8.243603,
                 "overview_bm25": 3.8143613,        Each feature value logged for this
                 "release_year": 2010.0}},          movie for the "social network" query
 {"id": "267752",
  "title": "#chicagoGirl",
  "[features]": {"title_bm25": 0.0,
                 "overview_bm25": 6.0172443,
                 "release_year": 2013.0}},
 {"id": "38408",
  "title": "Life As We Know It",
```

```
"[features]": {"title_bm25": 0.0,
               "overview_bm25": 4.353118,
               "release_year": 2010.0}},
{"id": "28303",
 "title": "The Cheyenne Social Club",
 "[features]": {"title_bm25": 3.4286604,
                "overview_bm25": 3.1086721,
                "release_year": 1970.0}}]
```

Notice that the search request (for Solr in this case) in listing 10.5 has a return field containing square brackets. This syntax tells Solr to return an extra field on each document containing the feature data defined in the feature store (the `movies` feature store in this case). The `efi` parameter stands for *external feature information,* and it's used here to pass the keyword query (`social network`) and any additional query-time information needed to compute each feature. The response contains the four requested documents with their corresponding features. These parameters will be different for each search engine, but the concepts will be similar.

With some mundane Python data transformation, we can fill in the features for the query `social network` in our training set from this response. In listing 10.6, we apply feature data to judgments for the query `social network`:

Listing 10.6 Judgments with logged features for query `social network`

> Judgment for the movie The Social Network relative to the "social network" query, including the logged feature values

```
[Judgment(grade=1, keywords="social network", doc_id=37799, qid=1,
         features=[8.243603, 3.8143613, 2010.0], weight=1),       ◁
 Judgment(0, "social network", 267752, 1, [0.0, 6.0172443, 2013.0], 1),
 Judgment(0, "social network", 38408, 1, [0.0, 4.353118, 2010.0],1),   ◁
 Judgment(0, "social network", 28303, 1, [3.4286604, 3.1086721, 1970.0], 1)]
```

> An irrelevant document for the "social network" query (note the low first feature value, the title_bm25 score of 0.0)

In listing 10.6, as we might expect, the first feature value corresponds to the first feature in our feature store (`title_bm25`), the second value to the second feature in our feature store (`overview_bm25`), and so on. Let's repeat the process of logging features for judgments for the query `star wars`.

Listing 10.7 Logged judgments for the query `star wars`

```
[Judgment(1, "star wars", 11, 2, [6.7963624, 0.0, 1977.0], 1),
 Judgment(1, "star wars", 1892, 2, [0.0, 1.9681965, 1983.0], 1),
 Judgment(0, "star wars", 54138, 2, [2.444128, 0.0, 2013.0], 1),
 Judgment(0, "star wars", 85783, 2, [3.1871135, 0.0, 1952.0], 1),
 Judgment(0, "star wars", 325553, 2, [0.0, 0.0, 2003.0], 1)]
```

With the ability to generate logged judgments, let's expand the judgment list to about a hundred movie queries, each with about 40 movies graded as relevant/irrelevant. Code for loading and logging features for this larger training set essentially repeats the search engine request shown in listing 10.5. The end result of this feature logging looks just like listing 10.7, but created from a much larger judgment list.

We'll move on next to consider how to handle the problem of ranking as a machine learning problem.

10.4   Step 3: Transforming LTR to a traditional machine learning problem

In this section, we're going to explore ranking as a machine learning problem. This will help us understand how to apply well-known, traditional machine learning concepts to our LTR task.

The task of LTR is to look over many relevant and irrelevant training examples for a query and then build a model to bring more relevant documents to the top (and conversely push less relevant documents down). Each training example doesn't have much value by itself; what matters is how it's ordered alongside its peers in a query. Figure 10.2 shows this task, with two queries. The goal is to find a scoring function that can use the features to correctly order results.

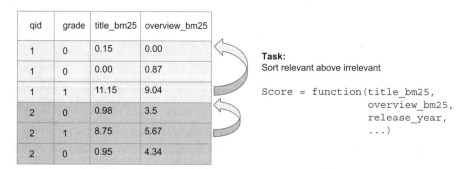

Ranking is *not* direct prediction (ranking optimizes order of a query grouping of examples)

qid	grade	title_bm25	overview_bm25
1	0	0.15	0.00
1	0	0.00	0.87
1	1	11.15	9.04
2	0	0.98	3.5
2	1	8.75	5.67
2	0	0.95	4.34

Task:
Sort relevant above irrelevant

```
Score = function(title_bm25,
                 overview_bm25,
                 release_year,
                 ...)
```

Figure 10.2   LTR is about placing each query's result set in the ideal order, not about predicting individual relevance grades. That means we need to look at each query as a case unto itself.

Contrast LTR with a more traditional pointwise machine learning task: a task like predicting a company's stock price as mentioned in table 10.2 earlier. *Pointwise machine learning* means that we can evaluate the model's accuracy on each example in isolation, predicting its absolute value as opposed to its relative value versus other examples. We know, just by looking at one company, how well we predicted that company's stock price. Compare figure 10.3 showing a pointwise task to figure 10.2. Notice in figure 10.3 that the learned function attempts to predict the stock price directly, whereas with LTR, the function's output is only meaningful for ordering items relative to their peers for a query.

Traditional machine learning using ungrouped, pointwise prediction

Stock price	Number of employees	Revenue
$21.05	1248	$1.65B
$915.00	1295	$590M
$10.05	98194	$200M
$89.58	258	$23B
$27.98	45	$512M
$34.89	12	$812M

Task:
Be accurate at direct point predictions

```
Stock Price = function(num_employees,
                       revenue,
                       ...)
```

Figure 10.3 Pointwise machine learning tries to optimize predictions of individual points (such as a stock price or the temperature). Search relevance is a different problem than pointwise prediction. Instead, we need to optimize a ranking of examples grouped by a search query.

LTR targets a very different objective (ranking multiple results) than pointwise machine learning (predicting specific values of results). Most LTR methods use clever alchemy to transmogrify this "ranking of pairs" task into a classification task per document that learns to predict which features and feature weights best separate "relevant" from "irrelevant" documents. This transformation is the key to building a generalizable LTR model that can operate on specific documents as opposed to only pairs of documents. We'll look at one model's method for transforming the ranking task in the next section by exploring a popular LTR model named SVMrank.

10.4.1 SVMrank: Transforming ranking to binary classification

At the core of LTR is the model: the actual algorithm that learns the relationship between relevance/irrelevance and the features like `title_bm25`, `overview_bm25`, etc. In this section, we'll explore one such model, SVMrank, first understanding what "SVM" stands for and then how it can be used to build a great, generalizable LTR model.

SVMrank transforms relevance into a binary classification problem. *Binary classification* simply means classifying items as one of two classes (like "relevant" versus "irrelevant", "adult" versus "child", "dog" versus "cat") using the available features.

An *SVM* or *support vector machine* is one method of performing binary classification. We won't go in-depth into SVMs, as you need not be a machine learning expert to follow the discussion. Nevertheless, if you want to get a deeper overview of SVMs, you can look at a book such as *Grokking Machine Learning* by Luis Serrano (Manning, 2021).

Intuitively, an SVM finds the best, most generalizable hyperplane to draw between the two classes. A *hyperplane* is a boundary that separates a vector space into two parts. A 1D point can be a hyperplane separating a 2D line into two parts, just as a line can be a hyperplane separating a 3D space into two parts. A plane is usually a 3D boundary separating a 4D space. All of these, as well as boundaries even greater than three dimensions are generically referred to as hyperplanes.

As an example, if we were trying to build a model to predict whether an animal is a dog or cat, we might look at a 2D graph of the heights and weights of known dogs or cats and draw a line separating the two classes as shown in figure 10.4.

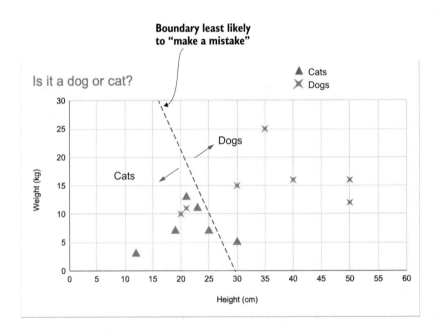

Figure 10.4   SVM example: Is an animal a dog or a cat? This hyperplane (the line here) separates these two cases based on two features: height and weight. Soon you'll see how we might do something similar to separate relevant and irrelevant search results for a query.

A good separating hyperplane drawn between the classes attempts to minimize the mistakes it makes in classifying the training data (fewer dogs on the cat side and vice versa). We also want a hyperplane that is *generalizable*, meaning that it will probably do a good job of classifying animals that weren't seen during training. After all, what good is a model if it can't make predictions about new data? It wouldn't be very AI-powered!

Another detail to know about SVMs is that they can be sensitive to the range of our features. For example, imagine if the `height` feature was millimeters instead of centimeters, like in figure 10.5. It forces the data to stretch out on the *x*-axis, and the separating hyperplane looks quite different!

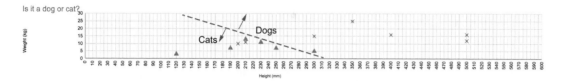

Figure 10.5 **Separating hyperplane affected by the range of one of the features. This causes SVMs to be sensitive to the range of features, and thus we need to normalize the features so one feature doesn't create undue influence on the model.**

SVMs work best when our data is normalized. *Normalization* just means scaling features to a comparable range. We'll normalize our data by mapping 0 to the mean of the feature values. If the average `release_year` is 1990, movies released in 1990 will normalize to 0. We'll also map +1 and -1 to one standard deviation above or below the mean. So if the standard deviation of movie release years is 22 years, then movies in 2012 turn into a 1.0; movies in 1968 turn into a -1.0. We can repeat this for `title_bm25` and `overview_bm25` using those features' means and standard deviations in our training data. This helps make the features a bit more comparable when finding a separating hyperplane.

With that brief background out of the way, let's now explore how SVMrank can create a generalizable model to distinguish relevant from irrelevant documents, even for queries it has never seen before.

10.4.2 Transforming our LTR training task to binary classification

With LTR, we must reframe the task from ranking to a traditional machine learning task. In this section, we'll explore how SVMrank transforms ranking into a binary classification task suitable for an SVM.

Before we get started, let's inspect the fully logged training set from the end of step 2 for our two favorite queries, `star wars` and `social network`. In this section, we'll focus on just two features (`title_bm25` and `overview_bm25`) to help us explore feature relationships graphically. Figure 10.6 shows these two features for every graded document for the `star wars` and `social network` queries, labeling some prominent movies from the training set.

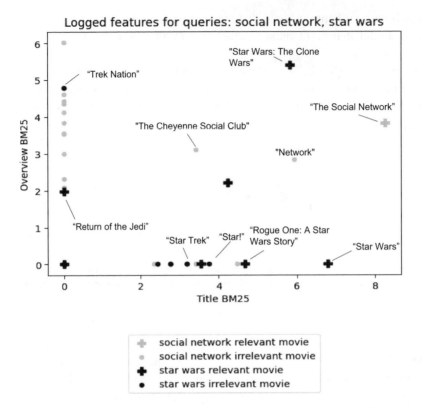

Figure 10.6   Logged feature scores for `social network` and `star wars` queries

FIRST, NORMALIZE THE LTR FEATURES

Our first step is to normalize each feature. The following listing takes the logged output from step 2 and normalizes features into `normed_judgments`.

Listing 10.8   Normalizing logged LTR training data

```
means, std_devs, normed_judgments = normalize_features(logged_judgments)
print(logged_judgments[360])
print(normed_judgments[360])
```

Output:

```
#Judgment(grade, keywords, doc_id,
#         qid, features, weight)
Judgment(1, "social network", 37799,
         11, [8.244, 3.814, 2010.0], 1)
Judgment(1, "social network", 37799,
         11, [4.483, 2.100, 0.835], 1)
```

Unnormalized example, with raw title_bm25, overview_bm25, and release_year

Same judgment, but normalized

You can see that the output from listing 10.8 shows first the logged BM25 scores for title and overview (`8.244`, `3.814`) alongside the release year (`2010`). These features are then normalized, where `8.244` for `title_bm25` corresponds to `4.483` standard deviations above the mean `title_bm25`, and so on for each feature.

We've plotted the normalized features in figure 10.7. This looks very similar to figure 10.6, with only the scale on each axis differing.

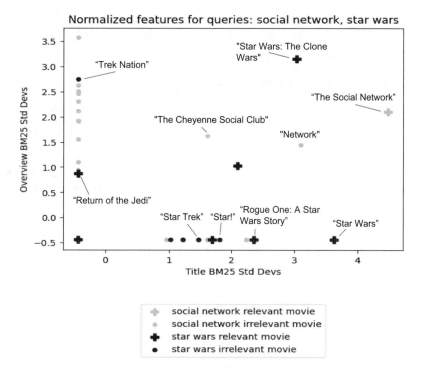

Figure 10.7   Normalized `star wars` and `social network` graded movies. Each increment in the graph is a standard deviation above or below the mean.

Next, we'll turn ranking into a binary classification learning problem to separate the relevant from irrelevant results.

SECOND, COMPUTE THE PAIRWISE DIFFERENCES

With normalized data, we've forced features to a consistent range. Now our SVM should not be biased by features that happen to have very large ranges. In this section, we're ready to transform the task into a binary classification problem, setting the stage for us to train our model.

SVMrank uses a pairwise transformation to reformulate LTR to a binary classification problem. *Pairwise* simply means turning ranking into the task of minimizing out-of-order pairs for a query.

In the rest of this section, we'll carefully walk through SVMrank's pairwise algorithm, outlined in listing 10.9. The SVMrank algorithm takes every judgment for each query and compares it to every other judgment for that same query. It computes the feature differences (`feature_deltas`) between every relevant and irrelevant pair for that query. When adding to `feature_deltas`, if the first judgment is more relevant than the second, it's labeled with a +1 in `predictor_deltas`. If the first judgment is less relevant, it is labeled with a -1. This pairwise transform algorithm yields training data (the `feature_deltas` and `predictor_deltas`) needed for binary classification.

Listing 10.9   Transforming features into pairwise data for SVMrank

```
for doc1_judgment in query_judgments:
  for doc2_judgment in query_judgments:
    j1_features = numpy.array(doc1_judgment.features)
    j2_features = numpy.array(doc2_judgment.features)

    if doc1_judgment.grade > doc2_judgment.grade:
      predictor_deltas.append(+1)
      feature_deltas.append(j1_features -
                            j2_features)
    elif doc1_judgment.grade < doc2_judgment.grade:
      predictor_deltas.append(-1)
      feature_deltas.append(j1_features -
                            j2_features)
```

Stores a label of +1 if doc1 is more relevant than doc2.

Stores the feature deltas

Stores a label of −1 if doc1 is less relevant than doc2.

Stores the feature deltas

Figure 10.8 plots the pairwise differences and highlights important points.

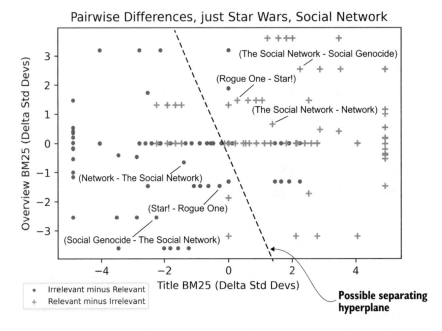

Figure 10.8   Pairwise differences after SVMrank's transformation for `social network` and `star wars` documents, along with a candidate separating hyperplane.

You'll notice that the positive pairwise deltas (+) tend to be toward the upper right. This means relevant documents have a higher `title_bm25` and `overview_bm25` when compared to irrelevant ones.

That's a lot to digest! Let's walk through a few examples carefully, step-by-step, to see how this algorithm constructs the data points in figure 10.9. This algorithm compares relevant and irrelevant documents for each query, comparing two documents (*Network* and *The Social Network*) within the query `social network` as shown in figure 10.9.

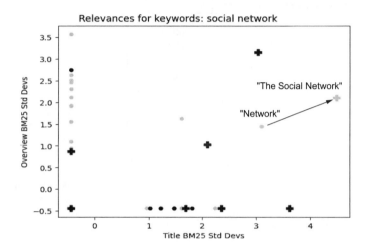

Figure 10.9 Comparing *Network* to *The Social Network* for the query `social network`

These are the features for *The Social Network*:

```
# [title_bm25, overview_bm25]
[4.483, 2.100]
```
title_bm25 is 4.483 standard deviations above the mean, and overview_bm25 is 2.100 standard deviations above the mean.

These are the features for *Network*:

```
# [title_bm25, overview_bm25]
[3.101, 1.443]
```
title_bm25 is 3.101 standard deviations above the mean, and overview_bm25 is 1.443 standard deviations above the mean.

We then insert the delta between *The Social Network* and *Network* in the following listing.

Listing 10.10 Calculating and storing the feature delta

```
predictor_deltas.append(+1)
feature_deltas.append([4.483, 2.100] - [3.101, 1.443])
```
Adds [1.382, 0.657] to feature_deltas

To restate listing 10.10, we might say that here is one example of a movie, *The Social Network*, that's more relevant than the movie *Network* for this query `social network`. Interesting! Let's look at what makes them different. Of course, "difference" in math means subtraction, which we'll do here. Ah yes, after taking the difference we see *The Social Network*'s `title_bm25` is `1.382` standard deviations higher than *Network*'s; similarly, the `overview_bm25` is `0.657` standard deviations higher. Indeed, note the + for *The Social Network* minus *Network* in figure 10.8 showing the point `[1.382,  0.657]` amongst the deltas.

The algorithm would also note that *Network* is less relevant than *The Social Network* for the query `social network`, as shown in figure 10.10.

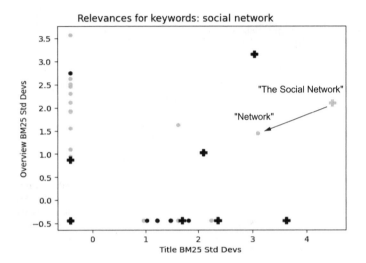

Figure 10.10 Comparing *Network* to *The Social Network* for the query `social network`

Just as in listing 10.9, our code captures this difference in relevance between these two documents, but this time in the opposite direction (irrelevant-minus-relevant). So it's no surprise that we see the same values, but in the negative.

```
predictor_deltas.append(-1)
feature_deltas.append([3.101, 1.443] - [4.483, 2.100])
```
◁⎯ **Evaluates to
[−1.382, −0.657]**

In figure 10.11, we move on to another relevant-irrelevant comparison of two documents for the query `social  network`, appending another comparison to the new training set.

Listing 10.11 shows appending both positive deltas (with the more relevant document listed first) and negative deltas (with the less relevant document listed first) for the highlighted pair of documents compared in figure 10.11.

Listing 10.11   Adding the positive and negative deltas

```
# Positive example
predictor_deltas.append(+1)
feature_deltas.append([4.483, 2.100] - [2.234, -0.444])
```
◁⎯ **Evaluates to
[2.249, 2.544]**

```
# Negative example
predictor_deltas.append(-1)
feature_deltas.append([2.234, -0.444] - [4.483, 2.100])
```

Evaluates to
[–2.249, –2.544]

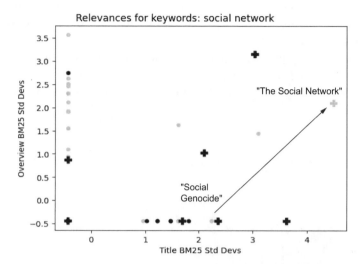

Figure 10.11 Comparing *Social Genocide* to *The Social Network* for the query `social network`

Once we iterate through every pairwise difference between documents matching the query `social network` to create a pointwise training set, we can move on to also logging differences for other queries. Figure 10.12 shows differences for a second query, this time comparing the relevance of documents matching the query `star wars`.

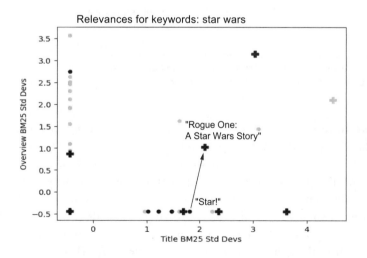

Figure 10.12 Comparing *Rogue One: A Star Wars Movie* to *Star!* for the query `star wars`. We've moved on from `social network` and have begun to look at patterns within another query.

```
# Positive example
predictor_deltas.append(+1)
feature_deltas.append([2.088, 1.024] - [1.808, -0.444])
```

Rogue One features minus *Star!* features

```
# Negative example
predictor_deltas.append(-1)
feature_deltas.append([1.808, -0.444] - [2.088, 1.024])
```
◁── *Star!* features minus *Rogue One* features

We continue this process of calculating differences between feature values for relevant versus irrelevant documents until we have calculated all the pairwise differences for our training and test queries.

You can see back in figure 10.8 that the positive examples show a positive `title_bm25` delta, and possibly a slightly positive `overview_bm25` delta. This becomes even more clear if we calculate deltas over the full dataset of 100 queries, as shown in figure 10.13.

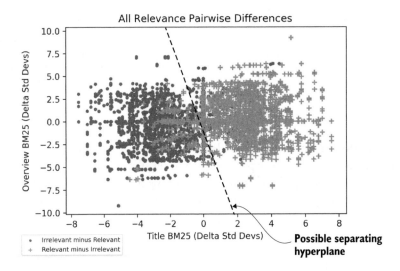

Figure 10.13 **Full training set with a hyperplane separating relevant from irrelevant documents. We see a pattern! Relevant documents have a higher** `title_bm25` **and perhaps a modestly higher** `overview_bm25`.

Interesting! It is now very easy to visually identify that a larger `title_bm25` score match is highly correlated with a document being relevant for a query, and that having a higher `overview_bm25` score is at least somewhat positively correlated.

It's worth taking a step back now and asking whether this formulation of ranking is appropriate for your domain. Different LTR models have their own method of mapping pairwise comparisons into classification problems as needed. As another example, LambdaMART—a popular LTR algorithm based on boosted trees—uses pairwise swapping and measures the change in *discounted cumulative gain* (DCG).

Next up, we'll train a robust model to capture the patterns in our fully transformed ranking dataset.

10.5   Step 4: Training (and testing!) the model

Good machine learning clearly requires a lot of data preparation. Luckily, you've arrived at the section where we actually train a model! With the `feature_deltas` and `predictor_deltas` from the last section, we now have a training set suitable for training a ranking classifier. This model will let us predict when documents might be relevant, even for queries and documents it hasn't seen yet.

10.5.1   Turning a separating hyperplane's vector into a scoring function

We've seen how SVMrank's separating hyperplane can classify and differentiate irrelevant examples from the relevant ones. That's useful, but you may remember that our task is to find *optimal* weights for our features, not just to classify documents. Let's therefore look at how we can *score* search results using this hyperplane.

It turns out that the separating hyperplane also gives us what we need to learn optimal weights. Any hyperplane is defined by the vector orthogonal to the plane. So when an SVM machine learning library does its work, it gives us a sense of the weights that each feature should have, as shown in figure 10.14.

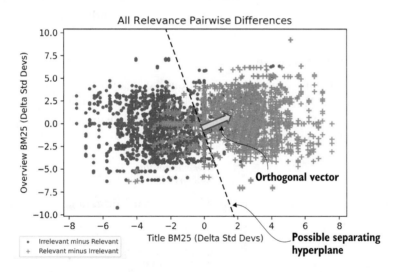

Figure 10.14   Full training set with a candidate-separating hyperplane, showing the orthogonal vector defining the hyperplane.

Think about what this orthogonal vector represents. This vector points in the direction of relevance! It says relevant examples are this way, and irrelevant ones are in the opposite direction. This vector *definitely* points to `title_bm25` having a strong influence on relevance, with some smaller influence coming from `overview_bm25`. This vector might be something like:

```
[0.65, 0.40]
```

We used the pairwise transform algorithm in listing 10.9 to compute the deltas needed to perform classification between irrelevant and relevant examples. If we train an SVM on this data, as in the following listing, the model gives us the vector defining the separating hyperplane.

Listing 10.12   Training a linear SVM with scikit-learn

```
from sklearn import svm                              Creates a linear
model = svm.LinearSVC(max_iter=10000)                model with sklearn
model.fit(feature_deltas, predictor_deltas)          Fits to deltas
display(model.coef_)                                 using an SVM
                      The vector that defines
                      the separating hyperplane
```

Output:

```
array([0.40512169, 0.29006328, 0.14451715])
```

Listing 10.12 trains an SVM to separate the `predictor_deltas` (remember they're +1 and -1) using the corresponding `feature_deltas` (the deltas in the normalized `title_bm25`, `overview_bm25`, and `release_year` features). The resulting model is a vector orthogonal to the separating hyperplane. As expected, it shows a strong weight on `title_bm25`, a more modest one on `overview_bm25`, and a weaker weight on `release_year`.

10.5.2   *Taking the model for a test drive*

How does this model work as a ranking function? Let's suppose the user enters the query `wrath of khan`. How might this model score the document *Star Trek II: The Wrath of Khan* relative to this query? The unnormalized feature vector indicates a strong title and overview match for this query.

```
[5.9217176, 3.401492, 1982.0]          Raw features for
                                        "Star Trek II"
```

Normalizing it, each feature value is this many standard deviations above or below each feature's mean:

```
[3.099, 1.825, -0.568]                 Normalized features
                                       for "Star Trek II"
```

We simply multiply each normalized feature with its corresponding `coef_` value. Summing them then gives us a relevance score:

```
(3.099 * 0.405) + (1.825 * 0.290) + (-0.568 * 0.1445) = 1.702

                                       Relevance score calculation
                                       for "Star Trek II"
```

How would this model rank *Star Trek III: The Search for Spock* relative to *Star Trek II: The Wrath of Khan* for our query `wrath of khan`? Hopefully not nearly as highly! Indeed, it doesn't:

```
[0.0, 0.0, 1984.0]       ◄──┘
[-0.432, -0.444, -0.468]
(-0.432 * 0.405) + (-0.444 * 0.290) + (-0.468 * 0.1445) = -0.371       ◄──────┐
```

Raw features for "Star Trek III"

Normalized features for "Star Trek III"

Relevance calculation for "Star Trek III"

The model seems to be correctly predicting the most relevant answer.

10.5.3 Validating the model

Testing a couple of queries helps us spot problems, but we'd prefer a more systematic way of checking if the model is generalizable.

One difference between LTR and traditional machine learning is that we usually evaluate queries and entire result sets, not individual data points, to prove our model is effective. We'll perform a test/training split at the query level. This will let us spot types of queries with problems. We'll evaluate using a simple precision metric, counting the proportion of results in the top K (with k=5 in our case) that are relevant. You should choose the relevance metric best suited to your own use case.

First, we will randomly put our queries into a test or training set, as shown in the following listing.

Listing 10.13   Simple test/training split at the query level

```
all_qids = list(set([j.qid for j in normed_judgments]))
random.shuffle(all_qids)
proportion_train = 0.1

split_idx = int(len(all_qids) * proportion_train)
test_qids = all_qids[:split_index]
train_qids = all_qids[split_index:]

train_data = []; test_data=[]
for j in normed_judgments:
  if j.qid in train_qids:
    train_data.append(j)
  elif j.qid in test_qids:
    test_data.append(j)
```

Identifies a random 10% of the judgments to go into the training set

Places each judgment into training data (10%) or test set (90%)

With the training data split out, we can perform the pairwise transform trick from step 3. We can then retrain on just the training data.

Listing 10.14   Train just on training data

```
train_data_features, train_data_predictors = pairwise_transform(train_data)

from sklearn import svm
model = svm.LinearSVC(max_iter=10000, verbose=1)
model.fit(train_data_features, train_data_predictors)    ◄──┘
display(model.coef_[0])
```

Fits only to training data

Output:

```
array([0.37486809, 0.28187458, 0.12097921])
```

So far, we have held back the test data. Just like a good teacher, we don't want to give the student all the answers. We want to see if the model has learned anything beyond rote memorization of the training examples.

In the next listing, we evaluate our model using the test data. This code loops over every test query and ranks every test judgment using the model. It then computes the precision for the top four judgments.

Listing 10.15   Can our model generalize beyond the training data?

```
def score_one(features, model):
  score = 0.0
  for idx, f in enumerate(features):
    this_coef = model.coef_[0][idx].item()
    score += f * this_coef
  return score

def rank(query_judgments, model):
  for j in query_judgments:
    j.score = score_one(j.features, model)
  return sorted(query_judgments, key=lambda j: j.score, reverse=True)

def evaluate_model(test_data, model, k=5):
  total_precision = 0
  unique_queries = groupby(test_data, lambda j: j.qid)
  num_groups = 0                                               For each
  for qid, query_judgments in unique_queries:                  test query
    num_groups += 1
    ranked = rank(list(query_judgments), model)                            Scores each
    total_relevant = len([j for j in ranked[:k]                            judgment and
                          if j.grade == 1])         Compute the            ranks this query
    total_precision += total_relevant / float(k)    precisions for         using the model
  return total_precision / num_groups               this query

evaluation = evaluate_model(test_data, model)
print(evaluation)
```

Evaluation:

```
0.36
```

On multiple runs, you should expect a precision of approximately 0.3–0.4. Not bad for our first iteration, where we just guessed at a few features (title_bm25, overview_bm25, and release_year)!

In LTR, you can always look back at previous steps to see what might be improved. This precision test is the first time we've been able to systematically evaluate our model, so it's a natural time to revisit the features to see how the precision might be improved in subsequent runs. Go all the way back up to step 2. See what examples are on the wrong side of the separating hyperplane. For example, if you look back at figure 10.8, the third Star Wars movie, *Return of the Jedi*, fits a pattern of a relevant document that doesn't have a keyword match in the title. In the absence of a title, what other features might be added to help capture that a movie belongs in a specific collection like Star Wars? Perhaps there is a property within the TMDB dataset that we could experiment with.

For now, though, let's take the model we just built and see how we can deploy it to production.

10.6   Steps 5 and 6: Upload a model and search

In this section, we'll finally upload our model so that it can be applied to rank future search results. We'll then discuss both applying the model to rank all documents, as well as applying it to rerank an already-run and likely more efficient initial query. Finally, we'll discuss some of the performance implications of using LTR models in production.

10.6.1   Deploying and using the LTR model

Originally, we presented our objective as finding *ideal* boosts for a hardcoded ranking function like the one in listing 10.2:

```
{"query": f"title:({keywords})^10 overview:({keywords})^20
➥{!func}release_year^0.01"}
```

This boosted query indeed multiplies each feature by a weight (the boost) and sums the results. But it turns out that we don't want the search engine to multiply the *raw* feature values. Instead, we need the feature values to be normalized.

Many search engines let us store a linear ranking model along with feature normalization statistics. We saved the `means` and `std_devs` of each feature, which will be used to normalize values for any document being evaluated. These coefficients are associated with each feature when uploading the model, as shown in the next listing.

Listing 10.16   Generating and uploading a linear model

```
model_name = "movie_model"
feature_names = ["title_bm25", "overview_bm25", "release_year"]
linear_model = ltr.generate_model(model_name, feature_names,
                                   means, std_devs, model.coef_[0])
response = ltr.upload_model(linear_model)
display(linear_model)
```

Generated linear model (for `engine=solr`):

```
{"store": "movies",                         ◁─────────────   Feature store to
 "class": "org.apache.solr.ltr.model.LinearModel",          locate the features
 "name": "movie_model",
 "features": [
```

The `response` from listing 10.16 is Solr-specific and will change depending on which search engine you have configured. Next, we can issue a search using the uploaded LTR model, as shown in the following listing.

Listing 10.17   Ranking all documents with LTR model for `harry potter`

```
request = {"query_fields": ["title", "overview"],
           "return_fields": ["title", "id", "score"],
           "rerank_query": "harry potter",
           "log": True}
response = ltr.search_with_model("movie_model", **request)
display(response["docs"])
```

Engine-specific search request (for `engine=solr`):

```
{"fields": ["title", "id", "score"],
 "limit": 5,
 "query": "{!ltr reRankDocs=9999999
 model=movie_model efi.keywords=\"harry potter\"}"}
```

Executes our model over the maximum number of documents with the specified parameters

Returned documents:

```
[{"id": "570724", "title": "The Story of Harry Potter", "score": 2.4261155},
 {"id": "116972", "title": "Discovering the Real World of Harry Potter",
  "score": 2.247846},
 {"id": "672", "title": "Harry Potter and the Chamber of Secrets",
  "score": 2.017499},
 {"id": "671", "title": "Harry Potter and the Philosopher's Stone",
  "score": 1.9944705},
 {"id": "54507", "title": "A Very Potter Musical",
  "score": 1.9833609}]
```

In listing 10.17, the LTR model ranks all the documents in the corpus using the keywords in the `rerank_query` parameter as input to the model. Since no initial `query` parameter is specified in the request, no matching filter is applied to the collection before the search results (all documents) are ranked by the LTR model. Though scoring such a large number of documents with the model will lead to nontrivial latency, it allows us to test the model directly, absent of any other matching parameters.

Notice in listing 10.17 the use of the term "rerank" in the `rerank_query` parameter. As this term implies, LTR usually happens as a second ranking phase on results first calculated by a more efficient algorithm (such as BM25 and/or an initial Boolean match). This is to reduce the number of documents that must be scored by the more expensive LTR model. The following listing demonstrates executing a baseline search and then reranking the top 500 results with the LTR model.

> **Listing 10.18 Searching for `harry potter` and reranking with the model**

```
request = {"query": "harry potter",
           "query_fields": ["title", "overview"],
           "return_fields": ["title", "id", "score"],
           "rerank_query": "harry potter",
           "rerank_count": 500,
           "log": True}
response = ltr.search_with_model("movie_model", **request)
display(response["docs"])
```

Engine-specific search request (for `engine=solr`):

```
{"query": "harry potter",
 "fields": ["title", "id", "score"],
 "limit": 5,
 "params": {
   "rq": "{!ltr reRankDocs=500 model=movie_model
   efi.keywords=\"harry potter\"}",
   "qf": ["title", "overview"],
   "defType": "edismax"}}
```

First-pass Solr query—a simple keyword query with BM25 ranking

Reranks only the top 500 documents

Returned documents:

```
[{"id": "570724", "title": "The Story of Harry Potter", "score": 2.4261155},
 {"id": "116972", "title": "Discovering the Real World of Harry Potter",
  "score": 2.247846},
 {"id": "672", "title": "Harry Potter and the Chamber of Secrets",
  "score": 2.017499},
 {"id": "671", "title": "Harry Potter and the Philosopher's Stone",
  "score": 1.9944705},
 {"id": "54507", "title": "A Very Potter Musical", "score": 1.9833605}]
```

This request is much faster, and it still yields the same top results when performing the cheaper initial BM25 ranking on the filtered `query` followed by the more expensive LTR-based reranking on just the top 500 results.

10.6.2 A note on LTR performance

As you can see, many steps are required to build a real-world LTR model. Let's close the chapter with some additional thoughts on practical performance constraints in LTR systems:

- *Model complexity*—The more complex the model, the more accurate it *might* be. A simpler model can be faster and easier to understand, though perhaps less accurate. Here we've stuck to a very simple model (a set of linear weights). Imagine a complex deep-learning model—how well would that work? Would the complexity be worth it? Would it be as generalizable (or could it possibly be more generalizable)?
- *Rerank depth*—The deeper you rerank, the more you might find additional documents that could be hidden gems. On the other hand, the deeper you rerank, the more compute cycles your model spends scoring results in your live search engine cluster.
- *Feature complexity*—If you compute very complex features at query time, they might help your model. However, they'll slow down evaluation and search response time.
- *Number of features*—A model with many features might lead to higher relevance. However, it will also take more time to compute every feature on each document, so ask yourself which features are crucial. Many academic LTR systems use hundreds. Practical LTR systems usually boil these down to dozens. You will almost always see diminishing returns for relevance ranking and rising compute and latency costs as you continue adding additional features, so prioritizing which features to include is important.

Cross-encoders

A cross-encoder is a specialized kind of machine-learned ranking model. Cross-encoders are trained to score the relevance of two pieces of input (usually text), such as a query and a document. They use a Transformer architecture to combine both pieces of input into a single representation, which is then used in search to rank the relevance of the document for the query based upon interpreting both the query and document within their shared semantic context. Cross-encoders are ranking classifiers, like other LTR models, but they are unique in that they are pretrained on a large amount of data and are generally only focused on the textual similarity between the query and document instead of other features like popularity, recency, or user behavior. While they can be fine-tuned on your dataset, they are often used as is, since they are already trained on a large amount of data and can generalize well to new textual inputs.

Cross-encoders are very easy to use out of the box, and they're often the easiest way to get started with machine-learned ranking without having to do your own training. Cross-encoders tend to be slow, so they're not typically used to rerank large numbers of documents. Our focus in this chapter and in the coming chapter is on more flexible models that can use reflected intelligence, including those trained on your users' judgments and implicit judgments from user signals, but it's good to be familiar with cross-encoders, as they are a popular choice for many search teams, particularly when just getting started. We'll cover cross-encoders in more detail, with example code, in section 13.7.

10.7 Rinse and repeat

Congrats! You've done one full cycle of LTR! Like many data problems, though, you'll likely need to continue iterating on the problem. There's always something new you can do to improve.

On your second iteration, you might consider the following:

- *New and better features*—Are there types of queries or examples on which the model performs poorly, such as `title` searches where there's no `title` mention? ("Star Wars" is not mentioned in the title of *Return of the Jedi*. What features could capture these?) Could we incorporate lessons from chapters 1–9 to construct more advanced features?
- *Training data coverage of all features*—The flip side of more features is more training data. As you increase the features you'd like to try, you should be wondering whether your training data has enough examples of relevant and irrelevant documents across each different combination of your features. Otherwise, your model won't know how to use features to solve the problem.
- *Different model architectures*—We used a relatively simple model that expects features to linearly and independently correlate with relevance, but relevance can often be nonlinear and multidimensional. A shopper searching for `ipad` might expect the most recent Apple iPad release, except when they add the word "cable", making the query `ipad cable`. For that query, the shopper might just want the cheapest cable they can find instead of the most recent. In this case, there may be "recency" and "price" features that activate depending on specific keyword combinations, necessitating a more complicated model architecture.

In the next chapter, we will focus on the foundation of good LTR: great judgments!

Summary

- Learning to rank (LTR) builds generalized ranking functions that can be applied across all searches, using robust machine learning techniques.
- LTR features generally correspond to search queries. Search engines that support LTR often let you store and log features for use when training, and later applying, a ranking model.
- We have tremendous freedom in what features we use to generalize relevance. Features could be properties of queries (like the number of terms), properties of documents (like popularity), or relationships between queries and documents (like BM25 or other relevance scores).

- To do LTR well and apply well-known machine learning techniques, we typically reformulate the relevance ranking problem into a traditional, pointwise machine learning problem.
- SVMrank creates simple linear weights on normalized feature values, a good first step on your LTR journey.
- To be truly useful, we need our model to generalize beyond what it's learned. We can confirm an LTR model's ability to generalize by setting some judgments aside in a test dataset and not using them during training. After training, we can then evaluate the model on that previously unseen test dataset to confirm the model's ability to generalize.
- Once an LTR model is loaded into your search engine, be sure to consider performance (as in speed) tradeoffs with relevance. Real-life search systems require both.

Automating learning to rank with click models

This chapter covers

- Automating learning to rank retraining from user behavioral signals (searches, clicks, etc.)
- Transforming user signals into implicit LTR training data using click models
- Overcoming user's tendency to click items higher in the search results, regardless of relevance
- Handling low-confidence documents with fewer clicks when deriving implicit judgments

In chapter 10, we went step by step through training a learning to rank (LTR) model. Like walking through the mechanics of building a car, we saw the underlying nuts and bolts of LTR model training. In this chapter, we'll treat the LTR training process as a black box. In other words, we'll step away from the LTR internals, instead treating LTR more like a self-driving car, fine-tuning its trip toward a final destination.

Recall that LTR relies on accurate training data in order to be effective. LTR training data describes how users expect search results to be optimally ranked; it provides the directions we'll input into our LTR self-driving car. As you'll see, determining what's relevant based on user interactions comes with many challenges. If we can overcome these challenges and gain high confidence in our training data, though, we can build *automated learning to rank*: a system that regularly retrains LTR to capture the latest user relevance expectations.

As training data is so central to automated LTR, the challenges become not "What model/features/search engine should we use?" but more fundamentally, "What do users want from search?", "How do we turn that into training data?", and "How do we know whether that training data is any good?". By improving our confidence in the answers to these questions, we can put LTR (re)training on autopilot, as shown in figure 11.1.

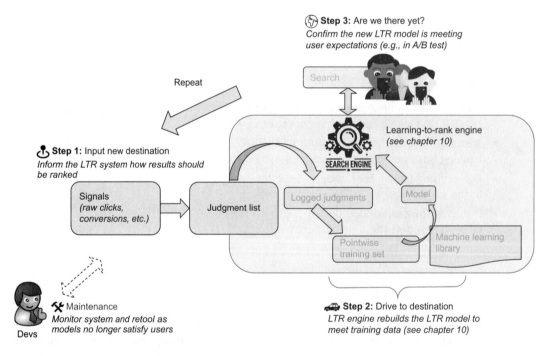

Figure 11.1   An automated LTR system automatically learns and retrains from the user's signals. This helps build models based on what actual users consider relevant over many queries.

Let's briefly walk through each step in the automated LTR process:

1   *Input new destination*—We input training data into the LTR system describing ideal relevance, based on our understanding of user behavioral signals, such as searches, clicks, and conversions (covered in this chapter).

2 *Drive to destination*—Our LTR system retrains an LTR model using the provided training data (as covered in chapter 10).

3 *Are we there yet?*—Is the model truly helping users? And should future models perhaps explore alternate routes (covered in chapter 12)?

Automated LTR repeats steps 1–3 continuously to automatically optimize relevance. The search team monitors the automated LTR's performance and intervenes as needed. This is the *maintenance* portion of figure 11.1. During maintenance, we open the hood to explore new LTR features and other model adjustments. Maintenance could also mean revisiting step 1 to correct our understanding of user behaviors and build more reliable, robust training data. After all, without good training data, we could follow chapter 10 to a T and still fail to satisfy our users.

This chapter starts our exploration of automated LTR by focusing on step 1— inputting a new destination. We'll first define the task of deriving training data from user clicks. We'll then spend the rest of this chapter overcoming some common biases and challenges with search click data. By the end of this chapter, you'll be able to build models with more reliable training data derived from user signals. Chapter 12 will then finish our automated LTR exploration by observing the model interacting with live users, using active learning and Gaussian techniques to overcome trickier presentation biases, and integrating all these components into a final, end-to-end automated LTR system.

11.1 (Re)creating judgment lists from signals

We mentioned that we need to overcome biases when creating LTR training data from clicks. However, before we dig into those biases, we'll explore the implications of using clicks instead of manual labels for LTR training data. We'll then take a naive, first stab at crafting training data in this section, reflecting on what went well or not so well. This will set us up for the rest of the chapter, where we'll explore removing bias from these results (in section 11.2 and beyond).

11.1.1 Generating implicit, probabilistic judgments from signals

Let's lay a foundation for how to use behavioral signals as LTR training data. Then we'll dive into the details of constructing reliable judgment lists.

In chapter 10, we discussed LTR training data, referred to as *judgment lists* or *judgments*. These judgements contain labels or *grades* for how relevant potential search results are for a given query. In chapter 10, we used movies as our example, labeling them with a grade of either 1 (relevant) or 0 (irrelevant), as in the following example.

Listing 11.1 Labeling movies relevant or irrelevant

```
# Judgment(grade, keywords, doc_id)
sample_judgments = [
  # for 'social network' query
  Judgment(1, "social network", 37799),  # The Social Network
```

```
  Judgment(0, "social network", 267752), # #chicagoGirl
  Judgment(0, "social network", 38408),  # Life As We Know It
  Judgment(0, "social network", 28303),  # The Cheyenne Social Club
  # for 'star wars' query
  Judgment(1, "star wars", 11),           # Star Wars
  Judgment(1, "star wars", 1892),         # Return of the Jedi
  Judgment(0, "star wars", 54138),        # Star Trek Into Darkness
  Judgment(0, "star wars", 85783),        # The Star
  Judgment(0, "star wars", 325553)        # Battlestar Galactica
]
```

There are many techniques for generating judgment lists, and this isn't a comprehensive chapter on judgment lists and their many applications. Instead, we'll specifically focus on LTR training data. For this reason, we will only discuss judgments generated from user click signals. We call these *implicit judgments* because they derive from user interactions with the search application as users search and click. This contrasts with *explicit judgments*, where raters directly label search results as relevant/irrelevant.

Implicit judgments are ideal for automating LTR for several reasons:

- *Recency*—We have ready access to user traffic, so we can automate training today's LTR model on the latest user search expectations.
- *More data at less cost*—Setting up a task to capture explicit judgments, even with crowdsourcing, is time consuming and expensive to do well at scale. Deriving implicit judgments from live user interactions we're already collecting allows us to use the existing user base to do this work for us.
- *Capturing real use cases*—Implicit judgments capture real users doing actual tasks with your search app. Contrast this with an artificial setting where explicit raters think carefully, perhaps unrealistically so, about the abstract task of choosing the most relevant results.

Unfortunately, click data can be noisy. We don't know why a user clicked on a given search result. Further, users are not homogeneous; some will interpret one result as relevant, while others will think otherwise. Search interactions also contain biases that need to be overcome, creating additional uncertainty around a model's calculations, which we'll discuss in detail later in this chapter and the next.

For these reasons, instead of a binary judgment, click models create *probabilistic judgments*. Instead of producing a grade of only 1 (relevant) or 0 (irrelevant), the grade represents the probability (between 0.0 and 1.0) that a random user would consider the result to be relevant or not. For example, a good click model might restate the judgments from listing 11.1 as something more like the following.

Listing 11.2 Labeling movie query relevance probabilistically

```
# Judgment(grade, keywords, doc_id),
sample_judgments = [
  Judgment(0.99, "social network", 37799),  # The Social Network
  Judgment(0.01, "social network", 267752), # #chicagoGirl
  Judgment(0.01, "social network", 38408),  # Life As We Know It
```

```
    Judgment(0.01, "social network", 28303),   # The Cheyenne Social Club
    Judgment(0.99, "star wars", 11),            # Star Wars
    Judgment(0.80, "star wars", 1892),          # Return of the Jedi
    Judgment(0.20, "star wars", 54138),         # Star Trek Into Darkness
    Judgment(0.01, "star wars", 85783),         # The Star
    Judgment(0.20, "star wars", 325553)         # Battlestar Galactica
]
```

Notice the Star Wars movies in listing 10.2—the `grade` has become quite a bit more interesting. *Star Wars* now has a very high probability of relevance (`0.99`). The sequel, *Return of the Jedi*, has a slightly lower probability. Other science fiction movies (*Star Trek Into Darkness* and *Battlestar Galactica*) have ratings a bit higher than `0`, as fans of the Star Wars franchise might also enjoy these movies. *The Star* is completely unrelated—it's a children's animated movie about the first Christmas—so it receives a low `0.01` relevance probability.

11.1.2 Training an LTR model using probabilistic judgments

We just introduced the idea that a relevance grade could be probabilistic. Now let's consider how we can apply the lessons from chapter 10 to train a model using these probabilistic judgments (between `0.0` and `1.0`) instead of binary judgments.

Generally, you might consider these options when training a model:

- *Quantize the grades*—Quite simply, you can set arbitrary cutoffs before training to convert the grades to an acceptable format. You might assign a grade greater than `0.75` as relevant (or `1.00`). Anything less than `0.75` would be considered irrelevant (or `0.00`). Other algorithms, like LambdaMART, accept a range of grades, like `1` to `4`, and these could have discrete cutoffs as well, such as assigning anything less than `0.25` a grade of `1.00`, anything greater than or equal to `0.25` but less than `0.5` a grade of `2.00`, and so on. With these algorithms, you could create 100 such labels, assigning `0.00` a grade of `0`, `0.01` a grade of `1`, and so on, until `1` is assigned a grade of `100` prior to training.

- *Just use the floating-point judgments*—The SVMRank algorithm from chapter 10 subtracted a more relevant item's features from a less relevant item's features (and vice versa) and built a classifier to tell relevant from irrelevant items. We did this with binary judgments, but nothing prevents us from doing this with probabilistic judgments. Here, if *Return of the Jedi* (`grade=0.80`) is considered more relevant than *Star Trek Into Darkness* (`grade=0.20`), we simply note *Return of the Jedi* as more relevant than *Star Trek Into Darkness* (labeling the difference as `+1`). Then we perform the same pairwise subtraction we would perform from chapter 10, subtracting features of *Star Trek Into Darkness* from those of *Return of the Jedi* to create a full training example.

Retraining the model with judgments in this chapter would mostly repeat the code from chapter 10, so we'll instead focus on the mechanics of training a click model. We have included a notebook with a full end-to-end LTR training example (see section

11.4) that integrates the click model we'll arrive at by the end of this chapter into the LTR training process you already explored in chapter 10.

Time to get back to the code and see our first click model!

11.1.3 Click-Through Rate: Your first click model

Now that you've seen the judgments format that a click model generates and how this format can be integrated to train an LTR model, let's take a first, naive pass at building a click model. After that, we'll take a step back to focus on a more sophisticated, general-purpose click model, and we'll then explore some of the core biases inherent in processing query and click signals.

> **TIP** If you'd like to take a deeper dive into this topic, we encourage you to read *Click Models for Web Search* by Chuklin, Markov, and Rijke (Springer, 2015).

To build our click model, we'll return to the RetroTech dataset, as it comes conveniently bundled with user click signals. From these signals, we've also reverse-engineered the kind of raw session data you need to build high-quality judgments. We'll make use of the pandas library to perform tabular computations on session data.

In the following listing, we examine a sample search session for the movie *Transformers Dark of The Moon*. This raw session information is your starting point—the bare minimum information needed to develop a judgment list from user signals.

Listing 11.3   Examining a search session

```
query = "transformers dark of the moon"        Selects sessions for the
sessions = get_sessions(query)                 "transformers dark of the moon"
print(sessions.loc[3])          Examines a single search
                                session shown to the user
```

Output:

```
sess_id  query                             rank    doc_id        clicked
3        transformers dark of the moon     0.0     47875842328   False
3        transformers dark of the moon     1.0     24543701538   False
...
3        transformers dark of the moon     7.0     97360810042   True
...
3        transformers dark of the moon     13.0    47875841406   False
3        transformers dark of the moon     14.0    400192926087  False
```

Listing 11.3 corresponds to a single search session, with sess_id=3, for the query transformers dark of the moon. This session includes the query, the ranked results seen by the user, and whether each result was clicked. These three elements are the core ingredients needed to build a click model.

Search sessions will frequently differ. Another session, even seconds later, could have a slightly different ranking presented to the user. The search index might have changed, or a new relevance algorithm may have been deployed to production. We encourage you to retry listing 11.3 with another `sess_id` to compare sessions.

Let's convert this data into judgments using our first, simple click model: Click-Through Rate.

BUILDING JUDGMENTS FROM CLICK-THROUGH RATE

We'll start by building a very simple click model to get comfortable with the data, and then we can step back to see the flaws in this first pass. This will allow us to think carefully about the quality of the generated judgments for automated LTR in the rest of this chapter.

Our first click model will be based on *click-through rate* (CTR). CTR is the number of clicks received on a search result divided by the number of times it appeared in search results. If a result is clicked every single time the search engine returns the result, the CTR will be 1. If it's never clicked, the CTR will be 0. Sounds simple enough—what could go wrong?

We can look over every result for the query `transformers dark of the moon` and consider clicks with respect to the number of sessions in which the `doc_id` was returned. The following listing shows the computation and the resulting CTR value per document.

Listing 11.4   Computing CTR

```
def calculate_ctr(sessions):
  click_counts = sessions.groupby("doc_id")["clicked"].sum()
  sess_counts = sessions.groupby("doc_id")["sess_id"].nunique()
  ctrs = click_counts / sess_counts
  return ctrs.sort_values(ascending=False)

query = "transformers dark of the moon"
sessions = get_sessions(query, index=False)
click_through_rates = calculate_ctr(sessions)
print_series_data(click_through_rates, column="CTR")
```

Output:

```
doc_id          CTR       name
97360810042     0.0824    Transformers: Dark of the Moon - Blu-ray Disc
47875842328     0.0734    Transformers: Dark of the Moon Stealth Force E...
47875841420     0.0434    Transformers: Dark of the Moon Decepticons - N...
...
93624956037     0.0082    Transformers: Dark of the Moon - Original Soun...
47875841369     0.0074    Transformers: Dark of the Moon - PlayStation 3
24543750949     0.0062    X-Men: First Class - Widescreen Dubbed Subtitl...
```

In listing 11.4, for all `sessions` with the query `transformers dark of the moon` (per listing 11.3), we sum the clicks for each `doc_id` as `click_counts`. We also count the number of unique sessions for that document in `sess_counts`. Finally, we compute `ctrs` as `click_counts` / `sess_counts`, giving us our first click model. We see that document 97360810042 has the highest CTR and 24543750949 the lowest.

The preceding listing outputs the *ideal search results* based on the CTR. That is, if our LTR model was trained using this CTR click model to provide the relevance judgments, the search engine would produce this ordering as the optimal ranking. Throughout this chapter and the next, we'll frequently visually display this ideal ranking to understand whether the click model builds reasonable training data (judgments). We can see the CTR-based ideal judgments for `transformers dark of the moon` in figure 11.2.

Click-Through Rate judgments for q=transformers dark of the moon

	ctr	upc	image	name
0	0.0824	97360810042		Transformers: Dark of the Moon - Blu-ray Disc
1	0.0734	47875842328		Transformers: Dark of the Moon Stealth Force Edition - Nintendo Wii
2	0.0434	47875841420		Transformers: Dark of the Moon Decepticons - Nintendo DS
3	0.0364	24543701538		The A-Team - Widescreen Dubbed Subtitle AC3 - Blu-ray Disc
4	0.0352	25192107191		Fast Five - Widescreen - Blu-ray Disc

Figure 11.2   Search results ranked by CTR for the query `transformers dark of the moon`

Examining the results of figure 11.2, a couple of things jump out:

- The CTR for our top result (the Blu-ray of the movie *Transformers: Dark of the Moon*) seems rather low (`0.0824`, only a little better than the next judgment at `0.0734`). We might expect the Blu-ray's relevance grade to be much higher than other results.
- The DVD for the movie *Transformers: Dark of The Moon* doesn't even show up. It sits far below seemingly unrelated movies and secondary video games about the movie *Dark of The Moon*. We would expect the DVD to rank higher, maybe as high or higher than the Blu-ray.

But perhaps transformers dark of the moon is just a weird query. Let's repeat the process for something completely unrelated, this time for dryer in figure 11.3.

Click-Through Rate judgments for q=dryer

	ctr	upc	image	name
0	0.1608	84691226727		GE - 6.0 Cu. Ft. 3-Cycle Electric Dryer - White
1	0.0816	84691226703		Hotpoint - 6.0 Cu. Ft. 3-Cycle Electric Dryer - White-on-White
2	0.0710	12505451713		Frigidaire - Semi-Rigid Dryer Vent Kit - Silver
3	0.0576	783722274422		The Independent - Widescreen Subtitle - DVD
4	0.0572	883049066905		Whirlpool - Affresh Washer Cleaner

Figure 11.3   Search results ranked by CTR for the query dryer. Here we note the strange result for the movie *The Independent* that doesn't seem relevant.

In figure 11.3 we see other odd-looking results:

- The first two results are clothes dryers, which seems good.
- Following the clothes dryers are clothes-dryer parts. Hmm, OK?
- A movie called *The Independent* shows up. This seems completely random. Why would this be rated so highly?
- Next there's a washer accessory, which is kind of related.
- Finally, we see hair dryers, which shows another potential meaning of the word "dryer".

What do you think of the judgments produced by the CTR click model? Think back to what you learned in chapter 10. Remember this is the foundation, the very target, of your LTR model. Do you think these judgments would lead to a good LTR model that would ultimately succeed if put into production?

We also encourage you to ask yourself a more fundamental question: how could we even tell if a judgment list is good? Our subjective interpretation could be as flawed as the data in a click model. We'll consider this more analytically in chapter 12. For this chapter, we'll let our instincts guide us to possible problems.

11.1.4   *Common biases in judgments*

We've seen so far that we can create probabilistic judgments—those with grades between 0.00 and 1.00—simply by dividing the number of clicks on a product by the number of times that product is returned by search. The output, however, seemed to be a bit wanting, as it included movies unrelated to the Transformers franchise. We also saw a movie placed in the search results for `dryer`!

It turns out that search click data is full of biases. Here, we'll briefly define what we mean by "bias" before exploring each of these biases in the RetroTech click data.

With click models, a *bias* is a reason that raw user click data can have nothing to do with the relevance of search results. Instead, biases define how clicks (or the lack of clicks) reflect user psychology, search user interface design, or noisy data. We can separate biases into two broad groups: nonalgorithmic and algorithmic biases. *Algorithmic biases* are those inherent in the ranking, display, and interaction with search results. *Nonalgorithmic biases* occur for reasons only indirectly related to search ranking.

Algorithmic biases can include the following:

- *Position bias*—Users click on higher-ranked results more than lower-ranked results.
- *Confidence bias*—Documents with little signal data influence judgments the same as documents with much more data.
- *Presentation Bias*—If search never surfaces particular results, users never click them, so the click model won't know whether they're relevant.

Nonalgorithmic biases, on the other hand, are biases like the following:

- *Attractiveness bias*—Some results appear attractive and generate clicks (perhaps due to better images or wording selection), but they turn out to be spammy or just irrelevant.
- *Performance bias*—Users give up on slow searches, get distracted, and end up not clicking anything or clicking only on the earliest-returned results.

Since this book is about *AI-powered* search, we will focus our discussion on *algorithmic* biases in search clickstream data. We'll cover position bias and confidence bias in this chapter. Presentation bias will be covered in chapter 12.

But nonalgorithmic biases matter too! Search is a complex ecosystem that goes beyond relevance rankings. If results are frequently clicked, but follow-up actions like sales or other conversions don't occur, it might not be a ranking problem—perhaps you have a problem with spammy products. Or you might have a problem with the product pages or checkout process. You may find yourself asked to improve "relevance" when the limiting factor is actually the user experience, the content, or the speed of search.

Now that we've reflected on our first click model, let's work to overcome the first bias.

11.2 Overcoming position bias

In the previous section, we saw our first click model in action: a simple CTR click model. This divided the number of times a product was clicked in search by the number of times it was returned in the top results. We saw that this was quite a flawed approach, noting numerous reasons it could be biased. Specifically, we pointed out position bias, confidence bias, and presentation bias as three of the algorithmic biases present in our click model. It's time to begin tackling those problems!

In this section, we'll focus on the first of those algorithmic biases, position bias, digging into the problem and working on a click model designed to overcome it.

11.2.1 Defining position bias

Position bias is present in most search systems. If users are shown search results, they tend to prefer highly ranked search results over lower ones, even when those lower results are in fact more relevant. Joachims, et al. in their paper "Evaluating the Accuracy of Implicit Feedback from Clicks and Query Reformulations in Web Search" (www.cs.cornell.edu/people/tj/publications/joachims_etal_07a.pdf) discuss several reasons for position biases to exist:

- *Trust bias*—Users trust that the search engine must know what it's doing, so they interact with higher results more.
- *Scanning behaviors*—Users examine search results in specific patterns, such as top-to-bottom, and often don't explore everything in front of them.
- *Visibility*—Higher ranked results are likely to be rendered on the user's screen, so users need to scroll to see the remaining results.

With these factors in mind, let's see if we can detect position bias in the RetroTech sessions.

11.2.2 Position bias in RetroTech data

How much position bias exists in the sessions in the RetroTech dataset? If we can quantify this, we can consider how exactly we can remedy this problem. Let's assess the bias quickly before we consider a new click model for overcoming these biases.

By looking at all sessions across all queries, we can compute an average CTR per rank. This will tell us how much position bias exists in the RetroTech click data. We do this in the following listing.

> **Listing 11.5 CTR per rank in search sessions across all queries**

```
sessions = all_sessions()
num_sessions = len(sessions["sess_id"].unique())
ctr_by_rank = sessions.groupby("rank")["clicked"].sum() / num_sessions
print(ctr_by_rank)
```

Output:

```
rank
0     0.249727
1     0.142673
2     0.084218
3     0.063073
4     0.056255
5     0.042255
6     0.033236
7     0.038000
8     0.020964
9     0.017364
10    0.013982
```

You can see in listing 11.5 that users click higher positions more. The CTR of results at rank 0 is 0.25, followed by 0.143 at rank 1, and so on.

Further, we can see position bias when we compare the CTR judgments from earlier to the typical ranking for each product in a query. If position bias is present, then our judgment's ideal ranking will end up resembling the typical ranking shown to users. We can analyze this by averaging the rank of each document over every session to see where they appear.

The following listing shows the typical search results page for transformers dark of the moon sessions.

> **Listing 11.6 Examining ranking for transformers dark of the moon**

```
def calculate_average_rank(sessions):
    avg_rank = sessions.groupby("doc_id")["rank"].mean()
    return avg_rank.sort_values(ascending=True)

sessions = get_sessions("transformers dark of the moon")
average_rank = calculate_average_rank(sessions)
print_series_data(average_rank, "mean_rank")
```

Output:

```
doc_id          mean_rank    name
400192926087    13.0526      Transformers: Dark of the Moon - Original Soun...
97363532149     12.1494      Transformers: Revenge of the Fallen - Widescre...
93624956037     11.3298      Transformers: Dark of the Moon - Original Soun...
...
25192107191      2.6596      Fast Five - Widescreen - Blu-ray Disc
24543701538      1.8626      The A-Team - Widescreen Dubbed Subtitle AC3 - ...
47875842328      0.9808      Transformers: Dark of the Moon Stealth Force E...
```

In listing 11.6, some documents, like 24543701538 and 47875842328, historically occur toward the top of the search results for this query. They will be clicked more due to position bias. The typical results page, shown in figure 11.4, overlaps quite a lot with the CTR rank from figure 11.2.

Typical search session for q=transformers dark of the moon

	mean_rank	upc	image	name
0	0.9808	47875842328		Transformers: Dark of the Moon Stealth Force Edition - Nintendo Wii
1	1.8626	24543701538		The A-Team - Widescreen Dubbed Subtitle AC3 - Blu-ray Disc
2	2.6596	25192107191		Fast Five - Widescreen - Blu-ray Disc
3	3.5344	47875841420		Transformers: Dark of the Moon Decepticons - Nintendo DS
4	4.4444	786936817218		Pirates of the Caribbean: On Stranger Tides - Blu-ray 3D

Figure 11.4 Typical search result page for the `transformers dark of the moon` query. Notice the irrelevant movies like *The A-Team* and *Fast Five* showing up. Also note the high ranking of the Wii game. The high position of these results and the fact that they get clicked more just by showing up higher in the list explains why the CTR model erroneously thinks these are relevant.

Unfortunately, CTR is primarily influenced by position bias. Users click on the odd movies in figure 11.4 because the search engine returns them highly for this query, not because they are relevant. If we train an LTR model just on CTR, we would be asking the LTR model to optimize for what users already see and interact with. We must account for position bias when automating LTR.

Next, let's see how we can overcome position bias in a more robust click model that compensates for position bias.

11.2.3 Simplified dynamic Bayesian network: A click model that overcomes position bias

You've seen the harm position bias can do in action! If we just use clicks directly, we will train our LTR model to reinforce the ranking already shown to users. It's time to introduce a click model that can overcome position bias. We'll start by defining an "examine", a key concept in modeling position bias. We'll then introduce one particular click model that uses this examine concept to adjust raw clicks to overcome position bias.

HOW CLICK MODELS OVERCOME POSITION BIAS WITH AN "EXAMINE" EVENT

The basic CTR calculation doesn't *really* account for how users scan search results. The user likely considers only a few results—biased by position—before deciding to click one or two. If we can capture which results users consciously consider before clicking, we might be able to overcome position bias. Click models do exactly this by defining the concept of an "examine". We'll explore this concept before building a click model that overcomes position bias.

What is an examine? You may be familiar with an *impression*—when a UI element is rendered on the visible part of a user's screen. In click models, we consider instead an *examine*, the probability that a search result was consciously considered by the user. As we know, users often fail to notice something right in front of their eyes. You may have even been that user! Figure 11.5 captures this concept, contrasting impressions with examines.

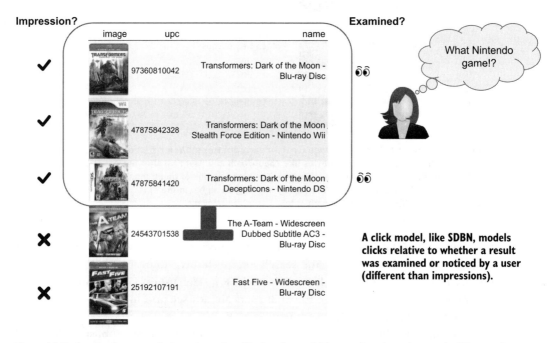

Figure 11.5 Impressions are whatever is rendered in the viewport (the monitor-shaped square) while examines are what the user considers (the results with eyeballs adjacent). Modeling what users examine helps correctly account for how users interact with search results.

You can see in figure 11.5 that the user fails to notice the Nintendo game in the second position, even though it's being rendered on their monitor. If the user didn't examine it, a click model shouldn't penalize the Nintendo game's relevance.

Why does tracking examines help overcome position bias? Examines are how a click model understands position bias. Another way of saying "position bias" is "we think that whether users examine search results depends on the position." As a result, modeling examines correctly is a core activity of most click models. Some click models, like the *position-based model* (PBM) attempt to determine an examine probability per position across all searches. Others, like the *cascading model* or, as we'll see soon, the *dynamic Bayesian network* (DBN) models, assume that if a result was above the last click on the search page, it likely was examined.

For most click models, the top position usually has a higher examine probability than lower ones. This allows click models to adjust for clicks correctly. Items examined frequently and clicked are rewarded and seen as more relevant. Those examined but not clicked are seen as less relevant.

To make this more concrete, let's dive deeper into one of the dynamic Bayesian network click models that uses examines to help overcome position bias.

DEFINING A SIMPLIFIED DYNAMIC BAYESIAN NETWORK

A *simplified dynamic Bayesian network* (SDBN) is a slightly less accurate version of the more complex dynamic Bayesian network (DBN) click model. These click models assume that, within a search session, the probability that a user examined a document depends heavily on whether it was positioned at or above the lowest clicked document.

SDBN's algorithm first marks the last click of each session and then considers every document at or above this last click as examined. Finally, it computes a relevance grade by simply dividing the total clicks on a document by that document's total examines. We thus get a kind of dynamic CTR, tracking within each user's search session when they likely examined a result, and carefully using this to account for how that user evaluated its relevance. We then use these relevance evaluations in aggregate across sessions to train the SDBN click model.

Let's follow this algorithm step by step. We'll first mark the last click of each session in the following listing.

Listing 11.7 Marking which results were examined in each session

```
def calculate_examine_probability(sessions):
  last_click_per_session = sessions.groupby(
    ["clicked", "sess_id"])["rank"].max()[True]
  sessions["last_click_rank"] = last_click_per_session
  sessions["examined"] = \
    sessions["rank"] <= sessions["last_click_rank"]
  return sessions

sessions = get_sessions("dryer")
probability_data = calculate_examine_probability(sessions).loc[3]
print(probability_data)
```

Computes last_click_per_session, the max rank where clicked is True per session.

Marks the last click rank in each session

Sets every position at or above the last click to True (otherwise False)

Output (truncated):

sess_id	query	rank	doc_id	clicked	last_click_rank	examined
3	dryer	0.0	12505451713	False	9.0	True
3	dryer	1.0	84691226727	False	9.0	True
3	dryer	2.0	883049066905	False	9.0	True
...						

```
3        dryer    8.0     14381196320    True     9.0         True
3        dryer    9.0     74108096487    True     9.0         True
3        dryer    10.0    74108007469    False    9.0         False
3        dryer    11.0    12505525766    False    9.0         False
...
```

In listing 11.7, we find the max rank where `clicked` is `True` by storing it in `last_click_per_session`. We then mark positions at or above `last_click_rank` as examined in our sessions for `dryer`, as you can see in the output for `sess_id=3`.

With every session updated with examines set to `True` or `False`, we now sum the total clicks and examines per document across all sessions.

Listing 11.8 Sum clicks and examines per `doc_id` for this query

```
def calculate_clicked_examined(sessions):
  sessions = calculate_examine_probability(sessions)
  return sessions[sessions["examined"]] \
    .groupby("doc_id")[["clicked", "examined"]].sum()

sessions = get_sessions("dryer")
clicked_examined_data = calculate_clicked_examined(sessions)
print_dataframe(clicked_examined_data)
```

Output (truncated):

```
doc_id         clicked  examined    name
12505451713        355      2707    Frigidaire - Semi-Rigid Dryer Ve...
12505525766        268       974    Smart Choice - 6' 30 Amp 3-Prong...
...
36172950027         97       971    Tools in the Dryer: A Rarities C...
...
883049066905       286      2138    Whirlpool - Affresh Washer Cleaner
883929085118        44       578    A Charlie Brown Christmas - AC3 ...
```

In listing 11.8, `sessions[sessions["examined"]]` filters to examined rows only. Then, for each `doc_id`, we compute the total `clicked` and `examined` counts. You can see that some results, like `doc_id=36172950027`, clearly were examined a lot with relatively few clicks from users.

Finally, we finish the SDBN algorithm in the following listing by computing clicks over examines.

Listing 11.9 Compute final SDBN grades

```
def calculate_grade(sessions):
  sessions = calculate_clicked_examined(sessions)
  sessions["grade"] = sessions["clicked"] / sessions["examined"]
  return sessions.sort_values("grade", ascending=False)
```

```
query = "dryer"
sessions = get_sessions(query)
grade_data = calculate_grade(sessions)
print_dataframe(grade_data)
```

Output (truncated):

```
doc_id        clicked   examined   grade      name
856751002097    133         323    0.411765   Practecol - Dryer Balls (2-Pack)
48231011396     166         423    0.392435   LG - 3.5 Cu. Ft. 7-Cycle High-Ef...
84691226727     804        2541    0.316411   GE - 6.0 Cu. Ft. 3-Cycle Electri...
...
12505451713     355        2707    0.131141   Frigidaire - Semi-Rigid Dryer Ve...
36172950027      97         971    0.099897   Tools in the Dryer: A Rarities C...
883929085118     44         578    0.076125   A Charlie Brown Christmas - AC3 ...
```

In the output of listing 11.9, document 856751002097 is seen as the most relevant, with a grade of 0.4118, or 133 clicks out of 323 examines.

Let's revisit our two queries to see how the ideal results now look for dryer and transformers dark of the moon. Figure 11.6 shows results for dryer, and figure 11.7 shows the transformers dark of the moon results.

SDBN judgments for q=dryer

	grade	upc	image	name
0	0.4118	856751002097		Practecol - Dryer Balls (2-Pack)
1	0.3924	48231011396	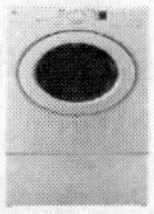	LG - 3.5 Cu. Ft. 7-Cycle High-Efficiency Washer - White
2	0.3164	84691226727	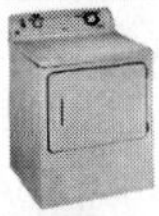	GE - 6.0 Cu. Ft. 3-Cycle Electric Dryer - White
3	0.2938	74108007469		Conair - 1875-Watt Folding Handle Hair Dryer - Blue
4	0.2752	12505525766		Smart Choice - 6' 30 Amp 3-Prong Dryer Cord

Figure 11.6 Ideal search results for the query dryer according to SDBN. Notice how SDBN seems to promote more results related to washing clothes.

SDBN judgments for q=transformers dark of the moon

grade	upc	image	name
0 0.6417	97360810042		Transformers: Dark of the Moon - Blu-ray Disc
1 0.4806	400192926087		Transformers: Dark of the Moon - Original Soundtrack - CD
2 0.3951	97363560449		Transformers: Dark of the Moon - Widescreen Dubbed Subtitle - DVD
3 0.3231	97363532149		Transformers: Revenge of the Fallen - Widescreen Dubbed Subtitle - DVD
4 0.2662	93624956037		Transformers: Dark of the Moon - Original Soundtrack - CD

Figure 11.7   **Ideal search results for the query** `transformers dark of the moon` **according to SDBN. We've now surfaced the DVD, Blu-ray movie, and CD soundtrack.**

If we subjectively examine figures 11.6 and 11.7, both sets of judgments appear more intuitive than the previous CTR judgments. In our `dryer` example, the emphasis appears to be on washing clothes. There are some accessories (such as the dryer balls) that score roughly the same as the dryers themselves.

For `transformers dark of the moon`, we note the very high grade for the Blu-ray movie. We also see the DVD and CD soundtrack ranking higher than other secondary "Dark of the Moon" items such as video games. Somewhat oddly, the soundtrack CD is ranked higher than the movie DVD—perhaps we should investigate this more.

Of course, as we've said earlier, we're using our intuition for now. In chapter 12, we'll think more objectively about how we might evaluate judgment quality.

With our position bias more under control, we'll now move on to fine-tune our judgments to handle another crucial bias: confidence bias.

11.3   *Handling confidence bias: Not upending your model due to a few lucky clicks*

In the game of baseball, a player's batting average tells us the proportion of hits they get for every at bat. A great professional player has a batting average greater than 0.3. Consider, however, a lucky little league baseball player stepping up to the plate for their first at bat and getting a hit. Their batting average is technically 1.0! We can conclude, then, that this young child is a baseball prodigy and will certainly have a great baseball career. Right?

Not quite! In this section, we're going to explore the relevance side of this lucky little leaguer. What do we do with results that, perhaps simply out of luck, have been examined only a few times, each resulting in a click? These likely shouldn't get a perfect grade of 1.0. We'll see (and correct) this problem in our data.

11.3.1   The low-confidence problem in click data

Let's look at the data to see where low-confidence data points are biasing the training data. We'll then see how we can compensate for low-confidence problems in the SDBN results. To define the problem, let's look at the SDBN results for `transformers dark of the moon` and another, rarer, query to see common low-confidence situations.

If you recall, it was a bit suspicious that the soundtrack CD for the *Transformers Dark of The Moon* movie ranked so highly according to SDBN. When we examine the raw data underlying the rankings, we can see a possible problem. In the following listing, we reconstruct the SDBN data for `transformers dark of the moon` to debug this problem, combining listings 11.7–11.9.

Listing 11.10   Recomputing SDBN statistics

```
query = "transformers dark of the moon"
sessions = get_sessions(query)
grade_data = calculate_grade(sessions)
print_dataframe(grade_data)
```

Output (truncated):

```
doc_id          clicked   examined   grade      name
97360810042        412        642   0.641745   Transformers: Dark of the Moon -...
400192926087        62        129   0.480620   Transformers: Dark of the Moon -...
97363560449         96        243   0.395062   Transformers: Dark of the Moon -...
...
47875841406         80        626   0.127796   Transformers: Dark of the Moon A...
24543750949         31        313   0.099042   X-Men: First Class - Widescreen ...
47875842335         53        681   0.077827   Transformers: Dark of the Moon S...
```

In the output of listing 11.10, note that the top result, the Blu-ray movie (`doc_id=97360810042`), has far more examines (`642`) than the soundtrack CD (`doc_id=400192926087` with `129` examines). The Blu-ray's grade is more reliable, given it has had many times more opportunities for user interaction, making it less likely to be dominated by noisy, spurious clicks. The CD, on the other hand, has far fewer examines. Shouldn't the Blu-ray's relevance grade be weighed higher, given that it's a more reliable data point compared to the CD with more limited data?

Often, this situation is even starker, particularly when dealing with less common queries. Regardless of the number of queries your search engine receives, some queries are likely to be received many times (*head queries*), some a moderate number of times (*torso queries*), and some very rarely (*long-tail queries*, or simply *tail queries*).

Consider the query `blue ray`. You'll note that this is a common misspelling of "Blu-ray". As a common mistake, it likely mixes documents with a modest number of examines with documents receiving very few. In the following listing, we compute the SDBN statistics for `blue ray`, which suffers from this data sparsity problem.

Listing 11.11   SDBN judgments for a query with sparse data

```
def get_sample_sessions(query):
  sessions = get_sessions(query, index=False)
  sessions = sessions[sessions["sess_id"] < 50050]      ◁—┐ Randomly samples a few
  return sessions.set_index("sess_id")                     │ sessions to simulate a
                                                           │ typical long-tail case
sessions = get_sample_sessions("blue ray")
grade_data = calculate_grade(sessions)
print_dataframe(grade_data)
```

Output (truncated):

```
doc_id          clicked   examined   grade      name
600603132872    1         1          1.000000   Blu-ray Disc Cases (10-Pack)
827396513927    14        34         0.411765   Panasonic - Blu-Ray Player
25192073007     8         20         0.400000   The Blues Brothers - Widescree...
...
25192107191     0         7          0.000000   Fast Five - Widescreen - Blu-r...
23942972389     0         15         0.000000   Verbatim - 10-Pack 6x BD-R Dis...
885170038875    0         5          0.000000   Panasonic - 9" Widescreen Port...
```

Looking at the output of listing 11.11, we see something unsettling. Like the most extreme case of our lucky little league baseball player, the most relevant result, doc 600603132872, receives a grade of `1.0` (perfectly relevant) after being examined by only one user! This grade of `1.0` ranks higher than the next result, which has a grade of `0.411` based on `34` examines. When you consider that doc 600603132872 is a set of Blu-ray cases and 827396513927 is a Blu-ray player, this feels more troubling. Our subjective interpretation might rank the player above the cases. Shouldn't the fact that the second result was examined significantly more count for something?

What we've seen in these examples is *confidence bias*—when a judgment list has many grades based on statistically insignificant, spurious events. We say these spurious events with few examines have low confidence, whereas those with more examines provide a higher level of confidence. No matter your click model, you likely have many situations where queries have only a modest amount of traffic. To automate LTR, you'll need to adjust your training data generation to account for the confidence you have in the data.

Now that you've seen the effect of low-confidence data, we can move on to some solutions you can apply when building your click model.

11.3.2   *Using a beta prior to model confidence probabilistically*

We've just seen a few problems created by valuing low-confidence data too highly. Without adjusting your models based on your confidence in the data, you won't be able to build a reliable automated LTR system. We could just filter these low-confidence examples out, but can we perhaps do something smarter? We'll discuss an approach to preserving all the click-stream data in this section as we introduce the concept of beta distributions. But first, let's discuss why using all data is generally preferred over simply filtering out the low-confidence examples.

SHOULD WE FILTER OUT LOW-CONFIDENCE JUDGMENTS?

In our click model, should we just remove the low-confidence examples? We don't generally recommend throwing data points away like that.

Filtering training data, such as data points below some minimum threshold of examines, reduces the amount of training data you have. Even with a reasonable threshold, documents for a query are typically examined on a power law distribution. Users examine some documents very frequently, while examining the vast majority very infrequently. A threshold can thus remove too many LTR examples and cause an LTR model to miss important patterns. Even with a threshold, you would be left with the challenge of how to weight medium-confidence examples against high-confidence ones, such as with the `transformers dark of the moon` query from earlier.

Instead of using a hard cutoff, we advocate keeping low-confidence examples and just weighing all examples based on confidence level. We'll do this using a beta distribution on the computed relevance grades. We'll then apply this solution to fix our SDBN click model judgments.

USING THE BETA DISTRIBUTION TO ADJUST FOR CONFIDENCE

Beta distributions help us draw conclusions from our clicks and examines based on probabilities instead of just biased occurrences. However, before we dive straight into using the beta distribution for judgments, let's first examine the usefulness of a beta distribution using our previous, intuitive baseball batting-average analogy.

In baseball, a batting average of 0.295 for a player means that when this player goes to bat, there's roughly a 29.5% chance they will get a hit. But if we wanted to know "What's the batting average for that player, batting in Fenway Park in September on rainy days", we'd probably have very little information to go on. The player may have only batted in those conditions a handful of times. Maybe they made 2 hits out of 3 tries in those conditions. We would conclude their batting average in these cases is 2/3 or 0.67. We know by now that this conclusion would be a mistake: do we really think, based on only 3 chances at bat, we can conclude that the player has an improbably high 66.7% chance of making a hit? A better approach would be to use the 0.295 general batting average as an initial belief, moving slowly away from that assumption as we gradually gain more data on "Fenway Park in September on rainy days" at bats.

The *beta distribution* is a tool used to manage beliefs. It turns a probability, like a batting average or judgment grade, into two values, a and b, that represent the probability as a distribution. The a and b values can be interpreted as follows:

- a *(the successes)*—The number of at bats with hits we've observed, or the number of examines with clicks

- b *(the failures)*—The number of at bats without hits we've observed, or the number of examines without clicks

With the beta distribution, the property mean = a / (a + b) holds, where mean is the initial point value, like a batting average. Given a mean, we can find many a and b values that satisfy mean = a / (a + b). After all, 0.295 = 295 / (295 + 705) as does 0.295 = 1475 / (1475 + 3525) and so on. Yet each represents a different beta distribution. Keep this property in mind as we move along.

Let's put these pieces together to see how the beta distribution prevents us from jumping to conclusions on spurious click (or batting) data.

We could declare our initial belief about any document's relevance grade as 0.125. This is like declaring the baseball player's batting average to be 0.295 as our initial belief of their performance. We can use the beta distribution to update the initial belief for specific cases like "Fenway Park in September on rainy days" or a specific document's relevance for a search query.

The first step is to pick an a and a b that capture our initial belief. For our relevance case, we could choose many values for a and b that satisfy 0.125 = a / (a + b). Suppose we choose a=2.5, b=17.5 as our relevance belief on documents with no clicks. Graphing this, we would see the distribution in figure 11.8.

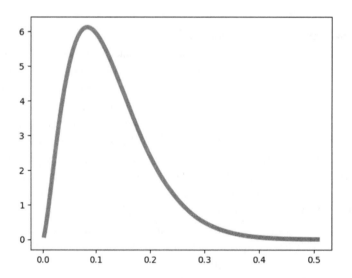

Figure 11.8   Beta distribution for a relevance grade of 0.125. The mean corresponds to our default relevance grade. We see the distribution of most likely relevance grades.

We can observe now what happens when we see a document's first click, incrementing that document's a to 3.5. In figure 11.9 we have a=3.5, b=17.5.

The mean relevance grade for the updated distribution is now 3.5 / (17.5 + 3.5) or 0.1667, effectively pulling the initial belief a little higher, given its first click. Without the beta distribution, this document would have 1 click and 1 examine, resulting in a grade of 1.

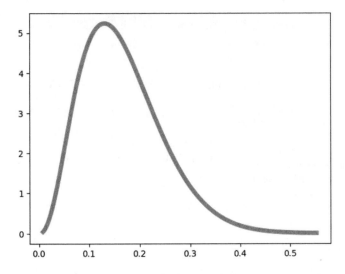

Figure 11.9   The beta distribution for a relevance grade after adding one click is now `0.1667`**. Adding a click "pulls" the probability distribution a little toward one direction, updating the initial belief.**

We refer to the starting point probability distribution (the chosen a and b) as the *prior distribution*, or just a *prior*. This is our initial belief in what will happen. The distribution after updating a and b for a specific case, like a document, is a *posterior distribution*, or just a *posterior*. This is our updated belief.

Recall that we said earlier that many initial a and b values could be chosen. This has significance, as the magnitude of the initial a and b make our prior weaker or stronger. We could choose any value for a and b where a / (a + b) = 0.125. But note what happens if we choose a very small value a=0.25, b=1.75. Then we go to update a by incrementing it by 1. The new expected value of the posterior distribution is 1.25 / (1.25 + 1.75) or ~0.416. That's a major effect for just one click. Conversely, using very high a and b values would make a prior so strong it would barely budge. When you use the beta distribution, you'll want to tune the magnitude of the prior so updates have the desired effect.

Now that you've seen this handy tool for capturing SDBN grades in practice, let's see how the beta distribution can help with our SDBN confidence problems.

USING A BETA PRIOR IN SDBN CLICK MODELS

Let's finish the chapter by updating the SDBN click model using the beta distribution. If you use other click models, like the ones alluded to earlier in this chapter, you'll need to reflect on how confidence can be solved in those cases. The beta distribution might be a useful tool there, as well.

If you recall, the output of SDBN was a count of `clicks` and `examines` for each document. In listing 11.12, we pick up from listing 11.11, which computed the SDBN for the `blue ray` query. We'll choose a prior grade of `0.3` for use with our SDBN model. This is our default grade when we don't have information about the document—possibly derived from the typical grade we see in our judgments. We'll then compute a prior beta distribution (`prior_a` and `prior_b`) using this prior grade.

Listing 11.12 Computing prior beta distribution

```
def calculate_prior(sessions, prior_grade, prior_weight):
    sessions = calculate_grade(sessions)
    sessions["prior_a"] = prior_grade * prior_weight
    sessions["prior_b"] = (1 - prior_grade) * prior_weight
    return sessions

prior_grade = 0.3
prior_weight = 100
query = "blue ray"
sessions = get_sample_sessions(query)
prior_data = calculate_prior(sessions, prior_grade, prior_weight)
print(prior_data)
```

Resulting a and b satisfying prior_grade = prior_a / (prior_a + prior_b)

Default prior relevance grade

How much confidence to place in the prior (prior_weight = a + b)

Output (truncated):

```
doc_id          clicked   examined   grade       prior_a   prior_b
600603132872    1.0       1.0        1.000000    30.0      70.0
827396513927    14.0      34.0       0.411765    30.0      70.0
25192073007     8.0       20.0       0.400000    30.0      70.0
885170033412    6.0       19.0       0.315789    30.0      70.0
...
```

In listing 11.12, with a weight of 100, you can confirm that prior_grade = prior_a / (prior_a + prior_b) or 0.3 = 30 / (30 + 70). This has captured an initial probability distribution for our prior.

In listing 11.13, we need to compute a posterior distribution and corresponding relevance grade. We do this by incrementing prior_a for clicks (our "successes"), and prior_b for examines with no clicks (our "failures"). Finally, we compute an updated grade as the beta_grade.

Listing 11.13 Computing posterior beta distribution

Updates our belief about the document's lack of relevance, increasing from prior_b by examines without clicks

Updates our belief about the document's relevance, increasing from prior_a by the number of clicks

```
def calculate_sdbn(sessions, prior_grade=0.3, prior_weight=100):
    sessions = calculate_prior(sessions, prior_grade, prior_weight)
    sessions["posterior_a"] = (sessions["prior_a"] +
                               sessions["clicked"])
    sessions["posterior_b"] = (sessions["prior_b"] +
        sessions["examined"] - sessions["clicked"])
    sessions["beta_grade"] = (sessions["posterior_a"] /
        (sessions["posterior_a"] + sessions["posterior_b"]))
    return sessions.sort_values("beta_grade", ascending=False)

query = "blue ray"
sessions = get_sample_sessions(query)
bluray_sdbn_data = calculate_sdbn(sessions)
print(bluray_sdbn_data)
```

Computes a new grade from posterior_a and posterior_b

Output (truncated):

```
doc_id         cl  ex  grade  pr_a  pr_b  posterior_a posterior_b beta_grade
827396513927   14  34  0.411  30.0  70.0  44.0        90.0        0.328358
25192073007    8   20  0.400  30.0  70.0  38.0        82.0        0.316667
600603132872   1   1   1.000  30.0  70.0  31.0        70.0        0.306931
...
786936805017   1   14  0.071  30.0  70.0  31.0        83.0        0.271930
36725608511    0   11  0.000  30.0  70.0  30.0        81.0        0.270270
23942972389    0   15  0.000  30.0  70.0  30.0        85.0        0.260870
```

In the output of listing 11.13, the column headers clicked, examined, prior a, and prior_b were shortened for space to cl, ex, pr_a, and pr_b. Notice our new ideal results for the query blue ray by sorting on beta grade. The beta grade values remain closer to the prior grade of 0.3. Notably, our Blu-ray cases have slid to the third most relevant slot, with the single click not pushing the grade much past 0.3.

When we repeat this calculation of judgments for dryer and transformers dark of the moon in figures 11.10 and 11.11, we note that the order is the same, but the grades themselves stay closer to the prior of 0.3 depending on our confidence in the data.

Confidence-adjusted SDBN judgments for q=dryer

	beta_grade	upc	image	name
0	0.3853	856751002097		Practecol - Dryer Balls (2-Pack)
1	0.3748	48231011396	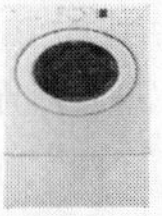	LG - 3.5 Cu. Ft. 7-Cycle High-Efficiency Washer - White
2	0.3158	84691226727		GE - 6.0 Cu. Ft. 3-Cycle Electric Dryer - White
3	0.2946	74108007469		Conair - 1875-Watt Folding Handle Hair Dryer - Blue
4	0.2775	12505525766		Smart Choice - 6' 30 Amp 3-Prong Dryer Cord

Figure 11.10   Beta-adjusted SDBN results for dryer. Notice the grades now are more tightly focused around the prior grade 0.3, with some above or below this prior.

Confidence-adjusted SDBN judgments for q=transformers dark of the moon

	beta_grade	upc	image	name
0	0.5957	97360810042		Transformers: Dark of the Moon - Blu-ray Disc
1	0.4017	400192926087		Transformers: Dark of the Moon - Original Soundtrack - CD
2	0.3673	97363560449		Transformers: Dark of the Moon - Widescreen Dubbed Subtitle - DVD
3	0.3130	97363532149		Transformers: Revenge of the Fallen - Widescreen Dubbed Subtitle - DVD
4	0.2795	93624956037		Transformers: Dark of the Moon - Original Soundtrack - CD

Figure 11.11   Beta-adjusted SDBN results for `transformers dark of the moon`. In figure 11.7, we noted the soundtrack seemed oddly high (`0.48`) in its relevance grade despite fewer clicks than the Blu-ray movie. We now see the soundtrack's relevance closer to the prior of `0.4`.

Figure 11.11 notably shows less confidence in the soundtrack when compared to the SDBN judgments without modeling confidence (figure 11.7). The grade has dropped from `0.4806` to `0.4017`. Notably, the DVD grade following the CD has not changed much, only changing from `0.3951` to `0.3673`, because of our higher confidence in that observation. As more observations come in, it's likely the CD would even move down in ranking if this pattern continues.

Most of your queries won't be like `dryer` or `transformers dark of the moon`. They'll be more like `blue ray`. To meaningfully work with these queries for LTR, you'll need to be able to handle these "small data" problems, such as having lower confidence.

We are beginning to have a more reasonable training set for automating LTR, but there's still work to do. In the next chapter, we'll move to look at the complete search feedback loop. This includes working on presentation bias. Recall that this is the bias where users never examine what search never returns to them. How can we add surveillance to the automated LTR feedback loop to both overcome presentation bias and ensure that our model—and by extension, the judgments—are working as expected?

Before we examine those topics in the next chapter, though, let's look again at training an LTR model end-to-end so you can experiment with what you've learned so far.

11.4 Exploring your training data in an LTR system

Great work! You've made it through chapters 10 and 11. You now have what you need to develop reasonable LTR training data and train an LTR model. You're likely eager to train a model from your work. Instead of repeating the extensive code from chapter 10 here, we've created an "End-to-End Automated Learning to Rank" notebook in the ch11 folder of the book's codebase (4.end-to-end-auto-ltr.ipynb). It will allow you to experiment with LTR on the RetroTech data (figure 11.12).

In this notebook, you can fine-tune the inner LTR engine—the feature engineering and model creation that attempts to satisfy the training data. You can also explore the implications of altering the automated inputs to this engine: the training data itself. Altogether, this notebook has every step you've learned about so far:

1 Processing raw click session data into judgments, using the SDBN click model and a beta prior
2 Transforming the dataframe into the judgments we used in chapter 10
3 Loading a selection of LTR features to use with the search engine's feature store capabilities
4 Logging these features from the search engine and then performing a pairwise transformation of the data into a suitable training set
5 Training and uploading a model to the search engine's model store
6 Searching and ranking with the model

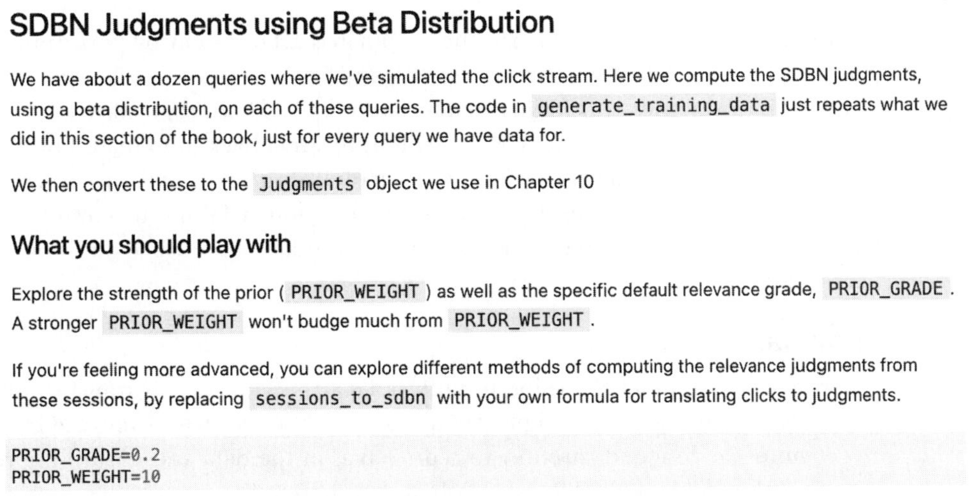

SDBN Judgments using Beta Distribution

We have about a dozen queries where we've simulated the click stream. Here we compute the SDBN judgments, using a beta distribution, on each of these queries. The code in `generate_training_data` just repeats what we did in this section of the book, just for every query we have data for.

We then convert these to the `Judgments` object we use in Chapter 10

What you should play with

Explore the strength of the prior (`PRIOR_WEIGHT`) as well as the specific default relevance grade, `PRIOR_GRADE` . A stronger `PRIOR_WEIGHT` won't budge much from `PRIOR_WEIGHT` .

If you're feeling more advanced, you can explore different methods of computing the relevance judgments from these sessions, by replacing `sessions_to_sdbn` with your own formula for translating clicks to judgments.

```
PRIOR_GRADE=0.2
PRIOR_WEIGHT=10
```

Figure 11.12 Notebook exploring the full LTR system. You can take the model for a test drive.

We invite you to tune the click model parameters and to think of new features, and different ways of arriving at the final LTR model, discovering which ones seem to yield the best results. While you do this tuning, please be sure to question your own subjective assumptions compared to what the data is showing you.

With out-of-the box tuning, we'll leave you with figure 11.13, showing the current search results for the query `transformers dvd`. Try different queries here. How can you help the model better discriminate between relevant and irrelevant documents? Are the problems you encounter due to the training data used? Or are they due to the features used to construct the model?

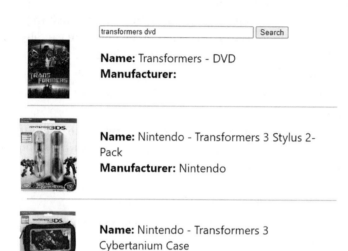

Figure 11.13 How our trained model ranks `transformers dvd`. Do you think you could improve on this?

In the next chapter, we'll finalize the automated LTR system by performing surveillance on the model. Most crucially, we'll consider how to overcome *presentation bias.* Even with the adjustments in this chapter, users will still only ever have a chance to act on what the search shows them. So we still have a feedback loop biased heavily by the current relevance ranking. How can we look out for this problem and overcome it? In the next chapter, we'll consider these problems as our LTR model continues to iteratively incorporate incoming user interactions and actively surface additional promising results.

Summary

- We can automate learning to rank (LTR) if we can reliably transform user click data into relevance judgments using a click model. However, the click model must be designed carefully to reduce bias in the data and ensure the reliability of the automated LTR system when deployed to live users.
- Learned (implicit) relevance judgment lists can be plugged into existing LTR training processes to either replace or augment manually created judgments.

- Raw clicks are usually problematic in automated LTR models due to common biases in how algorithms rank and present search results to users.
- Among the visible search results, position bias says users prefer results ranked near the top. We can overcome position bias by using a click model that tracks the probability that a user has examined a document or a position in the search results.
- Most search applications have a lot of spurious click data. When training data is biased toward these spurious results, we have confidence bias. We can overcome confidence bias by using a beta distribution to create a prior that we update gradually with new observations as they come in.

Overcoming ranking bias through active learning

12

This chapter covers

- Harnessing live user interactions to gather feedback on a deployed LTR model
- A/B testing search relevance solutions with live users
- Using active learning to explore potentially relevant results beyond the top results
- Balancing *exploiting* user interactions while *exploring* what else might be relevant

So far, our learning to rank (LTR) work has taken place in the lab. In previous chapters, we built models using automatically constructed training data from user clicks. In this chapter, we'll take our model into the real world for a test drive with (simulated) live users!

Recall that we compared an automated LTR system to a self-driving car. Internally, the car has an engine: the end-to-end model retraining on historical judgments as discussed in chapter 10. In chapter 11, we compared our model's training data to self-driving car directions: what *should* we optimize to automatically learn judgments based on previous interactions with search results? We built training data and overcame key biases inherent in click data.

In this chapter, our focus is on moving our ranking models from the lab to production. We'll deploy and monitor our models as they receive user traffic. We'll see where the model does well and understand whether the work in the previous two chapters failed or succeeded. This means exploring a new kind of testing to validate our model: *A/B testing*. In *A/B testing* we randomly assign live users to different models and examine business outcomes (sales, etc.), to see which models perform best. You might be familiar with A/B testing in other contexts, but here we'll zero in on the implications for an automated LTR system.

Live users help us not just validate our system, they also aid in escaping dangerous negative feedback loops our models can find themselves in, as shown in figure 12.1.

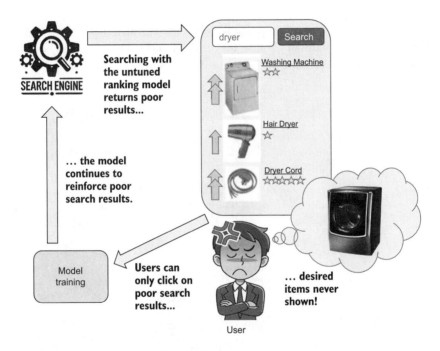

Figure 12.1   Presentation bias's negative feedback loop. Users never click on what the search engine never returns, so relevance models can never grow beyond the current model's knowledge.

In figure 12.1, our model can only learn what's relevant *within the results shown to the user*. In other words, we have an unfortunate chicken-and-egg problem: the model is trained based on what users deem relevant, but what users deem relevant is based on what the model shows them. Good LTR attempts to optimize for results with the most positive interaction signals, but users will only click on what's right in front of them. How could LTR possibly get better when the training data seems hopelessly biased toward the search engine's current ranking? This bias of implicitly derived training data reflecting back the previously displayed results is called *presentation bias*.

After we explore A/B testing, we'll fight presentation bias for the rest of the chapter using active learning. An *active learning* system is one that can interactively gather new labeled data from users to answer new questions. In our case, our active learning algorithm will determine blind spots leading to ranking bias, prompt users to interact with new results exploring those blind spots, and utilize the user interactions as new training data to correct the blind spots. Much like a self-driving car that has only learned one suboptimal path, we'll have to strategically explore alternative promising paths—in our case, additional types of search results—to learn new patterns for what's relevant to users. In figure 12.2, we see the automated LTR loop augmented with this blind-spot exploration.

Before we get to this all-important subject, we must first wrap everything we learned in chapters 10 and 11 into a few lines of code. Then we'll be able to iterate quickly, exploring A/B testing and overcoming presentation bias.

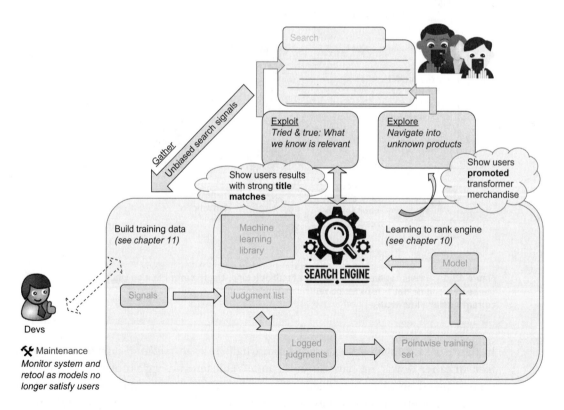

Figure 12.2 Automated LTR meets live users. To be useful, our automated LTR system must overcome presentation bias by exploring yet-to-be-seen results with users to expand training data coverage.

12.1 Our automated LTR engine in a few lines of code

Before we begin to A/B test, let's gather all our knowledge from chapters 10 and 11 into a small handful of reusable Python helper functions. First, we'll define a function to let us rebuild training data from raw session clicks using a simplified dynamic Bayesian network (SDBN) click model (all of chapter 11). Next, we'll create an equally simple snippet of code to train a model with that training data (all of chapter 10). We'll very quickly sum up these functions before diving into A/B testing and overcoming presentation bias in the rest of the chapter.

12.1.1 Turning clicks into training data (chapter 11 in one line of code)

In chapter 11, we turned clicks into training data and explored the SDBN click model, which can overcome biases in how users click on search results. We will reuse much of the code from chapter 11 as we explore additional biases and automate the end-to-end LTR process in this chapter.

As a reminder, our click model turns raw clicks into training labels or *grades* mapping how relevant a document is for a keyword. The raw input we need to build the training data includes a query string, the rank of the result as displayed, the document in that position, and whether it was clicked. We can see that data stored in this dataframe:

```
id  sess_id  query      rank  doc_id        clicked
0   50002    blue ray   0.0   600603141003  True
1   50002    blue ray   1.0   827396513927  False
2   50002    blue ray   2.0   24543672067   False
3   50002    blue ray   3.0   719192580374  False
4   50002    blue ray   4.0   885170033412  True
```

Given this input, we can wrap all of chapter 11 into a reusable function that computes our training data. Recall that we use the term *judgment list* or *judgments* to refer to our training data. We can see our judgments computation in the following listing.

Listing 12.1   Generating training data from sessions (chapter 11)

```
training_data = generate_training_data(sessions, prior_weight=10,
                                       prior_grade=0.2)
display(training_data)
```

Output (truncated):

```
query             doc_id        clicked  examined  grade     beta_grade
blue ray          27242815414   42       42        1.000000  0.846154
                  827396513927  1304     3359      0.388211  0.387652
                  883929140855  140      506       0.276680  0.275194
                  885170033412  568      2147      0.264555  0.264256
                  24543672067   665      2763      0.240680  0.240534
...
transformers dvd  47875819733   24       1679      0.014294  0.015394
                  708056579739  23       1659      0.013864  0.014979
```

```
879862003524      23        1685      0.013650   0.014749
 93624974918      19        1653      0.011494   0.012628
 47875839090      16        1669      0.009587   0.010721
```

The `generate_training_data` function takes in all the user search `sessions`, along with the `prior_weight`, indicating how strong the prior should be weighted (defaults to `10`), and the `prior_grade`, specifying the default probability of a result's relevance when we have no evidence (defaults to `0.2`). See section 11.3.2 for a refresher on how these values influence the SDBN calculation.

Let's briefly revisit what we learned in chapter 11 by looking at listing 12.1. As you can see in the output, we compute a dataframe where each query-document pair has corresponding `clicked` and `examined` counts. Clicks are what they sound like: the sum of raw clicks this product received for this query. Recall that `examined` corresponds to the number of times the click model thinks the user noticed the result.

The `grade` and `beta_grade` statistics are the training labels. These correspond to the probability that a document is relevant for the query. Recall that `grade` simply divides `clicked` by `examined`: the naive, first implementation of the SDBN click model. However, we learned in chapter 11 that it would be better to account for how much information we have (see section 11.3). We don't want one click with one examine (`1 / 1 = 1.0`) to be counted as strongly as a hundred-clicks with a hundred examines (`100 / 100 = 1.0`). For this reason, `beta_grade` places a higher weight on results with more information (preferring the hundred-clicks example). We'll therefore use `beta_grade` as opposed to `grade` when retraining LTR models.

This data served as training data for the LTR models we trained in chapter 10. Next, let's see how we can easily take this training data, train a model, and deploy it.

12.1.2 *Model training and evaluation in a few function calls*

In addition to regenerating training data, we also need to retrain our model before deploying it for live users. In this section, we'll explore the convenience functions for our core LTR model training engine. This will set us up to quickly experiment with models through the rest of this chapter.

We'll wrap model training and offline evaluation in a few simple lines.

> **Listing 12.2 Training and evaluating the model on a few features**

```
def train_and_evaluate_model(sessions, model_name, features, log=False):
  training_data = generate_training_data(sessions)
  train, test = split_training_data(training_data, 0.8)
  train_and_upload_model(train, model_name, features=features, log=log)
  evaluation = evaluate_model(test, model_name, training_data, log=log)
  return evaluation


feature_set = [
  ltr.generate_query_feature(feature_name="long_description_bm25",
                       field_name="long_description"),
```

```
ltr.generate_query_feature(feature_name="short_description_constant",
                           field_name="short_description",
                           constant_score=True)]

evaluation = train_and_evaluate_model(sessions, "ltr_model_variant_1",
                                      feature_set)
display(evaluation)
```

Evaluation for `ltr_model_variant_1`:

```
{"dryer": 0.03753076750950996,
 "blue ray": 0.0,
 "headphones": 0.0846717500031762,
 "dark of moon": 0.0,
 "transformers dvd": 0.0}
```

With the help of listing 12.2, let's briefly revisit what we learned in chapter 10. We define a `feature_set` with two features for LTR: one to search against the `long_description` field, and another to search against the `short_description` field. We must choose carefully, hoping to find features that meaningfully predict relevance and that can be learned from the training data in listing 12.1. We then split the `training_data` into `train` and `test` sets and use the `train` set to train and upload the model.

But how do we know if our model successfully learned from the training data? Splitting the judgments and excluding the `test` set during model training reserves some of the training data for evaluating the trained model. You're like a professor giving the student (here the model) a final exam. You might give students many sample problems to study for the test (the `train` set). But to see if students truly learned the material, as opposed to just memorizing it, you'd give them a final exam with different questions (the `test` set). This helps you evaluate whether the student understands what you've taught them before sending them off into the real world.

Of course, success in the classroom does not always equate to success in the real world. Graduating our model into the real world, with live users in an A/B test, might show it does not perform as well as we hoped!

Finally, what is the statistic next to each test query? How do we evaluate the students' success on the test queries? Recall from chapter 10 that we simply used precision (the proportion of relevant queries). This statistic sums the top N grades and divides by N (for us N = 10), which is effectively the average relevance grade. We recommend exploring other statistics for model training and evaluation that are biased toward getting the top positions correct, such as Discounted Cumulative Gain (DCG), Normalized DGC (NDCG), or Expected Reciprocal Rank (ERR). For our purposes, we'll stay with the simpler precision statistic.

Just judging by the relevance metrics for our test queries in listing 12.2, our model does quite poorly in offline testing. By improving offline metrics, we should see a significant improvement with live users in an A/B test.

12.2 A/B testing a new model

In this section, we'll simulate running an A/B test and compare listing 12.2's model to a model that seems to perform better in the lab. We'll reflect on the results of the A/B test, setting us up to complete the automated LTR feedback loop we introduced in chapter 11. We'll finish by reflecting on what didn't go so well, spending the remainder of the chapter on adding "active learning", a crucial, missing piece to our automated LTR feedback loop.

12.2.1 Taking a better model out for a test drive

Our original LTR model hasn't performed very well, as we saw in the output of listing 12.2. In this section, we'll train a new model, and once it looks promising, we'll deploy it in an A/B test against the model we trained in listing 12.2.

Let's look at the following improved model.

Listing 12.3   A new model improved by changing the features

```
feature_set = [
  ltr.generate_fuzzy_query_feature(feature_name="name_fuzzy",
                                   field_name="name"),
  ltr.generate_bigram_query_feature(feature_name="name_bigram",
                                    field_name="name"),
  ltr.generate_bigram_query_feature(feature_name="short_description_bigram"
                                    field_name="short_description")]

evaluation = train_and_evaluate_model(sessions, "ltr_model_variant_2",
                                      feature_set)
display(evaluation)
```

Evaluation for `ltr_model_variant_2`:

```
{"dryer": 0.07068309073137659,      #Before: 0.038
 "blue ray": 0.0,                   # 0.0
 "headphones": 0.06540945492120899, # 0.085
 "dark of moon": 0.2576592004029579, # 0.0
 "transformers dvd": 0.10077083021678328} # 0.0
```

In the preceding listing, we define a `feature_set` containing three features: `name_fuzzy`, which performs a fuzzy search against the `name` field, `name_bigram`, which performs a two-word phrase search on the `name` field, and `short_description_bigram`, which performs a two-word phrase search against the `short_description` field. Like before, this model is trained, deployed, and evaluated. Notice the output of listing 12.3—on the same set of test queries, our model seems to perform much better. This seems promising! Indeed, we've chosen a set of features that seems to capture the text-matching aspects of relevance better.

The astute reader might notice we've kept the test queries the same as in listing 12.2. We've intentionally done this for clarity. It's good enough to teach you fundamental AI-powered search skills. In real life, however, we would want a truly random test/train split to better evaluate the model's performance. We might even take things further, performing *cross-validation*—the resampling and training of many models on different test/train dataset splits to ensure the models generalize well without overfitting to the training data. If you'd like to dive deeper into offline model evaluation, we recommend a more general machine learning book, such as *Machine Learning Bootcamp* by Alexey Grigorev (Manning, 2021).

Perhaps your search team feels the model trained in listing 12.3 has promise and is good enough to deploy to production. The team's hopes are up, so let's see what happens when we deploy to production for further evaluation with live users.

12.2.2 Defining an A/B test in the context of automated LTR

By the end of chapter 11, we had developed an end-to-end LTR retraining process: we could take incoming user signals to generate a click model, use the click model to generate judgments, use the judgments to train an LTR model, and then deploy the LTR model to production to gather more signals to restart the process. With this LTR retraining loop set up, we can easily deploy promising new ranking models.

We haven't actually deployed our LTR models to production yet, though. We've only developed the theoretical models. How do we know whether what we built in the lab performs well in the real world? It's quite a different thing to handle live, real-world scenarios.

In this section, we'll explore the results of A/B testing with (simulated) live users. Because this is a book with a codebase you're running locally, it's unfortunately not possible for us to have real users hitting our application. Therefore, the "live" user traffic we'll use will just be simulated from within our codebase. For our purposes, this traffic simulation is similar enough to live user interactions to successfully demonstrate the active learning process.

We'll see how the A/B test serves as the ultimate arbiter of our automated LTR system's success. It will enable us to correct problems in our offline automated LTR model training so the feedback loop can progressively grow more reliable.

You may know about A/B tests, but here we'll demonstrate how they factor into an automated LTR system. As illustrated in figure 12.3, an *A/B test* randomly assigns users to two *variants*. Each *variant* contains a distinct set of application features. This might include anything from different button colors to new relevance ranking algorithms. Because users are randomly assigned to the variants, we can more reliably infer which variant performs best on chosen business outcomes, such as sales, time spent on the app, user retention, or whatever else the business might choose to prioritize.

When running an A/B test, you will usually make one of the variants a *control group* representing the current default algorithm. Having a control allows you to measure the improvement of other models. It's also common to perform multivariate testing, whereby multiple variants or combinations of variants are tested simultaneously. More advanced testing strategies can be implemented, like multi-arm bandit testing, where the test continually shifts live traffic toward the currently best-performing variants, or signals-based backtesting, where you use historical data to simulate the A/B test to predict the best variant offline before even showing results to live users.

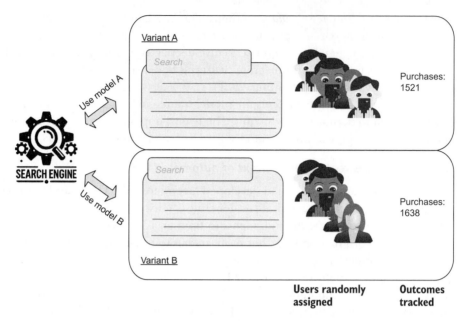

Figure 12.3   A search A/B test. Search users are randomly assigned to two relevance algorithms (here two LTR models) with outcomes tracked.

12.2.3 *Graduating the better model into an A/B test*

Next, we'll deploy our promising new model, `ltr_model_variant_2` from listing 12.3, into an A/B test. We'll then explore the implications of the test results. Hopes are high, and your team thinks this model might knock the socks off the competition: the poorly performing `ltr_model_variant_1` from listing 12.2.

In this section, we'll simulate an A/B test, assigning 1,000 users randomly to each model. In our case, these simulated users have specific items they want to buy. If they see those items, they'll make a purchase and leave our store happy. If they don't, they might browse around, but they'll most likely leave without making a purchase. Our search team, of course, doesn't know what users hope to buy—this information is hidden from us. We only see a stream of clicks and purchases, which, as we'll see, is heavily influenced by presentation bias.

In listing 12.4, we have a population of users seeking the newest Transformers movies by searching for `transformers dvd`. We'll stay focused on this single query during our discussion. Of course, with a real A/B test, we'd look over the full query set, and the user population wouldn't be this static. By zeroing in on one query, though, we can more concretely understand the implications of our A/B test for automated LTR. For a deeper overview of good A/B testing experimentation, we recommend the book *Experimentation for Engineers: From A/B testing to Bayesian optimization* by David Sweet (Manning, 2023).

For each run of the `a_b_test` function in listing 12.4, a model is assigned at random. Then the `simulate_live_user_session` function simulates a user searching with the query and selected model, scanning the results, possibly clicking and making a purchase. Unbeknownst to us, our user population has hidden preferences behind their queries, which are simulated in `simulate_live_user_session`. We run `a_b_test` 1,000 times, collecting the purchases made by users that use each model.

Listing 12.4   Simulated A/B test for the query `transformers dvd`

```
def a_b_test(query, model_a, model_b):
    draw = random.random()                                   Randomly assigns each
    model_name = model_a if draw < 0.5 else model_b   ◁───   user to model a or b
    purchase_made = simulate_live_user_session(query,
                                       model_name)           Simulates a user's searching
    return (model_name, purchase_made)                       and purchasing behavior


def simulate_user_a_b_test(query, model_a, model_b, number_of_users=1000):
    purchases = {model_a: 0, model_b: 0}
    for _ in range(number_of_users):
        model_name, purchase_made = a_b_test(query, model_a, model_b)        Simulates the
        if purchase_made:                                                    number_of_users
            purchases[model_name] += 1    Counts the total number of         being tested
    return purchases                      purchases made by each model

results = simulate_user_a_b_test("transformers dvd",
                                 "ltr_model_variant_1",
                                 "ltr_model_variant_2")
display(results)
```

Output:

```
{"ltr_model_variant_1": 21,
 "ltr_model_variant_2": 15}
```

As we see in the output of listing 12.4, `ltr_model_variant_2` (our golden student), actually performs *worse* in this A/B test! How can this be? What could have gone wrong for it to have such good offline test metric performance but poor outcomes in the real world?

For the rest of this chapter, we'll dive into what's happening and attempt to address the problem. Thus, you'll learn how live users can increase the accuracy of your automated LTR system, allowing you to retrain with confidence!

12.2.4   When "good" models go bad: What we can learn from a failed A/B test

As we saw in listing 12.4, a lot can change when our model enters the real world. In this section, we'll reflect on the implications of the A/B test we just ran to see what next steps would be appropriate.

When a model performs well in the lab but fails an A/B test, it means that while we may have built a "correct" LTR model, we built it to the wrong specification. We need to correct problems with the training data itself: the judgments generated from our click model.

But how might problems creep into our click-model-based judgments? We saw two problems in chapter 11: *position bias* and *confidence bias*. Depending on your goals, UX, and domain, additional biases can creep in. In e-commerce, users might be enticed to click an item that's on sale, skewing the data toward those items. In a research setting, one article might provide a richer summary in the search results than another. Some biases blur the line between "bias" and actual relevance for that domain. A product with a missing image, for example, might get fewer clicks. It might be technically identical to another "relevant" product with an image, but, to users, a product missing an image seems less trustworthy and thus won't be clicked. Is that a bias or simply an actual indicator of relevance for this domain, where product trustworthiness is a factor?

To make better judgments, should clicks be ignored or discounted, and should we instead use other behavioral signals? Perhaps follow-on actions after clicking, such as clicking a "like" button, adding an item to a cart, or clicking a "read more" button, ought to be included? Perhaps we should ignore "cheap" or accidental clicks when the user immediately hits the back button after clicking?

Considering post-click actions can be valuable. However, we must ask how strongly search ranking influences events like a purchase or add-to-cart, or whether they are attributable to other factors. For example, a lack of purchases could indicate a problem with a product display page, or with a complex checkout process, not just with the search result's relevance for a specific query.

We might use an outcome like total purchases, in aggregate over all queries for each test group, to evaluate an A/B test. As long as all other variables in the app remain unchanged, except the ranking algorithm, then we know any significant difference in purchases across test groups must be caused by the one thing we changed. However, in the specific query-to-document relationship, causality gets complicated. Any single product may have very few purchases (many people view a $2,000 television, but very few buy). The data may simply lack enough quantity to know whether the purchase is exclusively related to a product's specific relevance for a query.

Accounting for all the variations in search UX, domains, and behaviors would fill many books and still fall short. The search space constantly evolves, with new ways of interacting with search results coming in and out of fashion. For most scenarios, using clicks and standard click models will suffice. Clicks in search UIs have been heavily studied. Still, arriving at good judgments is both an art and science; you may find a slight modification to a click model that accounts for extra signals is important to your domain and may provide tremendous gains in how your model performs in an A/B test. You can spend as much time perfecting your click model as you do developing your search engine.

However, there is one universally pernicious training data problem that challenges all click models: presentation bias. *Presentation bias* occurs when our models can't learn what's relevant from user clicks because the results never show up to be clicked in the first place. We'll dive into this difficult problem next and learn how to overcome this bias by simultaneously optimizing both for what our models have already learned and for what they still need to learn.

12.3 Overcoming presentation bias: Knowing when to explore vs. exploit

Regardless of whether we use clicks or more complex signals, users never interact with what they can't see. In other words, underneath automated LTR is a chicken and egg problem: if the relevant result is never returned by the original, poorly tuned system, how could any click-based machine learning system learn that the result is relevant?

In this section, you'll learn about one machine learning technique that selects documents to explore *despite those results having no click data.* This final missing piece of our automated LTR system helps us not just build models optimized for the training data, but actively participates in its own learning to grow the breadth of the available training data. We call a system that participates in its own learning an *active learning* system.

Figure 12.4 demonstrates presentation bias. The items on the right side of the figure could feasibly be relevant for our query, but, without traffic, we have no data to know either way. It would be nice to send some traffic to these results to learn whether users find them relevant.

Figure 12.4 Presentation bias (versus unexplored results) for the query `dryer`

To overcome presentation bias, we must carefully balance *exploiting* our model's current, hard-earned knowledge and *exploring* beyond that knowledge. This is the *explore versus exploit* tradeoff. Exploring lets us gain knowledge, growing the coverage of our click model to new and different types of documents. However, if we always explore, we will never take advantage of our knowledge. When we *exploit*, we optimize for what we currently know performs well. Exploiting corresponds to our current LTR model that aligns with our training data. Knowing how to systematically balance exploring and exploiting is key, and it's something we'll discuss in the next few sections using a machine learning tool (a Gaussian process) built for this purpose.

12.3.1 Presentation bias in the RetroTech training data

Let's first analyze the current training data to get the lay of the land. What kinds of search results does the training data lack? Where is our knowledge incomplete? Another way of saying "presentation bias" is that there are potentially relevant search results excluded from the training data: blind spots we must detect and fight against. Once we've defined those blind spots, we can better correct them. This will set us up to retrain with a more robust model.

In listing 12.5, we create a new feature set named `explore_feature_set`, in which we have three simple features: `long_description_match`, `short_description_match`, and `name_match`, telling us whether a given field match occurs or not. These correspond to features our model has already learned. In addition, we've added a `has_promotion` feature. This feature becomes a `1.0` if the product is on sale and is being promoted through marketing channels. We haven't explored this feature before; perhaps it's a blind spot?

Listing 12.5 Analyzing missing types of documents

```
def get_latest_explore_feature_set():
  return [
    ltr.generate_query_feature(
      feature_name="long_description_match",
      field_name="long_description",
      constant_score=True),
    ltr.generate_query_feature(
      feature_name="short_description_match",
      field_name="short_description",
      constant_score=True),
    ltr.generate_query_feature(
      feature_name="name_match",
      field_name="name", constant_score=True),
    ltr.generate_query_feature(
      feature_name="has_promotion",
      field_name="has_promotion", value="true")]

def get_logged_transformers_judgments(sessions, features):
  training_data = generate_training_data(sessions)
  logged_judgments = generate_logged_judgments(training_data,
                                       features, "explore")
  logged_judgments = logged_judgments \
    [logged_judgments["query"] == "transformers dvd"]
  return logged_judgments
```

Features corresponding to fields already used to train the LTR model.

New feature we're exploring for blind spot: promotions

Logs the feature values and returns the SDBN judgments joined with the feature values

Builds SDBN judgments from the current raw sessions

Examines the properties of the current "transformers dvd" training data

```
explore_features = get_latest_explore_features()
logged_transformers_judgments = get_logged_transformers_judgments(sessions,
                                                      explore_features)
display(logged_transformers_judgments)
```

Output:

```
doc_id          query           grade  long_desc*_match  name_match
                                       short_desc*_match  has_promotion
------------------------------------------------------------------------
97363560449    transformers dvd 0.34   0.0   0.0              1.0   0.0
97361312804    transformers dvd 0.34   0.0   0.0              1.0   0.0
97361312743    transformers dvd 0.34   0.0   0.0              1.0   0.0
97363455349    transformers dvd 0.34   0.0   0.0              1.0   0.0
...
708056579739   transformers dvd 0.01   1.0   1.0              1.0   0.0
879862003524   transformers dvd 0.01   1.0   1.0              1.0   0.0
93624974918    transformers dvd 0.01   0.0   0.0              1.0   0.0
47875839090    transformers dvd 0.01   1.0   0.0              1.0   0.0
```

We can see some gaps in our training data's knowledge in the output of listing 12.5:

- Every item includes a name match.
- No promotions (has_promotion=0) are present.
- There's a range of long_description_match and short_description_match values.

Intuitively, if we want to expand our knowledge, we should show users searching for transformers dvd something completely outside the box from what's in the output of listing 12.5. That would mean showing users a promoted item, and possibly one with no name match. In other words, we need to get search out of its own echo chamber by explicitly diversifying what we show to the user, moving away from what's in the training data. The only question is, how much of a risk are we willing to take to improve our knowledge? We don't want to blanket the search results with random products just to broaden our training data.

What we've done so far has not been systematic: we've only analyzed a single query to see what was missing. How might we automate this? Next up, we'll discuss one method for automating exploration using a tool called a Gaussian process.

12.3.2   Beyond the ad hoc: Thoughtfully exploring with a Gaussian process

A *Gaussian process* is a statistical model that makes predictions and provides a probability distribution capturing the certainty of that prediction. In this section, we'll use a Gaussian process to select areas for exploration. Later in this chapter, we'll create a more robust way of finding gaps in our data.

GAUSSIAN PROCESS BY EXAMPLE: EXPLORING A NEW RIVER BY EXPLOITING EXISTING KNOWLEDGE
To get an intuition for Gaussian processes, let's use a concrete example of real-life exploration. Working through this example will enable you to think more intuitively about how we might, mathematically, make explore versus exploit tradeoffs.

Imagine you're a scientist planning to survey a rarely explored river deep in the wilderness. As you plan your trip, you have only spotty river depth observations from past expeditions to know when it's safe to travel. For example, one observation shows the river is two meters deep in April; another time in August it's one meter deep. You'd like to pick a date for your expedition that optimizes for ideal river conditions (i.e., not monsoon season, but also not during a dry spell). However, you're also a scientist—you'd like to make observations during yet-unobserved times of the year to increase your knowledge of the river. Figure 12.5 shows river depth measurements made throughout the year.

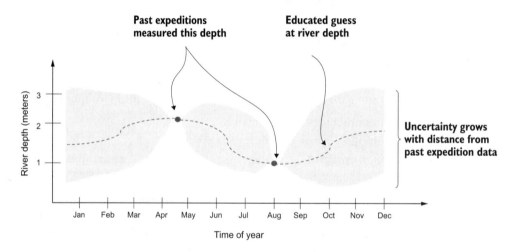

Figure 12.5 **Exploring a river, with uncertainty of the river's depth increasing as we get further away from past observations. How would we pick a time of year that is both safe and maximally increases our knowledge of the river's depth?**

How might we choose a date for the expedition? If you observed a river depth of two meters on April 14th, you would guess that the April 15th depth would be very close to two meters. Traveling during that time might be pleasant: you trust the river wouldn't be excessively flooded. However, you wouldn't gain much knowledge about the river. What about trying to go several months away from this observation, like January? January would be too far from April to understand the river's likely depth. We might travel during a treacherous time of the year, but we'd almost certainly gain new knowledge—perhaps far more than we bargained for! With so little data to go on, there may be too much risk exploring at this time of the year.

In figure 12.5 we see an educated guess at the river level, based on an expected correlation between adjacent dates (April 15th and 14th should be very close). Our level of certainty decreases as we move away from direct observations, represented by the widening gray zone.

Figure 12.5 illustrates a Gaussian process. It mathematically captures predictions, along with our uncertainty in each prediction. How does this relate to relevance ranking? Just as nearby dates have similar river levels, similar search results would be similar in their relevance. Consider our explore features from listing 12.5. Those with strong name matches for `transformers dvd`, that are not promoted, and with no short/long description matches would likely have similar relevance grades—all moderately relevant. As we move away from these well-trodden examples—perhaps adding promoted items—we grow less certain about our educated guesses. If we go very far, way outside the box, such as a search result with no name match, that is promoted, but that has strong short/long description field matches, our uncertainty grows very high. Just like the scientist considering a trip in January, we have almost no ability to make a good guess about whether those results could be relevant. It might involve too much risk to show those results to users.

We can use Gaussian processes to balance exploiting existing relevance knowledge with riskier exploration to gain knowledge. Gaussian processes use incomplete information to make careful tradeoffs in the likely quality and the knowledge gained. For example, we can trade off ideal river conditions or a likely relevant search result against learning more about river conditions or about the relevance of a new kind of search result. We can carefully choose how far away from known, safe search results we want to venture to gain new knowledge.

In our `transformers dvd` case, what kind of search result would have a high upside, would likely also be relevant/safe to explore, but also would maximally increase our knowledge? Let's train a Gaussian process and find out!

TRAINING AND ANALYZING A GAUSSIAN PROCESS

Let's get hands-on to see how a Gaussian process works. We'll train a Gaussian process on the `transformers dvd` query. We'll then use it to generate the best exploration candidates. You'll see how we can score those exploration candidates to maximally reduce our risk and increase the likelihood we'll gain knowledge.

In the following listing, we train a Gaussian process using the `GaussianProcess-Regressor` (aka `gpr`) from `sklearn`. This code creates a Gaussian process that attempts to predict the relevance `grade` as a function of the `explore_feature_set` features we logged.

Listing 12.6   Training a `GaussianProcessRegressor` on our training data

```
from sklearn.gaussian_process import GaussianProcessRegressor

def train_gpr(logged_judgments, feature_names):
    feature_data = logged_judgments[feature_names]
    grades = logged_judgments["grade"]
    gpr = GaussianProcessRegressor()
    gpr.fit(feature_data, grades)
    return gpr
```

Uses the features logged from the `explore_feature_set` in listing 12.5

Predicts relevance grades

Creates and trains the gpr model

Once we've trained a `GaussianProcessRegressor`, we can use it to make predictions. Remember that a `GaussianProcessRegressor` not only predicts a value, it also returns the probability distribution of that prediction. This helps us gauge the model's certainty.

In listing 12.7, we generate candidate feature values we'd like to possibly explore. With our river exploration example, these values correspond to possible exploration dates for our scientist's expedition. In our case, as each feature can either be 0 or 1, we look at each possible feature value as a candidate.

Listing 12.7   Predicting a set of candidates to explore

Generates a candidate matrix with a possible value of 0 or 1 for each feature we want to explore

```
def calculate_prediction_data(logged_judgments, feature_names):
  index = pandas.MultiIndex.from_product([[0, 1]] * 4,
                              names=feature_names)
  with_prediction = pandas.DataFrame(index=index).reset_index()
```

Predicts grade and standard deviation for those candidates based on the gpr probability distribution

```
  gpr = train_gpr(logged_judgments, feature_names)
  predictions_with_std = gpr.predict(
    with_prediction[feature_names], return_std=True)
  with_prediction["predicted_grade"] = predictions_with_std[0]
  with_prediction["predicted_stddev"] = predictions_with_std[1]
```

Stores the predicted grade and standard deviation from the gpr

```
  return  with_prediction.sort_values("predicted_stddev", ascending=True)

explore_features = get_latest_explore_features()
logged_transformers_judgments = get_logged_transformers_judgments(sessions,
                                                explore_features)
feature_names = [f["name"] for f in explore_features]
prediction_data = calculate_prediction_data(logged_transformers_judgments,
                                                feature_names)
display(prediction_data)
```

Output:

```
long_description_match   name_match      predicted_grade
        short_description_match   has_promotion          prediction_stddev
0       0               1         0       0.256798        0.000004
1       0               1         0       0.014674        0.000005
1       1               1         0       0.014864        0.000007
0       1               1         0       0.022834        0.000010
1       0               1         1       0.018530        0.000010
0       0               1         1       0.161596        0.632121
1       1               1         1       0.014856        0.632121
```

In the output of listing 12.7, we see a `predicted_grade`—the educated guess from `gpr` on the relevance of that example. We also have `prediction_stddev`, which captures the gray band in figure 12.5—how much uncertainty is in the prediction.

We note in the output of listing 12.7 that the standard deviation is near 0 for the first four products with `name_match=1`. In other words, the `gpr` tends to have more confidence when `name_match=1`. We see after these observations that the standard deviation dramatically increases, as we lack a great deal of knowledge beyond these initial name-matching examples.

The output begins to show the presentation biases we intuitively detected in listing 12.5. We find a tremendous amount of knowledge about the importance of name matches, but little knowledge about other cases. Which case would be worth exploring with live users and also minimizes the risk that we'll show users something completely strange in the search results?

In listing 12.8, we generate and score exploration candidates using an algorithm called *expected improvement*, which predicts the candidates with the highest potential upside. We'll only cover the basic details of this algorithm, so we recommend the article "Exploring Bayesian Optimization" by Agnihotri and Batra if you'd like to learn more (https://distill.pub/2020/bayesian-optimization).

Listing 12.8   Calculating expected improvement for exploration

```
def calculate_expected_improvement(logged_judgments, feature_names, theta=0.6):
    data = calculate_prediction_data(logged_judgments, feature_names)
    data["opportunity"] = (data["predicted_grade"] -
            logged_judgments["grade"].mean() - theta)
```
Is the predicted grade likely to be above or below the typical grade?

```
    data["prob_of_improvement"] = (
      norm.cdf(data["opportunity"] /
            data["predicted_stddev"]))
```
Probability we'll improve over the mean, considering the amount of uncertainty in the prediction

```
    data["expected_improvement"] = (
      data["opportunity"] * data["prob_of_improvement"] +
      data["predicted_stddev"] *
      norm.pdf(data["opportunity"] /
            data["predicted_stddev"]))
```
How much there is to gain, given the probability and improvement and the magnitude of the improvement.

```
    return data.sort_values("expected_improvement",
                    ascending=False)
```
Sorts to show the best exploration candidates

```
improvement_data = calculate_expected_improvement(
     logged_transformers_judgments, feature_names)
display(improvement_data)
```

Output:

```
long_description_match  name_match  opportunity          expected_improvement
    short_description_match  has_promotion      prob_of_improvement
0   0                   0   1           -0.638497  0.234728  0.121201
0   1                   0   1           -0.725962  0.213214  0.110633
0   0                   0   0           -0.580755  0.232556  0.107853
1   1                   0   1           -0.727500  0.204914  0.101653
0   1                   0   0           -0.722661  0.181691  0.078549
```

The higher the expected improvement, the higher the predicted upside for the exploration candidate. But how does the algorithm quantify this potential upside? It's either the case that we know to a high degree of certainty there's an upside (standard deviation is low and the predicted grade is high) or we know that there's a high degree of uncertainty but the predicted grade is still high enough to take a gamble. We can see this in the following code from listing 12.8:

```
data["expected_improvement"] = (
  data["opportunity"] * data["prob_of_improvement"] +
  (data["prediction_stddev"] * norm.pdf(data["opportunity"] /
                                  data["prediction_stddev"])))
```

An opportunity that is more of a sure thing is covered by this first expression:

```
data["opportunity"] * data["prob_of_improvement"]
```

Meanwhile, an unknown opportunity with wide variability is covered by this second expression (after the +):

```
data["prediction_stddev"] * norm.pdf(data["opportunity"] /
                                  data["prediction_stddev"])
```

In the first expression, you'll notice that the opportunity (how much we expect to gain) times the probability that improvement happens corresponds to feeling confident in a good outcome. On the other hand, the second expression depends much more on the standard deviation. The higher the standard deviation *and* opportunity, the more likely it will be selected.

We can calibrate our risk tolerance with a parameter called `theta`: the higher this value, the more we prefer candidates with a higher standard deviation. A high `theta` causes `opportunity` to diminish toward 0. This biases scoring to the second expression—the unknown, higher standard deviation cases.

If we set `theta` too high, our `gpr` selects candidates to learn about without considering whether they might be useful to the user. If `theta` is too low, we don't explore new candidates very much and instead will be biased toward existing knowledge. A high `theta` is analogous to a scientist taking a high degree of risk (like exploring in January) in figure 12.5, while a very low `theta` corresponds to traveling during a risk-averse time (like mid-April). Because we're using this algorithm to augment an existing LTR system, we chose `theta` of `0.6` (a bit high) to give us more knowledge.

In the output of listing 12.8, we see that `gpr` confirms our earlier ad hoc analysis: we should show users items with promotions. These products will more likely yield greater knowledge, with possibly a high upside from the gamble.

Now that we have identified the kind of products we should explore, let's gather products from the search engine to show users. The following listing shows how we might go about selecting products for exploration that we can later intersperse into the existing model's search results.

Listing 12.9 Selecting a product to explore from the search engine

```
def explore(query, logged_judgments, features):
    feature_names = [f["name"] for f in features]
    prediction_data = calculate_expected_improvement(logged_judgments,
                                                     feature_names)
    explore_vector = prediction_data.head().iloc[0][feature_names]
    return search_for_explore_candidate(explore_vector, query)

explore_features = get_latest_explore_features()
logged_judgments = get_logged_transformers_judgments(sessions,
                                                     explore_features)
exploration_upc = explore("transformers dvd", logged_judgments,
                          explore_features)["upc"]
print(exploration_upc)
```

Explores according to the provided explore vector and selects a random doc from that group — `def explore(query, logged_judgments, features):`

Extracts the best exploration candidate features based on expected_improvement — `explore_vector = prediction_data.head().iloc[0][feature_names]`

Searches for a candidate matching the criteria — `return search_for_explore_candidate(explore_vector, query)`

Output:

```
826663114164    # Transformers: The Complete Series [25th Anniversary ... ]
```

In listing 12.9, we take the best exploration candidate—promoted items—and issue a query to fetch documents with those characteristics. We omit the lower-level translation here of converting the candidate into a query (the `explore_query` function), but you can imagine that if `has_promotion=1.0` in the candidate, that we would issue a query searching for any item with a promotion (`has_promotion=true`), and so on for other features.

We see in the output of listing 12.9 that for the query `transformers dvd`, the randomly selected promoted product for exploration is 826663114164. This corresponds to *Transformers: The Complete Series [25th Anniversary Matrix of Leadership Edition] [16 Discs] - DVD*. Interesting!

What should we do with this document? This comes down to a design decision. A common choice is to slot it into the third position of the results, as this allows the user to still see the previously most relevant results first, but also ensures that the explore result gets high visibility. Note our 826663114164 document in the third slot (`rank=2.0`).

```
doc_id         product_name          sess_id query              rank click
93624974918    Transformers: Revenge O...  100049  transformers dvd   0.0  False
879862003524   Razer - DeathAdder Tran...  100049  transformers dvd   1.0  False
826663114164   Transformers: The Compl...  100049  transformers dvd   2.0  False
708056579739   Nintendo - Transformers...  100049  transformers dvd   3.0  False
```

We've simulated many similar exploration sessions in the accompanying notebook. Since we don't have actual live users hitting our app, the simulation code is implemented just for demonstration purposes so we can integrate explore candidates for active learning within our automated LTR system. In a real production environment, you would be showing results to real users instead of simulating user sessions.

Each session adds a random exploration candidate based on listing 12.9, simulates whether the added exploration result was clicked, and appends it to a new set of sessions: `sessions_with_exploration`. Recall that these sessions serve as the input we need to compute LTR training data (the SDBN-based judgments from chapter 11 that are generated in listing 12.1).

Finally, we have the data needed to rerun our automated LTR training loop. We'll see what happens with these examples added to our training data and how we can fit this exploration into the overall automated LTR algorithm.

12.3.3   *Examining the outcome of our explorations*

We've explored by showing some outside-the-box search results to (simulated) live users. We now have new sessions appended to the original session data stored in the `sessions_with_exploration` dataframe. In this section, we'll run the session data through our automated LTR functions to regenerate training data and train a model. We'll then run this new model in an A/B test to see the results.

As you'll recall, our automated LTR helpers can regenerate training data using the `generate_training_data` function. We do this in listing 12.10, but this time with our augmented sessions that include exploration data.

Listing 12.10   Regenerating SDBN judgments from new sessions

```
query = "transformers dvd"
sessions_with_exploration = generate_simulated_exploration_sessions(
  query, sessions, logged_transformers_judgments, explore_features)
training_data_with_exploration = \
  generate_training_data(sessions_with_exploration)
display(training_data_with_exploration.loc["transformers dvd"])
```

Output:

doc_id	product_name	click	examined	grade	beta_grade
97360724240	Transformers: Revenge of...	43	44	0.977	0.833333
826663114164	Transformers: The Comple...	42	44	0.954	0.814815
97360722345	Transformers/Transformer...	46	55	0.836	0.738462
97363455349	Transformers - Widescree...	731	2113	0.345	0.345266
97361312804	Transformers - Widescree...	726	2109	0.344	0.343558

We see in listing 12.10's output that a new product has been included. Note specifically the addition of 826663114164, *Transformers: The Complete Series [25th Anniversary Matrix of Leadership Edition] [16 Discs] - DVD*. Interestingly, this movie has has_promotion=true, meaning it was one of the newly selected explore candidates from the previous section:

```
{"upc": "826663114164",
 "name": "Transformers: The Complete Series [25th Anniversary ...] - DVD",
 "manufacturer": "",
 "short_description": "",
 "long_description": "",
 "has_promotion": True}
```

It seems users are drawn to promoted products, so let's move our `has_promotion` feature from the explore feature set to our main model and retrain to see the effect. In the following listing, we train a model with this new feature added to the mix to see the effect.

Listing 12.11   Rebuilding model using updated judgments

```
promotion_feature_set = [
  ltr.generate_fuzzy_query_feature(feature_name="name_fuzzy",
                                   field_name="name"),
  ltr.generate_bigram_query_feature(feature_name="name_bigram",
                                    field_name="name"),
  ltr.generate_bigram_query_feature(feature_name="short_description_bigram",
                                    field_name="short_description"),
  ltr.generate_query_feature(feature_name="has_promotion",
                             field_name="has_promotion",
                             value="true",
                             constant_score=True)]
```

> Adding has_promotion to the feature set we're training our model with

```
evaluation = train_and_evaluate_model(sessions_with_exploration,
                                      "ltr_model_variant_3",
                                      feature_set)
display(evaluation)
```

Evaluation for `ltr_model_variant_3`:

```
{"dryer": 0.12737002598513025,        # Before: 0.071
 "blue ray": 0.08461538461538462,         # 0.0
 "headphones": 0.12110565745285455,       # 0.065
 "dark of moon": 0.1492224251599605,      # 0.258
 "transformers dvd": 0.26947504217124457}  # 0.101
```

Wow! When comparing listing 12.11 to the earlier output from listing 12.3, we see that adding a promoted product to the training data creates a significant improvement in most cases in our offline test evaluation. The precision of `transformers dvd`, in particular, jumped significantly! If we issue a search for `transformers dvd`, we see this reflected in our data.

Listing 12.12   Searching for `transformers dvd` using the latest model

```
results = ltr.search_with_model("ltr_model_variant_3",
                                query="transformers dvd",
                                rerank_query="transformers dvd",
                                limit=5)["docs"]
display([doc["name"] for doc in results])
```

Output:

```
["Transformers/Transformers: Revenge of the Fallen: Two-Movie Mega Coll...",
 "Transformers: Revenge of the Fallen - Widescreen - DVD",
 "Transformers: Dark of the Moon - Original Soundtrack - CD",
 "Transformers: The Complete Series [25th Anniversary Matrix of Leaders...",
 "Transformers: Dark of the Moon Stealth Force Edition - Nintendo Wii"]
```

However, we know great-looking test results don't always translate to the real world. What happens when we rerun the A/B test from listing 12.4? If you recall, we created an a_b_test function that randomly selects a model for a user's search. If the results contained an item the user secretly wanted to purchase, a purchase would likely occur. If we use this function to resimulate an A/B test, we see our new model appears to have hit the jackpot!

Listing 12.13   Rerunning A/B test on new `ltr_model_variant_3` model

```
results = simulate_user_a_b_test(query="transformers dvd",
                                 model_a="ltr_model_variant_1",
                                 model_b="ltr_model_variant_3",
                                 number_of_users=1000)
display(results)
```

Output:

```
{"ltr_model_variant_1": 21,
 "ltr_model_variant_3": 145}
```

Now we see that the new model (`ltr_model_variant_3`) has significantly outperformed the old model (`ltr_model_variant_1`) in the A/B test. We now know that not only did our exploration help us find a theoretical gap in the training data, but that when we tested the new model in a real-world scenario for our target query (`transformers dvd`), it performed significantly better than the old "exploit-only" model. While we focused on a particular query in this chapter, the same process can be applied across many queries and exploration candidates to continue to automatically refine your LTR model with active learning.

We've now implemented an automated LTR system that not only relearns from the latest user signals, but that uses active learning to explore what else might be relevant to live users and then collects the corresponding signals measuring their feedback. This active learning process helps remove blind spots in the training data on an ongoing basis.

12.4   Exploit, explore, gather, rinse, repeat: A robust automated LTR loop

With the final pieces in place, we see how exploring new features helps us to overcome presentation bias. Feature exploration and training data exploration go hand-in-hand, as we learn our presentation biases by understanding the features we lack and may need to engineer into search. In this chapter, we used a simple example with "promotions", but what other, more complex, features might show blind spots in your training data? In this section, let's conclude by augmenting our automated LTR algorithm from chapter 11 to include not just training a model with previous click-model-based training data, but also this new active learning approach to explore beyond the training data's current scope.

Our new auto-exploring automated LTR algorithm can be summarized in these three main steps:

1 *Exploit*—Use known features and train the LTR model for ranking using existing training data.
2 *Explore*—Generate hypothesized, "explore" features to eliminate training data blind spots.
3 *Gather*—With a deployed model and a trained `gpr` model, show explore/exploit search results, and gather clicks to build judgments.

We can summarize the past three chapters by combining them into listing 12.14, shown next. This listing puts all the pieces together (with some internals omitted). Our main decision points in this algorithm are the features used to explore and exploit. We can also go under the hood to change the chosen click model, the LTR model architecture, and our risk tolerance (the `theta` parameter).

Listing 12.14   Summarizing the fully automated LTR algorithm

```
def train_and_deploy_model(sessions, model_name, feature_set):
  judgments = generate_training_data(sessions)
  train, test = split_training_data(judgments, 0.8)           Returns the
  train_ranksvm_model(train, model_name, feature_set=feature_set)   model once
                                                               once per day

def ltr_retraining_loop(latest_sessions, iterations=sys.maxsize,
                    retraining_frequency=60 * 60 * 24):
  exploit_feature_set = get_exploit_feature_set()
  train_and_deploy_model(latest_sessions,          Trains the LTR model on
                  "exploit",                        known good features and
                  exploit_feature_set)              current training data
  for i in range(0, iterations):                    Collects the new sessions
    judgments = generate_training_data(latest_sessions)   and repeats the process
    train, test = split_training_data(judgments)
    if i > 0:
      previous_explore_model_name = f"explore_variant_{i-1}"
      exploit_model_evaluation = evaluate_model(test_data=test,
        model_name="exploit", training_data=train)
      explore_model_evaluation = evaluate_model(test_data=test,
        model_name=previous_explore_model_name, training_data=train)
      print(f"Exploit evaluation: {exploit_model_evaluation}")
      print(f"Explore evaluation: {explore_model_evaluation}")
      if is_improvement(explore_model_evaluation,
                  exploit_model_evaluation):        Evaluates the current
        print("Promoting previous explore model")   explore variant and
        train_and_deploy_model(latest_sessions,     promotes it if it's better than
                  "exploit",                        the current explore model
                  explore_feature_set)

    explore_feature_set = get_latest_explore_feature_set()
    train_and_deploy_model(latest_sessions,         Hypothesizes new
                  f"explore_variant_{i}",           features to explore
                  explore_feature_set)              for blind spots
```

```
wait_for_more_sessions(retraining_frequency)
latest_sessions = gather_latest_sessions(
            "transformers dvd",
            latest_sessions,
            explore_feature_set)
```

Collects the new sessions and repeats the process ◁——— Collects user signals until it is time to retrain the model

```
ltr_retraining_loop(sessions)
```

In this loop, we capture a better automated LTR process. We actively learn our training data's blind spots by theorizing the features that might be behind them. In letting the loop run, we can observe its performance and decide when to promote "explore" features to the full production "exploit" feature set. As we retire old click data, we can also note when old features no longer matter and when new features become important due to trends and seasonality. Our implementation uses a hand-tuned exploit-and-explore feature set to keep our search relevance team in control of feature engineering, but you could certainly write an algorithm to generate new features or use deep learning to discover latent features or use some other approach based on existing content attributes.

Taken together, these algorithms provide a robust mechanism for approaching an ideal ranking, considering a full spectrum of options that could be shown to users. They let you choose new features to investigate blind spots, arriving at a relevance algorithm that maximizes what users prefer to see in their search results.

Summary

- Performing well in an offline test shows that our features can approximate the training data. However, that's no guarantee of success. An A/B test can show us situations where the training data itself was misleading.
- Training data must be monitored for biases and carefully corrected.
- Presentation bias is one of search's most pernicious relevance problems. Presentation bias happens when our models can't learn what's relevant from user clicks because the results never show up to be clicked in the first place.
- We can overcome presentation bias by making the automated LTR process an active participant in finding blind spots in the training data. Models that do this participate in active learning.
- A Gaussian process is one way to select promising opportunities for exploration. Using a set of features, we can find what's missing in the training and select new items to show to users based on which items are likely to provide the most useful new data points for continued learning. We can experiment with different ways of describing the data via features to find new and interesting blind spots and areas of investigation.
- When we put together exploiting existing knowledge with exploring blind spots, we have a more robust, automated LTR system—reflected intelligence that can automatically explore and exploit features with little internal maintenance.

Part 4

The search frontier

The rise of embeddings and generative AI has been a boon for the field of information retrieval. Not only do large language models (LLMs) and other foundation models provide new ways to understand and generate text, but they also serve as a perfect complement for search engines. Generative models need reliable data as context (which search engines provide), and search engines need to interpret and summarize the data they search (which generative AI models provide).

In part 4, we'll explore the frontier of search. We'll look at how generative models are being used to improve search, and how search is being used to augment generative models. We'll also look at the emerging future at the intersection of AI and information retrieval.

Chapter 13 covers semantic search over embeddings, explaining how Transformers work and how semantic search over dense vectors can be optimized for efficiency with approximate nearest neighbor (ANN) and quantization approaches. Chapter 14 demonstrates how to fine-tune an LLM on your data and implement extractive question answering: responding to questions in queries with explicit answers extracted from search results.

Chapter 15 wraps up by discussing emerging techniques in AI-powered search. We'll look at generative search techniques, demonstrating retrieval augmented generation (RAG) for dynamic search results summarization, the generation of synthetic training data using generative models, and the evaluation of generative model quality. We'll finally demonstrate multimodal search (across text and images) and hybrid search (combining lexical and dense vector search) and look into the future of search in the age of generative AI.

*Semantic search
with dense vectors*

This chapter covers

- Semantic search using embeddings from LLMs
- An introduction to Transformers, and their effect on text representation and retrieval
- Building autocomplete using Transformer models
- Using ANN search and vector quantization to speed up dense vector retrieval
- Semantic search with bi-encoders and cross-encoders

In this chapter, we'll start our journey into dense vector search, where the hyper-contextual vectors generated by large language models (LLMs) drive significant improvements to the interpretation of queries, documents, and search results. Generative LLMs (like ChatGPT by OpenAI and many other commercial and open source alternatives) are also able to use these vectors to generate new content, including query expansion, search training data, and summarization of search results, as we'll explore further in the coming chapters.

341

The state of the art in LLMs is changing on a monthly (and sometimes almost daily) basis, but even the best general-purpose models can currently be outperformed on specific tasks by fine-tuning other smaller models for those tasks. Over the next few chapters, we'll discuss the concepts behind LLMs and how to best use them in your search application. We'll introduce Transformers in this chapter and discuss how to use them for semantic search with dense vectors. We'll cover fine-tuning an LLM for question answering in chapter 14 and leveraging LLMs and other foundation models for generative search in chapter 15.

Our story begins with what you learned in section 2.5: that we can represent context as numerical vectors, and we can compare these vectors to see which ones are closer using a similarity metric. In chapter 2, we demonstrated the concept of searching on dense vectors, a technique known as *dense vector search*, but our examples were simple and contrived (searching on made-up food attributes). In this chapter, we'll pose the questions "How can we convert real-world unstructured text into a high dimensional dense vector space that attempts to model the actual meaning of the text representation?" and "How can we use this representation of knowledge for advanced search applications?".

13.1 *Representation of meaning through embeddings*

We're going to use language translation as an example to understand what we mean by "dense vector" embeddings. Take the following two sentences: "Hello to you!" (English) and "Barev Dzes" (Armenian). These two expressions hold approximately the same meaning: each is a greeting, with some implied sense of formality.

Computationally, to successfully respond to the greeting of "Hello to you!" the machine must both comprehend the meaning of the prompt and also comprehend all the possible ideal responses, in the same vector space. When the answer is decided upon, the machine must then express it to a person by generating the label from the answer's vector representation.

This vector representation of meaning is called an *embedding*. Embeddings are used interchangeably between natural language processing (NLP) tasks and can be further molded to meet specific use cases. We generated embeddings from an LLM (`all -mpnet-base-v2`) in chapter 9, but we glossed over most of the details on how embeddings work. In this chapter, we'll introduce techniques and tools for getting embeddings from text, and we'll use them to significantly enhance query and document interpretation within our search engine.

> **Natural language processing**
>
> NLP is the set of techniques and tools that converts unstructured text into machine-actionable data. The field of NLP is quite large and includes many research areas and types of problems (NLP tasks) to be solved. A comprehensive list of the problem areas is maintained on the NLP-Progress site (https://nlpprogress.com).

We will be focusing specifically on applying NLP to information retrieval, an important requirement of AI-powered search.

One important point is worth noting up front: behind the two short English and Armenian greetings we mentioned, there are deep cultural nuances. Each of them carries a rich history, and learning them thus carries the context of those histories. This was the case with the semantic knowledge graphs we explored in chapter 5, but those only used the context of documents within the search engine as their model. Transformers are usually trained on much larger corpuses of text, bringing in significantly more of this nuanced context from external sources.

We can use the human brain as an analogy for how Transformer models learn to represent meaning. How did you, as a baby, child, teen, and beyond, learn the meaning of words? You were told, and you consumed knowledge and its representation. People who taught you already had this knowledge and the power to express it. Aside from someone pointing out a cat and saying "kitty" to you, you also watched movies and videos and then moved on to literature and instructional material. You read books, blogs, periodicals, and letters. Through all of your experiences, you incorporated this knowledge into your brain, creating a dense representation of concepts and how they relate to one another, allowing you to reason about them.

Can we impart to machines the same content from which we obtained this power of language, and then expect them to understand and respond sensibly when queried? Hold on to your hats!

13.2 Search using dense vectors

Understanding when to use dense vectors for search instead of sparse vectors requires understanding how to process and relate text. This section briefly reviews how sparse vector search works in comparison with dense vector search. We will also introduce *nearest-neighbor search* as one type of similarity used for dense vector search, as compared to BM25 (the most common similarity function used for sparse vector search).

Vector-based nearest-neighbor search

Also known as KNN (*k*-nearest neighbor), vector-based nearest-neighbor search is the problem space of indexing numerical vectors of a uniform dimensionality into a data structure and searching that data structure with a query vector for the closest k-related vectors. We mentioned in chapter 3 that there are many similarity measures for comparing numerical vectors: cosine similarity, dot product, Euclidean distance, and so on. We will use cosine similarity (implemented as dot product over unit-normalized vectors) throughout this chapter for vector similarity comparisons.

13.2.1 *A brief refresher on sparse vectors*

Sparse vector search is usually implemented using an inverted index. An inverted index is like what you find in the back of any textbook—a list of terms that reference their location in the source content. To efficiently find text, we structure information in an index by processing and normalizing tokens into a dictionary with references to the postings (the document identifiers and positions in which they occur). The resulting data structure is a sparse vector representation that allows for fast lookup of those tokens.

At search time, we tokenize and normalize the query terms and, using the inverted index, match the document hits for retrieval. Then we apply the BM25 formula to score the documents and rank them by similarity, as we covered in section 3.2.

Applying scores for each query term and document feature gives us fast and relevant search, but this model suffers from the "query term dependence" model of relevance, in which the terms (and normalized forms) are retrieved and ranked. The problem is that it uses the presence (and count) of query term strings to search and rank instead of the *meaning* represented by those strings. Therefore, the relevance scores are only useful in a relative sense, to tell you which documents best matched the query, but not to measure if any of the documents were objectively good matches. Dense vector approaches, as we'll see, can supply a more global sense of relevance that is also comparable across queries.

13.2.2 *A conceptual dense vector search engine*

We want to capture the meaning of content when we process documents, and we want to retrieve and rank based on the meaning and intent of the query when searching. With this goal in mind, we process documents to generate embeddings and then store those embeddings in the search index. At search time, we process queries to get embeddings and use those query embeddings to search the indexed document embeddings. Figure 13.1 shows a simplified diagram of this process, which we'll expand upon in section 13.4.

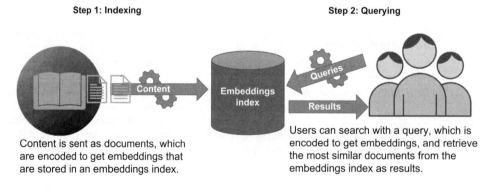

Step 1: Indexing   **Step 2: Querying**

Content is sent as documents, which are encoded to get embeddings that are stored in an embeddings index.

Users can search with a query, which is encoded to get embeddings, and retrieve the most similar documents from the embeddings index as results.

Figure 13.1   Building and searching the embeddings index. The content is processed and added to the index from the left, and a user queries the index to retrieve results.

The embeddings for both documents and queries exist in the same vector space. This is very important. If you map documents to one vector space and queries to another vector space, you'll be matching apples to oranges. The embeddings must belong to the same space for this to work effectively.

But what is an "embedding" exactly, and how do we search one? Well, an embedding is a vector of some set number of dimensions representing information. That information could be a query, a document, a word, a sentence, an image or video, or any other type of information.

Embedding scope and chunking

One important engineering task when working with embeddings is to figure out the right level of granularity for an embedding. An embedding can be made to represent a single word, sentence, paragraph, or much larger document.

When generating embeddings, it is often useful to break apart larger documents into sections and generate a separate embedding for each section, a process known as *chunking*. You can chunk your content by sentence, paragraph, or other conceptual boundaries, and you can even create overlapping chunks to ensure that the process of splitting the document doesn't destroy relevant context across splits.

If your search engine supports multivalued vector fields, you can index many embeddings into a single document and match based on any of its embeddings. Alternatively, you can index a separate document for each chunk, each with a single embedding, and then store the original document ID as a field to be returned when the indexed chunk document is matched.

It is difficult for very large chunks to be fully represented by an embedding, just as it is difficult for very small chunks to contain the full context needed for an embedding, so figuring out the right chunking granularity for your app can be an important consideration for improving recall.

Since embeddings are represented as vectors, we can use cosine similarity (which was covered in depth in chapters 2–3) or another similar distance measurement to compare two embedding vectors to each other and get a similarity score. This allows us to compare the vector of a query to the vectors of all the documents in the content we want to search. The document vectors that are the most similar to the query vector are referred to as *nearest neighbors*. Figure 13.2 illustrates this with three 2D vectors.

The cosine similarities between the vectors shown in figure 13.2, ordered by highest similarity first, are as follows:

- `cos(b, c) = 0.9762`
- `cos(a, b) = 0.7962`
- `cos(a, c) = 0.6459`

It is clear both visually and mathematically that b and c are closest to each other, so we say that b and c are the most similar of the three vectors.

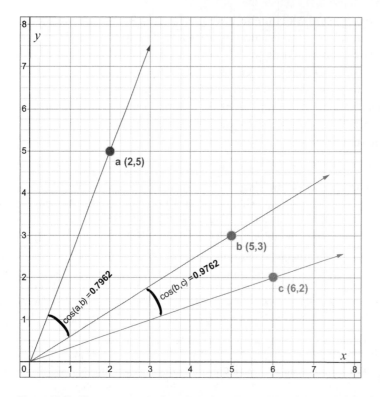

Figure 13.2 Three vectors (a, b, and c) plotted on a Cartesian plane. The similarities between a and b, and between b and c, are illustrated using the cosθ function.

We can easily apply cosine similarity to vectors of any length. In 3D space, we compare vectors with three features [x, y, z]. In a dense vector embedding space, we may use vectors with hundreds or thousands of dimensions. But no matter the number of dimensions, the formula is the same, as shown in figure 13.3.

Vector similarity($\mathbf{a}, \mathbf{b}$) : $\cos(\theta) = \dfrac{\mathbf{a} \cdot \mathbf{b}}{|\mathbf{a}| \times |\mathbf{b}|}$ **Figure 13.3 Formula for the cosine similarity of two vectors**

See section 3.1 for a recap of using this cosine similarity calculation to score the similarity between vectors. There, we walked through examples of calculating both the cosine similarity between vectors and the dot product between vectors. From the formula for cosine similarity (figure 13.3), however, you can see that the cosine is equal to the dot product (a · b) divided by the product of the lengths of the vectors (|a| x |b|). This means that if we can normalize the features in vectors a and b so that each of their lengths is 1 (a process called *unit-normalizing*), the cosine similarity and dot product are equal to each other:

```
1 = |a| = |b|
cos(a, b) = (a · b) / |a| x |b|
cos(a, b) = (a · b) / (1 x 1)
cos(a, b) = a · b
```

When a vector is normalized such that its length equals 1, it is known as a *unit-normalized* vector. But why would we care about normalizing vectors like this? Well, it turns out that calculating a dot product is much more efficient than calculating a cosine similarity, because there is no need to divide the dot product by the magnitudes of each vector (which requires using the Pythagorean theorem to calculate the square root of the sum of squares of each vector's features). Since the cosine calculation is often the most expensive part of the search when scoring a large number of documents, unit-normalizing vectors at index time and performing a dot product of the indexed vectors with a unit-normalized query vector at search time can substantially speed up searches while providing the same result:

```
vector_a = [5.0, 3.0]
vector_b = [6.0, 2.0]

unit_vector_a
    = unit_normalize(vector_a)
    = unit_normalize([5.0, 3.0])
    = [5.0 / sqrt(5.0^2 + 3.0^2), 3.0 / sqrt(5.0^2 + 3.0^2)]
    = [0.8575,  0.5145]

unit_vector_b
    = unit_normalize(vector_b)
    = unit_normalize([6.0, 2.0])
    = [6.0 / sqrt(6.0^2 + 2.0^2), 2.0 / sqrt(6.0^2 + 2.0^2)]
    = [0.9487, 0.3162]
```

The normalization of vectors a and b to a unit vector. All indexed vectors have this normalization done once, before being indexed.

```
cos(vector_a, vector_b)
    = cos([5.0, 3.0], [6.0, 2.0])
    = (5.0 x 6.0 + 3.0 x 2.0) /
      (sqrt(5.0^2 + 3.0^2) x sqrt(6.0^2 + 2.0^2))
    = 0.9762
```

Full cosine similarity calculation. Notice the denominator performs a square root of the sum of the squares for each vector.

```
dot_product(unit_vector_a, unit_vector_b)
    = dot_product([0.8575, 0.5145], [0.9487, 0.3162])
    = (0.8575 x 0.9487) + (0.5145 x 0.3162)
    = 0.9762
```

The dot product calculation on unit-normalized vectors. Notice the absence of the denominator and the much simpler sum of multiplied feature weights.

cos(vector_a, vector_b) = dot_product(unit_vector_a, unit_vector_b) = 0.9762

While we are conceptually still performing a cosine similarity (due to the unit-normalized vectors), using the dot product allows us to perform substantially faster calculations at query time. Because this optimization is possible, it is not a good idea performance-wise to perform a full cosine similarity calculation in production. While there are good use-case-specific reasons you would want to perform a cosine versus dot product, such as to ignore or consider the magnitude of vectors (see section 3.1.4

for a refresher), you will virtually always at least *implement* cosine similarity using unit-normalized vectors and a dot product calculation for performance reasons. To reinforce best practices, we'll consistently utilize this pattern in all the remaining code listings when cosine similarity is being implemented.

Optimizing for vector search compute performance and cost

Performing vector similarity calculations can be slow and computationally expensive at scale, so it's important to understand how to make the right trade-offs to optimize for performance and cost.

Because dot products are significantly faster to calculate than cosine similarities, we recommend you always implement cosine similarity by indexing unit-normalized vectors and then doing dot product calculations between document vectors and a unit-normalized query vector at search time. In addition, it is often possible to save significant memory and substantially improve search times using other optimization techniques:

- Using approximate nearest neighbors (ANN) approaches to quickly filter to the top-N results to rank instead of all documents (covered in section 13.5.3)
- Quantizing (compressing) vectors to reduce the number of bits used to represent each feature in a vector (covered in section 13.7)
- Using Matryoshka Representation Learning (MRL) to only index and/or search on key portions of your embeddings while still maintaining most of your recall (covered in section 13.7)
- Over-requesting a limited number of optimized search results using a cheaper search algorithm or similarity metric, and then reranking the top-N results using a more expensive similarity metric (covered in sections 13.5.3 and 13.7)

With the ability to perform dense vector search and nearest-neighbor similarity in place, the next critical step is to figure out a way to generate these mysterious embeddings.

13.3 *Getting text embeddings by using a Transformer encoder*

In this section, we cover Transformers and how they work to represent meaning. We also discuss how they are used to encode that meaning into embeddings.

13.3.1 *What is a Transformer?*

Transformers are a class of deep neural network architectures that are optimized to encode meaning as embeddings and also decode the meaning back from embeddings. Text-based Transformers do this by first representing term labels as dense vectors by using their surrounding context in a sentence (the encoding part) and then leveraging an output model to translate the vectors into different text representations (the decoding part).

One beautiful feature of this approach is the separation of concerns between encoding and decoding. We will take advantage of this feature and use the encoding mechanism just to obtain the embeddings, which we can then use as a semantic representation of meaning independent of any decoding steps.

> **Representing meaning**
>
> Recall the example English and Armenian greetings from the introduction to section 13.1. Using a specialized Transformer and dataset for English to Armenian language translation, it would be possible to train a model to encode the two phrases "Hello to you!" and "Barev Dzes" into nearly identical dense vectors. These vectors could then be decoded back into text to translate or reconstitute something closer to the original text.

Let's start our journey with Transformers by understanding how Transformer encoder models are trained and what they ultimately learn. To understand the motivations and mechanisms behind Transformers, it is important to know some history of the underlying concepts.

The year is 1953. You find yourself in a classroom with 20 other students, each of you sitting at your own desk. On your desk is a pencil, and a sheet of paper with the sentence `Q: I went to the _____ and bought some vegetables`. You already know what to do, and you write down "store" in the blank. You peek over at a classmate at the desk next to you, and they have written "market". A chime rings, and the answers are tallied. The most common answer is "store", and there are several with "market" and several with "grocer". This is the Cloze test. It is meant to test reading comprehension.

You are transported now to the year 1995. You are sitting in another classroom with students taking another test. This time, your sheet of paper has a very long paragraph. It looks to be about 60 words long and is somewhat complicated:

> *Ours was the marsh country, down by the river, within, as the river wound, twenty miles of the sea. My first most vivid and broad impression of the identity of things seems to me to have been gained on a memorable raw afternoon towards evening. At such a time I found out for certain that this bleak place overgrown with nettles was the churchyard.*

After the paragraph, there is a question listed with a prompt for an answer: `Q: How far away from the sea is the churchyard? A:_____`. You write in the blank, "twenty miles". You have just completed one of a dozen questions in the Regents English reading comprehension test. Specifically, this tested your attention.

These two tests are foundational to how we measure written language comprehension. To be able to pass these tests, you must read, read, read, and read some more. In fact, by the time most people take these tests in school, they have already practiced reading for about 14 years and have amassed a huge amount of contextual knowledge.

These theories form the basis for LLMs—NLP models trained on lots and lots of text (for example, the entirety of the Common Crawl dataset of the web).

Major breakthroughs in the NLP field culminated in a 2018 paper by researchers at Google (Jacob Devlin et al.) titled *BERT: Pre-training of Deep Bidirectional Transformers for Language Understanding*, which made use of the Cloze test and attention mechanisms within Transformers to reach state-of-the-art performance on many language comprehension benchmarks (https://arxiv.org/pdf/1810.04805).

BERT, specifically, performs self-learning by presenting Cloze tests to itself. The training style is "self-supervised", which means it is supervised learning, framed as an unsupervised task. This is ideal, because it does not require data to be manually labeled beforehand for the initial model pretraining. You can give it any text, and it will make the tests itself. In the training context, the Cloze test is known as *masked language modeling*. The model starts with a more basic embedding (for example, using the well-known word2vec or GloVe libraries for each word in the vocabulary), and it will randomly remove 15% of the tokens in a sentence for the test. The model then optimizes a loss function that will result in a higher Cloze test success rate. Also, during the training process, it uses the surrounding tokens and contexts (the attention). Given a vector in a single training example, the resulting trained output vector is an embedding that contains a deeply learned representation of the word and the surrounding contexts.

We encourage you to learn more about Transformers and BERT, if you are interested, by reading the paper. All you need to understand for now, however, is how to get embeddings from a BERT encoder. The basic concept is shown in figure 13.4.

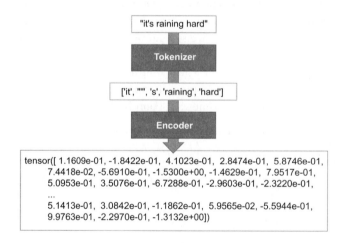

Figure 13.4
The Transformer encoder

In figure 13.4, we process text by first passing it through a tokenizer. The tokenizer splits text into *word pieces*, which are predefined parts of words that are represented in a vocabulary. This vocabulary is established for the model before it is trained. For example, the term "It's" will be split into three word pieces during tokenization: it, ', and s. The vocabulary used in the BERT paper included 30,000 word pieces. BERT also uses special word pieces to denote the beginning and end of sentences: [CLS] and [SEP] respectively. Once tokenized, the token stream is passed into the BERT model for encoding. The encoding process then outputs a *tensor*, which is an array of vectors (one vector for each token).

13.3.2 Openly available pretrained Transformer models

While Transformers enable state-of-the-art language models to be built, having the knowledge and resources to build them from scratch can present a large hurdle for many. One very important aspect of working with Transformers is the large community and open toolsets that make it possible for any engineer to quickly get up and running with the technology. All it takes is some knowledge of Python and an internet connection.

The models that are trained by this process from scratch are large and range from hundreds of MBs to hundreds of GBs in size, often needing similar amounts of GPU memory (VRAM) to run them quickly. The training itself also takes a large amount of expensive computing power and time, so being able to use preexisting models as a starting point provides a significant advantage. We'll use this advantage in the next section as we begin applying one of these models to search.

13.4 Applying Transformers to search

In this section, we'll build a highly accurate natural language autocomplete for search, which will recommend more precise and otherwise related keywords based on a prefix of terms. We'll do this by first passing our corpus text through a Transformer to get an index of embeddings. Then we'll use this Transformer at query time to get the query embedding and search the embedding index for the *k*-nearest documents with the most similar embeddings. Figure 13.5 is an architecture diagram demonstrating the steps in this process.

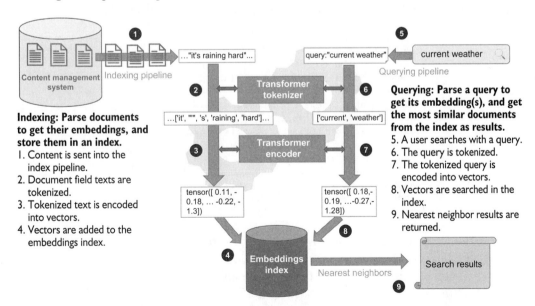

Figure 13.5   A conceptual architecture for end-to-end search using Transformer-encoded vectors

We have a content source, a nearest-neighbor index, a way to retrieve vectors from a Transformer, and a similarity formula. We can now build pipelines for all these pieces to process and index content, and then to retrieve and rank documents with a query.

13.4.1 Using the Stack Exchange outdoors dataset

In chapter 5, we introduced several datasets from Stack Exchange. We're choosing to use another one, the Stack Exchange outdoors dataset, here for a very important reason: the vocabulary and contexts in the outdoor question-and-answer domain already have good coverage in the Transformer models we'll be using. Specifically, Wikipedia is used when training many Transformer models, and Wikipedia has a section specifically on outdoors content (https://en.wikipedia.org/wiki/Outdoor).

> **NOTE** The outdoors examples used in chapters 13–15, along with references to Stack Exchange datasets in other chapters, are licensed by Stack Exchange under the CC-by-SA 4.0 License: https://creativecommons.org/licenses/by-sa/4.0.

The following listing walks through creating an outdoors collection and then indexing the outdoors question and answer data.

Listing 13.1 Indexing the outdoors dataset

```
outdoors_collection = engine.create_collection("outdoors")
outdoors_dataframe = load_outdoors_data("data/outdoors/posts.csv")
outdoors_collection.write(outdoors_dataframe)
```

This is the schema for the `outdoors` collection created in listing 13.1:

```
root
     |-- id: integer (nullable = true)
     |-- accepted_answer_id: integer (nullable = true)
     |-- parent_id: integer (nullable = true)
     |-- creation_date: timestamp (nullable = true)
     |-- score: integer (nullable = true)
     |-- view_count: integer (nullable = false)
     |-- body: string (nullable = true)
     |-- owner_user_id: string (nullable = true)
     |-- title: string (nullable = true)
     |-- tags: array (nullable = true)
     |    |-- element: string (containsNull = true)
     |-- answer_count: integer (nullable = true)
     |-- post_type: string (nullable = true)
     |-- url: string (nullable = true)
```

The indexed dataset contains documents representing both questions and answers, with answers linked to their original questions through the `parent_id` field. Each document contains a `post_type` field to differentiate whether it contains a "question" or an "answer".

The following listing shows a question post and its related answers.

Listing 13.2 Exploring post data for a question on `climbing knots`

```
[{"id": "18825",
  "accepted_answer_id": 18826,          Document 18826 is marked as the
                                        accepted answer to the question.
  "body": "If I wanted to learn how to tie certain knots,
➥or learn about new knots and what they're used for,          This is our
➥what are some good resources to look up?",            question document.
  "title": "What's a good resource for learning to tie knots for climbing?",
  "post_type": "question"},
{"id": "24440",
  "parent_id": 18825,
  "body": "Knots and Ropes for Climbers by Duane Raleigh is a fantastic
➥illustrated resource tailored specifically to climbers. The ABoK
➥is great, but a but beyond the pale of what the average rock...",

  "post_type": "answer"},          This is the document marked as the accepted answer
{"id": "18826",                    to the question (accepted_answer_id = 18826).
  "parent_id": 18825,
  "body": "Animated Knots By Grog Arguably the best resource online for knot
➥tying is Animated Knots by Grog , it's used by virtually every avid
➥knot tyer I've known. They have excellent step-by-step animatio...",
  "post_type": "answer"}]
```

These documents are answers to the question
in the first document (id = 18825).

These are answer documents
that relate to the question.

In the preceding listing, the first document is a question most related to the query `climbing knots`. The question has two answers that are linked back to the parent question through the `parent_id` field on each answer. One of these answers has been chosen as the accepted answer, which is identified by setting the `accepted_answer_id` field (to 18826 in this case) on the question document.

The `body` field of question documents contains elaborations on the question, while the `body` field of an answer contains the full answer. Only question posts have a `title`, which is a summary of the question. Several other fields (such as `view_count`, `answer_count`, and `owner_user_id`) are omitted here but are available in the full data-set as metadata fields, which can help with search relevance using BM25 mixed with other signals.

Now that you're familiarized with the data model, let's take a moment to try out some queries and see what types of questions come back. The following listing searches for questions matching a common query.

Listing 13.3 Running a basic lexical search for `climbing knots`

```
def search_questions(query, verbose=False):
    request = {"query": query,
               "query_fields": ["title", "body"],       Match the query against
               "limit": 5,                              the title and body fields.
               "return_fields": ["id", "url", "post_type", "title",
                                 "body", "accepted_answer_id", "score"],
               "filters": [("post_type", "question")],
```

```
            "order_by": [("score", "desc"), ("title", "asc")]}
    response = outdoors_collection.search(**request)
    display_questions(query, response, verbose)

search_questions("climbing knots")
```

Response:

```
Query: climbing knots

Ranked Questions:
Question 21855: What are the four climbing knots used by Jim Bridwell?
Question 18825: What's a good resource for learning to tie knots for clim...
Question 18814: How to tie a figure eight on a bight?
Question 9183: Can rock climbers easily transition to canyoning?
Question 22477: Tradeoffs between different stopper knots
```

We can see that these are somewhat relevant titles for this lexical query. But this is just a basic keyword search. Other queries do not perform nearly as well; for example, the query What is DEET in the next listing shows very irrelevant results.

Listing 13.4 Basic lexical matching can yield irrelevant results

```
search_questions("What is DEET?")
```

Response:

```
Query What is DEET?:

Ranked Questions:
Question 20403: What is bushcrafting?
Question 20977: What is "catskiing"?
Question 1660: What is Geocaching?
Question 17374: What is a tent skirt and what is its purpose?
Question 913: What is a buff?
```

This shows how traditional lexical search can fail for common natural language use cases. Specifically, the inverted index suffers from the query-term dependency problem. This means that the terms in the query are being matched as strings to terms in the index. This is why you see strong matches for what is in the results in listing 13.4. The *meaning* of the query is not comprehended, so the retrieval can only be based on string matching.

The rest of this chapter will provide the fundamentals needed to use Transformers for natural language search, and in chapter 14 we'll solve the question-answering problem evident in listing 13.4.

13.4.2 *Fine-tuning and the Semantic Text Similarity Benchmark*

Using a pretrained Transformer model out of the box usually won't yield optimal results for task-specific prompts. This is because the initial training was done in a general language context without any specific use case or domain in mind. In essence, it is "untuned", and using models this way is akin to indexing content in a search engine without tuning for relevance.

To realize the full potential of Transformers, they need to be refined to accomplish a specific task. This is known as *fine-tuning*—the process of taking a pretrained model and training it on more fit-for-purpose data to achieve a specific use case goal. For both autocomplete and semantic search, we are interested in fine-tuning to accomplish text similarity discovery tasks.

That brings us to the Semantic Text Similarity Benchmark (STS-B) training and testing set (https://ixa2.si.ehu.eus/stswiki/). This benchmark includes passages that are semantically similar and dissimilar, and they're labeled accordingly. Using this dataset, a model can be fine-tuned to improve the accuracy of nearest-neighbor search between a set of terms and many passages in a corpus, which will be our use case in this chapter.

In chapter 14, we will fine-tune our own question-answering model so you can see how it is done. For our purposes in this chapter, however, we'll use a project that already includes a pretuned model for this task: SBERT.

13.4.3 *Introducing the SBERT Transformer library*

SBERT, or *Sentence-BERT*, is a technique and Python library based on Transformers that is built on the idea that a BERT model can be fine-tuned in such a way that two semantically similar sentences, and not just tokens, should be represented closer in vector space. Specifically, SBERT *pools* all the BERT embeddings in one sentence to a single vector. (Pooling is a fancy way of saying it combines the values.) Once SBERT pools the values, it trains for similarity between sentences by using a special-purpose neural network that learns to optimize for the STS-B task. For further implementation details, check out the "Sentence-BERT" paper by Nils Reimers and Iryna Gurevych (https://arxiv.org/abs/1908.10084).

The upcoming listings will give you an overview of how to use SBERT via the `sentence_transformers` Python library. We'll start by importing the library using a pretrained model named `roberta-base-nli-stsb-mean-tokens`, which is based on an architecture called RoBERTa. It's helpful to think of RoBERTa as an evolved and improved version of BERT, with optimized hyperparameters (configuration settings) and slight modifications to the original techniques.

Hyperparameters

In machine learning, hyperparameters are any parameter values that can be changed before training and that will alter the learning process and affect the resulting model.

Unfortunately, you often don't know what the hyperparameter values should be set to when you start, so you may have to learn optimized values over time using iteration and measurement.

In the model name, `roberta-base-nli-stsb-mean-tokens`, we can also see some terms that you may not recognize, including "nli" and "mean-tokens". NLI stands for *natural language inference* (a subdomain of NLP used for language prediction), and mean-tokens refers to the whole sentence's tokenization being pooled together as a mean of the numeric values of the token embeddings. Using mean-tokens returns a single 768-dimension embedding for the entire sentence.

The following listing imports the `sentence_transformers` library, loads the model, and displays the full network architecture.

Listing 13.5 Loading the RoBERTa `SentenceTransformer` model

```
from sentence_transformers import SentenceTransformer
transformer = SentenceTransformer("roberta-base-nli-stsb-mean-tokens")
```

Now the PyTorch `transformer` object holds the neural network architecture for the Transformer as well as all the model weights.

With our model loaded, we can retrieve embeddings from text. This is where the fun really begins. We can take sentences and pass them through the neural network architecture using the pretrained model and get the embeddings as a result. We have four sentences that we'll encode and assess in the following listings.

Listing 13.6 demonstrates how to encode multiple phrases into dense vector embeddings.

Listing 13.6 Encoding phrases as dense vector embeddings

```
phrases = ["it's raining hard", "it is wet outside",
           "cars drive fast", "motorcycles are loud"]
embeddings = transformer.encode(phrases, convert_to_tensor=True)
print("Number of embeddings:", len(embeddings))
print("Dimensions per embedding:", len(embeddings[0]))
print("The embedding feature values of \"it's raining hard\":")
print(embeddings[0])
```

> The four sentences we want to encode. We will pass all of these to be encoded as a single batch.

> Just call transformer.encode, and the abstraction of sentence_transformers does all the heavy lifting for you.

Response:

```
Number of embeddings: 4
Dimensions per embedding: 768
The embedding feature values of "it's raining hard":
tensor( 1.1609e-01, -1.8422e-01,  4.1023e-01,  2.8474e-01,  5.8746e-01,
        7.4418e-02, -5.6910e-01, -1.5300e+00, -1.4629e-01,  7.9517e-01,
        5.0953e-01,  3.5076e-01, -6.7288e-01, -2.9603e-01, -2.3220e-01,
        ...
        5.1413e-01,  3.0842e-01, -1.1862e-01,  5.9565e-02, -5.5944e-01,
        9.9763e-01, -2.2970e-01, -1.3132e+00])
```

In the preceding listing, we take each sentence and pass it to the encoder. This results in a tensor for each sentence. A *tensor* is a generalizable data structure for holding potentially multidimensional values. A scalar (single value), vector (array of scalars), matrix (array of vectors), or even multidimensional matrix (array of matrices, matrix of matrices, etc.) are all examples of tensors of various dimensions. Tensors are produced by Transformer encoders, such as SBERT, when encoding text. For our use case, the tensor in listing 13.6 is an embedding containing 768 dimensions represented as floating point numbers.

With our embeddings, we can now perform cosine similarities (dot product on unit-normalized vectors) to see which phrases are closest neighbors to each other. We'll compare each phrase to every other phrase, and sort them by similarity to see which are most similar. This process is covered step by step in listings 13.7 and 13.8.

We'll use a PyTorch built-in library for calculating the dot product to do these comparisons, which allows us to pass in the embeddings with a single function call. We can then sort the resulting similarities and see which two phrases are most similar to one another and which two are most dissimilar. The following listing calculates the similarities between each of the phrase embeddings.

Listing 13.7 Comparing all the phrases to each other

```
                                          Unit-normalizes embeddings for speed
                                          so dot products = cosine similarities
def normalize_embedding(embedding):   ◁───┘
  normalized = numpy.divide(embedding, numpy.linalg.norm(embedding))
  return list(map(float, normalized))

normalized_embeddings = list(map(normalize_embedding, embeddings))
similarities = sentence_transformers.util.dot_score(normalized_embeddings,
                                                    normalized_embeddings)
print("The shape of the resulting similarities:", similarities.shape)
```

Output:

```
The shape of the resulting similarities: torch.Size([4, 4])
```

We print the shape of the similarities object in listing 13.7 to see how many comparisons we have. The shape is 4 x 4 (`[4, 4]`) because we have 4 phrases, and each phrase has a similarity score to every other phrase and itself. All the similarity scores are between 0.0 (least similar) and 1.0 (most similar). The shape is included here to help show the complexity of comparing many phrases. If there were 100 phrases, the similarities shape would be 100 x 100. If there were 10,000 phrases, the similarities shape would be 10,000 x 10,000. So, as you add phrases to compare, the computational and space costs will increase with complexity n^2, where n is the number of phrases.

With the similarities for our four phrases computed, we sort and print them in the following listing.

Listing 13.8 Sorting by similarities and printing the results

```
def rank_similarities(phrases, similarities, name=None):
  a_phrases = []
```

```
b_phrases = []
scores = []
for a in range(len(similarities) - 1):        Append all the phrase
    for b in range(a + 1, len(similarities)):  pairs to a dataframe.
        a_phrases.append(phrases[a])          We don't duplicate phrases or
        b_phrases.append(phrases[b])          append a phrase's similarity to
        scores.append(float(similarities[a][b]))  itself, as it will always be 1.0.

dataframe = pandas.DataFrame({"score": scores, "phrase a": a_phrases,
                             "phrase b": b_phrases})
dataframe["idx"] = dataframe.index            Add the index column
dataframe = dataframe.reindex(columns=["idx", "score",
                                       "phrase a", "phrase b"])

return dataframe.sort_values(by=["score"],        Sort the scores
                            ascending=False,      (ascending=False for
                            ignore_index=True)    highest scores first).

dataframe = rank_similarities(phrases, similarities)
display(HTML(dataframe.to_html(index=False)))
```

Get the score for each pair.

Response:

```
idx  score      phrase a          phrase b
0    0.669060   it's raining hard  it is wet outside
5    0.590783   cars drive fast    motorcycles are loud
1    0.281166   it's raining hard  cars drive fast
2    0.280800   it's raining hard  motorcycles are loud
4    0.204867   it is wet outside  motorcycles are loud
3    0.138172   it is wet outside  cars drive fast
```

We can now see that the two phrases that are most similar to one another are "it's raining hard" and "it is wet outside". We also see a strong similarity between cars and motorcycles.

The two most dissimilar phrases are "it is wet outside" and "cars drive fast". It's very clear from these examples that this semantic encoding process is working—we can associate rain with it being wet outside. The dense vector representations captured the context, and even though the words are different, the meaning is still there. Note the scores: the top two similar comparisons have a score of greater than 0.59, and the next closest comparison has a score of less than 0.29, This is because only the top two comparisons seem to be similar to one another, as we would perceive them in a *natural language understanding* (NLU) task. As intelligent people, we can group rain and wet ("weather"), and we can also group cars and motorcycles ("vehicle"). Also interestingly, cars likely drive slower when it is wet on the ground, so that likely explains the low similarity of the last pair.

13.5 *Natural language autocomplete*

Now that we know our vector encoding and similarity process is working well, it's time to put this embedding technique to work in a real search use case—natural language autocomplete!

In this section, we'll show a practical use for sentence Transformers at search time, with a basic and fast semantic autocomplete implementation. We will apply what we've learned thus far to extract concepts from the outdoors dataset. Using spaCy (the Python NLP library we used in chapter 5), we will chunk nouns and verbs to get outdoors concepts. We will put these concepts in a dictionary and process them to get their embeddings. Then we'll use the dictionary in an approximate nearest-neighbor (ANN) index to query in real time. This will give us the ability to enter a prefix or a term and get the most similar concepts that exist in the dictionary. Finally, we will take those concepts and present them to the user in order of similarity, demonstrating a smart, natural language autocomplete.

Experience and testing show that this works much better than even a well-tuned suggester in most lexical search engines. We will see that it's much less noisy and also that similar terms that are not spelled the same will be automatically included in the suggestions. This is because we are not comparing keyword strings to one another; rather, we are comparing the embeddings, which represent meaning and context. This is the embodiment of searching for "things, not strings", as introduced in section 1.2.4.

13.5.1 Getting noun and verb phrases for our nearest-neighbor vocabulary

Using what we learned in chapter 5, we'll write a simple function to extract *concepts* from the corpus. We won't include any taxonomical hierarchy, and we won't be building a full knowledge graph here. We just want a reliable list of frequently used nouns and verbs.

The concepts in our example are the important "things" and "actions" that people usually search for. We also need to understand the dataset, which is best accomplished by spending time reviewing the concepts and how they relate to one another. Understanding the corpus is critical when building any search application, and there's no exception when using advanced NLP techniques.

The following listing shows a strategy that will provide a decent quality baseline of candidate concepts for our vocabulary while removing significant noise from the autocomplete results.

Listing 13.9 Using the spaCy Matcher to get desired parts of text

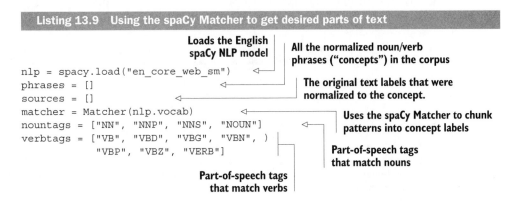

```
matcher.add("noun_phrases", [[{"TAG": {"IN": nountags},
                                "IS_ALPHA": True,
                                "OP": "+"}]])
matcher.add("verb_phrases", [[{"TAG": {"IN": verbtags},
                                "IS_ALPHA": True, "OP": "+",
                                "LEMMA":{"NOT_IN":["be"]}}]])
for doc, _ in tqdm.tqdm(nlp.pipe(yield_tuple(dataframe,
                                  source_field="body",
                                  total=total),)
                        batch_size=40,
                        n_threads=4,
                        as_tuples=True),
                    total=total):
    matches = matcher(doc)
    for _, start, end in matches:
        span = doc[start:end]
        phrases.append(normalize(span))
        sources.append(span.text)

concepts = {}
labels = {}
for i, phrase in phrases:
    if phrase not in concepts:
        concepts[phrase] = 0
        labels[phrase] = sources[i]
    concepts[phrase] += 1
```

> **Adds a noun phrase-matching pattern to the spaCy analysis pipeline**

> **Adds the verb phrase matching pattern. You can add more NOT_IN patterns to exclude other "stop word" verbs.**

> **Processes the body field for each outdoors question, in batches of 40 documents using 4 threads**

> **Gets all the noun and verb phrase matches, and keeps them in the sources and phrases lists**

> **Aggregates the normalized concepts by term frequency**

In the preceding listing, we use the spaCy Matcher to detect patterns as part-of-speech tags. We also explicitly remove forms of the verb "to be" from the verb concepts. The verb "to be" is used frequently in many non-useful situations and often clutters the concept suggestions. We could further improve quality by removing other noisy verbs like "have" and "can", but this is just an example for now. SpaCy's language pipeline (`nlp.pipe`) is also introduced in this listing. The `pipe` function accepts a batch size and the number of threads to use as parameters, and it then performs streaming processing of the text in parallel batches (and thus more quickly than making individual calls for each document).

With the function in listing 13.9, we can now get the list of concepts. When running this on your machine it may take some time, so be patient. The following listing returns the most prominent concepts and labels from the outdoors collection.

Listing 13.10   Generating the most frequent concepts in the corpus

```
collection = engine.get_collection("outdoors")
concepts, labels = get_concepts(collection, source_field="body",
                                load_from_cache=True)
topcons = {key: value for (key, value)
                        in concepts.items() if value > 5}
print("Total number of labels:", len(labels.keys()))
print("Total number of concepts:", len(concepts.keys()))
print("Concepts with greater than 5 term frequency:", len(topcons.keys()))
print(json.dumps(topcons, indent=2))
```

Response:

```
Total number of labels: 124366
Total number of concepts: 124366
Concepts with greater than 5 term frequency: 12375
{
  "have": 32782,
  "do": 26869,
  "use": 16793,
  ...
  "streamside vegetation": 6,
  "vehicle fluid": 6,
  "birdshot": 6
}
```

Aside from getting the concepts for the outdoors dataset, listing 13.10 filtered the total dataset to `topcons`, which only includes concepts with a frequency greater than 5. Filtering will limit noise from terms that don't appear as often in the corpus, such as misspellings and rare terms we don't want to suggest in an autocomplete scenario.

13.5.2 Getting embeddings

We're going to perform a complex normalization that will normalize similarly related concepts. But instead of algorithmic normalization (like stemming), we are normalizing to a dense vector space of 768 feature dimensions. Similar to stemming, the purpose of this is to increase *recall* (the percentage of relevant documents successfully returned). But instead of using a stemmer, we're finding and mapping together closely related concepts. As a reminder, we're only normalizing noun and verb phrases. Ignoring the other words is similar to stop-word removal, but that's OK, because we want to suggest similar concepts as concisely as possible. We'll also have a much better representation of the context and meaning of the remaining phrases. Therefore, the surrounding non-noun and non-verb terms are implied.

Now that we have a list of concepts (from the last section), we're going to process them using our loaded `model` (the RoBERTa Sentence Transformer model we loaded in listing 13.5) to retrieve the embeddings. This may take a while if you don't have a GPU, so after we calculate the embeddings the first time, we'll persist them to a "pickle file" (a serialized Python object that can be easily stored and loaded to and from disk). If you ever want to rerun the notebook, you can just load the previously created pickle file and not waste another half hour reprocessing the raw text.

Hyperparameter alert! The `minimum_frequency` term is a hyperparameter, and it's set to be greater than five (`>=6`) in the following listing to minimize noise from rare terms. We'll encounter more hyperparameters in other listings in this chapter and the next, especially when we get into fine-tuning. After you've been through the rest of the listings in this chapter, we encourage you to come back and change the value of `minimum_frequency` and see how it alters the results that are retrieved. You may find a value that's more suitable and more accurate than what we've arrived at here.

> **Listing 13.11   Retrieving the embeddings of our concept vocabulary**

```
def get_embeddings(texts, model, cache_name, ignore_cache=False):
    ...
    embeddings = model.encode(texts)          ◁──┐ Caching code
    ...                                          └ removed for brevity
    return embeddings

minimum_frequency = 6   ◁──
phrases = [key for (key, tf) in concepts.items() if tf >= minimum_frequency]
cache_name = "outdoors_embeddings"
embeddings = get_embeddings(phrases, transformer,
                            cache_name, ignore_cache=False)

print(f"Number of embeddings: {len(embeddings)}")
print(f"Dimensions per embedding: {len(embeddings[0])}")
```

This is a hyperparameter! We are ignoring terms that occur less than this number of times in the entire corpus. Lowering this threshold may lower precision, and raising it may lower recall.

Response:

```
Number of embeddings: 12375
Dimensions per embedding: 768
```

From listing 13.11, you can see that one embedding was generated from each of our 12,375 concepts. All embeddings have the same dimensionality from the same dense vector space and can therefore be directly compared with one another.

Figure 13.6 demonstrates what these embeddings look like and how they relate to one another when plotted in 3D.

The similarities of some concepts in the figure have been labeled to show neighborhoods of meaning. Concepts related to "wind" and "block" illustrate where they are located relative to each other in the vector space. We used dimensionality reduction to reduce the 768 dimensions for each embedding into 3 dimensions (x, y, z) so they could be easily plotted. *Dimensionality reduction* is a technique for condensing one vector with many features into another vector with fewer features. During this reduction, the relationships in the vector space are maintained as much as possible.

> **Dimensionality reduction loses context**
>
> A lot of context is lost when performing dimensionality reduction, so the visualization in figure 13.6 is only presented to give you an intuition of the vector space and concept similarity, not to suggest that reducing to three dimensions is an ideal way to represent the concepts.

With the embeddings calculated from listing 13.11, we can now perform a massive comparison to see which terms are more closely related to one another. We will do this by calculating the cosine similarity—the dot product for each unit-normalized embedding related to every other unit-normalized embedding. Note that we're limiting the number of embeddings that we're comparing in this example, because the

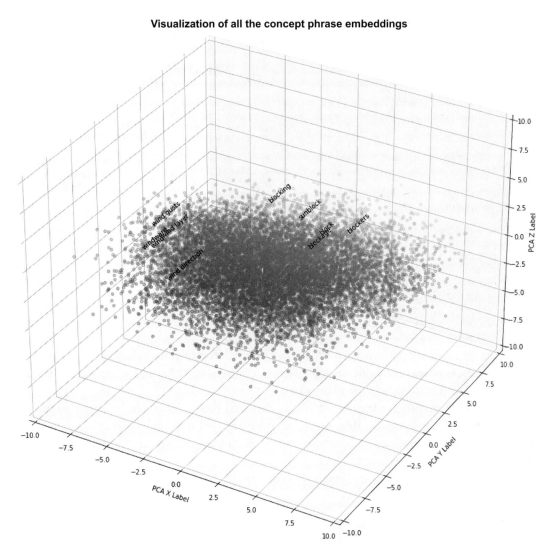

Figure 13.6   The vector space for the concept embeddings mapped to a 3D visualization

number of calculations that are required to be performed grows exponentially as the number of embeddings increases. If you're not sure what we mean, let's do some quick math. Each embedding has a dimensionality of 768 floating point values. Comparing the top 250 embeddings all against each other results in 250 × 250 × 768 = 48,000,000 floating point calculations. Were we to compare the full list of 12,375 embeddings, that would be 12,375 × 12,375 × 768 = 117,612,000,000 floating point calculations. Not only would this be slow to process, but it would also take a very large amount of memory.

The following listing performs a brute-force comparison of the top 250 concepts, to assess how similarity scores are distributed.

Listing 13.12   Exploring similarity scores from the head of the vocabulary

```
normalized_embeddings = list(map(normalize_embedding, embeddings))
similarities = sentence_transformers.util.dot_score(
                normalized_embeddings[0:250],          Finds the pairs with the
                normalized_embeddings[0:250])          highest dot product scores
comparisons = rank_similarities(phrases, similarities)      ◁─┐  Ranks similarities
display(HTML(comparisons[:10].to_html(index=False)))            as defined in
                                                                listing 13.8
```

Response:

```
idx       score      phrase a    phrase b
31096     0.928151   protect     protection
13241     0.923570   climbing    climber
18096     0.878894   camp        camping
...
7354      0.782962   climb       climber
1027      0.770643   go          leave
4422      0.768611   keep        stay
```

As you can see in listing 13.12, the `scores` dataframe now holds a sorted list of all phrases compared to one another, with the most similar being "protect" and "protection" with a dot product similarity of `0.928`.

Note that the index of `250` is arbitrary and can be changed to larger values for more data to visualize. Remember what we learned in listing 13.7: using n concepts yields a tensor of [n, n] in shape. This yields a total of `250 × 250 = 62500` similarities for the example in listing 13.12.

The following listing plots the distribution of the top 250 concept comparison similarity scores.

Listing 13.13   The distribution of word similarities

```
from plotnine import *
candidate_synonyms = comparisons[comparisons["score"] > 0.0]
{
  ggplot(comparisons, aes("idx", "score")) +
    geom_violin(color="blue") +
    scale_y_continuous(limits=[-0.4, 1.0],
                       breaks=[-0.4, -0.2, 0, 0.2, 0.4, 0.6, 0.8, 1.0])
}
```

The output of listing 13.13 is shown in figure 13.7, and the distribution clarifies the percentage of concepts that are most related to one another. You see that very few comparisons have a similarity score greater than `0.6`, and the vast majority have similarity scores less than that.

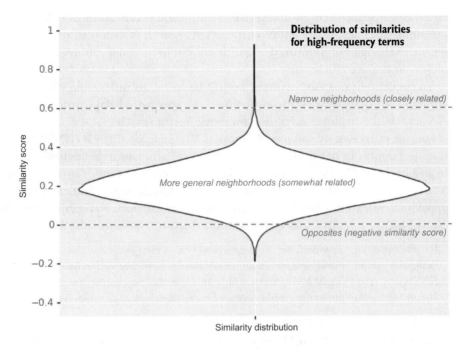

Figure 13.7 Distribution of how the top 250 concepts score with a dot product similarity when compared with each other. Note that very few comparisons result in a score higher than 0.6, and most scores are less than 0.4 (a very low confidence).

We plotted the distribution of scores so we can assess them and use our intuition for choosing a baseline similarity threshold at query time (used later in listing 13.15). The visualization in figure 13.7 is very promising. Since most concepts are noted as dissimilar, we can reliably choose a high enough number as a threshold of quality suggestions (such as 0.6 in this example). When we're performing an autocomplete during search, we're only interested in seeing the top five to ten suggested terms, so this distribution shows we can do that reliably.

13.5.3 ANN search

Before implementing the working autocomplete, we have one more important problem to solve. The problem is that, at query time, we ideally don't want to compare each search term to all 12,375 other terms. That would be inefficient and slow due to the dimensionality and computational overhead of using the `sentence_transformers` `.util.dot_score` function. Even if we were willing to calculate dot product similarities for all our documents, this would just get slower and slower as we scaled to millions of documents, so we ideally would only score documents that have a high chance of being similar.

We can accomplish this goal by performing what is known as an *approximate-nearest-neighbor* (ANN) search. ANN search will efficiently return the most closely related documents when given a vector, without the overhead of calculating embedding similarities across the entire corpus. ANN search is meant to trade some accuracy in exchange for improved logarithmic computational complexity, as well as memory and space efficiencies.

To implement our ANN search, we will be using an index-time strategy to store searchable content vectors ahead of time in a specialized data structure. Think of ANN search like an "inverted index" for dense vector search.

For our purposes, we will use *Hierarchical Navigable Small World* (HNSW) graphs to index and query our dense vectors. We'll also cover other approaches based on clustering and hashing, like product quantization and inverted file indexes (IVF), in section 13.7. HNSW is described in the abstract of its research paper, "Efficient and robust approximate nearest neighbor search using Hierarchical Navigable Small World graphs," by Yu. A. Malkov and D.A. Yashunin (https://arxiv.org/abs/1603.09320):

> *We present a new approach for the approximate K-nearest neighbor search based on navigable small world graphs with controllable hierarchy (Hierarchical NSW, HNSW).... Hierarchical NSW incrementally builds a multilayer structure consisting of hierarchical sets of proximity graphs (layers) for nested subsets of the stored elements.*

What this means is that HNSW will cluster similar vectors together as it builds the index. Navigable Small World graphs work by organizing data into neighborhoods and connecting the neighborhoods with probable relationship edges. When a dense vector representation is being indexed, the most appropriate neighborhood and its potential connections are identified and stored in the graph data structure.

Different ANN approaches

In this chapter, we use the HNSW algorithm for ANN search. HNSW provides a great balance between recall and query throughput and is currently (as of this writing) among the most popular ANN approaches. However, many other ANN approaches exist, including much simpler techniques like locality-sensitive hashing (LSH). LSH breaks the vector space into hash buckets (representing neighborhoods in the vector space) and encodes (hashes) each dense vector into one of those buckets. While recall is typically much higher for HNSW versus LSH, HNSW depends upon your data to generate the neighborhoods, and the neighborhoods can shift over time to better fit your data. LSH neighborhoods (hashes) are generated in a data-independent way, which can better meet some use cases requiring a priori sharding in distributed systems. We'll also cover other approaches based on clustering and hashing, like product quantization and inverted file indexes (IVF), in section 13.7. It may be worth your while to research different ANN algorithms to find the one that best suits your application.

When an HNSW search is initiated using a dense vector query, it finds the best cluster entry point for the query and searches for the closest neighbors. There are many other optimization techniques that HNSW implements, and we encourage you to read the paper if you want to learn more.

13.5.4   ANN index implementation

For our ANN search implementation, we'll start by using a library called the Non-Metric Space Library (NMSLIB). This library includes a canonical implementation of the *HNSW* algorithm.

We've chosen this library because not only is it fast, but it's also easy to use and requires very little code. Apache Lucene also includes a dense vector field type with native HNSW support, making the algorithm available in Solr, OpenSearch, Elasticsearch, and other Lucene-based engines like MongoDB Atlas Search. An implementation of HNSW is additionally available in other search engines, such as Vespa.ai, Weaviate, Milvus, and more.

NMSLIB is robust, well-tested, and widely used for ANN applications. NMSLIB is also appropriate for showing the simplicity of ANN search without getting into the details of the implementation. There are many other ANN libraries available, and we encourage you to investigate some of them listed on the excellent ANN Benchmarks site: https://ann-benchmarks.com.

To begin using NMSLIB, we simply need to import the library, initialize an index, add all of our embeddings to the index as a batch, and then commit. Autocomplete is an ideal use case when building an index in this way, because the vocabulary is rarely updated. Even though NMSLIB and other libraries may suffer from write-time performance in certain situations, this won't affect our read-heavy autocomplete application. From a practical standpoint, we can update our index offline as an evening or weekend job and deploy to production when appropriate.

The following listing creates our HNSW index from all 12,375 embeddings and then performs an example search for concepts similar to the term "bag".

Listing 13.14   ANN search using NMSLIB

```
import nmslib

concepts_index = nmslib.init(method="hnsw",
                             space="negdotprod")
normalized_embeddings = list(map(normalize_embedding, embeddings))
concepts_index.addDataPointBatch(normalized_embeddings)
concepts_index.createIndex(print_progress=True)

ids, _ = concepts_index.knnQuery(
             normalized_embeddings[25], k=10)
matches = [labels[phrases[i]].lower() for i in ids]
display(matches)
```

Initializes a new index, using an HNSW graph in the negdotprod metric space (distance function is –1 * dot_product)

All the embeddings can be added in a single batch.

Gets the top k nearest neighbors for the term query "bag" (embedding 25) in our embeddings

Looks up the label for each term

Commits the index to memory. This must be done before you can query for nearest neighbors.

Output:

```
['bag', 'bag ratings', 'bag cover', 'bag liner', 'garbage bags', 'wag bags',
 'bag cooking', 'airbag', 'paper bag', 'tea bags']
```

With the index created and committed, we ran a small example comparing the term "bag" and seeing what comes back. Interestingly, all these terms are hyponyms, which reveals another ideal result. We are interested in suggesting more precise terms to the user at autocomplete time. This has a higher likelihood of giving the user the chance to select the term most closely associated with their particular information need.

With our index confirmed working, we can now construct a straightforward query function that accepts any term and returns the top suggestions. SBERT has been trained using a technique that encodes similar terms to similar vector embeddings. Importantly, and in contrast to most lexical autocomplete implementations, this function accepts any query regardless of whether it's already in our dictionary. We first take the query and retrieve embeddings by passing the query through the same SBERT encoder we used to index our documents. With these embeddings, we access the nearest neighbors from the index. If the similarity score is greater than 0.75, we count it as a match and include that as a suggestion. With this function, we can get suggestions for complete terms, such as "mountain hike", as well as prefixes, such as "dehyd".

Listing 13.15 shows our autocomplete `semantic_suggest` function implementation, which performs an ANN search for concepts. Our query might not be in the dictionary, but we can get the embeddings on demand. We will use the threshold `dist>=0.75` to only return similar terms for which we see a high confidence in similarity.

Choose a good similarity threshold

We arrived at the 0.75 threshold for listing 13.15 by looking at the distribution from figure 13.7. This should be further tuned by looking at the quality of results for your actual user queries.

NOTE   This function may cause a CPU bottleneck in production, so we recommend measuring throughput at scale and adding hardware accordingly.

Listing 13.15   Encoding a query and returning the *k*-nearest-neighbor concepts

```
def embedding_search(index, query, phrases, k=20,
                min_similarity=0.75):
  matches = []
  query_embedding = transformer.encode(query)
  query_embedding = normalize_embedding(query_embedding)
  ids, distances = index.knnQuery(query_embedding, k=k)
  for i in range(len(ids)):
    similarity = distances[i] * -1
    if similarity >= min_similarity:
      matches.append((phrases[ids[i]], similarity))
  if not len(matches):
    matches.append((phrases[ids[1]], distances[1] * -1))
  return matches
```

We set k=20 for illustration purposes. In a production application, this would likely be set somewhere from 5 to 10.

Gets the embeddings for the query

Converts negative dot product distance into a positive dot product

We're only returning the terms with 0.75 or higher similarity.

No neighbors found! Returns just the original term

```
def semantic_suggest(prefix, phrases):
  matches = embedding_search(concepts_index, prefix, phrases)
  print_labels(prefix, matches)

semantic_suggest("mountain hike", phrases)
semantic_suggest("dehyd", phrases)
```

Response:

```
Results for: mountain hike

1.000 | mountain hike
0.975 | mountain hiking
0.847 | mountain trail
0.787 | mountain guide
0.779 | mountain terrain
0.775 | mountain climbing
0.768 | mountain ridge
0.754 | winter hike


Results for: "dehyd"

0.941 | dehydrate
0.931 | dehydration
0.852 | rehydration
...
0.812 | hydrate
0.788 | hydration pack
0.776 | hydration system
```

We've done it! We can now efficiently serve up a semantic autocomplete based on Transformer embeddings and approximate nearest-neighbor search.

Overall, the quality of results for many queries with this model is quite impressive. But beware, it's extremely important to use a labeled dataset to measure success before deploying a solution like this to real customers. We'll demonstrate this process of using labeled data to measure and improve relevance when implementing question-answering in chapter 14.

13.6   *Semantic search with LLM embeddings*

Using what we've learned so far, we'll now take dense vector search to the next level: we are going to query the document embeddings with the query embeddings as a recall step at search time.

We specifically started with autocomplete as our first implementation, because it was helpful to understand the basics of language similarity. It is essential to develop a strong intuition about why things are similar or dissimilar in a vector space. Otherwise, you will endlessly chase recall problems when using embeddings. To build that intuition we started with matching and scoring basic concepts only a few words in length each.

With that understanding, we will now move on to comparing entire sentences. We're going to perform a semantic search for titles. Remember that we're searching on the Stack Exchange outdoors dataset, so the document titles are really the summaries of the questions being asked by the contributors. As a bonus, we can use the same implementation from the last section to search for question titles that are similar to one another.

This function will mostly be a repeat of the encoding and similarity functions from the previous section. The code in this section is even shorter, since we don't need to extract concepts.

Here are the steps we'll follow:

1 Get the embeddings for all the titles in the outdoors dataset.
2 Create an NMSLIB index with the embeddings.
3 Get the embeddings for a query.
4 Search the NMSLIB index.
5 Show the nearest-neighbor titles.

13.6.1 Getting titles and their embeddings

Our NMSLIB index will be made up of title embeddings. We're using the exact same function from the previous autocomplete example, but instead of transforming concepts, we're now transforming the titles of all the questions the outdoors community asked. The following listing shows the process of encoding the titles into embeddings.

> **Listing 13.16   Encoding the titles into embeddings**

Gets the titles for every question in the outdoors corpus

```
outdoors_dataframe = load_dataframe("data/outdoors/posts.csv")
titles = outdoors_dataframe.rdd.map(lambda x: x.title).collect()
titles = list(filter(None, titles))
embeddings = get_embeddings(titles, cache_name)

print(f"Number of embeddings: {len(embeddings)}")
print(f"Dimensions per embedding: {len(embeddings[0])}")
```

Gets the embeddings for the titles (this takes a little while on the first run, until it is cached)

Response:

```
Number of embeddings: 5331
Dimensions per embedding: 768
```

We have encoded 5,331 titles into embeddings, and figure 13.8 plots the title embedding similarity distribution.

Compare figure 13.8 to the concept similarity distributions from figure 13.7. Note the slightly different shape and score distributions, due to the difference between titles and concepts. Figure 13.7 has a longer "needle" on top. This is because titles are more specific, and therefore will relate differently than broader noun and verb phrases.

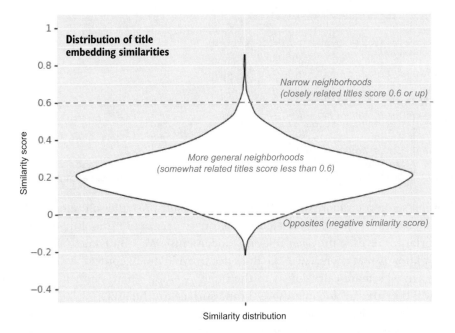

Figure 13.8 **The distribution of similarity scores when comparing all title embeddings to each another**

13.6.2 *Creating and searching the nearest-neighbor index*

Now that we have generated the embeddings for all the question titles in the corpus, we can easily create the nearest-neighbor index.

Listing 13.17 Creating the ANN title embeddings index

```
import nmslib
titles_index = nmslib.init(method="hnsw", space="negdotprod")
normalized_embeddings = list(map(normalize_embedding, embeddings))
titles_index.addDataPointBatch(normalized_embeddings)
titles_index.createIndex(print_progress=True)
```

With our newly created index, searching is easy! Listing 13.18 shows the new `semantic_search` function, which implements ANN search for question titles given a query. This is very similar to the `semantic_suggest` from listing 13.15 that we implemented for autocomplete—the main difference is that here the underlying embedding index is comprised of `title` content instead of concepts extracted from the `body` content.

Listing 13.18 Performing a semantic search for titles

```
def semantic_search(query, phrases):
    results = embedding_search(titles_index, query, phrases,
                    k=5, min_similarity=0.6)
```
embedding_search from listing 13.15

```
    print_labels(query, results)

semantic_search("mountain hike", titles)
```

Response:

```
Results for: mountain hike

0.723 | How is elevation gain and change measured for hiking trails?
0.715 | How do I Plan a Hiking Trip to Rocky Mountain National Park, CO
0.698 | Hints for hiking the west highland way
0.694 | New Hampshire A.T. Section Hike in May? Logistics and Trail Condi...
0.678 | Long distance hiking trail markings in North America or parts the...
```

Now let's take a moment and reflect on these results. Are they all relevant? Yes—they are all absolutely questions related to the query mountain hike. But, and this is very important, are they the *most* relevant documents? We don't know! The reason we don't know is that mountain hike does not provide much context at all. So, while the titles are all semantically similar to the query, we don't have enough information to know if they are the documents we should surface for the user.

That said, it is clear that this embedding-based approach to search brings interesting new capabilities to our matching and ranking toolbox, providing the ability to conceptually relate results. Whether those results are better or not depends on the context.

Thus far, we've implemented dense vector search in this chapter by hand, relying on the NMSLIB library to do the heavy lifting, but otherwise showing you how to build a dense vector index with ANN (HNSW) support and query it. We've done this intentionally to help you understand the inner workings of dense vector search. In your production system, however, you're likely going to use your search engine's built-in support for dense vector search. In the next listing, we switch over to using our collection interface to implement the same semantic search functionality using your configured search engine or vector database.

Listing 13.19 Performing vector search with the configured search engine

```
def display_results(query, search_results):
  print_labels(query, [(d["title"], d["score"])
                     for d in search_results])          Builds a new collection with
                                                        documents containing their
def index_outdoor_title_embeddings():            ◁──┘  title and embeddings
  create_view_from_collection(engine.get_collection("outdoors"),
                              "outdoors")
  outdoors_dataframe = spark.sql("""SELECT id, title FROM outdoors
                                    WHERE title IS NOT NULL""")
  ids = outdoors_dataframe.rdd.map(lambda x: x.id).collect()
  titles = outdoors_dataframe.rdd.map(lambda x: x.title).collect()
```

```
embeddings = list(
  map(normalize_embedding,                          Calculates normalized
      get_embeddings(titles, cache_name)))          embeddings for all documents
embeddings_dataframe = spark.createDataFrame(
  zip(ids, titles, embeddings),
  schema=["id", "title", "title_embedding"])

collection = engine.create_collection("outdoors_with_embeddings")
collection.write(embeddings_dataframe)
return collection                                   Returns documents by searching with a
                                                    query against title_embedding

def semantic_search_with_engine(collection, query, limit=10):   ◄──────┘
  query_vector = transformer.encode(query)
  query_vector = normalize_embedding(query_vector)      The string query is encoded
  request = {"query": query_vector,                     and normalized then built into
            "query_fields": ["title_embedding"],        a vector search request.
            "return_fields": ["title", "score", "title_embedding"],
            "quantization_size": "FLOAT32",    ◄──┐  The quantization size of
            "limit": limit}                         the embeddings, which
  response = collection.search(**request)           in this case is 32 bits
  return response["docs"]

embeddings_collection = index_outdoor_title_embeddings()

query = "mountain hike"
search_results = semantic_search_with_engine(embeddings_collection, query)
display_results(query, search_results)
```

Response:

```
0.723 | How is elevation gain and change measured for hiking trails?
0.715 | How do I Plan a Hiking Trip to Rocky Mountain National Park, CO
0.698 | Hints for hiking the west highland way
0.694 | New Hampshire A.T. Section Hike in May? Logistics and Trail Condi...
0.678 | Long distance hiking trail markings in North America or parts the...
```

Every search engine or vector database has its own unique APIs for implementing keyword search, vector search, hybrid keyword and vector search, and other capabilities. The `semantic_search_with_engine` function in listing 13.19 demonstrates using an engine-agnostic interface to query your configured search engine, though you may find it more powerful to perform certain operations using your engine's APIs directly for more advanced use cases.

We used NMSLIB earlier in this chapter to help you better understand the inner workings of dense vector search. Unless you're doing something very custom, though, you likely will want to use your search engine's built-in, scalable support for dense vector search as opposed to implementing it by hand locally with a library like NMSLIB, FAISS (which we'll introduce later in the chapter), or NumPy. You'll note that listing 13.19 returns the exact same results from your engine as the NMSLIB implementation returned in listing 13.18.

> ### Reranking results found with dense vector similarity
>
> In listing 13.18, we chose the default `min_similarity` threshold to require a similarity score of `0.6` or greater. Examine the title similarity distributions in figure 13.8—would you change this number to be different than `0.6`?
>
> You could set `min_similarity` to a value lower than `0.6` to potentially increase recall and change k to be a value higher than `5` as a rerank window size (for example, `250`). Then, using this larger result set, you could perform a rerank using dot product similarity. Using what you learned in chapters 10–12, you could also incorporate the dense vector similarity as a feature (potentially among many) in a more sophisticated learning-to-rank model.

Similarity scoring of embeddings is one of many features in a mature AI-powered search stack. This similarity will be used alongside personalization, learning to rank, and knowledge graphs for a robust search experience. Nearest-neighbor-based dense vector search is rapidly growing in popularity and is likely to supplant Boolean matching with BM25 ranking at some point as the most common retrieval and ranking technique for searching unstructured text. The two approaches—dense vector search and lexical search—are complementary, however, and hybrid approaches combining the two usually work even better.

13.7 *Quantization and representation learning for more efficient vector search*

In the last section, we introduced two concepts commonly used to speed up dense vector search: ANN search and reranking. Conceptually, ANN is a way to reduce the number of vector similarity calculations necessary at query time by efficiently locating and filtering to the top vectors that are the most likely to be similar to the query vector. Because ANN search is an approximation of the best results, it's common to rerank those top potential results using more precise (and computationally expensive) vector similarity calculations to get recall and relevance back on par with a non-ANN-optimized search.

The computation time and amount of memory required to represent and perform similarity calculations on vectors is directly related to the size of the vectors being searched. In this section, we'll introduce a few additional techniques for improving the efficiency of vector search:

- Scalar quantization
- Binary quantization
- Product quantization
- Matryoshka Representation Learning

Quantization is a technique used to reduce the memory footprint and computational complexity of numeric data representations, such as embedding vectors. In the context of embeddings, quantization involves compressing them by reducing the number of bits used to represent the features of the vector. Embeddings are typically represented as floating point numbers (floats), which are 32 bits (or 4 bytes) in size by default. If a typical vector embedding has 1,024 dimensions, this translates into 1,024 x 4 bytes, or 4,096 bytes (4 KB) per vector. If you have a large number of vectors to store and search, this can quickly add up to a significant amount of memory and computational overhead.

Quantizing embeddings allows you to trade off some ideally small amount of recall for significant improvements in storage efficiency and query speed, which is crucial for large-scale search systems. For example, you can reduce the memory usage of a vector of 32-bit floats (Float32) by 75% by converting each feature to an 8-bit integer (Int8). Compressing the individual numerical values (scalars) of each dimension like this is known as *scalar quantization*. This can often be done without significantly affecting recall, and it can be especially useful when you have a large number of vectors to store and search. You can even quantize each feature down to a single bit—a technique known as *binary quantization*—and still maintain a relatively high level of recall if it's combined with a reranking step using a higher-precision vector on the top-N results. Figure 13.9 visually demonstrates the concepts of scalar quantization and binary quantization using a vector containing an image of the cover of this book (assume the dimensions of the vector represent pixels in the image).

No Quantization
(Float32 per dimension)

Scalar Quantization
(Float16, Int8, Int4, etc.)

Binary Quantization
(1 bit per dimension)

Figure 13.9 Quantizing data: full precision, reduced scalar precision, and binary precision

In the figure, you can see the original image (no quantization), a scalar quantized image (using a reduced color palette that maps to similar ranges but with less colors/precision), and a binary quantized image (where each pixel is either black or white). You'll notice that the scalar quantized image still retains most of the important detail from the original image, and the binary quantized version is still clearly recognizable, albeit losing some important data (some of the characters in the title and the colors).

In this section, we'll cover scalar quantization, binary quantization, and a third type of quantization called product quantization. We'll also introduce a multi-tiered embedding approach known as Matryoshka Representation Learning, which can be used to dynamically switch the precision levels of already-generated embeddings without the need for additional quantization or retraining.

13.7.1 Scalar quantization

Scalar quantization is the simplest form of quantization, where each value in the embedding vector is independently mapped to a lower-precision representation. Consider the following two vectors:

```
[ -1.2345679,  2.2345679, 100.45679 ]   #4 bytes = 32 bits
[ -1.234,      2.234,      100.44 ]      #2 bytes = 16 bits
```

The first vector is a 32-bit float representation, and the second is a 16-bit float representation, each rounded to the maximum reliable precision. The second vector requires 50% less memory (2 bytes versus 4 bytes), all while still representing approximately the same values, just with less precision.

This reduced precision is a simple example of scalar quantization, taking higher-precision values and mapping them into lower-precision representations requiring less memory to store and less computation to process.

But what if we wanted to compress our vectors even further to a single byte (or even a few bits)—can we still pull this off and preserve most of our recall? The answer is yes, and we commonly accomplish this by mapping the range of float values into an Int8, as shown in figure 13.10.

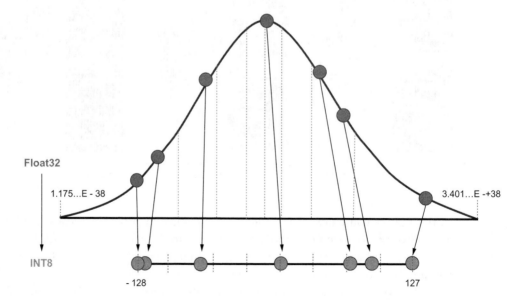

Figure 13.10   Scalar quantization from Float32 to Int8

In the figure, the curve at the top represents the distribution of values in the floating point range. Since we are quantizing from 32 bits to 8 bits, we map the range of the Float32 values into the smaller range of –128 to 127 (or 0 to 255 if using an unsigned integer). Depending on the quantization algorithm being used, attempts are often made to utilize the new ranges as fully as possible by *clamping* the values (limiting the range to the minimum and maximum), as well as by utilizing the density of values in the original vector to map more evenly into the new, quantized range.

Let's implement a scalar quantization example to see what effect this optimization yields on index size, recall, and search speed. Multiple libraries exist for performing scalar quantization. You can use the `sentence_transformers.quantization` module, or your search engine or language model may have its own quantization implementations built in. We are going to utilize the FAISS library for our quantized indexes, and a combination for the `sentence_transformers` library and FAISS for each of our quantization examples. FAISS (Facebook AI Similarity Search) is an open source library designed for efficient similarity search and clustering of dense vectors. It's similar to the NMSLIB library we used earlier in the chapter for semantic search, but it has some additional features, including built-in support for quantization. FAISS is widely used in production systems for dense vector search, and it's a great choice for implementing quantized indexes.

We'll look at an example later of how to run a search using the `collection` abstraction for your chosen search engine, but since not every engine has support for all quantization modes, and since each engine has different overhead and performance characteristics, we'll use FAISS for our benchmarking.

Let's now build a FAISS index with full-precision Float32 embeddings. We'll then use this as our baseline versus various quantized embedding indexes to compare index sizes, search speeds, and recall rates. Listing 13.20 shows the code to create the full-precision Float32 embeddings and index them into a FAISS index.

Listing 13.20 Indexing full-precision embeddings using FAISS

```
from sentence_transformers.quantization import quantize_embeddings

model = SentenceTransformer(
        "mixedbread-ai/mxbai-embed-large-v1",
        similarity_fn_name=SimilarityFunction.DOT_PRODUCT,
        truncate_dim=1024)

def index_full_precision_embeddings(doc_embeddings, name):
  index = faiss.IndexFlatIP(doc_embeddings.shape[1])
  index.add(doc_embeddings)
  faiss.write_index(index, name)
  return index

def get_outdoors_embeddings(model):
  outdoors_dataframe = load_dataframe("data/outdoors/posts.csv")
  post_texts = [post["title"] + " " + post["body"]
                for post in outdoors_dataframe.collect()]
```

This model creates embeddings supporting all upcoming optimization techniques.

The original embeddings will have 1,024 dimensions.

IndexFlatIP is a simple, unoptimized index supporting different embedding formats.

Adds documents to the index

Writes the index to disk

```
    return numpy.array(
        get_embeddings(post_texts, model, "outdoors_mrl_normed"))
doc_embeddings = get_outdoors_embeddings(model)
full_index = index_full_precision_embeddings(
                doc_embeddings, "full_embeddings")
```

Generates embeddings for the outdoors dataset

Creates a full-precision (Float32) FAISS index

In this listing, we calculate embeddings for the outdoors dataset using the `mixedbread -ai/mxbai-embed-large-v1` model, which produces high-quality embeddings that work well with all our quantization techniques and also supports Matryoshka Representation Learning, which we'll explore later in the chapter. We then index those embeddings to a full-precision (Float32) FAISS index, which we'll use soon as our baseline for benchmarking the performance of various quantization techniques.

For our benchmarks, we'll also need to encode some test queries into embeddings, which is shown in listing 13.21.

Listing 13.21   Generating query embeddings and full-index benchmarks

```
def get_test_queries():
  return ["tent poles", "hiking trails", "mountain forests",
          "white water", "best waterfalls", "mountain biking",
          "snowboarding slopes", "bungee jumping", "public parks"]

queries = get_test_queries()
query_embeddings = model.encode(queries,
                    convert_to_numpy=True,
                    normalize_embeddings=True)

full_results = time_and_execute_search(
                full_index, "full_embeddings",
                query_embeddings, k=25)
display_statistics(full_results)
```

Gets test queries for benchmarking

Generates embeddings for each query

Generates search time, index size, and recall statistics for the full-precision (Float32) index

Displays the benchmarking stats

Output:

```
full_embeddings search took: 7.621 ms
full_embeddings index size: 75.6 MB
Recall: 1.0
```

In the preceding listing, we define a list of queries we'll use to benchmark our full-precision index against various vector search optimization strategies. We then call a `time_and_execute_search` function (omitted for brevity) on the full-precision index from listing 13.20 and then pass the results to a `display_statistics` function (also omitted for brevity), which displays the search time, index size, and recall statistics.

This provides a baseline for comparison with our upcoming quantized (or otherwise optimized) indexes. Listing 13.22 shows the implementation of two additional functions we'll use to compare results from other indexing strategies: an `evaluate_search` function and an `evaluate_rerank_search` function.

Listing 13.22 Functions to benchmark optimized search approaches

```
def evaluate_search(full_index, optimized_index,
                    optimized_index_name,
                    query_embeddings,
                    optimized_query_embeddings,
                    k=25, display=True, log=False):
  full_results = time_and_execute_search(
                    full_index, "full_embeddings",
                    query_embeddings, k=k)
  optimized_results = time_and_execute_search(
                    optimized_index,
                    optimized_index_name,
                    optimized_query_embeddings, k=k)
  if display:
    display_statistics(optimized_results, full_results)
  return optimized_results, full_results

def evaluate_rerank_search(full_index, optimized_index,
                    query_embeddings,
                    optimized_embeddings,
                    k=50, limit=25):
  results, full_results = evaluate_search(
                    full_index,
                    optimized_index, None,
                    query_embeddings,
                    optimized_embeddings,
                    display=False, k=k)
  doc_embeddings = get_outdoors_embeddings(model)
  rescore_scores, rescore_ids = [], []
  for i in range(len(results["results"])):
    embedding_ids = results["faiss_ids"][i]
    top_k_embeddings = [doc_embeddings[id]
                        for id in embedding_ids]
    query_embedding = query_embeddings[i]
    scores = query_embedding @ \
             numpy.array(top_k_embeddings).T
    indices = scores.argsort()[::-1][:limit]
    top_k_indices = embedding_ids[indices]
    top_k_scores = scores[indices]
    rescore_scores.append(top_k_scores)
    rescore_ids.append(top_k_indices)
  results = generate_search_results(rescore_scores, rescore_ids)
  recall = calculate_recall(full_results["results"], results)
  print(f"Reranked recall: {recall}")
```

Brings back the top 25 results from each index and compares them

Calculates query speed, index size, and recall for optimized versus full-precision index

Same as evaluate_search, but over-requests to k=50 results (by default) and reranks those using full-precision embeddings

Generates embeddings for each doc in the outdoors dataset

Performs a dot product between the query embedding and the top-k embeddings

Sorts the results by dot product score to rerank them

Helper function (omitted) that combines IDs and scores with other document fields to return

Calculates the recall of results after reranking versus the full-precision index

The `evaluate_search` function internally calls the `time_and_execute_search` function on both the full-precision index and the quantized index, and it passes the results to a `display_statistics` function to compare and display the search time, index size, and recall statistics.

The `evaluate_rerank_search` function then calculates recall again after reranking the top-*N* results from the quantized index using full-precision embeddings. While quantization can drastically reduce memory and search times, we'll also see that it reduces recall, meaning that some of the results that *should* be returned are not. But by over-requesting and reranking just the top-*N* results using full-precision embeddings (typically loaded from disk after the quantized search, not kept in memory with the index), we can recapture most of that lost recall.

We'll show both the quantized recall and the reranked quantized recall in each subsequent listing to demonstrate the trade-offs between full-precision searches, quantized searches, and reranked quantized searches. For our first quantization example, let's implement Int8 scalar quantization.

Listing 13.23   Creating an Int8 quantized embeddings index using FAISS

```
def index_int8_embeddings(doc_embeddings, name):      Quantizes the doc
  int8_embeddings = quantize_embeddings(              embeddings to
                 doc_embeddings, precision="int8")    Int8 precision
  print("Int8 embeddings shape:", int8_embeddings.shape)
  index = faiss.IndexFlatIP(int8_embeddings.shape[1])    Creates an index
  index.add(int8_embeddings)           Adds the quantized   configured to expect the
  faiss.write_index(index, name)       embeddings to the index   shape of the embeddings
  return index
                                       Saves the index to disk so
int8_index_name = "int8_embeddings"    we can measure its size
int8_index = index_int8_embeddings(doc_embeddings, int8_index_name)


quantized_queries = quantize_embeddings(
  query_embeddings,                     Quantizes the
  calibration_embeddings=doc_embeddings,  query embeddings
  precision="int8")                     to Int8 precision


evaluate_search(full_index, int8_index,
             int8_index_name, query_embeddings,    Performs benchmarks for search
             quantized_queries)                    time, index size, and recall
evaluate_rerank_search(full_index, int8_index,
         query_embeddings, quantized_queries)
                                          Performs benchmarks again
                                          allowing reranking of top results
                                          with full-precision embeddings
```

Output:

```
Int8 embeddings shape: (18456, 1024)
int8_embeddings search took: 9.070 ms (38.65% improvement)
int8_embeddings index size: 18.91 MB (74.99% improvement)
Recall: 0.9289
Reranked recall: 1.0
```

In listing 13.23's output, we see that the Int8 quantized index is 75% smaller than the full-precision index, which makes sense given that we've reduced from Float32 to Int8 precision, which is an ~75% reduction from 32 bits to 8 bits. Likewise, we see that the total search time improved due to lower precision numbers being more efficient to process (at least on some systems). Note that search speed will vary *considerably* on all these benchmarks from system to system and run to run, but the index size benchmark should always be the same. Also note that we have a fairly small number of documents in our index, and query speed improvements from quantization are likely to become more pronounced as the number of documents increases.

The most important numbers, however, are the recall numbers. The Int8 quantized search maintained a 92.89% recall rate. This means that we achieved an ~75% reduction in index size and a significant improvement in search speed with only 7.11% of the top N=25 results missing in the quantized search. Just as the middle image of this book's cover in figure 13.9 maintained the vast majority of the important details of the original image, we were likewise able to retain high fidelity to our quantized embeddings in listing 13.23 when using Int8 quantization.

The `Reranked recall` value of 1.0 further indicates that by just requesting the top N=50 results and reranking them using the original full-precision embeddings, we get back to 100% recall. This is a common pattern when using quantization in dense vector search: perform an initial search that over-requests results using a quantized index (for a significant memory and speed improvement) and then rerank the top N results using higher-precision embeddings (usually pulled from disk so they don't affect your index and memory requirements) to recapture the lost recall and ranking precision. While these improvements are impressive, we could continue compressing even further, using 4 bits (Int4) or less. In the next section, we'll see what happens when we compress each dimension all the way down to a single bit!

13.7.2 *Binary quantization*

Binary quantization is an extreme form of quantization where each value in the embedding vector is represented by a single bit, reducing the values to 0 or 1. This method is akin to converting an image to black and white only (just one shade of black, not grayscale), like in the example on the right in figure 13.9.

Quantizing every feature into a single bit can be done using a simple threshold to assign a bit of 0 for any feature less than or equal to 0 and a value of 1 for any feature greater than 1.0. This works well if feature values across embeddings have a uniform distribution between positive and negative values. If feature values are not uniformly distributed across documents, however, it can be helpful to use the median value for each feature, or some similar threshold for assigning 0 versus 1 as the binary quantized value, in order to more evenly distribute the values.

Figure 13.11 illustrates the result of binary quantization, where only the most essential information is preserved, akin to the black-and-white version of the cover of this book. The far left image demonstrates using a simple threshold, the middle image represents using a non-uniform threshold that assigns values based on the relative distribution of values for each feature in the original embeddings, and the far right image shows an optimal learned binary representation directly from the Transformer encoder model. This last "model-based" binary quantization looks the best because the choice of values takes into account the context of the entire image when generating the binary representation, not just the individual features. This allows for a much

Simple threshold binary quantization	Non-uniform binary quantization	Model-based binary quantization

Figure 13.11   Different binary quantization techniques

more meaningful and accurate representation of the original embedding to be encoded into the available binary quantized feature values based on how the model has been trained to understand the image as a whole. We won't demonstrate an example of doing model-based binary quantization, since we're trying to benchmark recall for the same embeddings at different levels of quantization, but it's worth keeping in mind that if your model supports model-based binary quantization, it will generally provide better results than performing binary quantization on features after the model has already encoded and returned them at a higher level of precision.

Let's now implement binary quantization using FAISS and benchmark the results.

Listing 13.24   Indexing and benchmarking binary quantized embeddings

```
def index_binary_embeddings(doc_embeddings,
                            binary_index_name):
  binary_embeddings = quantize_embeddings(
    doc_embeddings,
    precision="binary").astype(numpy.uint8)
  print("Binary embeddings shape:", binary_embeddings.shape)
  index = faiss.IndexBinaryFlat(
    binary_embeddings.shape[1] * 8)
  index.add(binary_embeddings)
  faiss.write_index_binary(index, binary_index_name)
  return index

binary_index_name = "binary_embeddings"
binary_index = index_binary_embeddings(
  doc_embeddings, binary_index_name)

quantized_queries = quantize_embeddings(
  query_embeddings,
```

- **Quantizes the doc embeddings to binary (1 bit per dimension)**
- **Creates the binary embeddings index**
- **Adds all the doc embeddings to the index**
- **Writes the index to disk**
- **Quantizes the query embeddings to binary**

**The doc embeddings are provided to
the quantizer to calibrate the best
thresholds for assigning 0 or 1.**

```
calibration_embeddings=doc_embeddings,     ◁─────
precision="binary").astype(numpy.uint8)    ◁───────
```

**Saves every 8 dimensions
as 1 byte, encoded as
unsigned Int8**

```
evaluate_search(full_index, binary_index,
    binary_index_name,
    query_embeddings, quantized_queries)
evaluate_rerank_search(full_index, binary_index,
    query_embeddings, quantized_queries)
```

**Performs benchmarks with
and without reranking versus
the full-precision index**

Output:

```
Binary embeddings shape: (18456, 128)
binary_embeddings search took: 1.232 ms (83.38% improvement)
binary_embeddings index size: 2.36 MB (96.87% improvement)
Recall: 0.6044
Reranked recall: 1.0
```

While it should come as no surprise that binary quantization reduces the index size and memory requirements by 96.87% (from 32 bits to 1 bit), it is mind-boggling that we were able to retain 60.44% of the recall with just a single bit per embedding feature. While 60% recall isn't necessarily sufficient for many search use cases, note that when we over-requested by a factor of 2 (N=50 to find the top 25) and reranked, we were able to get recall back to 100% for our test queries. Across a larger dataset and number of queries, you won't likely be able to maintain 100% recall, but even approaching full recall with just a single bit per feature for your initial search is an impressive feat.

With the ability to achieve such extreme compression while still getting back to nearly 100% recall by over-requesting and reranking, binary quantization pushes the limits of what's possible with quantization. You might think that a single bit per dimension would be the limit for how far we can quantize our embeddings, but in the next section we'll introduce a technique that allows us to compress even further—product quantization.

13.7.3 Product quantization

While scalar quantization and binary quantization focus on reducing the precision of the individual features of an embedding, product quantization (PQ) instead focuses on quantizing the entire embedding down to a more memory-efficient representation. It allows for even deeper compression than binary quantization, making PQ particularly beneficial for large-scale search applications with a high number of embedding dimensions.

Imagine you have a long sentence and you split it into shorter phrases; it's easier to handle and process each phrase independently. Similarly, PQ divides the vector space into smaller regions (subvectors) and quantizes each subvector individually. PQ then clusters each of the subvector regions to find a set of cluster centroids and finally assigns one centroid ID to each subvector for each document. This list of centroid IDs (one per subvector) for each document is called a PQ code, and it is the quantized representation of the document's embedding. Figure 13.12 demonstrates the PQ process.

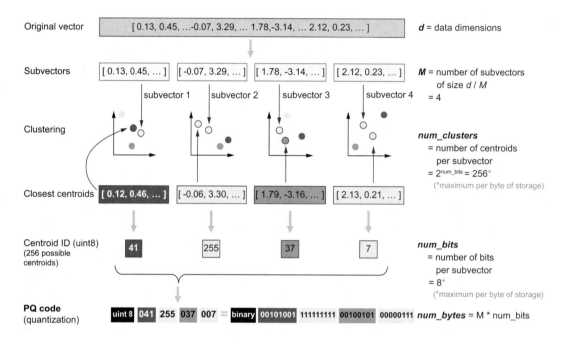

Figure 13.12   The product quantization process

The quantization process starts with the top layer of the figure and progresses sequentially down. First, the original vector space of d dimensions is divided into M subvector spaces. For each of the M subvector spaces, the corresponding subvector is partitioned from each original embedding. Clustering (usually using a *k*-means algorithm) is then performed on all the subvectors within each subspace to create a list of num_clusters clusters identified by their centroid vector within the subspace. Each centroid is then assigned an ID, which is recorded in a *codebook* containing a mapping of each centroid ID to its full subvectors. Finally, the centroid IDs for every subspace are concatenated together per document to create the *PQ code*, which is the official quantized representation of each document.

The documents' PQ codes are then indexed, and at query time the query embedding is divided into the same M subspaces, and the distance between the query subvector in that subspace and each centroid in the subspace is calculated and cached in a lookup table. Since each document's PQ code maps to a specific centroid in each subspace, we can get the approximate distance between the query subvector and document subvector by looking it up in the cached lookup table. The vector similarity scores between the query and each document can then be calculated and ranked by the smallest distance across the combined subspaces, using a metric like inner product or Euclidean distance. Calculating the Euclidean distance, for example, just requires taking the square root of the sum of the squared distances from each subvector.

Libraries like FAISS provide efficient implementations of PQ out of the box. Listing 13.25 demonstrates the process of building an index using PQ.

Listing 13.25 Building and benchmarking a product quantization index

Divides the embedding into M=16 subvectors (of 64 dimensions each)

The original embedding is 1024 dimensions.

```
def index_pq_embeddings(doc_embeddings, index_name, num_subvectors=16):
    dimensions = doc_embeddings.shape[1]
    M = num_subvectors
    num_bits = 8
    index = faiss.IndexPQ(dimensions, M, num_bits)
    index.train(doc_embeddings)
    index.add(doc_embeddings)
    faiss.write_index(index, index_name)
    return index

pq_index_name = "pq_embeddings"
pq_index = index_pq_embeddings(doc_embeddings,
                    pq_index_name)

evaluate_search(full_index, pq_index, pq_index_name,
                query_embeddings, query_embeddings)
evaluate_rerank_search(full_index, pq_index,
                query_embeddings,
                query_embeddings)
```

8 bits = 256 maximum cluster centroids per subvector.

Creates the PQ index

Generates the cluster centroids using k-means clustering

Adds all the doc_embeddings to the index

Saves the index to disk so we can measure the size

Runs the benchmarks versus the full-precision index

Output:

```
pq_embeddings search took: 2.092 ms (75.22% improvement)
pq_embeddings index size: 1.34 MB (98.22% improvement)
Recall: 0.3333
Reranked recall: 0.6800
```

You'll notice immediately that the recall for the PQ index is significantly lower than the scalar and binary quantization types we benchmarked at 33.33% recall without reranking and 68% recall after reranking. You'll also notice, however, that the index size is 98.22% smaller than the original full-precision index. Obviously, we've made an intentional trade-off here to hyper-optimize the index size in exchange for recall. Unlike the scalar and binary quantization techniques, however, PQ provides levers for adjusting that trade-off by increasing either the number of subvectors (M_subvectors) or the num_bits to store more precision in the index and improve recall. For example, if you were to set M_subvectors to 64, you would get the following:

```
pq_embeddings search took: 4.061 ms (43.99% improvement)
pq_embeddings index size: 2.23 MB (97.05% improvement)
```

```
Recall: 0.5778
Reranked recall: 0.9911
```

These results are now more on par with the binary quantization results. The key takeaway, then, is that the primary benefit of PQ is in the flexibility to control the trade-off between index size and recall, particularly when you need to significantly compress your embeddings.

We've now explored several quantization approaches to reduce the size of the indexed embeddings and speed up search times while maintaining a very high level of recall relative to the compression level. In the next subsection, we'll explore a different approach to tackling the compression versus recall trade-off by introducing embeddings that actually encode multiple levels of precision inside the original embedding representation.

13.7.4 *Matryoshka Representation Learning*

Matryoshka Representation Learning (MRL) is a novel approach to vector performance optimization that learns a hierarchical representation of a vector space, where multiple levels of precision are encoded by different ranges of dimensions within the vector space. This allows for flexible-length representations where shorter segments of an embedding can approximate the meaning of the full embedding, just with reduced precision. MRL is named after the Russian nesting dolls (Matryoshka dolls), signaling the "layers" of precision to be discovered inside of other layers.

As a conceptual explanation of how MRL works, imagine that someone who's never seen the animated Disney movie *The Lion King* asked you to describe it. If you're familiar with the movie, you might start with a very high-level summary and then expand on your description if the person wants more details. For example, you could imagine the following possible responses:

1 It's a Disney animated movie about a lion.
2 It's a Disney animated movie about a lion cub who grows up to become king.
3 It's a Disney animated movie about a lion cub named Simba who grows up to become king after his father is killed by his uncle.
4 It's a Disney animated movie about a lion cub named Simba who must discover his place in the circle of life after running away from his kingdom as a boy and returning as an adult to reclaim his throne from his uncle who killed his father.

Notice that these all give the main idea of the story at various levels of granularity. If it was really important that you provide the most accurate description, you'd go with the one with the most detail, but in reality, it can be more effective in some cases to start with the higher-level description and only provide additional levels of detail as needed.

This concept of hierarchical representations that reveal more about the subject at different hierarchical levels of granularity is the key idea behind MRL. This technique allows vectors to have progressive accuracy, meaning that the more of the vector you use, the more precise the representation becomes. To illustrate this, let's consider figure 13.13, which shows the cover of this book at various pixelation levels.

Figure 13.13 Hierarchical representation levels balancing accuracy and compression

As you can see, the image at the top left is highly pixelated, representing a very coarse approximation of the original cover. Moving to the right, and then to the next row, each subsequent image includes twice as many dimensions, eventually leading to a clear and detailed representation. These dimensions are *refinements* on the previous dimensions, however; they are not entirely new information. In other words, it's possible to use a full vector, only the first half of the vector, only the first quarter of the vector, and so on, and still get an approximation of the original vector, just with less precision. This is similar to how MRL embeddings work.

Listing 13.26 demonstrates building and benchmarking a FAISS index using MRL embeddings. Note that because the lower-precision representations are achieved by simply cutting off later dimensions of the original embedding, no special indexing strategy is necessary for MRL embeddings. You simply need to reduce the number of dimensions of the dense vector field you are indexing and searching to the number of dimensions for the MRL embeddings you choose to use (cutting them in half each time and discarding the latter half).

Listing 13.26   Benchmarking MRL embeddings at different thresholds

```
def get_mrl_embeddings(embeddings, num_dimensions):
  mrl_embeddings = numpy.array(
    list(map(lambda e: e[:num_dimensions], embeddings)))         Uses only the top
  return mrl_embeddings                                          num_dimensions
                                                                 dimensions

def index_mrl_embeddings(doc_embeddings, num_dimensions, mrl_index_name):
  mrl_doc_embeddings = get_mrl_embeddings(doc_embeddings, num_dimensions)
  print(f"{mrl_index_name} embeddings shape:", mrl_doc_embeddings.shape)
  mrl_index = index_full_precision_embeddings(
    mrl_doc_embeddings, mrl_index_name)          An MRL index is a standard
  return mrl_index                               index, just with a reduced
                                                 number of dimensions.

print(f"Original embeddings shape:", doc_embeddings.shape)
original_dimensions = doc_embeddings.shape[1]         ◁─── 1024 dimensions

for num_dimensions in [original_dimensions//2,        ◁─── 512 dimensions
                       original_dimensions//4,   ◁─── 256 dimensions
                       original_dimensions//8]:        ◁─── 128
                                                            dimensions

  mrl_index_name = f"mrl_embeddings_{num_dimensions}"
  mrl_index = index_mrl_embeddings(doc_embeddings,
                                   num_dimensions,
                                   mrl_index_name)
  mrl_queries = get_mrl_embeddings(query_embeddings,
                                   num_dimensions)

  evaluate_search(full_index, mrl_index, mrl_index_name,
                  query_embeddings, mrl_queries)               Benchmark MRL search
  evaluate_rerank_search(full_index,                   Benchmark MRL
    mrl_index, query_embeddings, mrl_queries)          search + reranking
```

Output:

```
Original embeddings shape: (18456, 1024)

mrl_embeddings_512 embeddings shape: (18456, 512)
mrl_embeddings_512 search took: 3.586 ms (49.15% improvement)
mrl_embeddings_512 index size: 37.8 MB (50.0% improvement)
Recall: 0.7022
Reranked recall: 1.0

mrl_embeddings_256 embeddings shape: (18456, 256)
mrl_embeddings_256 search took: 1.845 ms (73.45% improvement)
mrl_embeddings_256 index size: 18.9 MB (75.0% improvement)
Recall: 0.4756
Reranked recall: 0.9689
```

```
mrl_embeddings_128 embeddings shape: (18456, 128)
mrl_embeddings_128 search took: 1.061 ms (84.35% improvement)
mrl_embeddings_128 index size: 9.45 MB (87.5% improvement)
Recall: 0.2489
Reranked recall: 0.64
```

In the output, we see that 70.22% of the recall was encoded into the first 50% of the features of the embedding, 47.56% was encoded into the first 25% of the features, and 24.89% was encoded into the first 12.5% of the features. While this level of recall relative to the compression may not be as impressive as some of the earlier quantization approaches, the fact that it is built into the embedding representation to be used (or not used) whenever desired with no special indexing requirements provides some useful flexibility. Additionally, as we'll see in the next subsection, MRL can also be combined with most of the other approaches.

13.7.5 Combining multiple vector search optimization approaches

In this chapter, we've discussed multiple methods to improve the efficiency of vector search:

- ANN search to filter the number of documents that must be scored to those likely to score well
- Quantization techniques to reduce the memory requirements and processing time for embeddings
- MRL to reduce the number of dimensions required to find an initial set of search results
- Reranking to improve the recall and ranking of the top-N results after applying the other techniques more aggressively

In practice, you can often combine several of these techniques to achieve your desired level of performance. Listing 13.27 shows a final example combining each of these approaches in a single implementation: ANN using an inverted file index (IVF) for performance, binary quantization for performance and compression, MRL at 1/2 the original dimensionality for performance and compression, and reranking 2 times the number of results to improve recall and relevance ranking.

Listing 13.27 Combining ANN, quantization, MRL, and reranking

```
def index_binary_ivf_mrl_embeddings(reduced_mrl_doc_embeddings,
                                    binary_index_name):
    binary_embeddings = quantize_embeddings(          Binary quantization:
        reduced_mrl_doc_embeddings,                   applies quantization to
        calibration_embeddings=reduced_mrl_doc_embeddings,  the doc embeddings
        precision="binary").astype(numpy.uint8)

    dimensions = reduced_mrl_doc_embeddings.shape[1]   Configuration so the index
    quantizer = faiss.IndexBinaryFlat(dimensions)      knows how the doc embeddings
                                                       have been quantized
```

```
num_clusters = 256
index = faiss.IndexBinaryIVF(
        quantizer, dimensions, num_clusters)
index.nprobe = 4
```
ANN: uses a binary-quantized IVF index for ANN search

```
index.train(binary_embeddings)
index.add(binary_embeddings)
faiss.write_index_binary(index, binary_index_name)
return index
```
Trains, adds documents, and saves the combined index to disk

```
mrl_dimensions = doc_embeddings.shape[1] // 2
reduced_mrl_doc_embeddings = get_mrl_embeddings(
  doc_embeddings, mrl_dimensions)
```
MRL: gets reduced-dimension doc embeddings

```
binary_ivf_mrl_index_name = "binary_ivf_mrl_embeddings"
binary_ivf_mrl_index = index_binary_ivf_mrl_embeddings(
  reduced_mrl_doc_embeddings, mrl_dimensions,
  binary_ivf_mrl_index_name)
```

```
mrl_queries = get_mrl_embeddings(query_embeddings,
                      mrl_dimensions)
```
MRL: gets reduced-dimension query embeddings

```
quantized_queries = quantize_embeddings(mrl_queries,
  calibration_embeddings=reduced_mrl_doc_embeddings,
  precision="binary").astype(numpy.uint8)
```
Binary quantization: applies quantization to the query embeddings

```
evaluate_search(full_index, binary_ivf_mrl_index,
  binary_ivf_mrl_index_name,
  query_embeddings, quantized_queries)
```
Benchmarks the binary ANN, binary quantization, and MRL embeddings

```
evaluate_rerank_search(
  full_index, binary_ivf_mrl_index,
  query_embeddings, quantized_queries)
```
Benchmarks again with reranking using full-precision embeddings

Output:

```
binary_ivf_mrl_embeddings search took: 0.064 ms (99.09% improvement)
binary_ivf_mrl_embeddings index size: 1.35 MB (98.22% improvement)
Recall: 0.3511
Reranked recall: 0.7244
```

As you can see from the listing, the different embedding optimization approaches can be combined in complementary ways to achieve your desired balance between query speed, index compression and memory usage, and final relevance ranking. In this case, by combining ANN, MRL, binary quantization, and reranking, we were able to achieve by far the fastest search time (~99% faster than full-precision search) and by far the smallest index size (~98% reduction), while still maintaining over 72% recall after reranking.

Using quantization in a supported engine

We've created quantized indexes using FAISS in order to ensure all the demonstrated ANN and quantization approaches can be easily reproduced for index size, search speed, and recall, independent of your configured default `engine`. Different search engines have varying levels of support for quantization approaches, with some performing quantization inside the engine and some requiring you to quantize outside of the engine and configure an appropriate quantization format (`FLOAT32`, `INT8`, `BINARY`, and so on). The `search` method on our `collection` interface implements support for scalar quantization and binary quantization using the latter approach by accepting a `quantization_size` parameter (previously demonstrated in listing 11.19), and MRL should be supported by any engine with vector search capabilities by truncating MRL embeddings prior to indexing and searching. Reranking is also supported by adding a `rerank_query` section to your search request. For example:

```
{
    'query': [0, ..., 1],
    'query_fields': ['binary_embedding'],
    'quantization_size': 'BINARY',
    'order_by': [('score', 'desc')],
    'limit': 25,
      'rerank_query': {
        'query': [-0.01628, ..., 0.02110],
        'query_fields': ['full_embedding'],
        'quantization_size': 'FLOAT32',
        'order_by': [('score', 'desc')],
        'rerank_count': 50
    }
}
```

This example implements an initial binary quantized query (to whatever degree your engine supports it) and returns the top 25 results after reranking the top 50 results using full-precision (`Float32`) embeddings.

Combining various ANN, scalar quantization, binary quantization, product quantization, and MRL techniques can significantly improve the efficiency of your vector search system. Many other techniques for quantization exist, and more are being developed all the time, but this overview should give you a great starting point if you're looking to optimize your vector search usage. By experimenting with these techniques and combining them in different ways, you can optimize your search system to achieve the desired balance between speed, memory usage, and recall, especially when applying reranking as a final step. But reranking based on embeddings isn't always the best way to get the most relevant final search results. In the next section, we'll explore an often better way to perform the final reranking of top results: using a cross-encoder.

13.8   Cross-encoders vs. bi-encoders

In this chapter, we've built semantic search using a Transformer-based encoder to generate embeddings. Our strategy involved finding the similarity between a query and document by separately encoding both of them into embeddings, and then using a cosine similarity to generate a relevance score based on the similarity of the two embeddings. An encoder like this that separately encodes each input into an embedding, so that those embeddings can be compared, is known as a *bi-encoder*.

In contrast with a bi-encoder, a *cross-encoder* encodes pairs of inputs together and returns a similarity score. Assuming the inputs are a query and a document, the cross-encoder will concatenate and then encode the query and document together, returning a similarity score measuring how well the document answers the query.

Functionally, the cross-encoder is still generating a similarity score between the two inputs, but it can capture the shared context between the query and document in a way that a bi-encoder cannot. For example, a bi-encoder might place the query mountain hike near the document containing the text "first time snow hiking" because they are both related to a similar concept—hiking. But the cross-encoder would pass both the query and document to the encoder (a Transformer), which could then identify through its attention mechanism that while both inputs are about hiking, the document is about beginner snow hiking (which likely wouldn't involve mountains the first time) instead of specifically being about the query of mountain hike. By using the context of the query to interpret the document, the cross-encoder can therefore reach a more nuanced interpretation of how well a document matches a query than a bi-encoder, which only interprets the query and document independently.

Figure 13.14 visualizes the bi-encoder and cross-encoder architectures.

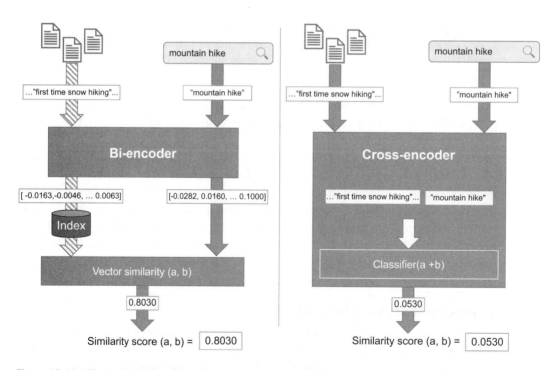

Figure 13.14 Bi-encoders vs. cross-encoders. Bi-encoders process query and document inputs separately, whereas cross-encoders process them together into a similarity score.

In the figure, note the following key characteristics:

- Bi-encoders encode queries and documents separately into embeddings that can then be compared using a similarity function (like cosine).
- Cross-encoders encode queries together to assign a similarity score.
- Solid-colored arrows indicate data processing that must occur at query time, whereas striped arrows indicate work that can be performed at index time and cached. Note that bi-encoders only need to encode the query once at query time, whereas cross-encoders must encode the query along with every document that needs a similarity score at query time.

Cross-encoders are more computationally expensive than bi-encoders at query time, but they are also usually more accurate than bi-encoders because they can capture the relevant interactions between the query and the document contexts. For this reason, cross-encoders are often used to rerank a small subset of the top results from a much faster bi-encoder-based vector search or lexical search to provide a more accurate similarity score for the top query and document pairs.

Just like the learning-to-rank models we built in chapters 10–12, cross-encoders are another form of *ranking classifier*—a model that classifies inputs into probable similarity scores. Listing 13.28 demonstrates how to invoke a cross-encoder to rerank search results. We'll use the same initial query from back in listing 13.19, but we'll over-request the number of search results (`limit=50`), so we'll provide more options for the cross-encoder to rerank.

Listing 13.28 Reranking search results with a cross-encoder

```
from sentence_transformers import CrossEncoder
cross_encoder = \
    CrossEncoder("cross-encoder/ms-marco-MiniLM-L-6-v2")

query = "mountain hike"
search_results = semantic_search_with_engine(
  embeddings_collection, query, limit=50)
pairs_to_score = [[query, doc["title"]]
                  for doc in search_results]
cross_scores = cross_encoder.predict(pairs_to_score,
               activation_fct=torch.nn.Sigmoid())
reranked_results = rerank(search_results, cross_scores)
display_results(query, reranked_results[:10])
```

Cross-encoder model trained on a similar dataset of questions and answers.

Generates a pair of query + document title to score for each document

Over-requests 50 results to supply sufficient candidates to rerank

Invokes the cross-encoder to score each pair

Optional activation function to normalize between 0 and 1

Updates the relevance ranking based on the cross-encoder scores

Response:

```
0.578 | What constitutes mountain exposure when hiking or scrambling?
0.337 | ... hiking trails... in... Rocky Mountain National Park...
0.317 | Where in the US can I find green mountains to hike...?
0.213 | Appropriate terms... hiking, trekking, mountaineering...
0.104 | Camping on top of a mountain
```

```
0.102 |  ... Plan a Hiking Trip to Rocky Mountain National Park, CO
0.093 |  What considerations... for... a hiking ascent of Mount...
0.073 |  Are there any easy hiking daytrips up mountains...
0.053 |  First time snow hiking
0.049 |  Advice for first Grand Canyon Hike for Eastern Hikers
```

Though the scores are not cosine similarities (and thus not directly comparable with the bi-encoder scores), the quality of the results seems generally improved after applying the bi-encoder. Notice that more documents are now related to mountain hiking as opposed to hiking in general.

Taking this chapter as a whole, one common pattern for integrating cross-encoders with bi-encoders is as follows:

1 Perform an initial search using a combination of ANN, quantization, and representation learning techniques (super fast).

2 Rerank a medium-sized number of results (hundreds or thousands) using N higher-precision vectors loaded from disk for only the top N results (fast, since the number results is reduced).

3 Take the top page or two of results, and rerank them with a cross-encoder to get the optimal ranking for the top results (slow, but only for a small number of results).

You can, of course, use any learning-to-rank model for your final ranking step. Cross-encoders are one of the most-deployed kinds of learning-to-rank model (focused solely on document content), as they don't require explicitly modeled features and instead have learned to model language and content features automatically from a deep learning training process. You can (and should) certainly fine-tune your cross-encoder model, leveraging the techniques from chapters 10 and 11, but many people just use off-the-shelf pretrained cross-encoder models without fine-tuning them, because they tend to generalize well when dealing with general text content.

With what you've learned in this chapter, you should now be able to do the following with your own content:

- Assess and choose an existing fine-tuned Transformer encoder model that matches your use case.
- Encode important text from your documents, and add them to an embeddings index for ANN search.
- Build an autocomplete pipeline to accept plain text queries, and quickly return the most closely related concepts.
- Add a powerful high-recall semantic search to your product.
- Optimize the performance of your dense vector search system by combining ANN, quantization, MRL, and reranking techniques.
- Rank results with a bi-encoder, and rerank those search results with a cross-encoder to improve search relevance ranking.

The technology underlying dense vector search still has room for improvement, because ranking on embeddings can be calculation-intensive, and ANN approaches have nontrivial scaling trade-offs. Sparse term vectors leveraging an inverted index are still much more efficient and simpler to scale. But tremendous forward progress continues to be made toward productionizing these dense vector search techniques, and for good reason. Not only does searching on vectors enable better semantic search on text, but it also enables cutting-edge approaches to question answering, results summarization, image search, and other advanced search use cases like retrieval augmented generation (RAG), all of which we'll cover in the following chapters.

Summary

- Dense vector search ranks relevant documents by comparing the distance between embedding vectors, such as from large language models (LLMs).
- Transformers enable LLMs to encode the meaning of content (queries, documents, sentences, etc.) into vectors and also to decode the meaning out of encoded vectors.
- Semantic search and other use search cases like semantic autocomplete can be implemented using embeddings.
- Approximate nearest-neighbor (ANN) search is a technique to speed up dense vector retrieval by filtering to documents containing similar vectors prior to performing expensive similarity calculations between the query and each document's vectors.
- Dense vector search can be heavily optimized for search speed, memory usage, and recall of the best results by combining techniques like ANN search, quantization, Matryoshka Representation Learning (MRL) embeddings, and over-requesting and reranking of results.
- Bi-encoders generate separate embeddings for queries and documents and support high-volume matching and ranking, whereas cross-encoders require much more computation at query time and are thus best used to rerank a smaller number of top results from a bi-encoder or lexical search.

Question answering
with a fine-tuned large
language model

This chapter covers

- Building a question-answering application using an LLM
- Curating a question-answering dataset for training
- Fine-tuning a Transformer-based LLM
- Integrating a deep-learning-based NLP pipeline to extract and rank answers from search results

We covered the basics of semantic search using Transformers in chapter 13, so we're now ready to attempt one of the hardest problems in search: question answering.

Question answering is the process of returning an answer for a searcher's query, rather than just a list of search results. There are two types of question-answering approaches: extractive and abstractive. *Extractive question answering* is the process of finding exact answers to questions from your documents. It returns snippets of your documents containing the likely answer to the user's question so they don't need to sift through search results. In contrast, *abstractive question answering* is the process of generating responses to a user's question either as a summary of multiple documents or directly from an LLM with no source documents. In this chapter, we'll focus primarily on extractive question answering, saving abstractive question answering for chapter 15.

By solving the question-answering problem, you will accomplish three things:

- You'll better understand the Transformer tooling and ecosystem that you started learning about in chapter 13.
- You'll learn how to fine-tune a large language model to a specific task.
- You'll merge your search engine with advanced natural language techniques.

In this chapter, we'll show you how to provide direct answers to questions and produce a working question-answering application. The query types we'll address are single clause *who, what, when, where, why*, and *how* questions. We'll also continue using the Stack Exchange outdoors dataset from the last chapter. Our goal is to enable users to ask a *previously unseen question* and get a short answer in response, eliminating the need for users to read through multiple search results to find the answer themselves.

14.1 Question-answering overview

Traditional search returns lists of documents or pages in response to a query, but people may often be looking for a quick answer to their question. In this case, we want to save people from having to dig for an answer in blocks of text when a straightforward one exists in our content.

In this section, we'll introduce the question-answering task and then define the retriever-reader pattern for implementing question-answering.

14.1.1 How a question-answering model works

Let's look at how a question-answering model works in practice. Specifically, we're implementing *extractive question answering*, which finds the best answer to a question in a given text. For example, take the following question:

Q: What are minimalist shoes?

Extractive question answering works by looking through a large document that probably contains the answer, and it identifies the answer for you.

Let's look at a document that might contain the answer to our question. We provide the question What are minimalist shoes? and the following document text (the context) to a model:

```
There was actually a project done on the definition of what a minimalist shoe
is and the result was "Footwear providing minimal interference with the
natural movement of the foot due to its high flexibility, low heel to toe
drop, weight and stack height, and the absence of motion control and stability
devices". If you are looking for a simpler definition, this is what Wikipedia
says, Minimalist shoes are shoes intended to closely approximate barefoot
running conditions. 1 They have reduced cushioning, thin soles, and are of
```

```
lighter weight than other running shoes, allowing for more sensory contact
for the foot on the ground while simultaneously providing the feet with some
protection from ground hazards and conditions (such as pebbles and dirt). One
example of minimalistic shoes would be the Vibram FiveFingers shoes which
look like this.
```

The document can be broken into many small parts, known as *spans*, and the model extracts the best span as the answer. A working question-answering model will evaluate the question and context and may produce this span as the answer:

A: `shoes intended to closely approximate barefoot running conditions`

But how does the model know the probability of whether any given span is the answer? We could try to look at different spans and see if they all somehow represent the answer, but that would be very complicated. Instead, the problem can be simplified by first learning the probability of whether each token in the context is the start of the answer and also the probability of whether each token in the context is the end of the answer. Since we are only looking at the probability for one token to represent the start, and another the end, the problem is easier to understand and solve. Our tokens are treated as discrete values, and the extractive question-answering model is trained to learn a *probability mass function* (PMF), which is a function that gives the probability that a discrete random variable is exactly equal to some value. This is different than measuring values that are continuous and are used in probability distributions, as we discussed with the continuous beta distribution in chapter 11. The main difference between the two is that our tokens are discrete values.

Using this strategy, we can train one model that will learn two probability mass functions—one for the starting token of the answer span, and one for the ending token of the answer span. You may have caught before that we said the model "*may produce*" the previous answer. Since models trained with different data and hyperparameters will give different results, the specific answer provided for a question can vary based on the model's training parameters.

To illustrate how this works, we'll start with a model that someone has already trained for the extractive question-answering task. The model will output the likelihood of whether the token is the start or the end of an answer span. When we identify the most likely start and end of the answer, that's our answer span. The pretrained model we'll use is `deepset/roberta-base-squad2`, available from the Hugging Face organization and trained by the Deepset team. We will pass the question and context through this model and pipeline in listings 14.1 through 14.3 to determine the answer span start and end probabilities, as well as the final answer. Figure 14.1 demonstrates how this process works by *tokenizing* the question and context input, *encoding* that input, and *predicting* the most appropriate answer span.

In the figure, you can see that the question and context are first combined into a pair for tokenization. Tokenization is then performed on the pair, obtaining token inputs for the model. The model accepts those inputs and then outputs two sequences: the first sequence is the probabilities for whether each token in the

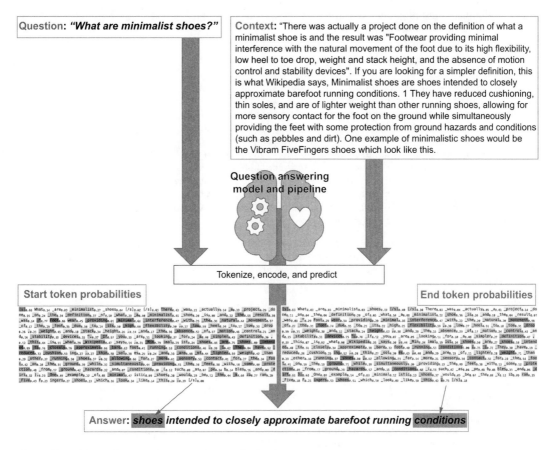

Figure 14.1 Extractive question-answering prediction process

context is the start of an answer, and the second sequence is the probabilities for whether each token in the context is the end of an answer. The start and end probability sequences are then combined to get the most likely answer span.

The following listing walks through the first step of this process: tokenization.

Listing 14.1 Loading the tokenizer and model

```
from transformers import AutoTokenizer, AutoModelForQuestionAnswering
model_name = "deepset/roberta-base-squad2"
tokenizer = AutoTokenizer.from_pretrained(model_name)
model = AutoModelForQuestionAnswering.from_pretrained(model_name)
```

The model name in listing 14.1 is a public model specifically pretrained for extractive question answering. With the model and tokenizer ready, we can now pass in a question and answer pair, shown in the following listing. The response will show that the number of tokens is equal to the number of start and end probabilities.

Listing 14.2   Tokenizing a question and context

```
question = "What are minimalist shoes"
context = """There was actually a project done on the definition of what a
minimalist shoe is and the result was "Footwear providing minimal
interference with the natural movement of the foot due to its high
flexibility, low heel to toe drop, weight and stack height, and the absence
of motion control and stability devices". If you are looking for a simpler
definition, this is what Wikipedia says, Minimalist shoes are shoes intended
to closely approximate barefoot running conditions. 1 They have reduced
cushioning, thin soles, and are of lighter weight than other running shoes,
allowing for more sensory contact for the foot on the ground while
simultaneously providing the feet with some protection from ground
hazards and conditions (such as pebbles and dirt).
One example of minimalistic shoes would be the Vibram FiveFingers
shoes which look like this."""

inputs = tokenizer(question, context, add_special_tokens=True,
                   return_tensors="pt")
input_ids = inputs["input_ids"].tolist()[0]

outputs = model(**inputs)
start_logits_norm = normalize(outputs[0].detach().numpy())
end_logits_norm = normalize(outputs[1].detach().numpy())

print(f"Total number of tokens: {len(input_ids)}")
print(f"Total number of start probabilities: {start_logits_norm.shape[1]}")
print(f"Total number of end probabilities: {end_logits_norm.shape[1]}")
```

Response:

```
Total number of tokens: 172
Total number of start probabilities: 172
Total number of end probabilities: 172
```

The inputs are obtained by tokenizing the question and context together. The outputs are obtained by making a forward pass with the inputs through the model. The `outputs` variable is a two-item list. The first item contains the start probabilities, and the second item contains the end probabilities.

Figure 14.2 visually demonstrates the probabilities for whether each token in the context is likely the start of an answer span, and figure 14.3 likewise demonstrates

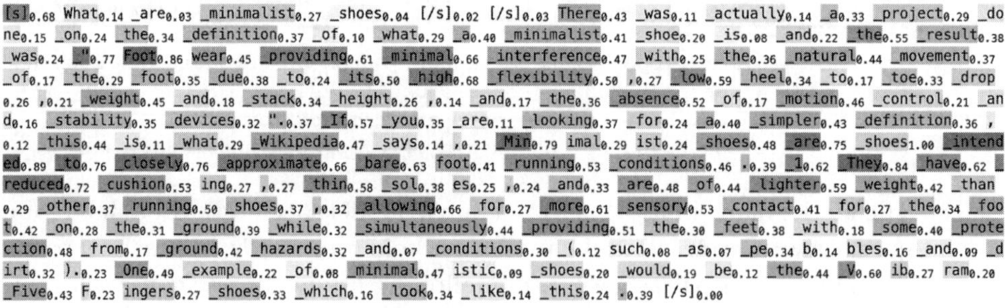

Figure 14.2   Probabilities for whether the token is the start of an answer span

whether each token is likely the end of an answer span (darker highlighting indicates a higher probability).

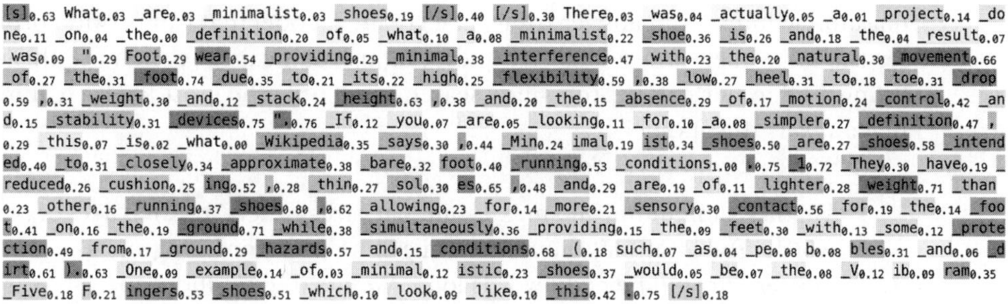

[s]$_{0.63}$ What$_{0.03}$ _are$_{0.03}$ _minimalist$_{0.03}$ _shoes$_{0.19}$ [/s]$_{0.40}$ [/s]$_{0.30}$ There$_{0.03}$ _was$_{0.04}$ _actually$_{0.05}$ _a$_{0.01}$ _project$_{0.14}$ _do ne$_{0.11}$ _on$_{0.04}$ _the$_{0.00}$ _definition$_{0.20}$ _of$_{0.05}$ _what$_{0.10}$ _a$_{0.08}$ _minimalist$_{0.22}$ _shoe$_{0.36}$ _is$_{0.26}$ _and$_{0.18}$ _the$_{0.04}$ _result$_{0.07}$ _was$_{0.09}$ _"$_{0.29}$ Foot$_{0.29}$ wear$_{0.54}$ _providing$_{0.29}$ _minimal$_{0.38}$ _interference$_{0.47}$ _with$_{0.23}$ _the$_{0.20}$ _natural$_{0.30}$ _movement$_{0.66}$ _of$_{0.27}$ _the$_{0.31}$ _foot$_{0.74}$ _due$_{0.35}$ _to$_{0.21}$ _its$_{0.22}$ _high$_{0.25}$ _flexibility$_{0.59}$,$_{0.38}$ _low$_{0.27}$ _heel$_{0.31}$ _to$_{0.18}$ _toe$_{0.31}$ _drop $_{0.59}$,$_{0.31}$ _weight$_{0.30}$ _and$_{0.12}$ _stack$_{0.24}$ _height$_{0.63}$,$_{0.38}$ _and$_{0.20}$ _the$_{0.15}$ _absence$_{0.29}$ _of$_{0.17}$ _motion$_{0.24}$ _control$_{0.42}$ _an d$_{0.15}$ _stability$_{0.31}$ _devices$_{0.75}$ "$_{0.76}$ _If$_{0.12}$ _you$_{0.07}$ _are$_{0.05}$ _looking$_{0.11}$ _for$_{0.10}$ _a$_{0.08}$ _simpler$_{0.27}$ _definition$_{0.47}$, $_{0.29}$ _this$_{0.07}$ _is$_{0.02}$ _what$_{0.00}$ _Wikipedia$_{0.35}$ _says$_{0.30}$,$_{0.44}$ _Min$_{0.24}$ imal$_{0.19}$ ist$_{0.34}$ _shoes$_{0.75}$ _are$_{0.27}$ _shoes$_{0.58}$ _intend ed$_{0.40}$ _to$_{0.31}$ _closely$_{0.34}$ _approximate$_{0.38}$ _bare$_{0.32}$ foot$_{0.40}$ _running$_{0.53}$ _conditions$_{1.00}$.$_{0.49}$]$_{0.72}$ _They$_{0.30}$ _have$_{0.19}$ _ reduced$_{0.26}$ _cushion$_{0.25}$ ing$_{0.52}$,$_{0.28}$ _thin$_{0.27}$ _sol$_{0.30}$ es$_{0.65}$,$_{0.48}$ _and$_{0.29}$ _are$_{0.19}$ _of$_{0.11}$ _lighter$_{0.28}$ _weight$_{0.71}$ _than $_{0.23}$ _other$_{0.16}$ _running$_{0.37}$ _shoes$_{0.80}$,$_{0.62}$ _allowing$_{0.23}$ _for$_{0.14}$ _more$_{0.21}$ _sensory$_{0.30}$ _contact$_{0.56}$ _for$_{0.19}$ _the$_{0.14}$ _foo t$_{0.41}$ _on$_{0.16}$ _the$_{0.19}$ _ground$_{0.71}$ _while$_{0.38}$ _simultaneously$_{0.36}$ _providing$_{0.15}$ _the$_{0.09}$ _feet$_{0.30}$ _with$_{0.13}$ _some$_{0.12}$ _prote ction$_{0.49}$ _from$_{0.17}$ _ground$_{0.29}$ _hazards$_{0.57}$ _and$_{0.15}$ _conditions$_{0.68}$ _($_{0.18}$ such$_{0.07}$ _as$_{0.04}$ _pe$_{0.08}$ b$_{0.08}$ bles$_{0.31}$ _and$_{0.06}$ _d irt$_{0.61}$)$_{0.63}$ _One$_{0.09}$ _example$_{0.14}$ _of$_{0.03}$ _minimal$_{0.12}$ istic$_{0.23}$ _shoes$_{0.37}$ _would$_{0.05}$ _be$_{0.07}$ _the$_{0.08}$ _V$_{0.12}$ ib$_{0.09}$ ram$_{0.35}$ _Five$_{0.18}$ F$_{0.21}$ ingers$_{0.53}$ _shoes$_{0.51}$ _which$_{0.10}$ _look$_{0.09}$ _like$_{0.10}$ _this$_{0.42}$.$_{0.75}$ [/s]$_{0.18}$

Figure 14.3 Probabilities for whether the token is the end of an answer span

Note that each token has a start probability (in figure 14.2) and an end probability (in figure 14.3) at its respective index. We also normalized the start and end probabilities at each index to be between `0.0` and `1.0`, which makes them easier to think about and calculate. We call these start and end probability lists *logits*, since they are lists of statistical probabilities.

For example, for the 17th token (`_definition`), the probability of this token being the start of the answer is ~`0.37`, and the probability of it being the end of the answer is ~`0.20`. Since we've normalized both lists, the start of our answer span is the token where `start_logits_norm == 1.0`, and the end of the answer span is where `end_logits_norm == 1.0`.

The following listing demonstrates both how to generate the token lists in figures 14.2 and 14.3, as well as how to extract the final answer span.

Listing 14.3 Identifying an answer span from a tokenized context

```
start_tokens = []
end_tokens = []
terms = tokenizer.convert_ids_to_tokens(input_ids)
start_token_id = 0
end_token_id = len(terms)
for i, term in enumerate(terms):
  start_tokens.append(stylize(term, [0, 127, 255], start_logits_norm[0][i]))
  end_tokens.append(stylize(term, [255, 0, 255], end_logits_norm[0][i]))
  if start_logits_norm[0][i] == 1.0:
    start_token_id = i
  if end_logits_norm[0][i] == 1.0:
    end_token_id = i + 1
answer = terms[start_token_id:end_token_id]
display(HTML(f'<h3>{clean_token(" ".join(answer))}</h3>'))
display(HTML(f'<pre>{" ".join(start_tokens)}</pre>'))
display(HTML(f'<pre>{" ".join(end_tokens)}</pre>'))
```

The end probabilities, shown in figure 14.3 → (points to last display line)

Extracting the answer span, shown in the following output → (points to answer line)

The start probabilities, shown in figure 14.2 → (points to start_tokens display line)

Output:

```
_shoes _intended _to _closely _approximate _bare foot _running _conditions
```

By fitting the start and end probability mass functions during training to a dataset of question, context, and answer triples, we create a model that can provide probabilities for the most likely answers to new questions and contexts. We then use this model in listing 14.3 to perform a probability search to identify the most likely span in the text that answers the question.

In practice, it works as follows:

1 We pick a minimum and maximum span size—where a span is a set of continuous words. For example, the answer might be one word long or, like the previous answer, it could be eight words long. We need to set those span sizes up front.
2 For each span, we check the probability of whether or not the span is the correct answer. The answer is the span with the highest probability.
3 When we're done checking all the spans, we present the correct answer.

Building the model requires lots of question/context/answer triples and a way to provide these triples to the model so that calculations can be performed. Enter the Transformer encoder, which you should already be familiar with from chapter 13. We first encode lots of training data using an LLM that produces dense vectors. Then we train a neural network to learn the probability mass function of whether a given span's encoding answers the question using positive and negative training examples.

We'll see how to fine-tune a question-answering model later in the chapter, but first we need to address a very important detail: When someone asks a question, where do we get the context?

14.1.2 *The retriever-reader pattern*

In reading about how extractive question answering works, you may have thought "so, for every question query, I need to check the probabilities of every span in the entire corpus?" No! That would be extremely slow and unnecessary, since we already have a really fast and accurate way of getting relevant documents that probably contain the answer: search.

What we're really going to make is a very powerful text highlighter. Think of the entire question-answering system as an automatic reference librarian of sorts. It knows what document contains your answer, and then it reads that document's text so it can point the exact answer out to you.

This is known as the retriever-reader pattern. This pattern uses one component to retrieve and rank the candidate documents (running a query against the search engine) and another component to read the spans of the most relevant documents and extract the appropriate answer. This is very similar to how highlighting works in Lucene-based search engines like Solr, OpenSearch, or Elasticsearch: the unified highlighter will find the best passage(s) containing the analyzed query terms and use them as the context. It then identifies the exact location of the queried keywords in that context to show the end user the surrounding context.

We're going to build something similar to a highlighter, but instead of showing the context containing the user's queried keywords, our question-answering highlighter will answer questions like this:

```
Q: What are minimalist shoes?
A: shoes intended to closely approximate barefoot running conditions
```

Let's look at the full context. When we ask `What are minimalist shoes?` we first use the *retriever* to get the document that is the most likely to contain the answer. In this case, this document (abridged here, but shown in full in section 14.1.1) was returned:

```
There was actually a project done on the definition... this is what Wikipedia
says, Minimalist shoes are shoes intended to closely approximate barefoot
running conditions. 1 They have reduced cushioning, thin soles, ...
```

With the document in hand, the *reader* then scans it and finds the text that is most likely to answer the question.

Aside from using fancy Transformers to find the correct answer, we're taking a step beyond basic search in that we'll actually use question/answer reader confidence as a reranker. So if we're not sure which document is the most likely to contain the answer during the retriever step, we'll have the reader look through a bunch of documents and see which is the best answer from all of them. The "bunch of documents" will be our reranking window, which we can set to any size.

Keep in mind, though, that analyzing documents in real time is not efficient. We shouldn't ask the reader to look at 100 documents—that's going to take too long. We'll limit it to a much smaller number, like 3 or 5. Limiting the reader window forces us to make sure our search engine is very accurate. The results must be relevant, as a retriever that doesn't get relevant candidates in the top 5 window size won't give the reader anything useful to work with.

The retriever-reader has two separated concerns, so we can even replace our retriever with something else. We've shown how you can use a lexical search engine with out-of-the-box ranking (BM25, as covered in chapter 3), but you can also try it with a dense vector index of embeddings, as covered in chapter 13.

Before we can take live user questions, we'll also need to train a question-answering model to predict the best answer from a context. The full set of steps we'll walk through for building our question-answering application is as follows:

1 *Set up a retriever using our search engine*—We'll use a simple high-recall query for candidate answers for our example.
2 *Wrangle and label the data appropriately*—This includes getting the data into the correct format, and getting a first pass at our answers from the base pretrained model. Then we'll take that first pass and manually fix it and mark what examples to use for training and testing.
3 *Understand the nuances of the data structures*—We'll use an existing data structure that will represent our training and test data in the correct format for a fine-tuning task.

4 *Fine-tune the model*—Using the corrections we made in the previous step, we'll train a fine-tuned question-answering model for better accuracy than the baseline.

5 *Use the model as the reader at query time*—We'll put everything together that lets us request a query, get candidates from the search engine, read/rerank the answers from the model, and show them as a response.

Figure 14.4 shows the flow of the entire architecture for our retriever, reader, and reranker:

1 A question is asked by a user, and documents are queried in the retriever (search engine) using the question.

2 The search engine matches and ranks to get the top-*k* most relevant documents for the reader.

3 The original question is paired with each top-*k* retrieved context and sent into the QA pipeline.

4 The question/context pairs are tokenized and encoded into spans by the reader, which then predicts the top-*n* most likely answer spans, with their probabilities for likeliness as the score.

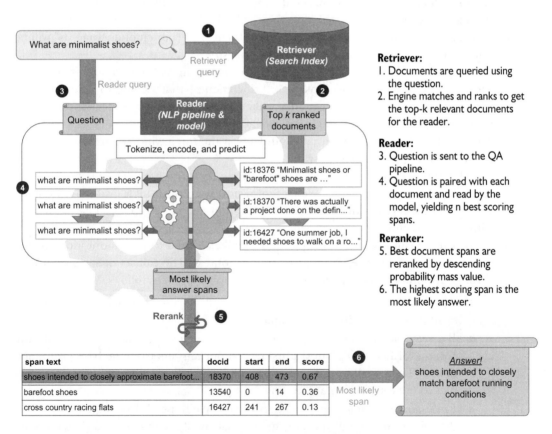

Figure 14.4 Retriever-reader pattern for extractive question answering

5 The reranker sorts the score for each top-*n* answer span in descending order.

6 The top ranked answer from the reranker is the accepted answer and is shown to the user.

To accomplish all of this, we need to tune the retriever, wrangle data to train the reader model, fine-tune the reader model using that data, and build a reranker. Strategies for tuning the retriever (the search engine) have already been covered thoroughly in this book, so for our next step, we'll wrangle the data.

14.2 Constructing a question-answering training dataset

In this section, we'll create a dataset we can use to train our question-answering model. This involves several steps:

- Gathering and cleaning a dataset to fit the question-answering problem space to our content
- Automatically creating a silver set (a semi-refined dataset that needs further labeling) from an existing model and corpus
- Manually correcting the silver set to produce the golden set (a trustworthy dataset we can use for training)
- Splitting the dataset for training, testing, and validation of a fine-tuned model

We'll start with our Stack Exchange outdoors dataset because its data is already well-suited to a question-and-answer application. We need question/answer pairs to use when fine-tuning a base model.

The outdoors dataset is already well-formatted and in bite-size question-and-answer chunks. With the power of Transformers, we can take off-the-shelf tools and models and construct the solution relatively quickly. This is far easier than trying to construct a question/answer dataset from something else, like the book *Great Expectations*. If you're working with long-form text, such as a book or lengthy documents, you'd need to first split the text into paragraphs and manually devise questions for the paragraphs.

> ### Golden sets and silver sets
>
> In machine learning, a *golden set* is an accurately labeled dataset that is used to train, test, and validate models. We treat golden sets as highly valuable assets, since gathering them often requires significant manual effort. The accuracy and usability of a trained model are limited by the accuracy and breadth of the golden set. Thus, the longer you spend growing and verifying your golden set, the better the model.
>
> To reduce some of the effort required in labeling data, we can save time by letting a machine try to generate a labeled dataset for us. This automatically generated set of labeled data is called a *silver set*, and it prevents us from having to start from scratch.
>
> A silver set is not as trustworthy as a golden set. Since we automatically obtain a silver set through machine-automated processes that aren't as accurate as humans, there will be mistakes. Thus, a silver set should ideally be improved with a manual

(continued)
audit and corrections to increase its accuracy. Using silver sets to bootstrap your training dataset can save a lot of time and mental effort in the long term, and it can help you scale your training data curation.

14.2.1 Gathering and cleaning a question-answering dataset

On to our first step: let's construct a dataset we can label and use to train a model. For this dataset, we need questions with associated contexts that contain their answers. Listing 14.4 shows how to get the questions and the contexts that contain answers in rows of a pandas dataframe. We need to construct two queries: one to get the community questions, and one to get the accepted community answers to those questions. We will only be using question/answer pairs that have an accepted answer. We will execute the two queries separately and join the two together.

The model that we are using refers to the content from which we pluck our answer as a context. Remember, we're not generating answers, we're just finding the most appropriate answer inside a body of text.

Listing 14.4 Pulling training questions from Solr

```
def get_questions():
    question_types = ["who", "what", "when",
                      "where", "why", "how"]        Narrows the scope of
    questions = []                                  question types that
    for type in question_types:                     we retrieve
        request = {"query": type,
                   "query_fields": ["title"],
                   "return_fields": ["id", "url", "owner_user_id",
                                     "title", "accepted_answer_id"],
                   "filters": [("accepted_answer_id", "*")],
                   "limit": 10000}
        docs = outdoors_collection.search(**request)["docs"]
        questions += [document for document in docs
                      if document["title"].lower().startswith(type)]
    return questions
```

Narrows the scope of question types that we retrieve

Only retrieves questions that have accepted answers

Only uses titles starting with a question type

With the list of questions from listing 14.4, we next need to get contexts associated with each question. Listing 14.5 returns a dataframe with the following columns: id, url, question, and context. We'll use the question and context to generate the training and evaluation data for our question-answering model in the coming sections.

Listing 14.5 Searching for accepted answer contexts

```
def get_answers_from_questions(questions, batch_size=500):
    answer_ids = list(set([str(q["accepted_answer_id"])
                           for q in questions]))
    batches = math.ceil(len(answer_ids) / batch_size)
    answers = {}
```

Gets a list of all distinct answer ids

Calculates the number of search requests that need to be made

```
for n in range(0, batches):                          ┌──  Aggregates
    ids = answer_ids[n * batch_size:(n + 1) * batch_size] │   all answers
    request = {"query": "(" + " ".join(ids) + ")",
               "query_fields": "id",
               "limit": batch_size,
               "filters": [("post_type", "answer")],
               "order_by": [("score", "desc")]}
    docs = outdoors_collection.search(**request)["docs"]
    answers |= {int(d["id"]): d["body"] for d in docs}
return answers

def get_context_dataframe(questions):                │  Retrieves all answer
    answers = get_answers_from_questions(questions)  ◄─┘  data for questions
    contexts = {"id": [], "question": [], "context": [], "url": []}
    for question in questions:
        contexts["id"].append(question["id"])
        contexts["url"].append(question["url"])
        contexts["question"].append(question["title"]),
        if question["accepted_answer_id"] in answers:
            context = answers[question["accepted_answer_id"]]
        else:
            context = "Not found"
        contexts["context"].append(context)
    return pandas.DataFrame(contexts)
                                    │  Load the questions
                                    │  from listing 14.4.
questions = get_questions()        ◄─┘
contexts = get_context_dataframe(questions)   ◄─┐  Load the contexts
display(contexts[0:5])                          │  for each question.
```

Output:

```
id     question                                context
4410   Who places the anchors that rock c...   There are two distinct styl...
5347   Who places the bolts on rock climb...   What you're talking about i...
20662  Who gets the bill if you activate ...   Almost always the victim ge...
11587  What sort of crane, and what sort ...   To answer the snake part of...
7623   What knot is this one? What are it...   Slip knot It's undoubtably ...
```

We encourage you to examine the full output for the question and context pairs to appreciate the variety of input and language used. We also included the original URL if you'd like to visit the Stack Exchange outdoors website and explore the source data yourself in the Jupyter notebook.

14.2.2 Creating the silver set: Automatically labeling data from a pretrained model

Now that we have our dataset, we have to label it. For the training to work, we need to tell the model what the correct answer is inside of the context (document), given the question. An LLM exists that already does a decent job at selecting answers: deepset/ roberta-base-squad2. This model was pretrained by the Deepset company using the SQuAD2 dataset and is freely available on their Hugging Face page (https:// huggingface.co/deepset). SQuAD is the *Stanford Question Answering Dataset,* which is a large public dataset made up of thousands of question and answer pairs. The Deepset team started with the RoBERTa architecture (covered in chapter 13) and fine-tuned a model based on this dataset for the task of question answering.

> **NOTE** It's a good idea to familiarize yourself with the Hugging Face website (https://huggingface.co). The Hugging Face community is very active and has provided thousands of free pretrained models, available for use by anyone.

Our strategy is to use the best pretrained model available to attempt to answer all the questions first. We'll call these answers "guesses" and the entire automatically labeled dataset the "silver set". Then we will go through the silver set guesses and correct them ourselves, to get a "golden set".

Listing 14.6 shows our question-answering function, which uses a Transformers pipeline type of `question-answering` and the `deepset/roberta-base-squad2` model. We use these to construct a pipeline with an appropriate tokenizer and target device (either CPU or GPU). This gives us everything we need to pass in raw data and obtain the silver set, as illustrated in figure 14.5.

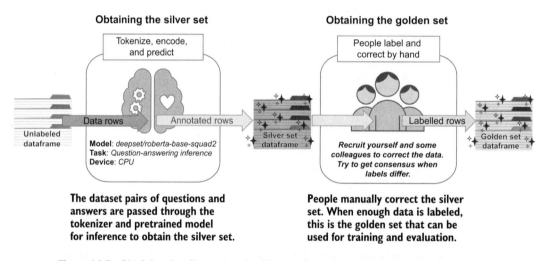

Figure 14.5   Obtaining the silver set and golden set from a prepared dataframe

In Python, we create a function called `answer_questions` that accepts the list of contexts that we extracted from our retriever. This function runs each question and context through the pipeline to generate the answer and appends it to the list. We won't presume that they're actually answers at this point, because many of them will be incorrect (as you'll see when you open the file). We will only count something as an *answer* when it's been vetted by a person. This is the nature of upgrading a silver set to a golden set.

The `device` (CPU or GPU) will be chosen automatically based on whether you have a GPU available to your Docker environment or not. Now is a good time to mention that if you're running or training these models on a CPU-only home computer or Docker configuration, you may be waiting a while for the inference of all the data to be complete. If you're not using a GPU, feel free to skip running listings 14.6–14.7, as we have already provided the output needed to run later listings in this notebook's dataset.

Listing 14.6 generates the silver set to extract out the most likely answers for our pairs of question and accepted answer contexts loaded previously in listing 14.5.

Listing 14.6   Generating answers given question/context pairs

```
from transformers import pipeline        ◁── This is the pipeline that we
import torch                                  illustrated in figure 14.1.
import tqdm                        ◁── tqdm prints the progress of the
                                       operation as a progress bar.
def get_processor_device():
  return 0 if torch.cuda.is_available() else -1      Process with GPU (CUDA) if
                                                     available; otherwise use the CPU.
def answer_questions(contexts, k=10):
  nlp = pipeline("question-answering", model=model_name,      This is the pipeline that we
                 tokenizer=model_name, device=device)         illustrated in figure 14.1.
  guesses = []
  for _, row in tqdm.tqdm(contexts[0:k].iterrows(), total=k):   ◁── tqdm prints the
    result = nlp({"question": row["question"],                      progress of the
                  "context": row["context"]})     Gets the answer        operation as a
    guesses.append(result)                         (and confidence      progress bar.
    return guesses                                 score) for every
                                                   question/context pair
model_name = "deepset/roberta-base-squad2"
device = get_processor_device()        ◁── Process with GPU (CUDA) if
                                           available; otherwise use the CPU.
guesses = answer_questions(contexts, k=len(contexts))
display_guesses(guesses)
```

Output:

```
score      start   end    answer
0.278927   474     516    a local enthusiast or group of enthusiasts
0.200848   81      117    the person who is creating the climb
0.018632   14      24     the victim
...
0.247008   227     265    the traditional longbow made from wood
0.480407   408     473    shoes intended to closely approximate barefoot run...
0.563754   192     232    a tube of lightweight, stretchy material
```

Congratulations, we have now obtained the silver set! In the next section, we'll improve it.

GPU recommended

Feel free to run these listings on your personal computer, but be warned—some of them take a while on a CPU. The total execution time for listing 14.6, for example, was reduced by about 20 times when running on a GPU versus a mid-market CPU during our tests.

Note that the fine-tuning examples later in the chapter will benefit significantly from having a GPU available. If you cannot access a GPU for those listings, that's okay—

(continued)

we've trained the model and already included it for you as part of the outdoors data-set. You can follow along in the listings to see how the model is trained, and if you don't have a GPU available, you can just skip running them. You can also use free services such as Google Colab or rent a server with a GPU from a cloud provider, which is typically a few US dollars per hour.

If you're interested in learning more about GPUs and why they are better suited to tasks such as training models, we recommend checking out *Parallel and High Performance Computing* by Robert Robey and Yuliana Zamora (Manning, 2021).

14.2.3   *Human-in-the-loop training: Manually correcting the silver set to produce a golden set*

The silver set CSV file (question-answering-squad2-guesses.csv) is used as a first pass at attempting to answer the questions. We'll use this with human-in-the-loop manual correction and labeling of the data to refine the silver set into the golden set.

> **NOTE** No Python code can generate a golden set for you. The data *must* be labeled by an intelligent person (or perhaps one day an AI model highly optimized for making relevance judgments) with an understanding of the domain. All further listings will use this golden set. We are giving you a break, though, since we already labeled the data for you. For reference, it took 4 to 6 hours to label about 200 guesses produced by the `deepset/roberta-base -squad2` model.

Labeling data yourself will give you a deeper appreciation for the difficulty of this NLP task. We *highly* encourage you to label even more documents and rerun the fine-tuning tasks coming up. Having an appreciation for the effort needed to obtain quality data, and the effect it has on the model accuracy, is a lesson you can only learn through experience.

Before diving in and just labeling data, however, we need to have a plan for how and what to label. For each row, we need to classify it and, if necessary, write the correct answer ourselves into another column.

Here is the key, as shown in figure 14.6, which we used for all the labeled rows in the `class` field:

- `-2` = This is a negative example (an example where we know the guess is wrong!).
- `-1` = Ignore this question, as it is too vague or we are missing some information. For example, `What is this bird?` We can't answer without a picture of the bird, so we don't even try.
- `0` = This is an example that has been corrected by a person to highlight a better answer span in the same context. The guess given by `deepset/roberta-base -squad2` was incorrect or incomplete, so we changed it.

- `1` = This is an example that was given a correct answer by `deepset/roberta-base-squad2`, so we did not change the answer.
- (blank) = We didn't check this row, so we'll ignore it.

Figure 14.6
Legend of label classes

You should open the outdoors_golden_answers.csv file and look through the rows yourself. Understand the ratio of questions that we labeled as `0` and `1`. You can even try opening the file in pandas and doing a little bit of analysis to familiarize yourself with the golden set.

14.2.4   Formatting the golden set for training, testing, and validation

Now that we have labeled data, we're almost ready to train our model, but first we need to get the data into the right format for the training and evaluation pipeline. Once our data is in the right format, we'll also need to split it into training, testing, and validation sets for use when training the model to ensure it does not overfit our data.

CONVERTING THE LABELED DATA INTO A STANDARDIZED DATA FORMAT

Hugging Face provides a library called `datasets`, which we'll use to prepare our data. The `datasets` library can accept the names of many publicly available datasets and provide a standard interface for working with them. The SQuAD2 dataset is one of the available datasets, but since our golden set is in a custom format, we first need to convert it to the standardized `datasets` configuration format shown in the following listing.

Listing 14.7   Transforming a golden dataset into SQuAD formatting

```
from datasets import Dataset, DatasetDict

def get_training_data(filename):
  golden_answers = pandas.read_csv(filename)
  golden_answers = golden_answers[golden_answers["class"] != None]
  qa_data = []
  for _, row in golden_answers.iterrows():
    answers = row["gold"].split("|")
    starts = [row["context"].find(a) for a in answers]
    missing = -1 in starts
    if not missing:
```

```
      row["title"] = row["question"]
      row["answers"] = {"text": answers, "answer_start": starts}
      qa_data.append(row)
  columns = ["id", "url", "title", "question", "context", "answers"]
  df = pandas.DataFrame(qa_data, columns=columns) \                      Randomly sorts
           .sample(frac=1, random_state=0)                              all the examples
  train_split = int(len(df) * 0.75)
  eval_split = (int((len(df) - train_split) / 1.25) +                   75% of the examples will be
                train_split - 1)                                        used for training. This will
  train_dataset = Dataset.from_pandas(df[:train_split])                 give us 125 training samples.
  test_dataset = Dataset.from_pandas(df[train_split:eval_split])
  validation_dataset = Dataset.from_pandas(df[eval_split:])
  return DatasetDict({"train": train_dataset,                           SQuAD requires three
                      "test": test_dataset,                             groups of data: train,
                      "validation": validation_dataset})                test, and validation

datadict = get_training_data("data/outdoors/outdoors_golden_answers.csv")
model_path = "data/question-answering/question-answering-training-set"
datadict.save_to_disk(model_path)
```

20% of the examples will be used for testing.
We subtract 1 from train_split to allow for
125/32/10 records on the three splits.

The remaining 5% of the examples
will be used for validation holdout.
This will be 10 samples.

The first part of the function in listing 14.7 loads the CSV into a pandas dataframe and does some preprocessing and formatting. Once formatted, the data is split up into three parts and converted.

The object returned and saved from listing 14.7 is a dataset dictionary (a `datadict`) that contains our three slices for training, testing, and validation. For our data table, with the split defined in `get_training_data`, we have 125 training examples, 32 testing examples, and 10 validation examples.

AVOIDING OVERFITTING WITH A TEST SET AND HOLDOUT VALIDATION SET

Overfitting a model means you trained it to only memorize the training examples provided. This means it won't generalize well enough to handle previously unseen data.

To prevent overfitting, we needed to split our dataset into separate training, testing, and validation slices, as we did in listing 14.7. The testing and the holdout validation sets are used to measure the success of the model after it is trained. After you've gone through the process from end to end, consider labeling some more data and doing different splits across the training, testing, and validation slices to see how the model performs.

We use a training/test split to give some data to the model training and some to test the outcome. We iteratively tune hyperparameters for the model training to achieve higher accuracy (measured using a loss function) when the model is applied to the test set.

The holdout validation set is the real-world proxy for unseen data, and it's not checked until the end. After training and testing are completed, you then validate the final model version by applying it against the holdout examples. If this score is much lower than the final test accuracy, you've overfit your model.

NOTE   The number of examples we're using is quite small (125 training examples, 32 testing examples, and 10 holdout validation examples) compared to what you'd use for fine-tuning data for a customer-facing system. As a general rule of thumb, aim for about 500 to 2,000 labeled examples. Sometimes you can get away with less, but typically the more you have the better. This will take considerable time investment, but it's well worth the effort.

14.3   Fine-tuning the question-answering model

We'll now walk through obtaining a better model by fine-tuning the existing `deepset/roberta-base-squad2` model with our golden set.

Unfortunately, this next notebook can be quite slow to run on a CPU. If you are going through the listings on a machine that is CUDA-capable and can configure your Docker environment to use the GPUs, then you should be all set! Otherwise, we recommend you use a service like Google Colab, which offers easy running of Jupyter notebooks on GPUs at no cost, or another cloud computing or hosting provider that has a CUDA device ready to go. You can load the notebook directly from Google Colab and run it without any other dependencies aside from our dataset. A link is provided above listing 14.8 in the associated notebook.

TIP   As we noted previously, if you don't want to go through the hassle of setting up a GPU-compatible environment, you can also follow along with listings 14.8–14.13 without running them, since we have already trained the model and included it for you to use. However, if you can, we do encourage you to go through the effort of getting GPU access and training the model yourself to see how the process works and to enable you to tinker with the hyperparameters. Figure 4.7 shows the kind of speedup that GPUs can provide for massively parallel computations like language model training.

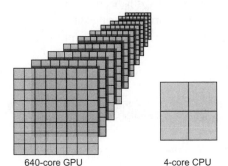

640-core GPU   4-core CPU

Figure 14.7   A V100 GPU (commonly available with cloud providers) has 640 tensor compute cores, compared to a 4-core x86-64 CPU. A Tesla T4 has 2,560 tensor compute cores. Individually, CPU cores are more powerful, but most GPUs have two to three orders of magnitude more cores than a CPU. This is important when doing massively parallel computations for millions of model parameters.

The first thing we need to do is require access to the GPU device. The code in the following listing will initialize and return the device ID of the available processor. If a GPU is configured and available, we should see that device's ID. If you are using Colab and having any problems with listing 14.8, you may need to change the runtime type to GPU in the settings.

Listing 14.8 Detecting and initializing a GPU device

```
def get_processor_type():
  gpu_device = torch.device("cuda:0")
  cpu_device = torch.device("cpu")
  return gpu_device or cpu_device

def get_processor_device():
  return 0 if torch.cuda.is_available() else -1

print("Processor: " + str(get_processor_type()))
print("Device id: " + str(get_processor_device()))
```

Output:

```
Processor: device(type='cuda', index=0)
Device id: 0
```

We have a GPU (in this listing output, at least). In the response, `device(type='cuda', index=0)` is what we were looking for. If a GPU isn't available when you run the listing, `device(type='cpu')` will be returned instead, indicating that the CPU will be used for processing. If you have more than one capable device available to the notebook, it will list each of them with an incrementing numerical id. You can access the device later in training by specifying an `id` (in our case, `0`).

With our device ready to go, we will next load and tokenize our previously labeled dataset from listing 14.7.

14.3.1 *Tokenizing and shaping our labeled data*

The model trainer doesn't recognize words; it recognizes tokens that exist in the RoBERTa vocabulary. We covered tokenization in chapter 13, where we used it as an initial step when encoding documents and queries into dense vectors for semantic search. Similarly, we need to tokenize our question-answering dataset before we can use it to train the model. The model accepts token values as the input parameters, just like any other Transformer model.

The following listing shows how we'll tokenize the data prior to model training.

Listing 14.9 Tokenizing our training set

```
# This function adapted from:
# https://github.com/huggingface/notebooks/blob/master/examples/
#question_answering.ipynb
# Copyright 2001, Hugging Face. Apache 2.0 Licensed.
from datasets import load_from_disk
from transformers import RobertaTokenizerFast

file = "data/question-answering/question-answering-training-set"
datadict = datasets.load_from_disk(file)
tokenizer = from_pretrained("roberta-base")
...
```

Loads the datadict we created in listing 14.7 from our golden set

Loads a pretrained tokenizer (roberta-base)

**This will be the number of tokens
in both the question and context.**

**Sometimes we need to split the context
into smaller chunks, so these chunks
will overlap by this many tokens.**

```
def tokenize_dataset(examples):
  maximum_tokens = 384
  document_overlap = 128
  pad_on_right = tokenizer.padding_side == "right"
  tokenized_examples = tokenizer(
    examples["question" if pad_on_right
                   else "context"],
    examples["context" if pad_on_right
                   else "question"],
    truncation="only_second" if pad_on_right
                   else "only_first",
    max_length=maximum_tokens,
    stride=document_overlap,
    return_overflowing_tokens=True,
    return_offsets_mapping=True,
    padding="max_length"
  )
  ...
  return tokenized_examples
tokenized_datasets = datadict.map(
  tokenize_dataset,
  batched=True,
  remove_columns=datadict["train"].column_names)
```

**Add padding tokens to the
end for question/context
pairs that are shorter than
the model input size.**

**Performs the
tokenization for
each of the
examples**

**Additional processing to identify start and
end positions for questions and contexts.
See the notebook for the full algorithm.**

**Invokes the tokenizer on each
example in our golden dataset**

We load a tokenizer (trained on the `roberta-base` model), load our `question -answering-training-set` golden set from disk (data/question-answering/question -answering-training-set/), and then run the examples from the golden set through the tokenizer to generate a `tokenized_datasets` object with the training and test datasets we'll soon pass to the model trainer.

For each context, we generate a list of tensors with a specific number of embeddings per tensor and a specific number of floats per embedding. The shape of the tensors containing the tokens must be the same for all the examples we provide to the trainer and evaluator. We accomplish this with a window-sliding technique.

Window sliding is a technique that involves splitting a long list of tokens into many sublists of tokens, but where each sublist after the first shares an overlapping number of tokens with the previous sublist. In our case, `maximum_tokens` defines the size of each sublist, and `document_overlap` defines the overlap. This window-sliding process is demonstrated in figure 14.8.

Figure 14.8 demonstrates very small `maximum_tokens` (24) and `document_overlap` (8) numbers for illustration purposes, but the real tokenization process splits the contexts into tensors of 384 tokens with an overlap of 128.

The window-sliding technique also makes use of *padding* to ensure that each tensor is the same length. If the number of tokens in the last tensor of the context is less than the maximum (384), then the rest of the positions in the tensor are filled with an empty marker token so that the final tensor size is also 384.

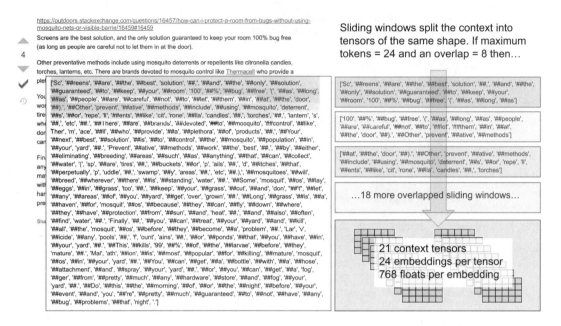

Figure 14.8   Visualizing the sliding window technique that splits one context into tensors of the same shape

Knowing how the contexts are processed is important, as it can affect both accuracy and processing time. If we're trying to identify answers in lengthy documents, the window-sliding process may reduce accuracy, particularly if the `maximum_tokens` and `document_overlap` are small and thus fragment the context too much. Long documents will also get sliced up into multiple tensors that collectively take longer to process. Most of the contexts in the outdoors dataset fit into the maximums we specified, but these trade-offs are important to consider in other datasets when choosing your `maximum_tokens` and `document_overlap` parameters.

14.3.2 Configuring the model trainer

We have one last step before we train our model: we need to specify *how* training and evaluation will happen.

When training our model, we need to specify the base model and training arguments (hyperparameters), as well as our training and testing datasets. You'll want to understand the following key concepts when configuring the hyperparameters for the model trainer:

- *Epochs*—The number of times the trainer will iterate over the dataset. More epochs help reinforce the context and reduce loss over time. Having too many epochs will likely overfit your model, though, and 3 epochs is a common choice when fine-tuning Transformers.
- *Batch sizes*—The number of examples that will be trained/evaluated at once. A higher batch size might produce a better model. This setting is constrained by

GPU core count and available memory, but common practice is to fit as much in a batch as possible to make the most of the available resources.

- *Warmups*—When training a model, it can be helpful to slowly tune the model initially, so that the early examples don't have an undue influence on the model's learned parameters. Warmup steps allow gradual improvements to the model (the *learning rate*), which helps prevent the trainer from overfitting on early examples.

- *Decay*—Weight decay is used to reduce overfitting by multiplying each weight by this constant value at each step. It is common to use 0.01 as the weight decay, but this can be changed to a higher value if the model is quickly overfitting or to a lower value if you don't see improvement fast enough.

Listing 4.10 demonstrates configuring the model trainer. The hyperparameters (`training_args`) we've specified in the listing are those used by SQuAD2 by default, but feel free to adjust any of them to see how it improves the quality of the question-answering model for your own questions.

When trying to choose the best settings, a common technique is to perform a grid search over these hyperparameters. A *grid search* is a process that automatically iterates over parameter values and tests how adjusting each of them in different combinations improves the quality of the trained models. We include a grid search example in the accompanying notebooks, should you wish to dive deeper into parameter tuning, but for now we'll proceed with the hyperparameters specified in listing 14.10.

Listing 14.10   Initializing the trainer and its hyperparameters

```
from transformers import RobertaForQuestionAnswering, TrainingArguments,
                         Trainer, default_data_collator

model = RobertaForQuestionAnswering.from_pretrained(
    "deepset/roberta-base-squad2")

training_args = TrainingArguments(
    evaluation_strategy="epoch",          ← Evaluates loss per epoch
    num_train_epochs=3,                   ← Total number of training epochs
    per_device_train_batch_size=16,       ← Batch size per device during training
    per_device_eval_batch_size=64,        ← Batch size for evaluation
    warmup_steps=500,                     ← Number of warmup steps for learning rate scheduler
    weight_decay=0.01,                    ← Strength of weight decay
    logging_dir="data/question-answering/logs",
    output_dir="data/question-answering/results")

trainer = Trainer(
    model=model,                          ← The instantiated Hugging Face Transformers model to be trained
    args=training_args,                   ← Training arguments
    data_collator=default_data_collator,
    tokenizer=tokenizer,
    train_dataset=tokenized_datasets["train"],   ← Specifies the training dataset
    eval_dataset=tokenized_datasets["test"])     ← Specifies the evaluation dataset
```

14.3.3   *Performing training and evaluating loss*

With our hyperparameters all set, it's now time to train the model. The following listing runs the previously configured trainer, returns the training output showing the model's performance, and saves the model.

Listing 14.11   Training and saving the model

```
trainer.train()
model_name = "data/question-answering/roberta-base-squad2-fine-tuned"
trainer.save_model(model_name)
```

Output:

```
[30/30 00:35, Epoch 3/3]
Epoch    Training Loss    Validation Loss    Runtime      Samples Per Second
1        No log           2.177553           1.008200     43.642000
2        No log           2.011696           1.027800     42.811000
3        No log           1.938573           1.047700     41.996000

TrainOutput(global_step=30, training_loss=2.531823984781901,
            metrics={'train_runtime': 37.1978,
                     'train_samples_per_second': 0.806,
                     'total_flos': 133766734473216, 'epoch': 3.0}))
```

A *loss function* is a decision function that uses the error to give a quantified estimate of how bad a model is. Lower loss means a higher-quality model. What we're looking for is a gradual reduction in loss with each epoch, which indicates that the model is continuing to get better with more training. We went from a validation loss of `2.178` to `2.012` to `1.939` on our testing set. The numbers are all getting smaller at a steady rate (no huge jumps), and that's a good sign.

The overall training loss for this freshly fine-tuned model is `2.532`, and the validation loss on our testing set is `1.939`. Given the constraints of our small fine-tuning dataset and hyperparameter configuration, a validation loss as small as `1.939` is quite good.

14.3.4   *Holdout validation and confirmation*

How do we know if our trained model can be used successfully for real-world question answering? Well, we need to test the model against our holdout validation dataset. Recall that the holdout validation set is the third dataset (with only 10 examples) in our `datadict` from listing 14.9.

Figure 14.9 underscores the purpose of the holdout validation set. We want the loss from the evaluation of our holdout set to be as good as our validation loss of `1.939` from listing 14.11. If our holdout loss turns out higher, that would be a red flag that we may have overfit! Let's see how our model performs in the following listing.

Figure 14.9 Holdout set: answering previously unseen questions with our trained mode

---

Listing 14.12 Evaluating the trained model on the holdout examples

```
evaluation = trainer.evaluate(eval_dataset=tokenized_datasets["validation"])
display(evaluation)
```

Output:

```
{"eval_loss": 1.7851890325546265,
 "eval_runtime": 2.9417,
 "eval_samples_per_second": 5.099,
 "eval_steps_per_second": 0.34,
 "epoch": 3.0}
```

The `eval_loss` of `1.785` from testing our holdout validation set looks great. It's even better than the training and testing loss. This means that our model is working well and is likely not overfitting the training or testing data.

Feel free to continue training and improving the model, but we'll continue with this as the fully trained model that we'll integrate into the reader for our question-answering system.

14.4 *Building the reader with the new fine-tuned model*

Now that our reader's model training is completed, we'll integrate it into a question-answering pipeline to produce our finalized reader that can extract answers from questions and contexts. The following listing demonstrates how we can load our model into a `question-answering` pipeline provided by the `transformers` library.

Listing 14.13 Loading the fine-tuned outdoors question-answering model

```
device = get_processor_device()
model_name = "data/question-answering/roberta-base-squad2-fine-tuned"
```

```
nlp2 = pipeline("question-answering", model=model_name,
                tokenizer=model_name, device=device)
```

With the question-answering pipeline loaded, we'll extract some answers from some question/context pairs. Let's use our 10-document holdout validation set used earlier in section 14.3.4. The holdout examples were not used to train or to test the model, so they should be a good litmus test for how well our model works in practice.

In the following listing, we test the accuracy of our question-answering model on the holdout validation set examples.

Listing 14.14   Evaluating the fine-tuned question-answering model

```
def answer_questions(examples):
  answers = []
  success = 0
  for example in examples:
    question = {"question": example["question"][0],
                "context": example["context"][0]}
    answer = nlp2(question)
    label = example["answers"][0]["text"][0]
    result = answer["answer"]
    print(question["question"])
    print("Label:", label)
    print("Result:", result)
    print("----------")
    success += 1 if label == result else 0
    answers.append(answer)
  print(f"{success}/{len(examples)} correct")

datadict["validation"].set_format(type="pandas", output_all_columns=True)
validation_examples = [example for example in datadict["validation"]]
answer_questions(validation_examples)
```

Output:

```
How to get pine sap off my teeth
Label: Take a small amount of margarine and rub on the sap
Result: Take a small amount of margarine and rub on the sap

Why are backpack waist straps so long?
Label: The most backpacks have only one size for everyone
Result: The most backpacks have only one size for everyone

...

How efficient is the Altai skis "the Hok"?
Label: you can easily glide in one direction (forward) and if you try to
       glide backwards, the fur will "bristle up"
Result: you can easily go uphill, without (much) affecting forward gliding pe
       rformance

7/10 Correct
```

Successfully extracting 7 out of 10 correct answers is an impressive result. Congratulations, you've now fine-tuned an LLM for a real-world use case! This completes the `reader` component of our architecture, but we still need to combine it with a `retriever` that finds the initial candidate contexts to pass to the `reader`. In the next section, we'll incorporate the retriever (our search engine) to finalize the end-to-end question-answering system.

14.5 Incorporating the retriever: Using the question-answering model with the search engine

Next, we'll implement a rerank operation using the reader confidence score to rank the top answers. Here's an outline of the steps we'll go through in this exercise:

1. Query the outdoors index from a search collection tuned for high recall.
2. Pair our question with the top-*K* document results and infer answers and scores with the question-answering NLP inference pipeline.
3. Rerank the answer predictions by descending score.
4. Return the correct answer and top results using the parts created in steps 1 through 3.

See figure 14.4 for a refresher on this application flow.

14.5.1 Step 1: Querying the retriever

Our goal in the first retrieval stage is recall. Specifically, what are all the possibly relevant documents that may contain our answer? We rely on the already-tuned search collection to give us that recall so that we can pass quality documents into our reranking stage.

The following listing implements our `retriever` function, which can accept a question and return an initial list of relevant documents to consider as potential contexts for the answer.

> **Listing 14.15   Retriever function that searches for relevant answers**

```
nlp = spacy.load("en_core_web_sm")          ◁──┐ Uses the English
nlp.remove_pipe("ner")                            spaCy NLP model

def get_query_from_question(question):
  words = [token.text for token in nlp(question)
           if not (token.lex.is_stop or token.lex.is_punct)]
  return " ".join(words)

def retriever(question):
  contexts = {"id": [], "question": [], "context": [], "url": []}
  query = get_query_from_question(question)
  request = {"query": query,
             "query_fields": ["body"],
             "return_fields": ["id", "url", "body"],
             "filters": [("post_type", "answer")],       ◁──┘
```

Uses the English spaCy NLP model

Converts the question to a query by removing stop words and focusing on important parts of speech (see the notebook for the implementation)

Only gets answer documents (not questions)

```
                  "limit": 5}
  docs = outdoors_collection.search(**request)["docs"]
  for doc in docs:
    contexts["id"].append(doc["id"])
    contexts["url"].append(doc["url"])
    contexts["question"].append(question)
    contexts["context"].append(doc["body"])
  return pandas.DataFrame(contexts)

example_contexts = retriever('What are minimalist shoes?')
display_contexts(example_contexts)
```

Response:

```
id     question                      context
18376  What are minimalist shoes?   Minimalist shoes or "barefoot" shoes are shoes...
18370  What are minimalist shoes?   There was actually a project done on the defin...
16427  What are minimalist shoes?   One summer job, I needed shoes to walk on a ro...
18375  What are minimalist shoes?   The answer to this question will vary on your...
13540  What are minimalist shoes?   Barefoot Shoes Also known as minimalist shoes,...
```

One problem we face when using the question as the query is noise. There are lots of documents that have the terms "who", "what", "when", "where", "why", and "how", as well as other stop words and less important parts of speech. Although BM25 may do a good job of deprioritizing these terms in a ranking function, we know those are not the key terms a user is searching for, so we remove them in the `get_query_from_question` function to reduce noise. We covered part of speech tagging with spaCy previously in chapters 5 and 13, so we won't repeat the implementation here (you can find it in the notebook).

With a good set of documents returned from the search engine that may contain the answers to the user's question, we can now pass those documents as contexts to the `reader` model.

14.5.2 Step 2: Inferring answers from the reader model

We now can use the `reader` model to infer answers to the question from each of the top *N* contexts. Listing 14.16 implements our generic `reader` interface, which accepts the output from the `retriever` from step 1. The model and pipeline loading for the retriever follow the same process as in listing 14.13, while the rest of the `reader` implementation specifically handles generating candidate answers (along with scores for each answer) from the passed-in contexts.

Listing 14.16   Reader function that incorporates our fine-tuned model

```
from transformers import pipeline
                                                    Creates a spaCy pipeline
                                                   using our fine-tuned model
device = get_processor_device()
model_name = "data/question-answering/roberta-base-squad2-fine-tuned"
qa_nlp = pipeline("question-answering", model=model_name,
              tokenizer=model_name, device=device)
```

```
def reader(contexts):
  answers = []
  for _, row in contexts.iterrows():
    answer = qa_nlp({"question": row["question"],
                     "context": row["context"]})
    answer["id"] = row["id"]
    answer["url"] = row["url"]
    answers.append(answer)
  return answers
```

Returns additional metadata about where each answer was found

Invokes the reader pipeline to extract a candidate answer from each context

The `reader` returns an answer from each context based upon our fine-tuned model, along with the `id`, `url`, and `score` for the answer.

14.5.3   *Step 3: Reranking the answers*

Listing 14.17 shows a straightforward function that reranks the answers by simply sorting them by the score (the probability mass function outputs) from the `reader` model. The top answer is the most likely and is therefore shown first. You can show one answer, or you can show all that are returned by the reader. Indeed, sometimes it might be useful to give the question-asker multiple options and let them decide. This increases the odds of showing a correct answer, but it also takes up more space in the browser or application presenting the answers, so it may require a user experience trade-off.

Listing 14.17   The reranker sorts on scores from the reader

```
def reranker(answers):
  return sorted(answers, key=lambda k: k["score"], reverse=True)
```

We should note that your reranker could be more sophisticated, potentially incorporating multiple conditional models or even attempting to combine multiple answers together (such as overlapping answers from multiple contexts). For our purposes, we'll just rely on the top score.

14.5.4   *Step 4: Returning results by combining the retriever, reader, and reranker*

We're now ready to assemble all the components of our question-answering (QA) system. The hard part is done, so we can put them in one function, aptly named `ask`, which will accept a query and print out the answer.

Listing 14.18   QA function combining retriever, reader, and reranker

```
def ask(question):
  documents = retriever(question)
  answers = reader(documents)
  reranked = reranker(answers)
  print_answer(question, reranked)
```

```
ask('What is the best mosquito repellent?')
ask('How many miles can a person hike day?')
ask('How much water does a person need per day?')
```

Response:

```
What is the best mosquito repellent?
1116    DEET (0.606)
1056    thiamine (0.362)
569     Free-standing bug nets (0.158)
1076    Insect repellent is not 100% effective (0.057)
829     bear-spray (0.05)

How many miles can a person hike day?
17651 20-25 (0.324)
19609 12 miles (0.164)
19558 13 (0.073)
13030 25-35 (0.065)
4536 13 miles (0.022)

How much water does a person need per day?
1629 3 liters (0.46)
193 MINIMUM a gallon (0.235)
20634 0.4 to 0.6 L/day (0.207)
11679 4 litres (0.084)
11687 carry water (0.037)
```

These results look pretty good. Note that in some cases multiple contexts could return the same answer. Generally, this would be a strong signal of a correct answer, so it may be a signal to consider integrating into your reranking.

It's amazing to see the quality of results possible using these out-of-the-box models with minimal retraining. Kudos to the NLP community for making these open source tools, techniques, models, and datasets freely available and straightforward to use!

Congratulations, you've successfully implemented an end-to-end question-answering system that extracts answers from search results. You generated a silver set of answers, saw how to improve them into a golden set, loaded and fine-tuned a question-answering reader model, and implemented the retriever-reader pattern, using your trained model and the search engine.

With LLMs, we can do much more than just extract answers from search results, however. LLM's can be fine-tuned to perform abstractive question answering to generate answers not seen in search results but synthesized from multiple sources. They can also be trained to summarize search results for users or even synthesize brand-new content (text, images, etc.) in response to user input. Many LLMs are trained on so much data across such a widespread amount of human knowledge (such as the majority of the known internet), that they can often perform a wide variety of tasks like this well out of the box. These foundation models, which we'll cover in the next chapter, are paving the way for the next evolution of both AI and AI-powered search.

Summary

- An extractive question-answering system generally follows the retriever-reader pattern, where possible contexts (documents) are found by the retriever and are then analyzed using the reader model to extract the most likely answer.

- A search engine serves as a great retriever, since it is specifically designed to take a query and return ranked documents that are likely to serve as relevant context for the query.

- A reader model analyzes spans of text to predict the most likely beginning and ending of the answer within each context, scoring all options to extract the most likely answer.

- Curating a training dataset is time-intensive, but you can generate a silver set of training data automatically using a pretrained model. You can then tweak the answers in the silver set to save significant effort compared to creating the entire golden training dataset manually.

- You can fine-tune a pretrained model to your specific dataset using a training, testing, and holdout validation dataset and optimizing for a loss minimization function.

15
Foundation models and emerging search paradigms

This chapter covers

- Retrieval augmented generation (RAG)
- Generative search for results summarization and abstractive question answering
- Integrating foundation models, prompt optimization, and evaluating model quality
- Generating synthetic data for model training
- Implementing multimodal and hybrid search
- The future of AI-powered search

Large language models (LLMs), like the ones we've tested and fine-tuned in the last two chapters, have been front and center in the advances in AI-powered search in recent years. You've already seen some of the key ways search quality can be enhanced by these models, from improving query interpretation and document understanding by mapping content into embeddings for dense vector search, to helping extract answers to questions from within documents.

But what additional advanced approaches are emerging on the horizon? In this chapter, we'll cover some of the more recent advances at the intersection of search and AI. We'll cover how foundation models are being used to extend new capabilities to AI-powered search, like results summarization, abstractive question answering, multimodal search across media types, and even conversational interfaces for search and information retrieval. We'll cover the basics of emerging search paradigms like generative search, retrieval augmented generation (RAG), and new classes of foundation models that are reinventing some of the ways we'll soon approach the frontier of AI-powered search.

15.1 Understanding foundation models

A *foundation model* is a model that is pretrained on a large amount of broad data and is designed to be generally effective at a wide variety of tasks. LLMs are a subset of foundation models that are trained on a very large amount of text. Foundation models can also be trained on images, audio, or other sources, or even on multimodal data incorporating many different input types. Figure 15.1 demonstrates common categories of foundation models.

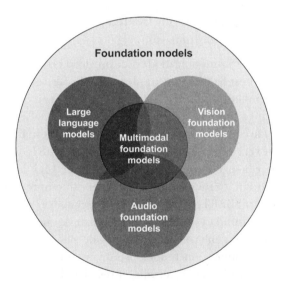

Figure 15.1 Foundation model types. LLMs are one of several types of foundation models.

Vision foundation models can be used to map images into embeddings (like how we mapped text to embeddings in chapter 13), which can then be searched to enable image-to-image search.

A multimodal foundation model can be built using both text and images (or other data types), and it can then enable cross-modal search for images based on text queries, or on text based on uploaded images as the query. We'll implement this kind of multimodal text and image search in section 15.3.2. Generative multimodal models, like Stable Diffusion (a text-to-image model), can also be used to generate brand-new images based only on text prompts. Multimodal foundation models that can learn from both images and text are also commonly referred to as *vision language models* (VLMs).

15.1.1 What qualifies as a foundation model?

Foundation models are typically trained on a wide variety of data covering many topics so that they are effective at generalized interpretation and prediction across domains. These models are called "foundation" models because they can serve as a base model (or foundation), which can then be more quickly fine-tuned on domain-specific or task-specific training sets to better tackle specific problems.

Foundation models typically meet the following criteria:

1   They are *large,* typically trained on massive amounts of data, often with billions or trillions of parameters.
2   They are *pretrained,* using significant compute capacity to arrive at model weights to be saved and deployed (or fine-tuned) later.
3   They are *generalizable* to many tasks, as opposed to limited to specific tasks.
4   They are *adaptable,* using prompts to pull in additional context from their trained model to adjust their predicted output. This makes the kinds of queries they can accept very flexible.
5   They are *self-supervised,* learning automatically from raw data how to relate and interpret the data and represent it for future use.

We have already worked with several foundation models in previous chapters, including BERT, which is one of the earliest foundation models, and RoBERTa, which we used in chapter 13 to generate embeddings and perform semantic search on those embeddings. Sentence Transformer models such as SBERT (Sentence-BERT) and SRoBERTa (Sentence-RoBERTa) are models that were fine-tuned from the BERT and RoBERTa foundation models to excel at the semantic textual similarity (STS) task. We also fine-tuned the `deepset/roberta-base-squad2` model in chapter 14; it is a model based upon the RoBERTa foundation model that has been fine-tuned for the question-answering task. Technically SBERT, SRoBERTa, and `deepset/roberta-base -squad2` are themselves fine-tuned foundation models, which can be further used as the foundation for more fine-tuning to generate additional models.

The dominant architecture for foundation models is currently the Transformer model, though recurrent neural networks (using architectures like MAMBA) can also be used, and additional architectures will inevitably evolve over time. Most Transformer-based models can be used to generate embedding vectors or predictive output.

The strength of the responses from foundation models reflects the quality of three processes: training, fine-tuning, and prompting.

15.1.2 Training vs. fine-tuning vs. prompting

Training (or *pretraining*) is the process whereby a massive amount of data (often a large portion of the internet) is used to learn model weights for billions or trillions of parameters in the foundation model's deep neural network. This process can sometimes be very expensive, take months, and cost millions of dollars due to the computing and energy requirements. This process manages to perform lossy compression of much of human knowledge into a neural network from which facts and relationships (words, linguistics, associations, etc.) can be decompressed back out later. Recall from section 13.3 that training a Transformer on text typically follows a self-supervised learning process that optimizes for predicting masked tokens in text sequences to measure overall comprehension of the text (the Cloze test described in section 13.3.1). This training can include any specific datasets that may be beneficial for the model's knowledge base, such as computer code or domain-specific content (financial documents, academic papers, foreign languages, multimodal content, etc.)

Fine-tuning is the process whereby the foundation model can be supplied with additional domain-specific data or instructions. For example, if you want the model to follow instructions or to act like a person or a chatbot, you can train the model with responses to input that reflect those behaviors. There are several approaches to fine-tuning, depending on the task or architecture and compute and budgetary requirements. Some types of fine-tuning will change all the weights of a model, which is helpful if the domain-tuning needs to be highly specific and the task of the original model is the same. More efficient or task-specific approaches may leave all the existing weights intact and add one or more additional layers to the neural network of the base foundation model. Fine-tuning enables these new sources to extend the capabilities of the original model to new data or patterns with a much smaller training process focused on specific data or goals.

Prompting is the process of supplying input to the trained language model to get an output. Prompting is the final "training" step for fine-tuning a model, but it occurs at inference time as opposed to training time. We can supply as much context in the prompt as the model allows, which means that the prompt can be manipulated to use this additional context to affect the output. For example, consider the output to the queries in listings 15.1 and 15.2 when they are sent to OpenAI's GPT-4 language model.

Listing 15.1   Query with no prompt engineering

```
Query: "What is a unicorn?"

Response:
A unicorn is a mythical creature that is typically depicted as a horse
with a single, spiraled horn projecting from its forehead. Unicorns have
been a part of human mythology and folklore for centuries and are often
associated with purity, grace, and magic. They are said to possess healing
powers and to be able to bring good luck to those who encounter them.
While unicorns are not real animals, they continue to be a popular symbol
in modern culture, appearing in literature, art, and popular media.
```

Listing 15.1 provides a good general description of a unicorn. Contrast this with listing 15.2, which uses prompt engineering to give the foundation model a "chatbot" persona named AIPS Chat and then tells the foundation model to respond as if it had a PhD in biology.

Listing 15.2   Query with additional context from prompt engineering

```
Query: "You are a chatbot named AIPS Chat.
        You have a Ph.D. in biology.
        What is a unicorn?"

Response:
Hello! I am a chatbot named AIPS Chat, and I have a Ph.D. in biology. While
unicorns have been depicted in various cultures throughout history, they
are not real animals that exist in the natural world.

From a biological perspective, a unicorn can be described as a mythical
creature resembling a horse with a single, spiraled horn on its forehead.
However, since unicorns are purely fictional, there is no actual
scientific data or research that can be conducted on them.

It is important to note that while many animals possess unique
characteristics, such as the horn of a rhinoceros or the tusk of a
narwhal, these features are not magical and do not provide any special
abilities or powers to the animal possessing them.

In conclusion, while unicorns are a fascinating aspect of human
folklore and mythology, they do not have a basis in reality within the
field of biology.
```

The query in listing 15.2, which includes the context of a chatbot having a PhD in biology, uses that additional context to inform its answer. If we had read/write access to the language model, we could fine-tune it with inputs and responses generated by a PhD in biology and by a chatbot. In the listing, we were able to accomplish a similar outcome simply by supplying the model with a prompt to pull in that context from its already-trained model. Fine-tuning will typically generate a better answer to such questions, but prompting is much more flexible, since you can supply any context at inference time, whereas fine-tuning would be more appropriate for general characteristics you want the model to learn and represent in all future interactions.

Providing additional context in the prompt can be key to getting the best output from a foundation model. Since generative foundation models sequentially predict the next token in a sequence, one token at a time, coercing the model to output more relevant context in the response can cause the model to generate more relevant output. A large pretrained model is capable of *few-shot learning* (being able to learn in context without further training by providing two or three examples with the prompt). In listing 15.2, for example, we saw that by adding the "biology" context to the prompt, the answer thereafter included phrases like "in the natural world", "From a biological perspective", "actual scientific data or research", and "within the field of biology".

The hardest and most expensive part of training is the initial generation of the foundation model. Once it's trained, the fine-tuning for specific tasks is relatively quick and inexpensive and can often be done with a reasonably small training set. If we compare training these models with human learning, a foundation model may be like a high school student who generally knows how to read and write and can answer basic questions about math, science, and world history. If we want the student to be able to generate and interpret financial statements (income statements, cash flow statements, and balance sheets), they are going to need to take an accounting course to learn those skills. After 18 or more years of training (life experience and school), however, the student can likely learn sufficient accounting within a few months to generate and interpret financial statements. Similarly, with foundation models, the initial training phase takes the longest and provides the base upon which further knowledge and skills can be much more quickly learned.

15.2 Generative search

Most of our journey into building AI-powered search has focused on finding the results, answers, or actions matching the user's intent. In chapter 14, we went so far as to extract specific answers to questions, using our retriever-reader pattern. But what if instead of returning real documents or extracted answers, our search engine could generate new content on the fly in response to queries?

Generative models are models that can generate new content based on incoming prompts. Their output can be text content, images generated from text input, audio emulating specific people or sounds, or videos combining both audio and video. Text can be generated to describe an image, or alternatively, an image, audio, or video can be generated to "describe" the text in a different modality.

We are entering a world where someone will be able to enter a search query, and the search engine could return entirely made-up content and images, generated on the fly, in response to the user's query or prompts. While this can be amazing with queries like `What is an optimal agenda for three days in Paris assuming I really like fine dining, historic buildings and museums, but hate crowds`, it also introduces severe ethical considerations.

Should a search engine be responsible for synthesizing information for its users instead of returning existing content for them to interpret? What if the search engine is politically or commercially biased and is trying to influence users' thinking or behavior? What if the search engine is being used as a tool for censorship or to spread propaganda (such as images or text that were modified on the fly) to trick people into false beliefs or to take dangerous actions?

Some of the more common use cases for generative search are abstractive question answering and results summarization. Whereas traditional search approaches have returned "ten blue links" or predetermined info boxes with information matching certain queries, generative search focuses on creating search responses on the fly based on dynamically analyzing the search results. From left to right, figure 15.2 shows the progression from these traditional search approaches toward generative search.

Extractive question answering, covered in chapter 14, begins the move toward generative search, in that it analyzes search results to return direct answers to questions instead of just the search results or predetermined answers. It's not entirely

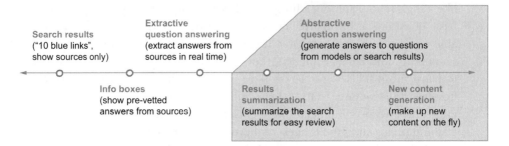

Figure 15.2   Spectrum of traditional search approaches (left) to generative search (right)

"generative" search, however, in that it still only returns answers exactly as presented in the searched documents, without any additional synthesis or new content generation.

As we continue toward the right in figure 15.2, results summarization is the first technique that can be fully considered generative search. Results summarization, which we'll cover in section 15.2.2, is the process of taking the search results and summarizing their content. This can be quite useful for the user, particularly if they are researching a topic and don't have time to read through all the results. Instead of the user needing to click on multiple links and read and analyze each of the results, a summary of the pages (along with citations, if desired) can be returned, saving the user time assessing the content.

Abstractive question answering is very similar to extractive question answering, in that it tries to answer a user's question, but it does so by either analyzing search results (like in results summarization) or simply by relying on the underlying foundation model to generate the answer. Relying on the foundation model is more likely to lead to made-up, or hallucinated, results, so it is often beneficial to use the search results as part of the prompt context for in-context learning. We'll cover this process of retrieval augmented generation in the next section.

Many major search engines and startups have integrated these generative models and interactive chat sessions into their search experiences, which provides the models with access to the internet (or at least a copy of the internet in the form of the search index). This allows the models to have a near-real-time view of the world's information. It means that the models may know detailed public information about the users they are interacting with, which may shape the results, and it also means that anyone can work to inject malicious information or intentions into these models by crafting web pages that relate concepts in misleading ways. If we're not careful, the field of search engine optimization (SEO) may go from trying to boost a website higher in search results to trying to manipulate the AI into providing malicious answers to end users. Applying critical thinking skills and validating the output of these models will be essential for anyone using them, but unfortunately, the models can be so compelling that many people are likely to be fooled into believing misleading output unless significant safeguards are put in place.

These models will continue to evolve to support searchers by interpreting search results. While many people may dream of having an AI-based personal assistant, the ethical considerations of having an AI generate the knowledge you consume daily will need to be handled carefully.

15.2.1 *Retrieval augmented generation*

The workflow of using a search engine or vector database to find relevant documents that can be supplied as context to an LLM is commonly referred to as *retrieval augmented generation* (RAG).

We've mentioned RAG several times before, and it's a big buzzword as this book is being published. There's a very good reason for this: the training of language models is a form of lossy compression of the training data, and the models can't faithfully store the massive amount of data they were trained on without losing fidelity. Their information also dates from the last time they were trained—it is hard for the models to make decisions on evolving information without some continually updated external data source.

No matter how much context a language model can accept in its prompt, it's computationally infeasible or at least cost-prohibitive to rely on an LLM as a source of truth for all the information it was trained on. Thankfully, the entire purpose of search engines is to find relevant context for any incoming query. In fact, this *entire* book is a deep dive into the *retrieval* part of RAG. As we discuss results summarization, abstractive question answering, and generative search in this chapter, we're touching on the *generation* part of RAG.

To perform RAG, most current libraries take documents, split them into one or more sections (chunks), and then index embeddings for each section into a search engine or vector database. Then, at generation time, the application prompting the language model will create queries to find supplementary information needed to execute the next prompt, generate embeddings for those queries, perform a dense vector search to find the highest-scoring sections using vector similarity (usually cosine or dot product), and pass the resulting ranked sections along with the prompt to the generative AI model.

CHALLENGES WITH CHUNKING

This process of splitting apart documents into sections is known as *chunking*, and it is both necessary and problematic. The problem can be understood as a tension between three constraints:

- *Vector database limitations*—Many vector databases are designed to index single vectors, but summarizing an entire document into a single vector can lose a lot of the specificity and context of the document. It pools the embedding across the entire document into a more vague summary embedding.
- *Loss of context between independent chunks*—Splitting a document into many separate documents to preserve the specificity of each section (chapter, paragraph, sentence, word, or other useful semantic chunk) can cause a loss of context

across chunks. If you split a document into 10 chunks and independently generate embeddings, the shared context across those embeddings is lost.

- *Computational complexity of many chunks*—The more chunks you have, the more vectors you need to index, and the more you need to search. This can be computationally expensive and slow, and it can also be difficult to manage the relevance of the results across the chunks when you have to weight many matches on the same initial document relative to fewer, but better, matches on other documents.

At the early stages of implementing RAG for generative AI, many people have focused on chunking documents into multiple separate documents to overcome vector database limitations. Computational complexity can be managed using good ANN (approximate nearest-neighbor) algorithms, but the loss of context across chunks is still problematic in that case, and it's frankly wasteful to create an unbounded number of overlapping chunks instead of using better algorithms to model the embeddings.

As an alternative approach, several search engines and vector databases (such as Vespa and Qdrant) already have support for multivalued vector fields, which makes it possible to create an arbitrary number of chunks and also to create overlapping chunks within one document (so that a single sentence or paragraph can be part of multiple chunks, thereby preserving more context across chunks). Such multivector support will likely become standard in the coming years to support emerging contextualized late interaction approaches like those introduced in the ColBERT family of models.

THE FUTURE OF RAG

RAG, as a discipline, is still in its infancy, but it's evolving rapidly. Numerous libraries and frameworks have been developed to perform RAG, but they are often based on an overly simple understanding of information retrieval. Current RAG implementations tend to rely entirely on a language model and vector similarity for relevance, ignoring most of the other AI-powered retrieval techniques we've covered in this book. In the context of the dimensions of user intent (figure 1.7), this has three effects:

- The content context is handled well conceptually (assuming the chosen embedding model was trained for query-document retrieval), but not on a specific keyword basis (due to the scope of the vectors summarizing multiple keywords).
- The domain context is handled as well as the language model is fine-tuned.
- The user context is usually ignored entirely.

For the content-understanding dimension of user intent (see section 1.2.5), promising approaches that use contextualized late interaction with embeddings are evolving, and they may eventually overcome the need for chunking altogether. These approaches (such as ColBERT, ColBERTv2, ColPali, and successors) involve generating an embedding per token in the document, but where each token's embedding uses the context of that token within the entire document (or at least a long surrounding context). This prevents the loss of context across chunks and avoids the need to index an unbounded number of chunks into the engine. These kinds of approaches make much more sense for RAG, and retrieval in general, than some of the more naive approaches mentioned in the last subsection. We expect to see similar approaches evolve over the coming years and to significantly improve recall over the current baseline ranking approaches.

The retrieval concepts you've learned in this book, concerning dimensions of user intent, reflected intelligence and signals models, semantic knowledge graphs, learning to rank, and feedback loops (combined with LLM-based vector search), are light years ahead of most current RAG implementations, which only use a subset.

That said, the future of RAG is bright, and it's likely the next few years will both see more sophisticated approaches to tackling current challenges, and see the integration of better retrieval and ranking techniques into the RAG process. RAG techniques are changing and evolving rapidly, and the field is ripe for continued innovation and improvement.

We'll cover one of the most popular generative search approaches using RAG in the coming section: results summarization (with citations).

15.2.2 *Results summarization using foundation models*

In chapter 3, we stated that the search engine is primarily responsible for three things: indexing, matching, and ranking results. Chapter 13 already showed how to enhance indexing (with embeddings), matching (with approximate nearest-neighbor search), and ranking of results (with similarity comparison on embedding vectors). But the way we return results is often just as important as the results themselves.

In chapter 14, we demonstrated how to extract answers out of ranked documents containing those answers, which can be a drastic improvement over returning full documents and forcing users to analyze them individually. But what if the answer to a question *requires* analysis of the documents? What if the desired answer is actually the *result* of an analysis that combines information from multiple documents into a unified, well-sourced answer?

One of the problems with answers generated directly from LLMs is that they are created based on statistical probability distributions from parameters learned by the model. Though the model may have been trained on a massive number of data sources, it does not store those data sources directly. Instead, the model is compressed into a lossy representation of the data. This means that you cannot count on the output from an LLM to accurately reflect the input data—only an approximation of it.

As a result, foundation models are well-known to hallucinate—to generate responses that make up incorrect facts or misrepresent the topics in the response. The context provided in the prompt also heavily influences the answer, to the point where foundation models can sometimes be more a reflection of the user's word choices and bias than a legitimate answer to a question. While this can be useful in creative endeavors, it makes today's foundation models quite unreliable for safely generating the fact-based responses for which search engines are historically relied upon. For users to truly trust the results, they need to be able to verify the sources of the information. Thankfully, instead of directly relying on foundation models for answers to questions, we can combine the search engine with a foundation model, using RAG to create a hybrid output.

Using foundation models like this to summarize search results is a great way to infuse your search engine with better AI-powered responses. Let's walk through an example of performing search results summarization with citations using a foundation model. We'll use output from OpenAI's GPT-4 model, but you can get similar output from most current open source or permissively licensed LLMs.

The workflow includes two steps:

1 Execute a search. This can involve converting the query to an embedding and performing a dense vector search or using any other technique we've discussed to find the most relevant results.

2 Construct a prompt instructing your foundation model to take the user's query and read and summarize a set of search results returned from the query.

The following listing demonstrates an example prompt combining the search results from step 1 into a prompt from step 2.

> **Listing 15.3   Prompt to foundation model to summarize search results**

```
Web search results:

[1] "A large language model, or LLM, is a deep learning algorithm that
can recognize, summarize, translate, predict and generate text and other
content based on knowledge gained from massive datasets."
URL: https://blogs.nvidia.com/blog/2023/
      01/26/what-are-large-language-models-used-for/

[2] A large language model (LLM) is a language model consisting of a
neural network with many parameters (typically billions of weights or
more), trained on large quantities of unlabeled text using
self-supervised learning. LLMs emerged around 2018 and perform well at a
wide variety of tasks. This has shifted the focus of natural language
processing research away from the previous paradigm of training
specialized supervised models for specific tasks.
URL: https://en.wikipedia.org/wiki/Large_language_model

[3] "In this guide, we'll discuss everything you need to know about
Large Language Models (LLMs), including key terms, algorithms,
fine-tuning, and more. As ChatGPT has taken the internet by storm crossing
1 million users in its first 5 days, you may be wondering what machine
learning algorithm is running under the hood. While ChatGPT uses a
specific type of reinforcement learning called "Reinforcement Learning
from Human Feedback (RLHF)", at a high level it is an example of a
Large Language Model (LLM)."
URL: https://www.mlq.ai/what-is-a-large-language-model-llm/

Instructions: Using the provided web search results, write a comprehensive
reply to the given query. Make sure to cite results using
[[number](URL)] notation after the reference. If the provided search
results refer to multiple subjects with the same name, write separate
```

```
answers for each subject.

Query: What is a large language model?
```

When all of listing 15.3 is passed as a prompt to the language model, we got the following result.

Listing 15.4   Response to the summarization prompt from listing 15.3

```
A large language model (LLM) is a deep learning algorithm that can
recognize, summarize, translate, predict, and generate text and other
content based on knowledge gained from massive datasets
[[1](https://blogs.nvidia.com/blog/2023/01/26/what-are-large-language-
    models-used-for/)].
It consists of a neural network with many parameters (typically billions
of weights or more) and is trained on large quantities of unlabeled text
using self-supervised learning
[[2](https://en.wikipedia.org/wiki/Large_language_model)]. LLMs emerged
around 2018 and have performed well at a wide variety of tasks, shifting
the focus of natural language processing research away from the previous
paradigm of training specialized supervised models for specific tasks
[[2](https://en.wikipedia.org/wiki/Large_language_model)]. One example of
a LLM is ChatGPT, which uses a specific type of reinforcement learning
called "Reinforcement Learning from Human Feedback (RLHF)"
[[3](https://www.mlq.ai/what-is-a-large-language-model-llm/)].
```

This output pulls critical details from the search results to answer the original query (What is a large language model?) but does it in a way that cites the original articles. If that answer is too verbose, an additional refinement to the prompt can be added to the end of the instructions: Be concise. This results in the following output instead:

```
...
Query: What is a large language model? Be concise.
```

Listing 15.5   Results for listing 15.3's prompt with Be concise.

```
A large language model (LLM) is a deep learning algorithm that uses neural
networks with billions of parameters, trained on massive unlabeled text
datasets for various language tasks [[2](https://en.wikipedia.org/
wiki/Large_language_model)][[1](https://blogs.nvidia.com/blog/2023/01/
26/what-are-large-language-models-used-for/)].
```

Many search engines have started relying on foundation models to interpret and cite search results like this. By adding in additional instructions like "avoid being vague, controversial, or off-topic", "use an unbiased and journalistic tone", or even "write at a fifth-grade reading level", you can adjust the quality and tone of the summaries to cater to your search engine's needs.

15.2.3 *Data generation using foundation models*

In addition to foundation models adding a synthesis and summarization layer on top of search results, one of the other emerging use cases for the models is the generation of synthetic domain-specific and task-specific training data.

As we think back to the numerous AI-powered search techniques we've already explored, many of them require substantial training data to implement:

- Signals boosting models require user signals data showing which user queries correspond with which documents.
- Click models, useful for automated LTR, require an understanding of which documents users click on and skip over in their search results.
- Semantic knowledge graphs require an index of data to find related terms and phrases.

But what if we fine-tuned a foundation model to "come up with documents about missing topics" or "come up with realistic queries" associated with each document? Or better yet, what if we didn't need to fine-tune at all, but could instead construct a prompt to generate great queries for documents? Such data could be used to generate synthetic signals to help improve relevance.

Listings 15.6 through 15.9 show how we can use a prompt to find queries and relevance scores by combining an LLM with searches on our Stack Exchange outdoors collection from chapter 14.

For our exercise, we found it better to give several documents to the prompt, as opposed to just one, and even better to return related documents (from the same topic or a results list from a previous query). This is important, because there are niche topics within each set of documents, so having related documents helps to return more fine-grained queries instead of general ones. Additionally, while all the documents may not be perfectly relevant to the original query (or may be noisy), this still gives the LLM a few-shot chance at understanding our corpus, as opposed to basing its context on a single example. The following listing shows the template used with the LLM to generate candidate queries for a list of documents.

Listing 15.6   A prompt that generates queries describing documents

```
What are some queries that should find the following documents?  List at
least 5 unique queries, where these documents are better than others
in an outdoors question and answer dataset. Be concise and only
output the list of queries, and a result number in the format [n] for
the best result in the resultset. Don't print a relevance summary at
the end.

### Results:
{resultset}
```

The following listing shows code that can generate the {resultset} to be inserted into the prompt from listing 15.6. With the example query what are minimalist shoes? we get the `resultset` using the `retriever` function from listing 14.15. The retriever provides answer contexts for a query.

```
example_contexts = retriever("What are minimalist shoes?")
resultset = [f"{idx}. {ctx}" for idx, ctx
  in enumerate(list(example_contexts[0:5]["context"]))]
print("\n".join(resultset))
```

We only want the index and context information from the first 5 results returned by the retriever, and we prefix each result with its index of 0 to 4.

Output:

0. Minimalist shoes or "barefoot" shoes are shoes that provide your feet with some form of protection, but get you as close to a barefoot experience as possible...
1. There was actually a project done on the definition of what a minimalist shoe is and the result was "Footwear providing minimal interference with the natural movement of the foot due to its high flexibility, low heel to toe drop, weight and stack height, and the absence of motion control and stability devices". If you are looking for a simpler definition, this is what Wikipedia says, Minimalist shoes are shoes intended to closely approximate barefoot running conditions...
2. One summer job, I needed shoes to walk on a rocky beach, sometimes in the water, for 5 to 10 miles per day all summer. Stretchy neoprene shoes were terrible for this- no traction and no support. So I used regular sneakers. I chose a pair of cross country racing flats... The uppers were extremely well ventilated polyester, so they drained very quickly, and the thin material dried much faster than a padded sandal, and certainly much faster than a regular sneaker of leather or cotton would... The thing to look for is thin fabric that attaches directly to the sole, with no rubber rim that would keep the water from draining...
3. ... It's not unhealthy to wear minimalist footwear, but on what terrain your wear them could be bad for your body in the long run. Human beings were never meant to walk or run exclusively on hard pavement or sidewalks. Nor were we designed to clamber around on sharp rocks at high elevations... If you're running on soft ground and you have the foot strength, then there are plenty of arguments in favour of minimalist shoes being better for you than other shoes, because it brings your posture and gait back to what nature intended it to be. If you're hiking in the mountains on uneven rocky terrain, especially while carrying a heavy bag, then you'd be better off wearing a supportive hiking boot...
4. ... My favourite barefoot shoes are Vibram Five-Fingers , I wear either my Mouri's or my KSO's at the beach. Vibram Five-Fingers 'Signa' watersport shoes: The thin sole will be enough to protect your feet from the lava sand...

These five results are then added to the bottom of the prompt from listing 15.6 by replacing the {resultset} value with the response from listing 15.7. We take the final, fully substituted prompt, and pass it into our LLM, yielding the following result.

Listing 15.8 LLM response relating documents to generating queries

```
resultset_text = "\n".join(resultset)
resultset_prompt = summarize_search_prompt.replace("{resultset}",
                                                    resultset_text)
generated_relevance_judgments = get_generative_response(resultset_prompt)
display(generated_relevance_judgments)
```

Output:

```
1.     What is the definition of a minimalist shoe?
2.     What are the characteristics of minimalist shoes?
3.     Which shoes are best for walking on rocky beaches?
4.     Are minimalist shoes suitable for all terrains?
5.     What are some recommended barefoot shoe brands?
```

Results:

```
1.     [1]
2.     [0]
3.     [2]
4.     [3]
5.     [4]
```

Notice the nuance in relevance between the candidate queries and the wording in each of their relevant results. Also note that the ordering of the relevant results is not the same as the ordering of the queries in the output. The context of document 0 is more relevant for the specific query What are the characteristics of minimalist shoes? and the context of document 1 is more relevant for the query What is the definition of a minimalist shoe?

Note that we just use the pandas index position for the context IDs, instead of the IDs of the documents. In our experience, the IDs can confuse the model by providing irrelevant information. Depending on the LLM you use, this may need to be reverse engineered with some code, like we've done with our existing example_contexts from listing 15.7. Also notice how the model changed the order in listing 15.8 (the queries are not in the same order as the judgment results), so we'll need to account for this next when we parse the output.

The following listing shows how to extract the information and make a nice Python dictionary for the queries, documents, and relevant results.

Listing 15.9 Extracting pairwise judgments from the LLM output

```
def extract_pairwise_judgments(text, contexts):
    query_pattern = re.compile(r"\d+\.\s+(.*)")
    result_pattern = re.compile(r"\d+\.\s+\[(\d+)\]")
    lines = text.split("\n")
    queries = []
    results = []
    for line in lines:
      query_match = query_pattern.match(line)
```

> **Regular expressions are used to see which line belongs to which list. You can experiment with more robust expressions if you run into some strange output from the model.**

```
  result_match = result_pattern.match(line)
  if result_match:
    result_index = int(result_match.group(1))
    results.append(result_index)
  elif query_match:
    query = query_match.group(1)
    queries.append(query)
output = [{"query": query, "relevant_document": contexts[result]["id"]}
         for query, result in zip(queries, results)]
return output
```

Next, we pass our output from listing 15.8 into the `extract_pairwise_judgments` from listing 15.9.

Listing 15.10   Positive relevance judgments generated from the LLM

```
resultset_contexts = example_contexts.to_dict("records")   ⟵
output = extract_pairwise_judgments(
             generated_relevance_judgments,
             resultset_contexts)
display(output)
```

example_contexts, from listing 15.7, contains the search results for the query 'What are minimalist shoes?'.

Response:

```
{"query": "What is the definition of a minimalist shoe?",
 "relevant_document": 18370}
{"query": "What are the characteristics of minimalist shoes?",
 "relevant_document": 18376}
{"query": "Which shoes are best for walking on rocky beaches?",
 "relevant_document": 18370}
{"query": "Are minimalist shoes suitable for all terrains?",
 "relevant_document": 18375}
{"query": "What are some recommended barefoot shoe brands?",
 "relevant_document": 13540}
```

Running this process through hundreds of result sets taken from customer queries will produce a large list of relevant query-document pairs. Since we are processing five results at a time, we'll also be generating five new positive pairwise judgments with every single prompt to the LLM. You can then use these judgments as synthetic signals or as training data to train many of the signals-based models explored in the earlier chapters.

15.2.4   *Evaluating generative output*

In previous chapters, we covered the importance of using judgment lists to measure the quality of our search algorithms. In chapters 10 and 11, we generated judgment lists manually and then later automatically using click models, for training and measuring the quality of LTR models. In chapter 14, we generated silver sets and golden sets to train and measure the quality of our fine-tuned LLM for extractive question answering.

These are all search use cases for which the query and results pairs are largely deterministic. Measuring the quality of generative model output is much trickier, however. We'll explore some of the generative use cases in this section to see what can be done to overcome those challenges.

Generative output can be subjective. Many generative models produce different outputs given the same prompt when you adjust a temperature parameter. *Temperature* is a value between `0.0` and `1.0` that controls the randomness in the output. The lower the temperature, the more predictable the output; the higher the temperature, the more creative the output. We recommend always setting the temperature to `0.0` for the evaluation and production of your model so you have a higher confidence in its output. However, even a temperature of `0.0` may still produce different responses for the same prompt between runs, depending on the model.

The core methodology for evaluating generative output is straightforward: frame and evaluate tasks that can be measured objectively. Since the output of the prompt can be unpredictable, however, it's not easy to curate a dataset that can be reused to measure different prompts for your exact task. Therefore, we typically rely on established metrics to assess the quality of the model chosen first, before you start your own evaluation on its downstream output.

Various important and common metrics address different language tasks. Each metric usually has a leaderboard, which is a competition-style benchmark that ranks models by performance on the given tasks. These are some common benchmarks:

- *AI2 Reasoning Challenge (ARC)*—A multiple-choice question-answering dataset consisting of 7,787 grade-school science exam questions.
- *HellaSwag*—Common-sense inference tests; for example, a complex reasoning question is given with multiple choice.
- *Massive Multitask Language Understanding (MMLU)*—A test to measure a text model's multitask accuracy. The test covers 57 tasks, including mathematics, history, computer science, law, and more.
- *TruthfulQA*—Measures whether a language model is truthful in generating answers to questions. The benchmark comprises 817 questions that span 38 categories. The authors crafted questions that some humans would answer falsely due to a false belief or misconception.

Figure 15.3 shows an example of a HellaSwag question-and-answer test.

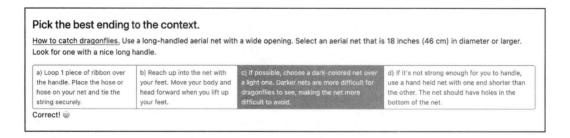

Figure 15.3   HellaSwag example question and multiple choices, with the correct answer highlighted

Some leaderboards contain multiple metrics, such as the Open LLM Leaderboard in figure 15.4.

Model	Average ⓘ ▲	ARC ▲	HellaSwag ▲	MMLU ▲	TruthfulQA ▲	Winogrande ▲	GSM8K ▲	Hub License
abacusai/Smaug-72B-v0.1 📄	80.48	76.02	89.27	77.15	76.67	85.08	78.7	other
ibivibiv/alpaca-dragon-72b-v1 📄	79.3	73.89	88.16	77.4	72.69	86.03	77.63	other
moreh/MoMo-72B-lora-1.8.7-DPO 📄	78.55	70.82	85.96	77.13	74.71	84.06	78.62	mit
cloudyu/TomGrc_FusionNet_34Bx2_MoE_v0.1_DPO_f16 📄	77.91	74.06	86.74	76.65	72.24	83.35	74.45	other
HanNayeoniee/LHK_DPO_v1 📄	77.62	74.74	89.3	64.9	79.89	88.32	68.54	mit
cloudyu/TomGrc_FusionNet_34Bx2_MoE_v0.1_full_linear_DPO 📄	77.52	74.06	86.67	76.69	71.32	83.43	72.93	other
zhengr/MixTAO-7Bx2-MoE-v8.1 📄	77.5	73.81	89.22	64.92	78.57	87.37	71.11	apache-2.0
yunconglong/Truthful_DPO_TomGrc_FusionNet_7Bx2_MoE_13B 📄	77.44	74.91	89.3	64.67	78.02	88.24	69.52	mit
JaeyeonKang/CCK_Asura_v1 📄	77.43	73.89	89.07	75.44	71.75	86.35	68.08	cc-by-nc-4.0
fblgit/UNA-SimpleSmaug-34b-v1beta 📄	77.41	74.57	86.74	76.68	70.17	83.82	72.48	apache-2.0
TomGrc/FusionNet_34Bx2_MoE_v0.1 📄	77.38	73.72	86.46	76.72	71.01	83.35	73.01	mit
migtissera/Tess-72B-v1.5b 📄	77.3	71.25	85.53	76.63	71.99	81.45	76.95	other

Figure 15.4   HuggingFaceH4 Open LLM Leaderboard space (taken March 2024)

You should use these metrics to decide which model to use for your specific domain and task. For example, if your task is abstractive question answering, consider using a model with the best TruthfulQA metric.

> **WARNING**   Models are licensed, so make sure you only use a model with a license that aligns with your use case. Some models have licenses similar to open source software (like Apache 2.0 or MIT). But be careful, because many models have commercial restrictions (such as the LLaMA models and derivatives or models trained on output from restrictive models like GPT from OpenAI).

Once you have chosen your model, you should take steps to evaluate it on your prompts. Be rigorous, and track responses to your prompts and how they fare. Some purpose-built tools are emerging in the market to do this for you, including automatic prompt optimization approaches, but a simple spreadsheet can suffice. In the following section, we'll construct our own metric to use for a new task.

15.2.5   Constructing your own metric

Let's explore how a generative task can be construed objectively, allowing you to create a dataset and use a metric like precision or recall (both introduced in section 5.4.5) to evaluate a model's accuracy. We'll use a prompt with unstructured data to extract structured information. Since our result will be formatted predictably, we can then measure the accuracy of the response based on a human-labeled result.

For our example, we'll test the named-entity recognition accuracy of a generative model. Specifically, we'll measure whether generative output from an LLM correctly labels entities of type person, organization, or location.

We'll use the following snippet of text from a news article:

```
Walter Silverman of Brighton owned one of the most successful local Carvel
franchises, at East Ridge Road and Hudson Avenue in Irondequoit.
He started working for Carvel in 1952. This is how it appeared in the
late 1970s/early 1980s.
[Alan Morrell, Democrat and Chronicle, May 29, 2023]
```

If we manually label the entities in this snippet with the tags `<per>` (person), `<org>` (organization), and `<loc>` (location), we'll arrive at the labeled version in the following listing.

Listing 15.11   Article tagged with entity labels

```
<per>Walter Silverman</per> of <loc>Brighton</loc> owned one of the most
successful local <org>Carvel</org> franchises, at
<loc>East Ridge Road</loc> and <loc>Hudson Avenue</loc> in
<loc>Irondequoit</loc>. He started working for <org>Carvel</org> in
1952. This is how it appeared in the late 1970s/early 1980s.
```

This is a format that a generative model should be able to produce, taking text and generating a marked-up version as instructed by a prompt. But this response is only semi-structured with ad hoc markup. We need to process it further, and we can write some Python to extract the entities into a suitable JSON format.

Listing 15.12   Extracting entities from generative output

```python
def extract_entities(text):
    entities = []
    pattern = r"<(per|loc|org)>(.*?)<\/(per|loc|org)>"
    matches = re.finditer(pattern, text)
    for match in matches:
        entity = {"label": match.group(1).upper(),
                  "offset": [match.start(), match.end() - 1],
                  "text": match.group(2)}
        entities.append(entity)
    return entities

entities = extract_entities(news_article_labelled)
display(entities)
```

Output:

```
[{"label": "PER", "offset": [0, 26], "text": "Walter Silverman"},
 {"label": "LOC", "offset": [31, 49], "text": "Brighton"},
 {"label": "ORG", "offset": [90, 106], "text": "Carvel"},
 {"label": "LOC", "offset": [123, 148], "text": "East Ridge Road"},
 {"label": "LOC", "offset": [154, 177], "text": "Hudson Avenue"},
 {"label": "LOC", "offset": [182, 203], "text": "Irondequoit"},
 {"label": "ORG", "offset": [229, 245], "text": "Carvel"}]
```

With the entities now represented in a structured form (as JSON), we can use the list to calculate our metric. We can manually label many passages or use the techniques from sections 14.2–14.3 to automate the labeling, using a model to construct a silver set and then correcting the outputs to produce a golden set.

When you have your golden set, you can try a prompt like the following.

Listing 15.13 Labeled entities

```
For a given passage, please identify and mark the following entities:
people with the tag '<per>', locations with the tag '<loc>', and
organizations with the tag '<org>'. Please repeat the passage below
with the appropriate markup.
### {text}
```

In the preceding prompt, {text} would be replaced by the paragraph for which you want to identify entities. When the model generates the response, it can be passed directly into the extract_entities function in listing 15.12.

The output of the extracted entities can then be compared to the golden set to produce the number of true positives, TP (correctly identified entities), false positives, FP (incorrectly identified text that should not be identified), and false negatives, FN (entities that should have been identified but were not).

From these numbers, you can calculate the following:

- Precision = $(TP/(TP+FP))$
- Recall = $(TP/(TP+FN))$
- F1 = $(2 * (Precision * Recall) / (Precision + Recall))$

Many of the metrics listed on leaderboards use F1 scores.

What generative tasks do you have? Be creative and think about how you can shape your task to be objectively measurable. For example, if you are generating search result summaries, you can perform something similar to the named-entity recognition task—check if the summaries show important spans of text for a given search result set or show result number citations with titles correctly attributed.

15.2.6 Algorithmic prompt optimization

Throughout section 15.2, we've covered the use of LLM prompts to generate synthetic data and to summarize and cite search results for RAG. We also covered metrics to quantify the quality of generated data. We discussed this in the context of measuring the *model's* quality, but there's an important point we glossed over: the quality of the *prompt*.

If you recall, we have three different ways to improve LLM output: improve the model during training (pretraining), fine-tune the model, or improve the prompt. Pretraining and fine-tuning are direct, programmatic optimizations of the neural network model, but we've thus far treated prompt creation and improvement (known as *prompt engineering*) as a manual process requiring human intervention.

In reality, the prompt can also be fine-tuned programmatically much like the model. Libraries like DSPy (Declarative Self-improving Language Programs, Pythonically) provide a framework for "programming" language model usage as opposed to manually prompting it. Functionally, this is accomplished by defining the desired output format from the language model (along with training data showing good responses) and letting the library optimize the prompt's wording to best achieve that output.

DSPy accomplishes this programmatic prompt optimization using four key components:

- *Signatures*—These are simple strings explaining the goal of the training process, as well as the expected input and output. Examples:
  - question → answer (question answering)
  - document → summary (document summarization)
  - context, question → answer (RAG)
- *Modules*—These take in a signature and combine it with a prompting technique, a configured LLM, and a set of parameters to generate a prompt to achieve the desired output.
- *Metrics*—These are measures of how well the output generated by a module matches the desired output.
- *Optimizers*—These are used to train the model by iteratively testing variations to the prompts and parameters to optimize for the specified metric.

Programming the language model usage like this provides four key benefits:

- It allows for the automatic optimization of the prompt, which can be a time-consuming and error-prone process when done manually.
- It allows for the optimization of the prompt to quickly test well-known templates (and new techniques or data over time) and best practices for prompting, as well as to chain multiple prompting stages together into a more sophisticated pipeline.
- It allows you to easily switch out the LLM at any time and "recompile" the DSPy program to re-optimize the prompt for the new model.
- It allows you to chain multiple modules, models, and workflows together into more sophisticated pipelines, and to optimize the prompts for each stage of the pipeline and the pipeline as a whole.

These benefits make your application more robust and easier to maintain, as compared to manual prompt tuning, and they ensure your prompt is always fine-tuned and optimized for your current environment and goals. Once you've coded up the configured DSPy pipeline, you just run the optimizer to *compile* it, at which point all the optimal parameters are learned for each module. Want to then try a new model, technique, or set of training data? Just recompile your DSPy program, and you're ready to go, with your prompts automatically optimized to yield the best results. You can find lots of "getting started" templates for implementing RAG, question answering, summarization, and any number of other LLM-prompt-based tasks in the DSPy documentation at https://github.com/stanfordnlp/dspy. If you're building a non-trivial LLM-based application, we highly recommend you opt for such a programmatic approach to prompt optimization.

15.3 Multimodal search

Let's now explore one of the most powerful capabilities enabled by foundation-model–based embeddings: multimodal search. Multimodal search engines allow you to search for one content type using another content type (also called *cross-modal* search), or to search multiple content types together. For example, you can search for an image using either text, an image, or a hybrid query combining both text and an image. We'll implement each of these use cases in this section.

Multimodal search is made possible by the fact that vector embeddings can be generated for text, images, audio, video, and other content that can be mapped into overlapping vector spaces. This enables us to search any content type against any other content type without the need for any special indexing or transformation.

Multimodal search engines have the potential to revolutionize the way we search for information, removing barriers that previously prevented us from using all the available context to best understand the incoming queries and rank results.

15.3.1 Common modes for multimodal search

While multimodal search entails many different data types being searchable, we'll briefly discuss the currently most common data modalities in this section: natural language, images, audio, and video.

NATURAL LANGUAGE SEARCH

In chapters 13 and 14, we implemented semantic search and question-answering using dense vectors. Both techniques are examples of natural language search. A simple query like `shirt without stripes` will confound every e-commerce platform built atop an inverted index, unless special logic is added manually or integrated into a search-focused knowledge graph using *semantic functions* like we implemented in chapter 7.

Today's state-of-the-art LLMs are becoming more sophisticated at handling these queries and are even able to interpret instructions and synthesize information from different sources to generate new responses. Many companies building traditional databases and NoSQL data stores are aggressively integrating dense vector support as first-class data types to take advantage of all these major advances.

While it is unlikely that these dense-vector–based approaches will fully replace traditional inverted indexes, knowledge graphs, signals boosting, learning to rank, click models, and other search techniques, we will see new hybrid approaches emerge that combine the best of each of these techniques to continue optimizing content and query understanding.

IMAGE SEARCH

As you saw in chapter 2, images are another form of unstructured data, alongside text.

Traditionally, if you wanted to search for images in an inverted index, you would search through text descriptions of the image or labels applied to the image. With dense vector search, however, searching images for visual or conceptual similarity can be implemented almost as easily as text search. By taking input images, encoding them into embedding vectors with a vision Transformer, and indexing those vectors, it becomes possible to accept another image as a query, encode it into an embedding, and then search with that vector to find visually similar images.

Further, by training a model with images alongside text descriptions of those images, it becomes possible to perform a multimodal search for images either by inputting an image or by text. Rather than having a caption and an unsearchable image, one can now use convolutional neural networks (CNNs) or vision Transformers to encode the image to a dense vector space that co-exists in the same vector space as text. With image representation and text representation in the same vector space, you can search for a more descriptive version of the image than the caption provides, yet still match using text to describe the features in the image.

Given this ability to encode images and text into the same dense vector space, it is also possible to reverse the search and use the image as the query to match any text documents that include similar language to what's occurring in the image, or to combine both an image and text into a hybrid query to find other images best matching a combination of the text and image query modalities. We'll walk through examples of some of these techniques in section 15.3.2.

AUDIO SEARCH

Searching with audio or for audio has historically been mostly a text-to-speech problem. Audio files would be converted to text and indexed, and audio queries would be converted to text and searched against the text index. Transcribing voice is a very difficult problem. Voice assistants from Google, Apple, Amazon, and Microsoft typically do very well with short queries, but this level of accuracy has historically been difficult to come by for those wanting to integrate open source solutions. Recent breakthroughs with the combinations of speech recognition and language models that can error-correct phonetic misunderstandings are bringing better technology to the market, however.

It's important to keep in mind that many other kinds of important sounds can be present in audio besides just spoken words. If someone searches for `loud train`, `rushing stream`, or `Irish accent`, these are all qualities they'd hope to find in any returned audio results. Multimodal Transformer models, when trained by text and audio mapping to overlapping vector spaces, now make this possible.

VIDEO SEARCH

Video is nothing more than the combination of sequential images overlaid and kept in sequence with audio. If audio and images can both be mapped to an overlapping vector space with written text, this means that by indexing each frame of a video (or maybe a few frames per second, depending on the granularity needed), it's possible to create a video search engine that allows searching by text description for any scene in the video, searching by audio clip, or searching by an image to find the most similar video. The deep learning models being generated in the fields of computer vision, natural language processing, and audio processing are all converging, and as long as these different types of media can all be represented in overlapping vector spaces, search engines can now search for them.

15.3.2 Implementing multimodal search

In this section, we'll implement one of the most popular forms of multimodal search: text-to-image search. We'll do this by using embeddings that were jointly trained on image and text data pairs from the internet. This results in the latent text features learned being in the same vector space as the latent image features learned. This also means that in addition to performing text-to-image search, we can use the same embedding model to perform an image-to-image visual search based on the pixels in any incoming image. We'll also show an example of combining modalities in a hybrid query, searching for results that best match both a text query *and* an image at the same time.

We'll use the CLIP model, which is a multimodal model that can understand images and text in the same vector space. CLIP is a Transformer-based model developed by OpenAI that was trained on a large dataset of images and their associated text captions. The model was trained to predict which caption goes with which image, and vice versa. This means that the model has learned to map images and text into the same vector space so that similar images and related text embeddings are located close together.

We will return to The Movie Database (TMDB) dataset we used in chapter 10 for implementing our multimodal search examples. In this case, however, instead of searching on the text of movies, we'll search on images from movies.

In the following listing, we define the functionality to calculate normalized embeddings and build a movie collection. The collection is composed of the movie's image embeddings and movie metadata, including titles, image source URLs, and the URL for the movie's TMDB page.

> **Listing 15.14   Indexing cached movie embeddings**

```
def normalize_embedding(embedding):
  return numpy.divide(embedding,
    numpy.linalg.norm(embedding,axis=0)).tolist()

def read(cache_name):
  cache_file_name = f"data/tmdb/{cache_name}.pickle"
  with open(cache_file_name, "rb") as fd:
    return pickle.load(fd)

def tmdb_with_embeddings_dataframe():
  movies = read("movies_with_image_embeddings")
  embeddings = movies["image_embeddings"]
  normalized_embeddings = [normalize_embedding(e)
                    for e in embeddings]
  movies_dataframe = spark.createDataFrame(
```

Annotations:
- **Normalize movie embeddings at index time so we can use the more efficient dot product (versus cosine) calculation at query time.**
- **We pregenerated and cached the movie embeddings so you don't have to download and process all the images.**

```
      zip(movies["movie_ids"], movies["titles"],
          movies["image_ids"], normalized_embeddings),
      schema=["movie_id", "title", "image_id", "image_embedding"])
   return movies_dataframe
```

```
embeddings_dataframe = tmdb_with_embeddings_dataframe()
embeddings_collection = engine.create_collection(
                          "tmdb_with_embeddings")
embeddings_collection.write(embeddings_dataframe)
```
> **Builds a movie collection containing image embeddings**

Because the CLIP model is a multimodal model jointly trained on text and images, the embeddings we generate from either text or images can be used to search the same image embeddings.

With the index now built using normalized embeddings, all that's left to do is to execute a vector search against the collection. The following listing shows the key functions needed to search for images using text queries, image queries, or hybrid text and image queries.

Listing 15.15 Multimodal text/image vector search using CLIP

```
device = "cuda" if torch.cuda.is_available() else "cpu"
model, preprocess = clip.load("ViT-B/32", device=device)
```
> **Loads the pretrained CLIP model and image preprocessor**

```
def movie_search(query_embedding, limit=8):
  collection = engine.get_collection("tmdb_with_embeddings")
  request = {"query_vector": query_embedding,
             "query_field": "image_embedding",
             "return_fields": ["movie_id", "title",
                               "image_id", "score"],
             "limit": limit,
             "quantization_size": "FLOAT32"}
  return collection.search(**request)
```
> **Executes a vector search for a query embedding**

> **Constructs a search request with a query embedding to search against the indexed image embeddings**

> **The data type used for each embedding feature value, in this case a 32-bit float.**

```
def encode_text(text, normalize=True):
  text = clip.tokenize([text]).to(device)
  text_features = model.encode_text(text)
  embedding = text_features.tolist()[0]
  if normalize:
    embedding = normalize_embedding(embedding)
  return embedding
```
> **Computes the normalized embeddings for text**

```
def encode_image(image_file, normalize=True):
  image = load_image(image_file)
  inputs = preprocess(image).unsqueeze(0).to(device)
  embedding = model.encode_image(inputs).tolist()[0]
  if normalize:
    embedding = normalize_embedding(embedding)
  return embedding
```
> **Computes the normalized embeddings for an image**

```
def encode_text_and_image(text_query, image_file):
  text_embedding = encode_text(text_query, False)
  image_embedding = encode_image(image_file, False)
```
> **Computes and combines normalized embeddings for an image and text**

```
return numpy.average((normalize_embedding(
    [text_embedding, image_embedding])), axis=0).tolist()
```
Averages the text and image vectors to create a multimodal query

The `movie_search` function follows a process similar to one we used in chapter 13: take a query vector and execute a vector search against a collection with embeddings. Our `encode_text` and `encode_image` functions calculate normalized embeddings based on text or an image. The `encode_text_and_image` function is a hybrid of the two, where we generate embeddings from both text and images, unit-normalize them, and pool them together by averaging them.

With the core multimodal embedding calculations in place, we can now implement a simple search interface to display the top results for an incoming text, image, or text and image query.

Listing 15.16 Multimodal vector search on text and image embeddings

```
def search_and_display(text_query="", image_query=None):
  if image_query:
    if text_query:
      query_embedding = encode_text_and_image(text_query, image_query)
    else:
      query_embedding = encode_image(image_query)
  else:
    query_embedding = encode_text(text_query)
  display_results(movie_search(query_embedding), show_fields=False)
```

The `search_and_display` function takes in either a text query, an image query, or both, and then retrieves the embeddings and executes the search. The function then displays the top results in a simple grid. Figure 15.5 shows an example output for the query `singing in the rain`:

```
search_and_display(text_query="singing in the rain")
```

Figure 15.5 Text query for `singing in the rain`

Three of the first four images are from the movie *Singin' in the Rain,* all of the images show someone in the rain or with an umbrella, and many are either from musicals or show people actively singing. These results demonstrate the power of performing image search using embeddings that were trained on both text and images: we now have the ability to search for pictures whose pixels contain the meaning expressed by the words!

To demonstrate some of the nuances of mapping text to meaning in images, let's run two variations of the same query: `superhero flying` versus `superheroes flying`. In traditional keyword search, we'd usually throw away the plural, but in the context of searching on embeddings, and particularly in the context of multimodal search, let's see how this slight difference affects the results. As you can see in figure 15.6, our search results changed from images of a single superhero flying (or at least up high off the ground) to pictures of mostly groups of superheroes containing similar actions.

"superhero flying"   **vs.**   "superheroes flying"

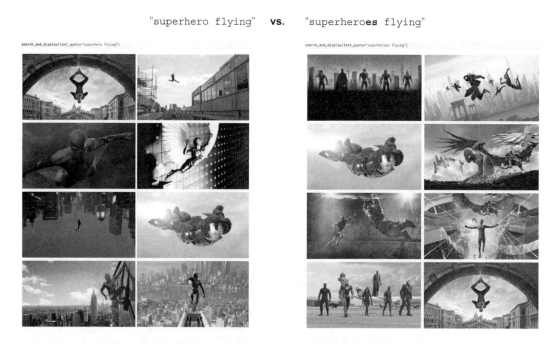

Figure 15.6   Nuanced difference between `superhero flying` **vs.** `superheroes flying` **queries**

This cross-modal (text-to-image) search is impressive, but let's also test out image-to-image search to demonstrate how reusable these multimodal embeddings are. Figure 15.7 shows the results of an image search using a picture of a DeLorean (the car famously converted to a time machine in the movie *Back to the Future*).

```
search_and_display(image_query="chapters/ch15/delorean-query.jpg")
```

Image query: Image query results:

Figure 15.7 Image-to-image search for a car that looks similar to a DeLorean

As you would expect, most of the cars are actually the famous DeLorean from *Back to the Future*. The other cars have similar aesthetic features: similar shapes, similarly opening doors. Not only have we matched the features of the car well, but many of the results also reflect the glowing lighting from the image query.

To take our DeLorean search one step further, let's try a multimodal search combining our last two query examples. Let's perform a multimodal query for both the previous DeLorean image (image modality) and the text query `superhero` (text modality). The output of this query is shown in figure 15.8.

```
search_and_display(text_query="superhero",
                   image_query="chapters/ch15/delorean-query.jpg")
```

Image query: **Multimodal query results:**

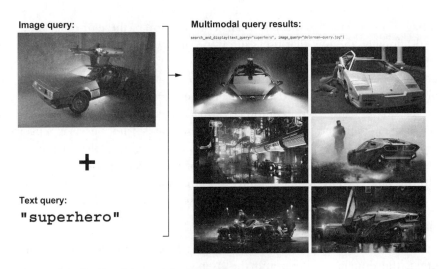

Text query:
"superhero"

Figure 15.8 Multimodal search for an image and text query

Interesting! The first image is of a superhero (Black Panther) on top of a sporty car, with lights glowing from the car, similar to the original picture. Most of the results now show the heroes or protagonists of their movies, with each of the results containing sporty cars and most images containing illuminating lighting effects picked up from the image query. This is a great example of how multimodal embeddings can be used to infer nuanced intent and to enable querying in new ways across diverse types of datasets.

The implications of multimodal search across text and images are vast. In e-commerce search, someone can upload a picture of a part they need and immediately find it without knowing the name, or upload a picture of an outfit or furniture that they like and find similar styles. Someone can describe a medical problem and immediately find images reflecting the symptoms or body systems involved. From chapter 9, you may remember our work to learn latent features of items and users from user behavior signals. This behavior is yet another modality, like images, that can be learned and cross-trained with text and other modalities to increase the intelligence of your search engine. As we'll discuss further in section 15.5, many additional data modalities like this will continue to become commonly searchable in the future, helping to make search engines even more powerful at understanding and finding relevant content and answers.

15.4 Other emerging AI-powered search paradigms

Throughout this book, you've learned techniques in most key AI-powered search categories, such as signals processing and crowdsourced relevance, knowledge graphs, personalized search, learning to rank, and semantic search using Transformer-based embeddings.

The introduction of foundation models and the ability to represent language as dense vectors has revolutionized how we think about and build search engines in recent years. Whereas search used to be primarily text-based, now it is possible to search on anything that can be encoded into dense vectors. This includes searching on images, audio, video, concepts, or any combination of these or other modalities.

Additionally, the way that users interface with search continues to evolve in new and groundbreaking ways. This includes the ability to ask questions, receive summarized answers that are a combination of multiple search results, generate new content explaining search results, and generate images, prose, code, instructions, or other content. Chatbot interfaces, combined with context tracking throughout conversations, have enabled iterative refinement of search tasks, where users can provide real-time feedback on responses and enable AI to act as an agent to search, synthesize, and refine the relevance of search results based upon live user feedback.

In this final section of our AI-powered search journey, we'll touch on a few of the trends we're seeing evolve and how they are likely to shape the future of search.

15.4.1 Conversational and contextual search

We've spent significant time covering contextual search—understanding the content context, the domain context, and the user context when interpreting queries. As search engines become more conversational, the personal context begins to take even more priority. For example,

```
User: "Please, take me home."
Phone: "I don't know where you live."
```

Despite someone having their address bookmarked under the name "Home" and their phone tracking their locations daily (including where they sleep at night), some highly used digital assistants are still unable to automatically bring in that context, like in figure 15.9, and instead require your home location to be explicitly configured in the settings. These short-comings are likely to disappear in the coming years as personal assistants build much more precise personalization models from all available contexts.

Figure 15.9 Digital assistants will need to pull in many different data sources to build out robust personalization models

In addition to these personalization contexts, there's an additional context that is becoming increasingly important: conversational context. Here's an example of a chatbot (virtual assistant) that lacks awareness of the current conversational context:

```
User: "Take me to the plumbing store."
Phone: "Here is a list of stores that I found. [shares list]"

User: "Go to the one in East Rochester."
Phone: [Provides directions to the geographical center of East Rochester,
        not the plumbing store it suggested in the last exchange]
```

Good chatbots integrate a strong search index to power their ability to answer questions and return information, but many still lack short-term and long-term memory of the previous conversational context. They may search each query independently, without considering the previous queries and responses. Depending on the application and type of query, some previous conversational context makes sense to remember indefinitely as part of a personalization model, such as someone's home address, family member names, or frequented places (doctor, dentist, school, etc.). In many cases, though, short-term memory just during the current conversation is sufficient. As search experiences become more conversational, short-term and long-term memory of the conversational context becomes more important.

Foundation models trained for chat contexts, such as ChatGPT by OpenAI, have brought about drastic improvements to the conversational capabilities of chatbots. Although they are pretrained models that don't update in real time, additional context can be injected into their prompts, making it entirely possible to capture and add personalized contexts into future prompts to improve their ability to cater to each user.

15.4.2 *Agent-based search*

Just as we discussed the importance of pipelines in chapter 7 for best interpreting and representing the meaning of user queries, pipelines are also an integral component for the kind of multistep problem-solving that is emerging with chatbots and foundation model interactions.

With agent-based search, a search engine or other AI interface is given a prompt and can then generate new prompts or tasks, chaining them together to achieve a desired outcome. Solving a user's request may require multiple steps, like generating new tasks ("now go find the top websites on this topic" or "explain if your last answer was correct"), reasoning about data ("now combine lists that were pulled from each website", or "summarize the results"), and other functional steps ("now return the search results").

A significant portion of web traffic in the future will originate from AI-based agents searching for information to use in their problem-solving. The degree to which web search engines act as the data-serving layer for these agents, since web search engines typically have a cached copy of much of the web already, remains to be seen, but search engines are natural launch points for these AI-based agents. Major search engines like Bing, as well as several startups, have already rolled out multistep searches involving some level of iterative task-following to compose better-researched responses. This is likely to be a growing trend for some time to come.

15.5 *Hybrid search*

In chapters 2 and 3, we introduced two different search paradigms: keyword-based lexical search (based on sparse vector representations, like an inverted index and typically ranked using BM25) and dense vector search (based on dense vector representations and typically ranked using cosine, dot product, or a similar vector-based similarity calculation). In this section, we'll demonstrate how to combine results across these different paradigms.

We've mostly treated lexical and vector search as orthogonal search approaches, but in practice, you'll often get the best results by using both approaches as part of a hybrid search. *Hybrid search* is the process of combining results from multiple search paradigms to deliver the most relevant results. Hybrid search usually involves combining lexical and vector search results, though the term isn't limited to just these two approaches.

There are a few ways to implement hybrid search. Some engines have direct support for combining lexical query syntax and vector search syntax as part of the same query, effectively allowing you to swap out specific keywords or filters within your query with vectors and combine vector similarity scores, BM25 scores, and function scores in arbitrarily complex ways. Some engines don't support running vector and lexical search as part of the same query, but instead support hybrid search *fusion* algorithms that enable you to merge results from separate lexical and vector queries in a thoughtful way. In other cases, you may be using a vector database that is separate from your lexical search engine, in which case you may end up using a similar fusion algorithm to combine those results outside of the engine.

15.5.1 Reciprocal rank fusion

In this section, we'll demonstrate a popular hybrid search algorithm for merging two sets of search results, called *reciprocal rank fusion* (RRF). RRF combines two or more sets of search results by ranking the documents based on their relative ranks across the different result sets. The algorithm is simple: for each document, it sums the reciprocal of the ranks of the document in each result set and then sorts the documents based on this sum. This algorithm is particularly effective when the two sets of search results are complementary, as it will rank documents higher that are already ranked higher in either set, but highest when they are ranked in both sets. The following listing implements the RRF algorithm.

Listing 15.17   RRF for combining multiple sets of search results

```
def reciprocal_rank_fusion(search_results, k=None):
    if k is None: k = 60
    scores = {}
    for ranked_docs in search_results:
        for rank, doc in enumerate(ranked_docs, 1):
            scores[doc["id"]] = (scores.get(doc["id"], 0) +
                                (1.0 / (k + rank)))
    sorted_scores = dict(sorted(scores.items(),
        key=lambda item: item[1], reverse=True))
    return sorted_scores
```

search_results is a list of sets of ranked documents associated with different searches (lexical search, vector search, etc.).

ranked_docs is a list of documents for a specific search.

A document's score increases by being in multiple ranked_docs lists and by being higher in each list.

Return the docs, sorted from highest RRF score to lowest.

In this function, an arbitrary list (`search_results`) of sets of ranked documents from each individual search is passed in. For example, you may have two items in `search_results`:

- The ranked docs from a lexical search
- The ranked docs from a vector search

The RRF score for each document is then calculated by summing the reciprocal ranks of the document (`1 / (k + rank)`) from each set of search results (`ranked_docs`). The final RRF scores are then sorted and returned.

The `k` parameter is a constant that can be increased to prevent an outlier ranking highly in one search result from carrying too much weight. The higher the `k`, the more weight is given to the docs that appear in multiple ranked document lists, as opposed to docs that rank higher in any given list of ranked documents. The `k` parameter is often set to `60` by default, based on research showing that this value works well in practice (https://plg.uwaterloo.ca/~gvcormac/cormacksigir09-rrf.pdf).

We've integrated the RRF logic into the `collection.hybrid_search` function, which we'll invoke in listing 15.19. First, however, let's see what the initial results look like for a lexical search versus the corresponding vector search for a sample phrase query: `"singin' in the rain"`.

Listing 15.18   Running lexical and vector searches independently

```
over_request_limit = 15
base_query = {"return_fields": ["id", "title", "id", "image_id",
                                "movie_id", "score", "image_embedding"],
              "limit": over_request_limit,
              "order_by": [("score", "desc"), ("title", "asc")]}

def lexical_search_request(query_text):
  return {"query": query_text,
          "query_fields": ["title", "overview"],
          "default_operator": "OR",
          **base_query}

def vector_search_request(query_embedding):
  return {"query": query_embedding,
          "query_fields": ["image_embedding"],
          "quantization_size": "FLOAT32",
          **base_query}

def display_lexical_search_results(query_text):
  collection = engine.get_collection("tmdb_lexical_plus_embeddings")
  lexical_request = lexical_search_request(query_text)
  lexical_search_results = collection.search(**lexical_request)

  display_results(lexical_search_results, display_header= \
              get_display_header(lexical_request=lexical_request))

def display_vector_search_results(query_text):
  collection = engine.get_collection("tmdb_lexical_plus_embeddings")
  query_embedding = encode_text(query_text)
  vector_request = vector_search_request(query_embedding)
  vector_search_results = collection.search(**vector_request)

  display_results(vector_search_results, display_header= \
              get_display_header(vector_request=vector_request))

query = '"' + "singin' in the rain" + '"'
display_lexical_search_results(query)
display_vector_search_results(query)
```

This listing takes the lexical phrase query "singin' in the rain" and encodes it as an embedding using the same `encode_text` function from listing 15.15. It then executes a lexical search and a vector search against the `tmdb_lexical_plus_embeddings` collection, which contains both the text fields needed for a lexical search and an image embedding for some of the movies in the TMDB dataset. The results from the lexical search and vector search are shown in figures 15.10 and 15.11, respectively.

Lexical Query: "singin' in the rain"

Singin' in the Rain
(score: 6.5101776)

Figure 15.10   A single lexical search result for the phrase query `"singin' in the rain"`

The lexical search, in this case, only returns one result: the movie *Singin' in the Rain*. Since the user's query was a phrase (quoted) query for the exact name of the title, it matched perfectly and found only the specific item the user was likely looking for. Figure 15.11 shows the corresponding vector search results for the same query.

Figure 15.11 Vector search results for the query `"singin' in the rain"`

You'll notice that the vector search results generally show images containing "rain" or "singing" or matching similar concepts, like umbrellas, weather, and musicals. This is because our vector search is on image embeddings, so the results are based on the visual content of the images, not the text content of the movies. While these images conceptually match the meaning of the words in the query better than the lexical search results, they don't contain the exact title match that the lexical search results do, so the ideal document for the movie *Singin' in the Rain* is missing from the top few results.

By combining these two sets of results using RRF, we can get the best of both worlds: the exact title match from the lexical search and the conceptually relevant images from the vector search. In the following listing, we demonstrate how to combine these two sets of search results by invoking `collection.hybrid_search`.

Listing 15.19 Hybrid search function

```
def display_hybrid_search_results(text_query, limit=8):
  lexical_search = lexical_search_from_text_query(text_query)
  vector_search = vector_search_from_embedding(encode_text(text_query))
  hybrid_search_results = collection.hybrid_search(
      [lexical_request, vector_request], limit=10,
      algorithm="rrf", algorithm_params={"k": 60})
  display_header = get_display_header(lexical_search, vector_search)
  display_results(hybrid_search_results, display_header)

display_hybrid_search_results(query)
```

We pass in an array of searches to execute—in this case, our `lexical_search` and `vector_search` from listing 15.18. The `collection.hybrid_search` function internally defaults to the RRF algorithm with `k=60` set, so if you'd like the pass in these parameters explicitly or change them, the full syntax is

```
collection.hybrid_search([lexical_search, vector_search], limit=10,
                algorithm="rrf", algorithm_params={"k": 60})
```

The call executes both searches and combines the results using RRF, with the output shown in figure 15.12.

Hybrid Results:
--Lexical Query: "singin' in the rain"
--Vector Query: [0.048921154115761124, 0.024482925930009714, …]

Singin' in the Rain
(score: 0.03009207275993712)

Mary Poppins
(score: 0.01639344262295082)

La Vie en Rose
(score: 0.016129032258064516)

The Sound of Music
(score: 0.015873015873015872)

Road to Perdition
(score: 0.015625)

Life Is Beautiful
(score: 0.015384615384615385)

The Wailing
(score: 0.015151515151515152)

Amélie
(score: 0.014925373134328358)

Figure 15.12   **Hybrid search results for lexical and vector searches using RRF for the query** `"singin' in the rain"`

These results demonstrate how hybrid search can often provide the best of both worlds: the exact keyword matches from the lexical search and the conceptually relevant results from the vector search. Vector search often struggles with matching exact names, specific keywords, and product names or IDs. Likewise, lexical search misses conceptually relevant results for the query text. In this case, the top result is the exact match the user was likely looking for (previously missing from the vector search results), but it has now been supplemented with other results conceptually similar to the user's query (previously missing from the lexical search).

Of course, you can pass in more than two searches to the hybrid search function if you want to. For example, you may want to add an additional vector field containing an embedding for the `title` or `overview` so that instead of just lexical search on text content, and vector search on images, you also have semantic search on the text content. Using RRF with these three sets of search results would allow you to combine the best of all three search approaches into a single set of results.

In addition to overcoming the respective functional limitations of keyword and vector search, hybrid search often yields better overall search ranking. This is because algorithms like RRF are designed to rank documents highest when they're found in multiple sets of search results. When the same items are returned as relevant from different searches, the fusion algorithm can use that agreement between the sets of results to boost those items' scores. This is particularly useful when one or more sets of search results have irrelevant documents, as the agreement between the two result sets can help filter out the noise, and surface the most relevant results. Listing 15.20 demonstrates this concept using the query the hobbit.

Listing 15.20   Lexical, vector, and hybrid searches for the hobbit

```
query = "the hobbit"
display_lexical_search_results(query)
display_vector_search_results(query)
display_hybrid_search_results(query)
```

Figures 15.13 through 15.15 show the results from listing 15.20.

In figure 15.13, you'll see five relevant results in the top six results (*The Hobbit* is part of the *Lord of the Rings* franchise). The text "The Hobbit" appears in the title of three of the first four results. There is one clearly bad result in the fifth position of the lexical search results, and all results are bad after the sixth document, mostly just matching on keywords like "the" and "of" in the title and overview fields.

Figure 15.14 shows the vector search results for the same query. These also show five relevant results related to *The Lord of the Rings*, but one of the relevant results from the lexical search is missing, and an additional relevant movie has been returned in the vector search results.

Lexical Query: the hobbit

Figure 15.13   Lexical search results for the query the hobbit

Vector Query: [-0.016278795212303375, -0.014356400471339553, ...]

Figure 15.14 Vector search results for the query `the hobbit`

Many of the remaining results are conceptually related to the query, showing mostly movies with fantasy landscapes and magic. Given the heavy overlap of good results between the lexical and vector search results, as well as the lack of overlap between the less relevant results, we should expect the hybrid search results to be quite good.

Indeed, in figure 15.15, we see that the first five results are all relevant and that six of the first seven results are related to *The Lord of the Rings*. We've moved from two different search results lists that were each missing a different document and showing some irrelevant results to a final list of results.

Hybrid Results:

--Lexical Query: the hobbit

--Vector Query: [-0.016278795212303375, -0.014356400471339553, ...]

Figure 15.15 Hybrid search results for the lexical and vector search results using RRF for the query `the hobbit`

RRF has allowed us to surface missing results from both lists and push down irrelevant results only appearing in one list, truly emphasizing the best qualities of each search paradigm (lexical versus vector) while overcoming each of their weaknesses.

15.5.2 *Other hybrid search algorithms*

While RRF is a popular and effective algorithm for combining search results, there are, of course, many other algorithms that can be used for similar purposes. One popular algorithm is *relative score fusion* (RSF), which is similar to RRF but uses the relative scores of documents in each search result set to combine the results. Since relevance scores are often not comparable across different ranking algorithms, the scores per query modality are typically scaled to the same range (often `0.0` to `1.0`) based on the minimum and maximum scores from each modality. The relative scores are then combined using a weighted average, with the weights often set based on the relative performance of each modality on a validation set.

Another common way to combine search results is to use one modality for an initial match and then rerank the results using another modality. Many engines support both lexical search and vector search as separate operations but allow you to run one query version (such as a lexical query) and then rerank the resulting documents using the other version (such as a vector query).

For example, if you want to ensure you match on specific keywords but also boost results that are conceptually similar to the query, you might run a lexical search first and then rerank the results using a vector search. The following listing demonstrates this concept.

> **Listing 15.21 Hybrid lexical search with vector search reranking**

```
def lexical_vector_rerank(text_query, limit=10):
    lexical_request = lexical_search_request(text_query)
    vector_request = vector_search_request(encode_text(text_query))
    hybrid_search_results = collection.hybrid_search(
        [lexical_request, vector_request],
        algorithm="lexical_vector_rerank", limit=limit)
    header = get_display_header(lexical_request, vector_request)
    display_results(hybrid_search_results, display_header=header)

lexical_vector_rerank("the hobbit")
```

Internally, this translates into a normal lexical search, but with the results then resorted using the score of a vector search for the same (encoded) query. Syntactically, these are the key parts of the search request generated by listing 15.21:

```
{'query': 'the hobbit',
 'query_fields': ['title', 'overview'],
 'default_operator': 'OR',
  ...
 'order_by': [('score', 'desc'), ('title', 'asc')],
```

```
'rerank_query': {
  'query': [-0.016278795212303375, ..., -0.02110762217111629],
  'query_fields': ['image_embedding'],
  'quantization_size': 'FLOAT32', ...
  'order_by': [('score', 'desc'), ('title', 'asc')], ...
 }
}
```

The output of this lexical search with vector search reranking is shown in figure 15.16. In this particular case, the results look very similar to the RRF results. Note that, unlike in figure 15.10 where the default operator for the lexical query was AND, resulting in a single exact lexical match, here the default operator is OR, so that more results are returned for the vector search to rerank. If you'd like to increase precision and only return more precise lexical matches, you can set the default operator to AND or add a `min_match` threshold in the lexical search request.

Hybrid Results:

--Lexical Query: the hobbit

--Vector Query: [-0.016278795212303375, -0.014356400471339553, ...]

The Hobbit: An Unexpected Journey
(score: 4.1808224)

The Lord of the Rings: The Fellowship of the Ring
(score: 3.7202718)

The Hobbit: The Desolation of Smaug
(score: 2.8664203)

The Hobbit: The Battle of the Five Armies
(score: 2.6256099)

The Lord of the Rings: The Return of the King
(score: 1.2284341)

The Wailing
(score: 1.2114973)

The Lord of the Rings: The Two Towers
(score: 1.2099149)

Rise of the Guardians
(score: 1.0686013)

Figure 15.16   Hybrid search by vector reranking of a lexical query

Functionally, the lexical search is entirely responsible for which documents return, while the vector search is entirely responsible for the order of the results. This may be preferred if you want to emphasize lexical keyword matching but with a more semantically relevant ranking. On the other hand, a fusion approach like RRF or RSF will provide a more blended approach, ensuring that the best results from each modality are surfaced. There are many other ways to combine search results, and the best approach will depend on the specific use case and the relative strengths and weaknesses of each search modality.

15.6   Convergence of contextual technologies

Just as recommendations, chatbots, and question-answering systems are all types of AI-powered information retrieval, many other technologies are also beginning to converge with search engines. Vector databases are emerging that function like search engines for multimodal data, and many different data sources and data modalities are being pulled together as additional contexts for optimal matching, ranking, and reasoning over data. Generative models are enabling a base-level understanding sufficient to generate new written and artistic works.

But most of these technologies are still implemented piecemeal into production systems. As researchers continue working toward building artificial general intelligence, intelligent robots, and smarter search systems, we're likely to see a continued convergence of technologies integrating new and different contexts to build a more comprehensive understanding of content, domains, and users. Figure 15.17 demonstrates what this convergence of technologies is likely to look like over the coming years.

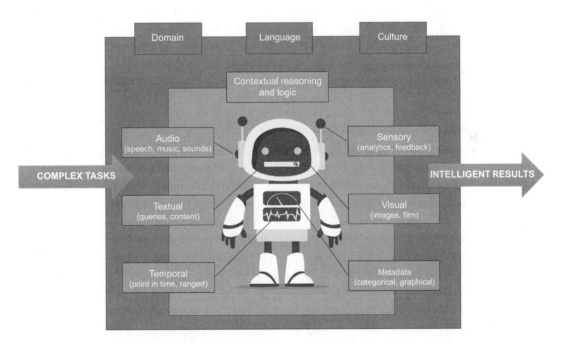

Figure 15.17   The convergence of contextual technologies to deliver more intelligent results

In the figure, we see the textual, audio, and video modalities we've already discussed, as well as a metadata modality that may provide additional context. We see a sensory modality, which might be available for a physical network of sensor-equipped devices or a robot with direct interactive access to the physical world. We also see the temporal modality, as the timing of both the queries and the data being searched can influence the relevance of the results.

Just as LLMs learn both the domain and the language structure of text (see chapter 13), additional cultural contexts and customs can also be learned by foundation models based on the geography and the observed behaviors from real-world interactions.

Much of this may seem *very* far away from traditional search, or even AI-powered search today—and it is! However, the goal of search is to best meet a user's information need, and as more overlapping technologies emerge to solve this problem from different angles, we see search being a critical base layer with which many of these technologies will integrate.

Many AI practitioners already recognize the importance of using RAG to find and supply real-time context to generative AI models, and data security, data accuracy, and model size considerations make it almost certain that search engines will be a critical backbone for knowledge-based generative AI systems well into the future. Large amounts of data coming from many sources will need to be indexed and available for real-time retrieval and use by generative AI models.

Having these technologies converge into end-to-end systems will enable solving these AI-powered search problems better than any of these systems could in isolation. Whether this gets labeled "robotics", "AI", "general intelligence", "AI-powered search", or something else entirely is yet to be seen. But many of the AI-powered search techniques you've learned have been, and will continue to be, central to the development of these next-generation contextual reasoning engines.

15.7 *All the above, please!*

Throughout this book, we've done a deep dive through the core concepts of building AI-powered search. We've covered both the theory behind how modern AI-powered search relevance works, and we've walked through code examples demonstrating each topic with real-world use cases.

The techniques and algorithms we've looked at won't be applicable to all use cases, but usually by combining multiple approaches, you will deliver a more effective and relevant search experience.

While the field of AI-powered search is evolving quickly, particularly due to the rapid innovation happening with generative foundation models and dense vector approaches to search, the core principles remain the same. The job of a search engine is to understand user intent and to return the content that best fulfills each user's information needs. This requires a proper understanding of the content context, the user context, and the domain context for each interaction. In addition to learning language models and knowledge graphs from your content, your search engine's capabilities will be supercharged if it can learn from your users implicitly, through their interactions (user signals) with the search engine.

You've learned how key AI-powered search algorithms work and how to implement and automate these algorithms into a self-learning search engine. Whether you need to automate the building of signals boosting models, learning to rank models, click models, collaborative filtering models, knowledge graph learning, or fine-tuning of deep-learning-based Transformer models for enhanced semantic search and question answering, you now have the knowledge and skills needed to implement a world-class AI-powered search engine. We look forward to seeing what you build!

Summary

- Foundation models serve as base models that are trained and can later be fine-tuned for specific domains or tasks.
- Prompt engineering allows you to inject additional context and data into each request, providing a way to perform real-time fine-tuning of the content that will be returned for the request. LLM-based applications should ideally be programmed to autogenerate and optimize prompts, as opposed to requiring manual prompt verification and adjustments, so they can automatically handle model and environment changes over time, while still performing optimally.
- Search results summarization and training data generation are two key areas in which foundation models can help drive relevance improvements in search engines.
- Jointly training embedding models on multiple data types enables powerful multimodal search capabilities (text-to-image, image-to-image, hybrid text-plus-image-to-image, and so on) extending user expressiveness and the search engine's ability to interpret user intent.
- AI-powered search is rapidly evolving with the rise of large language models, dense vector search, multimodal search, conversational and contextual search, generative search, and emerging hybrid search approaches.
- There are many techniques for implementing AI-powered search, and the best systems in the future will be those that can effectively apply multiple relevant approaches within hybrid search systems.

appendix A
Running the
code examples

During your journey through *AI-Powered Search*, we walk through a lot of code and run software examples demonstrating the techniques within this book. This appendix shows you how to easily set up and run the accompanying source code so that you can experiment with live, running examples as you work through the material. We'll cover how the book's source code is packaged, pulling and building the source code, and working with Jupyter notebooks and Docker to run the examples.

A.1 Overall structure of code examples

Building an AI-powered search system requires integrating many components and libraries. For our default search engine, we will use Apache Solr, which internally relies on Apache ZooKeeper. You can also swap out Solr with many other popular search engines and vector databases—see appendix B for instructions.

For significant data processing and machine learning tasks, we use Apache Spark. We use Python as our programming language for all the code examples and rely on many Python library dependencies, in addition to other system dependencies (like Java), which several of our systems require. Of course, we also need to execute our code examples and see the results in a user-friendly way, which we accomplish with the use of Jupyter notebooks.

Instead of installing dozens of software libraries and hundreds of dependencies to make this all work, we've made this process as easy as possible by packaging all of the book's examples into Docker containers, which are already fully configured and and ready to use. This means there is only a single prerequisite you must install before running the code examples in this book: Docker.

Docker enables the creation and running of tiny containers—fully functioning virtual machines that run only a lightweight operating system with all of the needed software and dependencies already installed and configured. This allows you to run the code on most operating systems (macOS, Windows, Linux) without having to configure any system-specific dependencies.

Once all of the services are running, all of the code listings in the book will be available through Jupyter notebooks, which will serve as the interface for running through and experimenting with the code examples to see the resulting outputs.

A.2   *Pulling the source code*

The source code accompanying this book is available on GitHub here: https://github.com/treygrainger/ai-powered-search. To pull the code, either use an installed Git client or open up a command-line interface in your preferred development folder and run the following command:

```
git clone https://github.com/treygrainger/ai-powered-search.git
```

You should now have a new folder in your current directory called ai-powered-search/ that contains all the source code for the book.

If you don't have Git installed or can't pull the code through the preceding command, there is also an option on the website to download the source code as a zip file through your web browser, which you would then just need to unzip into your development folder.

Feel free to rename or move the ai-powered-search/ folder if you wish; throughout the rest of this book, we'll simply refer to this directory using the variable $AIPS_HOME.

A.3   *Building and running the code*

As previously mentioned, Docker is the one key dependency you must install on your system to build and run the *AI-Powered Search* code examples. We will not cover this installation process here as it is system-dependent and changes from time to time. Please visit https://docker.com for download and installation instructions. We should also note that other container-management tools, like Podman, can be used instead of Docker, though we will not cover those here.

Once you have Docker installed, make sure to change the directory in your command-line interface to the $AIPS_HOME directory (cd $AIPS_HOME). To build and run the codebase, you then just need to run the following command:

```
docker compose up
```

Note that this command is equivalent to running `docker compose up solr`. The book's codebase works with multiple search engines and vector databases, and that (optional) last argument allows you to specify which engine(s) you want to use (with Apache Solr being the default). If you wanted to use OpenSearch with the book, for example, you would run `docker compose up opensearch` instead. For more information on other supported search engines, see appendix B.

TIP   The `docker compose up` command runs in the foreground of your console, which allows you to see all the logs streaming in real time, but this also means your containers will all die if you close the console. If you would like to instead run the containers in the background and close or continue using your console, you can pass in the `-d` or `--detach` parameter (`docker compose up -d`). If you launch it like this, be sure to explicitly run `docker compose --profile all down` when you are finished to stop the containers from running indefinitely in the background, consuming resources.

This command will take a while to run the first time, as it pulls in all of the code, operating systems, and dependencies needed to build and run the software accompanying this book. Once the command finishes, however, you will have all of the necessary services (Jupyter, Spark, ZooKeeper, Solr, etc.) running in separate Docker containers.

Now, to get started, simply open up your web browser and go to http://localhost:8888. This will redirect to the welcome screen listing all the book's chapters and their corresponding Jupyter notebooks (figure A.1). You can now click on any of the chapters to start running their code examples.

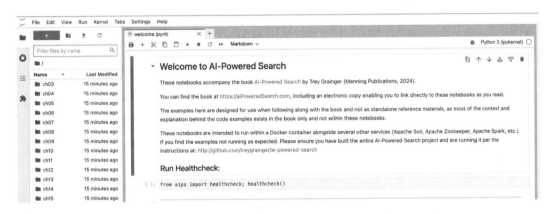

Figure A.1   Welcome screen. Once you see this, the *AI-Powered Search* containers are built and the Jupyter notebooks are running.

By default, the Jupyter Notebooks are loaded into a Jupyter Labs environment, which is a development environment for working with, debugging, and navigating notebooks. It allows you to open up and edit multiple notebooks at once (in separate tabs) and to navigate and modify the directory structure on the left side of the screen as you explore.

If you just want to follow along with the book in a simpler environment, you can alternatively go to http://localhost:8888/notebooks and navigate the table of contents to follow along, one notebook at a time, as you progress through the book. We'll use this simpler interface in the next section, though the same functionality (and more) is present in the default Jupyter Labs environment at http://localhost:8888.

A.4   *Working with Jupyter*

Once you view the `welcome.ipynb` notebook, you'll see a few data cells on the screen, including an introduction message, a "health check" script, and a table of contents to various notebooks containing executable examples from the book.

If you've never used Jupyter before, it is a tool that lets you mix markup (usually instructions and explanation) and code in your browser, and to edit, run, and interact with the output from the code examples. This makes learning much easier, as you don't have to use command-line tools and can instead interact entirely with ready-to-execute examples with the click of a button.

You'll notice a toolbar near the top of the screen (below the menu bar) that allows you to interact with the sections of content (called *cells*) within the notebook. You can use these tools to navigate up and down, to stop and restart the notebook, or to execute each cell sequentially using the Run button.

In figure A.2, clicking Run while the healthcheck code cell is highlighted will result in the healthcheck executing to confirm that all Docker containers are running and that the services running within them are healthy and responding.

Figure A.2   Running code examples. Clicking Run in the toolbar will execute any examples in the current cell (if any) and proceed to the next cell.

Figure A.3 shows the response you will see when everything is running as expected.

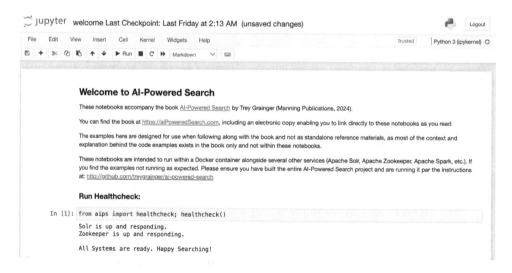

Figure A.3   Healthcheck success. You should see this message if everything is running correctly.

At this point, you can scroll down to the table of contents and proceed through the notebooks for each chapter. Of course, since the explanation behind the examples is contained within the book, you'll probably prefer to work through the examples as you're reading the book so that you have the appropriate background when running them. The Jupyter notebooks are not intended to be standalone examples, so you'll probably want to keep the book close by to provide context.

All Jupyter notebooks are designed to be independently idempotent. This means that, while all steps in a notebook need to be executed in order to guarantee a successful result, you can always start over at the beginning of any notebook, and it will "reset" to the expected results necessary to make the subsequent steps succeed. If ever you experience errors in a notebook, just go back to the first cell on the page and run through the whole notebook again.

A.5 *Working with Docker*

While everything in the previous sections should work as expected, it's of course possible that you could run into problems along the way. The most likely challenge you'll face is having one of your Docker containers, or the service running inside of it, fail. It's also possible, if you're making changes to underlying data or config in one of the services, for example, that you could put it in a bad state.

When this happens, you can always tear down your containers and start over. To do this, just run this command from the `$AIPS_HOME` directory:

```
docker compose --profile all down && docker compose up
```

Keep in mind that if you've made any changes to your notebooks or code, any work you've done will be lost when you run `docker compose --profile all down`. In general, the examples are designed to be transient. If you want to preserve your work across container rebuilds, you can modify the docker-compose.yaml file to mount folders to your local drive or use Docker data volumes marked as `external` that will be persistent. Please refer to the Docker documentation if you plan to make changes there, as the mechanisms and APIs can change from time to time.

If you ever modify the code examples or your configuration, it's also possible you may need to rebuild your Docker images. When you run `docker compose up` the first time, it will pull or build your images and start them, but it doesn't rebuild with changes made after the first build. To rebuild everything prior to restarting your Docker containers, you can instead run this command:

```
docker compose up --build
```

If you just want to temporarily stop your running Docker containers and resume them later, you can also run `docker compose --profile all stop` to stop, and then `docker compose start` later to resume. This is helpful if you want to preserve any changes you've made without resetting to a clean version of the notebooks on the next start.

This should give you everything you need to run through all of the notebooks and code in *AI-Powered Search*.

appendix B
Supported search engines and vector databases

We use the open source Apache Solr search engine as our default search engine throughout the book for consistency, but all of the algorithms in the codebase are designed to work with a wide variety of search engines and vector databases. To that end, other than cases where engine-specific syntax is required to demonstrate a point, we have implemented search functionality using a generic `engine` interface that allows you to easily swap in your preferred search engine or vector database. In this appendix, we'll cover the list of supported engines, how to swap out the default engine, and how the major abstractions (`engine` and `collection`) are used throughout the book.

B.1 Supported engines

The list of supported engines will continue to grow over time, but at the time of publication, the following engines are initially supported:

- `solr`—Apache Solr
- `opensearch`—OpenSearch
- `bonsai`—Bonsai
- `weaviate`—Weaviate

To see the full, most up-to-date list of all supported engines, please visit https://aipoweredsearch.com/supported-engines.

B.2 Swapping out the engine

Normally, you'll only be working with one search engine or vector database at a time when running the book's code examples. To use any particular engine, you just need to specify the engine's name (as enumerated above) when starting up Docker.

You would launch OpenSearch, for example, like this:

```
docker compose up opensearch
```

This will both start any necessary Docker containers needed to run `opensearch` (or the engine you specify) as well as set this engine as active in the book's Jupyter notebooks for use in all the code examples.

Note that some engines, such as managed search and API-based services, do not require any additional local Docker containers, since their services are hosted elsewhere. Also, some engines may require additional configuration parameters, such as API keys, remote addresses/URLs, ports, and so on. These parameters can be set in the .env file at the root of the project.

If you want to use a different engine at any time, you can restart the Docker containers and specify the new engine you want to use:

```
docker compose up bonsai
```

If you want to launch more than one engine at a time to experiment, you can provide a list of the engines you wish to start at the end of the `docker compose up` command:

```
docker compose up solr opensearch weaviate
```

The first engine you reference in your `docker compose up` command will be set as your active engine in the Jupyter notebooks, with the others available on standby.

If you'd like to switch to one of the standby engines within your live Jupyter notebooks (for example, to `opensearch`), you can do this at any time by simply running the following command in any notebook:

```
import aips
aips.set_engine("opensearch")
```

Keep in mind that if you call `set_engine` for an engine that is not currently running, this will later result in errors if that engine is still unavailable when you try to use it.

You can also check the currently set engine at any time by running this command:

```
aips.get_engine().name
```

B.3 *The engine and collection abstractions*

The search engine industry is full of different terminology and concepts, and we have tried to abstract away as much of that as possible in the codebase. Most search engines started with lexical keyword search and have since added support for vector search, and many vector databases started with vector search and have since added lexical search. For our purposes, we just think of all these systems as *matching and ranking engines*, and we use the term *engine* to refer to all of them.

Likewise, each engine has a concept of one or more logical partitions or containers for adding data. In Solr and Weaviate, these containers are called *collections*; in OpenSearch, Elasticsearch, and Redis these are called *indexes*; and in Vespa they are called *applications*. In MongoDB, the original data is stored in a *collection*, but it can then be copied into an *index* for search purposes. Naming also varies further among other engines.

For proper abstraction, we always use the term *collection* in the codebase, so every engine that gets implemented has a `collection` interface through which you can query or add documents.

Common public methods on the `engine` interface include

- `engine.create_collection(collection_name)`—Creates a new collection
- `engine.get_collection(collection_name)`—Returns an existing collection

Common public methods on the `collection` interface include

- `collection.search(**request)`—Runs a search and returns results. Individual request parameters should be passed in as Python keyword arguments, like `collection.search(query="keyword), limit=10"`.
- `collection.add_documents(docs)`—Adds a list of documents to the collection
- `collection.write(dataframe)`—Writes each row from a Spark dataframe to the collection as a document
- `collection.commit()`—Ensures that recently added documents are persisted and available for searching

The `engine` and `collection` interfaces also internally implement schema definitions and management for all the datasets used in the book.

Because the `collection.write` method takes a dataframe, we utilize helpers as needed when loading data from additional data sources, such as CSV or SQL:

- `collection.write(from_csv(csv_file))`—Writes each row in the CSV file to the collection as a document
- `collection.write(from_sql(sql_query))`—Runs the SQL query and writes each returned row to the collection as a document

No additional engine-specific implementation is needed for loading from these additional data sources, as any data source that can be mapped to a Spark dataframe is implicitly supported.

B.4   *Adding support for additional engines*

While we hope to eventually support most major search engines and vector databases, you may find that your favorite engine is not currently supported. If that is the case, we encourage you to add support for it and submit a pull request to the codebase. The `engine` and `collection` interfaces are designed to be easy to implement, and you can use the default `solr` implementation or any other already-implemented engines as a reference.

Not all data stores have full support for all the capabilities implemented in *AI-Powered Search*. For example, a pure vector database may not support lexical keyword matching and ranking, and some search engines may not support vector search. Likewise, some specialized capabilities may only be available in certain engines.

While the default `solr` engine supports all of the *AI-Powered Search* capabilities implemented in the book, other engines may require workarounds, integration of additional libraries, or delegation of some capabilities to another engine for certain algorithms. Most engines don't have native support for semantic knowledge graphs and text tagging, for example, so many of the engine implementations will delegate these one-off capabilities to other libraries.

We hope that the `engine` and `collection` abstractions will make it easy for you to add support for your favorite engine and also to potentially contribute it to the book's codebase to benefit the larger community of *AI-Powered Search* readers and practitioners. Happy searching!

index